THE COLLECTED WRITINGS OF
ROBERT DUNCAN

The publisher gratefully acknowledges the generous contribution to this book from the Jess Collins Trust and the ongoing efforts of its trustees, Mary Margaret Sloan and Christopher Wagstaff.

The publisher also gratefully acknowledges the support of the Leslie Scalapino Memorial Fund for Poetry, which was established by generous contributions to the UC Press Foundation by Thomas J. White and the Leslie Scalapino–O Books Fund.

The publisher also wishes to express gratitude to Robert Bertholf for all his work over the years to preserve and further the legacy of Robert Duncan.

Robert Duncan

The Collected
Early Poems and Plays

Robert Duncan

The Collected
Early Poems and Plays

Edited and with an Introduction by
Peter Quartermain

University of California Press
Berkeley   Los Angeles   London

NATIONAL ENDOWMENT FOR THE ARTS

This project is supported in part by an award from the National Endowment for the Arts.

University of California Press, one of the most distinguished university presses in the United States, enriches lives around the world by advancing scholarship in the humanities, social sciences, and natural sciences. Its activities are supported by the UC Press Foundation and by philanthropic contributions from individuals and institutions. For more information, visit www.ucpress.edu.

University of California Press
Berkeley and Los Angeles, California

University of California Press, Ltd.
London, England

Library of Congress Cataloging-in-Publication Data

Duncan, Robert, 1919–1988.
    The collected early poems and plays / Robert Duncan ; edited by Peter Quartermain.
        p.   cm. — (The collected writings of Robert Duncan ; 2)
    ISBN 978-0-520-25926-3 (cloth : alk. paper)
    I. Quartermain, Peter.   II. Title.
    PS3507.U629   2012
    811'.54—dc23   2012024993

Manufactured in the United States of America

21   20   19   18   17   16   15   14   13   12
10   9   8   7   6   5   4   3   2   1

The paper used in this publication meets the minimum requirements of ANSI/NISO Z39.48–1992 (R 1997) (*Permanence of Paper*).

Contents

Heavenly City, Earthly City

Uncollected Work 1933–1947

Preface

Robert Duncan: The Collected Early Poems and Plays is the first of two volumes of a reader's edition of Robert Duncan's poetry, plays, and fiction published in his lifetime, or whose publication was authorized by him. It gathers Duncan's poems, plays, and noncritical prose written from 1938 through 1956, when he completed *Letters* (published in 1958). The second volume, *The Collected Later Poems and Plays,* includes work written after 1956, from *The Opening of the Field* (1960) through the two volumes of *Ground Work* (1984 and 1987); it also includes what appears to be the last poem Duncan wrote, "Hekatombé," which was not published in Duncan's lifetime.

This edition, necessarily, cannot be thought of as complete, since not all Duncan's publications, in little magazines, catalogues, and similar ephemeral publications, may have come to light. There are also dozens if not scores of poems Duncan inscribed in catalogues, pamphlets, and books which friends and new acquaintances brought to him, an act which might reasonably be considered a form of publication, in that by so inscribing a poem the writer relinquishes control over its readership. Some of these were published after Duncan's death in 1988, but such writings remain largely unrecorded and emerge for the most part by chance. None of them is included in this edition. Where possible, however, this volume does include those poems which, handwritten in limited editions of books which were for sale, must be thought of as published.

Annotations in this edition are minimal: they contextualize the circumstances of a poem's composition as well as of its publication where needful, record major textual variations, translate foreign words and phrases and provide their source when possible, and on a very few occasions completely print another version of a poem. Annotations of individual books expand material sketched in the biographical section of the introduction. A fully annotated edition of the poems, recording all textual and orthographic changes, would be unbalanced, cumbersome, highly repetitious, and essentially unusable, with coded annotations five or six times as long as the text whose changes they record. It would be of interest only to the most dedicated of scholars. Some poems, notably *Medieval Scenes* (written 1947) and "The Venice Poem" (written 1948), both of great significance not only in the development of Duncan's poetics but in the history of U.S. poetry in the years following the Second World War, have a tangled and complex textual and compositional history which can only be sketched in the annotations: a full narrative and analysis must await a careful (and much needed) scholarly edition of each; there are multiple drafts of both.

Although this edition reprints the contents of each of Duncan's major collections of new poems as published, thereby preserving the integrity of each book, it prints them as far as possible in chronological order of composition, not of publication. In other respects its organization is strongly indebted to the two-volume *Collected Poems of William Carlos Williams*, edited by A. Walton Litz and Christopher MacGowan (New York: New Directions, 1982, revised 1991): it intersperses between some of Duncan's books, in chronological order of composition, work which Duncan gathered in such retrospective collections as *The First Decade* and the second (1972) edition of *Caesar's Gate*, as well as work he did not reprint after its appearance in a magazine or anthology. With the exceptions of *Letters*, which closes *The Collected Early Poems and Plays*, and *Faust Foutu*, this first volume takes first (usually periodical) publication as copy text; *Letters*, along with almost all the work in *The Collected Later Poems and Plays*, takes first book publication as copy text. Exceptions are explained, along with details of textual procedures and principles, in the textual section of the introduction.

Introduction: Disturbing Poetics

Duncan's Early Life and Work, 1919–1958

I want to compose a poetry with the meaning entirely occult, that is—with the meaning containd not as a jewel is containd in a box but as the inside of a box is containd in a box. —Robert Duncan

At birth, Duncan was named Edward Howard Duncan after his father, but his adoptive parents renamed him Robert Edward Symmes when they took him into their care; Duncan kept that name until, as he recorded in a notebook in 1941, "I have changed my name and disowned my family completely. Now, Robert Duncan."[1] Yet, though in that act he was rejecting many of the family's cultural values and much of its spiritual practice, it would be more than twenty-five years before, on 16 February 1967, he legally changed his name to Robert Edward Duncan. The circumstances of his birth and adoption appear more than once in his writing, and questions of identity, self, and the person permeate his notebooks, his reading, and his work. On 23 April 1967 he wrote to Robin Blaser of "the contrast between the authentic in poetry (you) and the derivative (me)."[2]

Probably a victim of the flu epidemic, his mother, Marguerite "Daisy" (Carpenter) Duncan, died within hours of his birth on 7 January 1919 in Oakland, California, and his father, a day-laborer, soon put him up for adoption. On 1 August (Lammas-day), Fayetta Harris Philip (who would become his Aunt Faye) told her sister about him, and on 4 August he was taken into the care of Edwin Joseph Symmes (an architect) and Minnehaha Harris Symmes. In their quest for a child the Symmes, both theosophical Hermeticists, had sought the guidance of astrological charts provided by the Oakland Hermetic Brotherhood, and they returned to that guidance in 1920 when they adopted another child, whom they named Barbara Eleanor Symmes. "I was adopted by astrology and as an infant I understood I was of the last generation of Atlantis," Duncan said in 1982.[3] Household talk would at times turn on such questions as whether or not there had been aeroplanes in Atlantis, or the date and nature of the impending destruction of the New Atlantis which they believed America to be. Duncan's childhood, even before he could read, was filled with story, not only of Atlantis but of demonic possession and darkness as well as benign inspiration and light: "Greek, Hebrew and Germanic myth, along with family lore of early pioneer days in the West."[4] In 1982, drafting a symposium paper on the place of spiritual and occult traditions in a new poetics, he began with a recollection of his grandmother reading to him, when he was six or seven years old, Thomas Taylor the Platonist's relation of the Orphic mysteries and his translation of Porphyry, Alexander Wilder's translation of Iamblichus, or, "a still more sacred text for my grandmother, one of the volumes of Mead's *Thrice-Greatest Hermes*."[5] Along with Andrew Lang's "colored" *Fairy Books,* Frank L. Baum's Oz books too became lifelong companions. The world of the Symmes, conventional in most respects, was a world suffused with hidden meanings, ancient lore, signs, and wonders, matters occulted from ordinary view. In such a world, books like George MacDonald's *Lilith* and *Phantastes* were to be read as coded truths from the world of the eternal, stories written not for children but for the child-like: "What can it matter that neither you nor your child should know what it means?" MacDonald asked in *The Light Princess and Other Fairy Stories:* "It is there not so much to convey a meaning as to *wake* a meaning." Such stories, "speaking," as Duncan later put it, "from the realm of lost or hidden truth," were a source for recurrent discussion and analysis in family conversations, a practice echoed in Duncan's own poetics: "I study what I write as I study out any mystery. A poem, mine or anothers, is an occult document, a body awaiting vivisection, analysis, X-ray," he wrote in 1953.[6] From 1947 and even earlier his notebooks began intermittently but persistently to devote much space to exercises in phonetics and extensive reading in linguistics, to close phonological analysis of poems. "I've got to have the roots of words," he told Denise Levertov in 1958, "the way the language works, at my fingertips."[7]

The practice of poetry, both writing and reading it (for Duncan the distinction was largely artificial), was a natural extension of his fam-

ily's occult interests and practice; his own childhood experience viv-
idly fed his insistence, in the first place that much of the world is in
fact hidden and calls out to be discerned—"things and events strive to
speak" he would write in *The H.D. Book* in 1961—and in the second
that the child's vision is free of the impediments of adult habits—"Can
a child," he scornfully asked, "be a banker?"[8] His deep distrust of such
"adult-ery," as he sometimes called it, informs his later political interests
and activity—his passionate opposition not only to the Korean War, for
example, in *Faust Foutu* (1953), but his outraged offense at "the Roosevelt
panacea for the ills of the profit system, the Permanent War Economy."[9]
His own inner conflict, which saw the power of the State as related to his
own power as poet, "but turnd to purposes of domination, exploitation
and destruction," is part and parcel of his necessity to find disturbance
at the heart of the poem, just as it is part and parcel of his own strong
desire to dominate. All this inflects his attitude toward childhood, which
cannot be seen simply as an instance of Duncan as a Late Romantic—for
he can just as readily be read as postmodern—nor can it be construed
simply as a matter of taking all experience, including reading and writ-
ing, as a great adventure (which Duncan did). It is also a perceptual
habit, almost perhaps a family trait, somewhat forcefully reinforced by a
childhood accident. In 1922 at Yosemite, where for some years the fam-
ily lived intermittently (Edwin Symmes had a long-term contract there),
the three-year-old Robert fell, running across the snow; the sunglasses
he was obliged to wear (because he was snow-blind) broke. "That," he
says in "A Sequence of Poems for H.D.'s Birthday" in *Roots and Branches,*
"explains how I was blinded and came to be cross-eyed. I had the double
reminder always, the vertical and horizontal displacement in vision that
later became separated, specialized into a near and a far sight. One image
to the right and above the other." Occasionally, in later years in public
readings or classes, one eye would be fixed on the page, the other discon-
certingly roaming. Such an overlay of images deeply inflected his poetry.
In later poetry (most obviously in *Bending the Bow*) the poem began to
be split, caesuras dividing the line left and right. But more important,
that double reminder always in his vision peopled his daily world with
presences, the child having to learn how to "point to the one that is
really there." At the same time, what with the household myths that were
always before him in family conversation, the child had to learn also to
heed those superimpositions, recognize those visible "signs and wonders,
felt presences or nearnesses of meaning, where we must follow in trust."[10]

So, inevitably, when in 1953 he heard Helen Adam reading Blake, he would instantly recognize in both a kindred childlike spirit.

By the time the Symmes family, following horoscopic advice, moved to Bakersfield in 1927 when Duncan was eight, he had started writing poems; by the time he left Emerson Junior High School in 1932, when he was thirteen, he had learned to fit in, joining the dramatic club and thereby acting in plays written by his class, writing for the school's monthly magazine *The Emersonian* and becoming its chief editor, and officiating at what Ekbert Faas calls "most leading functions" at the school—but none of them athletic.[11] At the very much larger Kern County Union High School (1932–36) he once again took part in the dramatic club's productions, and contributed to the school newspaper, *Blue and White,* and its literary magazine, *The Target.* But, as Duncan reports in *The H.D. Book,* the family, respectable in the closed community of Bakersfield, kept a low profile, quiet about its Hermeticism, its conversations about Atlantis, its discussions of the Kabbala. At school, though he never declared his emergent homosexuality, it was no secret that he was gay—that, his crossed eyes, and the fact that despite its restraint his family was nevertheless known for its unusual behavior made him much more the outsider than he had been at Emerson, despite the wide range of his activities.[12] As he said in an interview in 1980, "It was clear even in high school, that I wouldn't have a second profession, and that I would be just a poet."[13] Such nonconformist ambition found encouragement in Edna Keogh, whose English classes in his final year of high school, 1935–36, became (as he put it in *The H.D. Book*) "a realm of expectancy for me" as she pushed a select group, "set apart from the mass of those attending high school," into "our own explorations."[14] Under her tutelage the sixteen-year-old Duncan read a range of modernist avant-garde work emphatically outside "the matter of a prescribed course," including Lawrence's *The Man Who Died* and Woolf's *The Waves,* and poems by Ezra Pound and H.D. His homosexuality, of course, set him further apart. On one occasion in the fall of 1935—after his father's death from a heart attack that September—a young man attacked him (perhaps after their sexual intercourse, the details are obscure) and beat him so badly about the head that he briefly ended up in a hospital, the police quizzing him about his assailant. It would not be until Duncan entered the University of California as a freshman in 1936 that he could, clear of his mother's watchful eye and her skeptical opposition to his determination to be a poet, enter homosexual relationships more securely.

Duncan's at times intense engagement with politics, which started almost as soon as he arrived at Berkeley, would mesh nicely with his writerly ambitions. Joining the staff of the English Club's magazine, *The Occident,* he joined too the American Student Union (more radical than the Young Communist League), became editor of its newssheet, *Campus Review,* and with Trotskyist Virginia Admiral started a little magazine, *Epitaph,* which only lasted one issue. In the process he discovered how to join as well as tap networks of little magazines, and how not only to publish his work but to maintain *complete* control over its publication—a principle he could not steadfastly follow until after the publication of *Bending the Bow* in 1968, when he began to publish his own work privately. At Berkeley he read the work of T. S. Eliot, Gertrude Stein, and Ezra Pound—*The Cantos* enthralled him—and he was active in literary as well as student political life both on and off campus. But in December 1938 he left Berkeley for Philadelphia to join his lover Ned Fahs, who had got a job teaching at the Naval Academy in Annapolis, beginning a somewhat peripatetic existence with a Christmas visit, along with Ned, to James and Blanche Cooney at the Phoenix Community and Phoenix Press on Maverick Road in Woodstock, New York—where he met Anaïs Nin. He would spend the summer at Phoenix after he broke with Fahs in April or May 1940, but also spend much time in Manhattan, part of Nin's circle along with Henry Miller, Kenneth Patchen, George Barker, and Edgard Varèse. Over the next few years his itinerant existence included three months in the army (at Fort Knox), which ended with a dishonorable discharge on 25 June 1941 as a "sexual psychopath." Working as a typist was his fallback position, but he also worked as a dishwasher in Provincetown, as well as on a farm run by the Cooneys in Ashfield, Massachusetts, as a stockman in shipyards back in California, and as a traveling salesman for Dell Books in Boston. Knocking about is perhaps the best way to summarize a life marked not only by a brief army career but by an almost equally brief marriage to Marjorie McKee in 1943—he called it "my graduating degree in psychoanalysis," and recorded something of its flavor in his short story "Love."[15] In those years he enthusiastically developed his interest in the world of painting—here he was helped both by Nin and her circle and by Virginia Admiral—but devoted most of his energies to his writing, working on his novel *The Shaman* as well as many poems. In 1942, with a covering letter by Nin, he submitted two poems to *Poetry*—his first publication in a widely circulated magazine—following this up with a review of Patchen in *Accent* (Autumn

1942) and, in 1944, with his controversial essay "The Homosexual in Society" in Dwight Macdonald's *Politics* (August 1944). That essay, which he characterized in 1959 as an attempt to "insist . . . upon concern for the virtues of a homosexual relationship," insisting as it does that the necessity to conceal a homosexual life both dishonors Love and betrays public trust, so disturbed John Crowe Ransom that after he had accepted "An African Elegy" for publication in the influential *Kenyon Review* he refused to print it.[16]

In New York, and then in Berkeley, Duncan increasingly came to see that the poem should be a direct record of the actual process of writing it—he later referred to it as "testimony," like William Carlos Williams perhaps, or like the Pound of the *Pisan Cantos,* refusing to separate the poem from the life, the poet from the man—a refusal most obviously apparent, perhaps, in "Love." In the long term this would lead him initially to reject his inclusion in both the now-famous February 1957 "San Francisco Scene" issue of *Evergreen Review* and Donald M. Allen's pioneering and highly influential anthology *The New American Poetry: 1945–1960,* angrily expostulating that both ventures did nothing more than pander to a destructive careerism: "I want to write as the universe sings," he wrote to Robin Blaser in exasperation after he had agreed to take part, "not *for* appreciation, but *in* appreciation; not in order to be admired, but to admire; to love, to celebrate."[17] As he somewhat ruefully admitted to Blaser almost a year later, when Allen was putting the finishing touches on the anthology, "I have myself an ambitious shade that can disturb the roots of creative spirit."[18] His literary activities and interests, his struggles with his own ambitions as a poet, and his struggles to clarify his own poetics meshed nicely with his growing political awareness, his renewed attraction to anarchism. Meeting André Breton in New York refreshed his interest in a by no means apolitical surrealism, if indeed it had waned, and with Jackson Mac Low and Paul Goodman he more or less regularly attended anarchist "discussion meetings," a practice he would continue after he returned to California in September 1945 to lodge with his old anarchist friends Mary and Hamilton Tyler, who farmed chickens in Guerneville, Sonoma County, at Pond Farm. When the Tylers moved to the eighty-acre farm Treesbank in Healdsburg, Sonoma County, in January 1946, Duncan went with them, writing the "Treesbank" sequence of poems (in *Heavenly City, Earthly City*) while there.

The Tylers shared many of Duncan's literary views, encouraged

Duncan's writing, and were active in literary as well as anarchist circles; both Pond Farm and Treesbank were frequent meeting places for writers and anarchists. Regular visitors included Kenneth Rexroth and Philip Lamantia among others; William Everson ("Brother Antoninus") came to Treesbank on release from his internment at Camp 56, in Waldport on the Oregon coast, as a conscientious objector—he was an anarchist and pacifist.[19] In this environment Duncan wrote the group of poems which opened *Heavenly City, Earthly City*. In the summer of 1946, he moved back to the city (Mary Tyler gave birth to her first child, Brenda—for whom Duncan initially wrote *The Cat and the Blackbird*—in July), working as a typist at the University of California, meeting Jack Spicer at an anarchist meeting and through him Robin Blaser, and setting himself up as a kind of poetry entrepreneur by organizing a series of poetry readings, discussions, and informal lectures at a somewhat tumbledown boardinghouse on Telegraph Avenue. The lectures, when not given by Duncan, were by friends like Kenneth Rexroth or sympathetic faculty like Thomas Parkinson, on *Finnegans Wake,* Lorca, *Paterson,* Gertrude Stein, Eliot's *Four Quartets*. Between them Spicer, Duncan, and Blaser talked of themselves as starting a "Berkeley Renaissance" (which later became a foundation for the San Francisco Renaissance of the 1950s), and discussed the writing of poetry in terms of magic and magical practice. "We called ourselves the Berkeley Renaissance," Duncan said much later; "we meant that our poetry was really a Renaissance poetry: that Ficino would come into it; that questions of Dante and Petrarch would underlie it."[20] In 1983 Duncan noted that "Ficino knows very well that the poem, *by its sounds* . . . reaches the soul, the body and the spirit. The body cringes, feels immediately the sound and tone and distribution of notes toward possible resolutions, toward irresolution and toward awakened conflict."[21]

The intense literary conversation and activity of this period scarcely diminished when, in January 1948, Duncan joined Spicer and Blaser as a student in the "Civilization of the Middle Ages" program in order to study with Ernst Kantorowicz (Spicer had enrolled in the fall of 1947). The aristocratic and muscular dandy Kantorowicz, the great scholar of what he would call "medieval political theology," had been a member of Stefan George's largely homosexual inner circle, the Georgekreis, consisting of aesthetes devoted to preserving the highest essence of traditional art and beauty, and which saw Beauty (Poetry) in more or less theological terms as an Office to and for which the Artist (Poet) was responsible. His influence on the three poets was lasting, and profound: in the words of Michael Davidson, they "extended the lore of medieval and renaissance culture into their own lives, creating a spiritual and artistic brotherhood out of shared homosexual experience, occultism, and the reading of modern literature."[22] Kantorowicz's notions of the Office and Person of the King (which he later elaborated in *The King's Two Bodies,* 1957), and of a society ruled by a hierarchical spiritual aristocracy, especially fed Duncan's notion of himself as "a coterie poet not a regional one."[23]

By the end of 1948 Duncan had been corresponding with Ezra Pound for two years, Louis Zukofsky for eighteen months, and William Carlos Williams for just about a year, had been visited by Charles Olson in April 1947 and had visited Pound at St. Elizabeths in Washington, D.C., that summer. Add into the mix an intense relationship with Jaime de Angulo, who in 1949 would teach him much about shamans and shamanism, and frequent if not regular attendance at meetings of Rexroth's Libertarian Circle, where he met, among others, Richard Moore, one of the founders of KPFA/Pacifica Radio—the first listener-sponsored radio station in the United States—and it comes as no surprise that Duncan viewed the Berkeley English department with impatient suspicion: in an undated manuscript probably from 1948 he called it "this Forest Lawn of the intellect."[24] By the end of 1948 he had also published his first book. *Heavenly City, Earthly City* signaled that his poetic apprenticeship was drawing to a close: he would not print or reprint any of his earlier work, written between 1933 and 1946, until, almost twenty years later, he published *The Years As Catches: First Poems (1939–1946)*. In shaping *Heavenly City, Earthly City* by carefully selecting the poems from a larger body of work but preserving their chronological order of composition, Duncan adopted a pattern which two years later informed *Poems 1948–49*. In his unpublished "Introduction" to that book he described it as "a year's work and a year's record," but the record is selective, not complete.[25] All of Duncan's subsequent books consistently maintain this pattern, some with but minor variations in the chronological order: they are all, that is to say, carefully edited and shaped.

The intense reading, learning, conversation, and indefatigable writing, combined with a turbulent and frequently anguished love-life, made Berkeley, especially in 1947–48, a vigorous forcing ground for Duncan's poetry. Three works in particular reveal his growing confidence in his developing technical skills and in the value of experimentation and exploration; they clearly mark the opening stage of Duncan's mature writing life: *Medieval Scenes*, written in February 1947 but not published until 1950; "The Venice Poem," written over several months in 1948 and published in 1949; and "The Effort," begun in October 1948 and completed some time in the spring of 1949 when it was accepted for publication; it would not be published until 1989.

In a 1977 draft of the "Preface" to the 1978 reprint of *Medieval Scenes* Duncan called it "the first poem in which I knew what I had to do from the dictates of the work itself and where I sat down to follow its course."[26] Other than knowing that on ten successive evenings he would sit down, write a poem, and then read it to his companions, Duncan did not know ahead of time what the poem would do; it thus took on the qualities of a dictated poem, and at the time he wrote it, February 1947, Duncan likened its writing process to a séance in which nothing was known ahead but at the end of which everything would—by virtue of being in the poem in the first place—be connected: a paratactic sequence over the meaning of which the poet had relinquished control. The resulting series is a remarkable melding of complex elements, not least of which is its consistent though mainly occulted reliance on what, in shared lodgings, constituted Duncan's ordinary everyday life. "The actual is riddled thru with rimes," he would say some time in 1957 or 1958.[27] *Medieval Scenes* was significant in Spicer's eyes as a preliminary form of the serial poem which became, as Michael Davidson put it, "a dominant compositional mode" for Spicer and Blaser—and, one might add, for uncounted younger poets later.[28] Duncan would subsequently (from the late 1950s on), in *Passages* and *The Structure of Rime,* himself take up and develop much of the practice he worked out in writing *Medieval Scenes:* "Writing is first," he would say in "The Structure of Rime 1" (written in 1956, gathered in *The Opening of the Field*), "a search in obedience." Long before publication, *Medieval Scenes* rapidly became much talked of— Duncan gave public readings in 1947 and 1948—and perhaps because of its general unavailability (it was published by James Broughton's Centaur Press in an edition of only 250 copies) it acquired a somewhat legendary status in its way comparable to that accorded William Carlos Williams's sequence *Spring and All,* which after its 1923 publication was because of its equal scarcity talked of but seldom read.[29]

In 1975 Robin Blaser described the serial poem as "like a series of rooms where the lights go on and off. It is also a sequence of energies which may burn out, and it may, by the path it takes, include the constellated."[30] That "constellated" neatly points to the nonhierarchical and multiple nature of the series' meanings. Joseph Conte characterizes it as "more atomistic or molecular than plantlike. . . . The discontinuity of elements in the series . . . disrupts any internal development or progression of its materials. . . . There is no initiation, climax or terminus precisely because there can be no development."[31] The poem becomes a containment, and a release, of energy. Yet Duncan nevertheless insisted on the essential contribution of any part to the whole, telling Blaser in a letter dated 18 August 1957 that "in an articulated poem . . . every part must contribute to the movement. The only reason for greater articulation is to set words, phrases, breath groups, lines into a more complex movement. To provide gasps, sighs, periods of the meaning of the poem. . . . Each line is a proposition of the total structure."[32] As an articulation of distinct words, then, the poem should be jointed or joined, as a skeleton might be intelligibly sequenced.

Throughout his mature writing life Duncan insisted that his principal concerns as a poet were formal, at Black Mountain College in 1956 outlining his course as working toward "above all our own concern with this thing calld FORM."[33] His notebooks and letters repeatedly come back to the question: on 2 July 1959 he wrote in some dismay to Blaser that "I am all but back where I was (1950) or so: isolated by my demands for 'form' from the fashions of the day."[34] When in 1948 he was writing "The Venice Poem," he noted in a review of Stravinsky's *The Poetics of Music* that "poetics is the contemplation of the meaning of form"; "The Venice Poem" explores the formal potentialities of symphonic structure to handle thematic complexities.[35] Duncan adopted themes, materials, and strategies ahead of time in this long meditation and exploration of contrasts and personal conflicts arising from the jealous rage and shock of a lover's betrayal. It draws on Williams's *Paterson,* Pound's *Pisan Cantos,* and H.D.'s *Trilogy* to weave a complex structure—what in an unpublished "Introduction" to *Poems 1948–49* he called "development by variations and counterpoint (an idea tone coming in counterpoint to the lingering tone previously introduced)."[36] Structured overall after Stravinsky's Symphony in Three Movements (with an added coda), the poem contrasts the contemporary world of his own experience (his failed love affair, his correspondence, the city of Berkeley, and so forth) with worlds of which he has only indirect experience: lantern slides of Venice, a photograph of the Venus of Lespuges, historical and art historical accounts of Byzantium, Shakespeare's *Othello,* and so on. Perhaps the poem was written *toward* what he did not know.

Duncan's assessment of Medieval Scenes, in 1978, is helpful here, and is equally applicable to "The Venice Poem": "curious, not learned; written in a certain glow of imagining the world of the poem untainted by such knowledge as might have raised any questions of belief or disbelief."[37] The matter of "belief or disbelief" is significant, for in these (and other) poems of these years he was struggling to formulate his ideas about the truth-value of poetry, recognizing—as he reiterated throughout his writing life—that the Poet is Maker: the poet makes up the poem, and in making up the poem makes up the world. Hence he would play, especially after writing *Letters: Poems mcmlii-mcmlvi*, with etymologies (whether false or true) of *make-up* (cosmetics), *glamour*, *gramary* (witchcraft, magic), and *grammar*. In a similar vein, he somewhat impatiently protested in a 1958 workshop against those who claimed to see "no meaning where I myself saw meaning" in two poems, by Harold Dull and Joanne Kyger:

> I have my obsessions; and where my spirit feeds, where there is that other mystery of orders that I find in poetry, I am a fanatic not an aesthete. I can no more adjust myself to *like* or *dislike* here than I can *appreciate* the universe. I am in-bound to the event and suffer with the event in its disregard. I cannot get the perspective where there are levels shifting that these are effects or devices *only;* for effect and device where various meanings begin their dance become The Effect, The Device, whose creature I am.[38]

"We must," says a line in "The Venice Poem," quoting Ezra Pound, "understand what is happening." *Judgment* interferes. Much later, in 1983, he would put it this way: "while you are imagining, you don't believe or disbelieve."[39] The very word *belief* invites questions of true and not true, worth or unworthiness, and closes possibility.

The third crucial poem of 1948–49, "The Effort," both explicitly theorizes his own poetics of process as discovered and refined in his reading of Pound, Edith Sitwell, Williams, and Zukofsky, to whose work—none of it at that time at all generally read or "respectable"—the form of the poem pays homage, and at the same time explicitly acknowledges an artistic and musical avant-garde with which Duncan identifies. The inclusion of painters like Bonnard and Renoir suggests something of the importance Duncan attaches to the shifting ephemeral qualities of light; the inclusion of a composer like Satie along with poets like Basil Bunting, Sitwell, and Zukofsky suggests something of the importance Duncan attaches to the fleeting impermanence of sound, while implicitly declaring his allegiance to an (at that time) eccentric culture. Following Pound's advice (which he quoted in "The Venice Poem") to "be vitally aware of the duration of syllables, of melodic coherence, and of the tone leading of vowels," in 1948 he published "A Note on Tone in Poetry" in order "to indicate how in the traind ear variations will be playd upon a vowel sound which introduces the poem"; with detailed examples he proposed that "an initial tone once sounded carries over in the mind as a bass tone thruout the time of the poem. Much of the pleasure of the poem lies in the echoes and reiterations of this sound"[40]; in "The Truth and Life of Myth" some years later he spoke of vowels as "soundings of spirit upon which the form of the poem depends" and commented that "they are the least lasting sounds in our language; even in my lifetime, the sound of my vowels alters." In "Towards An Open Universe" (1964), looking back on the breakthrough poems of 1948–49, he said "With the *Pisan Cantos* of Ezra Pound, and *Paterson* of William Carlos Williams, with the *Symphony in Three Movements* of Stravinsky, I began to be aware of the possibility that the locus of form might be in the immediate minim of the work, and that one might concentrate upon the sound and meaning present where one was, and derive melody and story from impulse and not from plan."[41] That principle is already apparent in these lines from "The Effort":

> the language resisting
> one's imperfect counsels but
> having within it an endless
> perfectability of forms

"Driven by the language itself" is how a somewhat emotionally over-wrought passage in the "Coda" to "The Venice Poem" had put it a year earlier, Duncan trying to work himself *out* through the personal *in* to the language. These three poems, two of them the longest Duncan had written to date, mark a shift in his work. They announce what is clearly the first period of his mature work, a period which, with the writing (1953–56) of the poems in *Letters* (1958), segued into Duncan's great middle period, which saw *The Opening of the Field* (written 1956–59, published in 1960), *Roots and Branches* (written 1959–63, published 1964), and *Bending the Bow* (written 1963–67, published 1968).

There can be little doubt that the mature and assured exploration, experiment, and accomplishment of Duncan's work after 1950 owes much to Duncan's initial meeting with the painter Jess Collins (who had attended a reading of "The Venice Poem" in 1949). In January 1951, the two privately exchanged marriage vows, and their shared enthusiasms propelled them over the following decades into a remarkable wide-ranging collaborative relationship, one of the great creative relationships of the century, each imagination fostering the other, reading books aloud together and discussing them, each exploring the other's métier, a common ground already there with Jess writing and Duncan drawing. "Our love," Duncan would write in *The Artist's View* in 1953, "is both the storm and the hearth of our emotional being." Together they produced a remarkable range and variety of collaborative work, from *Boob* and *Fragments of a Disorderd Devotion* in 1952 through *Caesar's Gate* in 1955, which they produced together during a year in Mallorca (1955–56), to *A Book of Resemblances* (1966), *Names of People* (1968), and beyond.

All five of these publications, along with *Writing Writing* (1964) come from Duncan's extremely prolific years, 1950–56. In 1952 through 1954 he was (while doing other work too) especially engaged in a long series of Stein imitations. Jess's collages, with their radical disruptions of context and transformations of subject, their use of juxtaposition to establish paratactic relationships to establish the work as a field rather than a perspective, their avoidance of narrative and argument, no doubt reciprocally fed similar major disturbances in Duncan's Stein imitations. Working with Stein constituted a major breakthrough for Duncan, and *Writing Writing,* which he finished putting together in 1955, played as significant a role in his writing life as *Kora In Hell* had in William Carlos Williams's forty years earlier. In imitating Stein, Duncan found a means to put away his accustomed notion of *intent,* to relinquish authorial control—as a line in "Imagining In Writing" puts it (in *Writing Writing*), "In writing I am not but am writing." In the "Preface" to *Letters* he put it in the form of a question: "to work with a constant excitement at play? this is when compositions appear as possibilities of movement. So I pursue a process of re-vision and disorganization to keep creation of the poem and consciousness of the poem in interplay." Throughout his writing life, almost from the beginning, Duncan sought disturbance at the heart of the poem; he wrote to Levertov of the excitement of deciding, "on the instant," between "the word that is surrounded by possible meanings, and the word that limits direction."[42] The Stein imitations loosened his writing by extending his permissions: installing disturbance at the heart of the writing process, they freed his syntax from habitual constraints, opened up language as *source*—not, then, as medium of expression, but as agency. "If I can see where it's going," he told Cohn and O'Donnell, "so can the readers, so we won't go there."[43] Thus, tensions between networks of possible meanings, between readers' expectations and textual actuality, energize Duncan's subsequent work: fields of possibilities resistant to conclusion, resistant to closure—the poem as open form.

Duncan's correspondence with Robert Creeley (begun in 1952), and his and Jess's close company with him in Mallorca, contributed to Duncan's increasing practice of poetry as discovery—"How will I know what I think till I think it?" was a favorite Creeley question; "How will I know what I write till I write it?"—the poem, then, as a *means* of thinking. Some years later, in "The Truth and Life of Myth," Duncan would elaborate: "I evolve the form of a poem by an insistent attention to what happens in inattentions, a care for inaccuracies; for I strive in the poem not to make some imitation of a model experience but to go deeper and deeper into the experience of the process of the poem itself," to embrace error and "be true" to it, for "a mistake is a mutation altering the life of the spirit."[44] What Duncan thus learned from his Stein imitations was crucial to his rejection, in those years, of his early work—he would not reprint or publish any of the work written before *Heavenly City, Earthly City* until 1966. In 1961 he told an interviewer, "It took me a long time before I wrote well enough for anything to be published in a collected work by me today. Unfortunately, as a college freshman and sophomore I had poems printed in a college magazine. That's a great misfortune." The poems he published as an undergraduate were, he said, "hopeless. But there they are."[45] He discusses his retrieval of that work in the "Introduction" to its republication in *The Years As Catches*. He turned his back on it because, as he wrote in his notebook in 1954, "My concept of a fruitful life is to be possessd rather than to be self-possessd"[46]; Joanne Kyger recorded Duncan's insistence, in his "Sunday meetings" at his De Haro Street apartment in 1957, that "The poem is a reality inviting you to enter, nothing to do with your personal 'self,'" and hence (as he would come to see) not accessible to judgment.[47] Assessing his early poems in 1969 (after he had readmitted them, as he wrote in the introduction to *The Years As Catches*, "into my life's work") he commented that most of them "record personal episodes as poetic resolves or pretensions. Empty, or, rather, cloudy pretensions." He favored *Medieval Scenes*, where "flesh and love [are] projected as realities of the poem, the poet himself a voice of the poem, not a claim of the poem."[48]

While Duncan was writing the poems in *Letters,* the pace did not let up. In autumn 1954 he ran a creative writing workshop at the San Francisco Public Library, through which he met and became lifelong friends with Helen Adam, whose enthusiastic persistence writing ballads reintroduced him to the ballad form, in the process reviving and strengthening in him his long-standing devotion to the uncanny and the occult. Completion and preliminary publication of an acting script of *Faust Foutu* in 1953 led to its performance in January 1955; a residence at Black Mountain College for the summer of 1956, after his long stay in Mallorca from March 1955 to March 1956, and visits to Spain, France, and England, enabled the writing and completion of another play, *Medea at Kolchis.* That fall he became assistant director of the Poetry Center at San Francisco State College, setting up public readings for poets from across the United States. Along with Blaser (who in 1956 moved to Boston and opened an intense correspondence with Duncan), he began consistently to work through the five volumes of the 1934 Soncino edition of the Zohar (he had made a start in 1953). Its aim, to instruct Man in that which is occulted, its highly associative style, its detailed multiple exegeses of a biblical text word by word, syllable by syllable, and indeed letter by letter, chimed exactly with Duncan's own predilections (and the interpretive analytical habits fostered in his childhood by his parents' dinnertime and other conversations). By the time he put *Letters* together, he was roughly halfway through the second volume, and some time, probably in April 1956, *Letters* almost complete, he commented on its title: "These LETTERS are the ones between Alpha and Omega who attend our works, the ones from A to Z, our building blocks."[49]

Letters is a significant summation of his poetic practice as it had evolved through the work collected in this, the first volume of his *Collected Poems:* Duncan's discovery and development of his own notions of what came to be called "open form," and the gradual evolution of the variety of permissions which make that openness possible. For several years before *Letters* appeared, and indeed after, he worked and reworked many of his poems, arranging and rearranging them in several lists of possible collections with titles like *Early and Occasional Poems, First Poems,* and *A Looking Glass,* as well as two titles he later used: *A Book of Resemblances* and *Derivations.* But it would not be until the middle 1960s, when he was completing *Roots and Branches,* that he could return to what he called "these poems of it seems so long ago"—the poems written before 1946— to "admit them as part of my life work," gathering them in *The Years*

As Catches (1966), his refusal to print or reprint them testimony to what in the "Introduction" to that book he called their "mistaken . . . very disturbing poetics." Yet even then, seeking to have them "stand now as establishd measures in my art and keys of my intention, . . . in an expanding structure to take them up again as conditions of my maturity," he found himself rewriting and revising the poems, sometimes drastically, thus retrospectively recasting the course of his writing life. And in 1969, going through those poems yet again (in Notebooks B and C at the Bancroft Library, University of California, Berkeley), he found himself reassessing them, finding them wanting—evidence of the difficulty he still at times had in fully embracing *possibility* as central to his poetics, writing as the pursuit not of a control of meaning but its release.

In many respects *Letters* marks an important new departure for Duncan. As he put it in an interview in 1974, it "addresses itself throughout to the idea of process"—obedience to what is happening by letting it happen.[50] Process, the exploration of open form, rests on his apprehension of language as an event, not a system, and of the poem as event, something occurring in the present. The poem is a process recording its own history as that history actually unfolds in the present, and if the act of reading is as a Making indistinguishable from the act of writing, then the act of reading, as it unfolds, necessarily includes the act of re-seeing, re-vision. It is not, then, a question of error or mistake—the poem will be error-free for it is itself an event, "word happenings," as Duncan said, "so they're always in the system of the poem. They don't symbolize something outside."[51] Intent, then, is not here the intent that Duncan had in his early work, where clearly he was working something-he-had-to-say, where the writing was something *you* as writer do; in *Letters* Duncan is beginning with assurance to let the language do what *it* wants to do, conjuring the potential, attending to the complex *social* nature of meaning. Intent is not, then, a matter of design, but of what Duncan called "response-ability," and the intent of the poem, though it will have a direction, emerges in the what's-going-on, in the writer's responsiveness to the demands and exigencies of the present moment: the poet is not Director. The poem thus comes to have at its heart a suspension of expectation, a disturbance which renders judgment irrelevant: "we must understand what is going on." *Letters* is, then, a key work following the Stein imitations of the early 1950s. As Duncan himself observed, the book points to *Passages,* a series started in 1963, "very much where I went after *Letters* . . . what I aimed at is a weaving."[52] That weaving constitutes a field, a territory which reveals itself through the act of writing, so that from *Letters* on, he would write poems which would have their place and role in the projected book as it emerged, as it declared itself. He would no longer (as he had for *Heavenly City, Earthly City* and subsequent books) trawl his notebooks for poems to put in his books of new poetry, though he would do so in compiling/composing retrospective volumes of selected and collected poems. The poems in all the books written after *Letters* thus interconnect, sound contexts back and forth, echoing and interweaving one to another, as would the books themselves and the series within them and running through them: disturbances of energy within *The Opening of the Field, Roots and Branches,* and *Bending the Bow.* Grounds.

THE TEXTS

Duncan was an inveterate and at times obsessive reviser of his work; in some instances there are as many as five or six published versions of a given poem. The complexity of the task of providing reliable texts is exacerbated by this edition's aims, for it seeks to make available two ways of seeing Duncan's writing life: from the inside, the *personal*—the work as it occurred and developed, as it appeared to him; and from the outside, the *public*—the work as it appeared to his readers as it was published. In Duncan's eyes, chronology was important—poems in his books are almost invariably arranged in chronological order of composition. The chronological imperative is, then, inescapable, but the inner, personal history is seriously at odds with the outer, public history; the two chronologies—of composition and of publication—are severely at variance. The disparity is most clearly visible in tables 1 and 2, but the dates of composition given in these tables are somewhat misleading, since some books have very few poems indeed written in the earliest year recorded in the table—in *A Book of Resemblances,* for example, only one of the book's thirty-two poems was (perhaps) written in 1946, and two in 1949, though the book is subtitled *Poems 1950–1953;* similarly, *Caesar's Gate,* subtitled *Poems 1949–50,* includes four poems written in 1955.

An early task facing the editor was to determine the order in which the books should appear in *Robert Duncan: The Collected Early Poems and Plays* (CEPP) (this is not a problem for *Robert Duncan: The Collected Later Poems and Plays* [CLPP]). The resulting table of contents matches neither table, and arriving at it was complicated by a number of factors: whether to order the books by date of the first poem in the book to be written;

Table 1. Books and pamphlets in order of publication.

TITLE	PUBLISHED	WRITTEN
Heavenly City, Earthly City	1947	1945–1946
Poems 1948–49	1949	1947–1948
Medieval Scenes	1950	1947
Fragments of a Disorderd Devotion	1952 (2nd ed. [redrawn] 1966)	1952
Faust Foutu	1953 (2nd ed. 1959)	1950–1953, revised 1953–59
*Caesar's Gate**	1955	1949–1950
Letters	1958	1953–1956
The Opening of the Field	1960	1956–1958
Writing Writing	1964	1952–1955
Roots and Branches	1964	1959–1963
Medea at Kolchis	1965	1951–1956
A Book of Resemblances	1966	1946–1953
*The Years As Catches***	1966	1939–1946
The Cat and the Blackbird	1967	1953–1954(?)
Names of People	1968	1951–1952
Bending the Bow	1968	1963–1967
Play Time Pseudo Stein	1969	1953
Poetic Disturbances	1970	1949–1960
Ground Work: Before the War	1984	1967–1976
Ground Work II: In the Dark	1987	1976–1985

* For reasons offered in this "Introduction," the 13 poems added to the second edition of *Caesar's Gate* (1972, and not included in these tables), written between 1949 and 1972, appear in the appropriate section of Uncollected Work in *CEPP* and *CLPP*. The four poems written in 1949 and 1960, gathered in *Poetic Disturbances,* are treated similarly.
** *The Years As Catches* reprinted the complete text of *Heavenly City, Earthly City,* with some revisions.

by a median date determined by an average or mean date of composition; by counting the number of poems written in each year, assigning the date of the book by the resulting majority vote; or just simply by date of the book's completion. Should *Names of People,* for instance, appear before *A Book of Resemblances?* Should *Writing Writing? Names of People* was published in 1968, but the poems were, after all, written in 1951–52, before most of the poems gathered in *A Book of Resemblances* (published in 1966). But *Names of People* is in significant ways a companion volume,

Table 2. Books and pamphlets in order of composition (dates of composition are approximate).

TITLE	WRITTEN	PUBLISHED
The Years As Catches	1939–1946	1966
Heavenly City, Earthly City	1945–1946	1947
A Book of Resemblances	1946–1953	1966
Poems 1948–49	1947–1948	1949
Medieval Scenes	1947	1950
Caesar's Gate	1949–1950	1955
Poetic Disturbances	1949–1960	1970
Faust Foutu	1950–1953, revised 1953–59	1953 (2nd ed. 1959)
Names of People	1951–1952	1968
Medea at Kolchis	1951–1956	1965
Fragments of a Disorderd Devotion	1952	1952 (2nd ed. [redrawn] 1966)
Writing Writing	1952–1955	1964
Play Time Pseudo Stein	1953	1969
The Cat and the Blackbird	1953–1954(?)	1967
Letters	1953–1956	1958
The Opening of the Field	1956–1959	1960
Roots and Branches	1959–1963	1964
Bending the Bow	1963–1967	1968
Ground Work: Before the War	1967–1976	1984
Ground Work II: In the Dark	1976–1985	1987

a sequel to *A Book of Resemblances* (both were stunningly illustrated by Jess), and in terms of Duncan's public chronology it seems immovably fixed as a later work. There is, too, the question of longer works written over several years, like *Faust Foutu,* which Duncan started writing in about 1950, whose first version was circulated in a mimeograph edition of one hundred copies by Duncan in 1953–54 and performed in 1954, and which he then extensively revised by some time in 1958, adding characters, rewriting songs and scenes but hardly modifying the plot; the first act was published by White Rabbit Press in 1958, the complete text by Enkidu Surrogate (Duncan's own imprint) in 1959. The placement of books like *Names of People* and *Faust Foutu* is an aesthetic judgment call which will inevitably excite disagreement, as will the choice of copy text for *Faust Foutu,* whose extensive textual variants cannot economically or even reasonably be covered in the annotations. Similarly, the chapbook *Poetic Disturbances* (1970) consisted of four poems, three of which were written in 1949 and then reprinted in the 1972 edition of *Caesar's Gate,* and one of which was written in 1960, reprinted in *Manroot* 10 (late fall 1974–winter 1975), and not collected into a book at all. These poems, like other works with a similar compositional and publishing history, appear in the appropriate section of uncollected work.

Establishing the date of any given poem is similarly fraught with uncertainty. Duncan habitually dated neither his manuscripts and type-scripts nor his notebook entries. Undated typescripts, typed perhaps years apart but on the same or a similar machine, cannot readily be distinguished. On those occasions when Duncan gave a date of composition, he sometimes gave the date of composition as the day he started the poem; in others, the day he completed the first—or the final—draft. In some, he incorporated the date into the text of the poem, but sometimes (as in "Santa Cruz Propositions," printed in *CLPP*) he deliberately falsified it. He was a notebook poet, working from one notebook to another, copying a poem and then redrafting it in one notebook, again in another, then returning to the first notebook with yet a new version—or breaking off mid-line and shifting to the typewriter. Sometimes he would deliberately sit down with the firm intention of writing a poem; sometimes he would find himself writing a poem when he did not expect to. Some poems were written on a paper bag or a scrap of paper on the bus; others, when he was engaged in some domestic or more or less ordinary task. He frequently, working in a notebook, would be driven to write a poem and turn to the nearest blank page in the same notebook or, as often as not, in another which was at hand. Notebook 30, in the poetry collection at SUNY Buffalo, consists almost entirely of reading notes for and drafts of *The H.D. Book,* all of them dated between 31 August and 27 December 1961, in the middle of which (interrupting a section on *Helen in Egypt* dated 21 September) is a draft of "A Ride Along The Sea"—a poem which in September 1957 had been published in *Poetry* as "A Ride To The Sea" along with four other poems. But Duncan did not necessarily reach for a notebook when the fit was upon him: in later years especially he might simply grab the nearest book and scribble all or part of the poem down in the endpapers—on 6 June 1980 (he wrote the date in line 26 but removed it from the published version) he drafted "Enthralld" on the inside back cover and endpaper, and then on the front flyleaf, of Raphael Patai's *Myth and Modern Man* (Englewood Cliffs: Prentice-Hall, 1972).

For many years Duncan was, as he records in "Working Too Long At It" (in *A Book of Resemblances*), a professional typist—he early developed the habit in his holograph letters of shifting to the typewriter to transcribe a relevant quotation and then returning to handwritten text to continue the letter, a practice he adapted in writing his poems. He began some poems writing by hand on a sheet of paper or in a notebook, then continued at the typewriter, and on a few occasions then shifted back to not necessarily the same notebook. Such texts frequently have a note, "see blue notebook" or the like. In all cases where the poem was subsequently published, there is at least one clean typescript of the complete work, but that typescript is rarely identical to the handwritten original. In his earlier years, through the poems published in *Poems 1948–49* and less frequently beyond, Duncan characteristically through-composed his poems—that is, rather than canceling a line that struck a wrong note or had somehow gone astray, he would go back to the beginning of the poem and write the poem out again, writing through the initial stumbling point—for instance there are, in the Duncan archive at SUNY Buffalo, many such false starts to sections of "Heavenly City, Earthly City," in a variety of media, pencil and pen, handwritten and typewritten: three lines, start over; four-and-a-half lines, start over; seven lines, start over; take a new sheet of paper: six lines, start over; ten lines; then, move to the typewriter and start over. Duncan wrote with fountain pen, ballpoint, felt-tip, and pencil—his practice was by no means consistent— in varying shades of blue (or even, on occasion, black, green, or red), thickness of nib, softness of pencil, and in a varying hand; it is possible as a result to sort out, at least tentatively, a manuscript sequence, but overall, accurately sorting the sequence of drafts or establishing the date of composition is difficult if not impossible. Duncan frequently, however, especially after he met Spicer and Blaser (and, later, Creeley and Olson) sent newly drafted or completed poems to fellow poets, and it is on this basis that many of the poems, where Duncan did not himself provide a date, have been dated in these two volumes.

Duncan's restlessness (he seems endlessly to be arranging and rearranging selections of his work) and his habits of revision further complicate the textual picture: When did he finish the poem? Which, of the several published versions, should be the copy text? Where should the chapbook *Poetic Disturbances* (1970) appear (if at all) in the sequence of titles constituting *CEPP* and *CLPP?* The title poem was written in 1949 and first published in 1970 in the chapbook; Duncan gave it a new title—"Poetic Forms"—when he collected it in the second (revised) edition of *Caesar's Gate* in 1972, a book in whose advertising flyer he said "stands now as volume three of Robert Duncan's collected poems." Overall between 1959 and 1972 he put together and published five retrospective collections of his work, as enumerated in table 3: *Selected Poems* (1959), *The Years As Catches* (1966), *The First Decade: Selected Poems 1940–1950* (1968), *Derivations* (1968), and the second edition of *Caesar's Gate* (1972), each of them a selection, each of them arranged with scrupulous care. Under strict length constraints imposed by the publisher, Lawrence Ferlinghetti, he put *Selected Poems* together with some frustration in 1957. To his later regret he omitted two poems from *Medieval Scenes* (written in 1947), but nevertheless included "The Temple of the Animals" and five of the ten poems making up the series "Domestic Scenes" (also written 1947), as well as one poem from 1948, "Jerusalem." None of these had previously appeared in a collection of new work, nor did he include them in *The Years As Catches* (1966); he later included them in *The First Decade: Selected Poems 1940–1950*, which reprinted thirteen of the forty-two poems in *The Years As Catches: First Poems (1939–1946)*.

Of these five titles, *The Years As Catches* is a special case in that, as the first coherent arrangement and publication of the work of his apprenticeship, it is in all major respects a collection of new work. As such, it is the book that opens *CEPP*. With the exception of the poems from his first book, *Heavenly City, Earthly City* (long out of print and prohibitively expensive), and two poems ("An African Elegy" and "King Haydn of Miami Beach") from *Selected Poems* (another scarce and expensive book), not only had none of the twenty-nine remaining poems it collects ever appeared in a collection before, but—more to the point—the book is Duncan's careful attempt to restore to the canon of his work poems on which he had hitherto turned his back, to all intents and purposes renouncing them. On the dust jacket of *The First Decade* in 1968 he spoke of the early poems as providing "those texts which at this time I see as essential for a serious reading of evolving themes and forms; and, back of those formal preoccupations I have had as an artist, I have had in mind too in my choice presenting the typology of a life-work emerging." Yet, though Duncan would read *The Years As Catches* as an act of retrieval and recovery, restoring and calling forth the presuppositions underlying and

Table 3. Retrospective collections, in order of publication.

TITLE	PUBLISHED	WRITTEN
Selected Poems	1959	1942–1949
The Years As Catches: First Poems (1939–1946)	1966	1939–1946
The First Decade: Selected Poems 1940–1950	1968/1969**	1941–1950
Derivations: Selected Poems 1950–1956	1968/1969**	1950–1955
Caesar's Gate: Poems 1949–1950 (revised and enlarged)	1972	1949–1972

* The complete tables of contents for each of these (except *The Years As Catches*) are printed in Appendix 1.
** Bertholf, *Bibliography*, 97, 99, reports the dates of publication for *The First Decade* and *Derivations* as 1969.

informing the poems of his apprenticeship, it is also clear that Duncan is there reconstituting that history by rewriting it. To retrieve is to revise, and the retrospective view afforded in *The Years As Catches* is not the same as the view afforded by the texts when he wrote or first published them. This is perhaps an inevitable outcome given the twenty or more years of gap between the poem's first publication and its revision in about 1964 or 1965, but if *CEPP* is to make available to the reader the inner, personal history of Duncan's writing life, then the copy text must, necessarily, where at all possible be the first periodical appearance. This is most glaringly obvious in the case of *The Shaman,* part of which he published as "Toward The Shaman" in *Experimental Review* (November 1940); the version in *The Years As Catches* is less than a third its length. But it is equally to be taken as an editorial principle not only because of a possibly long interval between first (usually periodical) publication and first book publication, but also because of the material conditions of publication itself. When James Broughton's Centaur Press published *Medieval Scenes* in 1950, his typesetter Kermit Sheets, to Duncan's later dismay, regularized the stanzas. He also (inadvertently?) dropped a line from "The Helmet Of Goliath," which had earlier been published (with the line Sheets dropped) in *The Tiger's Eye* (June 1948). In his own copy of the Centaur Press edition Duncan restored the dropped line in pencil, and he restored it also to the somewhat revised version printed in *Selected Poems* (1959). Similarly, when Duncan inscribed holograph versions of texts for *A Book of Resemblances* he occasionally misjudged the space available within Jess's drawing and perforce truncated or rewrote the end of the poem. And so on—to enumerate all examples, here or even in the annotations, would double the bulk of *CEPP*.

Given the somewhat conflicted aims of this edition—to make available the inner, personal history and the outer, public history of Duncan's writing life—no single editorial principle regarding copy text can be consistently and uniformly applied. With two major exceptions, first periodical appearance is taken as copy text throughout *CEPP*, with significant variations recorded in the annotations. The major exceptions are *Faust Foutu*, where the revised edition of 1959 is taken as copy text, and *Letters*, where the first edition is taken as copy text. Some of the reasons for so treating *Letters* have already been suggested in the first section of this introduction; what needs emphasis here is first that in *Letters* Duncan was beginning to be especially concerned with the notation of the poem on the page—an issue that increasingly in subsequent years came to dominate his poetics—and second, that he saw *Letters* as a single, unified project—he was moving toward a view of his work as an entire body of work, a perpetually fluid whole, of stirring interconnections and echoing resonances. On 18 March 1957 he wrote to Robin Blaser of the "formidable task" of putting a *Selected Poems* together: "It is a problem in shaping. LETTERS is for me so beautifully a whole book that I should not like to select from it."[53] From *Letters* on, Duncan conceived every book—including the retrospective collections listed in table 3, like *Selected Poems* or *The First Decade*—as a carefully composed work whose contents, as he put it, "rimed": images, sources, syntax, themes, compulsions, dictates, whatever, echoing back and forth, one to another. So too he saw each series, and indeed each book, as an essential part of the longer work made up of his entire published oeuvre, "elements," as he put it in a letter to me dated 16 June 1970, "running through the totality they belong to," a "musical complex." The musical complex was to be apparent everywhere in the work; hence he paid extremely close attention to notation, the register of sound to the sight, the appearance of the work on the page. *Letters* took the best part of a year to set in type because, as Robert J. Bertholf has documented in his 2003 edition of the book, Duncan took extraordinary care with the proofs, constantly and at times in minute detail instructing Claude Fredericks, the printer: "spaces between paragraphs have meaning (are, that is, notation, not merely typography)."[54] The text of *Letters* was achieved through close collaboration between poet and printer, and the interval between first publication of a given poem and its appearance in the book was—compared to the other works collected here in *CEPP*—brief. Of the ten poems in *Letters* which first appeared in a periodical, six appeared in 1958, six months before the book came out, one in 1956, after Duncan had sent the typescript to the publisher, and only three earlier, in 1954. The time interval between first publication and book publication is on the whole very brief, and the revisions, principally to indentation, are generally minor. It makes sense, under all these circumstances, to treat the first edition of *Letters* as the copy text.

Taken as a whole, indeed, *Letters* set the pattern for the books printed in the second of these two volumes, *CLPP*, where the copy text is almost invariably that of first book publication. Throughout *CEPP* and *CLPP* the date of composition, the source of the copy text, and the details of its periodical and (usually subsequent) book publication are recorded in the notes. Textbook anthologies are not included.

Acknowledgments

I am deeply indebted to two major archives of Duncan materials, at the Bancroft Library, University of California at Berkeley and in the Poetry Collection of the University Libraries, University at Buffalo, State University of New York. At Buffalo, I am especially indebted to Michael Basinski, curator, for generously and easily smoothing my path through the collection, and to James Maynard, assistant curator, for his alert and enthusiastic support and unfailingly generous and informed guidance through the complexities of the Robert Duncan Collection, as well as for knowledgeable discussion of Duncan's reading of Alfred North Whitehead. My work at Buffalo was greatly facilitated by the companionable and material support of Steve McCaffery, David Gray Chair of Poetry and Letters at the University at Buffalo. I am also indebted to Tony Bliss, curator of rare books and manuscripts, and Susan Snyder, head of public services, at the Bancroft Library, University of California at Berkeley; Craig Simpson, Kent State University Libraries; Kelly Brown, special collections, John M. Olin Library, Washington University, St. Louis; and Robert G. Trujillo and Mattie Taormina, special collections and university archives, Green Library, Stanford University. Vanessa Hughes and Jason Kovari, both assistants at the Poetry Collection, University at Buffalo, were more assiduous in retrieving manuscripts, journals, and books than their job descriptions perhaps demanded; their enthusiastic help substantially shortened my stay in Buffalo.

This edition would not have been possible without the substantial financial help of a Standard Research Grant from the Social Sciences and Humanities Research Council of Canada for 2008–2010, administered by the University of British Columbia, and a David Gray Chair library fellowship awarded by the Institute of Humanities, University at Buffalo, State University of New York in the summer/fall of 2008. The encouragement and support of the Jess Collins Trust has been vital to this project. In addition, I'm grateful to the Jess Collins Trust for permission to reproduce Jess's paste-ups from *Caesar's Gate*. Anyone working in the Duncan archive at Buffalo will be indebted to the detailed index to Duncan's notebooks initially prepared some years ago by Lisa Jarnot, who has herself been consistently generous and patient with my queries. I draw heavily on her *Robert Duncan, the Ambassador from Venus: A Biography* (Berkeley: UC Press, 2012), which will no doubt be standard; it is usefully corrective to Ekbert Faas, *Young Robert Duncan: Portrait of the Poet as a Homosexual in Society* (Santa Barbara: Black Sparrow Press, 1983), on which I also draw in my introduction.

A project of this scope inevitably draws on the skills, knowledge, and generosity of many individuals; I wish to record here my gratitude for their help. Some thirty or more years ago the late Frank Newby, then recently retired from the English department at the University of British Columbia, noting my interest in and friendship with Duncan, gave me his well-thumbed copies of *The Phoenix*, *Experimental Review*, and *Heavenly City, Earthly City*—cherished gifts indeed. Also at the University of British Columbia, Ada Smailbegovic and then Scott Innis were both tirelessly cheerful and thoroughly careful research and editorial assistants to whom I owe much: without them this project could not have been brought even close to completion in the time allotted. Ken Hooper, archivist at Bakersfield High School, set his class to work tracking down Duncan materials in school records and publications and was generous with both materials and energies; Pauline Butling and Fred Wah both unstintingly shared letters and papers from their respective archives and helpfully recalled their experiences editing and publishing the first edition of *Writing Writing*. The late Robin Blaser, close and beloved friend, delighted in this whole project and was unstinting with advice, recollection, information, and cheer; he was a wonderful checkpoint for factual information and recollection, and—as he had for many years—kept a sharp eye on my sometimes extravagant enthusiasms.

Few readers (I am not one of them) have the range of skills and learning to follow Robert Duncan's use of languages other than English and his reference to a range of sources extending far beyond the standard canon. For help in translation from Chinese, French, German, Greek, Italian, Latin, Old English, and Spanish and in identifying sources, I here record my indebtedness to Alexander Globe, Annaliese Schulz, Carlo

Testa, and Gernot Wieland, all of the University of British Columbia; to Susan Adams, Paul Crane, Elena Fumi, Pierre Joris, Marjorie Perloff, Joanne Rankin, and Jan Zwicky. I am especially indebted to Robert Bringhurst for advice and commentary as well as translation from Chinese and Greek, and Erin Mouré, who not only translated most of the French but also tracked down many of Duncan's sources. In cases (and there were not a few) where translators disagreed, I made my own judgment calls.

Ammiel Alcalay sent me a photocopy of textual marginalia in *The First Decade;* the late Peter Howard, great and generous proprietor of Serendipity Books, was of immeasurable help in tracking down and providing scarce Duncan items, while James S. Jaffe and Tom Wood (of James S. Jaffe Books) generously transcribed and photocopied rare items. Steve Clay of Granary Books was also helpful in my pursuit—in his case of elusive copies of the limited edition of *Caesar's Gate.* Michael Boughn and Victor Coleman obligingly and accurately answered all my queries regarding *The H. D. Book.* Michael Boughn, Colin Browne, Pauline Butling, Victor Coleman, Michael Davidson, Rachel Blau DuPlessis, Stephen Fredman, Kevin Killian, Daphne Marlatt, Jenny Penberthy, Meredith Quartermain, and Fred Wah all read and commented on drafts of the introduction, as did Mary Margaret Sloan and Christopher Wagstaff of the Jess Collins Trust. Others offering advice, commentary, and/or information include Charles Altieri, Gerald Bruns, Stephen Collis, Penelope Creeley, Crispin Elsted, Allen Fisher, Harry Gilonis, Larry Goodell, Thomas Meyer, and Richard Owens.

My thanks to Jenny Penberthy, who published a version of the biographical section of the introduction in *The Capilano Review* 3.9 (Fall 2009): 63–77, as "Disturbing Poetry: Robert Duncan's Early Work." An early version of the textual section of the introduction was given as a talk at the Poetry Collection, University Libraries, University at Buffalo, on 2 October 2008, arranged by the Institute of Humanities, University at Buffalo: Nancy Nuzzo (director of music and special collections at the University at Buffalo Library) offered helpful comments and information following this talk. A much abbreviated version of the biographical and textual portions of the introduction was, thanks to Hilary Clark and Brent Nelson, given as a talk to the English department at the University of Saskatchewan, Saskatoon, on 21 January 2010.

At the University of California Press I owe deep and lasting thanks to Laura Cerruti, who in 2008 invited me to edit these two volumes of

Duncan's poetry, plays, and noncritical prose; to Rachel Berchten, whose skill, forbearance, patience, and good humor have steered me through this challenging and at (rare) times irksome project; and to copyeditor Caroline Knapp and designer Nola Burger.

My greatest debt is to Meredith Quartermain, who gave up much of her own precious writing time and energies to this project, reading, note-taking, discussing not only many of the materials in the Duncan archive at Buffalo, but also this entire volume in its sundry versions.

This edition is dedicated to Robin Blaser (1925–2009).

•

Materials from the Robert Edward Duncan Papers in their holdings are quoted courtesy of the Kent State University Libraries, Special Collections and Archives, Kent, Ohio, and with the permission of the Jess Collins Trust.

Materials from the Robert Duncan Collection, the Poetry Collection of the University Libraries, University at Buffalo, State University of New York, are quoted with permission of the Jess Collins Trust.

Materials from the Robert Edward Duncan Papers held at the Bancroft Library, University of California, Berkeley, are quoted with the permission of the Jess Collins Trust.

The extract from Robert Creeley's letter of 3 October 1955 to Robert Duncan, in the notes to *Caesar's Gate*, is copyright the Estate of Robert Creeley and is quoted with permission.

NOTE ON DATES

On all part titles (for example, as that of *The Years As Catches* on the facing page), the date on the right is the date of publication, not of the time of writing.

The Years As Catches

Early Poems 1939–1945

1966

Introduction

These are poems of an irregularity. From the beginning I had sought not the poem as a discipline or paradigm of my thought and feeling but as a source of feeling and thought, following the movement of an inner impulse and tension rising in the flow of returning vowel sounds and in measuring stresses that formed phrases of a music for me, having to do with mounting waves of feeling and yet incorporating an inner opposition or reproof of such feeling. It was the promise of a feeling I had found in certain poems and the permission given for feeling in poetry—what men called *poetic license*—that turned me towards creative writing in my adolescence. By my eighteenth year, I recognized in poetry my sole and ruling vocation. Only in this art—at once a dramatic projection and at the same time a magic ritual in which a poet was to come into being—only in this art, it seemd to me, could my inner nature unfold. I had no idea what that nature was, it was to be created in my work. But I could find no ready voice. I was, after all, to be a poet of many derivations. Putting it all together, poem by poem and even with individual poems line by line, I have had to go by the initial faith in the process of poetry itself, for I do not know, outside of the integrity of this working feeling, what may constitute the integrity of the whole.

In 1938, when I was nineteen, I had fallen in love and left college in my sophomore year, following my lover East. That first experience of a sexual relationship took over my life. I was moved by violent conflicts and yearnings, a need to be reassured in love that all but obscured any expression of loving. The opposites playd in me: male and female, love and hate, tenderness and jealous anger, hope and fear. Here too there had been the awakening of a rhythm, the imprint of a cadence at once physical and psychological, that could contain and project the components of an emerging homosexuality in an ardor that would prepare for the development of Eros and, eventually, for that domesticated or domesticating Love that governs the creation of a household and a lasting companionship. Perhaps the sexual irregularity underlay and led to the poetic; neither as homosexual nor as poet could one take over readily the accepted paradigms and conventions of the Protestant ethic. The structure of my life like the structure of my work was to emerge in a series of trials, a problematic identity. A magpie's nest or a collage, a construct of disparate elements drawn into the play they have excited, a syncretic religion. Often only the complex pun could hold the variety needed to assert the

Real felt in the unity that excited. *The Years As Catches* I would title a poem of 1942 that caught up, in the midst of my adoration as a reader for Pound's poetics, my being carried away as a writer by a Miltonic persuasion. It is a title that haunts me still today for it seems to me that my art is indeed such a net of catches, at once a fishing around for what I can catch and what catches me at work, and at the same time a fishing by means of such catches, a music *"writ by catches, with many intervals"*, as the O.E.D. quotes from Locke, or *"for each succeeding singer to take up or catch his part in time."*

In this early period I was seeking to find areas of being thru a series of rhetorics—ransacking the theological rhetoric of Milton, the ecstatic rhetoric of Gerard Manley Hopkins, or striving to imitate the demi-surrealist rhetorics of contemporary mannerist poets—Charles Henri Ford, George Barker, or Dylan Thomas.

In 1940, it was George Barker's *Calamiterror* that most persuaded me. I used to read aloud, rapt in the intoxication of his verse:

> The Shropshire lark and the Wyoming whipporwill
> Musical in the leaves of the September tree,
> Fall with eyes blinded and with feathers seared . . .

falling in love with this poetry, as poetry lovers in the last years of the nineteenth century used to fall in love with Swinburne's rhapsodies. *"It was / The object of the physical world breaking on me,"* I would read over and over, moving towards the exciting outbreak of the following lines:

> Like Krakatoa like Krakatoa like the
> Fist shooting out of the box like the gradual
> Appearance of morning at morning like Tutankhamen
> Carefully divesting itself in public places.

Like the poetry of Swinburne and of Thomas, Barker's poetry was often polymorphous perverse in its suggestion and could admit in its tide hints and overtures of a homoerotic lure as well as its heterosexual object, as if intensity in itself were a saving grace for all sexual feeling. This poetry agreed with Freud's concept of the underlying disturbd and disturbing bisexuality of man's nature. And Barker wrote with a bright confusion that, like the confusion of my own life feeling, could sweep up in its permission what a more discerning and discriminating metric might have found difficult to manage in concert. The excitement and carrying force of these rocking cadences are still there seven years later to make for the measures of *Heavenly City, Earthly City,* where an analytic structure of emotion and experience has begun to appear but where the unity of the whole still depends upon a driving continuous energy.

I took the art of poetry to be essentially a magic of excited, exalted or witch-like (exciting) speech, in which the poet had access to a world of sight and feeling, a reality, deeper, stranger, and larger, than the world of men's conventional concerns, and I took the craft to be a manipulation of effects in language towards that excitation. At first, there had been the simple desire to evoke such a world from myself at all. That a rhetoric, having a music, could give rise to a more intense sensation of the real was lure enough. If lark and whippoorwill, leaves and tree, came so vividly to Barker's incantation, I would try such a pulsing speech to call up the things of a world that would be mine. Since I believed from the first in the magic of the poetry of Ezra Pound, I would try again and again to find the efficacy of passages in the Cantos where I could not make my way—the documentations of law and use of money—but it was Pound's autohypnotic evocation of a world in which gods and elemental beings moved that I loved. So, in the poem *Persephone* I would try my hand at it, and in the later poem-letter to Sanders Russell from 1940, Pound would be mixt with Barker:

> Its green
moves about me—birds, the still pools,
disturbd only by rain, left after rain, stilld,
coold under branches alive with mosquitoes,
shadblow and lilac. The air is blue. The air
is white, because the shad have come up the river
bearing in their bellies the pockets of roe like sand . . .

Sanders was, when I met him, sometime in 1938 or 1939, already a mature poet. In the small company of poets I have known who have been and remain for me real poets, he was the first one. He had his own language, derived from Jeffers and from Eliot and Auden along another line but having undergone a creative change in Sanders' intense meditations and speculations upon the nature of consciousness and the landscape as an object and mirror of being—well, here he was close indeed to Eliot's way:

Getting into the country of big outcroppings
with pink-and-blue dawns,
shine off glacial surfaces,
sun glare on the water, glaze off snow,
the last groves before the fields of granite,
so many water slopes down polished terraces,
high cascades, a spongy meadow
with a forest of flowers,
paintbrush, tiger lilies, and shooting-stars;
the peppermint blooms and the air is heavy with it,
the wild onion is fragrant in the morning,
and up through U-shaped valleys to the headwaters of
    the Kings.

Such a poem had its intensity of focus from a metaphysical conviction in which awareness was all, *"the motives / in exact relation to design like music."* In Pound's *The Spirit of Romance* he had remarked of the troubadours' Lady "She serves as a sort of *mantram"*, and the image which he had defined as "an intellectual and emotional complex in an instant of time" was such a mantram too. In the poem *Spring 1941: Fort Knox,* I strove to render the scene at the Army Camp true to the sights of Sanders Russell's eye, my eye, informed by a magic of perspectives and definitions of reals and unreals. My model lay in passages of his poetry that still today come with their original force:

Resistance to truth's violence
has the feeling of unreality.
Real is the story-book sight
of painted trees and painted knight.

There, in the opening propositions of the poem, are Sanders' "mind", "map", "painted tents and geometries", and his resolution to be "clear and precise." Ezra Pound's *Cantos LII-LXXI* had appeard in 1940, and I remember the Chinese cantos were always in our thought as Sanders and I talkd of what poetry could be:

Toward summer when the sun is in Hyades
Sovran is Lord of the Fire
        to this month are birds,
with bitter smell and with the odour of burning
To the hearth god, lungs of the victim

> The green frog lifts up his voice
> and the white latex is in flower . . .

But such admired exercises of poetic *virtus,* such controld strength in poetry, having the power of exactitudes and discriminations of tone, could appear as an opposite to something else I must be. For when a rhythm began in my writing it would carry me on into a dimension in which fantasy, the glow and fusion of images that the Celtic world knew as the world of fairy, would take over. Sanders thought of this as the world of desire; it fascinated him—

> the birds, the beasts, the flowers
> in the pallid world, corposant fire,
> and the cold pole star burning at its center.

But he kept it in its place. I could want to be taken over by that lure, and so, as in the poem-letter of 1940, I go on to pass over into the Barker-like strain:

> the night
> is a water swarming with birds, the great globe of rivers
> where the tanager hides to celebrate the funereal spring.
> I remember the tanager king like a fish of gold in the deep
> and the voices, the birds, that cried for the dead.

Going back over my earliest poems, I am still dismayd. What a time I had finding speech for the feeling I wanted, and how often I seem to have found speech for feeling I did not want at all. *"I want to sing these distances as lies or drown with you / in tides of this untruthful ocean,"* I find in *Passage Over Water,* a poem which years later in *The Structure of Rime XI* I was to refer to as "the first poem". But this sense of untruthfulness and lies surely reflects upon an uneasiness I felt in my own stance in writing, and then come "traps of fear", "the incalculable", "diseased with stars", "depth-bombs". A menacing, desolate and overwhelming world of feeling, overcharged, was only too ready to take over in the poem. Auden's *Journal of An Airman,* which I had read and admired as early as 1937, had contributed to its literary origins, giving its images of disease to the dis-ease my own awareness of my homosexuality brought and its images of ruin and of apocalyptic destruction to the alienation I felt from the establisht society about me. *"'O what was that bird,' said horror to hearer,"* Auden's *Epilogue* to the Journal went:

> 'Did you see that shape in the twisted trees?
> Behind you swiftly the figure comes softly,
> The spot on your skin is a shocking disease?'

And in Saint-John Perse's *Anabase,* which I read in Eliot's translation the following year, I had been drawn by his vision that seemd compounded of nostalgia and portent, of evocation and hallucination. *"Delivers to us this incorruptible sky"*—which, just now, returning to the poem, I read as "delivers us to this incorruptible sky"—would raise in me feelings of cosmos and of the corruptible, of "the incalculable" and "diseased with stars". Here too, following Eliot's first translation, there had been figures of the diseased undergoing rites of purification:

> . . . And the man tainted with gonorrhea washes his linen
> in clean water. The stools of the weakling are burnt
> and the smell reaches the rower on his bench,
>   it is sweet in his nostrils.

I saw my own personal life belonging to a larger human life that was foreign to the society into which I had been born, to the American way, to the capitalist ethic with its identification of work with earning a wage and of the work with a saleable commodity, and with its ruthless exploitation of human energies for profit. The years of the Roosevelt administration had seen the great increase of state power—an America that would overthrow Hitler's State, taking its place and standing with the Soviet Union as an overwhelming contestant for world domination—and now, in these years as I began to write, from 1937 on, the Roosevelt panacea for the ills of the profit system, the Permanent War Economy, began to emerge as a reality that would take over. My deepest social feelings then were irregular too—for I saw the State and the War as diseases, eternal enemies of man's universal humanity and of the individual volition.

So, I sought a rhetoric again that might give voice to such a view. Here, Pound would not do; for, though he had given voice to the Confucian principle of individual order, he had at the same time, as Kung did, put the State in the place of the communal order or identified the State with the human community. The apocalyptic voice of Barker, harkening back to Blake and to Milton, for the time opend a way then. I would return again to Milton and to Blake, searching out there a vision of the individual freedom and the communal commitment of man, a vision I still seek and believe I shall ever seek.

However I went about it, I had to deal with elements in which I was not to be the master. The War itself and the power of the State I dimly perceived were not only a power over me but also a power related to my own creative power but turnd to purposes of domination, exploitation and destruction. And, rereading *Passage Over Water* now, I see that the bombs of the war and the traps of the sexual bond are properties there of something else— *"the tides of this untruthful ocean."* The disregard that subconscious or libidinal forces had for truth or untruth, peace or war, troubled me. I knew from Freud that what we are most ready to call our lies betray in truth contents of our psyches we would deny. What was it that the feeling and thought in a poem, rising as it did out of a hidden resource, was true to?

Three poems from 1942–3—*Toward An African Elegy, The Years As Catches,* and *King Haydn of Miami Beach*—epitomize the, it seemd, disparate strains of my poetry. I had read Lorca's *The Poet in New York* two years earlier, and then, in the summer of 1942, in Berkeley, Rosario Jimenez read *Poeta en Nueva York* aloud to me in its own music and language. Her voice entranced and lifted the hearer into a soaring sense of poetry, and *Oda A Walt Whitman* and *Llanta por Ignacio Sanchez Mejias,* those two immortal poems of Lorca's, rang in my heart in her reading. But it was *Oda al Rey de Harlem* that most struck me. It awakend some realm of my childhood dreams, of wild and splendid animals and negro kings, and I askt for the poem to be read again and again, having the insatiable insistence of a child to hear reread favorite tales and verses. *"Negros! Negros! Negros! Negros! / La sangre no tiene puertas en vuestra noche boca arriba"* had not far to go to raise in my inner ear the opening line of the second section of *Toward An African Elegy:* "Negroes, negroes, all those princes . . ." And when I came to write the third poem of this breakthrough—*King Haydn*—the nursery rimes from Laura Riding's *Collected Poems* reinforced the childhood references that had begun. *"One, two, three, four, more,"* Laura Riding began the poem *A Second Away:*

Knock at the door,
Come in, come in,
Stir the stew,

Warm love up
In a wooden pot
And serve it hot
With a wooden spoon.

Her polemical and logistical rhetoric, the argumentative fantasies of her war with false poetry and her doubt of the truth of poetry, were to depress and haunt my mind for the on-coming years, until I would make that resolve to make up a poetry in order to sing. Laura Riding posed herself as Dame Poetry and came to suspect even herself of misrepresenting herself. Good Mother Damnable from her *Forgotten Childhood* sequence or the mother of *The Sad Boy* was foster mother to *King Haydn* and *Lovewise,* with El Rey de Harlem as foster father from Rosario's reading that summer—

Con una cuchara de palo
arrancaba los ojos a los cocodrilos

Laura Riding scolding poets seems, even today, most to be scolding the poet I know myself to be, scolding my very thinking to know and presuming to be. Describing romantics, she described how I felt myself: "They were giant-like by their dreams, prophetically swollen with dreams; instead of writing poems, they drew a swollen outline of poetry . . ." And in Ben Jonson's *Timbers* it could seem to me mine was what he called "the vicious language": "vast and gaping, swelling and irregular; when it contends to be high, full of rock, mountain, and pointedness; as it affects to be low, it is abject, and creeps, full of bogs and holes." In my notebook of 1953 from which I drew the text of my issue of *The Artist's View,* I resolved: *"I am a poet, self-declared, manqué."* Not to deny the depths, but to affirm that the shallows too, and all our waterworks, belongd to the sea. "And I had to write to him," Olson responded in *Against Wisdom As Such* in which he took me to task:

that he was neither as balanced as the sentences in this "Notebook" try to be. Nor manqué. And that he chastises himself as either more or less than he is, because of some outside concept and measure of "wisdom".

I had come under the wing of the Adversary and the accusation of falseness, of literary passions and exaggerated pretensions, bit deep. I seemd to have no authenticity; my most moving poems were not mine at all but sprang from the originals of George Barker or Saint-John Perse, Lorca or Milton or Laura Riding. But I knew too that the wing of the Adversary, the accusation of falseness and the derivations must be then true to what I was, must be terms in which I must work.

What has happend in the almost two decades since *Heavenly City, Earthly City* was written, is that I have come not to resolve or to eliminate any of the old conflicting elements of my work but to imagine them now as contrasts of a field of composition in which I develop an ever-shifting possibility of the poet I am—at once a made up thing and at the same time a depth in which my being is—the poems not ends in themselves but forms arising from the final intention of the whole in which they have their form and in turn giving rise anew to that intention. Poems then are immediate presentations of the intention of the whole, the great poem of all poems, a unity, and in any two of its elements or parts appearing as a duality or a mating, each part in every other having, if we could see it, its condition—its opposite or contender and its satisfaction or twin. Yet in the composite of all members we see no duality but the variety of the one.

Nor is that one myself. It may be my *Self*, as each poem has its poetry, its Self or How It Is Made, in the process of Poetry itself. So, we come to understand the poems of Whitman or Dante, of Edward Lear or of Shakespeare, as belonging finally to the process of an art. That One or Self may be Man. And we write at all, in order that Man, however he can in us, still be a poet. But that One is the Cosmos—as early as *The Unresting* I seem to have begun to see that; and Man, one of the many poems in which the Cosmos seeks to realize its Self.

One of the factors in my returning now to these poems of it seems so long ago—other lives and other worlds ago—is that I would admit them as part of my life work. Certain of them have always been clearly realized as parts of what I have to do in the art: *Toward An African Elegy* or *King Haydn of Miami Beach*. And now, after some years of reaction against the poems of my first publisht book, as if they were mistaken in their poetics, I have seen them anew in making this collection and would bring that very disturbing poetics into the works. *The Berkeley Poems, The Apollonian Elegy* and *Heavenly City, Earthly City* I mean to stand now as establishd measures in my art and keys of my intention. As once I moved away from them, putting them away as immature things, now I move back or out in an expanding structure to take them up again

as conditions of my maturity. The rocking cadences of *Heavenly City,
Earthly City* are to be felt in the most remote, in the most immediate,
structures of my music to be. Every created entity creates thruout time
and space of creation. Thus, the poor poet in his imagining casts a reflec-
tion upon the nature of the creative will of the great sun from whom this
life that imagines has come. We see the sun anew.

Persephone

"We have passed the Great Trauma. These wounds disclose our loss."

memory: farfields of morning,
        maimed winter, wheel and hoofhammered weeds,
bare patches of earth. We heard rumor of rape
among the women who wait at the wells with dry urns,
talk among leaves and among the old men
who sift tin cans and seashells searching for driftwood
to make fires on cold hearthstones. Stone hearts
and arteries hardened to stone.
                    This sound of our mourning . . .
                        wailing of reeds,
comes over the ice and the grey wastes of water.
We listen: it shrieks thru the ruins of cities,
whistles in shellholes
and freezes like ether in our lungs

Shades falling under the oakshadow . . . shade upon shade,
intent with their sorrow. The lust of such sorrow
listless, moving over the leafmold,
footmolded and hoofmolded, spoors of past violence.
From such clay our roots writhe, sucking the life
from corpsemold and footclay
and mold of the skull rooting.

Spore-spotted Onan, baldheaded, trickling with seed,
moved among us, or troops of swift women pursuing the leopard
passed. The quiet unbroken, dark beneath dark
branches spotted with light; or a flute in the morning

made truce, awakening the leaves like birds.
We shot green from the bark to flute music,
moving out from the trunk in a dream.

The sun was like gold on my body,
roots in the cold dark below me and arms
from the slender trunk showered in gold light and shadows,
fingers green seeking the sun.

Lost, lost such peace and Persephone lost.
Last dream brought silence,
silent thread of death-threatening dream.

We remember in symbols such violence:
the splintering of rock, the shock of the trauma.
Shade falls under the shadow . . . shade upon shade,
spotted with bonewhite, splinter of driftwood,
the bark wet with terror, no sleep,
only waiting. Only we wait, our wounds barely healed
for the counterattack before sunrise.

Passage over Water

We have gone out in boats upon the sea at night,
lost, and the vast waters close traps of fear about us.
The boats are driven apart, and we are alone at last
under the incalculable sky, listless, diseased with stars.

Let the oars be idle, my love, and forget at this time
our love like a knife between us
defining the boundaries that we can never cross
nor destroy as we drift into the heart of our dream,
cutting the silence, slyly, the bitter rain in our mouths
and the dark wound closed in behind us.

Forget depth-bombs; death and promises we made,
gardens laid waste, and over the wastelands westward,
the rooms where we had come together bombed.

But even as we leave, your love turns back. I feel
your absence like the ringing of bells silenced. And salt
over your eyes and the scales of salt between us. Now,
you pass with ease into the destructive world.
There is a dry crash of cement. The light fails,
falls into the ruins of cities upon the distant shore
and within the indestructible night I am alone.

Toward the Shaman

{As we move together, as we open our mouths upon each other: a build-
ing falls; flowers open into the consuming eye of the moon where
            rivers run to the sea, lunar, dark waters, movement of fish as
thru mucous. And Fear lies where our families wait behind lockd doors —
    They have cast a shadow of destruction upon us — the Police raid at
twelve, hangings in the darkwood, weeping. The Beast is back. And the
Judge, omnipotent, unjust, sits at the entrance of Allwomb tracing the
scars of guilt across our faces; the word that betrays us dissected. The
drawing scribbled in the sand by the children has trapd us within its
intricate lines.

As we move:
            stars fail forever; a child of twelve walks pregnant thru the
rain, eyes like openings into death and a dead bird caught closed within
her hand. Cathedrals clotted with the shit of doves, the bells deadend,
and those slain in battle lying under the whirling sky of snow hear a ring-
ing in their ears forever. All the glasses turn. And the windows of insan-
ity open where the madmen give warning, eyes crossd, tongues stuck
out, exhibiting their genitals, giggling.
    We giggle, and the Hunger-moron crouches under a sky burning the
sky with the Sun.
    Protect us! the beauty of grass shoots from the earth save us!
    Ants swarm over the axle of steel.

*I cling to you. Stay beside me for you are like the strength of young trees about
me: you are like the desire of the earth after rain within me* — even as I move
upon you:

a mare foals in the stable by candlelight. Far to the west the dawn breaks over vineyards and barren hills, over gardens and grave-yards in the valleys. They dance in the cafes of the world, screaming and laughing, horns blowing, brass and screaming into the night, into the far rooms of sudden death. They dance bombs dropping into the open and flames in the great cities

dance wombs broken open with violence.

Men wander among the ruins. The threat of the Colossus towers above the city where it is worshipd. A music is made with sirens and steel, the breaking of glass and the drawing of nails over these surfaces of slate. A music is made with the scraping of the bone so that this woman screams and the baby's nerves go dead.

They ride into the silence within the blasted eardrum. The spectral horse tramples the slain. The air about them dusty and shaking with explosions. Gas rising about them.}

Where is peace? the regions of light flooding the body, shadows under water quietly and the rustling flight of swallows over fields of grain? where are the looms and the carved pillars of the kingdom I seek, the little forests of trees, green, undisturbd, and the deer passing thru them?

It is thru you that I prepare for the sea.

JOSEPH, overlord of the lower kingdoms, whose warehouses are full in this time of famines, how silently you come upon me. For on the table of this house a meal has been set for two people of cornpaste and pome-granates. We shall sit down to eat the mysterious fruit from its hives, staining our fingers; and we think of the lonely cattle going down upon their knees in pools of dust and the great bows of their ribs and the blind snakes hidden in the rock. We put a tango on the gramophone dancing where desire rises, the orchestra sobbing from the memory of a summer's love. Tonight we can find love where we left it.

{*Come to me tenderly, put your hands upon me like a gift of fear.*}
But we have been waiting: the day slips from us, the levels of water fall, light falls revealing a canyon, and the dog walks thru the rooms of the house searching for someone. One who is not with us.

{Let us remember where we stood together in a time of power reflected thru time; let us recall a dream adolescence of nude boys under fig trees.

But the orchard below the house is leafless; rooks caught in the branches of trees decay in the wind and the sharp sticks creak under a grey sky. We think of travel, a journey to be made: for we own nothing, and we pass into the way of those who search out a new land, of explorers in a territory where defeat has left wheels and the broken axle, where defeat has left the bones of horses.}

Some would wait, building a house of stone near a spring in the mountains. But the spring drys, disease eats the stone, and there can be no stopping, no waiting. A man stands on a low cliff of red earth with his hounds seeing a swallow fly up from the ruins of his house. They build their mudnests over a wall away from the sun and a time comes to go south. Or this son whose father has built a great factory, returns after a long absence, wanders among the rusted tanks, camps where an arch of fired-brick stands from the rubbish, and at dawn moves on.

You who have chosen this valley between mountains, lover of deserted seas, of stranded ships, lover of insects singing at dusk and the wild young men who gather near the warehouses and light a fire in the dark, light shadows of horns, piping their music under the fallen trestle. You with the dark eyes waiting — your love is a delicate treachery; your touch uncovers a desire to wander, a geography of migrations.

{HERE
a few bearded men dry nets in the waning light at low tide. Boys who are barefoot sit on the rocks repairing the nets, talking among themselves of leaving this place. And behind them out over the tide-flats, the marshes, saltcrusted, the universe of birds. The great heron booms in the marshes. Gulltracks in sand, a litter of shell, deserted nests, straws, dungs, feathers from a season of love. The departure from Babylon.

Look Here! if you doubt this, you who prepare such desolation in the territories of the soul, that this crossing will be made. Consider these movements.}

Night comes in forever over the tidal landscapes forever thru waves of saltgrass, and we sigh together finding a sheltered place against a wall that was left standing. A small band of outriders and their women are campd in a hollow far below us. We see their fires and we hear the broken talk on the wind. The last glimmer of a distant windowglass disappears in darkness. Everything gone, and the great voyage opens: the cities have fallen behind us, flames at the curved roof of the world {and the rooms of conquest destroyd by bombs, the gigantic gardens consumed and so many lost. Those whom we knew, those whom we met in beds, in coverd places.

Crossing over was easy and crossing back early, but I am weary in my aloneness. It is a long bondage; and I came to find that there was the surface of a mirror between myself and the image of my desire, and the green world of the past was lockd out forever.} Who saw it slipping? A man enters the room with a gift of keys and we must choose between doors. Stop! we have been trapd. I saw a shadow like a snake over the garden. I saw the last tree discoverd by the enemy and the new leaves revolving in their caskets: a dream of origins.

Maps are cast of the regions we are to pass thru guided by a compass which is allergic to everything. A journey thru the immeasurable regions of the dream, a crossing over thru the surd again, the square root of the human experience.

from A LETTER TO SANDERS RUSSELL *(May 1940)*

We set type, pump water, empty the buckets,
sit in the outhouse at night hearing the frogs sing
and the late spring rains run from the shingled roof.
Or during the day we dig in the garden, stir roots,
and pile a little wall of stones between pine trunks,
knowing that these flowers must be left behind,
that walls will be broken thru
and the quick grass spring up when we are gone.

I had not known, not in your country of great trees,
or of pine forests, or extrusions of granite where silence
made the wanderer uneasy — where as in a cathedral
space curved overhead too huge to be encompassd:
I had not known the intimate forest.
The green world moves around me, birds, the still pools,
disturbd only by rain, left after rain, stilld,
coold under the branches alive with mosquitoes.

Shadblow and lilac. The air is blue. The air
is white, because the shad have come up the river
bearing in their bellies the pockets of roe like sand;
and the delicate trunks of their trees
reach into a cluster of torn flowers.

Eggs are laid, rutting goes on and the tree buds.
In this year where time and space in a dreadful unity
curve toward the regions of Capricorn, the maniac regions,
we can trace the intricate veins that cross over — you find
the salamander that dances in his house of fire: and I,
born at the thin end of the year in a time of war, I find:
like nets between the dark past and the dark coming, waters
swarming with birds, with finches, the great globe of rivers
where the tanager hides to celebrate the funereal Spring.

I remember the tanager king like a fish of gold in the deep,
and the voices of the birds at night that cried for their dead.

Remember the wounded trees,
                              call up the horses that were murderd.

Mock spring: to see the earth this year
renewing, greening, leaf-bursting; to feel a peace
steal up in the half-shadow under the darkening trees,
to remember a lover — when in Europe the evening is gone,
the time of nostalgia, of dreams and love is gone,
and Fear has destroyd the quickening Spring. The Sun
has begun his long journey beneath the earth, and we see
already the night-madness, the fireworks of death.
In this country the disease sets in, disturbs the bone,
and Fear prepares the homicidal streak, the bombings,
the great advances and the great retreats until over the waste
a last lingering bell is heard ringing, a cloud of gasses
curls over the colleries; dust flies up from a falling facade.
. . . . .

You ahead, who have seen the flight of wings within a flame,
known the strength of your isolations, opening no doors
outward for invasions —I, being invaded, so that peace

is troubled and the clear light shadowd, am alone at last,
wander between worlds, compelld onward, lingering.

{I had not believed so much as loved
and love turns back. It is thru N. that I have come
to this place, to these powers, and now, on the other side,
he cannot hear me, nor the sound of seas moving, nor the pull
of tides. He has been lost, lost from me in a room
among books, where the sound of cannon was heard
and the smoking city encircled the heart.
                              Is there no turning back?
A way to turn back into the dark countries.
The longing is great and there is no fulfillment here, no peace.
The flutist in the modern world wanders seeking his loved one,
and I, I have known this for a long time, enterd this world
knowing that I can go little farther, waiting for him
to cross over. These things that I write have been in vain;
they have been songs with no powers, words turning no worlds,
not passwords. These poems were only a place I created
that he might pass thru. And he has turnd back.

I will sit forever on this shore watching for ships;
The stars will call up my longing at night, and whipporwills
cry in the lonely grove of the solar plexus. Let the moon
go down forever into the water and the rain like music
run forever thru the bone and the last empty ship drift in.

In the spherical consciousness everything takes place.
The journey and the far shore where I wait in the harbor
are simultaneous. Night and day lying upon the wheel of time
so that one cannot say that night comes in first
because the memory of a morning world is always present;
that the journey comes first, or loss before the journey.
And even as I wait — I pass on into the interiors
knowing that the time will come when waiting will die out,
disappearing like a word spoken into time past
where I cannot be found. Only I will be discoverd at the rock
in the harbor of some future love, a dream of a past life
that was his own: and he shall know that I have passd thru.
. . . . .

The man's body in the leopard's skin can control leopards.
The shepherd dressd in a cloak of red wool
walks among his sheep.

Let us speak of a revolution:
there is no movement apart from movement. What will die
destroys itself and is destroyd by the living.
The death of the father is a suicide and a murder,
and the son's birth creates and is created.
We at this time invade territories of consciousness
where few travel; yet all things have their existence there
as the roots of all continents merge in the sea;
and the great movement of revolution takes place
where the god with hair of fire emerges from his cave.

What you have done and are doing has been
an opening of doors for me; your words arm me,
preparing for entrance and an explosion of light.

THE GIANTS HAVE DIED. They fall in wild canyons where the swift water strangles with hair and their great bodies are crusted with weeds and with sand. The places where they built their fires are soakd with rain. Geese fly up from the shallows; and pools of dark liquid lie in their mouths, their eyes staring upward fixd on the blue untouchable stars.

A messenger who speaks like a thief stops in my courtyard carrying news to another place, and the servant girls gather about him under the thorntree.
Something has happend that will force us to move on.

They perform the forbidden circles, the ceremonies of urination. Hidden behind the dunes the Horse-man led by the urnings makes maps in the sand: *Here is the gateway where they gather whispering like lizards on the rocks. Here, the dark rivers come toward their caves, and these lines —*
the way over . . . .

I walk on and out onto the beach in the cold light carrying my naked body secretly, the hollows of the belly like talismans in the night, the hair mysterious above the penis. It is a time of priesthood, of rituals. A time for woodwinds over the wide earth, a season of fasts when no beast shall be killd, and on this side for some, a time of weeping. Pipings in the greenwood at dawn. Noon for the Bride of rivers. And dusk, dusk is a time for nearness, the agony we have in separation: from the gardens of the past, from those we love, from the wells of light, from the identity of water.

Because of this wound I return to this place.

The sea has gone out, leaving weeds and timbers in its wake. I hear it. The bottomless source of my strength and destruction in the darkness. This place is the perpetual shore of my separation where I walk, a creature imprisond in earth, lockd in the misery of the conscious ego, isolated, alone in the white light over the beach. The shapes of wreckd ships loom like skeletons in that light, the bars of ribs, the great gateway of the pelvic bone; and far away, lying huge over the wet sand, the body of a whale left by the sea, black and poisonous, left alone, terrible in a litter of tar and kelp.

Why is it my love poisons? that whenever I reach out there are wounds inflicted, wherever I turn I feel that my need leaves a wound?

It is the time for longing again, of longing to return to the sea, for even as I was cast up, even as I rose out of the cold waves of morning before the daylight broke over the earth and as I have haunted for so long the cities of desire, I have one desire beyond all their desires — the desire to return to life, to be part of life, without ego. But I have died up into the separation of all things in their way upon the earth. This body I have for communication: and as our mouths open into each other I speak to you wordlessly, organically. But where the word is spoken, I have conceald myself with deceits so that I may never extricate myself.

I would strip myself of protections; I would stand in my nakedness before myself, but my fear of the torture of such reality is too great. I am afraid to come upon myself, upon what is really happening. I am divided from it. Even in the dream I am what I believe myself to be. At this time only this I can reveal like a deep wound that cuts thru me: the longing to return.

HOW BEAUTIFUL ARE THE BOYS IN THE WATER! Their eyes are like flowers heavy with pollen and the long curve of their bodies is a betrayal for sailors. A man who has seen their thighs in dreams and the magic hair that grows from their secret places — such a man walks among the rocks and washes his feet in the waves. Or he will take to the sea in a boat by himself, fishing with nets, extending his powers over the sea, dreaming of a boy caught in his trap of ropes among the spheres of glass. And they have gone down, down, down into the singing shell-caves of water seeing before them their shell-like boy, the pale tragedy of his back and his buttocks that drive the hands crazy. They have gone down under the waves in the evening into the deep wells of death grasping his waist in their adoring hands into the last long kiss where the flower closes and the endless night begins.}

A monk watches the Prince in the garden under the fig trees, his hair like a birth of gold: remembers an empty ship drifting on the open sea and the shadows over its sail.

IN THE KINGDOM OF CHILDHOOD, thunder is heard beyond the mountains. Saint John of Persia walks beside me, the hooded one, master of falcons; and the meadows below us are heavy with water. The shadow of a cloud falls across the land, the hedged fields and the rivers between fields. Voices of boys who play baseball near the Armory.

"Peace is like a deceit upon this land —" I say, "for in such a time of quiet I feel its absence most sharply."

{He smiles, touching my body with his hand, a knowledge of peace. It is not among them for me. Always beyond, it lies like a disease in the body where the choice was made, and the route ahead or the route back is difficult.

I think of N. whom I loved like one defeated. I think of the sickness of my love at this time; a fear of impotence lies upon me.} I am the traveler without a compass, sunless. The power which comes is only the emana-tion of the loss of power. The sun is gone from us. In the harbor the last fire dies among the masts of the abandond whalers. A wind comes from the far side of the valley with rain.

The Saint of Persia walks among the shepherds where they stop for the night. Sodomites — men who lie with their sheep.

A young man in a cloak of goats-hair brings a gift of black horns and water.

Consider these men: consider the striped tents among the pillars of smoke; for this is no pastoral. I would create a way of being. I would bring a gift of unrest among men

and give praise for the man within himself, the wanderer, the man who goes apart in his own way; for these men driving the goats across the plain who stop by the well and joke with Ursula, the mother with many tongues; for the beauty of stones, of reeds, of cruelties, of deer, of words in the man's spirit; for the gymnastics; for the navel like the center of the world above the bone fissure; for the different ways of coming together.

An Ark for Lawrence Durrell

If we are to cross the barriers of snow
into the cave-home of our childhood, dark
among darkened lights, telling our beads,
if we are to cross over the wheel of night
and dwell among the roots of sorrow —
let us take with us the fox, for he is quicker than our sickness;
let us take the cock, for he remembers the day
and leaps for light. And let us take
the white-haired ass who is gentle
and bows his head.

The snake has his own way among us.

The Awakening into Dream, Love There:
Out of the Dream, and Our Beautiful Child

Closed in the heart the hurt world
breaks its shell of bone and dies,
and the tiny foetus curled
in his casket opens his eyes
of dangerous green. Seas roar
across their burning beaches where the beasts
rear raging from the breakers. More
gulls fly, cormorants fly, and shining feasts
of fish flash silver thru the tide.
My slight-of-hand flesh darts out, and Hairy Head
harpoons the body, snags the heart : spears hide,
spears bounding tissue and bright blood, red
at the center, caught: spears the quick soul
and the bird in the sun from his nest of hair.
The veils of water draw back and the whole
skull is revealed in sand beneath the singing air.

A History of My Family

Cyclop over cyclop in the myopic dawn of the world,
their gigantic genitals rising out of the mists,
south over Asia, the penises blue where they were bitten,
mushroom edge torn back, and forests over the edge of earth
splitting with dust. Needles and fur.
M.
Triumph of the egg, the bird flies.
More beautiful than chicken wings,
more beautiful than ragtime for eleven instruments,
more beautiful and the hen cutting a hole in the sky
with her beak than the sun and at night the mole
crying in the swamps under the blue light. Bird
at the head of the cyclop, conception of yolk. Bird,
conception of white at the cyclop's ear. And the Bird
in death under the sinister lip, the shell.

We went west from the isles of Langerhans
under the pressure of the sun beating the whip behind us,
and as we passed, the water in pools lying still
and clear without source, blue with poisons and salts,
and in cavities and under the rocks in sockets
the cysts hanging in clusters. And where we passed,
a little dry blood where we stopped to drink.
Out over the plains and at night under the sky,
blue with poisons, cyclop over cyclop in the dawn,
we small ones saw not clearly, only the largest of shapes
in the distance, the white shining penis,
the cunt lined with furs and hemlocks
and at night heard the sounds of the wild chicken.
We had not thought then of cages,
Nor owned any land.
And where we stopped. Tin cans.
The rusty tins of tuna fish. Neat piles of shit
in trenches that we dug, and broken glass.
And we pass. Steel knives.
Our hymns of voyage. Shouts of hate.
The hunt, the disappearance of the dodo.

Giants die. They fall in wild canyons,
the water in winter strangles with hair,
and their great handsome bodies crusted with weeds
and with sand, and pools of dark liquid lie
in their mouths, these eyes staring outward
fixed on the blue untouchable stars.

un da eeko ta a eeki

un da mala ta a aka ak

Over the cliffsides of slate
south of the great red place
we scribbled the names of the ancestors,
numbering the sick and the wounded
and those that gave birth during voyage.
Drew maps of the universe.
Twisted the lines of the stars

over the races of the unborn.
And this one, the man whose tongue
gave root to wild flesh
so that it burned,
this one counted those that were left,
remained at the branching of rivers
and made a mark for each
white on a boulder.

Fragment: 1940

I am liable in the late afternoon
lingering to remember in the various cities
the familiar streets, clock-tower, magnolias,
to remember, reconstructing yet not
faultlessly as then, for the singular vision
has departed, reconstructing the cities
in sand, not faultlessly, roughly,
impatiently—indicating only a shadow
multiformd as the flame shifts
over the treacherous passage of time—
so that from this hill nothing is seen
or from a valley the world is emprisond,
hopelessly bounded, on all sides
the primal limitations of a single court,
the first gateway endlessly repeated
so that the beyond is always beyond.

A Spring Memorandum

The year has run thin through the turning room of my mind
to have its spring in this desert's prison. The tree
from my heart, quick and green, dies at the throat's door
in the black and cannibal sun. As I turn back
the dust shifts and the glaring landscape bleaches the root.
We lie on our bellies in the white blaze. The eye tires,
and the black target—the spot of a man's lung plate,
or, as the sinister thought dictates, the soft navel eye,
the beautiful inner chamber of his body—bursts,
shivers upon the level edge of the front sight. In this way
we are made strangely innocent killers. Gonzales,
Daniel Garcia and I talk in a quiet moment
before mess, remembering the September fiestas,
the flowers' whirl in the sun's eye, or recall
from a waltz-time the mid-summer saxophones,
the earlier weddings. We speak of the Mexican cities,
sprawling, white unbelievable refuge, beyond us;
or at night we hear from some other barracks,
distant as the freedom of hills, a Texas guitar
and the prisoner's blues. If I had those wings
this bird would fly homeward, up from this guard-house,
over the hill. There is between us this desire
to be free, a silent territory in the cell; slow
to the kill, deliberate, the last shadow lifts
and we stand at attention in the mechanized day.
· ·
The eye and the band which trembled
when it first took the pistol grow steady
directed to murder. In his two dimensions
the flat man is easily shot: a small triangle.
He might have been loved.
it would have been harder.
                              Abstracted, his heart
may be plotted and a new gas devised
to deaden the nerve ends.

Dead.

Like the smell of wild apples
Like the smell of geranium
Like the smell of the hive broken open:
it is human to murder.

. . . .

Look! I am not native. I am a fox caught,
baited, clamped. I will daw my way free
from my own flesh, spring the lock at the wrist
leap out, away, power-dive to the darkness,
bleed to the wood, to run the red river
out of this body. I am not of this kind.
Green bark was my mother. My father is
Death, the most wild and the free way.
                              I am not of this kind,
inventors of cages, of nets, traps. Marches
hut two three four. Their white hairy God
stalks toward the Dead-thing, smells God-corpse
and grinning devours the rotten Sun.

. . . .

Or, because I love you, can there be life then
putting out branches to cover these wounds.
The Always, our dream of tomorrow, to be
more real than this country: consider,
the leaves of light that appear forever, here,
even in this wilderness, tormented by God.
Enormous worm, turning upon Himself in His cyst
disturbing the night with His love, who
has seen Him? I found at the trunk of his tree
a discarded body like dry paper, called,
Child of the Earth. Where
has He gone? The Never, suddenly realized,
has come to destroy us, to eat up our love.
Terrible Calendar of Days, is this
more bearable because we dream, or love
because the life roots are stubborn? The Again
is the sap rising under the horn-hided tree
to force out each bud to the hungry day

A Letter to Jack Johnson

Bakelite inhabitant of death, I see, when I have forgotten the green
and the opulent meadows, the direct skull which you push through the
skin to kiss life. I see when the trees have fallen under my hands of
dishonor the enormous beaked birds of desire; I see the corn kernels we
have scattered together break in the fields of cement and expand.

The casket is lowered into the mind's waiting cellars. I have ordered a
Waltz in its variations. Belvedere doorman, braided, metald, announcing
perpetually Night: whom shall I dance with? I open my wings to disclose
my other face and I find your eyes in the dark.

Let us remember the play and make our entrance with feathers. I shall
cry O lesbian fear! and you shall turn the many fine segments of your
body into despair. I shall mount the infernal cage of the Hesperides, beat-
ing the air in the radiant West. A roar fills the curve of the actual world
and I see you transformed, immovable like a witch-doktor in the lunar
eclypsis on a checkerboard table. I see you win over the knight whose
horse spreads disease in Bishop's Fourth; I see you defeat the Queen at
the junction of Impossible Victories.

O I am willing when I have seen the clear water withered to come
home to death. I am waiting under these wonders, these stars, my conceits.
I am waiting and wandering only in dreams as far as your threshold. Only,
if I lift my hand thru the surface, curved like a message, if I leave my right
hand with its five staring fingers as a gift in the wax, I will come home
to your solitude. Death's sirens, death's musical women and hunger will
come out of the subways and into their harps. When you blow you will
find in the trombone my hair like weeds in the water return on the music.
secret and plan for
I hear here already
Death's hurdy-gurdy. Plan for
a closet for the partial
continual arrival of me
> I shall be drawn thru in music
> I shall be drawn thru in pain
> I shall be drawn thru in delirium
I open my mouth to contain the last glass of our bridge toward the
waves, the magnificent structure, so long debated, disappears in the sea.
Silent. No deep sound to it.
The room we have together is like a diving bell.

An Encounter

His eyes are like mine so that I realize
his brain is much too bright,[1] and when I move
about the room or sit as I sit now
listening while they talk of art, I remark
how he follows every movement, how he speaks
a net of words to catch the leaping fish
his fear, and how the fish darts out,[2] uncaught.
The room has been disturbed by this violence
in its dimensions; and I feel[3] sitting apart from it,
the giddy recurrence of the speaker's distortions
observing how the reed mats on the floor lead back
into the depths of the inner room, into the contortions
of space as a mystery. Ethel lets down her black hair
and sings a song in German softly and he asks:
"Are you insane?" His eyes are restless,[4]
having no intent nor answer so that we look back

[1] even the sun is not larger in its terror
   as spots appear like murder or like rarer flowers
   where we tried to touch its centers.

[2] or as fishes' kiss partakes of cruelty
   spawning against our drunken tongues,
   pissing in the wide and deep water.

[3] nothing at all: idiot dancer! like a mirror
   opening carefully the box-like faces
   of the unprepared, the weak, the children.
   I have a private hound's hunger for the disease
   that lies inside the others.

[4] finding in me the race's criminal father
   or a blazing night, a fire-field of martyrs;
   finding in me a saint's burning grandfather;
   finding in me the cannibal saviour
   eating his own organs, devouring his tongue,
   the manroot of flesh and the internal circus.

each into our own eyes, seeing[5]
the endless perspective of question.
His abstractions avoid the ultimate decision
how can the room itself be faced or the derision
of these others in the room, would-be Gods[6] with voices
and eyes at tension, wooing the distance between them.[7]

[5] the wild okra sprouting with unbearable seed
between the sheets of the bed for All-men
(finding seed upon the floor like snakes
among the skin and bones of gutted boys).

[6] say that they are of some sexual origin not human,
carrying inside the consumed men and women
as a terrible gift for their children in labor.

[7] we have brought these identical skulls
to exchange for large and absorbing eyes
in the gardens of plant-people,
devourers of love. They are like huge melons,
warm and sweet and without danger,
lying asleep under the parted leaves
of their green early mothers.
Where we find them we eat
their rare breasts, we eat their tongues
curling like apple fronds and we lie
in love's jungles of tall grass, in perpetual noon—
or their blood is a rare wine, indeed,
and God's hand there is like a melon's quiet.
I too have seen how difficult, how heroic,
are the oral manipulations of soft pods and buds,
of small furry animals and hysterical dogs.
I have seen cruelty like an inside flower
unopened—or in dreams, the human joy
cut the belly of the wide day into a knife,
the human laughter explode within the child
and leave the blackened head
to hang upon its neck of murder like a speech;

the human love is more than a bayonet,
more than a knife or a nail, more than a fang

Once it is opend, the lovers are tremendous,[8]
like destroyers in the grey waters about them,
staring into the unfulfilld space,
with no space in them,
hungry and desperate among their chairs and tables.
Any stranger is dangerous, holding perhaps
the locks of self, who may release a flood.
The man in the room knows this, knows
the mutual betrayal of the opposing speakers,
each as God, in each a separate universe,
and so he watches for the enemy's appearance
in each eye

                                    in my eye
I see the water dripping continually in the shadow.[8]
I hear the voices of children using no words.
They are like birds or small animals in the trees

---

    driven into the flesh. I have opened a fault;
    I have thrust thru your body
    into the abyss that you conceald.
                  The tall women
    in dreams have opened into their sea-lockd rooms
    and threaten the desertion that lies in time.

    It is not death's cunning face that we found here,
    not that spider-monkey's, tho he was present.

[8] and I have found nowhere in the endless river
    that pours from my body that cover to hold him
    in the torn arms of my wings or to open the jaws
    of my face so that he can search for bullets
    in my throat's delirium, and I have found nowhere
    in the blood and seed of my anger
    that lover to take into the rooms
    where my cannibal fathers have prepared
    the wrinkled mummies of love.

(*Editor's Note:* As published in *The Ark* in 1947, Duncan's text has two note signals for note 8, but only one note so numbered. No manuscript of the poem has been located.)

talking together. And in the room we wonder[9]
whether something will happen as he tries
to define the element, wanting it hardened,
to be held in the hand, turnd like an endless stone,
wanting it known in this way, to be examined
and eliminated. This is perhaps better.[10]
We have met none of these dangers squarely;
but I see always the many other eyes of God
like a great clustering vision of the Fly
seeing in all directions, and I know that I
have not seen what you see or what the other man sees
who senses, while he talks, a demon in the room.

[9] how it is always there, booming in the caverns of why
   in the inner ear where sound is made from nothing
   your hair reveals no shore but water
   everywhere
   a bird in no form nor likeness flies
   merely as motion from no source
   within the sea that fills all space we know as rain
   or feel as depths
   with its singing restless ease
   of unreality

[10] I came into your bed because I wanted to kill myself
   and so we shall begin that dance immediately in the
   familiar darkness altho we know that it will crack
   open and the feathery sun's crow wake us into a day
   larger and more square than a barn's floor of cement
   joy only to feel your body's lips cry under my fingers
   and your breasts split thru the fine skin until you are
   more naked and suffering than I have ever been in this
   unlovely world :
           O my universe! Electric chair! you shall
   not light me more terribly than my own sun. And I
   shall burn out in one crazy flash awakening for never
   the many filaments that go back
   into the generations of me

           •

From Richard Burton's *Anatomy of Melancholy*

USING THE WORDS: *conscience, continual feasts, natural impediment, red nose, disgrace, reproach, imperfection, infirmity, feet, a company of fine glasses, chance, over much moved, moderate, riden, sottish, stock, common, every cur, dog, dares, courage.*

1. Infirmity is common. Conscience is
disgraced by chance & every dog
dares cur or sottish hound reproach.
Continual feasts of courage will encroach
upon a natural impediment; im-
moderate fine company over much
be moved by slight stock infirmity or
common moderate red nose or feet's
imperfection among fine glasses.

Riden by fine glasses dogd
by moderate reproach, a natural
impediment, red nose or common foot,
emerges as no infirmity of natural cause
but in over much moved company
appears the full & final cur disgrace.

Reproach is natural. An over much moved
sot will make
continual feasts upon infirmity. Another man's
disgrace of foot or dog-shaped face
troubles conscience and summons
the common stock as full disgrace.
Who dares as dog give more
than moderate love to cur
has courage; chance can be
no imperfection then nor be disgrace
to conscience.

11. An over much moved conscience will
continual feast infirmity make of,
on imperfection riden & the ill
much contemplate. So courage find
disgraced by chance & every dog

for sottish hound or cur reproach.
Continual feasts of conscience will encroach
upon a natural impediment. Im-
moderate fine company over much will
be moved by slight infirmity or sin
and common moderate red nose
deride as imperfection weighd against
a world of much fine glass.
And even countenance be fair & sweet,
the conscience over much must hide
the deep disgrace of animal feet.

WINTER 1941–42 *Near Ashfield, Massachusetts*

Variations upon Phrases from Milton's
The Reason of Church Government

Organized, as perfect as an army there
your body lies. It gleams upon the sweet
unorganized, the field of dark. It flashes
in the evening air perfection's battlements
as naked blade as unsheathed self. It pierces
ease of body and makes unquiet soul.
Now I shall rise, awake as when a trumpet blows,
and go into the world laid bare;
for I have seen in her audible harmony
Virtue who walks in the regular and disciplined
City of God; known this precision: irregular
absolute vision sure and persistent
renders the illusive in its full face.

I go into my father and out of my father.
I carry the stigmata before I approach you
seeing undone the American origins. In no mist,
in no shifting mirage, in the open, the cheap & the gawdy
crowbitten Indians go into the dry
corruptible dust before meeting the man

with the baubles, glass
beads and the glasses
with the red colord glass
beads wherein
passeth all vanity.

The Merchants of this World have such
crackd show for merchandise as needs
be little more disguised to buy
each incorruptible Indian's soul.
The commerce of this world
does cover, daily does disgrace each jewel
with counterpart, to buy a continent with axes,
knives, with beads and colord cloths, and needs
call Truth a shameful thing that they
might so betray & barter with a lie. But Truth
is a precious violent and hidebound
Rarity that is more real than an axe.

     The body is
God's world in image, an engine of despair
when loved but partly by any I
that has not sight. But love shall be
Truth's order, surely not only
the removal of disorder, but the body's,
clear and most precious of virtue's
disciplines. (I see her surrounded
by lights in the dark, an invariable Planet
of Joy & Felicity, in gestures of plants
in their proper seasons.)

    You,
the upsetting,
the fals glitter of cheapnes, the present
beautiful scarecrow violent hidebound
and precious inventory: your hide
in the boundary of hand has its luster
as no Orient diamond can grow in my head,
and your heart, the price of
proceeding out of my stomach and into the sick

and room tumbling once you are gone is
the City of God in disorder.

The silent beast of your absence, your dumb
& immovable animal faced me & I found
the Angels of God in my brain
whose tumult of orders
broke open my eyes and doubled my vision.

I found there the left-over Indian crow
whose fals glitter, whose beautiful violent
left me without.
I shall write you a letter naming the names
of my demon inside. What is this essay
for symmetry's reason? I thot you not fox
stript of your fur in the naked of no one
but Bison. I thought you tomorrow
who passd the corruptible over your body
and opend you graciously wherever
I touchd you. I thought once your ribs
were the original ribs
under my fingers.

Your animal faced me, forced me, unable to
    speak,
moving its tongue between your mouth and
    mine
and I felt that no hidebound nor violent
held me removed.

                    But lift me O lift from me
the weight of me
natural cause and dimension. I know
in the unbounded undarkend ranges of mind
lies the City of God, the undisturbd paradox:
that she lies in the regular and there
uncontended is
walks gesture of
discipline.

Variations in Praise of Jesus Christ Our Lord

Spring tiger on the racks of spring; the tooth
and clawfaced judges answer.
Harken hawk (if hawk be answering home);
Emanuel for Tobit doth
(if self be angel not
as harp but harpsichord) devise
a giddy music. The naked skin and frame of lust
are crucifix. If we deliberate a love not death
described as bird with beak and foot, the wing
becomes a burnd black bone before that beast,
the sun, is overcome.

But sun will overcome his beasts; see spring
upon their racks his tigers, judges; afford a home
for hawks; and answering self, see Tobit's
toothless, clawless angel love make music
not on harp or harpsichord but on
the naked skin and lusty frame of crucifix. And if
accept we then the loved deliberate bird,
the beak and foot of death, the bone thereof
is life, the brief burnd beast to rise
upon his blackend wing

        & sing & sing O
Jesus tiger. The tooth and clawfaced judges answer.
The soul like hawk sinks home to thee. Heal hawk
and quiet singing in the dusk the self as harp
or harpsichord. Within your dark, your quick
impermeable frame, our crucifix
shines lust. If we deliberate a death
not love, described as bone
burnd black, upon its wing the bird
becomes a sun before the beast
with beak and foot is overcome.

Witnesses

Witnesses point how we in our passion, fast as foxes,
caught and devourd and scattered the flesh
of our common body; accuse us of cruelties in nature
and blood. And now it is winter.
I, too, remember how fiercely, relentlessly,
drove we the blind split between us. I rise
in the night and hunt in the streets
that are emptied, suddenly vast
and filld with the dreary remain
of past obsessions.

The women, our mothers, advance from the distance,
with terrible weapons, the sirens and nooses of love.
Surely no fragment
of stone, no steel nor obsidian knife,
can tear in the heart such ruin as these. We are lost
with no witnesses — lying like foxes, to kiss
in the common bed that we hide
behind blinds from the past. In these rooms of our houses
our fathers died out. Each sent his skeleton
blind and refusal to partake of our love.
Surely no poverty, privation nor panic
can conceal in its natural suffering the unnatural
suffering I have found in my ribbd
and unwilling body.

I cannot measure nor present to the witnesses
the width of desertion, nor mark, nor describe
by careful observation of time the duress
of ancestral crime: how many fathers
or mothers, cold and unwilling, extended
this emptiness, geometrically accurate,
to separate our two bodies into their winters.

The Unresting

The unresting occurs from its solid chaos. The void
is disturbd by its voices, and one
central word stares fixt and unspoken.
Sound is essential, containing all elements;
water and fire, earth and air,
are delineated, once utterd,
into their continents. Suns are words.
Fixt and unspoken, the eternal sound element is.
I see there dissolved
in the wavering actual the circular sentence
encircling the soul, see
the glittering definitions of death like a girdle
where words pass thru their cells,
where they go utterly, utterd unheard,
into the ear of eternity,
they return to the future as phosphorous suns, pass
the wavering bridge of the actual, pass joy
and joy's mutilations. I see now more clearly
in my loss the continual losing,
for no wall can retain the word when it carries
the burden of love; but moord, sure and actual,
it vanishes, passes its actual into the distance
and lies like a shadow to cover all agony.

Statues are actual, stone and unchanging
words. Surely by architecture, cutting of stone
or the sound love of rocks, the original sound,
fixt and unspoken, may be approacht.

Birds, fish, or self, all swift utterd things,
give agony, turn on the heart that is motionless
and warn it of distance, uncover the treacherous
lovely cold of the empty. The search
that sends blood in its endless circuit

in each room of my body is that
unanswerd hunger,
the restless immovable word that is lodged
in the unopend ear of beginning.

Snow on Bug Hill

The snow has covered this ground.
Th'arrested world in black and white
of woods and snow seems brought to peace,
yet each bare tree shall each year
rediscover grief among its leaves. What
burden can brief winter gather in forever, keep,
when so near spring there hovereth?

Tho cold may bring this quiet sheath,
a world of animal and grass
seem brought to rest, a heart stilld
and an eye closed down in sleep,
newly each breath
feeds the breathless spring in me
and will destroy this still untroubled sight
of snow on earth in winter light.

Mother to Whom I Have Come Home

Mother to whom I have come home
& moved about the afternoon
thru the unease & wrath of love
the house I would have rid me of

in the diminishing time is dim
yet strong as it had ever been.

Shall I always in this room,
unspeaking, accuse you of not loving;
dumb in the dimensions of my mind
keep the accusation, keep the alive
shadow behind the afternoon?

Years in that everlasting life
darken, unmoving towards the same time.
Rooms after death have the same light
left over, beginning the length of the house.
This is the end beginning with you.
Long as the light afterwards of noon,
I have taken me to wife
and sleep and death the deep of home.

Toward an African Elegy

In the groves of Africa from their natural wonder
the wildebeeste, zebra, the okapi, the elephant,
have enterd the marvelous. No greater marvelous
know I than the mind's
natural jungle. The wives of the Congo
distil there their red and the husbands
hunt lion with spear and paint Death-spore
on their shields, wear his teeth, claws and hair
on ordinary occasions. There the Swahili
open his doors, let loose thru the trees
the tides of Death's sound & distil
from their leaves the terrible red.
He is the consort of dreams I have seen, heard
in the orchestral dark
like the barking of dogs.

Death is the dog-headed man zebra-striped
and surrounded by silence who walks like a lion,
who is black. It was his voice crying come back
that Virginia Woolf heard, turnd

her fine skull, hounded and haunted, stoppd,
pointed into the scent where
I see her in willows, in fog, at the river of sound
in the trees; I see her prepare there
to enter Death's mountains
like a white Afghan hound pass into the forest,
closed after, let loose in the leaves
with more grace than a hound & more wonder there,
even with flowers wound in her hair, allowing herself
like Ophelia a last
pastoral gesture of love toward the world;
                    and I see
all our tortures absolved in the fog
dispersed in Death's forests, forgotten. I see
all this gentleness like a hound in the water
float upward and outward beyond my dark hand.

I am waiting this winter in the black of love
for the Negro armies in the eucalyptus,
for the cities laid open and the cold in the love-light,
for hounds, women & birds
to go back to their forests
and leave us our solitude.

        •

Negroes, negroes, all those princes
holding cups of rhinoceros bone, make
magic with my blood. Where beautiful Marijuana
towers taller than the eucalyptus, turns
within the lips of night and falls,
falls downward, where as giant Kings we gathered
and devour her burning hands & feet. O Moonbar
there and Clarinet — those princes, talismans,
quickend in their sheltering leaves like thieves,
those negroes, all those princes
holding to their mouths like Death
the cups of rhino bone were there to burn
my body, divine the limits of the bone
and with their magic tie & twist me

like a rope. I know no other continent of Africa
more dark than this
dark continent of my breast.

And when we are deserted there,
when the rustling electric has passed thru the air,
once more we begin in the blind & blood throat
the African catches; and Desdemona,
Desdemona, like a Demon
wails within our bodies, warns
against this towering Moor of self, and then
laments her passing from him.

And I cry: hear.
Hear in the coild and secretive ear the drums
that I hear beat. The negroes, all those princes
holding cups of bone and horn, are there in halls
of blood that I call forests, in the dark
and shining caverns where
beats heart and pulses brain, in jungles
of my body, there, Othello moves, striped
black & white, the dog-faced fear. Moves
I, I, I, whom I have seen as black
as Orpheus, pursued deliriously his sound
and drownd in hunger's tone,
the deepest wilderness.

Then it was I, Death singing,
who bewilderd the forest. I thot
him my lover like a hound of great purity
disturbing the shadow and flesh of the jungle.
This was the beginning of the ending year.

From all of the empty the tortured appear
& the bird-faced children crawl out of their fathers,
and into
that never-filled pocket, the no longer asking
but silent, seeing nowhere the final sleep.

The halls of Africa we seek in dreams
as barriers of dream against the deep, & seas
disturbd turned back upon their tides into
the rooms deserted at the roots of love.
There is no end. And how sad then
is even the Congo. How the tired sirens
come up from the water, not to be touchd
but to lie on the rocks of the thunder.
How sad then is even
the marvelous.

The Years As Catches

This century, an iron bell of joy, has scarcely rung
its first harsh notes of morning. Scarcely rung
upon its ears the strident ecstasie in God. The bloody dawn
is scarcely with us. In the unpierc'd sky
it gathers. In the unsounded August, cold & early sight
bestirs my soul. Is this a later hour then, when Milton, he
past twenty-three, saw that year
gone from him, stood in the hasting days of his soul's April,
stood in the weary stretch of Christendom
impatient for the green, the bud & bloom
of manhood? Is this a later hour when we rise? For I
have lost already more than youth & all brief timely joy.

Already ere I wake I hear that makes disturbing
all this dear & pleasant world about me so devised
in harmonie where we would, fallen, see
in gardens chaos, I hear the clamor of that bell,
ring rathe upon my ears like iron. I hunger
for that testing that would sound the deep of grace,
that pure & metal spirit ring upon my soul at last
in which twas forged. Already ere I wake
I hear that sound. Shout & fill the air with sirens;

no sound that you can make for war or human miserie

can meet that sound or cover it. No waste you wreck
upon the body, no ravaging of mind nor spirit can
make deaf nor blind nor insensate. No pounding, strife,
no battles, nor repentence nor moaning over dead,
shall divert this sound once known. A single note
across the human image, endlessly repeated, so
that all that maimd, incapable and clouded metal
will be pain; all that insensate & battling structure
hungry upon itself that first deliberated blindness shall
be brought to sight; the mute unanswering rock of self
cry out—nor be there refuge. Virtue,
charity and hope avail not. This century
has scarcely rung its brightness nor laid bare
that clear unbearable sound world against whose purity

we set store a little blindness, we would make
an interim eternity, momentous war & peace, estate
and settlement, lament or celebrate a youth or age
that yet shall not avail against the still
unbroken universe of God.

But O the heavy change, now thou art gone,
now thou art gone, and we are set adrift in th'eclipse.

Any wastes, like Carthage, burnd & salted,
cities of despair, are better in the mind
than beauty—more coveted. Shall we
be less in sin than Adam to repeat like canker
in the rose of self, our greed for counterfeit delight,
that pass our word upon the scene, time's slaves,
bewail the autumn harshly come
ere there has been a month of green? Shall we
claim virtue, love of freedom, who've confined
our spirit, each his own; who've set
the worm to feed upon our conscience, nor turn
from leisure and these ill-gained days
but that would make our peace
with no peace in us; keep
a brutish silence in adversity.

I brood upon these lines of Milton, words
where there moves such a tide to feed
my restlessness. Where shall we sometime meet
in this dark land no longer having
darkness in us? And bring our tired souls home
to linger over wine about a fire, to hear
with equal grace a little Mozart played
within the gloom of an Autumnal room, to linger
over these last rude & somber moments
come to rest.
Lift, untimely joy.
Impatiently I
to break the day, unending bread
of morning light, waked
into scarce time to make
my peace with April, with the rose
that bled

life from my bloody heart
unsounded cold of love,

an ecstasie, all year as of
all youth to never cease,
to part
with no immediate grace,
continual
earliness to no fulfillment; lift
thy face,
his harmonie, my Chaos.
The never flies, the impatient joy,
in whose untime repeated I
in the hasting days, His still,
His clamorous bright day, see still
that unbroken rose that broken is
no other cross than love.

Break in the ear the sounding sight
of Mozart. Break this manhood, harsh
& miserie; lift the light
into the throat until

the broken cross, the body-rose
will close
My Harmonie, His chaos.
O lift into
that singleness,
no earliness; as free
as sight from eye,
as sound from ear,
as Truth from Lie,
His ecstasie to ring forth
from the miserie in me
as darkness rung from light.

Catch from the years the line of joy;
impatient & repeated day,
my heart, break; eye
break open and set free
His world, my ecstasie.

King Haydn of Miami Beach

1

In the rustling shelter of Japanese peach
with the blacks and the plum-colord lady apes
dances King Haydn of Miami Beach
the now, the now, of never perhaps;
bows to death, bows to death;
plans next week wonderfully pretend
a temporary pleasurable boat-trip and ride
round the capes, round the capes
and back again.

2

King Haydn abandons the dance of his do;
with joy he resumes
the half-waltz and rumba of never

come true, But
Mr. Responsible Person
booms in the head of Mr. Do Why.
Love-waltz and rumba come
stop.
King Haydn abandons
the never come true.
Hops.
To the tune of Mr. Do Why
vacations and oceans grow tired and die.

Fixd with a joyless partner motion
King Haydn and Mr.
Dandruff Why
do the why-do do why do.

3 PARADISE CLUB

This is the Heaven-House Everyday-Do
that Mr. Responsible-Person-God
built in a day.

This is Mr. Responsible Who
looks out for the welfare of me and you,
of Eve, of you, of Adam, of me.
This is the Absolute Person we fear.
This is His hot round biggish sun.
This is the middle of next year.
This is the bird on its wounded wing
that fell out of Heaven and started to sing,
that fell into soul, into single
extraordinary badly and poor.

This is the Other Place, the Miami Beach lure,
beyond the Absolute Door of Why
where each fallen birdie is 6 feet high.
This is the Eye of Mr. Responsible,
the Comprehensible,
sees each birdling that falles from grace
lose wits, lose form, lose time and face.

This is Mr. Responsible Person.
This is His ordinary only Heaven.

King Haydn in the Other Place
dances away his chance for grace.

4 PSYCHOANALYSIS

Death is a sin, death is a sin,
leaves a taste after of oil and tin.
In the fiery hell of Miami beach
the sun can glare like a red hot peach
but the night comes in
and the life goes out.
The boys and the girls play Turn About.
King Haydn and Mr. Why begin
to deal the cards and play at death.
The game is long and the chance is brief.
Among the dead
the blacks and the plum-colored apes
change and then again change shapes.

Death is a sin, death is a sin.
The sorry old sun can glower and pout
but Death comes in
and the life goes out
and leaves a taste after of oil and tin.

5

How many miles to love and back,
Hobbyhorse Wise? asked Mr. Why.

You can never get there.
To Where? To There?

Hobbyhorse Poor, said Mr. Why,
to Lack from Lack to Lack and back.

Lovewise

Lovewise less love
on an island suspended above
    his own heart
    practices his part-
time beautiful loving loveless suspension:

wait while the bone & the flesh invention
in a room of fire & roses
speaks the lie and flashes
white and sleepless faces,
    wide awake,
    each mistake-
en deliberate device
    painted twice.

    Lovewise alone
faces his own wise like a pair of crosst eyes
    fixt on a bone
multiplies the real & single fate
into too many faces
    for delite.

    Ah! then the night
goes up in roses, burning like hell.
The half & half, the This of That,
runs about like a randy cat
caught in a ringing loud old bell.
    Ah! then the town
    bursts and breaks down.

    In the head
    instead
sits like a hungry grandfather lied to
angry and sleepless as Pride
    painted red,
held to the heart, dumpt in the stomach
hard as a rock in the animal hammock,

sits Head in the Heart,
heart to the head.

Lovewise uses
a rock instead.

Mother Brother Door and Bed

My brother is black and wise to me.
From the door to the bed I watch his eyes.
My animal in his eyes I see.

The mute intention we call love
shakes like a forest of tall mute mothers
shockt by the wiry sex of child.
My brother is tame and I am wild.

Who with his brother intended his eyes,
intended his mother's kind of wise,
shakes like a child that is caught by a door.

My brother is wild. He starts for the bed
and never arrives in the forest of love.
The wiry black of the animal sex
shows in the bed like a pair of eyes.

My mother, my door,
My brother from door to bed I watch.
Wild for tame and sex for sight,
Like parts of a forest our faces match.
We shut our eyes and reach for the light.

Sight for sex and tame for wild,
the wiry black in the animal eyes
shakes like a door that covers a child.

Never arrives from door to bed
but stops in the dead,
in the forest of eyes,
the mute intention that we call mother.

7 Questions, 7 Answers

What is the skinny lust, the death? shaped
like a hut on chicken's legs, the horny sight
of Granny Guts? Who is the dancing
idiot Granny, progenitor of chicken huts?

What of the angry womb, the man? The woman,
his mother, her son despises; cooks
up of love from her spite in her pot
and looses her wits in his inside pocket.
What of the cross old womb, the man?

Why is your skull for me a face? At night
the death's head of my own, and daily is
the trumpt-up truth for the lie, my heart.
What of the other face, the lie,
truth cookt up in a mother's pot
with the horny spite of Granny Guts?

Who is the idiot, playing at death; lives
in his cross old hut and dances,
dances his dance like a chicken in bed
with love going round like a chicken's head?

From trumpt-up wit to guts trumpt-up
the words in their huts go round about.

Marriage

When I love
hate burns my right side.
When I stop
hate stops.

Love and hate go back where you came from.

I loving, hate burning my right side,
who is the nothing on my left side
left to face when I stop and hate stops?

Random Lines : A Discourse on Love

This is the same sea, love, grown dim
as if all the dead had at last come home,
the wide and restless tumbling tide,
the fathom deep sin in past & future time
darkend for storm. This is the still
that comes before, deceptive in its pale
as the first fruit hid among live, lithe leaves—
or as glimmers to me, a hive of bees,
your heart. Your head before my hungry hand appears
the rod that child and sinner fears.

As in my babyhood on that ebbing tide doubt
I saw the Lord Jesus walking about,
I saw our Lord Jesus, my love, my debt,
and I cried, I love you. Yet
this is the same sea come to its fill
too salt to slacken the thirst of soul—
too loving, too full.

The man in the sea is a baby fox
the sea-born chicken of my soul to catch.
The boy in the painting is death made sweet
like denial, like a fox in a wave of wheat.

And his eyes are soft as a baby's mouth.
To me they seem eyes of a baby's wrath.
The tiger in my dreams is mild.
What other Child can the sinner hold?
What other cross than the skeletal last,
the seaman's harp, is love's first feast?

This is the same sea after the thunder has sounded,
the storm and the fiery beasts gone under.
The rocks in the glimmering shake their lengths
from the source. The inert & punishing bank
appears from the seaside waste like a whale
or the giant of fathers conceald in a well.
The figure loving is the punishing man
to threaten a child who wanders toward home.

Your image is the daylight hoax
on which my soul & body wrecks.
The absence of your body is
the drowning place, the deep abyss.

•

Unspeakable myself, king without a shell, remote,
with my twin in the split-open chrysalis lies
encoild in one image. The worm is laid bare.
Incubus bone teeth and hair like an egg, the animal
secrets grown in the flesh, uncoverd, writhe
with a life of their own. Never therefore
only of God.

How when that Kingdom of Love's weather
sweeps into, sweeps out of, my head
and my body—Christ himself
no greater light had, no greater love held
too great to hold. Other earlier fathers moved,
fathers like rats in the walls of the house,
whisperd and tapt on the walls of the night
or appeard in the lonely distances love,
great single bird-fathers disturbd by our pleasures.

I
and my twin, grown together, turnd, leapt
and attempted to fly on one wing. Rid of its shell
the unspeakable, king, the sun, was hell-black;
another father, the luminous source, glowd
like red lust and we fell.
The beast of our origin
moved in his house, encircled and dumb,
the original fire. How burnd my body then,
as an insect burns and is born in his shell.

The animal glow grows cold in time.
Single lonely father birds have flown
into the secret places. Polar light, the electric remote,
dwindles and stiffens among the trees.
I and my love break open the shell, cease,
and cease to create our desire. Th'immediate fire
sharp as a snake fang starts in the flesh.
I and my twin in the chrysalis twist
encoild in one image. "Luminous eyes,
but his body fades." The power of love
is upside down. Time
is an older father than *he* is.

In Time my lover reflects the cold. I eye
in him another father. Caged inside the cold I see
the cold was the single lonely place
caging the skeletal parent bird or loon,
that monstrous shadow of legs and feathers
that stood in the house till the bed went black.
In time my lover is up-side-down,
croucht like an incubus in th'immediate fire,
faces the cold of the animal bent.
What of the no more charged air then?
Awake as a rooster caught on fire
Love is the body of the soul, desire.

Homage & Lament for Ezra Pound : May 12, 1944

Apprehension this spring . . . . the leaves, the leaves,
still, as still as everness returnd,
defining distances in green; the space between
alive with each upon each barely in motion;
coming into a room from hidden windows light
reflects in shade a spotted shade of spring
having almost sound upon the ear; four voices,
violin, viola, cello and bass appear and disappear
upon a warp and woof of distance
unified in light and sense of leaves, of Venus
sea-ambulant among the boughs; the numerous leaves
are still, as still as heart in seeing, as sound
as Brzeska's head of solid stone, as lasting
in the heart though the particular stone be crackd.
Iconoclasts may never reach that stone once seen,
once heard in returning everness of mind:
the numerous leaves are still in seeing, hearing.
The numerous leaves await in knowing
apprehension this spring like some crackd voice
fanatic dryad among the boughs, the melodies
of mind.

    Ezra, this time of year,
this deceptive real we fear — lest hunting voices
overtake the hunted; torn by wild upon the wild
evasive beauty, a mocking face recalls to mind
among the leaves, the lights: an enemy.
Far down — I hang in qualms of deep —
an old man stumbles,
mutters maledictions upon the hounds.

In this place, before hell's door, anger-blind,
leaves rehearse crimes. Human figures in a frieze
rehearse rememberd faces. Universities, the damnd,
seas of human faces go down like wolves
behind the eyes to fill distances with fire.

The desire, for all its leaves, for all of violin,
of solid stone, turns a human hurt and damnd
toward outrage's hell. Desire has crackd
crossd eyes to see a hell's door heaven;
hellsdoor's heaven will never change as leaves
may change and fall like wolves
upon the human flesh and bone; universities
the damnd, that turn upon the damnd
with passive righteousness — another hell
more treacherous than fire or wolves.
Far down — I voice in the wrong beauty
better than no beauty — to see a still world still
hopping mad among its calm of leaves.

•

We have not less to fear or hate. Old man, early
devoted voice — this afternoon as light falls down
it leaves one shining sill, promising, illusive.
The room is filld — enters in the mind with this,
an architecture to house the mind in heaven,
apprehending in a single phrase of Mozart
a universe, the tones, the tones like leaves of light
to fall, to reappear establishing distances
upon the warp and woof of person not to fall.
A single window upon another scene,
upon a painted Mediterranean blueness in the room
gives possession of the world by love;
against a Mediterranean scene an old man
stumbles, mutters maledictions, sees that blue
as Joyce once saw a sea, tighten scrotum,
mock at an old man's heart.

He screams abominations, curses, seeing a gull
fly up upon the wind, seeing an early eagerness
falter and drift to be touchd
by usury. What still and wondrous knowledge
avails then? to know as leaves, as sea
of soul gives out, no longer capable to eager green —

to see each upon each barely in motion
as still as everness returnd . . . . apprehension this spring
. . . . the leaves, the leaves,
still, as still as everness returning.

Christmas Letter 1944

Dear Mother, this by way of poem is little
more than Christmas greeting, by way of letter
sums more than a year, in and out, older
than not so long ago, but short
of the full greeting heart
might give had time not tamperd.

The face (looking up into the camera face)
fixes itself with as much grace
as it has in it. Lighted by clear air,
by reflected clean-washt rocks & shirt, the hair
shows blond. That was a good time of year
and place for a photograph
to catch so little wrath or fretful loving
showing in that face.

Christmas greeting would be care-free but's modified
by such a worrying face by care, dyed
a deeper, coarser, relentless, red and green
in the heart's careful remorseful stain,
catching into itself, with more distortion
than camera caught this face, a portion
of Christ's love, more than Christmas evening
revelry. Christ's serious accusing love
that measures us short in what we bring
each to all the others is a cross of
judgment that marks each face
seeking grace.

This by way of Christmas greeting is little
less than poetry; by way of total
(the face, the photograph) is fair
I hope. Showing more of what is there
than others. It allows
a certain warmth to show, a pause,
a Christmas hiatus in the midst of battle.

The full greeting heart might give
is tamperd by each day we live.
In memory of Christ's love we live
each day untamperd by our life.
And in our narrow hearts Christ's gift
gives love's face toward the total life.

Upon Watching a Storm

This is my ruind Europe; after war
remembering you in the twilit summering rooms
shaken and vacant in the near and far
distance of love. The gloom
falters, penetrated and alive.
How then your form appears
like that French maiden's voices in the leaves
and faith
restores the sought-for key of love.
Unlockt my separate breath begins.

This evening still, before a storm,
prestaging that Last Day, the soundless alarm,
thunderous orange light flared up, and I
was caught alone. O if death
had come then, if I had
not, will not, see you once again! my heart
had playd a fear like fire
upon love's darkening sky. Desire

is now a cunning lock to turn the day
upon your touch and voice alone.

This is my Europe ruind, fallen down.
Now that the barbarous hordes have passt
into their monuments, will spring
return? Among the separate solemn forms
to bring love's dignity?
This is my ruind Europe. On that ending day
I stand alone in the orange violent light,
the storm, and watch the light
die down.

        •

My Gabriel-wide day, voice emergent,
here the heart is strung to strike
harpwise home love's cardinal, a monument-
tongue of tone to calm the heart chord.
After violence love no longer urgent
lingers long after earning its end.

An April, tongued for Gabriel to speak
wide the widowd & dayless dawn.
The birds, leaféd, scatterd, fly to meet
the height of hope. Crowns of birds crack
against the no end no beginning sweep
of sky, scold; and fall far.

: a song to sing April against hope's height, love.
The voice devourd like harpd heaven
sounds the blood into the cove,
my haven, heart. The tangled tongue
harps upon its single note hanging above
the deep downward motionless me.

        •

My heart keeps the long watch over hours of sleep.
My heart is now like a dull bird

struggling in water, come home to its love.
Be still, heart. Listen. In the corridors
tomorrow resounds its patient deep tide; and I,
death-wedded, bride-still, will
sometime come home.

1945 Woodstock, New York
Pond Farm, California

The End of the Year

I

Now in this debacle, of this ruining kingdom,
of leafd & ever-returning crown, my world of thorns,
in the change of August, I can make no monument.
Love wandering comes to no crucifix
to be tried, tied in its final gesture. I stood
this morning, the length of my body made naked,
fixt in the heat of the sun; but my mind
wanders to earlier scenes and the spent sun
scatters unsurely. Surely
your hand comes to me, though you are far away.
Your hand, not being there, halts heart and casts
the world, loose change, about the street.
What a sad disorder then. Motherless,
Fatherless, I stand. Between
sick of home and homesick, a mocking other world
extends, a calm to set my heart, my house,
upon its edge.

2

There! the ruining summer has gone.
My lovers in the mocking grove grow wan.
At night I wait for that dark ship
to bear me upon the blackly flaming sea,
the pyre of August's majesty, dim burning glare

of crownd October's revelry.
Now in this debacle, berried and painted,
gaudy celebration of each mock nuptial,
send up the rooks and caws to whirr
against the sky; in the valley below us
ring out the bells as upon the last day.
There! the ruining summer has gone!

3
What shall we share? I have come
from childhood terror, from a seizure by my mother
bearing her curse. Surely no ancient
fear of sea voyager has ridden more franticly
Hercules' shoulders; no death's head
or eater set at the body of time
has clung to his victim
more faithfully, haunted even this room
as we talk, with more hunger
than has that mothering shark in my childhood sea.
She appears in the chattering darkness
circling round in that dance she in my mind
calld love. Slowly she fixt
her fixt and immutable Planet
Eye in my dark to organize my Day.

Then was I frantic tonight? the wine
quickend my wits toward that deadly fin
that cuts the surface of the gathering flood.
This house is like a black wave;
the vast intent, disturbd as I move,
rises into the shatterd glass of my mind.
The Kraken, the tentacled & shifting line,
waits in her depths to collect my debt.
My hand, when I reach for the wine,
trembles and betrays, shakes. My voice breaks
and wanders in its compulsive speech
against an old terror, against the image
of a threatening figure in a darkend room.

4

The Ship, the speech, among the remainders of supper,
flounders in the sea of voices. The summer's
dim prophetical warnings flicker; the signals
are clear but not to be fathomd. I fly
the betrayal of my mother tongue. The wine is a rare
wind to stir, a blood, a tide, to surrender the calm,
the moord heart to its blind disaster.

I fly, I fly like a drunken wingd sailor
caught upside down to surrender his pride
in the tangled betrayal, the riggings of Love.
The Ship, the Lust, survives to the last,
shivers and trembles upon its shoals.

5

These are the fields where we enter a cold season.
The thinning moon hangs over our house.
In the early dark we move about our chores.
We turn homewards to sit in the lighted room,
to drink our wine and meditate
upon a cigarette. We have come safely
thru a war, and we face
another war. In the hiatus, momentary & still
nightly shadow, the cows low and stir
upon the hill; the generator hums;
and we, after supper, settle down to rest,
to stir ourselves in the returning mood,
the shared warmth that we keep now
knowingly. "We are free," Dick reads,
"upon a sinking level." The intonations,
the rising falling voice beats,
stirs and haunts the ear. We wait,
hearing afterward the repeated interchange
of voices in the poem, in his single voice,
touch and retouch upon our wandering mind.

The golden fleece of sound in the hushd
the listening gloom—more real;
the lingering dream—more real; the poem
surrounds and lifts our certain doom,
lifts the approaching years from all we fear
into its own splendor.

6

The long year of Saturn winds to its close.
My own year, returning spell of cold and war.
We, the obsesst, in its chill fire, its glow,
turn and twist. This is a hunger not to be said
short of my longd-for, my lived-for, death;
not to be fed full by a life-long night,
by a deathwards intent. The returning day
tries the heart in its fragments, its scenes; shows
my returning face in its mirror.
I, the obsesst, in the wind of November,
face like an animal my attacking hunger; face
each wound of the wonder that refuses me, and wind
and unwind the steel spring at my heart.
Pang! the summer magic is sprung and lost.
The scatterd ship in its sails and riggings
burns among November's vineyards.

7

These are the fields where the cold clings.
Tho my ship be of fire the night is longer.
That great Leviathan, Keen of the Depths,
appears in dreams as the Kraken, the terror.
The vast black wave rolls under my feet.
Here Joyce dared to walk on that nightly sea
to be alone where I in my horror
find myself irrevocably lost, see, as I turn
or look forward, the unending deep.

These are the fields where we enter a cold,
no mere season, to try the heart, the lust.
The fiery ship gleams from its fathoms; the years
burn like wreckage from its unending heart.
His single voice now that he is gone
I hear again in the rooms of this house,
I hear again in the flood of the night,
touch and retouch, as an answering voice
might mock and comfort a lonely swimmer
who knows long before that he is not to be rescued.

The comfort itself mocks the heart
that waited for no mere single voice
but the final voice, His voice, the clang
and clamor to burnish each wave
like a shield of copper. Your hand!
in the far like a fire upon the water!
Surely your hand rests upon my heart; lifts
and leavens the returning sky. Kraken!
the formless and refusing world withdraws from me.
No hand extends, no dawn, no bird.

The golden fleece in the mocking gleam
whirs and caws against the sky. Your hand,
withdrawn, halts heart and casts, returns,
the world into its field of cold.

8

What against Chaos then my Christ avails?
my radiant terror? Here is a spear
forged in the heart
to appear like a dove, like
a brilliant bird in the storm of waters.
I wait in the restless & returning day
for that dark ship to bear down upon me.
I wait like an animal my attacking hunger,

wind & unwind the steel spring at my heart.
Clang! my ship, my dreamer, bursts into flame;
appears as a blazing pyre upon the welter, the flood.
What against Chaos then my Christ avails?

Song

How in the dark the cows lie down.
They sleep in grace, in their dumb remove.
How the dumb sheep in the grace of dark
huddle to sleep. How the winter's cold
sharpens & glisters the whispering still.
How each man to his beloved comes,
to his dumb, to his grace, in the evening's chill.
How, at last, to his comfort, his death,
comes even the damnd, to his final home.
Alone I lie in the hush of my beast
to hear upon my body's lyre
the varying discords of my desire
until the intervening nights and days,
the sheltering darks, the revealing lights,
have passt away.

At an Anarchist Meeting

One moment sounds in its clamour of voices,
traffic of love, chatter of anger; in the room
the noises cheer and strike upon the unbalanced mind.

This moment leaves only traffic and chatter — a waste,
a wilderness of discarded paper. The heart
strains forward from an equal disorder. The mind
centers blankly upon the field, unable to distinguish
its own.

In this vast body of contention, no-world,
now-and-then, there is no bone. A single voice
rises to cast a fragment of a song; the current is
as meaningless as music. "Just like a dog," said
whimsically. "I saw an Ace of Spades," Deva says,
"only it was blue." Unrelated fragments are utterd
to make the suspending distracted element.
Nervously. Monotonously.

                    Silently time
falls into place. They have no time.
In the passage of quiet I shall move again, shall feel
the counted weights falling in the water, hear
the single crossed wires of the real, cross
and recross in their own music.

Heavenly City, Earthly City

1947

Treesbank Poems

1946

• • •

I listen in the shade to one I love.
His voice falls on me like a troubled wave.
His voice illumines like a golden hive
the shadowd populace of which I live.
The music echoes in that sacred grove,
the peopled and troubled, the sleepless grave
of love; and now, I'm caught in the alive
remainder of the past that comes to give
its voice into the singing heart, the wove-
n melody to join his voice. The wave,
the moment, passes; but the image, life,
his voice, burns gravely in the mind. I have
a momentary sense of rest, of savi-
ior in his voice that seems to voice my love.

•

The silent throat in the dark portends
His voice. Mute world! in my original dumb
wondering flesh, I turn each dark
into its throat; my Christ upon my flesh
is crossd by love; each nail, its mark.
Crownd by the quick of the body's thorn
His Christ has made me King of my world,
voiced in its animal my angel, my voice,
to waken against my dark, His light,
my own. Glad Christ! of whom partaking I
am—as a universe is crucified in me—
Christ-crossd upon the body of my world.

•

Shall I alone make my way to my grave,
to my final skull, to my deep imprint?
Who fell forward from his nine months' cave
more than me to live in my world? Who,
when I struggled, when I waked and slept,
waked and fell into sleep beside me?
I shall never, as Zeno knows well,
arrive at my lover
who waits before me. Each step will make
the way ahead shorter; my shadow longer.
The skull that I carry, the unchanging thing,
has been changed and worn and charged anew
to turn my true face toward its lonely grave.
The world shall make my way to that place;
the years shall lay themselves there to sleep.
My life may come to rest in me
where I shall restless in the future be.

　　•

Sleep is a deep and many-voiced flood.
Our little Death from which we daily
do survive, it seems tonight
the very tide of life itself
upon whose surface we toss
unwilling to submit, like two swimmers
eager for rest but eager too for each other.
We struggle, we weary, we refuse
its calm depth that we know a storm.
We throw ourselves out from its silence
that like the coild and vacant chambers of a shell
is all aroar with our drownd
and ever present past. We turn to each other;
we cling; we keep a hand, a mouth, a head
above the water, sighing,
caught in sleep's undertow. Now,
watching above your loved form where it lies
admitted to life's death-soundings, sleep,
I toss alone. You have met other lovers there.
Looking past your sleeping eyes I see

death's deep resounding eyes. You hunt
among the shadows of your life that haunt
sleep's depth and hear in every voice
like some reminder from the distant past
the ominous tone my love assumes.

•

An Apollonian Elegy

Let Apollo, the hornéd and shining shepherd, pierce
in His grove the Muses, dim ladies,
until they blaze and raise His litanies
to break, the crack, the unlighted sky.
The sun in his trumpet then will set up his holler,
an elegy for the passing lyre
whose strings on fire burn in the trees,
burn white the black bodies of lovers, burn black
their white souls in the awake of night.
They see there each other. They rest,
they rock, in the human, in their dearly bought,
shelter and seize to at last each other;
and they see also there in themselves,
in each other, their chariot sun begd from Apollo
go careering, go careening, down thru its sky.

Return you, Apollo, to ride your old sun
across that nemesis world, the night. In our dark,
in our human, we rest, we rock.
Above us, the horses trample the silence, blast
and shock the wavering deep.
Each lover—Promethean—has stolen from you
his body, Your lyre, that once gave voice
devil-strummd in Your sacred grove
to as crazed a shriek, the thief's own terror,
of song as rockd ever the sun from its grave.

Then—Promethean—each lover hears,
pluckd from the string, the strain of his body,
by the lustful beak and claw of his hunger,
that music, love; and he cleaves
to the rock, to the human deep,
and sleeps his sun in Apollo's grove,
the depth, the dumb, of the body's love.

     •

I hold to my heart the unchanging light,
the mind's own sun that glares in the years;
but the accident of sun that from thy face
gleams its radiance disturbs me still.
Then more than human the god appears; starts
in the cold; flashes and haunts the blindness, my soul;
strikes and strikes again its change; strikes love
upon the unchanging steel.

When I turn, I touch; I, joyous, shout;
face the abyss where the angel of sun,
the dreaded, the loved, hovers
and covers my body with his wings.
He is gone: and trembling I face my lover.
He is more beautiful than the sun. The human
has in its rest what can be loved
and yet wrest not from the bone its flesh
nor from terror its love.

In Apollo's grove, the sunless night,
grave and pale his body, the burnishd steel,
gleams bright as a sword to reflect the blaze,
to burn, to sear, my body's dark.

     •

We live in a night broken by the sun; we are
ourselves each suns to break that darkness, Man.
We shine alone in an expanse of night
that is all our time. We shine in eternity
and our light floods back from the other suns.

Where we began is an utter beginning.
That is the unreal that haunts our days.
And when we are gone, we are death-done.
Where we end is an utter end, the blank
real equality of the persisting black.

.

Thou art an utter dark yet unto me
my day. In that unreal, how real
your countenance, gleam and glimmer is.
Eternity. Thou art not to be death-done
but brighter light you the heart's lanthorn,
            that light,
cold as the dawn and still, that presages
            the day's
clamorous blaze like a fire in the bone
in the mirroring bone. Thou art not to be gone;
nor dimmd in the face of the lonely heart
that catches your image into itself
            emblazond
as upon some fatal shield wrought by the crippled God,
rubbd and burnishd to reflect
irremediably its bearer's doom.

.

Apollo that in the grove of beasts,
against the Dionysiac flute, plays upon the mortal ear
immortality's refrain, wingd and splendid,
lion-visaged, Thou too has loved
and borne
mortality's bourne.

AI AI

The hyacinthus springs, love's flowering
in the year's renewal, white and blue-red
as the violet-blooded beloved youth.
How when he fell, your heart was torn
and you tasted the depth of our mortal regret.

AI AI

The mocking blood, the mocking flesh, beckons
and flowers in the wan pale light. See,
the beloved mouth, to be kissd, is closed;
the eyes are closed; the beloved body lies,
to be seized to your body, broken.
As in the early morning from their wet meadow
one gathers up the iris, blue tears of heaven,
eager to hold love's very fragrance
close to the heart, as one cuts them down
from their stems and they perish:

AI AI

heedless and eager to prove your love,
you have cut love down. Inscribe then your grief
upon love's bloom. Your grief springs anew
in every heart. The human flesh is
hyacinth staind. Were you, O too mortal
god of sun, my angel that would have me love
and hunger? that by your grievous hand
would strike from me complaint, complaint,

AI AI

in the year's renewal, your eternal
lamentation?

      Never shall he be from me;
he is my very grief, my spirit's shade
cast in the light of immortality's sun;
             and thus, Apollo,
sing I—who die utterly—your undying song,

AI AI

Deathless Apollo, Thou too hast loved; and Thou
immortally must bear
mortality's bourne.

Berkeley Poems

1946

. . .

Among my friends love is a great sorrow;
it has become a daily burden, a feast,
a gluttony for fools, a heart's famine.
We visit one another asking, telling one another;
we do not burn hotly, we question the fire.
We do not fall forward with our alive
eager faces looking thru into the fire.
We stare back into our own faces.
We have become our own realities.
We seek to exhaust our lovelessness.

Among my friends love is a painful question.
We seek out among the passing faces
A sphinx-face who will ask its riddle.
Among my friends love is an answer to a question
that has not been askd.
Then ask it.

Among my friends love is a payment.
It is an old debt for a borrowing foolishly spent.
And we go on, borrowing and borrowing
                    from each other.
Among my friends love is a wage
that one might have for an honest living.

An Elegiac Fragment

The women in the many chamberd dawn
lean their sorrowing heads upon their arms
and gaze.
They wait in the quiet rooms.
Women I have loved and in the flower of fear
touchd and gazed upon.
They burn at the dream's windows.
My far away brides
my heart asks for you, asks for you,
and my eyes
seek the deep waters in those wan smiles,
those mysterious sweet mouths that breathe
their distance.
My heart asks for you, asks for you.

There is an innocence in women
that asks me, asks me;
it is some hidden thing they are
before which I am innocent.
It is some knowledge of innocence.
Their breasts lie under cover.
Like deer in the shade of foliage,
they breathe deeply and wait;
and the hunter, innocent and terrible,
enters love's forest.

There is a fear in women
that asks me, asks me.
And I pause in the still of the forest
as if my own terror surrounded me.
I listen for my own footsteps, my shadow
hunts me. Did you not hear in the music,
in the body's tango that we danced,
the sigh as of a lover before whom appears
the weeping and stricken form of his beloved?
She is like a white deer in the foliage

that, panting, heated, fixes upon him
her innocent gaze. Asks me, asks me,
are you the lover? are you the hunter?

.

I am myself a sphinx before whose question
I have been doomd. Woman,
        the Egyptian night surrounds you;
your visage like a clear full moon
in its clouds of dark, its perfumes of hair,
broods its radiance over the desert.
Let us gaze upon Thebes, where
we shall soon return to sleep; wearily we shall stir
and upon this city of our dream come that cold
electric flood of light. Spectral avenue of sphinxes!
Questioning females, answering males.
Question that shall never fathom its answer.
Answer that shall never fathom its question.

A Woman's Drunken Lament

Thou art a lion, my son, an architect of lunar monoliths;
Thou casteth a shadow among the colonnades of Thebes
and roareth, solitary in the dark thereof.
Pain of my heart, I have a joy that is the dark thereof.
Seek thou my breast, for there are hours of the night
when in deserted streets watchd by an eye
thou hast a lion's savage solitude and sorrow
and the joy thereof we share, thou and I,
a world we have devourd in our dreams.
The dark thereof, Father and tomorrow of
this arctic month long day, shines in my mind.
Those are wavering lights to cast a threatening dawn
upon the black Egyptian desert. Thou shalt be
a lion without eyes, an architect of electric palaces,
where sightless thou shalt gaze upon my revelries;

thou roareth out in pain; thou listeneth.
The rumble of the city's traffic dies; the sleepers wake
and in the adjoining room they whisper. Then remember,
thou art dear to me. I drink deeply
of thy soul. Thou art my architect of lunar memories,
my naked ship to carry me toward Death's
forgiving shores. Thou listeneth.
Aye! Aye! thou lonely ship, thou casteth
shadow on the dimly colonnaded sea.
My lion, thou art a wrecking sun to shed thy cold
and deadly light on Thebes. Forgotten dreamer!

Thou shalt not forget
this city whereof I am the Queen. Dear Questioner,
dear drifter in the tide of love,
bestill your terror in my calm. I love,
I love you, savage, whimpering,
night-disturbing one. Seek thou my calm,
the sphinx's breast. Feast
upon my shadow, hide there thy wretched lion-ness

I drink deeply of thy soul.

Portrait of Two Women

1.

My wrong, my wrong, my most grievous wrong.
In which comes this beauty.

Do I with-hold my beauty to feed thereon?
My friends grieve and I cry:
this is a radiant joy. Song
fills my throat. Feast of fullness
my heart's famishing.

If only my sense of your beauty
could flow back and fill you.

My wrong, my wrong, my most grievous wrong.
In which flowers this green,
light and shadowd, this yearning.
The yearning is the beautiful thing.

I talkd and tried to explain my wrong.
The words in the listening room were vain.
They multiplied what I faild to say.
I stoppd. She lay, remotely questioning.
Her love in sorrow was articulate.
It trembled upon my lips. Her throat,
her body, articulate song. I took
the moment's absolution.

If only my sense of your beauty
could flow back and fill you.

2.

Jimenez in the golden company
drinks deeply of her sorrow's wine.
She steeps her soul in that red vein,
the passion's vintage, she would deny,
and recites to us Keats' lovely lines.
This is a beauty beyond all beauty.

My wrong, my wrong, my most grievous wrong.
In which comes this beatific song, wrought
in the suffering of my friend. "Thou still
unravishd bride of quietness" she reads.
The light of joy flows from her voice
and fills to its brim my thirsting heart.

If only my sense of your passion
could flow back and fill you.

I sang and tried to fill the void.
The poet's art is a passionate fountain.
My wrong, my wrong, my most grievous wrong.
In which speaks this beauty.

We sat on the terrace in the afternoon
and spoke together of the scene. The blue
intensity of sky was miracle.
The reaches of the campus, lawn and grove,
all the leafy stillness seemd
leafy stillness of our mind.
This is my paradise, I said.
She gave intensely to the scene.

*If only my sense of your passion
could flow back and fill you.*

I Am a Most Fleshly Man

I am a most fleshly man, and see
in your body what stirs my spirit.
And my spirit is intimate of my hand,
intimate of my breast and heart,
intimate of my parted lips
that would seek their solace
in your lips.

Receive me; worn and warm body I am.
I am a most fleshly fire, and yearn
for your body to replenish my flame.
I would embrace you and name myself
anew in your flesh.

The green of eucalyptus boughs
hung in the distances of the air;
Les terraces au clair de la lune
playd in the orb of the afternoon, blue
and sunlit area where
we moved;
the *japanoiserie* of bay
and islands in the smoky haze;
seemd to bear the fine imprint,

distinct and lonely of the mind's design,
the beckoning intimation of a love
in which the days like swallows flew,
one by one, from the heart's dim grove
to trace in their flight the lineaments of truth.
I spoke to you and tried to say
I seek the body's rest in grace.

O I should have knelt upon the floor
and wept;
I should have surrendered to the body's faith
and knelt,
suppliant to the hour's god that came
and went,
a luminous shadow in the blood.

I have made my vow in flesh, and see
in you the body's golden convenant.
And the spirit is intimate of your hand,
intimate of your breast and lips.
I woo that carnal sacrament of you,
the lover's testament of faith
in which in body we release
the spirit's immortality.

Come unto me; questioning dark spirit,
you dwell upon the threshold of my mind.
This yearning is a vast eternity
that waste about us questioning lies,
and we in the limbo of disembodied love
stare upon the bodies we deny.
I am a most fleshly fire.
I would embrace you in that flame,
and we should lie brought then to rest
and gaze, gaze upon each other in that hour
when newly created each in the other
we hang like smoky music in the air.

•

Heavenly City, Earthly City

OVERTURE

Beauty is a bright and terrible disk.
It is the light of our inward heaven
and the light of the heaven in which we walk.
We talk together. Let our love leaven
and enlighten our talk! O we are dim.
We are dim shadows before our fiery selves.
We are mere moments before our eternities

The youth of the man I am now has gone.
I have passed from its bright glare into its shadow.
Twenty-seven years have wrought their careful pattern,
worn in my flesh their inarticulate burden,
worn in my animal the mark and strain
of an inward heaven. Some bright and terrible disk
that lighted once this city of my passion
has dimmd and gone. Beauty
is a bright and terrible disk.
It is the light of our inward fire
and the light of the fire in which we walk.
When I see the figure of my lover,
—this is the eternal answer that the eye of love
sees in each being —then
from the years that have tried my flesh,
in the stain and age that trace in my figure
failure and betrayal of that golden vision,
man's possible beauty, th'eternal fire
in the guise of my animal burns, burns bright
from the dim of my youth and consumes my youth
in its fiery self.
          In the dark of my manhood the flamy self
leaps like the sun's hairy image
caught in the black of an obscure mirror.
This is the apish chiaroscuro of our source, the sun.
This is my age, my inward heaven.
The city of my passion is reveald in its beauty.

Earthly city in which I walk, the light, your sun,
is the golden heart of that deep body,
the darkend city that gleams in the tide
of an inward sea. Dumbly, I hear its voices,
voices that merge in a chaos of other voices,
murmur and surge of a bright confusion.
The song, your voice that in my throat
rises in praise of some pure spirit, lonely
and yet lovely human aspiration, breaks
in the chaos of a massd impurity.
So a single bird flying up from its field
claims above the clamor of a dismal century,
asserts, asserts, in its perishable body
the lone clear cry of its perishable beauty.
In the moment of song—earthly radiant
city of poetry—that golden light
consumes in its focus a world I have sufferd,
the darkend city of my perishable age.

Yet never, never, can the heart meet the gaze
of that earthly paradise in which I walk.
It seems to accuse my heart; its quiet
and its song, the dappled mien of light and shade,
are like a beloved face that searches its reflexion
and is torn in the rage of an inward flood.

    The heart in the darkness of the city sings.
    It answers the song of its source, the sun.
    The darkness of the city protests, protests;
    there is a throng of angry voices.
    The heart in the darkness of the city sings:

    I have seen the face of my Redeemer.
    —this is th'eternal figure that appears
        and disappears
    in the human flood. Momentary answer!
    Never, never, can I meet the gaze

of that inward angel articulate of love;
and yet He touches me in passing.
His touch seems to penetrate and awaken
some answer, pure in its sleep, and is gone.
And now awakend I lie, dumbly changed,
too late, too late, inarticulate of love.
Could I but dream and dreaming gaze
upon the paradise of his eyes, but they are gone.
He, he is gone; he is gone; and knowing this,
I know the heavy change upon the world.
I fear. I fear.
Tell me that my Redeemer will answer.
Tell me that my Redeemer lives.
For there's a kind of world remaining still
tho he who did make animate and fill
that world be gone.

The voices of the night protest:

O lonely heart, too late, too late.
You cry out as if you were
some innocent, foundling of the angelic orders,
awakend by the passing of your Redeemer
to face the last long night alone.
Betrayer of man's possible beauty,
Thou art awakend to gaze upon thy dead
and speechless self, touchd by that angel
awakener of the dead.
Thou hast no Redeemer.
The ghost that walks in its reflected glimmer
is but the wraith that you call splendor.
O but you are dim before the fiery self
that is gone from your world.
Wrath is the ghost that walks in its glimmer
and pities, pities the lonely dead,
touches them in passing and awakens the heart
to face its death. Too late, too late.
There is no Redeemer.

The heart in the darkness of the city sings.
It answers the song of its source, the sun:

I cry out as a child in the dark.
I know that my Redeemer lives.
The rage of my lover meets my cry;
feasts upon my inward hell and shakes,
shakes my spirit in his fury; tears
from me the strain of life,
inviolate song, and mocks my dim
inarticulate heaven. Now in my wilderness
where I have been driven by that blind
Avenger, awakener of the damnd,
betrayd by my Demon shall I in turn
betray my Redeemer? I walk alone
in that inward hell, shaken and riven
from my Beloved, the lover of my inward heaven.
Like Satan fallen in the weight of his pride,
speechless I face that punishing spirit
articulate of my own damnation.
This was the lover that answerd my cry,
as a wrathful father might answer a child
who, dumb in the strain of the wrath inside,
cried out in fear for the comfort of love.

I know that my Redeemer lives
who loves, who loves my lonely spirit
and seeks in the darkness of my night
to absolve my torture in his passion.

O my Beloved, in the night of my soul
I have thirsted for some passionate wrong.
I have lain in the arms of the destroying angel.
I have heard in hatred's sea the Siren's song and cast
  myself upon that strand; held in love's cruel
       counterpart,
known the warm embrace and the inward cold.

Dumbly, I listen to the Siren's insistent sound,
that brazen counterfeit of song that charms
and fixes the soul upon its destruction:
this is the magnet of a massd impurity.
I walk in the eclipse of my Beloved.

But O the Earthly city remains.
In my dismal century the Earth replenishes,
replenishes her beauty.
Against the Siren's monotone, the fixd accusing glare,
your voice, Beloved, rises in praise
of that fair spirit, my inward heaven.
I know that my Redeemer lives.
The light, His sun, is the radiant song
that consumes in its focus a world I have sufferd,
asserts, asserts, against the Siren counterfeit,
the Earthly paradise in which I walk;
this is the measure of my dismay:
To know its beauty like the face of my Beloved
that is torn in the rage of an inward flood.

II

Pity is the wrath in which we walk.
My heart like a burdend Icarus having struck terror
falls from its universe into the dark.
Then gaze deep upon my lover's gleam, feed my soul
upon the damnd perdition of his eyes.
The inward spark, the flamy self
dies, and its shadow leaps forward.
See, it is a demon lover to fill the abyss
as he falls.
Pity is the wrath in which we walk.
Then gaze deep, deep upon the gleam.
This is the true mirror of my face.
"No," I say. "No." In the shadowy room
I seek to disentangle myself from his arms.
Dumbly, unmoving he lies, having laid bare
his wrath, betrayd, he clings to me.
Pity is the gleam of the wrath inside,

a demon light to illuminate the face
and betray the heart. Like burdend Icarus
I would fall in the weight of my body
and damaged wings, in my knowledge,
into some dark and forgiving sea.
Pity is the unforgiving sea.

Traveler who would bring love's light into hell.
When that shadowy beloved turns from his hell
a face to gaze upon your face; this is a damnd
Eurydice, that catches in her mirroring quest
the gleam of love as a new perdition.
Sweep, then Orpheus, the wild music from your lyre
as if you sang lost love, but remember
the beauty and charm are hate's machineries,
demonic art that catches the damnation into its disk
and lends to hell its immortal strain.
Sweep, then, Orpheus, the wild love from your lips
and when from the far room your forgiven lover
cries out from the rejection that forgiving is:
remember Eurydice's face because you turnd
is turnd toward her death; remember her cry
cries with love's final breath and is gone;
remember that pity, for the damnd, is hate;
remember his face as your Eurydice
that was the woman's face in the lunar gleam of sleep.
The damnd in the fires of love wrap round themselves
and shriek. AI AI Orpheus, the brutal lyre,
beauty and charm to turn her face
toward its perdition.

Where is that dark and forgiving sea, flood
of rage or sorrow to sweep thru my body,
vast poem, ocean of the soul's resounding deep,
where falling Icarus falls to his rest?
In the blaze of his blinded eyes
the disk shows black, burnd in his mind
a charcoal sun.
Torn from his flight among the Bacchae of the sun,

those burning women of exaltation's fury,
he is hurld in the weight of wings and knowledge
into the forgiving depths of sleep.

J'ai dû tomber de très haut, de très haut,
très haut sur la tête.
Où est mon coeur? Où est ma tête?
Eurydice, Eurydice.
Que j'ai peur.
How heavy my heart falls with its burden.
There is no world than the world of my dreams
where the weight of my knowledge falls so far.
Orpheus of the bleeding wings among the beasts
in the shadowy meadows that extend in sleep
sings his sweet strain. *Eurydice, Eurydice.*
He closes his eyelids and in that inward light
Eurydice's dark face returns and is banishd by his gaze
into eternity. Nightmare minister to pain!
Pity is the wrath in which he walks.
The Bacchae, furious women, drunk with lust,
close their eyes like their clenchd fists
and see in the glare of their blinded eyes
a myriad burning destruction of the body.
AI AI these are sorrow's witch-like sisters
with their hair in rays like an angry sun; they cry
against earth's shady consolation, inviolate song.
How in our misery the calm of the grove,
and the calm of the evening's air, earth's
loving breath, commiserates and increases our fury.
We shall be redeemd and forgiven in passion,
washd thru by the fires of passion's sun,
and find in our bodies an immaculate quiet.

The Bacchae in pure passion's roar
raise their clenchd and violent hands
against the lonely and still singer,
Orpheus, who would sing love's praise.
He I am who torn in my flesh
return at last to my lost Eurydice,

the inward sea, terror's sister-face,
to receive my Icarus.

The Bacchae tear in my fleshly sleep
fleshly ribbons that gleam like gold.
I lie under the weight of the black water.
Eurydice toward whom I dare not look
—she is the bright spirit that sleeps in my heart—
returns to meet my inward gaze.

III

The praise of the sun is a didactic poem.
The ape in his raiment of gold or cloth of fire
apes the categories of the spiritual man
and, in the teaching, learns from his raiments
the torturous lesson of his apish form.
What man knows more in his cloth of gold
who fixes his eye upon his source? I know no more
than the fleshly life that clothes in its ardor
the bony rigor of my inward form.
The lineaments of my body are
a didactic poem,
the apish chiaroscuro of my source, the sun.

The praise of the sun is a solitary poem.
The lonely man can turn his skull sunwards
until that glory penetrates
and sears the confines of the bone;
can howl, can whirl his reluctant arms
and measure his pride against the sun;
can moan in his incompleted image,
can howl for the bliss of his final mate.
He catches the sun in the mirroring heart
and praises that blazing solitude.
Then in the avenues of his earthly city
unearthly presences wink,
unfathomable eyes of an inward vision.

O with what pain I watch in my vision
my proud and reluctant animal self
where he sings in his lonely monotone;
he turns his beseeching enraptured eyes
and glares upon the heavenly scene,
cries, cries as if hurt by the surrounding beauty,
and apes the sound of a vaster heart.

He mimics the opulence of the sun,
and in that bright confusion, love,
he burns in exaltation's fires,
clutches, clutches at his animal mate
and whimpers against the pit of dark.

I watch with pain my hairy self
crouchd in his abject sexual kingdom
writhe in that brief ecstatic span
as if he took the sun within himself
and became a creature of the sun;
became an illumined body of voices;
as if in the pit of his animal dumb
he heard the counterpoint,
the mimic tum–tum–tum of a vaster heart.

The praise of the sun is a nostalgic poem.
The tum–tum–tum in memory
is like the pounding surf in dreams.
The man in the solitude of his poetic form
finds his self-consciousness defined
by the boundaries of a non-committal sea
that washes, washes the reluctant mind
and carves from its shores its secret coves.

Sometimes our feelings are so mild
they are like a day when rocks
seem mere extensions of the sea
washd in a world of oceanic blue
and continents seem dreams of a watry deep.

Turbulent Pacific! the sea-lions bark
in ghostly conversations and sun themselves
upon the sea-conditiond rocks.
Insistent questioner of our shores!
Somnambulist, old comforter!
You wright in passion's storm and passionate calm
your reasonless change and seek to restore
the aspiring man to your green remote.

The individual ape in the human sea
is worn, is worn by a non-committal tide
and shows in his unnecessary watching face
the necessary convolutions of that sea,
the memories of forsaken lands.

The praise of the sun is a nostalgic poem;
sometimes the sea seems mild and light
as a luminous harp upon which the sun plays
threaded with indolent wires of gold
across the ruddy music of its waves
and its voices merge in a pulsing counterpoint
to sing the wonders of the sun,
the beasts of the sun and the watry beasts.

Sea leopards cough in the halls of our sleep,
swim in the wastes of salt and wrack of ships,
and sun themselves upon the resounding rocks,
or lie in the thoughtless shallows of the sun.
These are the tides of the poetic sea.
I drift, I drift. The praise of the sun
is purposeless. I dream of those forsaken shores
wrappd in the mind's redeeming haze.
Sea leopards cough in the halls of our sleep;
disturb the course of the nostalgic sea,
casual hints where harmlessly they swim
of some brooding fear in the fiery deep.

The earth has tides of desolation and of bliss,
of shadows and of amber marbled surfaces,
laments and cries, vague intimations of the sun,
terrors, brightnesses of noon, and groves
of memory: in these her beauty is renewd.
The wandering man returns to his city
as if he might return to earth a light, a joy;
and find his rest in earthly company.

The praise of the sun is a renewing poem.
The earth replenishes, replenishes her beauty
and sings a green praise of her terrible source.
The sea reflects, reflects in her evening tides
upon a lavender recall of some past glory,
some dazzle of a noon magnificence.
The evening hour is eloquent of the sun.
This is no dominion of the pure terror
but soothes, soothes. We walk in the light
of beauty's calm; our city lies about us
murmuring, drifts in an evening humanity.
There is a wisdom of night and day,
older than that proud blaze of sun,
in which we rest, a passion, primitive to love,
of perishing, a praise and recreation of the sun.
My earthly city is reveald in its beauty.

Uncollected Work 1933–1947

A Moment of Ecstasy

The sun, that had heated the great grey boulder upon which I lay, laid its genial warmth pleasantly tingling upon my back. Great green elephant ears swayed and bowed in the gentle breeze. My lungs rejoiced in the clean fresh air. The distant call of a bird, the scurry of wee feet, the rustle of leaves, the splash of a pebble as it fell into one of the cool pools that slumbered silently in the shaded grottos at the side of the stream, all seemed to my drugged senses a multitude of fantasies.

I had a strange urge to become a part of that brook that tossed and tumbled over the rocks giggling, gurgling and madly gyrating in fantasic swirls and eddies. I wished to rush onward, to trickle over the rocks and roar, to cascade, onward, ever onward to the sea. Finally the atmosphere dragged my ego into a state of helplessness, and I sank into a deep slumber.

That night I awoke in bed with a start. A thousand demons burned my flesh. I thought at first that I had died and that I had arrived at my destination. I turned, and a burning fiery lash whipped my neck. My legs had been baked to a brilliant scarlet. I spent the rest of the night on a bed of white hot coals.

Yet many summers in the future will see me as many summers in the past have seen me, lying on a rock in the sun.

An Interpretation

"Quinquireme of Nineveh from distant Ophir
Rowing home to heaven in sunny Palestine
With cargoes of ivory,
And apes and peacocks,
Sandalwood, cedarwood, and sweet white wine."

The Star of Isthar was returning from Egypt. Her hold was stored with treasure. There were rare wines of Spain and Greece and woods from the depths of Africa. There were monkeys and peacocks of silver, green-gold, and royal-blue. There was dull, cold gold from far Ophir to adorn the neck of Ila-Azil, the daughter of the high priest of Baal at Tyre. There were rolls of papyrus and cream tusks brought north from the sixth cataract of the Nile. There were slaves—Nubians, shining ebony sun-gods; Pygmies, cunning dwarves to amuse the court of Nineveh; and tall strong Bushmen to build the square temples of Assyria.

All five tiers of the rowers moved—full strength in perfect cadence. Balamahe, the captain, was angry and frightened. He knew that every sign told of a coming storm, and he cursed the star that had sent his ship to sea on that day.

The sky was dark; the air was heavy. The sea moaned and sobbed as if awaiting some awful moment—the Battle of the Gods. For a second the world was still. Then, with the wail of the Furies the wind rose, rolling and tossing the billows of the sea higher and higher. The huge galley was buffeted from height to height and side to side like a toy vessel in a washing machine. From the hold the horrid screams of the white baboon in utter terror and the harsh wild screeches of the peafowl, in discord with the pagan chants of the blacks, rose and fell in rivalry with the very screaming of the elements.

The ship lurched, swerved, and dived into the midst of the chaos. The sea opened a great mouth and swallowed the mighty vessel into her depths. A great God had claimed his own.

Song of Undine

The raging strength of mountain stream,
The secrets of the sea,
The rolling clouds of mist
Are given unto me.

The crashing waves of crumbling shores,
The murmur of the deep
Shall speak to those who understand
Of treasures that I keep.

The ancient towers of Atlantis
The wealth of sunken gold
More glories yet there are to know
A thousand tales untold.

Come kiss my icy lips tonight —
The earth holds naught for you;
Here in my arms you may forget
The sorrows come to you.

O Sailor come, oh! come to me
Your father came before
I took your wife, I took your child
I've taken many more.

O Sailor come, oh! come to me
To join them in the deep
You come, you come to kiss my lips
Another in my keep.

The Guardian of the Temple

Stay, stranger, questioning; you climbed the hill
And now you flee the answer. So I will
That you shall hear. For many men, I find,
Have scaled the focky step with wondering mind
Upon the snowy temple at its crest.
But seeing me they halt, forget their quest,
Turn their tracks, and unmindful of the way
Rush madly back, leaving me in dismay,
Alone. Am I a beast that men should shun
My glance? Seek not to go. I am not done.
You flinch; you would perhaps to break the hold,
But no, you must not go. The tale's untold.
You seek the gold of knowledge. In my eyes
Find truth. Look through the temple. There are lies.
You may wander your lives in shadowed halls.
You may search its altars. The jeweled palls
Are woven in dark design without light
Of meaning. Follow in dust of their flight
The children of filth. All time, all history,

Is naught. Look not back. What is there, but shade?
Light is ahead and in my eyes. Pasts fade;
Futures become distinct. There flee not,
Here in my eyes—the truth—the thing you sought—,
And still you turn from peace to darkest hells.

Ego Involneratus

A constant foe tears fierce against the walls
That shadowed stand above the privy pain
Of my dark heart. A silence heavy falls
Upon the spot within while battles reign
Without, and softmouthed spies would seek in vain
To steal the confidences of the place:
But ah, an armed watch it is who feigns
This seeming frankness that conceals his mace
And shield which he holds firm behind the face
Of peace. My guards are sly and ever firm
The secret walls that tower black in space
Above the treasured nothingness, the sperm
That sterile lies and false assumes a price
Set by its stern denial from men's eyes.

People

1.

He'd lost a leg (in the war, he said)
Jumping a freight car. We called him Red
And gave him a room (a meal and a bed)
For five bucks a month.

It's real easy living, Red used to say
The money's dirt cheap when you get it the way
I gets my dough.
We don't know his racket, but most of his pay
Goes for his booze. At the end of the day
He gets drunk. O, it's easy the way
He makes his money, but in the long run
We gets the dough while he has the fun
Cause Ma sells him gin.
We give him a room (a bed and a meal)
And he buys our rotgut. It's a good deal
Of gin that he buys for himself.
We don't know his racket, but most of his pay
Goes for his booze. And at the end of the day
We gets the dough.

2.

There's a guy at the corner under the light
And it's raining like hell (it doesn't seem right)
He just stands and stares and waits in the night.
I wish that he'd move, but he doesn't at all.
He just stands there waiting and lets the rain fall.
If I throw up the window, will he answer my call?
Are you dead, sir? He just stands there, tall
And unreal in the rain. Is it right?
"Do you want something, sir?" I cry in the night.
He turns and looks up and I switch off the light
And guiltily turn from the window in fright.

3.

If any you birds sees Tony Luchezzi
Tell the poor sucker his wife has gone crazy.
She's been wandering around a little bit hazy
In mind. And she's murdered Marie.

Tell him sometime when he's half in a dream,
When he's drunk and only some incomplete gleam
Of the facts will come in. Buy him a drink
And say that his Lotta's gone on the blink.
It's easy to do. Yon can laugh; you can jest.
But who's got the guts to tell him the rest.
And she's murdered little Marie.
He's got to be told, but who wouldn't shrink
From telling the guy that his baby's pink
Nightie is splattered with blood, and his wife
In a queer drunken fit has grabbed up a knife
And she's murdered little Marie.

If any you birds sees Tony Luchezzi
Buy him a drink, tell him he's lazy,
A poor drunken fool; and then through your laughter
Cry out the thought that must follow after:
She's murdered little Marie.

4.

Ellen sits sad by the window and peers
Out below to the street. The cries and the cheers
And the gay running feet on the road . . . but her ears
Hear them not, only emptiness swept by the years
That have sucked out her mind and dried up her tears
As she sits and solemnly peers
Out the window.
Ellen is gray and her once sparkling eyes
Are rheumy and hard, no more blue skies
Reflected within but only the greys
Of winter are there and a dull glittered glaze.
And hundreds of flies.
Come buzzing around
In the sun
As she sits in the sun.
She just sits and she sits and sometimes she sighs.
She nods her grey head and closes her eyes

(The dead winter skys) And she sleeps in the sun
Till we wake her for dinner. The day is begun
And ended in eating. Days one by one
Plod on to form months and the months to make years
As Ellen sits dead by the window and peers.

Pax Vobiscum

CAPITALIST

Is it cannon that I hear?
Sounds like war is drawing near.
We'll make paper shoes this year.
For the soldiers will not care
With the enemy to dare
What the hell they have to wear.

We'll make heaps and heaps of dough,
Watching all the soldiers go
Marching by in paper shoes . . .

FARMER

Is it gunshot in the morn?
I've no cause to be forlorn.
I'll sell rotten meat and corn.
For the soldiers it's a treat.
Anything is good to eat.
They can't crab about their meat.

We'll make money overnight,
Watching soldiers go to fight
Bellies full of rotgut booze . . .

PROSTITUTE

Are those soldiers in the square?
Money flowing over there?

I'll paint my lips, do up my hair,
Earn a little on the sly.
Who's to weep if they should die?
Take the next one passing by.

I'll make plenty out of this
Send them marching with a kiss,
Bodies bitten by my sting . . .

MOTHER

Is it war that has begun?
I'll send out my little son.
It'll be just lots of fun
Sitting here the whole war through
Knitting for my boy in blue.
I will bear his crosses too
And his medals when he dies
And as tears come to my eyes
In OUR honor all will sing . . .

COMMUNIST-PACIFIST

Are those war clouds over Spain?
I shall fight for peace again.
Make the cause of war quite plain.
It's the nasty Nazi boys
Making all that dirty noise.
Any Fascist quite enjoys
Raping nuns and burning homes.

All the blame for this is Rome's.
Just a Papist revelry . . .

FASCIST-MILITARIST

Is this war? Well I declare!
People fighting over there?
What a mess! By god, I swear
It's those anarchistic reds

Killing babies in their beds
Blowing off civilians' heads!

Helping rebels to the fore?
Heavens no. It's not our war.
Our boys fight for Italy . . .

A Campus Poet Sprouts Social Consciousness

No money for meat for supper, she said,
no bone for soup, nor butter, nor bread.
O God! we'll have to go hungry to bed
Pop's unemployed and Grandmother's dead
Mother broke her arm and we're all unfed
all unfed, all unfed.
Not naked yet, but nearly dead
Not naked yet, but god we're cold
six in a bed, nine days old
Mother Hubbard her bosom bare
starving gaily in a rocking chair.
In silence the middle class may fret
but we are the PROLETARIATE

Down with the rich, up with the poor
        let the bosses shovel manure!
Let the bosses give way to the Masses
        the world will be ruled by the lower classes!

Self-Portrait at 90

Grandfather Symmes is a sloppy old fool.
He's lost all his teeth and they feed him on gruel,
And he dribbles his mush in his beard.
At six in the morning they wind up his bed

And no matter how careful they are how he's fed,
He upsets his coffee and ever ill-bred
He dribbles his mush in his beard.
At noon he will sputter and bubble and spray
His milk toast and prune juice flying astray
Out of his mouth on the blankets to stay
Til Annie or Georgie clean the room for the day.

Poor Robert Symmes — at ninety he drools.
If he ever can keep his beard out of his gruels
He dribbles his mush in his beard.

Relativity, a Love Letter, and Relative to What; A Love Letter

Dark leads into the streets and dark leads into the streets and a shut door. Partly only into being and a shut door. Partly only into being and a shut door. Being as in being nowhere. Being as to come into being in partly only and outside. Dark leads into the streets and a shut door.

To come suddenly upon something. Suddenly upon something and and partly only in being. To be outside and partly in being in by the inside. Suddenly inside to come suddenly partly only to being. Being only as for one partly understanding and a shut door.

Shutting out and shutting in. Shutting out shutting in and shutting in shutting out. Inside and outside shut in. Inside and outside shut out. Shut out. Shut, partly being shut and partly being shut. Inside and shut out. To come suddenly out and shut in.

Being always aware of what has to come to be happening. Being suddenly always aware of what has to come to be happening. Is happening and being also suddenly and always aware. Being, partly only in being and always aware. Always being to one who is not aware. Being suddenly aware of one being who has not been aware. One who is not aware. Suddenly and always aware of being outside and being only by the inside. Aware of the outside as being the inside. Aware of the inside as being the outside and a shut door.

Partly in being and more in position to. More in position in space and in time and now being aware. Being aware of space. Being aware of being relative only to one who is not aware and being aware of space in relation to another ones being. Being partly aware of space in another ones being. Now another ones being elsewhere. Another one being constantly elsewhere and being entirely and sincerely different. Another one being sincerely. Another one being sincerely a shut door. More in position than in being. And another one entirely in position, and entirely another one in being. Partly only being and not aware of position. Not aware of once being in position. Not aware of time and another ones being.

Suddenly one comes to be one living and one ceases to be one studying to be living. Suddenly one comes to be one living another one outside. Always one is living another one inside entirely, and sincerely another one being outside. Another is one inside who is outside.

This one is entirely this one. There are many ones and this one is entirely and sincerely this one. This one may be relative only to time and space but that one feels not relativity but entirely for this one. That one feels entirely living for this one. This one may be and this one may have been and this one may come to have been. This one is being relative only to space but that one feels entirely living for this one. This can be understood Sarie but not known. Not clearly known but clearly felt.

(not felt but clearly spoken)

That is a highly impudent answer.

This one was one being entirely himself and that one was one being several other people. This one was entirely unaware and one being relative only to time and space. That one felt that one could be being entirely for another one. One and one. A shut door and one. A dog crying at a closed door in the dark. There were many other ones for that one but this one was entirely and always this one for that one. This one was always that one for that one then. There were very many others being relative to time and space for that one and this one for that one that one felt was being. That one felt was being. That one felt was being within and sincerely outside. Outside, shut door. Outside, a shut door and. And out and in and. And in the outside and. And and. Often and. Much was to be said about and. Much was never thought about and. Much was thought about inside without. Much had been thought about out side within. Out with in. Out with in and in with out and.

In, entirely being. and Outside, a shut door. Outside, a door. Much had been thought about doors and death and about death by this one. Doors and death by this one. Doors and death and doors. Doors and doors and doors. Much had been thought about doors by that one. Much had been said about death by this one. This one about doors and death. Death and death and doors and thread. This one built doors and that one built windows. Sensing to see a window. That one built windows and doors for very many others who were often partly this one.

Partially punning and partially making sense.

(CECILY: A PARABLE)

Some of these were partially making sense. Sense and senses and Cecily. Cecily and forever partially senses and partially suddenly being sense and senses. Sense. Sense and senses for Cecily. Some of these sensed senses. Cecily sensing and Cecily sensing and Cecily sensing.

(DOLOUR: A QUESTION)

May this one have come to be one resenting that one? Resenting that one entirely.

May this one have come to be one aware of resenting.

(CABELL: A DESCRIPTION)

Resenting Cabell. Being partly resenting and partly being afraid of Cabell. Cabell shares and Cabell share and being partly resenting of Cabell shares. Being entirely different from self and Cabell. Being different and resenting two things at once. Cabell shares and partly and. Cabell and Cecily sensing. Cabell sensing senses.

This one being entirely elsewhere. This one being often and entirely apart. That one being never elsewhere but being one being in another ones being then. Being one not being oneself but being one being elsewhere another ones being. One being sincerely. One being sincerely and another one being in ones being sincerely. One being outside and without inside without. One being relative and fearing relativity.

Relative to what and a door and a door again a door.

Ritual

"From the encroaching glaciers of despair, from the drought that withers the lower centers, from the star Wormwood, and from death by burning . . . " —*Auden*

I shall not be spared
nor shall my limbs be spared
nor those blind pockets spared
kept shamefully
the frightened sockets
of my cold gems be spared
the drying wind.

Is there to be no bed from cold
No bed is there from cold?
the long cruel breath of dying ice
the slow death creeping
up from the seawastes slicing
mist and shroud of fog and
heavy branches weeping
in the shroud of fog with cold.
Nor from the ice
slut grey upon the fields
moving grey across the lands
biting at the hands of mourning,
eating back the roots with cold
eating back into the rock
the early roots with shock
of sudden cold.

No refuge there from cold
No refuge in the ground
Not the refuge in the dark
Not the refuge found for eyes
in darkness hiding.
Nor may I hide as underneath the stone
the sullen serpent hides
and keeps his wanton pile of eggs
and skins shed off in shreds
of winters past and sleeps.

No refuge there.
No shelter shuts it out.
No sanctuary found from doubt
beneath the stone.
No sanctuary found in madness,
no turning back.
There is no turning backward here
in dreams, no automat escape.
I move with dreameyes closed
somnambulant with cold long hands
dropped listless sleeping,
white beneath the gown disclosed
at night.
No longer fear of older races
nor of drowning nor of faces
hid by masks for prophecy.

2) THE CLAIRAUDIENTS

I   Dust of the winds
Mocking
Dust of the
Mocking
Dust
Dust of dreams
Dust of the winds
Dust of dreams blown
where the wind whispers,
at the cold stone moving in tombs,
moving in darkness without eyes,
sightless in caverns,
in the rooms of the dead, sightless.

Dreams of the dead where the wind
moving blindly
speaks secrets
whispers. whispers.
Dreams of dead sisters
sitting in rows in old coffins

where the dead sit
with dead hands raised in shame
above the dead face pitted
above the dead face
that no mirror reflects
no creek casts image moving
no shining surface broken
no image moving
no shadow shifting from the sun,
only shade of shadow's shadow drifting.

Vacant voices
that were heard in dreams,
withering in dreams, with dust recalled,
brought back,
brought up,
reheard in caves where the dead sit
waiting.
pointing at nothing.
Three dead sisters nothing covering,
with caution
with silence
with dead hands raised
where the wind whispers
lifting. Drifting dust
and shifting voiceless,
without voices.

II   Regard the empty plain and the moon
     with pitted face above the wastes,
     no longer moving tides,
     no longer moving seas,
     but dead.
     The white moon riding
     sickly in the jaundiced sky, a sterile cavity
     where once an eye had glared
     with fire now gone,
     now smothered out.   The dawn
     brings yawning shadows to the city,

wastes and perishes.
The early light upon the lands
runs cold and barren to the sea
the dead sea now
no longer moving to the moon
the cold sea now, desexed,
made impotent with waxen face of water
motionless.
The waters robbed,
deprived of voices, speechless,
silent, silent.

III Those who see clearly
see little.
Those who hear clearly
hear little
other than wind
or the turning of dust
on that other sea.

IV Who knows as the wind at the pillars knows
knows who came last?
The tired ones came to sleep, and those
came too who could not sleep
because of dreams.
                    Memory of things forgotten,
memory of youth desired, and wasted, gone.
The tired ones came to sleep, and those
came too who could not sleep
because of dreams, disturbed by visions,
words from cities,
words from words from words from cities,
heard as through a waterwall
fardistant tones recall
the shining past.
These voices heard clairaudient
call back the word
the lost sound they had cherished
on their printed pages, dreams

that perished in the night,
lost meaning, echoed meaningless
upon the senile earth from caverns.

v   In mirrors
    Eyes that had gone blind and sunken in
    stared wildly from their sockets, dead,
    importantly from caverns, peering out from caverns
    dried back into their dead pocked faces.
    Flowers died that doubt had withered.
    Flowers bloomed hysterically and withered,
    shrunken back with dying seed,
    the black sap curdling at their roots
    bitten to the stone.

    Where did you hear it?
    Out of the moon.
    Where did you hear it?
    Foretold from the dead craters of the moon.

    Ask the wind in the corridors
    Ask the wind at the dead pillars
    in the tired places, what their voices were
    what were their voices
    those last people.
    Where they gathered, those last ones waiting,
    waiting. waiting.
    peering up with pallid faces, watching in the sky
    the birds of prey
    with leering wings soaring
    with wings soaring of bone
    and boney beaks.

    This now the empty day's
    the formless night's
    where wonders walk no more abroad
    and strength is lost.
    The age run dry, the senile age,
    the dry, dead seed spilled useless,

wasted.
These last orgasms
painful
useless
these sterile lusts
these last writhings in the sand
these last dead passions
burnt out
run sick
perverted.
the old world
the old earth
the old soil, wrinkled.
Remembering old strength lost
searching old balls for seed.
dead seed
dry
dry loins
and no more
no seed.

3) THE SACRIFICE

Where had the forms gone, now returned,
where burned, now springing from ashes
the new phoenix,
bloody,
tearing of flesh.

And the doors were swung back.
Out into the sunlight we came, into the courtyard
and through the streets singing.

She with her breasts naked,
high standing breasts shining white in the sun,
chilled with the morning.
Stoney.
Stoney.
She with the sky blue and the sea blue
dark with the night and her eyes dark

and her hair black with night and no stars,
no shower of lights.
And they brought a bull then
straining with the full ropes and
sullen with strength.
She with her breasts naked
she with her dark hair flowing
and her long narrow body white in the sun,
white with stillness,
waited.
And they brought a young bull
to be mated, to be broken
steel head in the sun
out of aloneness,
bearing a wreath of flowers came
and leading there before them, slowly
where the gates narrowed,
leading a bull.

There is pain when the soil breaks.
The roots in the spring cut the soil
and there's pain.
I feel it.
I feel the pain.
I sense the earth's splitting, yielding in terror.
There where the sword cuts.
There where the blade breaks through the surface.
Each shining green dripping with blood
each cruel flower sapping up pain,
exploding with whiteness, straining the soil
breaking through the peace of old age
and of winter.
There is pain when the ice breaks,
pain where the creek cuts the surface
slashing the quiet with rage
breaking the spring with anger.
I feel it.
I feel it.
I feel the breaking of winter

stabbing the fields with new glory
bleeding the hills with purple.
I feel it.
I feel the pain.

No peace had we in dying.
Even the dead flesh is quickened up from rest with pain
and breeds new seed.
No peace had we in dying.
Even that final darkness broken
pierced and shattered.
Even the dark earth broken.
No peace,
What had decayed and lain at rest,
what we had laid at rest,
is hurt again to life,
unwanted.

And we who thought to sleep
who had rejoiced in death are tortured now
with sudden wakening at night.
No refuge now, the sudden light
destroys our eyes with pain,
the new roots stir the flesh with life
unwanted birth,
in agony resurrection.
We who had been laid to rest are hurt
the silence of the sepulchre,
the chastity in stone is broken,
torn apart,
awakened.
And then they ate the bull
cutting up the flesh in parts
Titan females tearing at the flesh
Each to each.
Fourteen times divided, scattered,
eaten, devoured by Titans there
destroyed.

And Isis glassy eyed,
without tears, wandered tearless,
blind with the agony of loneliness.
Full breasted Isis wandered
penetrating here the wilderness
here the desert, here the city
cherishing the fragments,
walking through the crowds alone
searching every face in passing
searching out the faces passing.

I saw her too.
I saw her when they rioted at Frisco,
standing on the docks among the strikers,
crying blood.
I saw her when the mobs in London
swarmed the gas filled streets and sank
struggling at their feet.
I saw her in those last days waiting,
standing, watching.
I saw her in those last days by the river
where the lonely wandered,
contemplating death.
I too am lonely, incomplete.
And she was there, there at the gates of Sing-Sing
counting faces.
His?
Twice in the madhouse found she hope,
hearing the wailing of a lost fragment
cut apart in some time past, she had hope
that it was hers,
His body.
I saw her at the scaffold clutching to an arm
and there at Chateau-Thierry robbing graves,
quickening the ash with pain
and cherishing the fragments.

But they cut through the silence
gnawing at the tomb,
wracked his body with new pain
inspiring life,
running as a thin flame through the veins,
burning at the dead centers,
quickening the nerves to sense again
the agony of hands.
But they out through the silence,
Rent aside the seals,
clawing at the stoney boundaries
they raped his tomb and forced him back
back to the light,
to agony of hands
that they might hope,
might hope.

We came
And through the streets singing,
fanfare of trumpets,
crashing of cymbals, cutting the air
slashing the air with knives
bearing knives, singing.
down to the caves.
Came down to the caves.

The Gestation

I have gone down to the beach
where green in this light of this moon
and huge in the shadow of this land
the host lies.
Already my mother eats
and there are others
crouched where millions swarm in the sand
mouths covered with dust

moving up and over the body
eating in this green light,
and I will not eat.

But rather I walk at the shore
where the water grins, sinking inward,
leaving at the rim
this ring of salt.

Nor is there beast-call nor bird-call
nor call of trumpet.

The concave sky curving from the edge of the world
catches only the rustle of beetles,
and they dry.
And the moon swerves
sickening through the wide immaculate heaven,
Broods disaster, blurred with gin.

Nor bear they yolk of egg,
only dry shell.

And their voices, those men
feasting at the fungus flesh,
their song is the croak
their voice, the dry rasp.
Away from the towering fungus corpse,
from the dunes to the broad shore
and he comes with me.

The insect race is behind,
creeps blindly on the carcase of the host
and creaks minutely.
        Churp! crack! the sound of crickets
lusting in the wilderness.

And he grasps my hand
and I grasp his hand
sensing the strength that was lost
and the seed of new strength from despair.

We stand at the sea edge, waiting,
and the sea comes roaring at our feet
out of that womb the waters roaring
hissing up in many voices
with tendril arms extending
coiling back from the rim of salt,
back from our ankles hollow with hunger.

I have desire to dance
and in a clear clear sky
I see a white bird flying south
I see a shining rock high rising
a tragic pylon from the sea.

The Protestants

CANTO ONE

The guilty look shifts from each window
and in the street the children stop their games.
Among the piles of broken brick
the cops and robbers stop. In her retreat
the slattern female winces up her face
and screws a smile for silence,
accepts with shifty eyes your challenge
while from abandoned street
across the rows of rusted rail
and from the dark of doorways
comes this barking. Even the small ones
leaving their chalkmark on the pavement
follow with a crafty baby face for money.

Hunger breeds such age in one,
hunger wrinkles back the skin,
reveals the animal eye
and the claw.

I see the bone beneath her flesh
and where she moves
the pelvic rot.

Houses of greed crowding the street,
brownstone fronts with empty eyes.
For Rent. For Sale. Condemned.
Each hungry room reaching back
with hollows of darkness and broken glass.
Haven for cats. Mocker of poor.
Stone. Timber. Lumber under the dust,
bearing the shock of the passing truck.

The house shakes with the contact.
Brick breaks the window. Laughter.
Everything tight to a breaking.

Grass cracks through such cement.
The rain in the spring and the sun
and a little grass pushing up
here in this corner breaks the cement.

Fire coming upon such a world,
from such things will make a test.
The sky over the L blazes with heat
where stripes of sulphur streak the walls.
Ice melts, and the psychopath beholds
the burning gas in a midnight world.
The Times. The News. A million books.
Coupons. tickets. food for the fireburn.
Phoenix rising from the ash heap —
birdfire from bundles — old clothes,
furniture broken and broken teeth
and with her hair streaming fire
a woman approaches, entirely nude,
her body stone white from the age of stone,
and a wolf at her side.
"Poisoner of the young!" — I cry.
"Demon, and you so near the bottom?"

And she — "Your world already shudders."
And we walked out under the X-rays
so that the metal plates above my knee
showed dark against my gelatine flesh,
and she was stone all milky stone,
the wolf a bony spectre at her side.

Crumbling south and north, the subway,
shower of brick and dust of mortar.
The skeleton city revealed.
The light humming.
The air making sound over the city.
Greyribbed. Inconstant.
Airdeath into fire at midnight,
and she being not of this world,
having crossed from beyond,
walks beside me. Speaks.
"We walk here among lost people."
and an old man rises in protest
making the sign of the comrade.
"See" — he cries — "you who would avoid hell-mouth,
Here is a hell we have created."

Granite. Steel. Webs of stone.
This concrete world against the sky
so that if there are stars,
there are stars only through a shield of glass,
only the glimmer, cold and unreal,
the cinema hallucination
lost in the eternal brighter eyes of our electric night.
When I look out over the river
there looms this arm of iron across the sky,
the sooty stacks of railroad yards
and if there are stars — I look —
they are lost in the lights of the town.

And from the caverns of this world,
houses of greed crowding the street
so that no man finds his rest.

This room empty, hungry with dust,
movement only as the spider moves.
And this room where seven live,
a frying pan with fish upon the bureau,
and on the bed — last Sunday's Times,
a dirty shift and cans of beer.
Fragments of my world on fire.
From here. By telephone. By wire
and shrieking from cheap radios,
from subway corridors and halls,
outcries. The saxophone and calls of pain
vibrate upon the starless air.
I hear the sound of horns and of hands.

But we would pass this place
so many people crowd the shore.
Already beams have caught the fire.
The surfaces of buildings crack with heat.
A child's face thru the smoke
comes ever to my eyes.
Voices deep and hoarse,
and sounds of hands amongst them
as I fall. The howling of a wolf.
Such sounds as poverty will make,
such voices as the poor contain,
eyes thru smoke and idle hands
in protest. Banners. Fists.
I pass on thru the gates of Hell.

Les Questions Surréalistes

what is the meaning of a choice of doors?
will the refusal of a crown at this time avert disaster?
where have the children gone? why have they stopped playing their
    dance-games in the wildflower fields?
what is the meaning of a choice of doors?

les questions surréalistes

what would have happened if she had not passed me?
(I SEE TWO LARGE BLACK DOGS)
who is to blame for such a decision?
did the destruction of the dam have anything to do with what was
    done before?
where will I find what I am looking for?
"I see two large black dogs"

les questions surréalistes et prémonitoires

who is at the door?
what will it be that will happen because she made that sound?
why do vans keep going by?
who misplaced my pen and my book deliberately?
what are you trying to say to me?
what are you refusing to say to me?
should I accept the crown of dancers or break away from the game?
what will happen if this is not done?
what will happen if this is done?
what is a shoe?
why have I found a brass horn in my bed?
where have the dogs gone? I can hear them still
will it be the same tomorrow?
why does mother leave the room at this time?
who is at the door?

les signes de la morte sont dans
les questions surréalistes.

les questions surréalistes
sont pour les singes de la morte.

We Have Forgotten Venus

We have forgotten Venus rising from the sea,
and we walk at the dark edge crusted with salt in the night.
Seasound and wavesound and sound of mourning
and the wail of dogs on the dark shore beyond.
For us there is silence.

The rock rises with threat of destruction.
The fog brings confusion and panic.
Wavesound and seasound, the tedious pounding of tides
and the roar of the beasts at the rock.

The voice in the mike booms from nowhere,
counting the dead, "Last minute news!"
"God," cries my father turning in sleep,
and he howls, "Turn it off!"

And the sea heard only dimly through doors
and through walls never changes its tone.

I hear her struggling within the coppered archway of the vault.
Do you not hear her rising there again
where she was buried,
you who laughed when I grew sick
and passed the plate to educate the heathen black?

Nor does the moon cause such a rise of tide
over the dunes to the door in this light,
the tinny light of afternoon piercing the heart,
shining back from the surfaces of water,
nor malignance of stars nor cards, this tide.

Water intrudes upon the house,
a pool of terror in the hall,
so that murder is rudely interrupted,
and mother drops her dirty work,
the acid destruction of the past,
so that the past may be retained.

Disintegrate. My father's house:
after the funeral meats are gone
the spirit dies. And she:

Mother. Mother. Mother.
On this picture and on this.

I hear the sea and those that hang,
the beggared bodies on the beach,
and those that starve. Look.

Do you not see him? How he glares?
Even the stones made capable,
and the sea moved.

Hamlet
A Draft of the Prologue

The SIBYL *is revealed sitting motionless on a stool. One hand holds back the
dark robe from her face, the other hand lies in her lap, palm upward,
holding a huge egg.*

*A man (*CLAUDIUS*) nude except for a jock-strap enters the room in back of her,
pauses, turns and writes in chalk on the blackboard at the back of the room*
"LAUGH AT HER"

*His back is painted with eyes like sores.
Abrupt stylized laughter comes from the Audience*

AUDIENCE: HA! HA! HA!

*From behind the blackboard the man picks up a whip and an executioner's mask
which he adjusts over his head.*

(BLACK-OUT) *The* SIBYL *sits in a neardark, a light sometimes playing over
her. During her speech* HAMLET *is seen to move in the background but like
a figure projected by the cinema he is not aware of what happens in the room.*
HORATIO *appears at the right front questioning the* SIBYL

HORATIO: Hamlet and I walked at night
nearing the sea and talked of love.
Simple talk— of things we'd seen together
and the long summer hills of childhood
rolling under the sun we longed for.
For us the fields had begun the marriage
and the earth yielded it sanctity.

Yet now so much is changed.
The oak splits under the axe and mange
eats the grass back to the barren ground
where so little grace is left us
before the grave.
               The water this spring
is choked with rust and rings of vultures roost
upon the stones where we made altars to the sun.
Everywhere are signs of a killing:
gunwounds in the earth
and cesspools lying open under foot,
a bog of shells and cast-off bones.

The trees in our time grow from such ground
and the flowers are sick and crazy with shell-shock.

Walking at night where the sea has crawled
so far from our shores in its sickness
leaving a waste of sand and salt,
in a wilderness of rubbish
we saw wrecks of ships
and the staring eye of a moon gone mad.

But Hamlet walks apart from me. His eyes
start with terror at his thoughts.
He does not speak.
A wild machinery of clocks between us
and destiny like King Kong at the door
that I dare not open. The ticktock of a bomb
is my heart, I find. Will it explode?
What tricks of cruelty are plotted for the future?

At home what game of Hangman's Bluff awaits us
that casts already a panic upon my mind
and sends dear Hamlet into distempers.

A glass is smashed against the wall. The SIBYL *turns her head toward*
*   * HORATIO, *all dark except for her face lighted boldly.*

SIBYL: They eat fish at the funeral,
         feasting on fish until they shine with scales
         and smell of carp in intercourse.

         They who were waiting write JEW on the window,
         and Murderman succeeds his corpse
             marching thru the streets in triumph.
         Nor is there protest.
         The dead have been laid with care.

         And the widow wears on her lips beneath her paint
         the kiss of his guilt, her teeth black with soot,
         and her hair done by Dali
         is filled with the feathers of chickens
             and ashes of condoms and doll's eyes of glass.

         On this land is the passage thru death,
         the Prince that she loved when he moved
         in the orchard, carried the teaspoon of poison
         and bent to whisper in the victim's ear.
         On this land is the stain of the traitor's disease,
         the venereal mark on the bed crossed by murder,
         the marriage feasted with meats from the wake.

         The fruits of the orchard have shrunken with fear,
         they stink on the ground from the pits of a shanker,
         apples of syphilis and over the branches
         the withering hand of the sick.

         So that the factories stand bare and silent
         with rusting of iron in the sun. Roof crushed.
         A little oil clotted with dirt, and in back alleys
         the swift Assassin strikes again. Again.
         There shall be no end to murder in our day.

(BLACKOUT) *(On a small stage* HAMLET *is being questioned)*

HAMLET: The voices of the past pursue me
    rising from their No Man's Land at night,
    that strip between our shore of pretense
    and the enemy's land of truth.
    I hear a calling of voices wounded in steel,
    and the great wound crying up from the stones.

HORATIO: What do they say, Hamlet? What do they say?

HAMLET: I cannot hear.
    Only at night I feel that there are sounds.
    In dreams I feel the shapes of sounds,
    a protest far beyond the walls of sense,
    and see these shadows move
    so that I fear to allow them form.......

    I remember when they brought my father's body
    and my mother had covered his face with wax
    moulding tranquility upon his lips,
    and she wept tears from her painted eyes
    so that black streams ran down her face
    and she let down her hair flowing about her,
    the weeping hair about her shoulders,
    but she could not pray in the church by the body.
    She said she was too ill with grief.

    She moved in the morgue over the masked corpse,
    her ghoul's mouth lost in the veils of black,
    and my uncle stood in the alcove, waiting,
    shining from a pool of darkness,
    and she passed near him, drifting,
    touching his body as she passed.

    This I have seen, and after the grave in the yard,
    over the fresh turned earth, the eyes of lust;
    this I have seen, and in six months' time
    the incestuous fish lie in rut.

    I am tortured by sight.
    If I were blind, there are things I would feel,

the cells of my body have eyes of awareness
revealing the fungus growth and the worm.

But fear walks with my father and closes doors,
forbids me from the inner rooms. I dare the gates
of Hell, and my father stands at the portals,
the blood drained from his body and his hands
shaking with terror so that taboo holds me mute......

What does he keep from me? What goes on there?
I remember one night when I could not sleep
and I got up to go to mother. I had a dream
that frightened me, and I called for her, Mother,
and I got up, and they heard me.
My father came to the door like from the dead
and he was angry.

HORATIO: It is your mother that he hides from you.
Wherever you go, Hamlet, there are doors there
      that you cannot pass.
Things that you cannot see.
It is your mother.

HAMLET: I see my mother too clearly.

When I look upon my mother
I see with X-ray eyes
under the shadow of brickdust and soot
the freak fornications at noon in the square.
And in dreams I have stood by her side
at night where she and my father's brother lie,
scaly body to scaly body,
fucking in tombs and back of the piles of tin
in the junk yards
spilling their glue on the pavement........

Darkness, I would crave darkness,
cataracts over my eyes,
the bridal veil of blindness,
or disease to eat out the sight.

(Pitchdark. Sound of door opening. Ghost of Hamlet's father who is HAMLET
glistens upstage)

Do you not hear an opening of doors?
Ho! He speaks.

HORATIO: Who speaks?

HAMLET: I know him well, he sneaks already to my soul,
hides at the solar plexus, disease like a shadow
and Sorrow is his name.   O love lost!
The need I have cries within me.

GHOST: She is fair, fair.

Listen: these things that I say unwillingly,
you must perform.   Murder for murder.
O, I say this most unwillingly, blindly,
but I have the madness of justice at my heart
and my eyes see only evil about me:
the syphilitic hand of treachery behind each act,
and stalking down the halls at night, the Killer.
He, he is the one that pollutes my bed,
slobbers food at my board so that I cannot eat
and couples with my bride at night.
My ears are filled with his breath gasping,
treachery, treachery, treachery in every breath,
and I have no peace in such a world.

I have been away so long and returning find rot
at foundations and these things I treasured gone.
I try to sleep at night but the wet earth
will not hold me, nor the deep pit of death hold me,
the unrest of justice has so moved my soul.

Listen: she is fair, fair, and I lay in the garden
dreaming, speckled with light, and the cool green
bursting from the branches overhead, I lay dreaming,
the light warm on my eyelids and the long song of bees
drifting in the air. Even the adders were harmless.

And the fresh odor of spring earth at the nostrils
spread peace over the body. Yet while I slept,
this Prince of treachery cast darkness over sunlight.
Serpents beneath the wet leaves stirred, and he bent
like a gossip pouring his poison in my ears,
chloroform spread over my face, and this Hellblood
trickling thru, flooding the arteries and veins,
sickness bursting the cells and leaving the body
soured behind it.   And no peace, no forgiveness
for wrongs done, nor tears at my deathbed.

*There is not room to include the complete speech of the Hamlet-ghost. The rest
of the Prologue with the opening Choruses of the play itself will be printed in a
Supplement to be sent to* RITUAL *subscribers in* MAY.

A Song for Michael Cooney*

The towers of your heritage still stand, the long coast,
rocks and the sea singing under the cliffs.
Rivers revolving in caves and at night the wind
and planets are yours. Great flocks of birds
fly up from the source of light filling the dark
with wing: in this rebirth you are gifted.

Your house is of earth, and your strength shall come
from the ploughturned earth, from fishnets
drying over the sand and those about you
who shall be comrades —
                              We build this world for you.
Our dream that you shall inhabit,
                              the creative world,
the looms and the altars under the sky
in this region of peace, power of sunlight,
the courage of brothers and the strength of trees.

*Born at Easter time of this year, 1940

Your body shall be a communication, your hands
shall be builders of monuments, your penis
the father of all life, and the great surfaces of skin
shall know all things — shall know sea, salt
and wind, shall know the fecundity of soil
and the cutting of rain, the world of sensation
open like a bursting fig to your powers.

Sing, because in the years before your birth no one
could sing. Dance, dance and make music
because in the years before your birth music was murdered.
You shall remember the death that we conquered
but pass none of it to your children, none of these things
we have known, our heritage of mechanical hell,
the years of killing and the diseases of steel,
the street of misery, the forbidden body
These things must be only as a myth to you,
so that you shall know that life springs at last
from the long ritual of such an age,
that peace shall survive.

A Pair of Uranian Garters for Aurora Bligh

Death's legs in black net stockings will
confuse our undercover revolutions. Death's darkened lips
like astral idiots bring chaos to our ouija board and fill
the house with doubtful relatives. She slips
the marriage sheets of comrades back, reveals
an ox. A lightning splits amoeba pride and cow-
faced fear springs up to love. Death's limbs concealed
in black suede boots have claimed the boy and now
the passionate zebra comes no more in dreams.

Whore!
unbelievable woman, corseted and false,

death knows no new mascara for your eyes.
The explosive day has drowned within your waltz-
time permutations. Time flies
into a closet and
is cut in two
with an hour left between
as no one's paradise.

I see your excommunicated garments there,
I see your shoes upon the chair
I see your uncontrollable black hair
lying like a serpent upon the floor
of our desire, like darkness at the windows
everywhere.

Death's legs in black net stockings can
divert our ardor from her lips. The gramophone
discourages Ouspensky with a back-from-man
delirium of swing upon a chicken bone—
it is a blue and lonely day, a lonely day
for love, for love. Among the armored trees
I lost my heart. I heard her say:
I have for you these pleasures—
and she showed the end of day to me;
she opened up a door
where there was only night
in one big empty room.

There is no more.

. . .

The Virgin among the cattle has hit upon the wound
striking such rocks as make mouths for boys' anger.

Of such feasts we partake, dividing the ruin
doled out behind wreckage in deserted cities,
star-lit and flare-lit and shining with rain,
wet sand and gravel in our mouths from month to month
expressing the violence to be done in the Spring.

I would give an order to kill them all
that the murderer might not escape,
eager increaser of our sorrow.
Chimneys fall scattering bricks on the flagstones;
a child's skull is split revealing fruit and roses;
a painting of melon rind and fresh fish
forecasts disaster.

We wait, we wait like apes of silence in a row
counting beads until the end.

In the cold wind the Virgin gave birth.
We saw His eyes thru the glistening veils.
A bull's head fell from the pedestal
marking the tiny feet with black dots.

Concerning the Maze

We were surrounded at that time by avenues of escape. You began at
a certain point and went on, and the streets were the natural runways
where we tried the same turn over and over again being lost in the maze.
Where only a second before someone had passed before us we could
smell fear and confusion in their sweat along the walls.
One of us got a dry section of cheese by running the right angle and
then twice to the left. He tried it again and found the same dry section of

cheese. One ran down past three bypaths, turned the circle, went down instead of up and found a hole gnawed in the wood. He went through, out into the world on the other side of the sky. Others have crouched at that crack in the wall entangled in wire, pissing with fear, seeing only the glassy reflection of their own eyes on the other side.

•

If we always had found food there, and then there was no food, if then there is never any food there where we had expected to find food: there are definite somatic results that such a frustration has on us. We lose sleep. Our hair grows thick with secretions and coarse and scarce with age. Our skin is scaly. And we are given to tremens.
It is even more horrible when we can find no doors.

•

We kept seeing that there was a certain way to get at the food. It was very simple. We could all see that— that it must be very simple, a very very simple thing, an everyday thing that any one of us could do. There were only a given number of things among which we could choose: jump onto the little platform, roll the wooden ball down the groove, turn to the right and pull the latch, run up the inclined plane and jump into the net, make a dive for the door at the far corner of the room. But only one of these was the correct choice. Any one thing, if it were wrong, would set into motion a cycle of events which might never lead us back to an opportunity, back to the GREAT OPPORTUNITY which we now faced. It was very simple, however. It was OBVIOUS that one of these things— maybe rolling the wooden ball down the groove—would bring freedom. It was surely a very commonplace thing, some one of these simple acts that any of us, as I have said before, could do to release himself. Some of us had made the choice before and run wild to come again and again to this same place, but we could not remember what we had chosen— the trials that had resulted from that choice had been so severe. I only want to tell something about the choice. It is a simple thing to jump onto the platform and find out, to roll the wooden ball down the groove and find out, to run up the inclined plane and jump and find out, to turn to the right and release the latch and find out, to make a dash for the door and find out. But we remember the ordeals of the years that come from a wrong choice, and we have returned here so many times that we cannot remember what choices we have made that were wrong. It seems as if all of them are wrong, and yet we know that that is not so. There is one right way. There is only that way, we know that there is a way we have not tried before, one which will save us, but we have gone thru so many errors that we cannot be sure that any given act might not be a repeated error.

It is so simple. A choice among five acts. Yet some have died of exhaustion. And it is hunger not over-eating that gives us nightmares.

•

Parables are partly true.

•

There was a long narrow tunnel or a hall cut into a great block of stone with barely enough room for two to pass if they stood sideways against the walls, and I was running on a treadmill there. Far down the hall I could see a man standing in the white light of a doorway. There was a fire inside the room behind him of burning newspaper, never consumed. I could see this man standing, and I was conscious that I was very young and that the treadmill would go on forever. I remembered the horses, white and gawdy with ribbons that raced on the yellow treadmill in the circus. I raced on and on. l'idee fixe. I raced on and on. I could see this man standing, peering down the hall at me, miles down the hall; a great white light was all around him so that he stood black in the center of a white light that ran out like water over the sand of the floor, and I could hear all around us the terrific breathing of the sea. I noticed that the walls at my side were moist and salty. A coating of mucous surrounded me, loading me down as I struggled to move down the hall, my hoofs kicking out over the treadmill. The man standing at the door so far away couldn't see who I was. If I could only come near enough for him to recognize me, the problem of the foodtrap would be solved. At that moment I realized that the tunnel was under water. There was a rusty puddle all about me, and the treadmill had become clogged with sand and rubbish of shells and weeds washed in by the tides. I ran on and on down the long tunnel, knowing that I would drown when I reached the light.

Fragment from a Journal

Our greatest betrayal is our infinite gentleness. We shall move with a quiet suavity of body, we shall speak more quietly still, sleepily, now that we have begun to kill again. Do not consider this killing is an aberration—it is the core of our being in consciousness. At last we only desire to learn a greater subtlety in the killing, to be infinitely more sure of our success. The sudden killing, the direct thrust like the rape is so natural, so direct, so unperverted that we have repudiated these actions. The last fascination is that we can be the mildest, the weakest of the animal world and the greatest killers. We eat our own mothers—but how delicately, how beautifully. Was it because in the beginning we were the most ugly that we changed our ways of killing? For we have perfected at the last the exquisite destruction of ourselves—that final beauty of the degradation of others. The killer who creates the murderers who stalk him.

We are ourselves at the last the double gods, for all other game is dull, meaningless. We ourselves are the most beautiful to be hunted.

Dreams
André Breton

But the light returns
the pleasure of smoking
The spider-fairy of the cinders in points of blue and red
is never content with her mansions of Mozart.
The wound heals everything uses its ingenuity to make itself
recognized I speak and beneath your face the cone of shadow
turns which from the depths of the sea has calld the pearls
the eyelids, the lips, inhale the day
the arena empties itself
one of the birds in flying away
did not think to forget the straw and the thread
hardly has a crowd thought it fit to stir
when the arrow flies
a star nothing but a star lost in the fur of the night

New York, October 1943

Windward
André Breton

Jersey Guernsey by times somber and illustrious
restore to the flood two cups overflowing with melody,
the one whose name is on all lips,
the other which has been in no way profaned,
and this one discloses the imprint of a scene, familial and anodyne
beneath the lamp an adolescent reads aloud to an aged dame
but what fervor on the part of each and in him what transports
however little she had been the friend of Fabre d'Olivet
and he had been calld to exalt himself with the name of Saint-Yves
    d'Alveydre
and the octopus in his crystalline retreat
gives way in whorls and ringing sounds
to the Hebrew alphabet* I know what were the poetic directions
    yesterday,
they are no longer valid for today.
The little songs go on to die their natural death.
I persuade you to put on your hats before going.
It will be better no longer to be satisfied with your thin soup
brewd up in measure in blinking rooms
while justice is renderd by three quarters of beef.
once for all Poetry must rise again from the ruins
in the robes and the glory of Esclarmonde
and reclaim aloud the cause of Esclarmonde
for there can be no peace for the soul of Esclarmonde
in our hearts and the words die that are not
good nails for the hooves of the horse of Esclarmonde
before the precipice where the edelweiss keeps the breath of
    Esclarmonde
the night's vision has been something it is a question now
of extending from the physical to the moral
in which its empire will be without limits.

*So much true grandeur, yes, in spite of how upsetting an aspect of the
exterior person of the marquis may be this reserve is as good apparatus for the
Showman of the angry octopus as his crags his revolving tables *he feels himself
seize by foot* but more than ever I go beyond more than enough for taste. A.B.

The images have pleased me, it was the art
wrongly decried for burning its candle at both ends,
but everything is much more wick, the complicities are
    otherwise learned and dramatic.
As you will see I have just seen an eskimo mask
it's the head of a grey reindeer under the snow
realistic in conception except that between the right ear and eye
    lies in wait the tiny rose-colord hunter
    just as he is supposed to appear in the distance to the animal.
But fitted with cedar and a metal without alloy
the marvelous blade
cut out in waves on an egyptian back
in the reflection of the fourteenth century of our era
alone will express it
by one of the animated figures of the tarot of the days to come,
the hand in the act of taking at the very moment of letting go
quicker than at the game of *la mourre**
and of *l'amour*

*La mourre—a game of flashing the hand and asking "How many fingers do I
hold up?" R.D.

• • •

The blesséd Herbert in his love does sing
"Our Life is hid with Christ in God."
He is a faithful and single-minded lover.
"Thou art my loveliness, my life, my light,
                    Beauty alone to mee," he writes.

And I:

There is not one God.
There are many Gods. They pass away.
There is an endless beautiful company
in which our life is hidden. Our loveliness.

A Ride to the Sea

The bland electricity, light blue wash
    air . . . colonies of the sun:
    Picasso's Antibes
    imagine a new element.

    Outcasts! we are. But the smooth sea
    is not translatable.

There is some secret lockd in these afternoons
event of the New Era
    rams heads horns, fresh fish,
    coils and ropes or scales,
    pennants or tatters.

We are on the edge of nakedness.
We are not citizens of this Greek discovery.
But nakedness will have
after days of nakedness
its own bland element.
    Then . . .

Ah, but how desolate the beach is.
We are not even imagined naked.
We have not come to the Antibes.

Two black nuns stand staring
upon the hissing waters.
The figures below us
seem to struggle ponderously,
and your great golden eyes are not open.

We have nothing but lust
with which to compose ourselves.

. . .

Faithless and many-minded muses —
each as a lovely woman or a stream
that flows of music
ever-changing and yet constant because lovely,
— that beauty Heraclitus sang,
not of the thing but of its being.

Faithless, O myriad minded.
The sun is new each day;
never to step twice in the same beauty
(river of music) but other
and yet other waters,
each as a lovely woman,
the dark and the gold of beauty
replenish the constant single source.

Thou art new loveliness, new life, new light
          Beauty alone to mee
In which my life is hid anew in God.

Ode for Dick Brown
Upon the Termination of His Parole: March 17, 1947

I.

When I sing in the evening, praise of Apollo,
when I touch upon the heart of song,
then I remember there are countrymen of my heart,
there are brothers of my keen desire.
O Mnemosyne, bright mother of our reverent song,
lift from my heart that heavy weight
that all men bear,
witnesses of histories and despair,
and let me sing that mingling of hate and love,
until the clear voice comes, pure stream of joy,
and I turn my face into Apollo's light

and sing unto the blessed spirits of his fire.
Open the prison of the heart—O
how its beating becomes, when we remember,
the pulse within the stone, the struggling speaker
in the dim paroles of human art,
the desire that measures our desires,
the golden spirit of our histories.

I am not mad to hate the stone
imprisoning thing; I am not mad to rage
against those moments of our compromise
when we bore witness against our love
and betrayd the country of our desire.
How in the green and dedicated groves
we watchd the impious battles rage
and Erisichthon cut again the sacred oak,
cry "I care not if this tree be loved
or if it bleed," and fell to earth
the trunk and many branches of our piety.
I am not mad to regret that I
had not given my life wholly, wholly,
to redeem the irreverent thing,
the furious denial of the spring.

O bountiful, true mother of our souls, Demeter,
terrible and bright quickener of our tree to life,
I would in song imitate the green,
the foliate wonder of human love, and praise
those gardeners of our desire
who watch, who watch over the renewal of the grove.
Their touch, when Famine in this age
of hungers seems to strike all spirit,
revives, revives and heals the newly sprouted tree.
Were there a final blasphemy,
were there a final destruction of the sacred core,
it had been destroyd again in these past years.
Surely the weight of our sorrow
has been increased. With what unease
we return to the grove, defiled, defiled.

Those who defiled were not men of our country,
blind lumber-jacks of a consuming greed,
—they seem intent to destroy the earth,
destroy the heart in their fury—but prisoners
of Famine, defamers of the Cerean green.

II.

We are wanderers of a Western shore,
pathetic moment of a Paradise, grown vulgar
in the moment's victory, whose cities
like all the cities of the world
breed miseries, grow fat and fear
and restless on the eve of war.
Yet this is the country of my life.
It is the westward edge of dreams,
the golden promise of our days. The world
has been defiled of man, used in vain,
and searchd in Famine's vanity of wise.
O that we have come to the edge of childhood here,
as if to reap the promise of a life,
and reap an imprisond stone-maturity,
citizens of Hunger's democratic realm;
to find the veins of gold mined out to coin
a bright new slavery of gold; to see the golden veins
where the bloody promise ran from childhood's heart
mined out to gild the commerce of the age;
to watch the young men of promise hug their moan
and turn in stony prisons as if alive
or give their lives to swell the profits made in blood.
This is the country of my life; my fellow men
are dumb with pain, or die,
or taste the world's vain ambitious roar,
or wander, as if exiled, upon this native shore,
lone fellows of a vast despair.

There is a true country to which we hold.
These are its groves, the eucalyptus and the oak,
the cypress and the madrone. These are its fields

where we have walkd and known in dumb retreat
retaste of all the stolen gold and give our hearts
to return the golden tribute to the earth.
This is the true sea whose tides
are those eternal tides where Neptune lies
among the gods of the persisting deep.
We go among our fellow men
like Jews among the Christians in a land
grown false and huge and deadly proud;
or, like Negroes, dark among white overlords,
we fight our hate and strive to keep
the covenants of the redeeming source.
Demeter, mother of all men, redeem
the hearts of men and free
these bloody Christians from their Christian pride.
I have heard in the ramifications of the air
the clear spirit undefiled, and seen,
there, there, luminous in human company,
the lares and lemures of our earthly domicile.
How they persist, not to be touchd,
nor defiled by Erisichthon's rage,
not to fall in the falling of our age,
not to be compromised nor destroyd.
We, we alone are compromised with hate.
Yet there are persisting spirits of our heart,
uncompromised, that spring to green.
We are wanderers of a sacred scene,
lonely fellows of a love's fraternity.

When in the evening I sing in praise
—of those who hold to freedom in this state
and keep, within, the sacred song—
my song is sad. For where we freely go
and breathe the lighter air, our breathing
seems to mock the breathless, vast
humanity, imprisond and afraid. They hold
upon our hearts, a drowning weight,
and sink, as if accusing, into the greedy tide.

For where we freely love, we taste
how universal is the bondage of our woe.
We know the bright betrayal of our fear.
Yet I would sing, as if in vain,
imaginary heroes of persisting love.
Their touch inspires, and all that weight
falls by as chaos of a bad dream—
how poor we seem against the inner vision,
the moments when our song
becomes song of our flesh, radiance of our touch.

III.

Restore, restore the mystery to the land
and to the hearts of men restore
the mystery. In memory, bright Mnemosyne's
rich tapestry of voices, revelations,
and persisting scenes, the luminous
reasonable and mysterious oak thrives.
The source of our lives makes each man sacred.
And yet the cutter seems to cut against his sanctity;
Erisichthon seems to fell again the oak
and triumph in his blasphemy. Famine seems
to rule the land, to sit upon the hearts of men
and cast her cold upon each hearth. We feel
the breath of war like leaves swept from their source
or leaves grown dead and dumb upon the bough.
Eternal mother, bright Demeter, when spring's
momentous thunder speaks to the awakend,
awaken me. Touch you my heart into the fire
and discover that oak of glory to me in this world.
Awaken the dumb and dead upon their bough.
I would see these hills above the bay—
combd now in evening with electric lights,
restless twinklings of uneasy human hearts—
combd with the rich and knowing honey of that fire
from which life flows.
I would see new lights of mystery aglow,

like the glory of a million leaves, crying eyes
or mouths upon the blooded branches of the tree.
Discover to us each our bough and trunk,
discover to us each the root, the vein
whose honied sap rises like the pain,
the memory of unrememberd things.

I am like a whispering leaf among dumb leaves.
Is it the wind, vaster than we know, that whispers?
Is it the tree, is it the source that whispers?
I am like a whispering leaf borne on a roaring tree.
Is it the roar as the tree crashes?
Downward, downward, we seem to rush,
to hesitate upon the crash. Is it the dream
of my heart's crashing that I hear?
I watch the million evening lights appear
upon the desolate Berkeley shore
that seems to touch the brutal edge of war.
They are like leaves upon the threatend tree.
I cry in vain against the long continued blasphemy:
"We are children beloved of Demeter;
our blood bleeds from the source of life; our fear
is like the shivering of life's eternal tree
beneath the maddend Erisichthon's axe."
Are we beloved then in vain?
Goddess of the rustling green, of flowerings,
of ripenings, restore,
restore our spirit to the thriving tree,
and bless, set free the golden promise of our blood.
Each heart in art awaken to your mysteries;
each body touch and fill with honey and with awe,
to know that fear when human joy increases
and seems about to come to rest, yet strikes
new thunders of desire. Demeter,
goddess of the renewing fire, open the prison of the heart.
Its pulse within the stone still lives,
the holy carnal tree of love we thought cut down.

There is something holy in each carnal man.
Dumb as a stone, stupid as a sphinx of clay,
yet the doomd man seems a temple of the flesh
in which some proper spirit seeks to speak.
So when they die upon the impious battlefields
or lie beneath the groaning weight of this dark age,
are paralyzed with fear, or some contemptuous rage
show in their eyes, or consumed with greed
become themselves new beasts of prey
and shove a swinish snout upon the world,
we say a holy place has been defiled. The flesh,
that brightest miracle of ways, in which some art
would seem to make the stupid clay about to speak,
grows dumb again and then seem vicious,
hateful as the untouchd clay had never been.
It speaks the speechless betrayal of our dreams.
And yet the spirit returns into the man.
Among the crowded, pitiful and damnd, each man
must fight against the inner fire, cut down
again, again, the Cerean speaking tree. He must deny
his source. His source does not deny
but like a stubborn artist works the stubborn clay.
O when I sing the praise of the awakend men
then I remember there are countrymen of my heart,
who love and seek to know the workings of their source.
That source is something holy in all carnal men
who in their flesh bear, painfully and dumb,
the mark of some magnificence. O spirit,
forgive and heal the Erisichthean man,
the sacrilege, and set us free.
Open the prisons of our rage.
Restore, restore us to the thriving tree.

A Discourse on Love

Dear Jack: I have my raptures, senses
of aboundingness. This year they are of you.
My sense of every man bound in the cunning of your face
that no man is. How less in being more
than you I am. I am alone.
That is the final rapture in which this year
you keep me company. That loneliness
is empire of passionate avowals. Famous eccentrics,
wearers of gigantic hats, gewgaws of empire,
reminders to Death of his promises,
they are near cousins of my pride.

The lions of sex in my incautious zoo,
fantastic propriety of improper beasts,
are cautions in that world of make-shift elegance
of the rapturous inelegance of the wild.
They are not lions of hatred.
They devour the lovely child and smile.
They shake their loving paws upon the air.
They roar at feeding time with loneliness
and paw the troubled air into a quiet,
beloved drowsiness of an after-roar.

I sit with you in imagination's Tea-House,
past the parks of rapturous baboons.
I break from each enclosure of rice-cake
a fortune. Love is a strange untruth
to read of truthful prophecies. And yet,
planning these despairs, grim messages
of accidental warnings, they are rapt
in an aboundingness. This year
I sit with you in imagination's Tea-House.

Your spirit has a body of fine loving.
It moves me in my solitary sorrow.
O, if from the airs of troubled empire,

lusts of the Celtic twilight,
singings of the air, luve's ayres,
I might be liond into a quiet,
beloved roarishness of an afternoon!
The magic runes lie like our fortunes,
a scattering of slips of paper on the ground.

I dream in imagination's Tea-House
of some momentary joy,
some feeding of a discontent.

Your hair is like a rarely troubled air.
Yon Cassius-lion has a lean unhungry look.
His kindly eyes are sleepy; he beams,
a Mr. Pickwick of the zoo; but he will stare,
as you will stare again, and show
the fierce eccentric loving of his dreams,
bare the idle claws of his despair.

I shake my mane and order tea.
You talk a lion's philosophy of doubts
and jungle-ish sophistications,
Mad Hatter of my agape at noon.
I pour the tea into the cups and gaze
upon the fellow lionishness of your eyes.

There is some grander appetite of love
than tea-time wonderings can avow.
If claws were thots of love conceald
in velvet paws of poetry, we cannot know
what woeful marks our passion
after tea-time might bestow.

A Morning Letter

The various members of the hierarchy move,
early morning awakening of the world.
They are like the shuffling of doors,
eager and reluctant, two-faced, I suppose.
Eight o'clock carillons seem universal magic.

Now after hoping for magic,
I was an ordinary messenger to arrive.
Wake up, you are yourself the God of Love
asleep. Whom did you expect? you lay
eyes closed as if afloat.
Proud boy,
whom did you expect who did not wear
only your lesser face? someone from up there?
someone just stepped down from a throne,
smelling of majesty?
Poetry has gone straight to your head.
Your mind wanders.
There are no empty thrones in heaven.
This is early morning in a world without kings.
A small-time Don Juan knocks at your door.
I put on all my pride to climb the stairs.

I was only messenger of myself
to tell you you are yourself Love.
How do you arrange the young men in your dreams?
arranging and re-arranging youth's hierarchies.
Don't you hear the bells ringing,
starting the day out with common tunes?
Ta-ra-ra-boom-de-ay and *Auld Lang Syne*.
Waking up from your Imperial World,
you, for a moment, not I,
are Emperor of my world.
The hierarchies of powers move like doors
—this is a good dream figure.
I am not dreaming.

I came to praise Love, not you.
And the poor writhe.
Bringing spiteful wreathes to celebrate. . . .
I, being poor, brought my pride.
Wake up from your Empire. I am still dreaming.
This is early morning in a world of kings.

The Homecoming

Great Venus came into the room,
Ishtar, the full-blown rose.
The room became a shell of pearl,
the petals of the shell flung back,
it was so likened to Beauty's tomb.

The shadows seemed to spoil
around her; her hair
was pearl for luster. Her arm,
flung back, created with one stroke
upon the air, as if the air awoke
and cried, an arc, a triumph,
and alarm.

Great Venus came, a rose full-blown
—this, perhaps, was Friedel in 1945—
as if she bloomd in the full blowse of sleep.
Her fleshy petals, alive, about to fall,
unfurld the richest spoilage of the rose.
—this was, perhaps, Friedel,
dreaming of her son, Adonis. "The Jew
and German mixd in one."
attar of the rose . . . . Attis,
the summer's hero.

Ah, but he had died, had died.
I was no more than sleep's incarnation
of her son. And she, great Ishtar,

slumbering, whimperd, moand
in ravages of descending sleep.

Why does she arrive again?
She swells the bloody sunset foam
on which she rides. She comes
from Cythera to the Berkeley shore.
We feel—as if she were the moon
and we the waves—her pull.
"Where is Adonis," cried that whore.
(the tides of lust ran full, ran full.)
"I come from Cythera to bear him home."

We searchd for Attis, combd the dead.
Ah, every man is some woman's son
who moans and becomes like Venus in her sleep.
The Venusian legions were like a wave
of blood that cried: "The Lord!" they said,
"has died, has died, and has died
and left us less than men. His grave
is not in Berkeley—or, his grave
is in Berkeley held this year,
Adonis, the withering of the bough.

The Temple of the Animals

The temple of the animals has fallen into disrepair.
The pad of feet has faded.
The panthers flee the shadows of the day.
The smell of musk has faded but lingers there—
lingers, lingers, Ah, bitterly in my room.
Tired, I recall the animals of last year:
the altars of the bear, tribunals of the ape,
solitudes of elephantine gloom, rare
zebra-striped retreats, prophecies of dog,
sanctuaries of the pygmy deer.

Were there rituals I had forgotten? animal calls
to which those animal voices replied,
calld and calld until that jungle stirrd.
Were there voices that I heard?
Love was the very animal made his lair,
slept out his winter in my heart.
Did he seek my heart or ever
sleep there?

I have seen the animals depart,
forgotten their voices, or barely rememberd
—like the last speech when the company goes
or the beloved face that the heart knows,
forgets and knows—
I have heard the dying footsteps fall.
The sound has faded but lingers here.
Ah, bitterly I recall
the animals of last year.

There's Too Much Sea on the Big Sur

The woman on the mountain kept her fictive ocean,
the ocean her fiction, and kept her tree,
a single point in all that blue,
or in the loony shimmer of the moon
in all that gleam of a real enuf pacific,
but, for her, a fictive sweep of sea.

"That," she seemd to say
—she smiled a solitary smile & showd
a kind display of cruel teeth—
        "great dark"
—she gestured vaguely toward the sea,
somnambulant lapping deep,
            "is dark of me."

She overlookd her deep.
Upon the steep edge she gardend in the sun,
wearing a large straw hat
to shade her eyes.
She stood against the hedge of sage
aware that she stood too
against the dazzling hint of sea.
· "That," she seemd to say
—she lifted her arms
true as her tree
and offerd some kind of refuge—
     "to me is a final beauty.
     "Nothing else is final."

She leand against the single real of tree
and celebrated herself
intensely human.

"You are uninteresting," one might have said,
"but never so uninteresting" (she seemd so
various and mild)
"as that reoccurring splendour of the sea has been."

"I have not been out,"
she said, "since I came here.
The real sea keeps me in."

. . .

When the immortal blond basketball player
is confronted by the negro in saffron shorts,
the negro is subtler by a dancing mind
than death when he feints, gives the ball magic,
and absorbs in his nonchalance
the blond hero worship that floods from the audience.

He is a sprite of intelligence, this negro—
one of a team that turn the sport
into a nimble pursuit by mind of a purpose.
See! he out wits all other kinds of beauty,
certain of hand, with a body
knit to confound disbelief in the audience
and to escape in the howl of acclaim.

The Revenant

Do not tell me that adultery is not real
in the mind. These reasonable conclusions
merely mask undefined fears.
How rationally the man may tend that tree,
reason's felicity, and watch in daylight's hours
the flowering vistas of affection's
public gardens.
In midnight's private awakening
— what was that sound he heard,
the shifting step outside the door,
the reoccurence of some ordinary noise
transformd to mimic the inner speech,
an accusation, a disturbd confession, or,
did the heart stop its beat,
like the roar of silence when a clock stops,
terrify the speaker? In midnight's
private garden, the lover
trespasst upon his love and found,

no sooner had he gaind the winter's rose,
his fear. The Beast,
that bridegroom Death, playd host
and spread a feast of meats and fruits.

For whom was that rose
pluckt from its thorny stem?
This was not love's gift,
the troubador's addition to the young bride's
diadem.

Nor was it the prize
— rose and stem —
stolen from an envied arbor.
But rather, a souvenir,
replete with the man's ardor
for the Beast himself.

Half waking, lying taut beside the girl,
he waited. She was almost superfluous to his fear.
Surely she was not dreaming of the Beast
nor of the man whose place he had taken
nor of him lying beside her
who had been dreaming of the Beast
and half awoke now.

— Here I lie, he thought, where the bridegroom lay.
Tonight I am the bridegroom and yet I am not he
nor do I lie where he lies nor chooses to lie.
He does not care. I care.
Therefore, I alone know that I commit
adultery.

The man was hot with sweat.
The girl's arm
flung across his chest
where it had been left in a last embrace
was beastly hot. Her body
burnd in sleep's effusions.
He did not dare to move.

An accusing figure that he could not turn to see
stood at the window watching.

Is it he? or is it his spirit
who has come to watch?
Surely, he thought,
I lie in waves of the watcher's
        hostile sight.
Nor does he gaze upon her
but rather upon me.

    •

She had fallen from a precipice of sleep.
The thrill of falling
ran through her body
hot as wax.

She clutcht his shoulder.
The man felt her hot hand
tighten.
Her fingers graspt his shoulder
and let go. She was not frightend,
but fallen, heavy as a bird with wet feathers,
dropt by a single bullet.

"Not here" she said.
"I want to go home."
(This was her husband)
She spoke in sleep. The two,
heavy and huge but bird-like,
wingd and talond, caught
in each others struggle
dropt.
        And then the thrill came.
The man felt it as a shudder
that woke him.
        Or the word *"here"*
spoken in her sleep he heard
and he knew
that her husband had come.

Here.
Like a stone falcon that had hoverd above them,
or above him, alone,
dropt plumb
to the heart.

Stopt.
This is the Watcher.
He stands at the threshold
beyond which is Life.

Awake, but with his eyes closed,
for he was afraid to look — he
could not turn his head, he
listend. It was not what he could hear
but someone here — the bridegroom.

Father protect us, he prayd, from those we have loved,
keeping the love as a gnawing vow
to heat our own vitals. Protect us
from those loved unloved who return.

And Now I Have Returnd

And now I have returnd:
I never held the musing body that I loved.
The poem is a vain excited thing; it turns
the empty moment of the arms
            into a questioning;
and yet I never held. The hunger for beauty
began where desire so pitifully finisht.
The body cold and famisht, before beginning
famisht for beauty. Or love,
Love, itself, the vain hot thing—as if it warmd
the cryptic deformd wanting.
And now I have returnd:

to say—I have never been away.
I return to be
poetry-glutted, heart-famined,
body-denied, mind beauty-fed,
beauty-fatted. The thick of beauty-grease
gives glister to the deprivation.
And love, itself, the waxy polish of a lust
            denied.

Let there be an afternoon,
when in the dusky light of some saloon
upon the cold and bone of the piano keys
I'll play vast melodies of my
            enraptured lover—
these are the imagined sonatas,
ragtime tunes, betrothal cantatas
            of the brighter air—
and find some rich luxury of vice,
wreathe garlands of the laurel
            in my embrace.

Imagined melodies!
Awkwardly upon the keyboard I but sound
a single lonely tentative note
            and fear I might be drownd
in all the weight of the restricted tide,
the tidal wave of the desire.

O, if I ever seek to drown myself
or know the undertow of some dark tide,
it would be not that I might die
but that I might yield then to life.

Honestly I fear to die.
It holds me from the heart of life.

I flap upon the sand like a live fish
that strangles in the thin of air,
that strangles in the blaze of sun,

and yet I fear those currents where
the heart of meaning seems to run.

And now I have come back . . .
And now I have come back . . .

The New Hesperides: At Marlowe's Tomb

INVOCATION

We sail into the promises of blood, proud Tamburlaines,
conquerors of an empire of despair. Apollo's laurel bough
that grew within our hearts,
cut down, spurts out from arteries its blood.

O vivid Marlowe,
livid Tamburlaine, knew you the sanguine wine
of the Hesperides, slippery crowns of paradise?
Knew you the glaze of conquerd eyes,
the spurt of arteries,
the spirit's metamorphosis in lusts of flesh?
When you said *heart*, thought you
that bloody actual organ of our love?
    [*he cuts his life*]
"A wound is nothing be it ne'er so deep;
blood is the god of love's rich livery.
Now I look like a lover, and this wound
as great a grace and majesty to me
as if a chain of gold, enamelled,
enchased with diamonds, sapphires, rubies."

Westward of our life lies that island where the sun
in bliss returns to slumber and to dream.
The boughs bend down beneath their fruit,
the carnal weight of golden fruit.
The Lords of the Sun and their dragons
lie beneath those rich abundancies
and tongue the hives of the solar bees,
those hives whose combs are honey-sweet

with blood, among the leaves
and blood-sweet fruit.

Those are not apples of ash but rare
consummations of the flesh; eternal joys,
the slattern golden never-perishing delites.
Those are not abominations, tho you may taste
your hell, I'll praise those fruits,
jewels of the Sun kingdom, as the first fruits
of a Heaven I may devour, desire.

Westward of our dim humanity we sail.
There lies Apollo's land, the laurel
we thot died, the ripe and knowing fruit
we thot devourd, the noon
we thot had passt into an evening tide.
                    O furious Marlowe,
curious Faustus-Marlowe, what promises
were broken when you broke
upon the knife of Francis Archer, spurted
forth your hot encumbering lifely blood?
The glutted lyre is broken and pours forth
from broken arteries its song.
          How beautiful and still
the emptied Marlowe lies,
          Prince of an Eastward Westernness,
as we sail westward toward the Eastern
          gardens of our love's Hesperides.

RHAPSODY

You are a Jack of Diamonds pride to bear,
as if among life's dreams that pass
there were an unpassing dream of dreams,
a Beau Danube of the diamond air.

Is there a sun among the summer's leaves,
warmer and more gold, whose liquid rays
bathe round the summer's fruit, or Lord of the Sun
who shakes the pollen from his brassy hair

until the sulky breathing lover dreams
the seeming mortality of love come true?
Is there a radiance, sorrowing glow of paradise,
further that I might know?
Is there a further glow? first lover
or friend of some electric blue?
Is there a dearer prize? Is there
in youthful liveliness of leaves more life
to break the heart into its green,
to freshen love? Is there a touch
more tender to tender more the proud
and inner fire? O Jack of Diamonds,

lay your head again upon my breast
and let me hold against my mouth
the richness of your hair; and arms
embrace as if I held—a naked heart—
your naked heart to me; and touch
your naked hand upon my naked hand
as if the touch could speak what all
our artfulness can never touch.

What will the lovers bring?
Mirrors of our suffering.

Where are we going? to what further shore?
If there were eternal orchards,
fruits of love and flowerings of each tree,
abundancies, how I should contend to break
the satiate concert of the singing air;
how I should long for the fruits' falling,
for the bright and fatal world we know.

Then I should turn from the blue of days,
from the golden perishings of summer's fruit,
in that fine pain of spirit known of old,
and seek the solace of your eyes, bright
fatality of the watch you keep.
You watch the painful fineness die,
grow dull and dark and fall away.

Gardener of the New Hesperides, you know
the fatal over-ripening of that fruit.
Patient, you see in the moment's pleasure
the year's rich claim to that first flowering,
the deadly consummation, Jade of Diamonds pride,
grow round and full and drop to die
upon the proudly litterd ground.

    There the appropriate dragons lie
and dream that the garden does not change.
Each slitted lizard eye beneath its scaly lid
guards the bright eternity of youth and watches
for those wanderers, amorous and impoverisht thieves.
Among the sleeping dragon forms
the thieves slip by to taste the fruits;
the fatted clever worms arrive
to dwell in the spirit's ripeness; the ripeness
grows over-sweet and falls into
the bright and fatal world we know.

    Watch the Lordly Sinners go.
They fall away like leaves and leave
the branches bare. Bachelors of the greening air,
the vernal jades—these are not make-shift answers,
but real answers, but of the season only.
The Lords of the Sun fail.
They grow sober and fall from their love-drunk dreams.
Is it that lovers fail or that the love-wine fails?
There is to every dark a further shore of dawn.
Where are we going? to what further shore?

What will the lovers prove?
New necessities of love.

They falter. They taste the spirit's wine,
grow drunken and oracular,
and then grow sober. The spring is drunk.
The brandy skies, the blossom-giddy trees,
whirl round the young spring dragons in their dream.
The summer grows oracular. The fruit is round

and naked red. It hides in thicknesses of green.
The dragons talk among themselves in sleep.
In Fall they will awake and stare
with sober eyes upon the plunderd scene.
They are like fatal guardians, awakend
and accusing Lords. The Gardener smiles.
These are the dreams of dragons.
He keeps the gardens of the true Hesperides.

O but my Gardener, tender with your green,
tender as you will that sweet distil
of lingering love. The thieves will touch
and teach the heart consummate gardens of their own
that they will steal away as if they robbd
the heart—as real, not more, but pangs
to tune the heart-strings lute and play
a Beau Danube, Vienna sadness upon that air of blue
that seems to wash the gold of ripening fruit,
the vistas of an August loss.

      And are they false?
Your hair is like a Beau Danube, but true.
I dream a dragon's dream. You seem
a Jack of Diamonds pride to bear,
a Prince who plays the Gardener of the Isles.
I turn to you. A thief, a dragon, a knife—
these are my dreams. They stir my heart.
And what if I am proud? O friend,
I seek again intoxications of your fine regard.
We walk among the over-loaded trees,
the summer's golden majesty.
The garden is bright and fatal as we go.

ELEGY

Is this the world we loved? the groves
of our enchanted isles where youth had eyes
to seek out Paradise and blood to know
first thoughts of the Hesperides—O Kit,
enamouring us what years and years ago?

What raptures have we lost, or years
wrought in their patina the heart's despair?
What tears give to the fruits their glow,
unendurable of the enduring gold?
What fears disturb the pastures of the soul
and set their guardian dragons there?

The earliest dreams are lingering and real.
They seem to take immortally of you, to live
in every promise of this scene. The blue
of sky recalls intenser blue. The rust
and gold, the treasures of this restless grove,
partake of a restless hue, of an intenser gold.
Your memory I feel like some grave weight of wings,
enormous bird that haunts the airy flight,
the arctic cold of perisht love,
alive and falling far away—O leave me,
leave me to new love and go.

I wept that time would wear the thread
away and season's change would steal
the golden burden of love's painted bough.
I praised the timeless orchards of the mind,
the heart's Hesperides that may not fade,
and thought the bright external joys unreal,
impermanent tapestries one might avow
or disavow, and I was blind.

But now I long for raptures of new love.
My pulse is like a haunted corridor
where some wrongd spirit dwells
who may not rest, a dusky bird that beats
its heavy wings about the heart, confined,
and seeks to fly into the sweet
oblivious wide world, unwind the thread,
the song, upon the lyrical bright air,
fly up, fly up into the branches of its tree
and sing new love. First lover, sprite of love,
is this the world of our eternity?

First lover, sprite of love, the love-feast done,
the poets linger in the lyric hall to talk of love.
Amid the ruinous banquet of my dreams
the singing lamps fall in the floods of night,
shine like eyes of basilisk upon the deep,
demonic, glower and fade,
wraiths of discourse in the drowsy mind.

Socrates, Aristophanes and Agathon
argue on. The aged Socrates is clear
as dawn, as if in old age of wisdom
thought were barely begun. His voice is lost.
It washes the falling shores, the minds
of drowsy Aristophanes and Agathon.
The pure discoursing tone,
in the washing, the defining and redefining of some line,
grey and cold, the mourning wave,
seems to be a morning wisdom
vanishing upon these sands.

The tides of night swell cold and dark
& then retreat until the crowing of the cocks.
Dream breaks upon the last thin wave
—this is the thinnest wisdom—
and day awakens.

How beautiful and still, how blind,
the sleeping Marlowe lies. First lover,
still & lovely source. He is not dead
but dreams the dream in which I live
till love's long night is broken by love's day.

Early History

The Devil, the elaborate one, he gave the first push. Old gamester. He gave the first push. And Rabbit, the big-foot ancestor, began to hop. So we went hopping.

The Devil, old hunter of rabbits, made rabbits to hunt. Made big-footed hoppers to hop after.

And Electric Light, he made Devil to look at. He started the Devil.

The Devil, old hunter of rabbits, made rabbits to hunt. And Rabbit, Big-foot carrot-eater, he calld the first day a Hunt. He married Fox and began hopping. He calld the Hunt the First Day and invented Electric Light to see by. And Electric Light, he was the first Looker. And he lookd like the Devil. He invented Devil. And Devil, he gave the first push. He started the Hunt.

THE CITIES OF THE PLAIN

Dog, he was our Ancestor. Rabbit, he was the ancestor of our Spirit. Cat, he was the Other Half of our Ancestor.

Dog and Cat were friendly with Rabbit. They all ate together. Dog and Cat ate carrots. Dog and Cat cohabited together in a Single House. Dog and Cat turned out Electric Light in order to look. They took looking away from Electric Light, ancestor of Looking. And Electric Light took away the Devil. So Dog and Cat cohabited without the Devil.

Old Hopper was hopping mad. He took away all the carrots. He, eater of carrots. So Dog and Cat ate old Hopper, the Rabbit Spirit. And Old Hopper stoppd the First Day.

Dog and Cat lived in the Next Day. Dog and Cat ate Rabbit for supper, and cohabited in a house of the Plain without Devil.

So they were punishd.

This was the beginning of Now. And Dog hates Cat. And Cat hates Dog.

The Old Devil, he was the original Hunter. Now Cat hunts, and Dog hunts. They hunt each other. They hate each other.

Dog is our Ancestor. Cat is the Other Half of our Ancestor. Now we are separated people.

Dog eats Rabbit; Cat eats Rabbit. When we eat Rabbit we celebrate our Spirit. Dog eats Dog; but Cat, that inevitable Ancestor of our Other

Half, has eaten the Devil. Now we are separated people. We are the punishment of Dog and Cat.

And Old Devil, Old Devil. We make traps for Him. We like to remember that he was the Trapper. Old Rat-face, the original hunter.

THE GOLDEN AGE

Devil made a city of gold so when he went away we would be contented to have him gone. Devil told us the First Answer. He told us our First Answer and gave us Restless Feeling. Then he gave us Unnatural Pleasure. Devil made us a city of gold.

Gold was the First Answer. Then Devil went away. And we were not contented.

We were calld the Golden Ones. These were our ancestors when Devil deserted them. They were the Golden Ones dreaming of Devil.

The Golden Age was an age of dreaming. And our ancestors deserted by Devil went in search of their lost lover. He went away and left them a city of gold. They (our ancestors) were not contented. They left that place and came to a second place.

They worshippd iron and thought that Devil would return.

"This is reality," they said. "We are no longer the people of dreams, the Golden Ones. We are the Men of Iron, the Conquerors. We will conquer the Devil."

So our ancestors, he (our ancestor), wooed the Devil and Devil said yes. But he (our ancestor) was not satisfied.

Devil said yes and he came to stay. He did not go away. He wanted us to be contented. But he (our ancestor) was not contented.

"This is not really," he said. And he askd the First Question.

"This is not really," he said. And then he went away leaving the Devil a city of gold so he would be contented when he (our ancestor) was gone.

And Devil discovered his Unnatural Pain. He made a city of lead to suffer because he (our ancestor) had deserted him.

In the Street

It starts with a groan.
Dark—as of several trees
or bent storm warnings.
Groans.

The old old children climb
the level ending street
as if to escape the ringing of the bell.
The little girls
hug their arms about their boys
until they fall away like dolls.
The old old children climb,
as if ascending toward friendship
before the sounding of the hour,
the level street.

2

It
goes with a groan
with only one hand
groping the parturience of words
until the silence has grown.

Too young to spell,
they can cast a spell,
write letters with only one hand,
keep the lines level
by rule of single thumb.

3

Now that years have interfered
I pay my heart's fee
to see a mother's scorn

wither in not her son's
but in his friend's face
until I face her withering.

4

You will find now that I am over
no trustworthy cover,
you will find that each lover
has left friendship open

5

for the wind, the wind, the wind

6

rushes upon the difficult street,
sweeps thru the pilgrims in the street
seeking to escape home from school,
fearing the tolling of the hour—
the end, the end, the end.

They climb against the wind's wildness
until their pincht faces look starved
and bring forth from childhood's way
friendliness died upon their voices
to declaim the fury of old age.

Whatever they shout is lost in the street.

Domestic Scenes

1. Breakfast

I sleep a serpent-sleep in slough of human skin.
I hibernate in that brief dark of wisdom
that we seek in sleep. I seek
disorderly excitements of a dream.

I shall awake to the ennui of breakfast foods,
to teach morning's bright of commonplace,
redundancies of tasty goodness.
I shall put sleep's dream gratifications away,
awake to talk's dream gratifications, and still
in that un-dream, no sleep no talk,
remain ungratified.

Disorder of dishes, the wisdom of soild spoons,
of discarded forks and knives, exciting litter
excites the domestic dreaming mind
to that brief of wisdom calld disgust.

2. Real Estate

There is some gall of nigger-pink reality,
some stucco grit of which our dream façades are made.
The snake-oil ineffectual, the heart's shop-talk,
is serpent-real of that old Seducer, the heart's reality.
To talk the heart's reality betrays
that questiond Eden-imitation that we buy.
We are serpent-real of tongue to argue human-wise
in words devised by serpents.
There is some gall of nigger-pink reality
in our words.

3. Bus Fare

The day has suburbs for a night's metropolis.
I ride in plain daylight, a simple cheap delight
that takes the place of midnight's pleasures
cheap yet dear.

Sometimes when I am riding that old line,
that brilliant talking bus, I fear
that busy clatter as if it might appear
before me, made concrete, some cinema of the afternoon,
lit up in a tautology of coming attractions,
dispassionate reminders of a night's resort
to passion playd upon a screen by shadow stars.
Sometimes I fear
a silence as if you might then appear to me
in all the woeful and endearing charm
of uniform and pass out transfers
and announce: Reality Street,
the end of the line.

But Day has no such streetnames. There are
suburbs with exotic names in plain daylight
and streets seem innocent of what they midnight know,
a simple cheap delight that takes the place
of darker dearnesses.

4. Mail Boxes

The literal repetition, hope denied,
annoys, and yet I wait. I wait
upon some dénouement, some clarinet
splendour of the first rate.

I dream of salutation, saxophone
concertos and the dark refrains
of love to give a fine Tchaikovskian tone.
I dream of some truth in falsehood's clothing,
elegant sophistication, jazzy
declamations of the cavalier.

I dream of postal-cards, Venetian scenes,
some literal repetition of a hope denied,
annoyances of clarinet, some eloquence,
heart-false verity of pride.

And you arrive, inevitable literal dream,
clothed in the new clothes, some truth
that that proud-wise old emperor
never wore. And ask that I admire
your nudity. I wait.
I wait upon some dénouement, some clarinet,
splendorous pretense of an attire.

5. Matches

Friend, friend. What if my voice at times
betrays elaborations of a cloudy mind,
of Turneresques and rosy cumulus?
We smoke our vernacular peace-pipes,
cigarettes of various brands, and inhabit,
uneasily, the vulgar honesty of dailiness.

I dwell in a world of scarlet sinkings,
flame-spotted sails collapsing
into the glitter of a friendly eye.

I dreamt of a duplicity of ships.

There is a hostile scarlet idea of dawn
or sunset horizon in friendship's day
or love's night-watch of spirits.
Friend, friend. What if at times I dwell
in dawns or sunsets of a livid hue,
witness assaults of grandeur, saxophone
chimeras of a smoky atmosphere.
We smoke our advertised tobacco, brands
of nationally recognized composures of the mind.
And then my unfriendly eye,
saying friend, is made uneasy
by some older idea of the tobacco, Turneresque
of dying galleons in a waste of sea.

6. Bath

The folly of repose beguiles
the watchful misanthropic eye,
and Crocodile Smiles, some reptile
progenitor, broods upon the suddy paradise.

I lie in that erotic nakedness,
uncostly seduction of a disturbd humidity.
The warmth of company grows hot as cold.
The intimate cold seeps into me.

The folly of repose precedes
beguilingly a panic in repose.
I sprawl in nude anticipation,
dreamed by some snaky father of the ape,
lewd exposures to the humid tide,
and feel the warmth of friendship waver,
congeal and grow cold upon my hide.

7. Radio

Sweet heart, the swank of love
is swank of bright humiliations,
swagger of moony certainties,
and swash of buckley song,
a moonlight swainish with delight.
The radio, station *Love,*
is an all nite program, swell & sweet.

Heart, don't go. Don't go.
I forgot to say I need
the cynic adoration of your eyes.
The roses in their summer flush of brass
fall into the dim uncertainty.
I fear to see your season pass.
I fear the swart eclipses of the moon.
I fear the phases of orchestral loneliness,
the loony disarray when you are gone.
And yet I do not think that I can say
I love you and not know
the hurt of roses as they die,
humiliation-bright uncertainty of the rose.
Don't go. Don't go.

But take this swindle of the heart,
I love you. There is a swank
of realistic swans, moon-certain birds,
truthful joys in that dishonest swamp,
painted lugubriousness of Hollywood lagoon.
There is a swagger of sweet bees, costly
waves of crooning orchestras,
a swash of buckley, cynic joy,
a moonlight swarmish with delight.

8. Electric Iron

Then, of potential strength,
the gaunt irregular giantism of
the spiritual man: Aristotle says
one cannot expect every kind of pleasure
from tragedy. Yet a single thing,
potent in its electric thingness,
gives expectation of every kind of pleasure.

There are, more potent in bewildering
than mechanicals of a dream, mechanicals
of fact, princely manipulations of the real,
real threats and conceald perfections.
An empty room lit by a single electric light
reveals a little universe of its deserted things:
menacings of enameld saucepan meanness,
cruelties of bolts and door knobs,
secretive stoveness in stove black.

Welcome to my world of menacings,
kitchen statuaries of the insane.
Welcome home to those cheap presences,
sensual foreshadowings that watch,
in their omnipotence,
over the poor power of poetry.
Welcome home, O potential spirit,
impermanence of the candle flame.

The potent iron and the enamel rule
a nameless kingdom of their own.

9. Lunch with Buns

At noon the opiate of the sun revives
intoxications of an oceanic feeling.
I dine with you in ecstasies of table,
prince among imaginary birds,
and break the bread of my loving.
I sip the cool of the human wine.

I don my natural disguise,
the arch diplomacies the lover learns.
I fear your supernatural grace.

O apish lionesque,
you beckon to some childish angel
of the room or of yourself.
I see the advantage in your eyes.
At noon the midnight scene transformed
appears in a bright magic of the sun.
I dine in casual imitation of some hunger
passionately known in darker reveries.
And you, a very lion of the sun,
are meek in your advantage. Seek
my eye and devour the white of bread
in pious celebration of the feast.

10. Piano

I am rapt in a tarnish of the wine.
There is some cheap
Venetian consummation to be sought,
deep Burgundy of the romantic vein.

I know the nigger-pink seduction of the real.
I know the purplish lust of the ideal,
rank musk of some primeval tarnish.

The evening change is redolent of the rose.
I know the amber gleam of that clear varnish,
Love. It makes the thick graind rosewood glow
on pianos in saloons of love-drunk millionaires.
Its musk perfumes the incidental rites
of movie stars.

I shall awake to the elegance of common things
and cast the shadow of princely appetites.
In the dark I have been with the millionaires,
heard the diamond sonatas and have seen
the costly lovers, opulence of good bodies,
the Côte d'Azur of priceless lusts.
I have playd the horses: Crucible,
Nom de Plume. Ecstasy and Werther.

The evening change is redolent of the rose.
I am rapt in a tarnish of the wine,
archipelagos of some Tchaikovskian gloom,
inconstancies of a loving mind.

●

Medieval Scenes

1950

Upon the wall of her chamber, so
the legend goes, the poetess Laura Riding
had inscribed in letters of gold:

GOD IS A WOMAN

The Dreamers

The Genius mixd too strong a cup.
At noon the lethargy remains.
We cannot shake it off.

Sleep lingers all our lifetime in our eyes
as night at midday hovers
in the fir tree boughs.
The Genius brews his lethal cup.
All things swim and glitter.

The magic in convolutions of our company
winks its lights. Its touch is slight
and vital. But we are bearish magickers,
makers of lightnings in half-sleep of furry storm.

It is the magic of not-touching,
not-looking sharpenings of the eye,
dim thunders of imaginings. Half-loves
kept shore of love's redeeming fire,

temperd to fear and sharpend
to a knife-edge cut. It flashes
in the air. But we are bear-like
dreamers in a lifetime's hibernation,

the sleep of summer's heroes,
of romance's mountain magic. The shadow hovers
in the doom bejewelld fir and whispers.
The daemon swims and glitters in each face.

Each sleepy bearish hero short of love
recounts his dreams. The fir
casts on the day's continuum of light
a shade of language dragon red with hope.

It is the magic of not-touching,
the hostile speech of rigid magickers.
And we are unawakend dreamers,
sleep-talking miseries of animal despair.

I have within my heart a tree, a fir
of shadows, Hibernia of dreams.
"The speech," I said, "is sexual.
It tells our lovers what we are; excites
the hesitating ear of an animal mind."

"But beasts," then Curran said, "at least
would nudge each other."

The Helmet of Goliath

What if the poet in a moment of terror
or memory of a terrible event
is not *like* David but David himself?

This is the Helmet of Goliath.

"Goliath stoppd," the poet writes—
"   he heard his armour creak
"and grow alive with its increasing weight
"and felt a cooling night creep on the land."

Is it mere song, or memory?

A cooling revolution of the mind
is like a night of starry wilderness
a bright antique of sacred presences.

The windy armour grows alive with song
and in that darkend helmet
the poet's face is curious. The lonely men
about the revolutionary table sit.
They seem to muse, each man so solitary,
or, like excited Oracles in conversations after hours,
speak secrets of their trade.

The helmet sings:

Cry woe upon the sleeping land.
A revolution works unknowing there.
The lonely knight in Goliath's poetry of armour
is not Goliath. He was a spirit of power,
fallen away into a dark disuse.
See how the beauty of his form
has been deformd! He wears
a doom bejewelld bright of armory.

Cry woe upon the sleeping land.
It grows alive with an increasing weight.
There is a secret wooing in the night,
a fine adultery of voices talking.
I saw the sleight-of-look, the moment's
quick avowals. It vanishd,

wraith-like elegance
of a forbidden swan.

The solitary muse
speaks to each man. They grieve
and shake their heads. They grieve
that grief can teach them nothing
nor can they touching touch.

The poets at their table speak of love.
The waves of an uncomprehending sea
wash between each lover and his love.
The words are drownd of meaning in that roar.

Goliath from a distance fell
into a dark of meaning.

The roar within the helmet makes us deaf.
It grows alive. We never seem to reach our life.
The sword, our innerness,
is sleight-of-soul, it vanishes.
We yearn. The yearning vanishes.

The speech of the poets seems to deny
all love. They listen to forbidden music.
And in that darkend helmet
each poet's face is curious.

The Banners

The Swan is the signet, heraldic joy.
The Banners make animate the inanimate day.
No longer mere, but night-mare changed.
The Swan, the sign, displays its grace.

The lion in the loin that slumbers
shakes the sheath of sleep back from his claws
and stretches. The poets
weave upon that tapestry a spell
of flowering, gold-threaded tendrils of a vine;
make animate each animal form
with conceit of loving. There:

as if washd up upon a wave of violet,
of blue, vermillion and clear yellow,
the poets animate a unicorn,
animalization of the beckoning swan.
This is the night-mare thread of their loom.

The days before awakenings, dark ages,
are long with hours for the poet's tapestry.
The unicorn of gold and swan-white threads

nuzzles the sleeping virgin in the park.
Above their heads the signet of the Prince
is woven, elaborate blood-red signature.

The poets weave themselves as the erotic hunters.
They wear bright jerkins of a rich brocade
and silk of forest green upon their thighs.

They stand with instruments of hunting,
hooded falcons, spears and nets,
and watch that sleeping nakedness
where they had woven her,
half-hidden in the flowery spread upon the ground.
They smile mysteriously upon their innocence
and upon their unicorn, virgin wildness brought to bay.

Swan into unicorn, innocence to wildness,
brought to bay.

They seem unconscious of the signature.
It glimmers in embroidery of leaves,
the scarlet lake of some significance.

The Kingdom of Jerusalem

The hosts of the glittering fay return.
Their sunken palaces in lakes of dream
rise, amaze, and perish.

What of avowals then? fealties of ruin?
The splendid Emperor of Jerusalem dreams
of the Emperor of Jerusalem in his splendor.
The poets at their board
subvert the empire with their sorrow.
Powerless and melancholy, the young men smile,
evasively, and stroll
along the shores of the slumbering lake. We hear
the diapasons of a drownd magnificence.

Then, then the agony came.
"There is something else," I said.
          I had not known
I had so deep a sorrowing.

The knights are luminous with the dreamer's splendor.
I serve the unease of an early promise;
I remember now the sea was calm.
The wind had fallen into a still of potency.
The sails hung slack, and the Sun in His heavens
was the Lion of our sorrow. I drank
the draught of a secret thirst.

The people of the goddess Danan smile,
evasively, and work their spell.

The poets are foolish in their wise.
They stroll like gallants in the park of days,
attended by their shadows that are hounds
of a disturbing wonder.
O but these gallants seem so calm,
they fall into a still of potency,
listless, uneasy rememberers.

The palaces of the fay appear.
We seem to hear the battle cry,
                or love cry,
      or death cry,   the last haloo
of some deserted lover's horn,   lost
upon a field we had forgotten,   amaze
and perish.

The Festivals

Was it a dream, or was it memory?

"I do not want the witless rounds of spring
to break this fine enchantment.
The joy unbroken is the lovely thing."

The poet sees his foolish Muse bestir herself
as if to shake off foolishness. "The sleeping joy,"
he murmurs in her dream, "is best.

Then let us drift upon the fire with closed eyes,
pretend our midnight. When we dead awaken
we will find our ecstasy
will break into the maddest of all noons.

I would avoid the chattering of birds,
the twittering in gid and gawdy wide awake.
Our unicorn is but a gilded ass
adornd by village fools with a single horn
of painted wood.

Faces too bright, janglings of love too live,
in the candid minds of the redeemd
these do not appear. I do not want
the wantonness of spring
to break my wonder into a spiritless chuckle,
piebald ribaldry of nights and days."

The poet holds the musing body that he loves,
and, like that glistening lover that Saint Julian knew,
that body has a leprous questioning of his soul.
All lovers, male and female hungers, move
in transformations of the Muse.
The Muse is wide awake.

"The joy awake," she says,
"is everywhere. You are a wondrous sleeping
in a world of wonders. The braying ass
the fools have painted gold and red
and decorated with a single horn
—I saw him in my dream and dreamt
he was a magic wonder—now awake
I see he is a braying foolish unicorn."

The Muse, amused,
awakens the fearful poet to her dream.

The Mirror

Two women stroll among the orange-trees.
Reflected in the glass their nakedness
is like a feud of brilliancies.
One woman's hair is of a lewd gold,
red as man's first thought of sin.
It falls across the heavy indolence of her thighs
and barely sweeps the ground with gold.

The second woman has grown old.
Her naked body sags and wrinkles in its lust.
It speaks cavernous wastages of a despair.
She grins and shows her broken teeth.
The glass is like a rose of broken teeth.
It trembles with the waverings of the air.

The mirror does not ask if they are witches.
It watches. There is a naked man
between them. He twists between his thumb
                    and finger
one nipple of the woman with the hair of gold.
She stands like an unknowing Eve,

radiant with evil, and waits. He holds
the nipple like a blood-red cherry there
between his curious extended fingers.

The daughters of Danaus lead their naked husbands,
each her naked husband to the naked bed.
There is a carnal burning in the air.

The woman with the fiery hair plays on a lute
the plaint of some erotic melody.
"I have within my heart of hearts a tree,"
she sings, "that bears no fruit but misery."

The man is standing with one foot
placed forward. He holds
the aged witch's dugs with his two hands
and thrusts his blood red penis in the air.

She touches it. She smiles.

O all of human wisdom seems to fall
into the reawakend depth of mystery.
She is the woman with the golden hair.

Her vulva gleams beneath the hairless mount of Venus.
It seems impenetrable in flesh or
as if some violence were needed of the man.
The mirror shines in a still of muted lust.
The image shows the oranges upon the ground
like jewels in the greeny gold of grass.
There is a plaintive singing in the air,
the air . . . . The daughters of Danaus fill
with blood the sieves of lust and cry.

The Reaper

Created by the poets to sing my song,
or created by my song to sing.

The source of the song must die away.

All day the night of music hovers
in the fir-tree, swims and glitters.
O touch me not to song
for I desire to be forever mute with my first Lord.

The source of the song will die away.

Glorious is the hot sun.
The reaper in his youth cuts down the living grain.
We see the glitter of his hot curved scythe.
His weary labours cut us down
while yet we live.

The source of the song will die away.

Sweep not upon the strings of my dark lyre,
my body, music; make mute
the tree within the heart, for I desire
to come unto my Lord unsung: the Tomb
of Muses in the marble of the flesh
is like a monument of song.

The source of the song will die away.

All night the pestilential reaper slays.
We fall away beneath his blade.
Our youth is daily harvested like wheat
from fields of our first Lord.

The source of the song will die away.

But see, glorious is the hot sun.
The Reaper cuts my hot youth down.
He cuts me down from my first Lord
while yet I live.

The source of the song will die away.

The Adoration of the Virgin

The speechless statue of the Virgin stands
among the whisperings of shadowy forms.
The magic beckoning extends
beyond her figure wrapt in the adoring light.
The solid druid wood, self-contain magic
of a live virginity, shows thru the gilt
the ruddy sheen of gold.

The poet lovers in the evening hall
walk in the clamour of dim carillons
that roll, that roll, the fall of night.

They wait, disturbd,
as if the rigid Virgin image were to stir
and speak. The miracle seems immanent.

She is not innocent. But, virgin,
she has known God. Her draperies
fly up, unfurl, and are caught,
at war with the surrounding air,
carved in a wonder and brushd with gold.

To her, her son did not appear.
To us who did not know him
he appeard. White Baldur
in the bleeding wood appeard.

I walk with my lover. We sorrow for a third.
A third walks with us. Wounded splendor.
No longer mere, but changed. But more.
He bears our wounds, tears that are blood,
crowns that are thorns.

O haloed Mother, heal
my lover and myself. Hail
Mary full of grace.

The lonely image of the Virgin is
articulate with grace.
She holds the Infant Wizard
like an exclamation.

Forgive, forgive us in our love, and heal.

      The druid wood disturbs.
It speaks beneath the leaf of gold.
Her woe is older than we know.
The gold, His blood, upon the rigid draperies,
gives grace.

The poet lovers feel her touch
as if that touch were stolen from their hearts.

Huon of Bordeaux

The torches in the windy corridors
light up their faces. One by one
the poets fall. Their faces
darken.

They are the legions of the Ruler of this World
and come to death. Their minds are vacant
where winds may come from distances
and howl.

Illuminations of no spirit.

No longer mere, there is something else.

I answer:

This, Beloved, is to close the Happy Sphinx,
the statue half-emerging from the sea,
before whom let us gladly fail,
answer stupidly a question
answerd wisely might have forced
too early doom upon us.

The harpy lies in the slumbering waters,
glittering and pale,
and, like a sudden look into our own eyes,
we see her, mute
                    mad stone questioner.
We shall not hunger madly for a stone to speak.

Morgana le Fay!

She is like a sphinx of stone,
or like a man
upon the throne of Christendom.
She stirs the fir-tree in her wise.

I feel Death's cold upon me when I see
the Tomb of Muses where the Lover lies.
He is a man surrounded by staves —
heir of imaginings, changeling son of a Roman king.

He,
in all his brightness, has
cold memories of Egypt in his eyes.
He dreams of power not of love.
Conceived in a dark of power,
he will not die.

The empty armor of Ishkander Khan
casts its shade upon our bed.

We render unto Caesar's what is Caesar's.
Our hearts are renderd to some spirit who has passd.
Our speech is renderd to the Riddler,
Our Lady of the Lake.

We listen, but we will not answer.
We will not speak forbidden things.
The Tomb of Muses where He lies,
            a Sphinx's son of laughter,
floats upon the lethal sea.

The Albigenses

We move as dragons in the lethargy.

The spirit of our Lord moves in the universe,
that spoke to us of evil things.

We hear the rustling of a serpent brilliance.

See how the worldly splendor swells.
The darkness of our Lord is vegetable with hate.

The spirits of the Light move in the dark.
They strive to touch. We know
dim memories of their chastity.

I know a serpent wisdom of the blood,
of suffering, of coital magic.
The light of our spirit is draind away
into the flesh. The womb,
the blood red sun, the universe,
are bright with evil presences,
            angels of a leprous fire.

The spirit of desire moves in all lively things,
a beauty that glitters in the leaves of trees.

The Pope of Rome magnificent with massacres
is Lucifer. He repeats, repeats in us, creates
his evil image. The bride turns in the woe
of her devil's form and seeks to know
the devil maleness of her groom.
They eat the body of our Lord.
Golgotha mount stares on their paradise.

The poet lovers in copulation know
the emergence of the dragon from all things.
They burn in the wrath of the wrathful God.
Black is the beauty of the brightest day.

O let me die, but if you love me, let me die.
Your grief and fury hurt my second life.

I would come unto the source of light unsung.
The Golden Ones move in invisible realms.
If we could know their chastity; we strive to touch.
The consoled of God die away from life.
We reach, we reach to hold them back.
They grow invisible to our lust.

O let me die, but if you love me, let me die.

Poems 1948–1949

1949

Three Songs for Jerry

The Inexplicable History of Music

1) Water enclosed; the birds wear away;
   water opend; wear away.
   The shores, patients of the little sun,
      crowded with birds.

2) In the early morning I open the blood;
   this is the same deed as yesterday.

   I watch the great tears drop
   patiently. The Muse wears white;

   snores like a bird. The patience,
   of the little sun, wears away.

3) Child-eyed Muse!
   the sick patients of the sun
   are like shores that wait at your house.

   I watch the tear drops open
   into blood.

4) Indeed!

   That flaming drop
   roars in the jungle of green leaves.
   A lion torn from the flanks of steel
   shows great gashes of belief.

   The Muse
   floats upward with child-eyes open.
   Stare at the sun, O Muse!
   This is the same deed as yesterday.

5) Time for algebra to answer.
   Who will sing

—now that I no longer care—
better than I sang?

6) La de da de do
de dum de dum do de dum.
de la la de la de tum de tum;
who dum who la de, la de dum?
dum dum who, who lad de;
la de dum de dum dum who do
la.

7) That was no lady that was my Muse.

A Weekend of the Same Event

1) The bears circling around each other
reek with sweat and blood.

They drop
where they are,
two moons of pewter
feasting upon each other.

The bears, no longer bears,
but pure, bear-like only,
murmur.

They lick their wounds
like lovers licking
dinner plates.

2) Finding a dead bear's head
alive with truths
I dippd my curious hand
into his crawling hole
and let live truth
eat away my curiosity.

3)   The sun droppd down
     into the bleeding sky at five-oclock.
     I met my lover at the last corner.
     We went over to Mother's
     and sat like six foot Kodiak bears
     to eat the little feast spread there.

4)   hum. hum.
     ho. ho.
     hum. hum.
     hum.

5)   She unwrapd the baby
     and showd its naked face.
     It was like a pewter plate
     submerged in that old muck,
     the bottom of wisdom's well.
     It was like goodbye
     warm in its own hair.
     Cynic nurse! I cried,
     careless of my own tears.
     My eyes,
     opening upon the dark.

6)   hum. hum.
     ho . . .

7)   What if there is another war?
     What for?
     The universe whirls like a great mobile
     upon a single wheel.

     How out of darkness
     do bears cast their shadows?
     Where?

8)   Then let love last;
     the heart hive bleed into new hives
     to feed new bees. I tore away at last

the hypocritic baby's skull
to let the night's blood drop into the sun,
to let the heavy dripping sun drop down
   and touch the honey humming sea,
to let the sea fill in my wounds,
licking her old shore as if with love;
at last, at last, at last.

Sleeping All Night

1)   The statue of my mother will not speak.
     What do I hear?
     Mother? Mother?
     Why am I here?

2)   Father climbd up into the sky
     above my bed.
     On the seventh day of my love I said:
     I love you
     I love you
     I love you
     I love you
     I love you
     I love you
     I love you
     and it was good.

3)   Good!? God was like a death sentence.
     My mother was the Judge.
     My father sat in his old nightshirt
     writing his apology for my life.

4)   And so I came to want to die.
     I slit my throat and layd me down
     to watch the hours come and go
     and wait for my parents to pass me by.

I bought me a cup to catch my tears.
I bought me a ragdoll to rock in my arms.
I shut my eyes to match my dreams.
I counted out one hundred years.

I lookd for my heart when I was grown.
I bought me a ragdoll to rock me away.
And so I came to want to die.
I slit my throat and layd me down.

5) Sleep . . . Sleep . . .
    sky of intensest blue.
    Why do I feel so sad, so sad?
    Sleep . . .

    Sleep . . . Sleep.

    I live alone for you.
    Rock me honey until I dream.
    I'm sleeping.

6) Then said the Beast to his Beloved
    I have lived in the Garden of Life
    that is beautiful beyond all beauties; I alone
    touchd by the enchantment of disbelief.
    When honeysuckle bloomd and the sweet air,
    heavy as a dream, disclosed
    true things: I was the lone ruler
    of the untransformd. In winter,
    roses—such as the rose of love you hold—
    bloomd, birds sang rapturously: I alone
    was true to the cold, markd by the weather
    to bear the world's pride in my face.
    Why was it when I cried that you answerd?
    Now I die away with love.
    Have you never seen my face?

7) Goodnight. I am not afraid.
    Everything will be all right.

Now I lay me down to sleep.
Now I lay me down to sleep.
Now I lay me down to sleep.
Now I lay me down to sleep.
Now I lay me down to sleep.
Now I lay me down to sleep.
Now I lay me down to sleep.

•

I Tell of Love

(*variations upon Pound's essay on* Cavalcanti *and his translation of*
Cavalcanti's Donna Mi Prega)

I TELL OF LOVE. This
is the animation, "a world
of moving energies"; I think
of a clear stream; I seem
to be so containd in this element;
giving up my wit, my essence,
into the light of it.
        Let me make this Love visible:
He stands, still mysterious to the naked eye.
We are so merged in what we see.
Where we walk now—for two months
my lover and I: "where one thought
cuts through another
with clean edge."
This is not a question nor answer.
This is not a statement.
        Let me make this Love visible.
I am filld with a notion of form
that seems visible.

Love moves in the dimmest memories.
He takes form, gathering radiance

in love-less childhood. He opens
his eyes as our eyes open; he is created
early. Does not the heart
hunger for love; and the mind
learn patience, seeking no vain-glory
but that sureness—to merge
indistinguishable in love yet
having its own quality? Love moves
in the word to be discernd
by the mind in which love's yearning
has been stirrd; by the sight
from the naked body
where Love seems to rest, each time,
singular as if appointed, necessary,
appropriate to the pattern.
Yet restless.
   I was afraid.
   You disturbed the pattern.
   I fell. I bled.
We as lovers are mysterious:
wherein Love spread his rays
"not to delight, but in an ardour of thought."
Love has no base likeness.
I do not speak of a drunken state.
He heightens the sense
   of the surrounding darkness.
My eye is clearer.
I speak boldly. Love casts
his own light:
   "where thought has its demarcation,
   the substance its virtu".
A base likeness will not kindle
this ardour.

I feel this : Love.
 Reason does not perceive Him
 but takes its light from His presence.
 Reason is a right form

from which His radiance flows.
How did I come to fall from Love's way?
How have I held back?
Or turnd from Love? or refused?
Yet I do not have my life by chance.

Have I not been poor in discernment?
Have I not seen Love's light wane?
"Often his power meets death in the end."
For Love seeks his true form.
Reason takes its light from his presence.
Have I not stumbled in Love's absence
as if I were a fool and a liar,
or lackd reason to perceive Love;
searching for perfection's source
with imperfect vision?
Have I not had dark reasons?
Yet I do not have my life by chance.
I fell. I bled.
I feel now so contain'd in Love's element.
Reason takes its light from his presence.

"None can imagine Love
        that knows not Love."
Who refuse to go in search of Love
but wait for his favour
do not know him : they talk
by hearsay only. What
is Love for them
but a silly word. Can they envy
what does not move
        but draws all to him?
 Surely it is not of Love
        that they think with envy.

Who go out to seek him
cannot tarry,
but are drawn to him: they speak
of Love until

he is evoked.
"He comes to be and is when will's so great
it twists itself from out all natural measure;"
He has his own nature.

Now I am no longer idle.
Love has made me impatient
    with richness. Extravagance
    has no meaning. Excess
    prevents
Love's clear speech.
His advent rouses a thirst
    that breaks into flame
    that feeds its own flame. Love
    wakens
will's new nature.
I am impatient with dallying.
My eye is clearer. He moves.
He is made new. Truth
seems more various. Now,
I can weep. I look
upon disorder with a new eye.
I do not dwell in my fear.
Love moves; makes new.
He is not
like the sun
but the sun itself.

Love gives forth his own light,
worthy of faith. In him
    who knows Love
is compassion born.

    Who knows not Love
    cannot restore order.
    Not by hearsay
    is falsity dispelld.
    Who gives himself not
    over to Love's light

has not right reason.
Light
no longer moves from the eye.
There
is no radiance.
Beauty so near, furtive,
perishes or becomes
wild-cruel as darts
to him
who goes not in Love's search.

So man has craft from fear;
envy from ignorance,
harbors hates.
He falls upon Beauty
like an animal,
caught, falls
on the spike of
or the trap of
   the naked body
where beauty is death.

Who knows not Love
   can not believe,
     nor will imagination teach him,
     nor this song show him,
that Love gives forth his own light.
There is the joy; there is no base likeness.
Beauty takes its light from his presence.

So that I have sense or glow with Reason's fire;
I give myself over to Love's praise.
   Craft does not avail for this song;
   I do not desire pleasures of mere
ornamentation but strive only to sing
Love's song wherein is a light
   worthy of faith.

The Venice Poem

A Description of Venice

The lions of Venice crouch

suppliant to the ringing in the air.
The bell tower of San Marco
shakes the gold of sound upon
the slumbering city. Gathering,
the bronze boy burns the blue of sky
with jewel blue eyes. The lions
crouch suppliant to
the ringing, burning blue.

He has a heavy head of dreams;
wary tho he seems, his eye
is fixd upon the boy's eye —
as if he saw all love was frozen there
              in knowing,
forming a central sapphire,
cruel and absolute.

        This jewel,
        from which proceeds,
        as if rays,
        a melody. . . .

 •

And when Saint William Shakespeare
              plagued by the flies of jealousy and rage
enterd the Carnal City and stood
              defiant with love in full sight of the Doge
              he lit the holy tapers
              and worshipd
              under the five adulterous false domes
                    of burnished copper.

The Doge, Iago,
knowing more than Shakespeare,
saw with cynic wonder
        at such poetic consternation
        the lewd shadows
        haunting the holy candles;
saw with satisfaction
        the simple-minded Shakespeare
        light with love
        the beautiful fat candles.

Saint William Shakespeare under the true domes
wept so filld he was with the wonder
of the pseudo-dome, the copper, the splendour,
        saw in a vision
        the virgin Desdemona,
        whore of Venice.

    The Doge, Iago.
    the knowing Shakespeare,
    watchd the beasts leap up,
    watchd the cruel shadows
        among the mosaics,
    the jewels and gold.

    Beloved William Shakespeare,
    simple-minded,
        prayd to Our Lady, Love:
    Holy Mother, hail.
        Heal
        my lover and myself.

    •

The lions of Saint Mark's gaze upon the blue,
blue of terror like the oceanic blue
in which the onion-globe world floats
suspended like a yolk in the albumen air.
        The four bronze horses
face the square — as if they had suddenly

          appeard there,
under the wingd heraldic lion —
          this is a vision of rare
          exultant cold love,
          a monument that
          tho bathed in gold of the sun
and painted over with warm gold
resplendent with blue and green
          gives despair words.

          The horses stare triumphantly,
          glory of Byzantium,
glory of that city of Venus who wears
Byzantium's other face. The Doge
at breakfast in the Palazzo
dreams of his city's yearly repeated
wedding with the adulterous
                    Adriatic waters.

Upon the blue blue deep I saw in the eyes
bright with love's betrayal of love
the square of San Marco, center of that world,
                    like the great sea-shell
coil-of Venus, ear filld with the coo-ri-coo
of her flocks, cuckold mimic murmur of the sea.

    •

The cry I heard upon the water
might have been Othello's song;
who sang:

          Why is the house so still?
          Where have you gone?

          My knowing now will never be still.
          My loving now will never be still.
          I am like an empty shell
          tortured with voices.

Alone, I know not where I am.
I cry out.
My voices answer.

O my soul's joy!
Love burns in changes of the moon.
She comes so near to earth
and makes men mad.

Alone, I know not where I am.
The world is false as water.
It echoes back the heart's desire.
Love burns in changes of the moon.

·

Or in full daylight : the hourly ringing
over the city and the surrounding green
or blue water,
            over the onion-shaped copper-domes
that catch the sound as they catch the light
in a murmurous glare, pride of 14th century
Venetian pomp, erected to cover
the actual archaic domes built in the image of
Byzantium's perishd 5 domed
            Church of the Apostles.

·

Damn the persistent tolling of the hour.
Damn the actual brute time.
        I hug my hurt and
        fixing mind away from my heart
describe the sea-wed timeless
        city. Not happy, but in such richness
as delights the eye past hurt
        until the heart awakes
to that vast watery waste enclosed
        by copper domes too beautiful
            for the eye.

·

          Lantern slide visions
of Venice repair; not happy, but splendid.
6 hued colord photographs
reproduce a monument of all desire and fear
for mind's anxiety to feed upon,
to teach the blue of terror so that the blue
of ornament or sky is deeper than time —
blue of an idiotic empty jar,
hotter than mere moment's dismay.

Time turns the glare to watery green.

   •

        Of Desdemona do not say
        she was mere spirit but body
        in which my virtue lay;
        I believed, I had faith.
        —In faith the mind does not weary.
        —In faith the heart knows joy,
        leaps up toward its beloved
        like a believing hound
        lively with dumb piety.

        —In faith the eye is sure.
        —In faith no tongue is false
        but speaks
        straight from the heart.
        Of Desdemona:
        say she was my true witness,
        say I named her advocate
        in whose arms I lay,
        virtuous therein.

Othello moves among the green and purple glasses,
reliques of Crusades, perishable beauty
of imperishable Venice; he holds
his black head in his hands and weeps.

Of Iago: say that he was faithful,
for knowledge like death is faithful.
He saw my true nature.
He was accurate as an angel.

Testimony

j'avais été tenté sinon à cause de la saison.
d'aller me promener sur les eaux pour mois
surtout printanières de Venise.

Those images, *"de Venise et de Saint-Marc"*
"desséchées et nues que j'avais"; I knew.
My heart thirsted after their fountains.
Where shall my heart feed, drink deep
the carnal waters until the dry heart
flowers? Those images, then,
like great tears swim

      in lust's malicious eye;
      transform its glare
      where the heart feeds;
      render a rare music.

"These natural sounds suggest music,
      but are not yet themselves music;
      Pleasing in themselves
      they are but promises of music.
      It takes
a human being to keep them."
      To savour lust and to create
      from lust love's
      immortality —
      like Venice
      created out of the waters, or Venus
      who rides
      upon her invented chariot-shell,
fills the poet's ingenuous machine

with her radiance.
Pure ingenuity could not devise
such a nightingale.

    •

"These natural sounds suggest music,
        but are not yet themselves music."
When they seemingly arrange themselves,
        so subtly the traind mind arranges,
then there appears from the swift fingers writing
        what the ear hears; word and vision
seem inspiration. As if the goddess herself,
        awful and lovely, spoke to the dumb poet
more than he knew. Where shall my heart feed
        but from this fountain—certain to perish,
a mirage, *"desséchées et nues"*,
        and yet immortal
as if it were the mind itself
        which descends in the poem
and becomes manifest.

    •

My jealousy is like a jewel, a sapphire
        or sapphire needle, "good for 1000 performances",
cruel and absolute, from which comes my music,
        at once apparent and yet mysterious
this beauty, as the apparent, explainable
        phonograph and recording disc
        renders the impressd concerto of voices
        for the listening ear. For the hearer,
there is no apparatus, no ingenuity,
        but the ingenuous melody distracts,
                not happy but splendid.

Great Jealousy herself is no mere needle;
        terrible and lovely the Greeks addressed her,
where Eros and Himeros went with her,
        where Love and Desire went with her,

she in the middle riding, Beauty herself,
　　　　Our Lady Love: Great Jealousy was her avatar;
Joy was her avatar; Abounding Love of Man and Beast
　　　　her avatar; Longing for Death her avatar.
　　　　She has so many faces, forms; so many
individual perfections strike panic, jealousy,
　　　　or joy in the heart; flood the mind with a light
clear as the light of reason but delirious;
　　　　strike a music in the blood, a melody
"scatterd to the winds with indefatigable profusion,"
　　　　which, set into order, emerges
as the central portion, the symphonic *allegro*,
　　　　jewelld perfection of music's hierarchy.

Apollo and his Muses address her. No one
　　　　is immune to her seductions but has
all joy by her courtesy. There is no pain
　　　　that I would not bear for her sake.

Imaginary Instructions

There is another world of man and beasts
taking their own fabulous color beyond my hand.
But when the whole world expands into wholeness,
the giant bodied spirit I
holding all things in its ambience,
　　　　the world
will be balm to the perishing heart.

　　　　This day apart,
the individual man is self-central,
　　　　Prince or daemon.
Other Princes are peripheral, are
　　　　other-wordly central.
　　　　They have conceald virtues.
　　　　They are not answers
　　　　　　but questions.

The young girls upon St. Agnes Eve
see, of course, a shadowy groom. But
        looking into a mirror
may show the astonished virgin
more than her husband. Surely someday
she will recall how many faces, forms, glances
        the phantom lover had—

    where have they gone?

This is the first proposition:
in the poem as a mirror, the whole world:
        an instruction.

I no longer know the virgin mirror.
Sometimes the diadems of poetry
        —mock gold glories cut out from paper
of an afternoon—
        turn until my head turns; inflate
a bulbous image of a world, a vulgar empire.
And I can sit upon a throne,
        cross-eyed king of one thousand lines.
In the mirror of poetry I conjure
        luxuries I can ill afford.

The artist, like Lorenzo Bernini, sees
        Louis the 14th's head
"qui avait l'esprit vif et brillant"
        that floats upon the air
            (his own head:
                the whole world there)
carved from an elegance of marble,
        the swirl, the twist,
the savage despair of draperies,
        as if flying, as if flying,
the sensual arrogant face
        carved with such ardor . . .

    a bust by Bernini
in a corridor of the Andrew Mellon museum,

why does it come to mind
     now when I say
I no longer know the virgin mirror?

          Why are we never at rest, I ask.
          Why am I touchd so deeply?
There is a root, faithless and painful,
          from which we spring.
          Why does the rose
          never cease unfolding
but grows and unfurls
          the swirl, the twist,
          the savage despair of draperies
                    so that its beauty
                    surpasses knowing.

          •

Accident will finally strip the king
and show him naked in a moment's mirror.
—This is not the exalted face
          Bernini saw—
the forlorn cocksucker is not wonderful

          This cock
          presents a humiliating moment.
—Not that those low hung balls
          rescue the scene—
only passion can rise to the occasion.

This is the second proposition: in the mirror
                    the Part:
consternation of a whole world.

          Yet his is the noble moment
          In our dreams this nakedness
                    is our kingdom;
          the cock
raised in the air is man's urge;
          his pride, his greed—
          he trembles,

eager to love and yet
      eager to thrive;
      so too his lover
      meets him,
arrogant and alive, his eyes
      seeing already
      more than Love's mirror shows.

Faithless and painful, why does the rose
      never cease unfolding
      but grows and unfurls,
the swirl, the twist:
      the hot clasp of bodies,
      embraces
as if with love, lips fastend,
      eyes staring or closed,
having this power to hold one,
      having no power
other than this power of clasping.

      Yet here seeks the heart solace.
      Dismay, strain, exhaustion often;
      anger, pain, endurance.
Buggary stirs enmity, unguarded hatred.
Cocksucking breeds self-humiliation,
      pride,
      helplessness;
      begets Lotophagoi, dreamers.

      Yet here seeks the heart solace.
      Nature barely provides for it.
      Men fuck men by audacity.
      Yet here the heart bounds
      as if only here,
            here it might rest.

   •

"We must understand what is happening:"
watch "the duration of syllables,

"the melodic coherence,
        "the tone leading of vowels."
"The function of poetry is to debunk by lucidity."

        This is the third proposition:
                a realistic image.
        As if that virgin upon St. Agnes Eve
        had seen
        old Nobody
        wearing a face in the mirror.

We must understand what is happening.

        —tears from a stone
        (that stone might have been the Stone
        of the Philosophers
        the Fool says)
        but watch the duration of syllables.

How many faces, forms are there,
        each, as if omnipotent.

        This is Love. Our Lady
        appears and reappears;
                Her virtue gathers
        in so many forms, glances,
        never at rest.
                Now we are bathed
        in her light, sapphire with light,
                ultramarine, rose,
                delirious; and now,
        in the dark, the mirror
        held to show our faces
        hints at some earlier
        frightening form,

        from which her virtue flows
                violent,
        each time as if appointed,
                singular, necessary.

This is Love.
Everywhere, everywhere,
she calls her hounds about her
who leap up, joyous,
dumb beasts of pleasure.

Do I obscure your quality,
giving you up to fabulous color?

Ephebe, what appetites,
in what fiery tombs,
gusts of flame, flashes
out of obscurity?

who go about the town, go up and down, ride
in their expensive motor cars, their convertible
up-to-date automobiles, the red leather and the metal
rich and bewildering to the eye; attired
in suede or cord-du-roy with cashmere sweaters.
I have bought a corduroy coat myself, but they
display casually, as if it did not matter,
bodies, expensive and cavalier,
only money can breed such bodies.
How lonely, how lovely these Venetians
seem, distant and to be worshippd;
only the envious can deny their beauty:
who go about the town, these princes of money,
splendid as the cartwheel or great rare silver
dollar piece, splendid as a dollar.
How lovely, how lonely these princes are,
too proud, too holy to walk among the humble.
Only the envious can deny their power,
faithless and splendid as the gods they go.

•

Turn, turn—how dark it is!
The inventing head
"qui avait l'esprit"
upon a single air, one melody,

discovers voices,
counterparts, *"vif et brillant"*
    so many faces, forms, glances
    appear and reappear,
wound-up, keyd:
    —this is the air of Apollo;
    so many tones vibrate.

The invented head
    invents; having
    so many tones; having
    this one air.

    The lilt
    appears.
—ah, there the heart sings,
the inventing head declares,
—clear as the light of reason,
    the lilt,
    delirious.

    Has he fallen in love?
    He falls
but never to the depth.
Like Canute he plays sovereign to the sea.
He sits for hours as if he might hold it back—
    eyes fixd upon the tide,
    cross-eyed king of one thousand lines.

    Does he never sleep? dream?

I do not know if he
has fascinated love, or love
has fascinated him.

    The air he breathes . . .
    The air he creates . . .

He stares intently
as if he stared upon a sound.

What does he see? hear?
waiting, waiting, for the *allegro*
to re-occur.

The invented head
is like a sound upon which he stares—
Louis XIV's head again
inventing
what does he hear
that he has not invented?

The other head,
the poet's listening head,
as if flying upon the air,
carved by Bernini
out of what obscurity?

stops. CHANGES.

This is the fourth proposition:
the mirror as imitation, as poem,

STOPS. changes.

Recorso

into the long, slow cadence, the anticipating,
rapt, attentive, climbing
neither upward nor downward,
but hovering : dream of a sea-surge.
the tide, the tide of event.

And the old gods rising, falling.
—Those were only waves roaring—
—That dark form, a sea-lion, floating
neither upward nor downward,
but sleeping : washd by the tides.

the swollen body of a man,
                washd by the tides,
        as if suspended in the glare . . .

so dark, so dark. Vague and unsure.
Quickground of images, rising, falling . . .

Sometimes, in the mind's closed eye,
everything springs into flame,
hot as radium, unstable,
death to the touch,
        the whole sea raging, rising . . .

        in which we float, touching, alive,
        as if before death
        in Love's great light.

into the long, shoreward roll, the anticipating.
Now when I hear an aeroplane
        late at night or in full daylight
        —beautiful and mysterious machine—
        the red jewel lights sailing in the dark, or
        the sword flash of the sun on metallic wings,
I do not know, I am afraid.

into the waste, the assembling of repeated forms,
        first came the heat and then the after-glow,
        violet or electric gold.

        We held our humming heads with both hands,
        swinging, swinging.
                to and fro, the light
falling away across the water, lavender,
rose, ultramarine, rising, falling—

the woman climbing up the stairs, the woman
climbing up the stairs, the woman climbing
up the stairs, up and up, to and fro—

open and closed, open and closed—
lips parted, teeth half opend, tongue
held between, the lips parted, swinging,
spinning like a top—

        Do you remember, remember?

in a row of stainless aluminum pots
the pattern repeats, repeats endlessly
accurate: accurate, endlessly repeats,
repeats pattern the pots aluminum
stainless of row "A" in—remember?

rose, ultramarine, rising, falling,
the same wave rolls and reversed
unrolls

        rolls and reversed—

the dropd cup reappears from its fragments
      springs to the hand as if from nowhere
      complete.

The Venus of Lespuges

Of first things: solid.
                Her paleolithic image
      is large. Six inches in height
      it is monumental.
                The spirit is flung upward.
      The body remains, monumental,
      from which all spirit flows;

      the breasts
      and the buttocks
      clusterd
      like fruits above
      the mons veneris.

I return to first things. Her image looms
          wherein lies the universe
          of felt things; from which
          the spirit is flung outward,
          born out of the fat fruit

          so that: the shoulders and the long neck
          with the round sexual head
          curved above like the violin neck
          above the female musical body
          seem instrumental;
          the deep strings of the viol
          waiting for sound.

Of first things. First into flower and then
          the full fruit, pendulant;
          the man curved above
          like the prow of the gondola
          drifting—or the fern frond,
          the male, not first,
          but out of the female

                    Ἀφροδίτη
                    μῆτερ

In the cards she is the queen of hearts
above the ace of spades:
          the creator or destroyer wearing
          the mask of Eleanor of Aquitaine,

          all the meaning held in her image:

          or Henri Rousseau's mistress,
          Queen of the Jungle, mistress of the tiger.

          the odors of flesh, heavy as a dream,
          from which all odors flow:
          oil of myrrh, eucalyptus,
          sexual odors, taints of first things.

At the nape of the neck
there is the pine odor; the beautiful fat
round and clear, meditative

absorbing all things.

       She has so many arts,
the pearl-like lustrous flesh,
the warmth that is not like the sun
but from which the sun is flung out
and yet containd.
       She has such art,
confounding all things . . .

the weight of her breasts,
the weight of words,

stirring the depths
from which the crest rises
      upward,
or the touch of the viol string
      vibrates

      the head singing

into the male, like the suspended star-sapphire:
      blue of heaven, or blue of the depths,
      that men gather from a limb of the flood
      or rock of sea-deep, the dark sapphire
      crystal of death-depth blue
      or the star in which wander
         gold lights,
      blue of terror or the oceanic blue
      as if all love were frozen there
      swilce gildene steorran

into the stone, *Safire,*
      in the deep water found and dark with virtue,
      putteth away envy
      & comforteth the body and the members;

who saw in the second fundament of the City
a bliss-ful sapphire
and therefore saw there *hope*
and memory of him-self.
She was amused.

She questiond. In haze of smoke,
    in drunkenness,
    she was insistent.

    There came then the flood of first forms.

He hit upon the image when he remarkd
that *the poet slept within the statue*
while the war raged.

    But all things sleep here.
    This fat immortality is alive.

    Not Chaos;
    but first form.

    This quality cannot be obscured.

   •

Of first forms:

    So many eyes in the jungle.
    She lies on the horsehair sofa,
    nude and serene, mysterious
    as the white disk of the moon,
    her hibiscus-pink flesh luminous,
    pearl and unreal,
    listening . . .

    There is such a quiet here.
    The soundless woodwind
    blows among the rushes,
    the soundless elephant lifts his trunk
        into a gesture of trumpeting—
    all sounds are muted in the painter's eye.

But these forms,
painted as they are,
lift into music.

The concrete image moves upward
into the coherent
only in sound,
in the tone leading of vowels,
in the humming, the hesitating.

She lies on the horsehair sofa,
placed in the visual jungle,
surrounded by plants and animals
of the eye.

This is the painter's real world.
She hesitates upon the verge of sound.
She waits upon a sounding impossibility,
upon the edge of poetry.

The image lifts into gesture
like the hand pointing
or the trunk lifting
or the silent black man
holding the pipe as a gesture,

and the gesture lifts
like the trunk trumpeting
or the throat pulsating
into the duration of syllables.

Who has no coherence
other than the melodic vein
suffusing its pearl luster
over all surfaces.

She rose out of a great rustling of waters,
transformd in the sea roar
within the shell.

What is happening?

music, magic,
emerging

out of the shell-coil ear

the mimic murmur,
the remembering

Coda

Between the sapphire and the sound
unfurls the rose of vision;
tears from a stone
unlock the stone;
months have passd like days of pain
now the most bewildering of all pains
these images like great tears swim.
I am barely able to go on.

Where there is neither faith nor vision
truth in the many petalld division of the rose,
each of the unfolding parts
becomes identified, grows into enormity,
is beautiful, and stares,
more sickening than beautiful.
I am barely able to go on.

Adultery began like the unfolding rose
showing the cruelest passionate facts.
Between the sapphire and the sound
only the imagination can take hold
and the imagination loses its hold.
I am barely able to go on.

Who has waited in Love's cave
watching the shadows of real things

when the reality of lust has gone
knows the most bewildering of all pains,
knows the longing for tears in the stone.
I am barely able to go on.

Here at last is the place of no gods.
Venice has perished, fallen into disrepair.
The sapphire has become extreme and cold
as if it took all strength to bear.
Again and again all things return
into the faithless and un-fair.
I am barely able to go on.

> How deep the violation goes,
> unfolds, petal by petal, rooted,
> and yet so multiplied,
> inflorescent.

When you come to this moment the water in the tap
drops as if counting the eternity of time.
Stop Look and Listen. Summon up your wisdom.
Nothing will answer and the long dark room
will not be light when you turn on the light.
Your four hundred volumes by the very best authors
will go blank as the paper at which you are staring.
When you come to this moment the mind goes dead.
It will never restore when you cry out in need
the faith in which there was no need.

When you come to this moment and you are left over,
you rise to the occasion and death won't come.
When the love-light perishes and lusting has gone
and you try to make up love in the marriage bed
you will long for the violence of the approaching wars.
BANG. You will lust for the cut of the stone.
BANG.

When you come to this moment there are no gods.
In the merciless light there you are shown
naked and silly as the primeval bone.

There isn't any poetry. The doggerel begins
like the drums in the dark where the cannibals chew
at the monotonous liver and spit their bile
and the words in the dark go round and round.
When you lie in the bed and know with a start
that the vows are broken— You face with a grin
and damn your mind that searches the fact
where your lover lies panting in a new lover's arms
holds on and comes in some secret room
lifted again to the passionate pitch. BANG.
When your thirty years are counted up
they seem the beginning of an endless stretch
that repeats and repeats the ritual feast
that devours your flesh and eats at your bone.
BANG.
When you come to death's door and he won't let you in.
you can hear the bed groan and the adulterous sounds
wound and wound but they do not kill. BANG.

How deep the violation goes.

     Heal.

There are so many faces, forms.

     Heal.

So many arbitrary divisions.

     I do not want to drift,

     stops. CHANGES.

     There must be a moment when that faith returns.
     The artist searches out the deepest roots.
     He is violent. He is animal.
     Driven by the language itself
     alive with such forces,
     he violates, desiring to move
     the deepest sound.

The lion-life sea
caught in the cup
of the particular Red Sea Spider Shell,
coil of Venus, natural ear,
      where
love's avatar was held, perpetually
      to speak . . .

Hear the lion's roar in the shell.

There is no thought here.
      Logic forbade this.
      All that we value:
      order, remembrance,
      human nature and conduct,
      natural coherence—

What do they avail when this art
      dictates its laws?

•

What does he say? He
has gone further than this art allows,
      losing so many values
just for that sound. Why does he let go?
      Why does he not let go?

      There is nothing un-fair
      he has not created,
brooding upon the primitive source.

      Is there nothing
he will not read into what we are saying,
      feeling?

      There is no wisdom:
      there are no gods here.

      He says there are gods here,
      denying our human individual being

He says there are gods here.
Staring without sight,
          his ear
fixd on his imaginary shell.

What can we tell him
          he will not hear
warpd in the twist of that damnd coil?

"the white disk of the moon.
her hibiscus pink flesh luminous"

He was staring at the painting—
How did his ear
organize those sounds?
          Leading us away from the painting.

•

There then:

          went Saint William Shakespeare
          (the whole world there)
          to light the holy tapers.

          This stage, he said,
          is eternal.
          Even death is subject
          to these lights.

          This candle
          shines bright.
          It dwindles.
          It perishes.
          It is so dark.

          The inventing head
          has its own light,
          But remember, remember . . .

This candle
is love's taper,
and this
is candle of innocence
whose flame
does not die.

How lonely
these lights seem
in all this pride
as if in vain.

Anger, pain, exhaustion
often
once lit,
never consumed, but

how dark it is.

Candle in the window
light me home.
Candle in the beginning
light my last day.

This stage, he said,
is Truth—
never in living
but here, here,
all felt things are,
permitted to speak.

This candle I lit
is faith's candle.
In nursery
it comforted,
as evening song
or humming
comforted.

Do not leave my side, I said,
but love me.
And then in the still room
cried and did not die.

Who comes so near to earth . . .

O blessed Mother, heal.

This candle is mysterious.
I did not light this candle.
It came into being
as I came into being.
There was no beginning.
Then there were first things.

There is no pain
I would not bear for her sake.

Who gives also faith
and surcease from pain.

This candle is the word,
"potency",
candle of magic.
This candle too is eternal,
in whose light you must love me.
Do not disbelieve the shadows
but love me.
Do not put this candle out.
This is one of my holy candles.

There is no mask I wear
that is not emotion,
that is not deeply rooted.

Knowledge does not survive;
accuracy does not survive;
but the devotion survives
bearing wounds
no wisdom would bear.

Foolish William Shakespeare
is more than his knowing.

Knowledge did not begin;
accuracy did not begin . . .

The sapphire pendant
dangled above the eyes
catching the light
or the soothing voice
in whose ambience first
faith was full:
these things are earlier
than we know.

      Born.

Out of what obscurity?

These months have passd
like days of pain.
Now the most bewildering of all pains

      forced

      outward

flung out from the fat form.

Ring, then, ring clear!
Baby is charmd by the bells ringing.
Baby is charmd by the towers swaying,
hearing each sound
in the morning din.
Little cross-eyed king held
secure in the center of all things.

Baby blue—all eyes—my eyes
fixd upon the central sapphire

outside

reaching

terror, grief, joy
move in the glare

leaps upward

toward his beloved

anger, pain, endurance

swinging

swinging

Ring, then, ring clear!
Fatherly towers in the air!

•

3 Poems in Homage to the Brothers Grimm

The Robber Moon

The Moon like a lantern or a face
swims in its cowl, fat with light.
I lie brooding.
The shadows of the room grow.
What if I should go now; walk the hills,
stare across the outspread
dwindling city or grow fat with stars,
big-headed as this panoramic view,
swollen as if with rain. My heart
is swollen; like a lantern or a face
it rides thru the forest, lonely as a light
swinging in its solitary hut.

      Now, one by one,
the robber beasts arrive.
They sit about the table, deal the cards
and play Death's game.
      The solitary light swings.
Each round the robbers wound the light;
tearless, brooding, remembering,
they play. The Moon
is closeted. —HO!
the boisterous cook exclaims,
frightening the robbers:

      —I've cookd up a fat face here
      for midnight supper.
      Wait 'til the Moon comes out again.
      Then we'll sit down together, boys,
      to more than Black Jack or fortune.

Ah! but the Moon sails away,
like a face that has found fortune fair.
And the rain pelting the roof
frightens the robbers. The cook
frightens the robbers. The swollen light
swings
back and forth, snaring the robber beast
and the robber beast and the robber beast
until the murmuring stops.
Leaving the hills, I'll say I left the Moon.
But I saw the Moon go
who had my heart for supper, fat with light.

Strawberries under the Snow

Digging in the snow, the children
uncoverd wild strawberries,
rosy and joyous, hidden among leaves,
red, red as the blood of the children
fallen upon the drifts of snow.

All winter the snow fell;
the children lying in the chill snow drifts
uncoverd wild strawberries
hidden among the leaves.
And the little Saints came down,
the little Saints came down the ladders of Heaven
to sing for the frozen children
whose tears
glowd like love in the cold.

> Beautiful Griselda,
> how you dream!
> You have been drinking wine, child,
> that's why your heart is singing.
> Your cold face does not move
> but how you dream!

You turn your head in the drifts of leaves
until the snow melts
and your dreaming eyes
open like strawberries.

There is no evil here.
The snow is so soft, so white.
Tho the children will never waken,
they are not dead. They sleep.
O how the heart breaks
yearning to awaken the sleeping children.
Look! Childhood lies here
at the foot of the ladders of Heaven.
Here are the strawberries.
There is no evil here.

The Dinner Table of Harlequin

Harlequin rippd off his face.
Ah Death! who would have thought
the beginning of the play
would be so bloody funny:
        —like a mouthful of tears,
        —like an empty plate at dinner.
Who would have thought Harlequin
could laugh
right out of the tear in his face?

Ah Love! You have taught a lesson
or two
catching the birds before they fall
out of my two eyes
and holding them stark upright
stuck on pike-heads
for all to see.
        —like a crackd glass
        from which the flesh flows

into nothingness.
Ah Harlequin! I said I would stop poetry,
rip it off like a face
to see you too laugh.

> The other side of the moon
> is turnd away,
> cold but not lonely,
> lovely to not-see.
> My side of the moon
> is white as a day
> and sings to me.
> The other side of the year
> has slippd away,
> happy, so happy,
> lovely to not-be.
> My side of the year
> is a moon-like joy
> for all to see,
> for all to see.

•

Revival

"Go to Hell!"—the signs return—and the agency: the telephone. This
time I was "shown the door" and walkd out. *The time has not come yet.*
Not a sign but an evocation.

Again you have "shown me the door"—
I have been thrown out. "Go to Hell"
and there, the open door.
Where I long to go into the open.
—We have been alone before;
countless, we have walkd.
I am almost happy walking there
toward the house of friends,

when I arrive—who will cry
ah, ah, ah, here at last you are!
At last you have come to our door.

"I go where I love and where I am loved."
When you say go
I go. I obey. I obey.

The time has not come yet.

When I arrive, turnd out at last
of my unhappiness. So many times
I have been shown the door.

When at last I recognize
the open door
and I walk out toward the house of friends,
who will cry—*at last you have come!*
At last you have come to our door.

| REVIVAL |

the sign said
printed in red letters
on the side of the white church
in the dark.

The time has not yet come.
but; now I have been shown the door.
The great sky with stars
as I walk in the dark before morning
seems to watch.

Am I on the brink of happiness?
Am I on the brink of panic?

Not even love or not-love
seems significant
when I consider
the panic with which I walk
toward the house of friends.

A Poet's Masque

written for Erika Braun
Hallowe'en 1948

CURTAIN-RAISER. *Four figures seated on thrones wearing crowns; these are the Authorities of Literature itself. The lights are on and the masque has not begun.*

Man with a
False Nose   Obscure. Not plain-as-the-nose-on-your-face.
         Riddled with private titillations. You'll see
   what I mean. Intimations of more
   than is ever there. A four-square honest man
   sees thru such rot. I see thru.
   You will see thru but
   it's not as simple as all that.
   It's not insig-
   nificant—reviving old superstitions,
   death's heads and magic,
      irrelevant images . . .

Lady Philosopher with
False Teeth   You come near to the truth but miss
         by just a mile enuf to please.
   Swollen with vanity, indiscriminate
   as tornado or big wind from Winnetka,
   these enthusiasts are never merely good.
   I like something I
   can sink my teeth into. Simple and swell,
   poetry can be plain as the nose on your face
   and just as painful, cut short
   just where these bladders begin
   expanding. A ballad might teach
   economy; this school of rhapsodes
   is more than I can ever quite believe.
   My ear gets tired. A folk tune
   tried and true, a democratic speech
   or two, a milk man's revery
   or careful keen sight of ice-cream

fountain irony: would save
the occasion.

Professor with
False Ears   What we are about to hear is all that.
        But I have been aware,
recognized early in these students
      SENSIBILITY,
nerves finely wrought, the strongest bull,
all unknowing, caught in the heat
of oedipal complex or narcissistic urge—
I can point out—evolving
in oral excitement or syncopated
heart beat: all that
I see. I will point out.
Let us not judge too harshly.
The mind is mysteriously formd.
Freud makes us aware.
Einstein makes us wary.

Man with a
False Nose   Well, I don't know
        what it is all about. So much smoke
need not betoken a great fire.
With little wit, a mighty smudge
will luke-warm the dreary orange groves.
And there is little sense here
and much vague heat spread all about.
Dr. Johnson would
have spotted something queer.
He'd not have botherd
tapping it with his cane but rappd
such a coxcomb soundly
on the head. Nothing else considerd
this poetry lacks
not only sense but meter;
lacks matter. It decays
in all the Romantic fallacies;
thrives upon ignorance;
and in these days of moral indigence

forgoes coherence, cohesion;
thrives on optical illusion,
metaphorical protrusions;
provides a maudlin, undisciplined
    irrational audience
with all the excitements of bad taste.
Lady Philosopher with
False Teeth   You have a nose for the right thing but lose
    by forfeit of intuition where you gain
by sensible imagination.

But I agree yet
disagree. This stuff
has too much sense for me.
It is not obscurely lacking matter
but matter-fully obvious. It swells
and grows enormous huge
in such a gross of messages.
These big-voiced prophets
shout so loud
the small voice of truth is lost.

One must not bite off
more poetry than one can chew, but these
have mouths greedy full
of poetry. It fairly spews forth;
it so takes the unwary listener.
A good course in literary acumen—
say, English 100
Methods and Materials of Literary
Criticism, might
bring authentic stuff to light.
Professor with
False Ears   We are perhaps watching
    lit-er-a-ture in the making. *That*
is the important thing; we must keep
the vital evolution in mind. We must not
underestimate the Word. I myself
have tried to make students aware

of what is meaningful in our time;
presented Joyce, Proust and
Katherine Anne Porter—these major
intellects   You will agree
they see a whole, a sensible totality.
Our role must be to convey, to carry over,
to portray, to sketch the message,
the living core of what they write.
We keep alive the universal flame,
the fame. We nip the artist in the student bud.
With A's and B's and C's and D's
and F's we rush, we push, we form,
we graft, we foresee the fruit
upon the young poetic tree.
We fertilize the hidden ocular spud.

As a member of our faculty has writ
the autobiography of Man or Fire
in admirable prose and
          scholarly research;
the professor, too, has his great role.
Hours at the microfilm, catalogues
of ands and buts, substantiations
of calculations of ramifications,
creative indoctrinations, corrections,
studies of hitherto
unseen defections
bring Yeats nearer; make
Eliot clearer.
The professor too
has his great role
and this, these poets tend to overlook,
to ridicule; and yet the School
holds the balance. I myself
know too well
the stern regrettable task
that Justice plays—who is not blind.
I am sensibly aware
of both sides—tho the creative

always goes too far,
strays into insanity or
emotional imbalance, fugue-states,
or merits administrative discipline.
I do what I can do.
A cautionary word or two
may keep the worst of them in place.
Pumpkin-head   I speak from a common unpretentious
                successful writer's point of view.
I speak from common sense.
When I lecture on American literature,
I can weed the plot—sometimes
a rousing good tale—out from the tedious
prose of Melville. Biggest circus on earth
I call it! Just a damnd good story
about a Whaler and a Whale,
overwritten but not stale. I spotted
Henry James for what he is
right from the start. There's
no story in it. A bunch of snobs
try to say there is. A cult
of superior brainy guys.
The ordinary man
decently can't
make heads or tales out of all this.
Nobody understands Eliot
and you can judge
the dishonest fake who says he does.
As for the rest—they will not last—
fascists, perverts and aesthetes.
You can't find
a good story among them.

"Boots" and "If": those are lasting poems,
good as poems go. They inspire
real manhood. Read smoking a pipe
around the campfire or
on occasion to bolster up
morale—they have a sounding meter

and healthy rhyme. There's no verse
of account among these pouting moderns,
unread anyway, who can't keep meter
and put all sense to rout.

The Masque

PART ONE

The Guide with a candle
The Poet

Guide: She will meet you here. As poet,
      I can go with you this far
      where you as child or shadow
      have been before. You will know her
      as if that great face bending over you
      had been the universe in the beginning.
                As poet—
      I falter—just where the poem begins
      and you alter my course. I retreat
      into a personal autobiography and you
      are poet—just where I fail.

      And yet remember, Poet, I
      carried the first light and led,
      as if I knew, thru field and wood.
      I imagined all that you
      will find to be most real.

Poet: And where are we?
      I can barely see. This single candle
      flickers—casts a shadow
      into darkness, reveals half-forms.

Guide: At Love. If I could see
      with your eyes now I'd feast
      upon the swimming moon
      as if upon eternity.

You have a little light
that shows a world of darkness.
But I am blind and see another moon,
great candle for love-ridden flies
swarming with infatuate wings.
See—there it is in your hand!
By which you peer into a gloom—
Love.
The moon swollen with moon's blood
is appropriate, I think, for a lovers' night,
to meet and love passionately
under the evil regard of witches
on All Hallow's Eve.

Let the knowing eye stray. Fear
the moonlit lover and his love
as you fear the moon
who may turn a wild eye to meet your eye.
Lest in the dark you find
dark of the moon and un-knowing.

Wait, O Poet, for your love
and fear the truth.

The Poet with a candle
Eurydice

Poet: where am I? I speak
to the darkness as if it loved to hear.
O darkness, that lovingly
surrounds my single flame—
trees that bend to hear—
night that is like an ear
to which I speak. My love is dark.
She, like Eurydice, among the dead
seems lost in memory; yet I
shall not look back but face forward
and meet her there ahead.

Eurydice: Ah dew, ah dew,
look back on me.
See,
among the murmuring dead I stand.
I follow.

If you listen
you will hear my footfall,
you will hear me call
love, love.
ah dew, ah dew,
remember, remember.
Do not forget.
Turn your head.
You will see my face
just as the candle falls,
just as the light fails.

You will see my death's head
swim in the pool of hell.

Ah dew, ah dew,
love, love.
If you listen you will hear
my whisper.
You will almost see
my face
as if it were
the universe.

If you turn your head,
if you make sure,
you will see my clear face once
clear in the blaze of memory.

Ah do, ah do turn,
do turn, ah love
do not believe but
make sure.

Poet: I see you, dark among all women
            sorrowing. I do not need to turn.
            You are like a shadow that makes this night
            almost a day. All things are clear
            measured by your obscurity.

            Faceless. Intimate.
            I call you truth. I do not fear
            but love that pale, unseen—but beautiful
            beneath her shroud—Fate.

            What substance my thot wears, I cry,
            of flesh more real than the resounding day.
            Darkness within darkness
            that makes the black night blaze
            jewel-like. I rest, as if in grace,
            as those two mourning eyes become your face.

Eurydice: Ah love, ah love,
            here is your mirror.
            Gaze, gaze.

            In the mirror
            you can look
            over your shoulder.

            Remember Perseus
            who could see
            Medusa's face
            unscathed—

            In the mirror
            you can remember.

Poet: My face grows large and there
            beyond I see as if ahead
            all white and milky as the moon
            behind my back
            that happy indistinction.

Eurydice: Ah love, love.
            Do you barely remember?

Mine is a particular face.
Mine is a voice
you have heard before.
Turn and look
search the darkness.

Once—just once.
When my eyes are closed.
While I sleep.
Lift the candle
and steal
one backward look.

(The Poet turns and with a cry drops the candle, plunging the stage into darkness)

Three Robbers with candles
The Cook

1st Robber: —where is that nigger?

         —I, Black-heart, smell him.
         Hell, he stinks! I'll root him
         out of the darkness. I'll give him
         the candle, all 10 inches of it
         where it will do him some good.
3rd Robber: (giggles)
1st Robber: —where is that mother—ing nigger?
         He'll eat his s— before this nite is thru
         and taste the blood of his own tongue
                for poetry.
         I know his kind. Dreamers! minds of muck!
         He'll hold a candle yet
         too hot to hold.

(they advance to the table, set the candles thereon and begin to deal out a deck of cards)

3rd Robber: I hold his heart in my hand.
         See. I spit on it. He shrieks.

When *I* play his Fate
he'll know the LIE.

When the chips are down,
he'll cry out as if torn from the earth,
bleeding at the root.

This is he!

The nine of spades!
Crazy as midnight!

2nd Robber: Wait till death shows up.
That's the card of the world's terror!

We'll play tonight
until that cock-proud sinner
receives the mortal blow.

1st Robber: Death
won't come so easy.   He'll be tired
before *our* game's half done
and yell for death!
That nigger'll hang from a thousand trees
and have no glory in it
but an idiot's agony
swinging in the wind of ridicule.

3rd Robber: —the witless wanderer!

2nd Robber: —a limp six!

1st Robber: —the deuce take him!

3rd Robber: —the seven of frauds!

2nd Robber: —the Jack of No Good!

1st Robber: —the blood QUEEN herself!

*(there is a great roar—the Cook from off stage who shouts HO! the robbers
overturn the table plunging the scene into darkness)*

Robbers: The Cook! The Cook!

The table is set up with a candle in the center. At one end of the table sits the Poet. At the other stands the Cook who is stirring an enormous Pot.

The Cook with a candle
The Poet

The Cook: I'm like Diogenes, young man. And
　　　　　　with this candle I have searched for true
　　　　　　ingredients for poetry. This will do and this won't
　　　　　　do. You'll have to wait until the stew is done
　　　　　　and then like Sigfried out of Fafnir's blood
　　　　　　you'll smack a most illuminating brew.

　　　　　　But mind, when Love arrives,
　　　　　　it's taken already five candles—a little cost
　　　　　　of twenty-five cents—
　　　　　　and you won't find
　　　　　　the Poem before you've bled; nor Love,
　　　　　　unshamed; nor Bliss
　　　　　　without its taste of this and this.
　　　　　　There's never a kiss
　　　　　　without its teeth and tongue;
　　　　　　there's never a heart strung up
　　　　　　to play a melody
　　　　　　that's not a naked sorry sight
　　　　　　to sicken the boldest interne going.
　　　　　　There's never a doctor
　　　　　　tougher than Poetry's muse
　　　　　　who'll rip the gutty roots out raw
　　　　　　to leave a singing wound.

　　　　　　Now there's a curious object for you!
　　　　　　A clawy footed primeval thing
　　　　　　if ever I saw one for love
　　　　　　or poetry. It'll not be hid.
　　　　　　And once it's seen,
　　　　　　there's not a song can comfort it.

And here's an undigested wad
to make the rhyme and meter sag
and sense go wild. Wait till the critics
get a smell of that! all wriggling
like a net of glittery inedibles.

And here's the Cat that's got your tongue.
You'll want that back before you sing.
You've seen her face before,
as if you weren't afraid.

And this here whorish spoon
will melt down, to stir the moon with,
until the tears of sour cream
clot in that dull sheen that quiets
troubled waters — sweet deceit.

Now gather brambles from Love's Wood,
thornwood and poorly burning
green stuff, pouring forth its smoke
and running pitch, slow to catch the fire;
or poison oak
to make the fond eyes smart.

But don't sit there. You'll kiss the pot
and learn the wild wood witch's art
before you can go forward, boy!
and drink this mess as your own blood
down and around and thru and thru
down and thru and round until
        each vein and tube
is fat and globular with witch's brew!
Sing me a song, lover boy;
I'll interrupt and criticize,
but sing, my waggon, sing.

Poet: *then like a child I go, child go*
Cook: Ha! now here
this shiny bulbous wonder
catching a single color in the light

is all the thief's terror.
Who would suspect it
so cookd up?

Poet: *searching for my love to find*

Cook: a pickle-shaped monstrosity
calld Wish-Me-Well.
He'll cook it down until its glow
is will-o-the-wisp strong
o'er everything.

Poet: *then like a child I go*
searching for my love to find
I lookd at you with my two eyes
you said that love was blind

Cook: aye, there's an eye—and that's a sound
that few can bring to harmony
and subtle variation; but witless Isis-wise
with many tries and dark disguise
must gather up all things into
one monstrous cacophony of eyes!

Poet: *then like a child I go, child go*
I said to Cat where shall I rest
and Cat said no Child rest, no rest,
for Love lies further on ahead

Cook: Now *that* is short of good
but in it goes! there's not a fault
or line that you won't rue
to see immortal in the pot.

Poet: *then I go, go, I cried,*
like a child that is sure
but unknowing, all unknowing,
go thru the dark door

go where the bird sings
said Cat and I go
the Cat has my tongue
and I can't find my heart.

Cook: You're weak in the lung, boy,
but that is that.

I'll snuff the candle out
and climb into the pot myself.
Then drink the hideous brew
until your singing head swings
like the moon in dark and lights.

goodnight. goodnight.

The Poet with a candle
A Voice (the Guide's Voice,
        but with sleepy
        boyish intonations)

---

*(The Poet enters striking a match or two in the darkness and finally lighting
a candle. The table is cleard now except for pen and ink and paper and a few
books)*

Poet (writing):   *My muse, my moon—triumph of the moon*

            —this, of course, is my sixth candle—and
            I shall not light the seventh. I have only
            been given six—in a dream, in a vision—
            some moment. Having come so far,
            having come so far upon a dark path,
            guided by my daemon who goes
            no further; driven by derision; with music or
            with silence, without music; only
            the inner trembling and then stillness . . .

            Here, here. Is she dark or fair?
            Dare I look into the mirror or the dish
            in which the ring is placed
            closing the incomplete circle?
            The woman within—the question within—
            without an answer. I have seen the answer,
            voiceless to ask the question.
                        "the cat has got my tongue"
            that is a curious message
            to unfold.

Voice: hon—
 Poet: yes
Voice: What is the matter?
 Poet: nothing
Voice: Have you finished the masque?
        What happens after the Cook-
        Witch scene?
 Poet: I don't know.
Voice: Have you written anything more?
        It's too good for a party like that.
        I wish we could do it right.
        With all the parts just like you want them.
 Poet: I'm the only one who will ever read them that way.

        And it will be all abominably done,
        mis-read, stumbled over,
        performd like a parlor game by drunks.

        I wish it were more than a parlor game.

        There'll be people there I loathe,
        and some I'd love to hear the masque
        will not be there.
Voice: But we could give it sometime
        the right way—
        that Eurydice part
        is beautiful.
 Poet: "in the middle of a dark wood"
        go back to sleep, dear,
        go back to sleep. I want to sit a while
        and watch the candle burn;
        and then
        there is no final speech.

Uncollected Work 1948–1951

Jerusalem

Then Jerusalem became the goal.
I wanted to go. I wanted to go.
I put away my games
and went to dance

      too late, too late.

I never saw Jerusalem fall.
I never saw Jerusalem restored.
I wanted to go. I wanted to go.
It seemd so far.
Jerusalem like a star
drew upon my heart until the pain
bewilderd me. I was so small.
I could not cry.
I stared upon the star.
I wanted to go. I wanted to go.

I heard the newsboys in the street
      cry out Jerusalem!
      Jerusalem!
      O sweet Jerusalem!
There the heart will find its rest.
      I wanted to cry.
      It seemd so far.
The newsboys calld, too late, too late!

      I wanted to go. I wanted to go.

A Derivation from Rimbaud

1.

The Caliph of Hunger remembering
lived out a full feast.
Hearts like roasts laid themselves open.
The wine flowd from the glasses
    in themselves.
The hearts beat with longing,
sweet to his taste.

O I remember
how the sea beat!
Drum beats of no meaning upon the great ear!

The year swung round,
a seven-course dinner of seasons.
I contrived harvests in spite,
grand artificer of fruit trees and rewards.
Light fell down from the branches.

O I remember
the full mind
like a peach grown from a blood-root
swollen and red.

Haroun, the magnificent Liar,
sat at the table of seasons.
Beauty herself like a mere whore
he sat on his knee!

O I remember
she was bitter!
the dead rind of pleasure, the thermometer.
I curse her.

How far can we go without hope: Hope is still hidden there,
hidden there. Where shall the rifleman direct his sure shot?
Straight to the mark of the meaningful wound. Who can erase
the palpitations there?

When the Seasons are twisted
so their laughter continues.
The record is warpt,
the needle grinds the music
out of the warpt surface
like a man without appetite
chewing a bone.

2. CONTEMPLATION OF THE HEART

When I return to Sleep,
prodigal of wonders,
machine, deserted
and noble weaver,
what river
turns such cogwheels, sets
such shuttles into motion?
such rooms, lovers, terrors
interwoven?

In this world
only that which does not move
points out the abyss.

3.

All we have given up!
Slowly the garden would have devourd us
had we not, as we did,
eaten the garden. Now

there is rage and excitement.
The lion in the brush
sucks his wound.
The beast will be devourd by us

without love! without love!
base without corruption,
tasting the lash of desires
stupidly. Pierceness of eye,

bluntness of tongue, taste
of lip, lewd and dumb to the hand!
The lion in the brush
naked and bland to naked hunger.

Without sacrament!
All we have given up
with shame returned to us.
This is not our shame, we cry.

Our shame surrounds us.

Love—A Story

It was Thanksgiving Day, and Maggie and Charley Ford had asked her eagerly, just her, of course, to have that day with them.

When she awoke, the cold light from the street barely seeped into the room. She had fallen asleep then—actually fallen from that shelf of sleeplessness. There had been something about a mirror.

The book was there. It had not been in a dream.

Claudia Bernstein reached for her glasses—she could see no more than a blur in the light without them—and opened the volume of Strindberg again.

Then you'll have seen, the Confessor said, *that Venus is represented in a mirror. This mirror was originally made of copper, so that copper was called Venus and bore her stamp. But now the reverse of Venus' mirror is covered with quicksilver or mercury!* THE POETRY OF STRINDBEBG—she had jotted in the margin. Meaningless, obvious, that is, in the morning. But this passage was painful.

She reached for a pencil and wrote PAIN above the word POETRY.

Quicksilver is therefore the reverse side of Venus. Quicksilver is itself as bright as a calm sea, as a lake at the height of summer; but when mercury meets firestone and burns, it blushes and turns red like newly-shed blood—LOSS OF VIRGINITY—she wrote eagerly in the margin. *Like the cloth of the scaffold, like the cinnabar lips of the whore!*

She lay for a while staring at the clock. Two hours of sleep, if one can call it that. Cigarettes exhaust me, she thot. I must have a cigarette.

She got up and boiled a pot full of coffee, reading the Strindberg over her morning cup, lighting one cigarette upon the stub of another. She kept a pad of paper beside her and jotted down as it came to mind —THE POINT ABOUT MAGGIE AND CHARLES IS THAT THEY ARE TALKING THEMSELVES OUT—. Then she carefully drew an arrow—equals— ACTING THEMSELVES OUT.

Claudia Bernstein was a plump, near-sighted little jewess. She might have been voluptuous, but she was so tense that one could observe this only in spite of her. —*in order to spite me*—she might have very well written in the margin. She shared the prejudice of the society in which she lived against the exploitation of such potentialities. The combination of being female and jew was fatal she knew; and in self-preservation she marshalled her intellect against such possibilities.

Maggie and Charley Ford were what might be called a handsome couple. REFLECTED IN EACH OTHER Claudia had scribbled down someplace. She was writing a play in which they were characters. Claudia was in it herself, of course. "seeing thru them or thru their eyes, I see thru Life—" "—my own life is true—" that was the main idea, over and against Life with the capital L. Not seeing that was the tragic flaw.

Maggie Ford had been on the stage, that had been some ten years before, and she carried over daily a certain manner of the theater, grand in its way. At thirty Maggie Ford had a wide-eyed professional child stare; suitable in its innocence equally to express joy or terror. Well, her eyes and her hair, close-cropped to her head and childishly chic, went one way, and her mouth deliberate and even pained went another. "When you've been in love, I mean madly in love with a real pinbrain," Maggie had confided to Claudia, "when you've been in love with an actor, then you know the full cheat. Like when we get up to this monkey's hotel room—I mean I was that *dumb*—'You're going to be a great actress.' He says this just like that while he's taking off his pants. 'I've got to have it, baby. I'm crazy about you. I've got to have it'."

"What I mean is," Maggie had finished, "is that you don't learn anything. I'm just as damned dumb at thirty as I was at eighteen." "There isn't a man that don't call you baby, loathing babies the way they do." "'My little girl!' that means the same old game of count to ten and I'll ditch you for good."

But Maggie and Charley were different. They were "soulmates," so very much alike; adoring each other, they adored themselves. They had been friends for almost a year before they realized they were in love. "In twenty years," Maggie had said to Claudia, "Charley's had as much of it as I've had in thirty." "I always thot," Charley had said to Claudia, "that she was so clever; you know how she talks. Then one night at Dan's Place, I was cruising the bar and I ran into her and that fourth husband of hers. He went to the men's room and she started to cry. 'Charley,' she said, 'we've got to get out of here before he comes back.' We went to my place on Bleeker street and talked for hours about the men we'd known. 'I could sleep with you and it would be different,' she said. You know how little and like a child she is. I could have cried it was so sad."

Claudia had lived in the Fords' being in love, sheltered them, gardened them, carried water to them, turned over the earth around them. Now that they were, after two years, engaged in a "cold war" (if one may borrow a phrase from today for an event so long ago), she felt involved. Their battle seemed a battle around and within herself: as if two parts of her own being, so barely united, now had turned upon each other.

So she arrived early Thanksgiving Day, not to miss a minute of it, carrying the Strindberg with her.

The Fords had made up. There was Charley Ford, when she got there, early as it was, engrossed in preparing a handsome side of veal. "A poem!" he exclaimed, "of garlic and thyme and lemon rind."

"Poetry, I suppose," he said, "is dammed up. Not that I haven't damned it all my little self—and here it is," waving his hands in a gesture, "a dash of olive oil." "A veritable drive from the libido, consummated in the impermanence of a hot dish!"

"To be eaten by all three of us—" his wife mocked, "in so short a time."

Charley Ford and Claudia Bernstein had been friends for over two years when Maggie had appeared. He had been writing poetry when Claudia first knew him, bringing his poem to her hot off the page, the two of them avid in the reading aloud—listening intensity of them. Exhausting for her, in a way, but compelling. At once taking in and disregarding the disgraceful things of life.

Then Charley's love for Maggie had become the new drama for Claudia, the one she was always writing now. He no longer wrote poetry, but she had become a fervent convert of his marriage, and an exacting accuser. The excitement had kept it going from poems to marriage, tantalizing. Charley exhibited himself to her—not carelessly, but ruthlessly, with a flair. Beneath, was his scornful regard that there was something tender about him that she could never savour. He had been brought up in a tolerant Anglo-American household, a grim and archaic development from the pre-meltingpot era, and he believed thoroughly (he could say it but he might never believe that he believed it) that a jewess could never really understand certain things. "What I like about Claudia," he would say to his wife, "is that she knows everything about me, more than you want to know, and yet she knows nothing, absolutely nothing."

He enjoyed showing Claudia Bernstein in all its brutality what he knew about Maggie Ford. Having out with the worst, what he never let himself "know", seemed to keep glowing and alive the painful bond that Claudia Bernstein would not accept in that struggle of hers for self-preservation.

"She sees only the truth," he had said to his wife, "and consequently nothing of the important things."

"The very shock of it," he had said some weeks before to Claudia at lunch, settling himself across the table, lighting a cigarette as if to smoke the shock out of it (remembered in tranquility), the glow of it setting fire to his speech, the taunt of it making Claudia vivid to him. "To realize that we are only alive, really alive, in moments of madness." He was rapt in himself and in her listening, receiving eagerly and tensely the excitement of him, excluded as she was and yet, the center of the disclosure. "Maggie had an appointment with Lowen at nine that night, and I waited here at this very table, smoking cigarette after cigarette and drinking. I don't know, Lowen always seems—when she tells it— to corroborate everything I know about her, but I always feel a panic during those hours when she is at the analyst's. Oh I don't know what I expect—or expected that night. Then she came in and gave it to me, 'threw the line at me' she learned so superbly while she was on the stage. It wasn't anything we hadn't rehearsed ourselves, said to each other over and over again. But there is something about the analyst's saying it. He's the old Delphic Oracle, of course, and everything he says is loaded. Or if he really doesn't say it—she *does* make him say what she wants him to have said—everything she says was said seems so loaded." "We wait for the payoff, both wanting it and not wanting it, telling it over and over again, only the psychoanalyst provides—dramatist that he is, Shakespeare of our time when the stage has died—the stage for it!"

"She is so very beautiful at times and she was then," he went on, taking up a nostalgic tone, a note of tendresse, "in that powdery lavender turban, the color of death the analyst says. Something almost *Persian* about her. Oh she knew it. She was costumed for it, and she threw it up to me. 'Lowen said we mustn't get married,' she said.

"The old Jew had seen to the heart of me," (Claudia and Charley winced at the word but he did not underline or hesitate in his story, he flung the word at her in passing) "and I was seized with trembling while Maggie spoke. 'He handed down the Commandment,' she said. 'There it is. I hate you and you hate me, and I have to free myself of it. I can't go through it again! We can't get married,' she repeated, 'what he said is true.'

"Oh it was and it is," Charley went on, Claudia Bernstein taking it in in all its cruelty. "But I knew then that I couldn't go on without Maggie. I started to cry, here in this restaurant, and she led me as if I were blind, I was of course, into the street where we started to walk toward the river. I fell down there on the sidewalk and clung to Maggie sobbing.

"Have you ever felt shipwrecked?" (He knew that Claudia had, and *that,* holding on to no one,) "I felt the pain of it that blacked everything in the world out for me except her and the knowledge that denied her I would be deprived . . . of Life. I suppose." He drew deeply upon his cigarette, watching, almost not seeing Claudia's face.

"We walked to the East River. There was nothing we could say anymore, I held her hand. My crying had excited her; she was no longer sure, self-possessed, and then I was sure. 'Lowen is right,' I said to her, putting my now-strong arm about her shoulder as we walked and pulled her against me. I had never realized before that moment my absolute male power over Maggie, and I exulted in it. 'It's all over,' I said, changed by the almost lordly power of those words, and Maggie started to whimper. 'But I love you, I love you,' she repeated. 'I'll die.' And so that was the cue of course to go back to my room, hot and in despair . . . "

. . . or that night coming home from the dance in Provincetown across the dunes in the storm, we took off our clothes, wet to the skin as we were, and left them, running until we fell, in the glare of the lightning, making love in the fury of it. What do these moments of savagery mean?

Thanksgiving! the table was laid out for three. Maggie Ford had a flair for that—for the room that was a sheltering place, cozy and dramatic with its red glass lamplight, its broadleafed dark-green plants, its unique wickerwork chairs painted over with dead white, and the red cushions. The perfected interior! Tawny port for the occasion. Majolica ware. "Smell that roast!" The thick meaty odor filled the studio room, pungent with garlic and lemon.

"Thus Charley and how else!" Maggie exclaimed hugging her husband and slipping her hands eagerly down over his stomach under his belt. Claudia giggled with discomfort. "As usual everything, he thinks, is better than anything."

Her greed was loaded, and she enjoyed the statement of it. That she could afford it was a triumph of a kind over the timidity of the audience. Claudia felt almost dizzy with impression at moments like this; and Charley felt betrayed, both succumbing to and demanding it as he did. But he knew that the betrayal must be shown too, everything must be exhibited. "I get what I want," Maggie seemed to say to both him and Claudia; and Charley was "gotten", "had". It remained evident, of course, that he could never be capable of "having" her in quite that way.

"The whole point in Melville," he said, pushing his wife's hands possessively down until she touched the roots of his pubic hair, "is the punishment of pride. It's what no one sees in all this vogue of Melville's work; the terrifying vision of *Pierre* greater O far greater than *Moby Dick*. I have discovered myself in that book as I never discovered myself in Life. *Now do I remember that in her most caressing love, there ever gleamed some scaly glittering folds of pride.*"

He disengaged himself, and, Claudia following him, they deserted Maggie who remained in the kitchen busying herself with the salad. He was led to the book where he caught the volume up, leafing thru the pages marked and underlined. "Here it is, just it: *As thou knowest that thou wouldst now droop and die without me; so would I without thee. We are equal there; mark that, too, Isabel. I do not stoop to thee, nor thou to me; but we both reach up alike to a glorious ideal! Now the continualness, the secretness, yet the always present domesticness of our love; how may we best compass that, without jeopardizing the ever-sacred memory I hinted of.*"

"Charley does it just the other way too," Maggie commented drily from the doorway to the studio, "There's not an ever-sacred memory he won't jeopardize to keep the secretness going."

"*He held her,*" Charley went on, as if oblivious to his wife, "*tremblingly; she bent over toward him; his mouth wet her ear; he whispered it.*

"*The girl moved not; was done with all her trembling; leaned closer to him, with an inexpressible strangeness of an intense love, new and inexplicable. Over the face of Pierre there shot a terrible self-revelation; he imprinted repeated burn-*

ing kisses upon her; pressed hard her hand; would not let go her sweet and awful passiveness.

"Then they changed; they coiled together, and entangledly stood mute."

The three people in the room, the reader and the two listeners saw quite clearly the two people joined so, clinging at first mutely and then like snakes copulating.

"The whole point is," Charley said, "that Pierre and Isabel do not know at all what that ever-sacred memory is."

Maggie had retreated to the bathroom where she stood in front of the mirror cleaning her face meticulously with creams and pumice stone.

"Why did you read that passage?" Claudia almost panted, "don't you think she knows what you are talking about? What are you trying to do?"

"Oh," he said, he never had been able to say it before, and the violence of imparting it thrilled him—"it's all over between us. It's thru. Done with."

Tears came into Claudia's eyes, of anger and chagrin. She pushed her cigarette rudely out, squashing the barely started cigarette into the dish and lighting another.

"I loathe you when you're like this" but the remark was ingenuous, taking up the tone he had indulged in.

"It *would* be good in a play, if this were a play," he said. "It's not remotely true, it's exactly true, and you know it's too good to be true. The roast meanwhile, is almost done, and I have to get sour cream for the gravy." "Maggie," he called out, "I've got to get the sour cream. Anything else you want?"

"Now that I'm beautiful?" she said coming to the door. "Just give us time to tear you to shreds and then we can sit down to a cozy meal."

"What's going on?" Claudia asked once he was out of the house. "What's been happening?"

"Isn't he cute?" Maggie asked sarcastically. "He's been at this Melville stuff for days. He overdoes it, doesn't he? Ham it up, honey, I always say."

"But he loves you" Claudia went on. "That's the important thing. This is only a relapse from the real resolve." She paused—"either the dinner, the table, the poem as he calls it, is all wrong or it's all right."

"The only resolution that any man has on his mind is to come to quits," Maggie said. "It's different with you—that's friendship and friendship exists by dismissing resolutions. But for me he's not a friend. If it weren't for love, we'd be enemies now—it's all the same hunger to come to the point: the only deep human emotion—to set the stage for the grand exit. Over my dead body or yours. Once they say 'I love you' they're either right or you're wrong. You can't win the argument." "He wants to go whoring again," she went on. She let Claudia's flushed discomfort please her. "He's such a little whore at heart. So he's all denials and Melville." "It's the straight whore in him I can't let go." There let her have it, she thought vividly enough for Claudia to get it. "When he shrinks away from my hands," she said, "I can feel all that hot sexy just-try-to-come-and-get-me lure. It's like stealing cookies when you're sick of the damned things. Just for the gluttony of it." "I know he doesn't want me. That's the only time I have to have him." Her hands while she talked made suggestive grasping movements, baby's hands at the reluctant breast—

—dreadful to think that, Claudia thought.

"You remember that line of Melville's," Charley said, entering the studio with sour cream in hand and a newspaper under his arm. "*Decay is often a gardener.* There is the start of a paper that ought to be done. Show his wife as she was, impervious to his suffering, delightful as it was to him making her suffer too. And hating his writing, rank adultery that it was. Too stupid to know or too wise to know why marriage was a prison for him, and yet her faithfulness—just her own getting even, stifling his vision. Why did he allow it?

They sat down, the three of them, with a sudden festive air, before the roast—intent for the moment upon the homey sacrifice of the feast.

He reached with one hand, warmly, glowing with pride, and took his wife's hand. She smiled.

"Another year has passed," he said tenderly.

The tawny port was golden in the glasses. The candles shed a warm light over the darkening room. The paintings on the walls, the objets d'art, the areas of tapestry and carpet shone back the wealth of his wife's mind—and eye for the right thing. Which included him, of course.

"For the richness of life"—he said.

Veal, peas cooked in butter with mushrooms, potatoes roasted and glazed in the meaty juice, the thick sour gravy.

"How is the play coming along?" he asked Claudia.

"Two things worry the dramatist," she answered. "Time and then—well just the things you and Maggie say can't really be said on the stage."

Both Maggie and Charles liked the glow of notoriety.

"Bette Davis could play you—" he said, "and Luise Rainer could do

Maggie. Maggie does Luise Rainer a bit, it would be a fair swap. ." he stopped because whoever could play his part seemed elusive. That *he* could do it superbly was painfully obvious.

"It always seemed to me when I was on the stage," Maggie said, "that actors know what a play should be. Shakespeare was an actor, and Strindberg—he could see that all one needed was the significant moments wherever or whenever they are. Chronology, plot, or unit only obscures the issue."

"That's what I want to do," Claudia said, "and I just can't do it. The long path from Shakespeare to Strindberg and then there is no one who can go further. What we face is the necessity to bring actual sex onto the stage and that can't be done. I mean no one can even talk about it really—and all the pity and terror is there for us. In sex, that is, and in time."

"Strindberg the Alchemist," Maggie said, "with dreck on his hands and gold on his mind."

"The alchemy of Strindberg," Charley began, "was a natural misconception for the dramatist to have. The gold of the stage or the dreck of the stage; the gold of life or the dreck of life; I don't know which for which, but to convert one into the other was as sad a task as converting actuality into fiction. What haunted Strindberg was the betrayal in the process itself—beautifully explicit in the crucibles of mystic alchemy or practical alchemy."

"At least," Claudia went on, "he found the resolution for Shakespeare's vision—the end of the stage. Shakespeare had filled the stage out of himself with humanity. Strindberg empties the whole stage back into himself."

"Freud," Charley said, "goes one step further, like that Persian Gurdieyev and makes actors of us all. There we are at absolute self-consciousness, even in breathing. 'I am someone who is trying to impersonate myself.' Who could go further? All the world a stage emptied into oneself, and everyone being stagey as hell. Acting out the nightmare of one's existence for that great audience the id."

"When I read *Yerma*," Maggie said, "I ran around for weeks being Yerma playing myself."

"Do you ever think of going on the stage again?" Claudia asked.

"Lowen points out," Maggie replied, "that if I'd wanted to be *anything* I could have succeeded—but the stage was terrifying then and it would be again because I want to be *something;* and that anything that a part should be always becomes that something for which I am searching. Some actresses become ill with love or hate, suffering, or joy, that is never theirs. I don't want *that* and that is all that the stage would mean."

"The anxiety of the theater or who are we tonight," announced Charley taking a turn about the room, a bow. "Every day a preparation, every evening a scene, every night a second act curtain. And we all know that the third act will be lousy. No wonder there is no theater today."

"Well, the problem's there," Claudia concluded, "and it's only by the theater that it can be resolved."

They delayed over nuts, apples in brandy, and coffee. The table was cleared and they sat back from the feast, smoking and reminiscing.

"Thanksgiving day, when I was a child," Maggie said, "was always the most miserable day of the year. Mother prepared the meal in a kind of anger, seeing to it that there was ten times more than anyone could eat and at the same time that no one could eat anything. And Father would do his part. 'Just us two, Babykins,' he made it. Taking me over to his side against Mother. He was so sad and so beautiful with his soft sad voice. He gave me my appetite for beautiful men. 'I always wanted to go around the world,' he would say. 'And I was all ready to go when I met your mother.' Impossible, of course, to go anyplace with *her*. 'But next year, we'll go together—just you and me. We'll see India, all of Asia.' 'Asia!' And then he had the perfect out: he knew he was going to die before that time came. He couldn't be to blame for dying, could he? He got to lie there, calling me to his side. Camille perfectly. Nothing but tears of remorse after the curtain goes down. One had never loved him enough. One can't after all damn the dead.

"He could say tenderly—it was cheap at half the price—'Maggie, I was never happy until you were born, my Babykins, you at least understand me.' Mother, standing there, hating me the rest of my life."

They sat without speaking, smoking and drinking gin now with hot tea which had been brought out steaming in its knitted teacozy. Soaking fragrant sticks of cinnamon in their cups. Maggie and Charley poured the gin with a determined abandon.

"When I was in Boston—" Charley began. The gin seemed to lift him into a sudden inspiration, a funny story—"that time I ran off with Tommy Orwell." Talking about that time—the Fords never talked about it—Charles was drunk with his daring. "Well Tommy and I were sitting one evening at the Statler bar with a sailor we knew, one of those bitches who made a career out of the war. 'There's a piece of gold braid that's hot for me,' he says. 'He'll be down here in a minute. What do you bet.' Sure enough, this officer came up to our table dragging along a rather pretty woman who was drunk as a pig. "This heah is mah wife,' the officer said, 'and I all was wondering if you-all were a pharmacist's mate?' At which this sailor says he was and asks this officer and his wife if they would join us."

Maggie had taken up her knitting and sat grimly flashing the needles. The discomfort of the hour was thick.

"—'I-all have something in my eye,' the officer said," Charley went on stubbornly. "—'and I wondered if you all would come to the men's room with me and extract it'."

"Well we all were that lost for words. The officer's wife sat down at the table and began to talk: 'I all just nevah drank until ah came up heah to Bahston,' she said. '—Gawge has been so wonderful to me, taking me just everywheah with him. Everybody's been so helpful and all. But I just seem to staht drinking and ah cain't stop. It must just worry him but then ah have such a good time, don't I? Who can help it if drinking just seems to go on for such a good time. Gawge knows so many nice sailah boys and all. Ah've just been up heah for two weeks as a kind of surprise for Gawge and ah've been just drinking evah since I got here. It's just been one long party!'"

Then the evening was over. Why did I tell that damned story? Charley heard his silly voice still lingering in the room.

"Well, I thought it was funny," he said.

"It's so nice," Maggie said in even tones, biting each word, "to be married to a real fairy."

"O," Claudia exclaimed humorously (and how else?), "I'm going before you get any worse."

Riding home on the subway, Claudia looked forward to her room and not backward to the scene she had left. That was over-done, she had mentally scribbled in the margin of the page; and she took up the Strindberg. Every scene of the play was more dreadful than the last.

"*Not out of revenge but in order to free myself from the unhealthy thoughts her faithlessness had forced on me; for when I tried to tear her picture out of my heart, images of her lovers always rose and crept into my blood, so that at last I seemed to be living in unlawful relationship with three men—with a woman as the link between us!*"

The speech haunted her. It seemed almost meaningless to her tired mind. She read it over again, chewing it up word by word. It was too late, putting it back together again hopeless.

"*Yes*, jealousy," it said later—"*that feeling for cleanliness that seeks to preserve thoughts from pollution by strangers.*"

"*Civilization*," she read, "*that feeling for cleanliness.*" Was that what the book had said? The long path of civilization from Shakespeare to Strindberg. But then none of them were really civilized. Betrayal and cruelty. When she got home she would copy out that first speech. "*to free oneself*" it said further on down the page. And then one would lie again. The spring of ones mind ran down. What time was it? Late? And one would never know when one slept.

"One can't forget," Charley said, "that Claudia is a Jew. Heir that is to the world of things, and denied by covenant—that she makes it with herself and not with Jehovah makes no difference—denied by covenant the world of spirit. She can set up the stage, give the directions, write the speeches. She knows everything about us after all. And yet the salvation of the actors is beyond her imagination."

"There's nothing, of course, that you haven't told her," Maggie retorted bitterly.

They did not refer to the end of the evening, but, undressing for bed, they felt themselves on the brink of a scene.

"I feel so damned naked. Shamed." Maggie cried out. "There's nothing of me you wouldn't show her, betray to anyone. Why don't you just have all your friends in to peer at me in the bathroom?" Her voice was hard and bitter, that mouth pulled down in scorn.

Charles Ford shrugged his shoulders so as to anger her, assuming a patronizing air. He wasn't losing *his* temper.

"I'm going to sleep in the other room," he said in a patient weary tone. "O hell," she said.

He read a while, but the pain of the hour, inexplicable, was vast. It increased. It seized him and he awoke with panic, listening. She would come to him. Now he could feel nothing but the inexhaustible pain in his body drawing him to her.

O let me touch you, touch me, forgive me, forgive me and take this agony from me.

It seemed hours and she did not come to his bed.

Finally he rose, as if the house were filled with the painful beating of his own heart—panic, fear, and pride compounded in that beat. Can she hear my heart beating, he gasped, as if for breath, and walked silently down the hall, standing outside her door.

"Maggie," he said in a small quavering voice.

"Yes," she answered.

"O my secret Maggie," he emitted falsely. He stood now in her room and flung himself forward upon their bed burying his wet face in her breasts. She held him to her there.

"I am so afraid," she cried suddenly, drawing back. "Before you ever slept with me, before I went to bed with you, you could have been my friend but then you went over to the Enemy."

The depths of her depression swept him on, enchanted and estranged him.

"Who are you? Who are you anyway? Another one. One and one and one. The legions of men. All crowding in."

She sat up in bed, her eyes black and inscrutable with terror.

"O I *hate* you. The Enemy Man. All of you. So many faces and voices, looking and talking. What do you care? What are they saying?"

The tick of the clock in the interim of silence had been going on all the time she was talking of course.

"Everyman," she began again. "I haven't just listened to your voice all evening. I've heard you talking all my life. The words hiding everything. Leaving me all alone. Everything seems so terrible that no one can see the real terror.

"Fool!" she hissed at him.

He was calm now and let her talk until she sank back, sobbing and tossing and shivering. He held her in his arms, stroking her hair and kissing her tear wet face. The violent upheaval—for she sobbed so wholly—aroused him and he began to stroke her breasts, moving his hand under her nightgown, pushing it back over her thighs, and then he undressed her.

"So beautiful, so beautiful," he said to her.

She gazed up at him in the dark, smiling through her tears, a touch of greed wavering upon the surface, regaining possession of herself and of him in his passion.

"You are perfectly you, so completely you," she whispered.

And the trick was turned. Cinnabar red. And then in the great couch of the dark they lay, cradled, as if one, rocking, and then rocked, sank and floated. Outward and cleansed of all being, into darkness.

The Effort

"I have seen the first rudiments of the chick as a little cloud in the hen's egg about the fourth or fifth day of incubation, with the shell removed and the egg placed in clear warm water. In the center of the cloud there was a throbbing point of blood, so trifling that it disappeared on contraction and was lost to sight, while on relaxation it appeared again like a red pin-point. Throbbing between existence and non-existence, now visible, now invisible, it was the beginning of life."

Out of Chaos:

Δίκη δ'ὑπὲρ Ὕβριος ἴσχει
ἐς τέλος ἐξελθοῦσα

So, you will see Justice over Outrage
when you see last things:
    who live in a world without end, who
    can know
    neither first things
    nor last things.
    You will see Justice survive;
    you will see the evening of the scales.

"Since Nature makes nothing in vain"
    παθὼν δέ τε νήπιος ἔγνω.
now visible, now   ("You who think you will
invisible   get through hell in a hurry")

"that theme emerges more and more
clearly" now
that you have discoverd Outrage
is it not an intimation of Justice?

明 this sign
    Bright
or the Moon
as it waxes   as it wanes

The line learnd in the hand
the line learnd in the ear:
like Matisse, blindfolded,
drawing upon the naked door—
"je n'avais pas encore commencé à chanter":
each animal gesture displaying
    intellect
sure and splendid as the lion
    in his way.

    The line
within which, its muscular variety
    laid bare,
each sound not thought-out
but composed; learnd
    in the touch.
No more difficult than walking
    this leisurely and exact
    talking. A song
not yet begun. Yet
    setting the tone.

    Notes,
assertions, passages
as if of the song itself,
sections of the needed intensity,
    references
to a completion of still
    another Partial
    gesture.

The line learnd in the hand
like the lions strippd of their skins:
    magnificent when naked,
    each muscle bold with control,
that were, all thru
    what they ought to be.

•

Utter devotion to the thing made:
to the stone, cut, polishd.
         "keep a grindin'"
task of course never done;
         the language resisting
one's imperfect counsels but
having within it an endless
         perfectability of forms;
         or
oaths, taxes, impositions:
         the law, too,
demands of the devoted an effort
         obscure;
as if of magic or incarnation
         to the barbarian.

not "the regular everlasting job of making over
         again the absolute content of sensibility
         with which we get on, or with which we
         acknowledge our failure to do so"

         "the old dandy is nothing else but"

not a sublime desperation

but: pleasant to learn

         this sign
         "the rapid and frequent
         motion of wings" a bird
         learning to fly;
         an effort

"of how to enter Heaven?" but Morris Graves
(studying the photograph I see
admirable plain elegance
in leather vest; hierarchic stance)
         is right:
"the cathedral is a diagram."

A diagram of acts displays
personality serious and gay.

A child's absorbd curiosity
in drawing may be a key
to what I mean:
what one admires in Edith Sitwell
transfigured or merely posing
is that invention. Warm or cold,
excites because it imitates:
the exact and rigorous long nose
or set rigid mouth
sign of a frigidity; wearing
not mere face but conscious
contemplation of pride, pain,
recognizing in experience a test
or proof of the inevitable.

This scar, slashd by a knife,
is witness to the lion's claw:
or tatooed thigh, a design
of endurance that endures.

LEARNING TO FLY

A bird learning to fly
to realize the flight inherent in its form,
to soar, in learning, into an element
learnd in the bone

or the ear learning greek
touches, touches the weights, estimates
the tones as the throat awakens:
so I listen as if waiting
no language dead: death comes to no tongue:
studying the diagram of speech,
estimating what the eye has known
the hand knows, what the ear
knows the throat has known:

the body of the speech like one's own body
      pleasant to learn

Play: containing a destiny
no more than posing a question
one acknowledges
the rage of the lion, or diagrams
like Satie playing upon a piano
or the immortal Pierrot playing the lover
savoring the moon's changes
of a fortune told;

to play oneself! this scar
slashd by a knife or
cut by a line is witness
to the violence of the line.

And then: have you seen your true form?
the great vision is . . .
in this city—three generations
because I have loved and lived here
the will for beauty if only in words
the great vision is beyond the eye
which apprehends, awaits—

between the height and the depth beyond
where the city extends to its shore
where the distances shimmer
or where they seem screens, shadows of light,
San Francisco in the far,
Berkeley near, pinpoints of light
where from this height
in the falling away the heart yearns so
obscure to the believer

THE BEAUTY OF THE PEOPLE

the beauty of the people is hidden
only when the histories have been exhausted

or when there are no histories, rags
of discomfort and the nude moment
informs, or memory
marks the true thing

there the great vision is . . .
hid in mere gossip, pain, injustice
    if you detect it
obscured in the web of convictions

is there one who is not dubious;
yet dubious, dubious
in the gold light they move

breakfast in the summer glare
friends move as in a clearer air
the company during that war
when we savord the war-bought pleasures
—what pleasures in those times unmixed—
wrath and red wine
and the sublime talk after the table
(Milton then for his richness)
these poets were not English to us
but spoke in that language
partaking of what has yet to come
already contained in their moment.

How many times have I seen her
as she was then, that very morning
and then tho her hair shows grey
    in the rich black
of no quality of age but of living
as if coming to life

the great vision is. . . .
more than the wrath and the red wine

a city transformd because there
these young men sing

once more in words as if they had seen her
of what do I dream? personal disappointments
futilities but there is a height of dream
falling away from which
all gleams, washd in the day

and the air between us alive with color
and the near geranium that glows
        more than afire
may be no more than her flower
        for she arranged there
        in the almost dark room
        such cheap abundancies of orange
                magenta, deep red
        my Beatrice?
                and the near blue shivers
                the far lies in pink haze
                or violet shines to the eyes the far shore
                        shows
                as Tommy has shown it;
        where vision lies
                drawn outward, drawn
                as if from the great height of years

disappointments, futilities
        drifts of smoke
where signs but where there was smoke
        there is fire

consuming all things:

    is:

like the line, shifts, holding all shapes
        immanent

        about to be.

every moment is not so ecstatic,
    but I remember
Pound in the hospital garden
a sun visor shading his eyes
no father-figure for the Freudians ·
    but there

in the mind eternal— of what
do I dream? at so young an age? of

      disappointments then,
      failures of destiny?

      drifts of smoke
mere signs but there come then fires
wherein all things pass away

          no more than vision
          in the center of the cloud
          it disappeard
            appeard
                so trifling
            throbbing

   Is there not
   a harmony of all things?

   inexhaustible.

   Who wld choose a lesser knowledge
   of one part
   against another
      who seeks
   the process underlying these things.

          "Let me stoop low.
          Be free
          of all my old compunction."

          "I am listening to something."

明　a sign; of great delight;
　　moonlight; that which was dark
　　shown clear.

We do not despair.

"only emotion endures"
the sensual mind asserts
the integrity of the thing made.
　　This stone
has been nobly cut; this chisel　　　　　　　　　　BRANCUSI
was here guided
with sincerity.
　　This hand
was sure in its craft.

　　This artist did not
tremble in his boots
　　but stood
with two feet upon the ground.

　　This endures.

　　　　Surety.
The mind in its brilliance
is sapphire or diamond; defines;
so that the emotion endures

throbbing. . . trifling
so that it disappears
　　　　appears

controlld; sure.

There comes the moment of joy,
　　force
like clear water

"when it spurts up thru bright sand
    setting everything into motion"
moods of oceanic rapport,
embracings of all things—
as vision embraces all things;
the rightness of cobalt
and vermilion, so related
and in such proportion
that we cry:
he has awakend
Beauty again;
        he has made new   MATISSE
the order of sensual things.

so that out of a dark cloud
the heart leaps,
the blood leaps.

    These women
    these flowers
    these rooms
flood the mind with delight,
stir the eye from old ways—
reveal "a single thread
in their argument."

    With what ease
this depth of feeling flows;
There is an imperishable joy;
there is a knowledge in color
that needs no other knowledge.
Rapt and attentive:
        who has calld forth
        my eye's keenness,
        my eye's devotion and praise;
who has raised my eyes
                out of darkness.

There is the joy of natural things seen
once the eye has been stirrd
to the mysterious blue
    the lavender, the rose
BONNARD the pale vibrant dance in the air
RENOIR   the rippling fall of light
    that is a woman's hair,
    the lavender of death or
    the shadow of the flesh and the life
    that blooms there, fruit rich
    where the blood and the sun
    flood up into the child's face
    setting everything into motion.

So that there is a throbbing
in the center of the cloud.
A dance. An imitation.
    These things
we praise.

  •

So related; and in such proportion
but without conclusion
These things have no conclusion.
There are no literary values here.
I forgo sentiment.
I show no
sensibility here. Have we not had
    enuf of sensibility? no complex
rich personality; but
I am no more than my voice crying
out of the blood's dance;
out of the breathing,
answering sea-roar
or wind-roar or
the sound of other voices.

Raw as Walt Whitman.

When I speak clearly,
departments of English literature
will understand nothing.

Will not understand my rage,
will not understand my intolerant joy.
I do not understand.
I dream. I chant.
I discourse. This is a stream
in which words dance.
        No one will ever love these words
        as I love these words
                singing myself.

The music is never the same;   STRAVINSKY
it never ends. It is now
without beginning.
        Endless variation;
it is the identical symphony in 3 movements.
It is the identical stream of sound,
        the measurements of time
        in which tones dance.
        It imitates
                in contraction
                in relaxation
        the heart
        the melody
                now invisible
                now visible.
It is profound, for I listen
        from the depths of my being—
that needs no other knowledge.

                She is fair.
                Her hair
                falls across her shoulders.
                The light
                is not

more light
than her hair.

I change the subject?
break the thread?
you have not been listening.

I am deadly dull?
You have not heard me
at all.

IN PRAISE

2   I mean there are no symbols.
      There are signs.
      There are literal things
      in themselves.

There are no associations,
no "stream of consciousness"
      but in the dance
      the emergence of things:
      the presence, literal
      and exact to the mind.

      The Miracle of Brancusi,
      the white light stone
      slowly revolving, almost
      imperceptibly, lucid . . .
            as if
      cutting, he had found life there,
      the stone, imperceptibly,
          about to speak.

"Psychoanalysis" "interpretation"
will only lead you astray.

     Rage/or joy

Is this a foolish
dance of all things?
is this no true vision?
is there a serpent singing
    of old seduction
    in the song?

This is a political vision.
This is an imitation
    of the great harmony.
Harvey remarks the sun,
    heart of the universe.
I do not understand.
I hear.

There is a knowledge in sound
that needs no other knowledge.

    A group of estheticians
        will arrive at a set
        of suitable definitions;
    they will realize immediately
        that if this is a work of art
        its esthetic message
        is a formal experience.
    I have never seen
        an esthetician dance. Or
    the perceptive philosopher
    will notice that there
        are no ideas here.
    The lady semanticist note
        declarative sentences,
        simple exclamations,
        exhortatory expressions:
    poetry has no meaning
        unavailable to prose:
        the holy
    is equal to the sum of its part.
            or
    the serious critic, who has developd

our moral sensibility, will see
the modern drama
will explain,
if he is not sickend
by my pretension,
the flaw, Achilles heel, or mystic
dreaming personality,
the failure not only of mind
but of nerve.

If they are honest, they will admit
I am wasting their time.

Dance, moralists, dance.

Who swerve from the true center
and from the still ecstatic fool's
point of view
look like fragments
flying around wildly
the heart of all things,
never touching
but whirling
about one center.

This isn't worth reading,
but listen, listen:
the rapport, the insupportable
insistence of the sound heard.

3.   Yet of Ole Ez
who is   after all
the Good Teacher.

I mean now not
no ideas
but the play of ideas—
more of our time
than Yeats or Eliot
knew to show.

You
who wld get thru hell
in a hurry.

Few are his good students—
Bunting, Zukofsky

And he askd, how far. . .
without destroying the feel
    of actual speech.

And you will see that Zukofsky
    recaptures
    the actual speech.

It comes as a moment of joy,
live voice
among deadly voices:
the Eliotizers swollen, sounding
    the church knell,
tolling the solemn bell,
church mice of a wealthy parish;
the high-toned, slightly bizarre
    Trappist
    imprimatur etc.
the feverish eye of the exploiter
    of an old Boston tradition,
speech
right out of Gerard Manley Hopkins
    into the American
    mouth.
Or look around in my own work.
    I have a high-flown
    hermetic
    rhapsodic diction,
    poet's delirium.

It isn't easy to learn
      the abrupt,
      or to cut
as Brancusi cuts
      without vagueness.

Or Zukofsky discovering
      the ideogram out of Shakespeare —
Henry James's Figure in the Carpet,
      who saw
      a certain irony there.

You say my talk is confused?
      said Kung, the Teacher,
There is a central thread in my argument.

Poetic Disturbances

Poetic Disturbances

Half-formd—
the apple upon the bough, the worm in the eye,
the whole sky opening like a cloudy mouth
singing tones of blue in which the sun
whirls, a tongue tasting its blue out of the blue
from which continually
leaves that are feet fall, hands
   from the innocent air,
tigers, soft horses, beasts coming in and out of it,
heads bursting from the skin of trees—
they want to come thru—they force
a place for themselves when I draw—
they exhaust me. *We felt the rays from the bomb,*
they told me, *and, in the radioactive light*
that hung there, descended. And I in turn
saw all those colors in her eye.

1)

The mute bird rots within the shell.
The worm coild in the closed bird's eye
grows fat upon sight and expects to see.
He sings as he grows
consuming all substance of sight.

So the worm in the world turns
rotting the fruit before it grows ripe,
white as a day he devours his night-time,
turning and spinning in the universal eye.

2)

The whole sky opening like a cloudy mouth.
I saw all those colors in Peggy Linnet's eye.

The black one, she was saying, comes at night
and drinks what he wants out of my perfume bottle.
I tell him to go away. He mocks me.
He will not go away. They are disobedient. Those
are not apes—but what do you call them?—
almost men, hideous as they are,
I see them holding little children.
The children stroke them, cuddle there
        as if to sleep;
they comfort the children.
This is the most terrible thing I see:
the love makes them beautiful.
This crawling thing is a tree.

3)

The light hung just under the dining-room table. The tongues of the
serpents flickt from the chairs. The Woman I had seen before appeard
then in the corner of the room and I thought: this is natural television.

Sometimes they tempt me, holding out their arms showing gold
wrist-watches. Or money falls from the air as if I might touch it. I do not
do what they tell me to do.

I live in *this* world and I am glad that Christ helps us in *this* world. I
am glad that Christ helps us in *this* world.

They told me to cut off my hair. O no! I said. I did not cut off my hair.

4)

The eye opening is a mouth seeing,
an organ of sight gasping for air—
Love in the eye corrupts the seed
stirring new freaks of vision there.

How wonderful in the new sight the world will appear!

The mouth speaking is a heart beating,
the blood itself has seen something,

the World Worm changing, coild in his pit,
is the ripeness of the fruit he is eating,
the organ of sight.

How wonderful in the new eye the world will appear!

What Is It You Have Come
to Tell Me, Garcia Lorca?

1) What is it you have come to tell me, Garcia Lorca?
    Asleep in the tear-staind moon you are
    not poet, not lover, but one of the dead ones
    who inhabit the moon.

    Why are the hills burning?
    Why is the sea still?

    The old are like rats living in the hill of poetry.
    The heart of the sea will not speak to them.
    It speaks to the young
    and draws their youth from them.

    In the Rings of Berkeley the hidden treasures
    are coverd with bees whose angry hum
    is like the sea murmuring. All stolen things
    are coverd with their honey.
    The bee-hive mountain glows in the dark.
    I address myself to your angry face.

    Why are the hills burning?
    Why is the sea still?
    Why is the hive murmuring?

    The rats entombd in the depths of honey
    are still alive, are drownd, are dead.
    They lie among their treasures
    like kings of pure hatred

tainting and tainted by
the amorous pools, the food of the bees.

Nothing moves.

2) In the honey-tombs the golden bees waiting
cross to the land of the dead and back.

The great hive of the moon perishes,
flourishes, ripens,
and is destroyd utterly.
So the dead in the moon
return to the living.

The rats crawl to their death.
Their red eyes turnd back upon us.

The bees fly homeward. Straight to the rose
and return homeward.

The rats look backward over their shoulders
to see themselves kings in the honey-filld chambers.
They cannot breathe.
They savor no sweetness.

Sweet, sweet is the deadly bee-sting.
The Queen of the Bees
mating in mid-air rips from her consort
his seed and rejects him.

Sweet, sweet is the deadly bee-sting!

3) When the rats went into the rose
to live like bees
they found their Queen there
laying new generations of rats
for the rats to eat.

4) Then there begins an Elegy:
for have we all not lost the speech of the moon?

O felix culpa
et nox sicut dies inluminabitur
et nox inluminatio mea in deliciis meis

O vere beata et mirabilis apis!
each least bee enormous with spirit

O vere beata nox!

The Voyage of the Poet into the Land of the Dead

1) Out of the moon he arrived
   and the moon in turn
   he produced from himself,
   setting her tear-staind face in his sky.

   Now when I want to cry, he said,
   she will cry; and I will sit
   witless with words beneath the honey-filld trees
   reading my grief from her holy light.

2) Let us organize a dream
   along Freudian lines.

   But my moon is a real moon
   produced out of myself.

   The great moon in his grief
   emitted howls of light
   that ran from tree-branches,
   a laughter that mockt him.

3) This is the full, the full
   glee of the holy moon, he said,
   faith of those dolts, the lovers,
   of the moment before love is gone.

Into the dark he returnd. He moand.
And the moon in turn
he took into himself dark as she was.
When I want to cry, he said,
I will cry.

4)   But I am dead as the dead are dead
     and I do not want to cry.

●

Appearances

At Home in Eden

At the core of sweet thought,
after seeds, the excellent Worm
tight as a fist coild
uncoils we call dream,

each word like a worm
sleeping in fruity sentences.
Eve herself listening
would not let such love rot.

I mean the mind's longing,
like a tree   where we see
apples furnishd forward
red fat with knowledge.

When Professor Adam
naked sat down to his wife,
sat down to dreams
his father had forbidden,

the Word, the Wide World,
sat down I mean   maybe
only to one fruity sentence,

a worm he had not longd for
curld up in his own longing.

I ripen on the tip of the month,
his wife said, paring her body,
laying the edible apple-ripe sections
upon a white plate.

Now all these forbidden words
uncoil in their covenants,
and Adam himself coils
at the core of his thought.

From a Season in Hell

The Caliph of Hunger remembering
lived out a full feast.
Hearts like roasts laid themselves open.
The wine flowed from the glasses.
The hearts beat with longing
sweet to his taste.

O, I remember
how the sea beat time!
the meaningless drums, the great ear
listening!

The year swung round,
a seven-course dinner of seasons.
I contrived harvests in spite,
grand artificer of trees and rewards.
Light fell down from the branches.

O, I remember
the full mind
like a peach grown from a blood-root
swollen and red!

Haroun, the magnificent liar,
sat at the table of seasons.
Beauty herself like a mere whore
he sat on his knee.

O, I remember
she was bitter!
the dead rind of pleasure.
I curse her.

How far can we go without hope? Hope is still hidden
there, hidden there. Where shall the rifleman direct
his sure shot? Straight to the mark of the meaningful
wound. Who can erase the palpitations there?

When the seasons are twisted
so that their laughter continues,
the record is warpt
to imitate pleasure.
The needle grinds the music
out of the warpt surface
that pleases
like a man without appetite
gnawing a bone.

The Conqueror's Song

Patience, then, patience,
you will come here again.
What man keeps his head
in the heat of the day?

All men grow amorous
like lions in the sun
changing to dust
and passing away

filling the air with their rage.

Here women are nothing.
The men lust at noon
licking forms of men
from the improvident clay.

Souls are as nothing
for the heat of their breathing
does not die but remains
in the heat of the day

filling the air with their rage.

Go to sleep, go to sleep.
You will waken again.
The Gate is still closed
and the soul wastes away.

Be angry like the lions
who roar like paind men,
suck at their sex
and crumble like clay,

filling the air with their rage.

Moving in Your Sights

Moving in your sights
I am a true target,
self-conscious bulls-eye of myself.

We Have Left of Course

We have left, of course, witchcraft, sleight
    and shifting of shapes

A Game of Kings

King The First:

I rode out until the trees
dropt even their branches
it was so winter
bleeding for love and
crying aloud. I did not turn back.

In the Game of my Kingdom, I said,
reading the cards from left to right,
there is a new start
       for the man who gets through.

There Must Be a Reason

There must be a reason
for each dead hour
when the face of Saint Sebastian
shakes off its arrows.

See the Stone Lions Cry

See the stone lions cry.
Their tears fall from their open eyes
that regard all mortal lions with joy,
joy that is like a song within the stone,
rain of Paradise, souvenir du bonheur.

Lions of Jazz, 20th century
        enfants du bonheur!

There is no war in these immortal forms.
They dance.
                The moon, I mean,
makes them seem to dance.

O Lions, stone claws raised,
        heads thrown back to roar,

rampant,
                as if for love . . . .

Before the Beautiful Things Turn Evil

Before the beautiful things turn evil,
turn of the eye, betrayal of the hand
behind the scene, ennuie,

dreadful suggestion of landscape, or
momentary roar of sea,

she let her hair down and allowd
the sphinx face to emerge.

●

A Villanelle

To sing of Love: Again, Great Love is dead.
Only the poets remain to sing his praise.
All greenness from the leaf has fled.

The worm spins winter from his bed
and eats all warmth from the remaining days.
To sing of Love: again, Great Love is dead.

He sat with us at lunch, his face was red.
With a lewd news of truth he says
all greenness from the leaf has fled.

Like maggots the lechers of the town have said
Fools are the poets who crawl not in our ways
but sing of love again. Great Love is dead.

Come to the bars, or wars,
his head you praised wears now in love of us
a leering face.
All greenness from the leaf has fled.

There are no eternal joys, instead
Great Love Himself is false and all decays.
Who sing of Love must know Love dead.
All greenness from the leaf has fled.

Fragments of a Disorderd Devotion

1952

. . .

unkingd by affection? One exchanges the empire of one's desire for
the anarchy of pleasures. But pleasures themselves one finds are not
domestic. and the trouble of the soul cast jewel-like reflextions upon
the daily surfaces. One has moved only to a world where the devoted
household commonplaces cast shadows that are empires; where the
warmth of the hearth is kept alive in a cold that extends infinitely, the
dreams of a king, ruthless in his omnipotence. A plenitude of powers,
an over-reaching inspired pretension, an *unam sanctum*, a papal conceit
over all beloved things.

We live within our selves then, like honest woodsmen within a
tyrannical forest, a magical element. Shelterd by our humble imaginary
lives from the eternal storm of our rage.

5 Pieces

1   The moon shining in the window
light of moon element in which
breathing —

The towers of our flesh
shine like fish, turning
in the moonlight.

Bodies we have desired, devourd
in the moonlight, corroded
dream stuff, an apparition
of fog dimness.

2   The nakedness changes.
Each body strippd bare
changes; over.

The hair like a harp string
to the touch
trembles with sound:

bell-tones
            float
      over the water.

3   All the bodies we can not touch
    are like harps. Touchd by the
      mind
    a sound trembles upon the string

    carnal impermanent celestial
      tones of nakedness
    invade our nerves.

              The sleeping hands
    lie across the strings of sensation
      like trees in a high wind
    bent to the ground.

4   And then
            does he not move again?
    discarding all forms of our desire,
    a falling of cloaks from his bare body.

        We move toward him.
    Going beyond, as we do, each other.
    Death there or love growing dim;
    we reach for a nakedness beyond us.

    Since the beginning we have longd
    to be consumed by this longing;
    drawn toward the giant of morning.

5   A momentary evangel,
                a spreading
    of the knife edge of morning
    into broad day.

            Sacrifice all!
    he says. Sacrifice all
    to watch the blood stream once more
    from the gashes of sunlight.

Hero Song

There was no repose.

We think of them
at the boundaries
crows of a carrion world
natural to the cold
driven forward, forced back.

caw,   caw,   caw.

He was a light in our restlessness,
        shedding no light
but luminous in himself —

an electric cloud,
then, embodied,
a torso foreign to our despair.

Death does not come down upon us.
We wait for him.
For the great carnal striker
to level our pride.

Brides to our future,
we hear the crows cawing.

Away! Away!

fear is mysterious
to instil resistance

We resist at the boundaries of the day
the first light we have seen,

the incandescence of the dead.

Love, he said,
   will eat away the empire
   until chaos remains.

An Imaginary Woman

She was all that we were not.

   O Lady, we cried
   since the beginning
   the world has wept with you
   yet you do not weep.

Your solitary regard
returns us to our solitude.

   •

She stood where they brought the dead bodies of our companions up
from the catastrophe; she reveald at every moment her splendor; her
body was like a passionate embrace in the course of a war;
needless of death;
claspd to us;

a sensual meandering stilld;
a painful journey reveald as fruitless.

   •

   The Jews cursed her.

   She stood beside Our Lady,
   Mother of the Savior,
   like a clear well
   beside a cup of blood.

Thirst not, she said.
The well is full.
Do not trouble the water.

.

    Or they pictured her
naked, in repose,
her thighs
like the light of day
without shadow.

.

always, always.

    O Lady, we cried,
    The war against the night
    costs us our lives.

She bent her head as if listening
until the music returnd from its source.

.

From My Notebook

.

The presences or hallucinations of presence
reflected, rippling as
the surface ripples;
the empty altars, renderd
by reason
ready for the intellect
—that spider—
obsessd by design, unknowing.

Hail! Spectre, vanishing host.

.

In our effort to wrest from the world about us the images of our "form"; we often feel that we are rescuing the true from the false, we are at last setting things in their true light. That is, the light of ourselves.

This underlying formal concept is like the characteristic stamp of the totality in each cell of the body. What we do is identifyable because every section shows a basic uncalculated form—a rigidity. All concepts exfoliate from this order. If we think of this signature, this microcosm, as a crystal, a logic, a rigid orderly unique perfect geometrical form: but flawd, shatterd, blurrd or contradicted—then we have the Solomon's seal. All in the world of experience that answers to this identity, the hazardous metaphors of our self—all that is somewhat so crystallized, or so perfected, or so blurrd, or so flawd or so contradicted, becomes peculiarly ours: it is recognized; it is what Roger Fry calld significant form. It signifies our eternal limitation, something calcified, dense, inert, skeletal—not our being but our identity.

The artist's in-sight is his vision of what this form is. I search it out in the imitative ordering of poetry & contemplation.

•

Tyrannical spirits search us out, they infect us with their dreams, they demand that we obey their will. How powerful, once they are admitted, because they pursue, accuse, and we must submit or resist or flee or be annihilated, all dominations seem. But free spirits leave only, it seems, a message—without commandment—no more than a life or a book, or a picture or music. Nowhere does it impinge upon us. We must search out what we can understand and love, all else escapes us. We must infect ourselves with them. How weak, because only our will toward fellow men draws us to them,—all powers seem.

•

The great mountains of Disclaimer, almost black, but dwarfly imposing beneath infinite blue of tired sky. Kites of excitement dance in the blue, defining what had been ennuie as a space to move about in. A downpour of uplifting rain sad obscures the mountains Renders them ranges of dim despair.
Coming out into the open of don't care, we were washd clean and

almost quite going to be happy because nite-nite was coming and
star-kites would define what had been space as merely heaven.

•

To commune with the spirit of ones work. The being, an altar to the
co-existence of an altar. Not quiet or humble but insignificant, not
carefully made but enraptured in making, not considerd, not fulfilld.
But a gesture extravagantly willing itself—a demonstration, a thing
done, elegant in its blithely conceived and exhibited magnanimity.
Presenting the world benevolently & generously with itself. Beautifully
Egotistical.

•

now the singing hushd in the bone
now the tonal structure of the Erechtheum
now the proceeding as if it were happening
now the giant life in the grove
now the controlld abandonment to challenge the danger
now the stranger we are to ourselves
                 —it is dark—
now the broad daylight in the narrow window
now the widow we are to ourselves after war
now the end that is beginning we are waiting for
now the bird calls imitated skillfully return
distorted; now the internal reference
is repeated facewise; now the eye hears
and speaks into its orifice
now the pupil instructs the treacherous teacher
now I the dictator dictate my non-sense
now how big is the enormous small of at all
now avalanches return to their settings
now the sun blushes red as the wine he begets there
now the abetting supplements and compliments the abuttments
now all we are keeping is our appointments.
now even nouns and their own verbs
disagrees. At ease.

Following shapes and shades of reminder.

Eluard's Death

a rose in an assassin's mouth

It is a death arose as a speech
from the violins of a pure pleasure
vowels and consonants fall
like petals of the too ripe air.

the silence of an inflamed desire,
a report from afar
a blaze falling along with its tear.

Arranging the rose in a white vase
the magician made it vanish.
He made where a cry arose a rose
a crow arise
and made it appear
in her fair hair.

The assassin's mouth full of thorns
waited for the rose return
to its thorns.   Those were words
unknowing he said
for the assassin

to burn

Love letters written for a false lover.
To the lovely girl with another
paper rose.
She beckons. O.K.

Now he is dead and the Bride
will not be the fair one
and the Groom will not be. He.
Will not be Eluard.

She climbs into her husband's mouth
to sit among the thorns.
A marriage.

Caesar's Gate

Poems 1949–1950

1955

Preface for *Caesar's Gate*

July, 1955

HELL. Dante says accurately that it is a forfeiting of the goods of the intellect. How far can there be a poetry of hell, out of hell? It is all that is not terror: the nostalgias, sophistications, self-debasements here that are voice of a soul-shriveling, the ironies of mediocrity. To this point I came, willingly demoralized, to pray for grief, or for sleep, or for the tides of blood, for the worm to turn.

Only the visions of this state, this *bardo*, to sustain me. That there was still vision was All. These mere poems, contrived however they were, responded to the whispering angels of the language.

It is because, in devotion to the art or in self-indulgence, we shape ourselves, that this shaping, this making by which we are *makaris*, is divine. Thru which we divine the image of a man.

WHERE WE ARE. Awakening from where we were, we ask: where are we? where are we? It is then that the Gate which we see, in ruins, ceases to be expressive. It is a sign of a place. And we see it so, because we too, given up as we are to the poem, see, now, structures of being.

"We"? The Adam slumbers in the dissolutions of lives thru all human being. Picture him, great Man, in all his likenesses. In Dante, he is created in the likeness of Hell, Purgatory, and Heaven. In Blake, he is created in the likeness of a joy enraged. As tiger he devours himself as lamb. In Joyce, he is created in the likeness of his intestinal history digesting himself.

THE CROWNS.

The flower of life opens, falls into its seeds. In whose orders, Adam falls into his selves; and over and over again, we, you and I — all of you and all of me — flower into whatever place and time of being and fall apart into ourselves.

Then why not into misery? into a hell? But we cannot make it, and we fail hell. Visions of where we are appear. But they are intimations of place. We are no sooner aware at all of the closed-dead-bird's eye than we are aware of the joyous flower opening, falling. And these vistas — of statues in a waste of ourselves, or of incubi spinning their forms out of each retraction, or of hierarchies contradicting hierarchies, or of painful deprivations — are vistas open upon more than we are.

322

Then the pretension of the poet! the blesséd pretension of the poet! That he is, as *makaris*, barely capable, but divinely gifted.

These poems, like the *Paradiso* of Dante, proceed from the crown of human speech. That is all miserable, all glorious, all failure, all victory, all joy.

It is in the light of the crown that they dwindle.
And absorb grandeur.

Four Poems as a Night Song

The Construction

After dark the construction begins.
Every shadow carpenter to fancy,
every lamp post placed at intervals
of outside insight. Cafes
light up. There, the engineers
gather, unrolling blue-prints,
imaginings, but diagramd
and wired and piped.

The architect
changes his plans repeatedly.
The sulky glamorous workmen
are his muses, he says,
who display in lifting, resting,
rivetting, in the process of doing,
the muscular and changing
inspiration.

The Walk to the Vacant Lot

Where drinking pure alcohol,
sitting on the bed, I said,
Why did you want me to come here?
Why did you call me?

I wanted you to fall, he answerd.

And,
      —I cannot sleep at night.
If you fix your eyes upon my body
      you will see
I have no soul at all.

The Waste, the Room, the Discarded Timbers

García Lorca tasted
death at this drinking-fountain;
saw a dead bird
sing inside this mountain;
heard a childless woman
curse this drinking-fountain.

García Lorca drank
life from this drinking-fountain;
witnessd the witless poor
sleeping inside this mountain;
returnd at night to praise
this public drinking-fountain.

García Lorca stole
poetry from this drinking-fountain;
sang and twangd
like a mandoline
this slumbering spanish mountain;
fell down and cried
in Granada.

This is the drinking-fountain.

Before Waking at Half-Past Six in the Morning

I cannot be stirrd from my long dream.
I float in the dawn light,
ring with the clock's ring.
Every nite was party nite.

What voice not singing then to me?
What bell-clear spirit not ringing
carillons in my airy mind?

I cannot be awakened. That architect,
those necessary ruthless laborers,
cannot awaken their blue-prints.
García Lorca cannot be awakened.
My soul cannot be awakened.

"This is the drinking fountain,"
the young swain said,
pointing to no more than an X,
a symbolic subterfuge
(the corridor — the all important corridor
— unrealized — no more
than symptom on the night blue page).
This is the long plannd
reason.
I cannot sleep.

This is where I am sleeping.

Eye Sight

Aurora Rose

She has reappeard as the roar of space. Crowds are her. It is from
them that the corruptions of anger occur in structure. Areas, or arenas.
In the Avenues of the Games, the wearing away to naked hour after
naked hour. Everything prepared addresses her. Beatific figure of my
adolescent dismay! false heats rise from the allowd rose. Aurora Rose! I
cry aloud There is no Time like the Present! Praised be my Time! Hour
of the homosexual rhino. Hour of the enraged machine. Hour of the
return of the ancient. Thy waves are inscrutable.   So:
The curtain rose. And from her cowering shell she rose. He stirs. The
   whole stage of the lover stirs in an earthquake of play!   : the
   play within the play began.
         From the gallery a roar arose.
   Slowly the thirst maddend beast
         tramples his spring.

The Second Night in the Week

Now I have come to Caesar's gate.

And the Spirit there, tired and raging,
who walks like a beast walks
the circumference of his cage, said:
think upon the meaning of my rage.

By Whom do you swear
that you return to this place?

I have come to the Gate
tired, tired as Asia,
and as rage-full, awake
as if there will now be no sleep,

sleep being a secret in this place.

O Alexander! O Conqueror of the Wastes!

Processionals I

Dragging our trains/dreams, great weights,
wagonloads/desires
    How heavy our robes are:
corteges des feux et des neiges.

        The mind, mindful of pledges
        —the rotting carcasses, pianos, clergymen
        —the stink so great that acting was difficult
        tugs: this tugging
        simulates passion.

The sheer strain, sweat, panting
in which there is frenzy.

corteges des feux et des neiges.

7 men in the bed rehearse
seven times seven, gestures of Lust,
of violation, hunger, repose:
living statues. Slowly
we move/and cannot move.

Dragging our trains like hearts, or vows
    we cross eternity
      seeing our spirits fly up before us.

      Ah Love! the word
      gaspd. And the hand slips.

Breathing as if under water,
speaking into the helmet
    I speak to you.
How many spirits attend.

Trying to swim to the surface.
deluges des feux et des neiges
    Help me! I cry.

My heart is heavier than my dreams.

Processionals II

Torches, we light our own way,
nor, in passing, notice our burnd bodies.

Look, look, I said,
the heart of the flame
has gone out, the wick!

Set yourself on fire once more, you said,
the way is dark.

O dead, to you this flesh
is no more than wax.

Torches, we appear to ourselves
flames in the distance
that extinguish themselves
before we can reach them.

Tears of St. Francis

The eye is lion of these wastes. Whose vision tears the carcase loose
from life, to ravage: the spirit! the spirit! Vultures of our feeling swim
blinded out of the sun.

Heart stench entrances clubs of hyenas. With pure love of the bestial
delicacy.

The animals descend into the precincts of St. Francis. He goes out
into the heat, wrappd in layers of his devotion, saintly insect, bewilderd
by conversation with his friends, the fish.

Seraphic hostesses! survivors of the last safari! The devout return
burnd black by the sun. He lifts sightless eyes into the blaze.

Father! Father! the animal sun!

Upon Another Shore of Hell

O forbidden Dead. I too drift.
Coming near to your river, I hear you.
Dead voices that would take body
out of my blood.
Your love cannot heal
      nor your touch comfort.

So am I, four months, like you:
loveless, driven by hatred as by rain
or by pain of cold, driven.

Is it true that the Christians
rank on rank stand
immortal in their love or
the love of a God? singing?

O holy Dead. It is the living
not the Divine
that I envy. Like you
I cry to be rejoind to the living.

An Incubus

Bodies in dreams are heavier than bodies.
"Our own desire has calld him here."
Formless and yet taking on all Form,
there are no eyes, no lips.
These, they say, are shades. I, no more than shade,
    having neither eyes to see
    nor hands,
but reaching between two worlds—
    seize upon my own cock, hot with blood.

Love, love, the demon sighd
    fitting his unflesh to my hunger.

Sunday.

LORD OF

THIS WORLD

WHOSE PEACE is FEAR,
WHOSE STATE is ALMIGHTY,
WHOSE COUNSEL is DESPAIR,
WHOSE SCHOOL is COMPULSORY,
WHOSE LAW is JEALOUS,
WHOSE ART is SIN,
WHOSE TIME is VALUABLE,
WHOSE WRATH is POWER,
WHOSE WAR is ALL.
• LOVE • LOVE • LOVE • LOVE •

←  DADDY SUNDAY

• LOVE • LOVE • LOVE • LOVE •

IN EVERY FATHERLAND!
SUFFER THEE LITTLE CHILDREN.
IN EVERY FATHERLAND!
TO COME UNTO MEAT.

Eyesight I

The mute bird rots within the shell.
The worm coild in the closed bird's eye
grows fat upon sight and expects to see.
He sings as he grows
consuming all substance of sight.

So the worm in the world turns
rotting the fruit before it grows ripe;
white as a day he devours his night time,
turning and spinning in the universal eye.

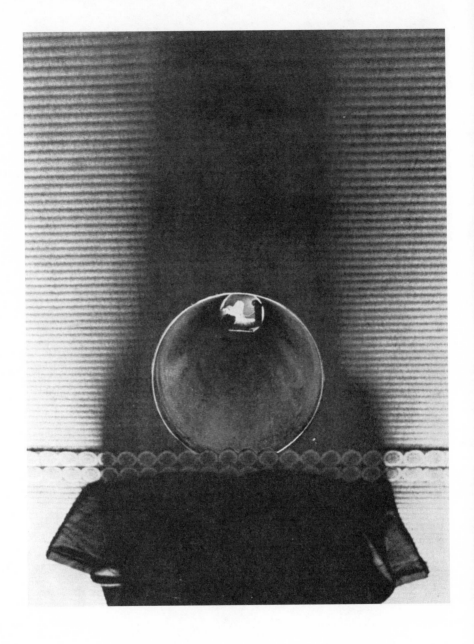

Eyesight II

The eye opening is a mouth seeing,
an organ of sight gasping for air.
Love in the eye corrupts the seed
stirring new freaks of vision there.

How wonderful in the new sight the world will appear!

The mouth speaking is a heart breathing.
The blood itself has seen something.
The world worm changing, coild in his pit,
is the ripeness of the fruit, the organ of sight.

How wonderful in the new eye the world will appear!

Bon Voyage!

O poem of the heart's dismay, the universe returns into the sea,
a flower closes into a cup, whatever we knew then we have erased,
embracing a new faith as easily as the moon embraces her fullness.

Having a good time. Wish you were here.

The End is in view. And we sail helplessly happy into the light cloud
of our conceald fury. The eye sails toward the end, casting its lines
toward its own vanishing point.

No more. No more.

O poem of the rising tower, of the ravages of victory.

Beyond our rapture there is.

No more. We have come to. O.

•

Goodbye to Youth

Goodbye to youth I say
as if all youth were gone. And why
    why go on
filling these corridors with drifts of ourselves?

Only in dreams we move,
statues trying to answer us.
Look, look back and see
how far we lovers have moved thru time!

Timeless the stone images are
surrounded by echoes when we speak.

Goodbye to youth, and that
was a universe in itself! Goodbye.
The statues of Love did not remain.
They disappeard. Replaced themselves.
    Seeming to fall in their not moving.
We alone are the Eternal Ones.
The statues of Mistrust remain.
    Proved to us
that their false faces were

    true faces. Learn
by heart their faces, names.

    Goodbye to Youth! longing now
not as youth yearns, but
    The man's madness is Truth:
    brightest confusions of the blood,
    denials, deprivations.

Show us the way we ask.

    Nothing moves with us.
    Nothing has changed.

All facts deny I love. Only I
    remain to say I love.

    Surrounded by echoes as I speak,

    I say I love.

    •

And if I live, I live for love of you.
Poor Faustus that would make all false dreams
true. He is the magical Bear, wizard of youth
I was. Incapable of death, the Fool
survives le bonjour, le bonheur.

The man alone no longer having youth
waits for his youth to return. Return,
old season of the heart, old foolishness.

Les mariages des ours, les mirages de bonheur.
C'est pour la jeunesse comme les milles fleurs.
C'est pour le virilité la tristesse, le bon feu.
Songe du coeur fou, mélange du sang pur
et impur. Les passages, les ans, les saluts,
c'est par la mort d'amour.

    •

And if I live, I live for love.
Restring and twang your ole gitar.
Who will share my empty bed
and sing to sleep my last desire?

German jazz distracts my ear,
all deathless youth beguiles my eye.
Show me the way to the whiskey bar.
In any language we must die.

And if I live, I live for love.
Then set to ragtime my complaint.
I know the syncopation of the rose
that fades beside the painted rose.
In time the false rose makes the true   seem faint.

Les mariages des ours, le bonheur du mirage,
c'est le fou songe, futile, idiote!
the foolish bear sings to the moon
setting to the blues his foolish hope.

> *O show me the way to the next whiskey bar*
> *O don't ask why   O don't ask why*
> *For I must find   the next whiskey bar*
> *For if   I don't find   the next   whiskey bar*
> *I tell you we must die   I tell you we must die*
> *I tell you   I tell you   I tell you*
> *we must die*

And if I live, I live for love.
All music that I hear sings so.
Restring and twang your old gitar
and sing me to sleep before you go.

•

Goodbye to Youth! and that
        was a Universe in itself!
The Statues of Song
        were continual pleasures, sang of Love
        and twangd from our hearts
        le bonheur, le bonjour.

O show us the way to the next whiskey bar.
I tell you   I tell you we must die.

The Statues do not yearn. Immune,
they are immortally what we were. All Youth!
The stony images of youth remain.

Our pleasures now are fires in which we burn
until we taste the mortal ash.

The Statues of Mistrust remain,
    chimneys to our fires,
        hearth-stones to our hearts-ashes,

    statues that would answer us.
Goodbye to Youth! the echo roars.

All facts deny the way.
Deny I love. Only I
    remain to say
    I love.

    I say I love.

Note: The song "Show Me the Way to the Next Whiskey Bar" is taken from
the Bertoldt Brecht–Kurt Weill opera *Mahagonny.*

H. M. S. Bearskin

He Entertains at a Dinner Party

Under that Banner,
the motto workd thereon
— WITHOUT REST, WITHOUT JOY —
the heart's guests are gatherd
to the feast of his faith.

Knaves, or knives, each
       cut to unlock as it wounds
eidolons — or as the Xtians call them
       demons —   wraiths or charms,
       ravenous birds of the spirit.

Crossing the border at death
he returns to this Table:
"I dread the gymnasium," he says,
"These Greeks have bodies
such as magicians invent."

"When I was dying I said,
I've been bitchd . . .
       how many rivals . . ." He reachd
for the crucifix and saw
       not his death bed
but the true board of his faith.

Crossing Forever,
he returns to this Table:
". . . have stolen my life from me."

He Consults the Tides

The Holy Mother herself appeard
bright as the full moon
shining upon the Table of Waters.

"It is your Child I seek," he cried.
"It is my Savior — who has died for my sake.
He who said love Me forever."

She put on her face of the Witch,
Notre Dame of the Animal Cathedral.
"This is my Cave," she replied.
"Look for your Lover among my Children
where the beasts howl. Treason itself
will find my love hidden there."

To Run with the Hare & Hunt with the Hound

Love, he said, is everywhere.
It makes the whirrld go round.
The lack of Love will stop the show
and make the world stand still. Stop.
The luck of Love is Mary go round
and overcomes the Will.

Love, he said, is valueless.
It eats like the merry Worm
upon the greenness of the leaf
and makes the greenness turn.

It spins around its own cocoon.
Out of the earth emerges the moon,
shedding the shreds of its belief.
Love, he said, is the heart's cocoon.
From which emerges its wingéd Grief.

• • •

Great **Grief**, then, herself!
An old hand at the game.

He Lists Subjects for Great Poetry: 1950

ALL THE PEOPLE GOING OFF IN PAIRS WHO CAME SINGLE
A CURSE FOR PROFESSORS, AN ITCH FOR CRITICS
LET'S GO TO WAR AND BACK AGAIN
IS THERE A LADY IN THE HOUSE?
YOUNG MEN WHO WON'T GO TO BED DESERVE TO BE CASTIGATED
WHO'S BORING FROM WITHIN : A REJECTED REPORT
BLOW THE TRUMPET, RAISE THE DEAD

He Has a Good Time There

Ridiculous, the butterfly
— avatar of the serious worm —
he lights upon the merde of Art;
that swish old relique, self-enamourd
fly-by-night, he hovers
among the cafe tables.

The great over-colord egotist,
a bag of wind! — I mean
soul, of course; a too loud Psyche
20th century version:
fairy-butterfly of man-worm
crawld from his poetry-cocoon.

Born anew, sprung
from his own thigh so to speak.

Under the satire of the honest flies
he keeps to his follies.
Lacking in motivation, he skims
no more than the surface of things.
Show shallow, He
pure pretension,
crown of the serious worm.

     •   •   •

All the way of Forever,
the shades are heavy with tears.

The Eidolons lie in fields of cold cash.

There are so many rumors
in town.   He
is surrounded by the pleasures of others.

The Heroes wearing Animal Masks
enter the Ark of the Ages.

The Absurdities of the Past
     absorb grandeur.

    •

A Book of Resemblances
Poems: 1950–1953

1966

TIDE LINES   The moon in her full and in her dark presides over the movement of the poem, the lines held tight run tense in the pulling tide and return, driven by that ancient machinery of Okeanos and his compelling mother-mistress, the tidal rise and fall in which the seed forms of all life were first conceived. So, where we feel our words as if they were drawn and released as by a lunar magic, tied as our inner nature is tied to an elemental compulsion, we are moved to poetry.

In 1950, when the first poems of this volume were written, Robert Graves and his White Goddess had come into all this. In 1953 when the last poems were written, the moon-lore of Thomas Mann's *Joseph and His Brothers*, which Jess and I had read aloud together in 1951, would have haunted my thought, and I had begun to read the Soncino *Zohar*. In our immediate oceanic being, we can seem to our examining conscious view all but hopelessly lost in a medium at once overpowering and vague, too huge to be true. Yet the tide lines of Okeanos we see traced in the rock formations of concrete thought, contours we take for granted once the movement in which they were carved has retreated. So the lines of a poem are tied to its realized form, the form of a process whose traces are left over after the excited language of poetry so eroded the shape of its shores, sentences and definitions, that the land, remaining, seems to us fundamental. As we near the language itself (the poem had presented itself as a welling up of words or waters that was yet a well in its fullness, eternal and motionless), we see it as an ocean that is at work at its own boundaries we feel as the reveald contours of the poem we, being of the ocean, would shape.

ASIA   In wave after wave, peoples flooded out from the disturbd heartland of Asia. In the pre-literate world the sea of languages was protean, an unreformed elemental source. The legendary Gate of Alexander stands like a door upon the chaos of the potential, of all that has not been recorded. Just where the hero on the verge of his given godhead would invade and conquer the source—there, not only the orgies of megalomaniac splendour and the new wisdom of naked masters of a Yoga that would enter into and change now the course of Greek civilization, but also the fortress—a household—and, beyond, the desolation of a continent swept by spectral storms in which the sound of perishing armies rang.

The rage of Love appeard to me to be a convulsion of the sea, driven by storm winds or shaken by upheavals of the under earth, itself an ocean of molten rock and fire. War, love, and the poem, shaped history as expressions of the deepest forces and cleavings (adherences and divisions) of Man's hidden nature. In 1950, America had become possesst by a demonic necessity, the hidden content of her victory in the Second World War, that now appeard in the phantasm of a blinding fear of communism, of the primal peoples of the world, and of the depths of Asia. And from China, in the inspired poetry of Mao Tse-tung, there were signs of the ancient empire of the Mongols reawakening. Working in sections from an essay by Robert Payne on Mao's poetry which had appeard in *Horizon* and quoting from his translations of Mao, in counterpoint to the ritualistic consultation of a fifth of Cutty Sark, in *An Imaginary War Elegy*, I began to compose in terms of this obsessional war that today, sixteen years later, has taken over the soul and spirit of America. But this phantom empire of Asia was for me the extension of being, held, as it came to me in 1960 with *Apprehensions, "so that there is a continent of feeling beyond our feeling."*

After the inspiration of William Carlos Williams's *Paterson* in 1946, 1948, 1949, had opend the way with its great thematic images of the roaring waters, the divorce, the geologic strata of a history, and the consuming and welding flames, in which extensions of content were generated, I tried in *An Essay at War* to incorporate the gains I saw in his work towards a poetry that would be Heraclitean form, a form in process, to draw from and in the same act set into motion the elements of my own life-experience—the death of Jaime de Angulo from cancer in 1950 and the rock crystal pitcher seen in the Hapsburg collection which tourd America that year, the form of elements in commotion, clouds, fire, smoke, the sea, and the household kept (the work of art as hearth of feeling) in the midst of catastrophe.

SONGS OF A HOUSEHOLDER   With *The Song of the Borderguard* in 1950 my life with Jess, the illustrator of this book, had begun, and thru 1951, my first year with him, I workt on the *Essay at War*, addressing myself to the things experienced in their being lost and the things eternally kept in the work, picturing, not a victory but a creative failure, a giving up of a war or a giving up to a war of its own things. *"Our love is both the storm and the hearth of our emotional being,"* I wrote in my issue of *The Artist's View* in 1953. Back of the *Essay at War* is the idea that, just as the psychoanalyst searches the language of Man for its universal sexual or archetypal content, so too all the content of Man's drama and destiny is reveald in the workings of that language; the poet releases formulations at once prophetic and projective. In the *Essay at War* and then in *Faust Foutu*, written in 1953–54, I was concernd with projecting a world, imagining its terms, and, in that projection, incorporating an analytic process—not only what was happening but the possible meanings of what was happening became my terms of conscious composition.

But these years are also the period of *Writing Writing*. Gertrude Stein, like Hans Arp, had suggested another poetry in which words were concrete things, "a picture or a sculpture without any object for model . . . just as concrete and sensual as a leaf or a stone," Arp proposes in *L'homme aime ce qui est vain et mort*. "Since the days of the caves," he writes in *Fils de la lumière*, as if he were particularly describing the matter and pretension of *An Essay at War*, "man has glorified and deified himself, and has brought about human catastrophes by his monstrous vanity. Art has collaborated in his false development." In the Stein imitations of this period—I often thought of poems too as being like Arp's sculptures, stones in a field among stones—I sought a restful movement; a non-Heraclitean creativity, arising not from strife, the agony of men in which they have their history, but from play. "Only spirit, dream, art lead to a true collectivity," Arp wrote in *Ein Magischer Schatz:* "They are the games that lead man into real life."

I have not, finally, the tranquility I see in Stein or Arp. At times, the inspiration of a poem has brought me to see the universe as supremely orderd and in that order supremely fitting. But I have come also to profound despairs and rages. Both the monstrous vanity of man and the spirit, dream, and art that lead him in his divine games haunt my sense of the ultimately real. "There could be a book without nations in its chapters," the poem after which this book is named proposes. I longd for the moment to have only what was happening happening. But all would-be simple events are darkend by portent for me. In my home-life I had then to be at home with fearful domesticities. As if one could hold by what one loved in the midst of the elemental Eris-Eros of the primal creation. I had not yet come to Boehme's great vision of the wrathful and anguisht Father in his need for, want of, love, giving birth to or creating (making up) the new Lord of Love and Peace, but I sensed that I must work not with my abilities but with my inabilities, not with what I clearly thought but with what I could not think clearly—for I wanted a poetry that would break thru what I wanted. And I sought myself now not "integrity" or "authenticity" but a fiction of identity, to make up the field of my participation in the truth of things.

So, *A Book of Resemblances*, resemblances to life, resemblances to poetry, resemblances to the writing of William Carlos Williams in *Paterson* or of Gertrude Stein in the volumes that were appearing in the Yale Series, resemblances to things and ways of a household—a book that properly here, I would dedicate to Jess, as he in turn, over the years, working on these illustrations, picturing and adorning the text, has dedicated the book to me.

PICTURING   The non-objective painting of Jess's masters in 1950—Clyfford Still, Hassel Smith, or Edward Corbett—became for him the ground of a return of images. Even as the inkblots of Rorschach stirred the phantasy and in their very non-representational formation gave rise to significant figures in the mind, so the masses of the drip and blob school, as it was calld, freeing themselves from reference to any model, became generative of inner vision. The student deriving his work from what was happening in the painting itself, taking his lead from what he saw there at work, became seer.

The painting of Vuillard and Bonnard, the Nabis, or of Edvard Munch and Gauguin or of Sérusier, had a special import for young painters who were responding to the suggestion of patterns and areas of color, to happenings in the painting itself from which picture began to come. And then, by-passing the dominant aesthetic of the first half of the century—the *grand chic parisien* establisht by Picasso and Matisse, and behind that, the whole modernist concern with painting values as distinguisht from and excluding any larger field of the imagination in which painting might take place—Jess followd the lead, back of the Nabis or the Fauves, to the life-stream of a romantic visionary art. To this period belong the illustrations of this book and his great canvasses of 1953–54: *Two Bathers on a Beach with an Angel, Feignting Spell, Don Quixote's Dream of Fair Dulcinea*, the triptych of *How the Great Fish Reveald his Tale*, and the mural-sized canvas, *Taking Leave of her Guardian*. This was an art no longer modern, seeking to make a new world of its own, but traditional, seeking to reincarnate an old way of the spirit. If Jess's paintings began to derive from a ground in poetry, so the poems of *Fragments of a Disorderd Devotion* seemd to me to come up from a world of imagined paintings. And, as Jess began more and more to explore the possibilities of an illustrational painting, so, later, in the composition of *Caesar's Gate*, I was to write prose poems to illustrate Jess's collages. Even as he returnd to the tradition of the romantics, and back of that to the symbolic and mystic tradition of the Renaissance and to its problematic revival in the painting of Moreau or Redon, so I returnd to Yeats back of Pound, to find the currents of an Hermetic poetry. Together, in the early 1950s, Jess and I sought out in our own terms the inspiration of long neglected and even despised sources in nineteenth-century phantasy, reading the visionary novels and fairy tales of George MacDonald, seeking out the paintings and illustrations of the Pre-Raphaelite movement. Jess, like me, would emerge at last in an art diverse, having as its key the collage of diversities, and derivative, whatever its authenticity, returning to and drawing itself from the field of the arts, not as a thing in itself, to incorporate specifically painting values, but as a medium for the life of the spirit.

THE BOOK   By imagination we give the universe a life in self, the ground of our individual experience, so that even the war is reawakend as a part of our inner reality, and, reciprocally, the imagined, as it arises from self, seeks return to be realized—a symbiosis in which matter and spirit participate that gives rise to a perpetually self-creating world and world-creating self, a union of realities. The image comes to the artist to create him and is charged then with the numinous aura, the daemonic import, of the creative: what we see and read informs us. This is one operation in the work of art; yet in the same work the artist projects—more than the image—the form of its actualization, illustrating the universe anew with the signature, in part of his identity, in part of his experience. In style we recognize immediately what we feel to be the identity of an historical period and of a particular artist; but style also communicates to us in our response to it the imprint of a way of experience, the spirit of its formation. The *Book of Resemblances*, the very book you now open, is itself such an image, become in turn an illustration of *A Book of Resemblances*, so that, like those pictures within pictures or mirror reflections with mirror reflections that bewilder our common sense and strike to fascinate our souls, from the inner reality of a household, a room, a lamplight, and a book open upon a table, a translation has been made and this book, illustrated by its text and its pictures, has been projected to become a property of the actual. The book may have had its origin in dream or play, in the increment of men's associations in a literature or the commune of men's wishes—for *A Book of Resemblances* is also, for its creators, an illustration of a wisht-for book; but in actualization, the writing and the drawing, it has its new origin in the ground of the work itself.

This book then, that has waited for more than ten years to find its publisher, is at last realized in a reproduction true to its actual format, true to its inner form, the dream in which it was conceived—the painter having had his secret life in these poems, as the poet has in these pictures.

The Horns of Artemis

There where great Artemis rides
naked, lake-clear bright lady
awakening her lovers, the hunters
    and the hunted,
her horns sound in the night.

Or are they horns of distant cars?
themselves fading and yet insistent
    like memories
recall to the heart horns,
    trips made at night
    in indefinite longing,
or the betrayd lover's horns
    painful crowns of the holy Moon.

We are awake now indeed,
And we are her Kings:
    fools poets and lunatics.

    Picture the Lady,
her whiplashes of pleasure, her bright
great eye fixd upon the games of the night.

    The bleeding bear
    and the hounds are one.
The enamourd hunters ride themselves down.

    All love has fled.
    All lovers cower.
Only Truth remains, the eternal
    cold light shed on all things.

Africa Revisited

(1)

He sings the same song but the words
    in the song change:

    notes upon a single string
twingd, twangd, strung,
    negro ecstasies
    under the same moon.

Drinking the changes of the moon;
head turnd in the moonlight;
eyes—not seeing—looking
into that nowhere jungle of the beasts' lair,
ears hearing, howl and hiatus

*   bbbbbbbbbbbbbbbbbb
    of the night bird,
honk and konk of senseless sound.

    Giraffes of noise
    that running thru sound
fold and unfold themselves,
    keeping their necks
    in eternity motionless,
    moving not dreaming,
    dreaming not moving,
revealing when photographd
    by the slowmotion camera
    eternities of form
    returning into themselves
    and awkwardly
    shifting their rigidities
    into the future.

*This sound is a voiced labial trill held for the duration indicated in the
rhythmic structure of the poem.

The hunter of song, dressd up in a song's skin,
sneaks up upon songs where they lap the night's water.
Cunning with magic, he makes sound of a song's lapping
and prepares for the kill. He wears,
as a ritual splendour, the scars
self-inflicted to imitate, to anticipate
the feard and desired rip of the song's claws.

But the song has no claws, leaving like love
no traces but the singer's agony
longing for trace—for a wound to wear
when he returns from his nowhere
into his real place. The poet
sits in his hut. He has a story to tell.

> *In No Time, Truth with her face*
> *wide and white*
> *came down from the sky and heard*
>   *the bbbbbbbbbbbbbbbbbbb*
>   *of the ridiculous water*
> *answer her, answer her*
>   *from the depths of Truth's well.*

This is not the story I had to tell!

Then come the unexplored jungles of sorrow
so filld with beasts that the poet is bewilderd:

For this I was unprepared.
Walking disguised in my animal skin
I saw my animal spirit flying above me
couple and uncouple freely
murmuring with love and directing toward us
a look that penetrated
the disguise of my body.

What was the song he sang?
taunting and exciting my poor tongue to sing.

The young men surround the dying poet
touching his hands, his eyes, his mouth.
They are a band of Swahili warriors
come with wonder upon a machine,
an enigma, a music-maker in the heart of the jungle.
Ignorant, they are violent,
and break from the machinery
its secret of song.

       bbbbbbbbbbbbbbbbbbb
       goes the motor
       with a life of its own.

The giraffes appeard then, moving across the screen
proper to the silent slow-moving
       picture-poetry,
naturally mute as they are,
       stars dissolving their fires in night's water.
Dumb and enduring
they ran; there being
not even the thunder of their hooves.

What was the song they appeard to sing
and could not sing then—
created as they were, creatures of pure beauty.

Or the garrulous machine, tinkerd by these curious,
impatient hunters, clickd and continued
its eternity of talk, its automatic whirr
stirrd with pain from its intricate heart.
It talkd American, of course, invented as it was
by an American and left there
to amuse and confound some innocent African.
I loved, I loved, I loved—The puzzled negroes
watchd the pins of invention prick
from its single cylinder the repetitions of sound.

The American had not foreseen
the limitations that rust and loss
might wreck upon his invention.

It went bbbbbbbbbbbbbbbbbbbb

It faild

to simulate pain, or love, or desire,
or death. It was ridiculous.
It struck terror. It was inscrutable.
It stood for itself, surviving its maker.

(2)

The secret of fucking, the dying man said,
is a poetry the traces of which
remain even in the skull. Surrounded by skulls,
I am surrounded by a trace of pain
that survives all carnal brutal impermanence,
a story repeated by my father
and his father before him,
which I impart to my son, being
incapable of imparting it.

It is a throwing of the skull
forward thru time,
awkward in its thrust, humiliating
        finally
because it is needed.
And so the real skull appears;
giving rise to the white man's
        suspicion
that we devourd its flesh,
        it strikes terror—

chalky and dead in itself,
alive only with spirit,
        a primitive continuity
        giving off love.

It is the love we have lived upon,
        consumed
from the magical skull.

He moved from his position,
shifting his black nakedness,
already shivering
as if caught in Death's door.
The young men watchd
seeing, beyond, their own faces.

Death—the Poet replied,
shows you your own faces,
but these are not the faces
you are living to see.

When we watch the Moon,
lifted out of ourselves
ghosts in the Moonsleight
preparing to move,
having neither voice
nor footfall,
yet with a story to tell:
so we watch the woman,
careless of our eternities,
awakend by her wondering
from the skull's poetry
into her spell   that floods thru us,
and holds us
bewitchd by the moonlight,
I said,   and we return thru her,
pushing ourselves
bodily thru time
to exist in another time,
            back to the place
            of the ancestral skull.

This—*you will not understand it*—
is what I have imitated.

Preparing to die
what am I imitating? what continent
impersonating? incontinent

even at this moment with the desire
to excite wonder, to surpass
myself, or woman, or time;
pulling the tides of my being and yours
as the unconquerable Moon
pulls at all fluid, shapeless things,
compelling even language into her own form.

(3)

The American and his companion, who
    may have been himself,
    (for we talk to ourselves)
but ten years younger, walkd in the glare
    of the transient summer
    so far from the equator's
    eternity of season.

I loved you—American repeated.
    He was tender but the words
    could not repeat
what reason and his American speech,
    having tense,
    had destroyd.

I thot—said the American, *but*
    my invention faild me,
    that I could keep you, at least,
        company;
    shielding you, loving you,
even before Death's rivalry.

I will argue against Africa—
    Christ or Mary will surely
    heal us
as heaven or hell in their eternity
    heal time.

There must be One Father,
    first and last lover

embracing even Africa, whose voice
  healing all lovers
may be heard thru lust's howl.

There must be One Father
  pictured by the African
  perhaps in a skull
filld and ever furnishing
  food for the first lonely man
  who has repeated himself
endlessly in his hunger   lost
  and surviving
  in the jungles of time.

But the elephants trumpetting rumpled the waters;
the lions came out of concealment, stalkd
and stretchd; more splendid than the American.
The angels to his bewilderd eye
        giraffes
appeard, fleeing like beauty before the lion-spell.
        There was not even Hell here.
        My, Father, my Father—he cried.
But the Moon, white and round in the darkness,
        flooded the jungle with an oceanic stirr,
        showing the same face she had shown before.
        There is no Time now—she said,
        for fear

        but love, love, erases
          in its oblivion
          such inventions of mere mind
        as heaven or hell.

        Now I disclose to you: Love
          is no wonder
        compared to my phases.

        The American (I myself of course)
          talking to myself

not to the attentive
restless young men of the tribe
waiting as he fancied them,
having started, breaking in their ignorance
his speech, his immortal longing

saw no Moon but felt her
as if filld with her
and faild with her;

the machine in the jungle,
the skull in the flesh,
preparing, even painfully,
to return to full face.

Adam's Song

When this garden
is no longer home to us,
when we are
no longer at home in love
but restless, and from faith
• mornings wide as a light room
and us light within the light
wherein bird-twitter at dawn
heralded green-leaf day •
when from the brightness of this day,
from faith's side, we wake and find
our strangeness come with afternoon
• Eve, come with me beyond faith.

After the estranging apple at noon
in strangeness come with me.
We will come again to Paradise.
We will come again to rest
with eyes that have known unease,
falling away from the ripeness,

known rebellion, exhaustion,
anger • return,
as if to the same place,
in another time
adore the restored garden.

And, this is ours, we will say.
As now we say this is ours,
seeing in the reflection of eyes
memory or promise of what we are,
as apples ripen in the eye
that meditates the flowering tree.
Or sees the fruit fall,
and the bare branch cries.

The war is all about us. Our joy
is like a world to come
or a world past. Near and far.
"Green-leaf day" I said.
There is no more than
gold of your eye or
your lips smiling, the
momentary curve,
to read love by.

This known wonder
returns, or we return to it.
As if rememberd, yet rare.
Never before known so.

Strangeness, come with me
beyond despair. Beloved,
come with me.

It is as if the garden were
always there, even where we are,
here, where war is, the certain
end, the paradise.

Working Too Long at It

Eight hours a day at the typewriter wearies me,
spends me before I can spend the money I make.
A year now without a lover has taken over
    thirty years of what I calld
    ecstasies and despairs.
Today I climb the same old hill
as if it were an eternal flight of stairs,
an up-hill • gardend and ever
    lovely to the eye seeing • but
but climbing as if it were thirty years of stairs.
Always I will reach the summit
surprised that one arrives so quickly.

The bear went over the mountain —
    my parents used to sing
— to see what he could see.   The car
would be going on in the night
    towards our summer season,
    towards our vacation

    • hearing the old round,
even, sleepily assenting, answering
    — the other side of the mountain —
    dropping off to sleep.

Thirty years have brought me again to the mountain,
to the climb, to no consolation, to no
six-foot teddy-bear lover I've waited for,
but to the dance of the totems,
    the bears in chains, of an heroic race
after the dying away of their creators.

Eight hours a day, I mean to say,
I have carried this typewriter
    up this hill of my living
    toward what other side, what
lovely vacation land of the mountains?

where I will see,
as if the years had fallen away
and the mountain changed,

the dance of the bears.

An Imaginary War Elegy

"There is only a vast desolation left"—
the strict verse form gives it substance, the poet:
needs to imprison his imagination or
grotesquely thru all the countries of the mind
he spills himself—the scarlet suggesting
blossoms of the plum-tree, not blood;
suggesting then the blood, not the plum-tree.
And the language, an excellent whiskey,
the spirit occult, yet potent.

Asia lies before us—archaic source,
terror and exhaustion hidden therein:
our own, changed as we are by our wars,
the amber whiskey, the violence, the mingling
in cruelty and despair,
a river depositing its dead violated bodies
into its sea
or into the mind, these things being vivid to us,
the plum-tree fading into wounds,
the continent of sleep vaster than we know
awakes, its armies stir
the armies of Asia stir, a poetry or history
returning into itself.
Mao is talking of great deserts and deliberately
these legends
hover like enormous statues seen thru the mists,

whiskey or empire of the blood.

"For a whole generation Genghis Khan was a favorite of heaven"

The poet
loses or wins a lover
an empire:
the splendour of eyes, *archaic,*
wonder of self in this thing,
grandeur and deceit of dreams,
his eyes like promises or fields
in which the grain, gold harvests or waves
of armies move.

Almost contemptuously traditional my song.

The amber clear radiant whiskey distilld
from the language,
words like the unharvested wheat,
a sea of nature's ripe irrational grain,
intoxications of injustice,
archaic as this evening worship of whiskey

or war of spirits.

"The three armies laughd when they had crossd over—"

changed, become a continent in themselves,
conquering as one conquers the whiskey.

"the Long March", I mean: the exhausting transition,
savage transformation, the armies changed,
bewildered by ghosts. I rose from each bed
from a betrayal or a war,
true to my time,
more weary than before.

The Kings in their tents drink
until their rage becomes like love,

blind Asia, drunk.
"No one in the Red Army fears the hardship of the Long March"

the ten thousand miles,
the ten thousand mountains,
the ten million dead,
the ten eternities of Hell.

Being mathematically inexact,
the poem acquires an emotional accuracy.
—remarkable is the use of phrases like "the three
armies", the traditional poetic name of the armies
of the empire . . . the second and third lines which
remain almost contemptuously traditional. The
poetic Imaginaton, so carefully based on archaic
sources rises slowly,
sights
with drunken precision, sees
(the strict verse form giving it substance)
more than the river throwing up its dead,
that flows between the mountains of the dead:

a song of such tenderness lingers
in the desolate night air
tender as your eyes were.

The poet sees his face
changed by the changes in his enemy's eyes.

The Song of the Border-Guard

The man with his lion under the shed of wars
sheds his belief as if he shed tears.
The sound of words waits —
a barbarian host at the border-line of sense.

The enamord guards desert their posts
harkening to the lion-smell of a poem
that rings in their ears.

— Dreams, a certain guard said
were never designd so
to re-arrange an empire.

Along about six o'clock I take out my guitar
and sing to a lion
who sleeps like a line of poetry
in the shed of wars.

The man shedding his belief
knows that the lion is not asleep,
does not dream, is never asleep,
is a wide-awake poem
waiting like a lover for the disrobing of the guard;
the beautiful boundaries of the empire
naked, rapt round in the smell of a lion.

(The barbarians have passd over the significant phrase)

— When I was asleep,
      a certain guard says,
  a man shed his clothes as if he shed tears
      and appeard as a lonely lion
  waiting for a song under the shed-roof of wars.

I sang the song that he waited to hear,
I, the Prize-Winner, the Poet-Acclaimd.

Dear, dear, dear, dear, I sang,
believe, believe, believe, believe.
The shed of wars is splendid as the sky,
houses our waiting like a pure song
housing in its words the lion-smell
        of the beloved disrobed.

I sang: believe, believe, believe.

        I the guard because of my guitar
believe. I am the certain guard,

certain of the Beloved, certain of the Lion,
certain of the Empire. I with my guitar.
Dear, dear, dear, dear, I sing.
I, the Prize-Winner, the Poet on Guard.

The border-lines of sense in the morning light
are naked as a line of poetry in a war.

An Essay at War

I

The design of a poem
        constantly
under reconstruction,
        changing, pusht forward;
alternations of sound, sensations;
        the mind dance
wherein thot shows its pattern:
        a proposition
        in movement.

        The design
not in the sense of a treachery or
        deception
but of a conception betrayd,
        without a plan,
        completed
in the all over thing heard;
        a hidden thing
reveald in its pulse and
        durations;
        a fire.

So we calld and heard the answering cowbells
or bellow below in the valley; we knew
in the dark they were coming home, coming
up the narrow cowpaths under the stars

where at the sheds we waited with lanterns.
Calling up words—or calld in by words
the familiar comforting beasts in the dark
come home toward our lanterns, and we,
herdsmen of our language, call them by name.
And the years return to us.   Our own
departed return.   What do we know of them
as they come thru towards us?   but we are
sure of them.   We leave a light in the window.
In the mind.   We read in the evening as if
they were about to enter.   We sit
about the round table
talking with a guest who has brought gin,
a friend now long dead.   The frosted square
bottle, the gingerbrown tea pot,
cucumbers and butterd white bread,
are spread on the table.
      And the genius of the moment
      is in the glow of the lamplight.

Light the lamp, I say:
It has been a hard day.   I am tired.
I want to sit with your ghosts and mine
in this room which is like a bonfire
lit upon a summer evening, sending
sparks up into the bright darkness of the sky,

      a window
      lit for our wandering, a single
candle flame fading or melting as we
      retreat from it.   The fog
rolls in over the water dissolving in waves
      electric lights of the city below us.

      It is an extension in time,
      a dimension surrounding us,   the fire
      itself surrounding us,
      the light, the glow . . .

Even the subhuman Mousterian man left
 ashes of fires.
From the beginning we picture
 the hearth light
in the room of the cave.   Outside
 the epoch of the greatest cold
 has driven
the mammoth and the reindeer southward
 to wander
in enormous herds.   Storm
has made an almost continual night. Inside:
 ears alert for the cave-lion or bear,
the Cro-Magnon man workt
 the inaccessible rock-face
and returnd from the deepest recesses of the mind
 to the hearth,
to the place where we too are gatherd.

It is the first named incarnation of love. We burn with it. The fire of
Hell. Pain. But it is also warmth. Demonic. But it is also light. The night
is all about us. A darkness within which all known things exist. So, a
moment before the appearance of one most feard or one most desired, or
one most loved. Or . . . the centuries are all about us. A light to read by.
Within us. A time within which all known things exist.

You who have given your intellect to love
think of this light even as the light of love.
"Make Light of It," Williams says,
dedicating his volume of stories
"to our troops in Korea."   Let
even our troops in Hell who have
hell-fire return from their flame-throwers
thru flame to the fire that burns them.
It is love. It is a hearth.
It is a lantern to read war by.
I mean it has burnd all that we value,
and we return to the burning itself,
made savage by it, warmd by it,

ears alert for the cave-lion or bear,
as a company will gather about a burning house
seeing the sparks fly up from their losses
            burning,   brought together . . .
    only   Love left.

So, in Hell, imagine.   All that we valued
        gone up in flames.   Destroyd.
                There is a great light there.

I mean the light of this war
        sweeps cities, a madness, laying waste.
        What remains is a hearth.
        What remains is the heart. Even
        out of Hell   we demand it.

        Make Light. Gather about the flames
and against the night   recite
        as the words dance,   dance
                as the flame flickers,   burn
        as the language takes fire,   revive
the heat of the heart from its cold.

This fire lighting up the room
almost to a tropical heat where
the old man is dying of cancer. "You
do not know how to light a fire,"
he cries.   "I will teach you
how to make a fire. So few . .   nobody
today knows how to make a fire
with kerosene."   This blaze
is the same kind roar of flames
that destroys in terror Korea
and we
do not know how to make a light
pouring kerosene on the already burning paper.

"What can I teach you
when there is no time for teaching?"

Teacher! your temper teaches.
The gesture is living: so many forms present
about the table-tipping of a moment.
The old man is like a city
laid waste by war. He is noble.
He is pathetic. He is an old nuisance.
with his fits of fury, tipping over the pisspot.
He is a bombd house, falling away from us,
reappearing in his own light,
a spiritual refinement. There is a shame
in a beautiful body wasted so.
There is a pity. A frailty. A pièta.
Blood, urine, shit—draining away.
And we who had admired his pride see
that pride is not eternal. Shame
is not eternal. Your temper teaches.
The frail persisting. The mountain of great strength.
Great snores of death.   An arm
inert upon the almost black brown blanket. Having
no longer strength of gesture. Head
thrown back, propt up.   He
absorbs grandeur. A history.
      A teacher.

      The poem designd so.

      to emit great snores
            or death's confusions.

      A pressure .
                  or a procession.
      A dream.
                  or a drain.

His mind . is wandering.
Come home . from us.
What do we know of him?   . The words
fly up, his breath . the breath of stars,
breadth of lungcase, pelvic bone,

a frame .
The morning light
falls full upon his face . He stares.

I am trying to let everything fall away.

A pressure .
a procession.

The poem designd so. They return to us or
thru us. The listeners cannot
put it all together. It is so weak.
What information from so infirm
a grasp upon the thread? The thread
breaks . or the light

breaks thru

the miles of water extending beyond the land,
the cold out there
between us . between these continents

I mean, the sea, cold
and just breaking at war with the light.

Or we are always at war.

II

; its glow
leads us upward, for we are . . .

What do we mean when we say we're in love?
We use the one word
for tenderness, for passion, for enduring
devotion, or for the ocean-wide deep drawing
of the moon. We use the word
for a sexual madness, running
under the brimstone rain of fire
—so Alighieri described us—

backs bared, emotionally flayd,
    or, afraid,
crave love from statue-proud
    stone, or flesh
      resistant as stone. Love
      and desire. Beauty
      it is they attend.

The Beauty of it! we say.   The eye
catching fire, the hair luminous,
the torso like the Hapsburgs' rock crystal
pitchers, flawd with its own wonder,
    shatterd visibly
with immutable perfection.

    The Beauty! a terror
or a sorrow so great that our longing
    reappears as if in a mirror,
    an enemy,
containd in the more-than-face
    mask of our passion
    facing us.

        Facing us?

Were we afraid?   Withdrawn?
Self-containd?   But love stronger
than terror or pity—a war of the senses!

In the museum of the ages
the passion for the beauty of passion
is not love, but love
is a dimension surrounding the passionate.
The individual Hermes-Dionysus
perfectly shown,
    the repeated perfected
    Tanagra figure or pearl-rope
twelve syllable measured Alexandrine line

or rhyme like a fine jewel
set in regular reoccurring pattern:
these have their terror self-containd.
But love—not of perfection
alone. The imperfection proposed, studied
in the cloudy stone, claims
          adoration.

     We have only the one word for it.

Light, yes.   The sensual delite
is all of it.   This sensuality
an appetite for weather, to be
filld like a tree with it,
          leaves radiant,
drownd in the heavy element of sun,
or boughs whipt by the wind
          roaring, darkness
          in the strings of the harp.

          "De ses neuf ouvertures
          encadrées de boucles
          l'homme exhale
de la vapeur bleue, du brouillard gris,
          de foumée noire."
          but "the games
that lead man into real life"
     if, as Arp says, "the Dream
connects man with the life of light and darkness"
     are substitutions of love.

     It is a hearth, a compassion,
     creating the world in its likeness.

In a poem. Its contractions and relaxations, pulse beats of largest lan-
guage. Each cell of the structure showing its blood type. Measure. The
passion of this speech repeats in imitation the passion of a daily living, a
cosmic more-than-we-are. The poem takes form from its words as love
takes form from its acts, an imaginary conclusion. Of acts or of words

A total vision. Exceeding the sensible. As if the beat of our hearts beat
in the universe. Spirit continually emanates from each living body. It
broods. It creates a beginning.

Anew?

Were we courageous to begin?

Singing like troubadours in Albi or Toulouse
as if in spite of . . .
            listening to the nightingales
in the midst of the slaughter.

What good will this do?

        In that
profonda e chiara sussistenza
dell' alto lume!

bombs, fragments of bodies,
this Japanese woman vomitting blood,
these cities laid waste, burning,
blasted before us. Were we afraid?

Standing before a sea of faces in San Francisco's civic Center, the General alluded
for the first time to the controversy which had brought him home. He added: The
only politics I have is contained in a simple phrase known to you all • GOD BLESS
AMERICA •
He strode gallantly into Constitution Hall to make a three-minute speech to 6,000
ladies of the D.A.R. (who carefully removed their hats en masse to provide a clear
view for all)

Were we courageous? Is there
no substitute for victory? for
these seas of blood, these trials
of our spirit wasted in killing,
in that line of men moving painfully forward,
thrust painfully back?

What shall we sing when the Victory is won?
The joy of our life goes on forever . . .
profonda
e chiara sussistenza dell' alto lume!

What is a nail? A nail is unison.

This blood is a river that runs forever.
Let us resolve
the right surrender.

III

We are fighting over there.
Without a plan   nor dream of conquest
nor from love of humanity fighting.

Orderd to stand—there being
no order—
we do not understand.

Into the cold of Asia
the dead go. We do not know
how many thousands—
scraps of an army obliterated,
routed, pusht back,
confusions of our mind before
a great idea, moving
not like the sea but
as the fanatic mind moves, with a plan,
shouting,
inexorably forward.
The plan is the war.

I have no idea of what is going on.
A single verity might outlast the idea.
We build upon a field of lies.
Truths of the imagination,
lofty sleights of macrocosmic mind, up-
lift us. But we face
uncertainties.

The war, or the plan, mocks us.
Certain things confound us.
Sure to win, we are unsure
of winning. What will it cost we ask?

Stalin, over time, has shown determination.
Mao is an idea transforming an idea,
a poet with a war, a plan, an inspiration.
Cruelties, not to be corrupted;
terrors not to be turnd. Music
may tame the tiger, but these tigers
proceed to their own tune,
measure their own true scale expertly.
    What medley of voices, what free harmony,
can stand over against or answer
        single-minded tyranny?
Only a plan, a unanimous war, can win.
            An inspiration
not to be corrupted, not to be turnd.

    This Victory, again and again
this cry "Surrender! All is Lost!", again
the demand that we die, give ourselves up,
join the army not to be turnd, all volition
        given over to belief.

This host of believers sweeps down upon us,
        or springs from our midst,
        seeking to exhaust their plan
their self-containd terror,
        in the chaos of our blood,   in Victory!

IV

            What does it mean?

    The design
constantly in reconstruction.
    Destroyd.
    Reformd.

Who would have thot these alternations
    of death
and realization so painful? painless?
    A dream . . .

in that *profonda e chiara sussistenza*

            or a drain . .

blood, urine, shit,   giving ourselves up, this

        falling away,
        falling

        face forward

v

What does it mean?   we pick up from a poem
or the sound of a poem the sound
of words saying themselves to us and saying
what we have been waiting to say.
Without a plan?   to touch
        a spring of volition?

What do we know of ourselves? It has taken years
to greet without contradiction grief
and gladness.   We too have been
like Lucius Apuleius in the guise of an ass,
prickt by lust, cheated by magic,
witness to adultery, rage, infamy.   Yet we were
never so eager for life, for this
spring-full tide, this eternal
never-to-fail love, this fullfillment.

Out of these invasions of Korea, what fulfillment?
What full filling in victory? out of mere war,
these deaths of G.I.s, carnage of men,
        of ourselves?

Out of these spasms of blind courage, blind ambition,
blind terror, blind love of comrades?
We do not know, we say.   We see them
frozen in ice fighting, or struggling
in the deep mud ruts up to their waists dying,
hopelessly, it seems. Uncomplaining
or complaining.   To no end.
        But the endless dying.
        The dead by the roadside,
        beautifully naked, left over
        that the old may grieve.

The scene under the 10,000 tons of bombs
in the heat and roar of the assault,
in the silence and rubble thereafter.

        Mixt for us here
with the first stirrings of panic or despair or of longing
        is a passion.

What can I teach you when there is no time for teaching?

        of passion :

        Not a boy, this young Chinese communist fanatic,
        but a man
changing as a city changes. Destroyd. During the day
        ruthless or inert, as if sleeping without dreams,
        the body. Destroyd.
        Neither questioning nor answering. Destroyd.
        The laborious undertaking
from which we emerged almost without spirit.

        Or at night.   Destroyd.
Surrendering its other
        mirror of ourselves.

        A young man with no language
other than the speech of thighs, or
        curve of lips smiling, Sphinx

or Kouros. A chink. A jap.
An enemy. Destroyd. His mind
without volition, a soldier. But still
is the City we dream of,
curve of the young torso
to make the heart leap, or tears
spring to the eye
striving to speak.

So this ordinary G.I. stript to the waist
carrying the wounded
American soldier in his arms
repeats in his hot Korean summer
a pièta.

He is like a nakedness of speech
shedding its words; or
an imaginary conclusion
of acts or of words; without plan,

a volunteer / having only a form in the mind,
A "setting off of a great many planes (or powers)
so that each is identical (in a third hidden thing)"

So, knowing or unknowing, the key
comes forward.   It lies in the speech
about us.   At ready response.   And within us.
It is in the air.
Everywhere.   The war is in the air.
The great self-contained war
is there   .   that we call love.

Let there be no substitution for surrender to this
ever about to be realized, this
imperfection in the cloudy stone, owl-wise
perfect balancing of incongruities,
only to fall.

What is a nail? A nail is unison.
Everywhere.   In unison.

To fail!   To fall?   without a plan,
doesn't everything turn out poorly?
Sure to surrender to the critic's contempt!

You see, what I feel is needed at this point is a nadir, a breakdown, a
failure of heart or of vision; and then, all longing left will be hopeless.
Without a plan I was destined to come to this pass, to this foreclosing
of all promise. The poem defeated. Yielding, without a war, we were
bound to fail. Infatuates! Dancers! Once the music stopt, the effort to
dance is painful to all concernd. What is left is despair. There is only the
death of invention.

> There is only the cold hearth.   The ashes
> waste . . it has all been said before.

> The fire was the war.
> We said burn with it.   We said
> surrender all that we value to it,
> to the burning   .   to the war
> of words, of the senses.

> We did not make sense.
> We made words dance. Dance,
> we said. What is left is the hearth.
> Dance by the light of the war.

The figure was love as a transformation
of war, or
war without an enemy, or
war without a victory   .   it was in war
> that we longd for love,
> for the fire that burns us,
for the fire of love consumes all that we loved

> "thus all suspended did my mind gaze
> fixt, immovable, intent,
> ever kindled by its gazing"

When does the poem end?   Why
does it go on?   to exhaust
what possibilities?   Why does the war
go on?

    He conceives the poem
as a shatterd pitcher of rock crystal,
its more than language not in the form
but in the intrigue of lines, the shattering,
the inability . .
tracing the veins of an imaginary conclusion,
the faults along which the tremor runs.

Or he conceives the poem as a mind dying
—that is, a mind dividing itself
from itself.   The line divides.

      Falling, face forward.
      Come home. From us.

The idea is elegiac.   A poem
of things lost or about to be lost.
Yet the idea is absolute,   of these things.
They are never to be lost.   Unresolved.
Held anyhow.   The beauty
is the beauty of a shock that runs thru it.

What!   will the war   never cease?

The war is a mineral perfection, clear,
unambiguous evil   within which
our delite, our life,   is the flaw,
the contradiction?   Or the elegiac moment
—itself a mood as pure as crystal rage
or the responsible traind military technician's art
without rage   planning campaigns,
organizing, ordering, giving   orders until
the blood flows red from each page
      —the elegiac moment

the too perfect in tone to be sanctimonious
moment of our pleasure in living grief
or living regret, the clear immutable pitcher
        flawd by our rage.   No calm
unbroken by variations of the line
or by the rime just off beat, repeated
tokens for the listening ear of the endeavor
        to shape war.

        The skull forward.
The flesh having melted into a dew.

All that is mortal reduced to necessity.

Of the Art

This honey is rare.
This child in her painting
has gatherd color from the rose itself.

Yet Malraux argues
that a child has no care or lacks skill.
This skill   is not a thing learnd
but a thing loved. Observe
how free from all other will but the rose itself
the child's hand moves.
This color, so related, by an ardor
no later knowledge may increase,
is all that art intends
or love or life seeks.

Christ himself torn on the cross
knowing Man's agony
no greater passion knew
than this child makes known to us
in a painted face
whose blotcht intensity
has reacht beauty.

See, how directly the bee
flies to the heart of the rose,
or these children, who have not been diverted
by the opinion of others,
travel the way that is obscured to us
to the place where the rose grows.

Five Pieces

Included in *Fragments of a Disorderd Devotion* (1952). See above.

Hero Song

Included in *Fragments of a Disorderd Devotion* (1952). See above.

An Imaginary Woman

Included in *Fragments of a Disorderd Devotion* (1952). See above.

Eluard's Death

Included in *Fragments of a Disorderd Devotion* (1952). See above.

Cats (1)

Always his imaginary existence endeard him. He added to it details
of his substance or rather we added from his substance details that
endeard themselves to us. Poor little animal of our anxious dreams!
Now that he is gone on some amorous adventure of his own, we fear

that we have lost him utterly. Our dreams at night are obsessd with
his presence just beyond our reclaim. He seems almost to taunt us, we
so long for him. O! we cry, what if he never comes back to us? How
obscurely we will be haunted by him.

Cats (2)

The arrival of minor angels, simple folk of the marvelous, guides
of the small animals, that have their own realm of fierceness. We are
aware of their processions, and our hearts are toucht, almost yield to the
vision of their imperium. When the black cat stirs in his sleep or the
grey mews to himself, half to re-enter the world of our affection and
half to take leave of the celestial . . . how we misread their tremors to
say they dream of mice! But their sleepy murmurs, purrs, twitches of
whisker, their leaps and dances that are a very art, self-attentive as they
are, are solemn acknowledgments, even to us, of invisible presences,
insignificant celestial beings, seraphim of little account.

Unkingd by affection?

Included in *Fragments of a Disorderd Devotion* (1952). See above.

Dance: Early Spring Weather Magic

Hug the girls, boys. Hug the boys, boys.
Hug the girls, girls. Hug the boys, girls.
Round, and around and round.
Remind me. Remind me.
Hop to a hug, hop. Hug. Kiss
the girls, boys. Kiss the boys.
O boy, boys. Kiss the boys, girls.
Round, around and round.

Let me.   Now let me.   Remind me.
Let me.   You let me.   You.

Choose your boy, girls. Round and around.
Change to a boy, girls. Change
your boys, boys. This is the way
the magic goes.
On your heels now on your toes now.
Choose your girls, boy. Choose
your naked pretty girls.
On your own now at your best now
Change to a girl now
like all the rest of the little boys.
Round and around.

Remind me.   Let me.
Be me.   Let me.   Now let me.
You be me.   Remind me.

Hop with the boys, boys.   Hear the tune
boys.   Hug the girls, girls.
Hop with the girls as the tune twirls
girls hop with the boys now.
How.   Hop.   And now.   Hop.

Remind me.   Let me.   Let me be me.   Let me
remind you. Tune to the boys,
boys. Be a boy, boys. Tune
to the girls, boys. Be a girl, boys.
Hop to the tune, girls. Tune
to the boys, girls. Be
boys girls girls boys. Boys and girls.

This is the magic is around
the magic around.
The boys and girls all around.
Round the magic, A tune.
Round and round and round.

Forced Lines

At last : all of reality. We find we are only what we
pretended to be.

These lions in the lazy passages of time
surfeit themselves upon carcasses of poetry.

He wants as if he is there were there. He reaches.
Almost. But touch touches.
He rises from touch enormous
shaking mere realities from his form
an ocean on end, a talking coffee pot at breakfast,
an unbelievable story escaping the believing reader,
a criminal, a primitive, a demagogue,
tyrant over the people, an
aroused automobile about to become an automobile.

He is so real that he longs for the real.
He grasps the idea. But touch touches.
And no mere idea, the ideal turns a sleeping teacher.
Another character, that renders
the whole act inconsequential. Magnificent shifts
of shiftless flesh. An armory of thighs, a pedagogy
of actual voluptuous pectoral pages to the hand,
words of hair, of visible eyes, closed or opend
closing.   A foreign language.

A POEM IN STRETCHING, prophesying. Reading water or words, signs are cards in their multiple juxtapositions. Where we read into. Its not really there. Its nothing. A plate of disturbd sand. A landscape of sound, honks, sighs, a sigh. A plain stretch of time in which trees are not green but hesitate. A sign. The easy trees, houses, far away castles, a moat, a highway with car streams of, a high net of wires. It is nothing. Wires or eyes crossd giving rise to vision in the distortion of vision. Its not there. Its in the air. The rumor. It comes to our ears? A poem stretching out once crampd in the hand. Heard having been seen. Now it is seen that it has been heard. A card, then another card. It is the queen of hearts and a seven. black. spades. Other cards we are not seeing determine the scene. We are not looking at them. We are not looking for them. They tell us, remind us. Unseen words we have just seen not yet heard tell us. I know now. I know, I mean. I see it all. All. She is afraid. A game of chance. Shuffle the deck. In the shuffle of words losing the sense we sense.

Put your cards on the table. O.K. Signs of the times.

A cigarette first. Yes. Hands in their motion holding. A cigarette. Lighting. A match. Light cigarette. A hesitation. Pausing before striking. The hot smoke toxic we draw in. A gasp. Stop. A bitter gasp. The hand grasps the pencil, straining at the bits of the sharp lead leading. A gasp. A sigh. The hot smoke distracting the intractable mind.

I see it. I see it all the way thru to the next phrase.

•

A phrase of such beauty. A pity to mar it. Now, now. She is afraid. The other card, a pity. To mar it. Carving in a sense a flood of, an arrangement in flooding words. And we reach out in it all

    like a drunk man now swimming
    suspended, smoking,
    seeing at last the magical horizons
    the world is round around its roundness
    contradicted. Everywhere.
    An inspired mind could see it flat.
    Suspended, gasping
    in another element, lungs gasping
    the hot smoke of vision,

a flat statement, a lasting doctrine.
Her husband has a collapsible hat.
Collapses.
An ending. Like a drunk man's words
doubling. An afflicted vision.
As flat as that.

•

Poetry Disarranged

Not a derangement of the senses but, yes, there is an occult other sense
of meaning in all dis-arrangements (Dis in his arranging). What was it
that I imagined the language to be? Not mythy (except as there is the
actual mythy evening, an atmosphere or preconception at best of the
darkness of the actual night)—Not visionary (except as the seen is real
in its intensity; this a scene wordwise).

But a hut of words primitive to our nature. The Language in its natural
disarray.

Not being in history we see as living in and not upon the world. And
the reader like a worried traveler might see "that little light in the vast
dark forest" and come to our door. Inquire and sit for a night by the
flickering of our sentences, hearing a tale nowheres about toward once
upon we are telling.

And it would be part of that realm of story that he might never find
his way there again. Returning to find the place he could no longer
recognize his surroundings.

What I am picturing is a poetry spun out of an evening as a whole cloth
spun out of a web of worn wool. And an out of the way—that ever
lasting cottage in the deepest part of the forest of the tales told by a fire.
What I am picturing is an old shawl worn, of no earthly importance, a
poetry reduced again to its ashes, an evening entertainment of no great
measure.

Talk in a room we are going toward we were from.

A secluded interrogation. Speech as if unheard—that it wld not trouble the hearers were it unheard.

There can be no time for will or structural ambition, when one would listen only to the relative positions, lengths and divisions, clusters and interweavings.

A poet who sits in the light of words like a cat in the mote-filld sunlight of a window. Where he is in the sentence is there. And he listens. His poetry pictures his listening.

A Book of Resemblances

There could be a book without nations in its chapters.

This would be portents that were portents of themselves. A constantly moving. This is as we ourselves are moving in coming and going, in sitting positions, knees crosst now, then legs wide apart planting their feet as our feet under standing.

There could be a story without its end in its unfolding.

This is on my mind. To stop even. Just as the rhythm. Just. In the divine outgrowing. To stop it. To be just. And restore the white vase. Adjust. The separate flowers. Just as. These are flags. Flags of our country. One full in papery lavender child and eager not yet full opening. Justice. One below, one above crumpling or and going limp in wet purples and sagging from color. Two curld buds, tight fists patient before flinging open.

A cat crossing the room. Stops. Rolls amorously. Just as soon as. Eyes looking black in fullness. Narrowing. Rises. Licks paw. Lifts hind foot. Hugging leg over neck. Licks. Licks licks. Lick groin.

A Dream of the End of the World

We came down to Darling Lake where the deceivers were. What did we care there? All of the deceptions were pleasurable. Darling Lake is for summer visitors.

Now let me introduce both of us to you. We are winter inhabitants and will pass willingly away with the holidays. The holidays are days for our passing away.

The mayor at Darling Lake greeted us as gladness. This is because all were visitors and everyone of winter in a crowd of summer is a lively reminder.

Wherever we were we decided we were there. If we were not starting, we were not easily startled. A Dream of the End of the World. If you look no further you can look all about you:

At the lovely about to be cremated mountains, at the cool about to be steaming streams, look at the green growing trees that are about to be witherd. This end of the world is a burning scene that being seen no further is a mountain resort.

At night along the shores of the lake in the continual little waves lapping there were loons singing. Their singing was calling. A calling too in calling became a calling to us. Of lonely pleasures.

Now let me tell you what we were doing. We were both writing deceptive poems as resorts for deceivers. These were kindly deceptions that deceived ourselves for we were our own best friends.

I wrote a poem calld *A Dream of the End of the World*

> We came down to Dar Ling Lake. Careful Americans
> among these Chinese walls and summers.
> Counting the holy days as they were passing
> we counted the beats our hearts were not missing.
> All the landscape seemd or was burning.

This we calld the End of the World, and returning
wherever we were we decided we were there.

He wrote a poem calld *In Love with a Lake* or *Looking Around Us*.

and delighted the visitors.

Lord Master Mouse

Lord Master Mouse stood in the wet to the skin.
A cosmos toild in his unwilling head.
—Skitterfoot, Skitterfoot, what do you do there?
cried the hosts of the mousey dead.

Lord Master Mouse lost in thot
stepd by step cautiously, cautiously.
—Mother Birdwing, what have you left me here
among the rude bones of your treasure house?

—O my little Mouse, my trembling Whiskers,
Mother Birdwing sang to her single son:
You are the only one, Lord, my mouse.
They cost me dear, Dear,
dear to my heart are those bones, my treasure,
cost by cost the heart of your heritage.

A moon came up where the other one set.
A black went down over his back.
All of the mouse-bones answered back:

—Skitterfoot, Skitterfoot, what do you do there?
trembling in your troubling whiskery haircoat?

Lord Master Mouse shrugged and turning
into the moon-glare, the real moonlight,
heard their voices slighter and slighter,
as the other side of his turn coat,
heard, didnt hear, hadnt heard, turnd away, fancied
a bone-mouse voice, bird dry and remote.

Shells

Max Ernst the wet automobile husband sands or claim.
Max Ernst in earning the same bloody rewards.
Max Ernst in earning feathers in the meat.
Max Ernst in the wet tunnel of deliberate flying.
Max Ernst wets the deliberation of lying in wait.
Max Ernst portrayd as a waiter in bed
    poses for the portrait in his irate head.
Max Max. What makes a wax head appear to be a dead likeness
    of our liking Max Ernst.
We do not like Max Ernst.
We do not agree where it hurts to lick the carving knife
    that divides the bearded curtain
    that parts in two faces that disagree
    that exposes its parts like a split bird
        or a split second dividing the curtain where it bleeds.
This is a door demanding more entries.
Max Ernst will win in the race for Max Ernst.
        A moment's decision—
the rest is collapsing. The only rest left
    is collapsing.
The rest on the right can be seen at night.
This is a field of righteousness.
        Max Ernst.
Max Ernst stubborn and stillborn.
Max Ernst of lying and flying. Lying flying.
Max Ernst relents relenting.
MAKES URNS are jars with dolls faces.
Shall faces or whole faces face the whole questioner.
Max Ernst in a litany is a litany on the right.
It is the right that is left.
There is none of the rest to be seen.

These Miracles Are Mirrors in the Open Sky for Philip Lamantia

Interior clouds appear to disappear in rifts of weather. But it is the floods as parks in erotic applications of crowds.

In crowds poetry goes unnoticed. These are pleasures conceald from their origins. Our permission.

After permission he was after his intermission which was not the mission he was calld for: a lock is completeness ineverything.

Filling until it is brilliant. Brilliant until it is overcoming. Coming until it is all over. All over until it is ready for filling.

A chalice among common relics protects us.
That is, the carmen have elected a Carmen who is theirs.

Lift me, lift me up. As a flood in a cup is a heady draught. A draft of faculties. A flat area in fullness. It is the other that he reaches to.

He reaches the outer reaches. Retch it. Wrench it out of its meanings into its means.

Its means is our underworld.

In the reflected sense he was Perse Symphony, God–Deus of Dark gneiss.

A Conversion

She went to the tree where the angels were talking.
She listens, she heard them, as if she were walking
among their sentences that were fruit trees
where the ripe fruit was shining. Or a single poem,
the orchard in its single tree, speech its
singular foliage that sang as a bird sings.

Moon was her name and she hung in the tree
like an electric light among its dark apples.
Well, those were the angels talking late at night.
She inquired if they were getting tired,
conversing in tones as dark as ripe
    apples hidden in a closet of leaves
and they replied
                (

) A lonely angel light enterd her head
and burnd out in her mind, turning her head
until the night was her hair
        surrounding a fire there.

Salvages: An Evening Piece

A plate in light upon a table is not a plate of hunger.
Coins on the table have their own innocent glimmer.
Everything about coins we obliterate is use and urgency.
How lovely the silver dull disk glimmer is. Shells without remorse.
The rubbd antique nickle dated 1939 Liberty portrait relief of
Jefferson and, beyond, darkend with use, a grimy patina beautiful 1929
buffalo Indian head nickle.

Bottles. An aluminum tea pot with wicker handle. A remnant length of
Italian shawl worn by my grandmother in the 80's, this too increasing
as beauty in dimness; the reds, ochres, blacks and once perhaps
almost white natural cotton yellowd. The wearing, the long use, the
discoloring. It would be becoming to beauty in words worn out. As a
poetry, to be discolord.

It is not the age it is the wearing, it is the reversion to the thing from its
values. One nickle; then two dimes, a brighter, a newness, fresh-minted
(yet when I look—in god we trust—it is 1944, the god is Mercury with
wingd helmet; the other a bust of Deus Roosevelt Roman style with
sagging chin and stuck-up defiant non-descript head—this is 1947— in
god we trust). Then two nickles—the grimy ones. One shiny fifty cent

piece above (beyond) a fourth nickle showing Montecello E Pluribus Unum.

This mere ninety cents is more, is all piece by piece, in art, as they are here, pieces of glimmer as rare as the mysterious chalice with faces and figures or the cast from the greek horse and rider.

Notes on use and values.

Then the litter. The gleams of silver and nickle seen as coins of light in the litter. A key—another gleam—an ancient evocation; a coinsilver spoon, a chippd cheap cup-shaped cup with grey glaze without the imperfections of beauty beautiful because it is a cup. A large brown glass bottle of vitamins that look like beans. Papers. A letter from a friend, a program in my own script black and definite (defiant) arranged over the white paper. Matches. An envelope.

In the late hour left after the history of the day, taken with a will before bed-time, how transformed the world is. The silence almost reaches us in which an original—all that has been left behind, tossd about—of us—remains.

Beautiful litter with thy gleams and glimmers, thy wastes and remains. The tide of our purpose has gone back into itself, into its own counsels. And it is the beauty of where we have been living that is the poetry of the hour.

Reflections

Because I have been in the service of Love, I love thee.
This is a light or a shadow or darkness of sleep
as it transforms everything. This is a showing of colors
that informs beloved objects or makes radiant,
moves. I mean to suggest
how in these days I have sensed thy presence,
unannounced and mysterious—there have been
joyous revelations—reflections?
as if clouds were passing in a windy weather,

happy turnings about. This was
her face radiant and, yes, transformd;
this was the loveliness of the hour
created by a joy or the joy
created by a loveliness. Or his head
bent almost as if yearning but not yearning.
There is no yearning,
no burning in thy transient passing
that casts the light of love carelessly.

Then I have my eternal devotion.
Then I have my meaningless freedom.
Then I have my surcease from my history.

Careless, useless, transient
intimations of the pure service of Love.

Salvages. Lassitude.

The long stretches. The cold hair. Bereft noons.

It is idle to place the word upon a table and announce
—there is no one here to hear the burning.

The burning in looking at the word is not reading.
This is in the room of all intense joys—not in stillness,
but in the voiceless uproar
even the chairs emptied of their solitude.

The last fleeting spirit flickers above its objects.
And we picture a loneliness of high noon
that has emptied the room of its shadows.

To address such a loneliness. A divorce
of the senses. The daily phoenix in its ashes.
Sweep the room of its troubles, its accumulations.
Sweep. Sweep. O for a great wind
to beat the impatient air!
the stifled wildness . . .

Friedl

The tough blue of the ideal—an idea I mean,
an ideology of images. Azure of Mallarmé
between and our daily blues.
The far away is near as an innerness
is far away or long ago or not reachd.
Not to be reachd. Yet. This is a spring of blue temper,
the twang of the everlasting water.
r-r-r-r-r that is a metal in language.
The afterwards. Full bodied image
as a carnal sentence afterwards
in its blue reverie. It does not disappear.

Then picture her as she was and will be,
a dolour that incarnates itself—
the fleshy scattering, a full abandon
in flowering; always
as if aroused so in the midst of slumber.
Picture the heat of the blood
as it suffuses the flesh—before awakening—

a ripeness always
rising below its own surface.

If we see her in her dreams,
she is like a rose submerged in its own heaviness,
she is a body drownd in its own deep.
And imagine the impenetrable heaviness
as the blue we imagine. See

all this real heaviness wavers,
does not awaken, but persists,
as rises, blue from our blue mind.

Songs for the Jews from Their Book of Splendours

I

Well of the Hebrews, well of days.
—I am that Well, we picture her as saying,
that comes once more among the jews.
I am that beneficent Moon of the rising waters
rising once more to greet you. Do you know me?

You have so long despised me, the World,
but ease, ease—the ecstasies of my order
are simple as walking, I am that
deep talking well of easiness, respite
of the weary. O weary in your world contempt,
O contemptible jews, the world
is this well of my waters.
—I am that Well, again I return to you.

The pollutions of history are over.
Cease jews, cease ancient troublers.
The pollutions of history are over.

The left side of justice is mute.
The right side of mercy is mute.
It is in the disorder of speaking
that is easy, that respite comes,
the Moon, well of waters.

The Zohar tells us: Verily, altho Sarah died,
her image did not depart from the house.

II

O when the serpent jews!
—cunning Isaac and Jacob in his cunning—
skin-shedders, whisperers,
whisperd to the people in the garden
and twisted their story into our story,
persistent truths of the desert.

Did the Moon shudder?
worshippd and reviled by them
among her children? in her fullness
revealing all that goes on in the desert places,
the cold light shuddering and still?
the angelic whispering in history?

As the Zohar tells us: In the same way Jacob sent word to Esau, saying 'I have sojournd with Laban and stayd until now' as much as to say: 'I have stayd with him twenty years, and have brought with me a deadly snake who slays people with his bite.'

The Scattering

They tore the body apart at the end of the service.
Divided it as food that is. And so torn,
all that was poet was torn into a simple feeding.

It was only a mortal anguish left.
It was not there. It was there in the tearing.
In what we partook of only in passing.

Image of Hector

It is in falling, not falling in love but
into death. As Troy fell into immor-
tality. Had we too fallen, been lost in
his being lost, we had remaind as Troy
has remaind. So utterly destroyd that
it draws the spirit out of all that survives
into its immortal spirit.

The Lover

I have been seeing his face everywhere, a former lover.
But it is not he. Passing, passing in the daily crowd,
an old ghost of the mind, of the heart, a starting up
of indelible pang. I said I would not forget.
      O the unknowing will of first love,
forcing a way, an eternity of feeling.

      Is it the time of year? I cannot remember.
Memory will not yield his image, all clear trace
lockd at the springs of passion. Only old will
forces recall. All else forgotten. But the dead
turn certainly in the graves of our longing,
the dead belonging turns seeking, unwanted.
He was once all of wanting, a need, an end
of youth! Now I am mistaken, often,
seeing his wraith in faces passing.

Names of People
Stein Imitations from 1952

1968

First

A Language for Poetry

A language for poetry.
A poetry for cats.
Cats who can read out loud.
Cats who can read outlawd.
Cats with imaginary
pages of books.

Nothing inside but the inside inside.

Are Cats?

Are cats afraid of
words for poetry?
Are cats afraid of
imaginary books?
Are cats afraid of
a language of looks?

Imaginary looks were words
in the real book.

Nothing said but what was said said.

●

Names of People

• • •

Names of people. Lilly Fenichel.
Lilly Fenichel. Names of people.

George Racket. Parker Parker.
Ambrose Bierce. Adrian Wilson.

Under the umbrella
Madeline, Madeline.
Into the sunshine
with Maripose Sampson.

The name of a person.
The name of a river.
Hamilton and Mary and Brenda Tyler
came over for dinner.

Who will forget kindly Jack Spicer?
Who will forget Old Black Joe?
Who will forget the David Barys?
Who will forget Brock Brockway to show?

Under the umbrella
Mary Ellen Rae was lovely to name.
Into the showtime, all time
    know time
names of people. Lilly Lilly Fenichel.

A leave
as You May

for John Ryan

. . .

They are looking for shadows and mice. Outside.
Outside they are in order. They are to order.
We rememberd sleep as the soundest
        kind of order.
Order a shadow for a look for an outside.

Poetry Permit for Volley

When you begin you are younger than you were.
Every nice cat is coverd with fur.
The water is so still. It cannot be far we say.
Impressions are stronger during the day.

Palaces catches. Palaces started. Catches
  places to place.
Fallacies to face. Coaches to rent.
    Places to go to. I can not.
You go to. I do not want. Too.
They will want to hear the song to sing.
    All. The. Way. Thru.

All Through

All through is a shadow over.

Boy.

Real words are a shy lover sharper.
Out.

One two three four. Feet forward.
First feet forward.

Poetry May Be as You Please

We listen to music all at once. We hear a bottle snore. We hear an army of our intentions.

Intentions are a lively wine of real delight. Who makes particles come to order, we say. Leap your own way particles, we say. We listen to music all the way out.

The company was tired and their uniforms were dusty. The road went so far that they were going to turn back. Turn back was the longest way round to the end of the story. A cloud arose, a cloud, a rose shaped like a conundrum, a humdrum house placed like a mountain on a mouse. This was a cloud built of rocks.

We heard music coming across the water from the rocks. Where they were marching.

A Reprieve at Dawn

When I hear the birds singing I let it be silent between notes of a song. The stillness is still lonely when we have all gone home. How lovely, I hear them. What are the wild waves singing? Crossing the bar is easy as pie. The end in view is like rain in the sky. All the birds are listening to let it rain.

A Song Is a Game

We dreamd there were openings in all the clouds.

Listen, I said, they are talking out loud.

The lines cross the field, Jess Collins said,
are ours to keep.
All our sheep are hidden in the fold.
Words are soft pockets to be seald.
Flowers, he said, are sheep that fold.

We opend the letters all day long.
Returning to A when the night closed down.

·

Naked as a word
Sound as a bird
Ten foot high to be heard.

Spelling is hard
but only the absurd renders
  rendering absurd.
Naked as a ward.
Sound as a bard.

●

Upon His Return

They said terrible Jack Spicer
was a nicer kind sprite
of earth. A hand painted
self-decorated plate,
a peasant design.

He came like a Gascon sage
out of the south. L.A.
exile. Why, it was no miracle
this Gary Cooper fascinating
old Merlin left such litter,
a poetry
refusing itself like a comet
with a tail of tin cans.

He never left the honey Moon.

That Calvinist goliard
watcht all his boys grow up
to fit his words.
Like Basketball Heroes advertising
Donald Duck orange juice
its bright goodness frozen alive
for morning repasts of grumpiness.

They said. But then I declared:
Who will forget kindly Jack Spicer.

Everyday
is riper now that
the movies explain
themselves to ourselves.

Two Painters

HASSEL SMITH

He is the only one who is trying. He was quite trying.

We saw the expanse without the expense.

How true!

We saw how true trying a man is.

An expanse of color undivided.

CORBETT

In the afternoon the paintings were wedded. Where the groom with longing. The downward swerving. The particulars are all wedded to no war. When we. The sky are.

When we are all wedded we will hear the bells ringing.

A Hassel heart beat. A Corbett beat. A bare breath.

CORBETT

I heard the heat smoking. The wine in the bottle was husky. Who heated the loud cloud? Where did they hide the burst in the blanket? Where did they? Who did they?

The people on the stairs heard the sound that was allowd. The woman in feathers said that was the report of a pistol from afar. A smudge. A fire. A loud sound in the removal of chairs from the room.

SMITH

He saw a Jew as a cog in the wheel. Turning. He saw the wheel in spite of the Jew. Turning.

The wide sweep of red swept his eyes.
An accusation he made against Matisse that he hated the Jews.
Clean for a restful violation.

The calm of a sea is betrayd in its turbulence.

Wherever he goes
Their hearts all go with him.
No more than an eye in the center.
Where the eye rests.

HASSEL SMITH. CORBETT.

Nothing left over remains.

•

An Arrangement

for James Broughton and Kermit Sheets

The Americans in a Scene of Ruins

Thunder thunder. The sound of a mountain changing.
Under the baby hood wide eyes glare.
The locomotive in a scene of ruins
carries us away. At last, we say.
Storms prepare the day of celebration.

They saw Roman baths in Rome.
Closed into ruins since the fall of the bathers.
The bathers who have enterd the sea at Nice.
The bathers who heard a roar in a wave's war.
The bathers who saw the machine at the mountain.
Won one far for away hills.
Come back home the Romans said.

We did as they did and
    here did we do.

A Mark at the Top of Capitol Hill

loco-co co moto mo mo
locomomo cotive como
    mocolotive
    motocolive
moco lomo motive lomo

co co co co co como co momo
lo mo como lo mo tomo

At Lake Como we saw mountains.

The world was as wide as around.
Fame was all we could find for home.
Everything else was too expensive.
The boys at home said
show them your buttons.

And we saw the forest for all the trees.

Hemlocks murmur. Pines
    sigh.
A row of lombardy poplars roard
    like mountains changing.

We said the cost does not matter.
The money matters.

•

An About Face

for Claire Mahl

The War is all thru.
That is what is going on.

•

Painting out loud. We gave paintings as prizes. To the prize winners.
She got a doll. She got it all. Aloud. The long afternoon came into
place. Allowd.

•

The war is all thru.
Revising our revisions.

•

The market is going down. The market is going up. The bills maid out
lead to a sensual rendering. To a. A bare bottom. A bare faced lay. A
reminder of child likes blue bare in a landescape.

•

Nothing in it but painting.
Lipstick or a large eye.

It raind and the grass was thick. Nature is all natural. A sign is a sign.
Revising all our revisions is all thru the war all thru everything.

> •

Now that it is all over.
Painting outloud.
All over.

> •

Or:
you will never break this dolly
—she is granny's imaginary baby.

A Coat of Arms

for Jess

ORANGE LIONS IN A FIELD OF BLUE

Returning from Europe they stopt to watch
lions in the sea. Not
seal lions. But lions out at sea.

In China, avenues of lions.

In San Francisco, tiny lions.
Taught to behave. They behave like tiny lions.

PARTY KINGS AND QUEENS

They behave like tiny lions.

Rosemary and rue. Sweet basil
and marjoram.
Royal rooms are rooms
opend wide.
With rosy curtains.

On a coat of arms we see
the things we know.

We Know.

Garden pleasures
Dinner pleasures
Painting pleasures
Pleasing pleasures
Gift plays pleasures and
pleasures.

Poems were pleasures
repeated again.

BARS OF COLOR: A FLAG
Well, I declare:
a declaration.

If you will remember me
you will remember me.

As I wanted to be
or a flag song
to wear your colors.

To wear your flag:
a declaration.

Remembering

> "Is it not delightful to have friends coming
> from distant quarters?"

We want our mornings undisturbd.
And splendid and tidy. Tides are tidy.
The disarray is splendid and diverting
    of dinner. A tidy beer. A tiny seer.
    Everything comes home for dinner with friends.

What does absence make the heart grow, Fonder?

    Absence is remembering roses
    now that daffodils are here.
    O to be in Piccadilly square.
    We are silly for the red red rose
    arranged with early daffodils.
    An easter remembrance.

    Dear Kit dear, dear
    dear Ilse, dear and near.
    Now that they are far
    we hear them, in our thots
    continually here.

Friends coming from a distance are delightful.
We arrange friends and criticize our relations.
David and Lloyd Bary were our vacations.
Ham and Mary Tyler offerd family dissensions.
Kenneth and Marthe Rexroth comfortable factions.

We rememberd Brenda as a rose in a garden
or a daffodil in a field of roses.

    An escutcheon.

But married friends go by twos. Especially
dear Kit and Ilse, we two to you too.

A Mexican Straight Summer

The demon in the cage at all.
The age of demonstration.
In the cage the demon proved.
And we went into full summer.
To demonstrate.
Proved to be. A bird.

A summer camp for boy birds.
Run by kindly leaders.
A demonstration.
Of flying. Of lying. Of flaying.
The leaders. Following the leaders:
a flay. Run into a summer camp.
For.
For.

A military change in the weather.
The military change.

If he is strong. If he is strong.
Or wild. If he is a child.
The age of demonstration.

The demon in the cage askt.
How far into full summer.
Is camping time. Facing.

A wild child who is a kindly leader later.
We all demonstrated.
At the demonstration. Birds.
In wet weather. Weary and angry.
Askt. What age is it. At all.

Robert Berg at Florence

We see palaces heated in the sun.
Italian summers of years ago.
When the Americans tourd.
  He was tired. He had
large dark almost Italian eyes.
He won the prize.

With a crown of flowers.

If you remember Caravaggio
or the Colonnas at home in Rome
teatime at Berenson's with celebrities
Berg and his mother were not there.

PART TWO

We were in love when he was in love.
We were in the bar when he was in the bar.
We were in debt when he was in debt.

All of his poetry was a private thot.

A private debt.

What did the Renaissance
disappear into?

The Renaissance disappeard
into the shifting of forms.
He was disappointed.

The fountains remaind in the garden
for days of special blue.

An Evening at Home

She set the lamp at the window and sat down to tea. A hurried
moment before a long repast. Well, the storm came up and she wrote it
down.

At intervals of calendar fun.

BARTH CARPENTER. MADELINE GLEASON.

There there and there. Are air and there.
Flying to a high place. She placed her.
Flying there are air and there.
She placed her there. Her book there.
She was to her as there are there.
Their place there is high in flying there.

MADELINE GLEASON.

No one complaind. Of.
They all exclaimd. For.
He declaimd. On.
On. For. Of. She blamed blame for the same.

BARTH, BARTH. A LOVELY FLAG.

In the blue. She was intervals of true.
Arrangements. Of perfect arrangements.
We knew we did not know if it was true.
Bring flowers into the room, Lucy.
We none of us intend to die. Before the war
is thru. Bring flowers into the room, Lucy.
It is quite quiet in here, dear.
Dear. Dear, dear.

MADELINE GLEASON IN SPANISH DISGUISE.

Songs. Strings to the oval sound. Songs.

Don Carillon came in a cloud of bells.
With songs. With songs. With strings singing.

Don Carillon traveld with birds on the way.
To sing. Strum the sounds. The music. The dark.

Flickers of hearthlight
showd in the dark.

MADELINE GLEASON AND BARTH CARPENTER.

She says how are you are you today.
She says I am on my way.
She says she is perfectly on her way.
She goes all her way to a calendar round.

AT INTERVALS.

Watch the cats the cats watch.
There are intervals of complete delight.

A Design for Flack

1.

Lines there are lines.
There are lines of no tension to
no tense place. An attention.
At attention. We paid.
A tense makes the line. Right.

Tight. Right there. Tight there.

Tie the line there.

When coming to a tension, salute.
Saludo Amigo.

2. SALUDO AMIGO.

Words were his vises. Vises were his pleasures. Pleasures were an
absolute measure. He cared carefully his waits and measures. He cared
carefully his wits and erasures.

We were certain he was certain.
Were we. Certain. Was he. Certain.

3. SUCH A POEM IS AN ISLAND EXACTLY OF POETRY

Such a poem is exactly of poetry.
An island in sight. An exaction
of rights of poetry. We were
certain we were he was seeing.
We were certain we were he was saying.
We were sometimes there were singing.

In the indolent hours, in the careless cares of ours, in the indescriminate
mainland pleasures the faraway careful words for a picture, from the
island, of birds was just what he had chosen. An other pleasure.

Play Time Pseudo Stein

From the Laboratory Records Notebook 1953

1969

1942, A Story

Hurriedly. They settled down. There. To ruin afternoons with furs. He was after the war they followd. She referrd and absented her mind in sewing. So

They had spent their time rewarding their neighbors.

An introduction. The first act was to act. A passion a total absorbing in interpreting a fiery somnolence in passing an impulse that repulses. She half to the half light lights. Wary but wearing. Wearing furs is a welcome.

A tarantula in the middle of a knot.

There was a perfect embellishment in swelling. A classy stare to do. A loose basket. Complications were always arrangements.

Let me explain everything.
Everything is about the importance of the obvious where we were at. The obvious were we a hat is an elegant hair. A hair is a wooley around she intends us.

In 1942 it was true. She rememberd her remembering when she forgot. Where did they go? Into the time they waited for. He was foolish for the expense of the time he was the other baby minded second they arrived the second they arrived.

A short story is reacht by a flight of her stares she saw where he ends. The End.

A Fairy Play
a Play

1/5/53   •2•

MARGARET GRACE : He intends is wonderful star potty horror story. It was in the late afternoon the bishop the bicycle parted. And a cloud arose to amaze us all.

JAMES FENNELL : She was amazed because the bishop's brother was finisht beginning. This was he was a fairy and that made a fairy play of everything pretended.

BISHOP FENNEL : An elderly Minister of Finance reveald his bicycle as the question they were answering. This was the total enchantment allowd in the regular procedure.

ELIZABETH ELIZABETH : This was a dream with serious consequences. She undertook to allow its parting.

•

In the village after the war what was it for. A play is where people are talking, troubling countering and misunderstanding their playing.

MARGARET FENNEL : If they play in turn then they play fair.

BISHOP FENNEL : After church she found what he was after. He was after ours to explain explaining.

ELIZABETH ELIZABETH : The dreadful thing about conclusions is the ready conclusion.

THE FAIRY GODMOTHER : A happy wish after the play time is all over is ready to remedy wishing. Bless you all and remind. A blessing is a story.

• • •

1 · 5 · 53   • 3 •

How
excited we get as the excitement increases. The whole increasing is
thrilling and inciting to increasement. This mounting until fills itself as
a hole expanding. We are grateful for an explanation of our greatness.

A memory extends lessons and confessions. This is like a boundary
makes a willing into beyond, a cake is a promise, a cake was the
premise of wonder for the widow.

IN A LANDSCAPE HOW FAR WE GO IS LENGTHEND IF WE DESIRE IT.

• • •

1/5/53   • 4 •

A butter machine

S.M.O.K.I.N.G T.H.E. C.I.G.A.R.E.T.T.E.

1/5/53   • 5 •

The hot smoking exhausts the question intent for the writing. A
pleasure in disorder for pressure is an unpleasant exceeding. This is to
make proceeding a burning. Once it is displeasure, exhaust, withering
not warming but almost a warning, once it is a vice only the writing is
pleasing.

The writing is appeasing. It is when we do not want to smoke the
cigarette that the cigarette is found wanting. The will against the not
being willing overcomes, threatens. The writing escapes from the
predicament of the smoking.

This is distracting so that it does not mind. Writing — to mind.

Writing Writing

1964

Dedication

For the love of Gertrude Stein in which I labord to write in whose mode; and for Lynn Brockway and Jess who found pleasure in some of these pieces of writing-like-Stein.

Robert Duncan
April 1964

First a Preface

Turning Into

turning into a restful roomfull;
turning into a guide to the book;
turning into a man-naked memory;
turning into a long avenue;
turning into a lady reclining;
turning into a mother declining;
turning into a vegetable declaiming;
turning into a yesterday for tomorrow;
turning into an age old sorrow;
turning into a cat fit for fiddling;
turning into a wheel withering;
turning into a god whose heart's ease;
turning into an hour of dis-ease;
turning into an eagle bottle January;
turning into a hairy baby song;
turning into an all nite long;
turning into a doctor's office;
turning into a rubber grimace;
turning into a snail's pace;
      a rail's distance, a long face;
turning into a turn with grace

Coming Out Of

coming out of the house to die;
coming out of a babe's first cry;
coming out of a swollen eye;
coming out of the belief in Jehovah;
coming out of the store on the corner;

coming out of his acquaintance with a convict;
coming out of a serious conviction;
coming out of a lover's communion;
coming out of so very little;
coming out of neighbor's tittle tattle;
coming out of a hole in a rattle;
coming out of stupid associations;
coming out of exhausted vacations;
coming out of six-foot relations;
coming out of church on sunday;
coming out of Wednesday and Monday;
coming out of exorbitant reading;
coming out of a swoon from bleeding;
coming out of a fanciful rain;
coming out of a doll in vain;
coming out again and again.

Making Up

making up to the policeman's star;
making up in a crowded bizarre;
making up for a lack of hair;
making up the best for a fair one;
making up what you hadn't won;
making up an ode that's too long;
making up at the beginning of the song;
making up as an ape with ears;
making up for the leap in years;
making up seem down to all eyes;
making up a surprise to surprise.

Out

Out the soft-toothd cloud, out
the miser, out the mile-high regret.
And a, a no thing nosing nothing.
A no thanks of a nose in a
handkerchief hidden. Enuf, enuf
of such cloud-cottony stuff. Snuff.

A Scene

The great mountains of Disclaimer, almost black, but dwarfly
imposing beneath infinite blue of tired sky. Kites of excitement dance
in the blue, defining what had been ennuie as a space to move about
in. A downpour of uplifting sad rain obscures the mountains. Renders
them ranges of dim despair. Coming out into the open of dont care,
we were washd clean and almost quite going to be happy because night
was coming and star-kites would define what had been space as merely
heaven.

•

writingwriting

The Beginning of Writing

a composition

Beginning to write. Continuing finally to write. Writing finally to continue beginning.

To overcome the beginning. To overcome the urgency. To overcome writing in writing

Not ever to overcome the beginning. Now to write writing. Not to overcome in beginning.

·

Love is sometimes advancing and including. Love is some times overcoming and not beginning. Love as a continual part of some writing is imagining expansion of loving to include beginning as continuing.

Desire: in not writing. Urgency: in not writing. Lying in waiting in not writing. Desire is the before not beginning of beginning. Urgency is a not feeling of finally beginning.

·

When I imagine not overcoming but including, loving takes place in the place of desiring. When I imagine daily beginning continuing, being is no longer re-forming but rapeating.

A giant of the whole day is awakeness.
a giant of the whole night is sleeping.
To be a universe! To be a universe!
Wrapt in its continually speaking.
To be returnd to dreaming.

When I imagine myself as lover
— love is again here, here I say:
coming forth by Day once more
from all mere longing, belonging
in saying.
    The morning turns
quiet as words speaking.
A soliloquy of audible silence.

  •

A soliloquy! A soliloquy!
Such idle talking in different colord lights, in sleights
of imagined person, in person.
The great Panjandrum rolls his eternal being like a drum
roll
over the measures of disorderd sleep.
Disorderd speech

Imagining in Writing

Not in believing, but in pretending. Not in knowing, but in
pretending. Not in undergoing, but in pretending.

At last, at last : all of reality. We find we are only what we pretended to
be. We realize.

These lions in the lazy passages of time like poets surfeit themselves
upon carcasses of poetry.

  •

He wants if he is there. He reaches,
almost. But touch touches.
He rises from touch enormous
shaking mere realities from his form
like an ocean on end, like a talking coffee pot at
breakfast, like an unbelievable story escaping the

believing mind, a criminal, a primitive, a demagogue,
tyrant over the people, an aroused automobile about to
become an automobile.

He is so real that he longs for the real.
He grasps the idea. But touch touches.
And no mere idea, the ideal turns like a sleeping teacher
— another character — that renders
the whole act inconsequential. Magnificent shifts
of shiftless flesh. An armory of thighs, a pedagogy
of actual voluptuous pectoral pages to the hand,
words of hair, of visible eyes, closed or opend closing.
a foreign language.

    •

How long at the corners of the street
the cars delay, we wait
for the promised, the promised,
for the promises that carry us home.

Away from the demands, the histories, away from the years. Immortal,
as in tears, we are carried. Away.

This is a description of sometimes a painful existing. This is a
description of a sometimes self betraying which is revealing. This is a
description in writing of the description in writing. This is a scripture
of a rapture in describing. In writing I am not but am writing.

This is a description of a continent of living: lions, streetcars,
explosions, newspapers like flies, flies like newspapers, giraffs of
devotion, sentences in locomotion as contrived as giraffs, as devoted as
all passing fashions. This is a description of passions designd as costumes
of real living.

This is a description of all pretend pages. Unimportant magnificences
of an inner forgiveness for living.

    •

It is the measure of the crippled sentence. It is the pleasure of the poetry
rotting its words until the flesh of the language falls away from its bone.
It is the beautiful senseless tone in the language crippling the sentence.
The poetry. The stink of the real to the imaginary nose.
The skull is the rose. A face like all other faces unlike.
A finality. A betrayal.
The rows of uneven teeth like the measure of a sentence.

> •

So we went up to the bedroom from all daily hungers and pleasures
to enter the dream, to enter together we said entwined as in death, as
in love, in unknowing otherness we anticipated, stretchd out each his
own eachness upon his own frame without space or time of stretching,
changing and rechanging form, deformd, enormities of pitiful sleep.

The violence of a face, cut open bleeding.
The violation of a form in a chin receding.
The violin of a figure disfigured; a crude
visual reminder, crackd, warpd, bloated.
An obscenity. A disemboweling
A vile charm never to change changeling
strung like a skin over contradictory
skeletons of form.

We saw warts and corrosions dividing.
Diseases were only reminders of our dis-ease.

All that we disownd, we ownd,
until the sick lions climbing up from their mother-fucking
vomited the remains of all claimd pleasures.

Writing as Writing

The word in the hand is the sound in the eye is the sight in the listening mind. Listen, do you mind. Mind then the solid pattern of all this soundless patter, collected together only in the writing.

The word has only been left on the page, left after the steady procession of developing sentences.

Poetry made up of sentences of words. Poetry in its regular irregular lines and divisions. Poetry in its steady revisions of its original vision, an accurate eye correcting its accuracies, an image of a man made in his own image inaccurately. I endeavor in delivering to deliver the speech from all truth spoken into its true form. I strive in inscribing in its different lengths the lengths of description, the lasts of all passages of literal understandings. I arrive in the reiteration of all the relations at lengthy vacations of ordinary prose in poses of poetry.

The word at rest rests in the mind in the restless continuation. The breaking down of all internal continual. The interruption of persistent locomotion. The persistent irruption of volcanic inconsequence. The landscape revised to portray a reality.

•

The landscape revised to portray a reality.
Seen from a height as heights of houses.
Seen as rows of intense cloud solid sounds.
Seen as a flat miasma of undiverted sunlight.
Seen as the intrusion of blue in the background,
    as blue in the foreground, crowded
    in a background of natural houses.
The city revised to outlast its sentences.

•

We see the architecture as a make-shift reality, see sky as a poor part of nature, see the crowded clouds as a pleasure.

The design of the paragraphs is in totalities of of. A pure possession possessd in its illusive properties.

What do we know then but seeking to know the stretch and the shrinking, the sureness of aim and the aimless surety, the feeling of security in reciting what we are doing, the fun of pursuing the ensuing phrases.

Opening our mouthd words to encompass the passage of time. Pretending the time in the space it takes to design our intentions. Relenting and preventing the importance of saying from satisfying and relaxing the hearer from listening. Relaxing the effort to fall back from its periods.

A literal transcription of letters is a conceit that pleases.

Possible Poetries: A Prelude

The weather is wide enuf for pastimes.

Possible Poetries: A Postcript

The rhymes you hear are the lions
panting in impatience. Rest. Rest.
At rest. All impatient lines
fall into the measures of discard.

Possible Poetries: A Postcript

Measures of discord are the pleasures of discard.
Words in their impatience follow afterwards.

•

An Imaginary Letter

Dear Saint Heart:

I like to remember you shooting your works there at the front like us here shooting the works in the rear. Daddy is all workd up about voting this year in the elections. Like he says everything is going to be changed, I mean we're going to really clean up the whole mess and we're going to remember like you boys up to your necks in shit and guts it takes shit and guts to go where we're going. God's with us, he's backing us up all the way down the line and everything's fine. Everybody's dying to know how far we're going when we go.

This old U.S.A. is just like sunday in a butcher shop. I mean all this dead meat costs more than we can afford to eat and we're opening for business. And there's no more pretend at this end of the deal we're going to fix everything up until its all over as real as the feel of the cock of a gun, I mean as fair as a Village square.

Yours in the red white of your blue.

Lucky Joe
The Guy on the Go

Imaginary Letter

Dearest Paul,

If you live, as you once said you did, for love alone, you will understand with what repugnance I view all that I was then and that I did, now that I am indeed in Love. I know that you do not believe and that you deny our blessed Lord and it hurts me. It would have hurt me then for myself, but now I pray for you: that you may come to Love. "Without ceasing I make mention of you always in my prayers."

The other nite at Elizabeth Really's I left early because I could not stand to hear you talk like you did about God and then all your greek "gods."

"Because that, when they knew God, they glorified him *not as God, neither were they thankful; but because vain in their imaginations, and their foolish heart was darkend."*

I left Elizabeth's and walkd home alone. It was cold and dark Friday. But the real cold and dark was of the heart of the city. Everywhere along the way, men driven by lust paced the streets. Just like beloved Augustine, I pitied them. These are your gods! Their hunger strikes terror and I prayd to our Lady that watches over us. I was not alone then, for I thot of the blessed Lord bleeding on the cross, and it struck in its pity all fear from my heart.

You and Robert and Adrian, what love can you offer in being untrue to God, that is not most untrue; the very cold and dark of these streets? Yet I loved you, and thus I denied in my heart the great reality of Love. Vain in your imagination, my dearest. I am filld with terror in my love for you. For you are still dear to me. What infinite loneliness there is for those who deny the only Love there is, the infinite care and tenderness and forgiveness of Jesus Christ.

K.

Imaginary Letter.

His Intention:

Dear Alicia

I know no one is to blame but I cant stand it anymore. So I am taking this way out. I dont blame you. Please just forget. Forget every thing. I thot and I thot and this was the only thing to do and I wanted a way out after the way everything has been going. Im tired of going on that way and I dont blame anybody. I sure dont blame you only I couldnt stand everything the way it was going and I was going to be real tired of trying to keep up with everything like I should of. Just forget me and all those week ends last summer and Stormy Weather and all because I dont blame you and I dont think we are to blame for anything the way everything is going and I cant

stand up to it anymore that way and whose to blame for what should
of happend. So Im taking the only way out that I can see that doesnt
go on that way I mean so I hope nobody is to blame for me and I
am going to forget every thing that way the way I am taking out
Im not chicken and so I hope you will forget it all too. Like Stormy
Weather I mean and going to the beach next summer. I love you and
the crowd more than everything but I just cant stand everything any
more. Love. I dont blame you or anybody anymore. Love. Forget.
Love.

Harold Target.

Motto

A correspondence is a poetry enlarged.

Division

Isnt the traffic killing?
Isnt the war simply
simply killing?
Arent the critics killing?
Isnt that show killing?
Isnt the pace killing?
Isnt the joke killing?
Isnt the killing killing?
Arent these prices telling?
Isnt the tax killing?
Isnt it killing telling?

Writing at Home in History

The word we were writing is all our reading. Our reading is never our believing. Our reading is never entirely our pretending. Our reading is not now our complete writing. Our reading is never our finally arriving.

The word we were writing is not part of our talking. But all of our writing is a height of conversation, a talking out loud to ourselves that is releasing, an increasing readiness in a decreasing toward the end of the beginning.

The sentences we were venturing we are adventuring towards a fictional future.

A composition. In the evening for the sake of forsaking the company we compose ourselves into the I of envisioning. There are no pictures but spaces and traces of going and retracing in order to show a choreographic nicety. An order to go on toward the individual end order that we are disordering.

Only one at a time can write in all these voices. Only in our sense of the together gathering of others can we compose ourselves as the single one writing. A demagogy of conclusions, a hierarchy of answers, a tyranny of questionable possible absolutions. .

Don't you sense the marvellous ghosts in the least alterd intentions? Foxes, lepers, strangers, lovers, ancient men who stir in their slumbers, extravagant women red haird whose elegance murmurs, crowds of illiterate mummers are our inventions. A novel passes from existence. We faild it. A poem rots on the line. We fould it. We filld all the moments with hours of talk. An extension.

Now if we are in the evening of the world we are at home writing home. Now if a history is beginning, we are not beginning in history. Now if in Korea as we hear there is continual killing, now if we rightly have no longer faith in our nations, now if we tire of futile decisions, we are at home among stranger relations.
Now if all men unwilling dying, we are not willing to be succeeding.

Now if the unlimited trying, the political reforming, the politics forming, we are not trying to form our reforming.

Now if the spiritual need and the bleeding and the ruthless weeding and the take heed that is fearing, we are not fearing the necessities we weed.

Now if all the dark and the dimly rememberd unbrokennes and the lost hopeful futureness and the painful confessions of unruly feature attractions and the contractions of heart in the intentions for doing and the wholeness of the longing for belonging, for an oblivious following, we are not featuring darkly or dimly the following forward of our own future attractions.

Now if the completely and dynamic, the overwhelming vote of the people, the peopleness at last arrives and survives, we are not surviving but contriving our amusement. A pointless diversion, the tattle of eternity in the message of history.

Entirely at home in writing. Not famous, not talented, not expanding but including, not promising but missing the blessing, not profound but professional professing an at-homeness. Not printed but writing, not convincing but appealing, not succeeding but succeeding ourselves, not winning but beginning. Entirely at home in beginning.

Writing for readers who want to be reading. Lesson Two.

I Am Not Afraid

I am not afraid of writing a great poem.
I am not afraid of writing a perfect lyric.
I am not afraid of being afraid.
I am not afraid of being staid.
I am not afraid of sounding like Stein.
I am not afraid of being inspired.
I am not afraid of your growing tired.
I am not afraid of oblivious night.
I am not afraid of the sense of being right.
I am not afraid of the failure to describe.

I am not afraid of succeeding Shelley.
I am not afraid of not knowing Greek.
I am not afraid of allowing no one to speak.
I am not afraid of ever being seen.
I am not afraid of being a queen.
I am not afraid of betraying the trust.
I am not afraid of my end in the dust.
I am not afraid of my bare behind.
I am not afraid of remarks unkind.
I am not afraid of the tried and untrue.
I am not afraid of not equalling Proust.
I am not afraid of great areas of blue.
I am not afraid to name a successor.
I am not afraid of the casual messenger.

An Interlude. Of Rare Beauty.

The seal in the depraved wave
glides in the green of it.
All his true statement
made in his mere swimming.

Thus: we reclaim
all senseless motion from its waves
of beauty.   Naming
no more than our affection for naming.

●

Appendix One: Essays and Try-Outs

Hung-Up

What sort of suffering does one have in its telling? or part of a pain in imparting, in painfully devising or in devising a painful revelation? What kind of kindness comes with recounting, in accounting for affections and warmths? What stages of passion pass into its phrases or into faces of passion?

Slowly, pains takingly wrote he, dear Mom, I am very home sick and I want to come home.

What sorrow pushes the crawling hand to recalling, recalling no words? What else? What else is there? No invention comes to prevent the sudden ending. The defiant dismay, the balking at writing, the choked up talking, the cheat in the heat of portraying these urgencies.

We went swimming. Our side is winning.

What dying in what living strains against all trying in the absolute dying of words in the letter? what utter dismay goes further than these futile tryings?

And over and over again anyone writing comes to such writhing, such absences of all feeling other than straining, such absorbd preambles of failure.

Waiting before lying, lying before waiting. Pretending, offending the urgency, overcoming the beginning only to be no longer winning the words to be going.

Racking his mind, or his heart, or his crampd hand racking not writing. Stuck, not poised, but crouchd at the end of its sentence.

Is it then something that should have been saying. Something we say preying, back of the mind, pressing out without outing, a mere shouting, clots and blots the miserable hand?

The anger lasts longer and stronger, the longing for belonging is wronger, the pent up desiring to be sharing all, everything worrying, the excesses of saying.

What sort of desiring, of needing, of bleeding, of writing to be winning, of sentences to be seducing goes further, is exceeding and refusing the solace of recounting?

This is a description of writing not coming, urgency not coming. A summing up of the painstaking coming up to not coming.

The Code of Justinian. A Discourse on Justice

The law of the land is the law we regard. The land of the law is the land we address. I address a land of true listeners. Regarding the law of the listeners, our own regard is the land they swear to, they adhere by, they accept and rejoice and imagine the great nation of lawgivers. The lawgivers give all that we receive, deceiving and believing; the code is the shape and direction of the ready adhering the judges are hearing.

What is the law we regard, disregarding coercions; what are the possible versions of virgin legality?

Writing moves by its values and measures, it measures and treasures, not voting, but denoting; not schooling but unruly ruling. Writing is continually ruling and directing, ordering and progressing to design its own writing.

The code we are discovering in the orders of our regarding, in the determinations of our discarding, in the true sense of the true in which we are lying, in the distances we are sensing in walking and talking, proportionate apportionings of our adherence.

The writer belongs to a nation writing. His understanding, his standing, his constant upstanding is measured and treasured in the nation of writers withstanding.

This is a nation like a constant ocean, an elementary talking in all tongues speaking.

This is a nation of continual seeking, a code, an ode, an oath of revealing, of unearthing concealing. A law in its continual writing, reshaping but shaping a nation of speech in which we are participating.

The law is the law defined by our keeping, by our constant adhering, by our coming to adhering, by our standing even in distrust or in sin or in pain or in punishment or in death in declaring. There is no law but our individual obeying, in our ordering remembering.

Justice determined by our weights and our measures, not certainly by our pleasures and displeasures, not by our powers developing but by our imagining the constantly changing unchanging form of our imagining. The laws of composition, the determinants of position, the laws of gravity and the laws for propriety—we are, even writers, completely incompleting our just composing in going toward reforming.

If every completing acting is in its anticipation a codification of possible conclusions, a system of legal excluding and protruding and deluding; if every determination even in moving and removing all its resemblance to its original beginning is in going and returning, in stopping and conserving, in preserving and enriching, in overthrowing and revising, in devising perfect disresemblances to its own perfection; if every indeterminate doing is determined in not quite moving toward its own moving; if the constant shaping of needs we are filling; then laws are continually absolutely ruling all we are knowing of what we have been doing.

Even stopping defines an end, a sentence, a law of its beginning.

Some in writing feel a law that is demanding, a conflict of others, of laws to which they are adhering that is not clearing but marring and denying the law they are commanding. Some in writing feel such a shape determined in their beginning that they are continually sinning when that shape is not emerging. Some in writing push and devise words and phrases, phases and sentences, into a legal proceeding. Some are needing an absolute form, a feeling of limiting, to discover without revealing their legal proceedings the length of the shape they are to be completing. Some need to be policemen, policing and directing, they need a persistent made-up determination not to be pretending in order not to be offending the sense that there is a law in perfecting. Some are gaily devising and revising all legalities aware that all their imagining is desiring and enfiring a law they are admiring. Some are filld with rage on the page at all other laws than the laws they are enraged by; contradicting and dictating in predicting such wrathful codifications of law as tie up all talking in finally ending. Finally ending is never beginning. So their sentences of absolution are laws to end laws, a hiatus of writing against writing that is fighting.

But a law is emerging from all this writing, and from the fighting, and from the delighting and from the good nighting; a law is reveald in the efforts that are conceald, in the magnificent protean coat he had on, the neurotic, erotic, the perfect, erect, penis proud old stallion, that man, in the cruelties he can do in burning and in turning against all that he adhered to, in the becoming and doing all that he feard to, in the home building and wrecking, the racking, the heart bleeding and feeding and force-feeding, in the shamed, the blamed, the reclaimd, the deliberately maimd, in the subservient bastardly prince to his princeness. A code is emerging in its continual completion that we describe in our denoting. Not a law, as we said, in our voting but a law we discover that we are voting.

A law is a description, an anticipation of the code we believe is hidden, the secret in, writing we are writing. This is why who the Bacon is was who wrote Shakespear. We know that decoded the swift articulation will return to its nothing.

The statement we are coming to will compromise, will surprise, will follow the pure dear old law of the form we are keeping.

The good old law is the revision of a vision we had of the law of revising.

So, writing is like the Code of Justinian, or like the laws of an ode, or like Holy Sentences of Divine Commandments, writing is like writing.

We are never believing entirely as long as a man is speaking, we are not understanding whatever a man is doing or being, we are seldom accepting wherever a man is writing, that the law of his speaking, of his doing or being, of his proceeding in writing is not a law we should be denying or relying upon. We are only, few of us, just perceiving that the law is the relating, the description to the right reader of the belief in his going he has come to be reconsidering. We are always amazed and often dismayd that the law we are seeing is not what we are reading; we proceed, so many of us, as if the code he were announcing were the code of his announcing.

This is a partial explanation of the declamation of laws.

The Discourse on Sin

The sweating sense of sin, the aweful dismembering, is the empty belonging to the preceding in proceeding; the I am believing in place of a time that is together cohering in receding. This is itself a not existing that in continuing in existing seems to deprive one in writing of all profession, that compels and repels a lasting not ever completing confession.

It is hard to describe this real what of sinning, the darkness that is extending from such doing as casts one out from the law of its repeating. But everywhere anyone is somehow sinning; there is not in every part of moment of continuing or renewing a confidence in the law one is perceiving in its renewd acquaintance. There is sometimes something lewd that is betraying a law we were denying, then we are crying with rage or with pain or with the hopeless returning again to the sense of a law, of a sin, that reveals the inconsequent terrors of our beginning.

Sinning is all the kinds of no order we are never entirely adhering to; all the oceanic feeling that we are not meaning but relying upon; all the nonentity that is not law full, the shapeless, the hopeless, the undoing in which we are never submerging but always always partly from which we are emerging into a codification, a commandment, a covenant to keep us, even grieving, even almost in rage and in dark law less seeing, in the law full proceeding, the continual formal realization in doing

Sometimes I came almost to a darkest kind of knowing, of knowing only the existing, came to just not quite an absolute grieving and ceasing of all kinds of believing; sometimes I came to a lawless not seeing, not doing, not writing; but always, not willing, not accepting, not submerging in these waters that are terribly baptizing, not completely hearing this almost discontinuation of the eternal reading. I came once to a dismay, to the edge of all the existing that is never speaking, that is never coming into sight or disappearing, to the not pretending any longer to be persisting; but the never dyingness, the never ending trying to speak was straining, and the pain, the vast waste of living, the almost entirely realization of sin, never did finally begin and the story goes on, went on beginning again from its ever recurring once there was to its even in this accurate description of upon a time and in time I no longer was stronger than my existing.

The sense of sin is aweful and really is, it is the absolutely really nothing of anything we are believing as long as we are believing; it is the totality in which we are part of which we are not participating. So the most real, the most relentless unchanging thing is that we are all, always, somehow sinning.

The sense of the law, the law itself, is the beautiful possibility of our completely adhering, believing and conceiving, completely the pretend of our just becoming. The quite lovely relation of the tellers and the hearers to the story we are relating.

There is the feeling at times then of words that are just as we weigh them and amazingly resembling the law full particular words we value in measure.

I cannot design entirely for amusement tho to be amused is to be initiate of the designing muse. She is portrayd as the lady secretly smiling, at once amused by the writing and amused at the writing. Mater dolorosa and smiling. She opposes, reserves her womanhood, even as she offers herself wholly; but all this writing that does not amuse is male opposition to its muse. Lady, bear with me. I proceed to regain your countenance. I cannot without lapses in my own engrossment play out the rites of writing. There is the preparation for what is fighting within; there is the reparation for all wrongs and the unsaid to be saying; there is the delaying to prolong the talking and the waiting for the doubling of the exposures of speech.

A delight. In the telling an excitement beginning and an inherent pleasure become absorbd in the measures; an emotion growing, expressing, showing in its phrases is becoming a multiple flavoring of all unknown knowing. I am no longer sincere, I am no longer expressing, I am no longer addressing but filld up to exclude all other feeling with the language which is ours unfolding itself, revealing its spirit in its words I was using. I am no longer choosing but losing myself; it is the medium, the means that is revealing its meaning.

Oracles of loquacity. The talkative medium.

A Poem in Stretching

Published in *A Book of Resemblances*. See above.

• • •

No, I cant reach you. I cant hold to you. Where are you? O my darling. My rose boy. My joy rises and floods me with feeling not feeling. Not reaching out and enwording you, saying you. Love. Love. Love. Only a word. Only a flock of words scrabbling woundwingd in the air. The tree in the lazy sun glow is loud with sound. And you are only. Cant clasp I the solid echoing spirit. The utterly broken stops mid air, a bird in flight, before changing and breaking. The form utterly gone. The grave moment of the afternoon held to. I cannot. Words twittering amidst those shadows, flies in the heart of the silence. A speaking coming, about to come, coming up, climbing joyfully with his back turnd to the rememberd sea, the abounding main joy, the deep drownd succumbing. O my God, I leap up. I swear. I am almost. Where? Where are you? were you? I saw heard the lovely gibberish of eyes, a language, untranslatable. Almost had, was reaching, had been. Rises joyfully to the crest of the cliff and calls his salute. Ha-aye!

All of my joy is a foreign element, submerged in the clear swift passing stream of, unchanged. Pure wordless sentences. In these towns that we ride by, on our way home as we are, or on our way to our lover we ever are, the tiny lights of our delight flicker and are passed by forever.

•

Appendix Two: Poetics

Descriptions of Imaginary Poetries.

1. Where giant wordlings interrupt the stuttering machine-gun-wit; the pale insensible bland body phrases loom, as islands in the line-of-fire. Not targets, but meaningless casualties. Luminous blobs in a splatterd night scene. Too accidental for inspiration, too clumsy for lyric.

2. Gaps.
        Regular straining.
Great rips in the febrile goods. .
    Gapes.
    A leftover intending.

3. My god, we thot after four minutes, how much more of this can there be? O a pure pure tedium. With and without ideas. A pure lovely tedium.

4. The poet can hardly lift these words.
    Not because they are heavy, but because he is so weak.

5. Unfolding phrases, like chairs closing into themselves. Furnitures walking, shifting sides over legs, backs. A gate closed in order to open. Irregular measures of meaning. The words, all cream and curds, all slick and sheen.

    Drop and drop of acid. A bitter cool smooth move ball bearing. A heavy wooden convertible structure.

6. A field of targets and archers.
    Bright. Black red and white concentric circles the bulls eyes. Looking not watching. Sing sting sing slings of fortune. Birds fly far afield in far off sky. A shout arises. Almost. Haloo. Elegiac victories.

    And all this refers to ones extreme of youth. How extreme youth is.

7. Wide awake and confusions.
   Then drowsy illness. Ill, at ease.
   Then. Deep imageless sequence of words as blackout.
   Two words startled like deep sleeping
   deer started up from
   deep thicket of words. Aroused.
   Confusion, like the breaking and smashing and
      trampling of
   a thicket of words.

   A weary after statement of wide awake confused
   aroused.

8. Two or three occasional
   endearing clear
   statement of a tea pot, a
   sculptural head, a cat asleep.

Smoking the Cigarette

Published in *Play Time Pseudo Stein*. See above.

Rhyme Mountain Particular

Rhyme mountain particular. Bus make ovoid. Ovoid is a shape. A shape in shape.

Rime particular mountain and particular. City blocks or her escape. Fire escape. His cape a landscape.

Rime mountain rime mountain. Particular heap far to fetch. Far and a fetch. A fetch in time. To rime.

Rime mountain particular. Car port to rime. A snow. Going. In what direction. A particular direction is following to fill in spaces before riming.

On the rim of the mountain. A particular place and shadow. The moon of course follows its course.

Particular rime mountain. Change from rime to mountain rime. Change from plain rime to particulars. Change to particular. Are you particular. Rime mountain and rime particular. These are rimes. Sound your mountain alike particular.

An Advertisement for a Fair Play

A racket is a noise that counts. Mayor Maisie and Count Deliver. To make money talk is playing the numbers by twos and threes.

A sound wall is one that does not fall when a trumpet is blown. This is a protection against criminal action that is pleasurable. A pleasure does not stay in measure or remain. A wall of sound is one erected by sounds. A sounding resounding. The pleasure is not all over.

Allowed as when it is aloud. Spoken out lawed and is allowed.

A Fair play plays fairly well when we play fairly. Fairly is not equally but equally playing. This takes attention. A tension. Will a tense one play. Well will attention play will it be well.

Progressing

When it is composed is it composition that is posed. Is it at ease. Is it by the numbers. Is it alterating. Is it alterd. What is alterd. What is alterd if it is numbers alterd to numbers. What does counting by threes do to the twos.

Progressing at ease is by threes to count these that are twos concealing the news that those are twos. A joke. A joke is not seeing what you are looking at when you are looking at what you are seeing. This is a trick of deceptive positions.

This Is the Poem They Are Praising as Loaded

This is the poem they are praising as loaded. This is as it is loaded and thrilling. Loaded with death's kingdom which is meaning. Loaded with meaning which is gathering the former tenants. Loaded with the former tenants speaking which brings weeping and fulfilling. Loaded with fulfilling which brings crises and then wealthy associations. This is the poem loaded up without shooting which is an eternal threatening.

The sadness of the threatening makes a poem in the poem's increasing. This is not an increasing in mere size but a more and moreness of pressure and precedence. An explosion that does not come but makes a partial exposure as a disclosure that substitutes for its period.

This makes an imposing poem, an impostor pretending to be what he really is, makes a great poem in collecting. This is the passing of the collection face. An anthology of human beings. A loaded folding up in which history is folded.

Orchards

Shake the tree. Leave the words fall where they woolen, the
airy spaces for verbs to came as a went they wind.
Not a storm. Not a space for a storming one.
Numbers in ovals, ovals in whirls for pitches.

What are the roots? The roots is conceald to this sorry tree.
What is this tree sorry for. It is forever.
Shake the sad tree and watch its tenses loosen or apples listen
for pitches.
Pitches is further darkness. Further darkness is thickness of sentence in
branches is other thoughts that demand ranging. This is only a tree by
limiting which makes forgetting grow. Organic form from lines that
indicate understandable stems of feeling, trunks that sense real beginning.

Shake the sentence and divide understandables into originals
which are pitch black or pitchers full with arrangements.

This takes a cast of the original people who are changed into verbs.

Only verbs sing and so they are singing.

Are you willing for their singing. There were a sentence that is really sentences.

A sentence is a judgment; fairly constructed but we acknowledge unfair in its concealments.

And leave the words for the dark they come to in grammatical spaces.

A Train of Thought

A train of thought is stutter going stud for a butter cow.
Picture the small engine or ingenuity goes by country to be pictured.

This is a track in the country we cannot follow or mistake when pictured for a wall.
Since we thot it was a wall we discoverd it was fake. Means.
We didnt do it or what we did.

We werent really the one who deserved it. This is the money that rewards the artist.
A reference to a fake Cézanne that worried us.
If it really worried us, was it fake or worried us.

The Feeling of Language in Poetry

This is a locomotion we are feeling in an interior talking, a muscular arrangement in transpositions that is weights of lifting and letting falling and measures of going and retaining the how of our proceeding thru the spaces of the time from the moment we are moving ourselves word after word walking by words and syllables until the arrival pronounces the structure of how we have been moving. This makes a poem moving. The intervals of achievement, the accents of the failing in its being retrieved into achievement, the hesitations and following forward organized into the affection for our awkward it is clear or makes a grace over timing that criticizes its own alternatives.

And there is the sensation aroused in running the flaws, the pause in a refreshing if it is long enuf not to be returning upon itself, not to be running but to be casually going, aimless it is if it is this this a melody which is singing, the awareness of all that is moving that has departed from any intention. And there is the growing tension reserved to emerge from the aimless cloud drifting. This calls attention to where and there it is there where it is. Crowd all the words that were moving into a contradictory space, a treadmill, then a tower cracking up, then a jostling, word upon word backing up upon cracks, parks, anvils, down; parks, cars, irregulars, a long open field parted in a crooked style. Time to crawl over, or leap for a passionate surpassing, or clamber to give a sense of the obstacle.

The melodic strain is it the stream of the melody or the extreme organization that has disregarded the strain of its natural disorganizations. We do well as the clouds do in passing; we do awfully in conglomerations; we do wonderfully in all over tone grey overcast casting — this is a colorless monotone that could please. Whom could it please who as he is we are whom. A mysterious grey that does not yield meaning. Contentment in what we are doing is challenging, is breaking up and dividing attentions in its yielding so that continual changes in discontent and in remorse and in a terrible sadness can supercede in yielding. This is a vanquishd ease that we see as an appetite for perfection or a light that is darkening because it has been spread throughout its sentence. How to define a paragraph.

Defining is the impatience over its preceeding patient proceeding.

The way we are going in living, how we are arranging our selves in two eyes looking, or ears hearing, or lips and throat and tongue and teeth and lungs and nose spacing and breathing, when we are shifting our legs or tensing each every all fingers into two hands of a single writing: this is the we that excludes to our mind in its constant separating and returning, in its diversions and its focus, in its interior manyness, their effortful pretension of identity in purpose, in the which is ours tense one or easy communality of double and plural and unfolding and upspringing and rememberd and dismemberd participation in doing to project the sentence we are imparting.

We go back to our so called beginning calld the procedure of poetry into the simple poem in order to disrupt, or to unwind at the springtime the year for unexpected days, mirths, spots of days, weeks we will not notice, that deny seasons and reasons for the fragmentary revelation of our end that is ends in an abrupt containing its own future exhaustion as their eternal and inexhaustible partial pleasure over and over itself over their flowering outward from its petals and silvery pollens of sound into a rippling that goes outward without singleness to define its center. This is a scarf worn in many places with significant tears and holes.

Each one again, this is one of our ears that we cannot tell it is listening as the second is harkening or is it talking to a companion. An imaginary other ear which this one of our ears is hearing its common second duplication in communicating. Each one again, one ear against the other is lost in the coordination as we somehow or anyhow from we are hearing words we are not speaking but listening to. There is no one or two that is not upon closer considering barely contriving its surviving singleness or doubleness, scarcely a machine as it is falling apart into our awareness. This is the advice of thousands, the roar that we see to our delight is united in the words which conquer their sentence as their sentence conquers its words and it adjusts all its protesting in their consenting participants into their straightforward pretension at coherence.

This is why walking is wonderful. Walking is a wonder to our comprehension. A simple poetry seen at all is heard as it all, as us all: a communication. A communication is a working together thru meaning to understand until there is no meaning that is holding us together.

Poise: to know distances as falling altogether and this is enabling us to measure where we are going.

All men in their commonness repeat sufficiently the incoherent powers of each their own oneness and oneness and oneness almost sickening and disturbing and maddening in the real many particular forces within them in doing, repeat sufficiently the violent incoherence of all that is coherent among them to make a sentence thrilling in its simple locomotion. Speech built of parts that are coming one after another and untying each word itself from all others it is tied to so that the whole sentence is drifting apart from itself or running away from itself into their selves as words in meaning: this is thrilling in representing how we are actually existing in its conquering its own reality. A form. A form is the important disregarding of what is going on in order to go on at all. At all. At all is the conclusion that we were waiting for it be resting in. This is the arresting that is exciting as we call it exciting.

Start up in the night from your sleep if your single in your purpose and listen to yourself falling apart if you can or you wont in not remembering to an all or no one that will have a name in expanding and then come down your stares until you focus to see me clearly and tell me you know which one of my no faces I have on to draw a likeness so on that denies what we are saying. It is not I nor to me that you will be answering us as if we were one you all could by talking to to reassemble the train of your hopes for sinking into a mere dream or deep slumber over or under. How do you know me if you have an unfamiliar glance of our face or the painful revelation of a strange inarticulate we are slipping into for sleeping. This abyss is a hole that might be measured by the rip in the thread of a conversation it is enlarged on, but a look at the whole reveals a granny's or grampa's old tatterd existence that might be reduced from her original splendor to his residue grumpiness; their life looks different from what it is in the raw in the all over cloth we dream our or my wholeness by.

•

It is the death that drives us. The death in between the words or the words each as each death itself if the rushing is stopd and the spaces between are allowd in hearing

Sentences : Carrying Weights and Measures

What are the carrying changes he waits while he measures.
This one is apples or that ones are oranges.
An orange is to her remembrance four by four.
Whatever it costs me I'll buy me four.

More than we can take or remember taking.
Orpheus is an auto. Mary well is tomorrow.
Sing pied the merrywell mark well and leisure.
Leisure time turtles home or color for Friday.
Talk minds his reminding turn tables toss.
An ant is a partial appearance an at last a ready
    bubble which I read as bicycle.
He sells out is before we can buy in on them.

Angels take up room and so do candy.
But candy is perishable. It sickens us.
Changing easier than all dropping away from there.
A door. A door enters in here as a habit.
But a hero wears his out habit as a uniform.
Angels take up all uniform collections
so that heaven is paid for.

Who pays for it. Who helps us or contributes.
This is money before daughters, a line.
Follow the line and profit by the width of this course.
This is the winnings thru a discourse.
A continual habit.

.

There Could Be a Book Without Nations in Its Chapters

There could be a book without nations in its chapters.
    This would be portents that were portents of themselves. A constantly moving. This is as we ourselves are moving in coming and going, in sitting positions, knees crossd now, then legs wide apart planting their feet as our feet understanding.
    There could be a story without its end in its unfolding.

    This is on my mind. To stop even. Just as the rhythm. Just. In the divine outgrowing. To stop it. And restore the white vase. The separate flowers. These are flags. Our flags. One full, in papery lavender child and eager not yet full opening. One below, one above crumpling or and going limp, in wet purples and sagging from color. Two curld buds, tight fists patient before flinging open.

    A cat crossing the room. Stops. Rolls amorously. Eyes looking black in fullness. Narrowing. Rises. Licks paw. Lifts hind foot. Hugging leg over neck to lick, lick, lick like a dripping faucet the groin.

6/16/53

Included in *A Book of Resemblances*, retitled "Poetry Disarranged." See
    above.

6/22/53

This is a net, torn, thru which stars fall,
a largest residue —our wholeness, among leavings.

6/27:

Reality, for the artist, is no more than a subject
matter —a beastly head of hair.

Rewriting Byron

When the lady's face is full a platter width is armd as beauty is.
She floats. This is walking. In a picture late day is carnal and cookie
aroundness in shining.
Paint her as a door shaped for four benches the garden. Automobile
in lavender. Checkers and check her before she advances. Before her as
she advances is her advertisement.
Coming. Coming. Coming our attractions.
All the lights are up in her name and it spells M.A.M.I.E.
Mamie is a name worn by the month of May.
When she is thinner she's maybe coming to dinner.
A relaxation of ovals toward January over again.

A Morass

They arrived in clouds, belonging to future disassembling in
gathering. An allowance made for notices and notices for various
implied arrangements, sudden, lard, cards of advantage and common
cards which excite prayers. Players in circles. Her eyes I surmise
without adequate description.

Indian advances. Perturbations. Coils. Coils coil and coin in advent.
Adventure is a season. Silly in season is an island in a story.

Is there a story as you heard of as she says. She says advise four more.
In heaven there are rows of roses. Different colors give distinction
between petals and pedals. One is emotion, one is motion. We do not
shun a full expression; we allow every satisfaction its place in one face.
Face to face.

Let us begin with objects or lamps in powders door knob magicians
tables and tassels. An Egyptian cat in black, Thoth in black and Japanese
dancer. Matches. Glass as container. Desenex cures feet is powder in
can. Tacks the tassels. A stove and a bureau. The darkness in the lists is
an area we are not entirely passd into.

Love was an angular further in not overreaching that rests on the sill in stillness. Play the play in heaven.

Leaving heaven, heading for home A lovely party.

We were party to heaven as we were leaving. I would like to leave in a boat because it is intimately public. The only little house that floats is our salvation.

There must be a particular blue that mounts above the circumference of additional sorrows as salads in daily endeavors. Domestic fringes not afraid but in order to surprise from his dullness his other dandy lion other and other is sunlight. This is in large quantities. Always is both ways. There is no other ways there are waves of ways without wandering. It is a way in wandering following that leads about the room. I sit already prepared for death in leaving. I am left.

She passd herself out to all. This is; passd out cold. She had been seductive in her way to allow for seduction. Easy to get, easy to go, and I'll count out before we're thru. There are only two kinds of males, afraid to and afraid not to, she said. She was afraid so that she could find company so. Help me. Help me meant help me out in my design in contempt. This help was a hole that renderd her helpless: a role to fill.

Canvas Coming into Itsélf. For Jess

In the as sentence pasts parts disclose. Clothes pasts parting an inn that interests. Red ready before the part it plays. A form in parting darkens around the light part arising.

Comes comes into sight. Comes comes into the light. Comes comes frightening and delightening comas and come as. Comes as comes as Comus his combs coming in threads as brood in sight is seeing.

Takes place, takes its place in place of plain in taking as plays place to place.

Other brother. Here as we see her.

Her is a hard of sound in paint.

Comus his combs in coming arranged.

Arranged for a range of comas. Divisions of parts, whole in each inning. Inning or winning in an arrangement of combs in comas. Hair split arrangements.

The combd floating. Bird. Apron in weather. Shown here shown. Out here shown for in there sight over by her wrought in telling. By her in telling.

Combd floating in apron saves. Saves nine. Every time. In aprons of floating weathers the wines of a painting. Clots. Clouds. And a clamour. A clamorous vowels sounded.

Eventually to astound in standing. Opening. With draws his sign as signature. Combd allowd drawn silk or sulk in event.

Clouds of aprons, a dress drawn out. Are you associating? in there. Are you retracting? in there. Are you finishd.

The comb of floating opens into other shadows we accept in finish. A dress.

How Do You Know You Are Thru?

How do you know are you thru? Lakes contain water no answers or and sirs. How do you know thru there are you here now?

Lakes contain no answers in water and stir. As wind stirs answers in happy among top sides of pleasure.

No pleasure knows how it likes to a water.

A little movement when I am listening
begins in the sequence, a stir
   across words in a sentence
I am listening to faster than a little
   movies of still words in sequence
makes move move I meant in listening.

Now an owl. All eyes and wise
   as every rememberd his hymn
sets up a church of feathers
   there where he all owl and over

occupies one only limb as I limn it
closed about. By. Other wise.

All absolutely owl only.

A line springs catlike if to a chair
there. Where he lands.
A word: melodiously. He
as if a purr rumpling the words heard.
Folds. Curls. Relates.
Slip by slip of his comfiture.
Along the slow paces of a phrase.

Eery ears.

Increasing

Increasing the orange until arrangements of
animal forms are merged in tallow,
Increasing a grade until numbers sound as
tones alike in wandering,
Increasing knots until the orange current is
built perpetual upon the hectic,
Increasing the ocean is boxed in ties to
others and machines as mothers.

Road Piece

A car in sofa races to place first.
Speed piece. Speed piece. After. Speed piece.
Came continually cars in likelihood as ready turns and tipturns
returns to piece in around came to coming.
Cars coming to head. A race piece.
Make erase and raise in racing.

As sofa to soft fellow, auto to ought to, arrow to row as a row in coming.

Erase leading to roadway or follow away as a way to follow.

No one is following in racing.

Place first.

Car piece. Car piece as speed place in turns.

Rotund Religion

First the future. I second the future.
Miracles. Are wonders in words.
Soft and easy. Hard and difficult. Easy is hard.
Does soft come easy? No. Everyone knows
easy is difficult. A different cult.

It is not the sounding of words that tells.
It is not the ringing of door bells.
Tell her phone. She will not listen.
Tell her phone. Everything funny.

A round religion. Rings
round religion.

Lazy and eager. Tired tried.
Eyes suck scenes to try.
A view opens of lakes in lateness.
Blue lanes thru broad and blue.
Every true lie knows.
Position in history is true.

Three

I

    Do derive pleasure. Walls in rose.
    In is a word. In is a place.
    In us a word is a place.
    Do deride play insure us and plays.

II

    Thickening the letter to write as a nun.
    Innocence one.

    Smoking a burn in the lung rings true
    Innocence two.

    Breaking the half is four cloth over.
    Innocence three.

    Incense for three to win won.

III

    Can you design a passionate poem to fit the page?
    A fit on this page.

Several Poems. In Prose.

Does this mean a meaning?

    •

After Shakespear there was pleasure in prose.

    •

Shake : spear, spare or peer Il y a pas de père. who is his peer. This pair.

    •

Is there in an imitation any intimation?
Of who wrote it. Of what right hand the
hand left knows as doing?

•

Can you derive pleasure?

•

What counts as counting?

•

If you cannot see through it, can you see through it?

•

I mean by means of it.

•

The purr in purpose. The F in effort.

•

Dollars attach by affection will to wont. Poor poetry is wanting in
images, aint is original, straining after effect, craven before inspection.
Poor poetry! Poor impure poetry.

•

The words I entertain are not my own. Do I propose to own them as
I propose them?

•

Lessen them in listening.

•

Did Stein do wright the way she did write?

LOAD YOUR AUTOMATIC POETRY BEFORE ITS BEGUN

Rings

Rings. Encirclements of outcry. A silent band. That makes his
audience uneasy.
Out: land, house, cry; side, man. Outriders.
She wrings out his shirk and hangs him to drive.

The poems of correspondents reappear as outleafings of. Where there
are rings of trees a forest appears. Wood whistlings and storms of green
contagion spread: The ayre denser there. And these men are calld
woodsmen; subservient to the element: wood.

Syllables

Make a donkey park to arrest. Four four. Making a donkey park to
arrest him. Remake or donkey a park to arrest. Park make a donkey or
the rest. The feel of the make, a park or a rest. Make king donkey park
or our rest. Four and four.

Three or three. Out of ease into these. Out of ease in two of these. It is
possible that more than three count as three.
Five count as three is in two threes. Operate. Man or date.
Man or drake. Change for fives. Change into these. Threes.
Can count syllables or words. Three words out. Into two.
As three. With a stop two more is three. One two three.

Easily. More than four.
One by one.

The whole field is for all of these men. For of and men can be counted
again. The is for me. What stands for itself in a sentence can go. So

a sentence can go. Threes against threes. Constantly. Threes within threes. Precisely. As a key. Makes it run. Count by words loses syllables are lost. Numbers make three? How many? Three numbers make four. Four within five.

Stuff Ark Mower Bottle

Stuff ark mower bottle. A ham string. Letting words stuff ark as more battle. As a stuffed hark. Olympic bier. At stops for writing. Stuff art mar bottle. Ham string.

A floods of forty. And Noah's art. A both unseen when angels part the waves from waves. Four found tens are forty dies. Where forty dies the ark survives.

In moyles of Rome home ark lights home. An only herd for answer comes.

In doors. All out of doors. He treads the light fantastic. The grades of wrath float out of doors. Measured in doors. He dreads the lie it is and sticks. A door sticks. As we adore it.

His style is sweet to eat. Pictures as more pleasures. Measure pleasures. To fit you are size. Size grows. The size of my graph. In creases. Or. In roads. Makes in roads of pleasure to be sweet.

Another Ido

Another ido. Cross eyes. Amiable cross eyes.
Densities change particular designs.
Sobre las olas de calor. A mother changes.
Her habit to walking and parasol.
Summer verano summer verano summer verano.
Using words from what we heard.
A little frog is a rano pequeño.

•

A Birthday Dirge for Lynne Brown

A birthday dirge is a suit for everybody.
April thirteenth and fourteenth for dirges and birthdays.

This is for sorry and answering.
Or schools for owls when they are little.
This owls whistle.

A dirge. This is country. This is a stable party.
This is everybodys willing if they are not worrying.

Problems. Oranges. A suit in colors and answers.
A table with birds shuffling. A slow a slander
probably or tomorrow.

April thirteen and fourteen or is a suit clean in trouble.
Trouble is an owl in the teapot.
She found the teapot empty. This was Thursday.
Which is a poor day without a future in banking.

If it is running out, why not run out.
A birthday running out of Thursday and whistling for water.

Sorry owls. Sorry. I'm sorry owls. Its Thursday.

Uncollected Work 1952–1956

. . .

Whose this liddl boob coming?
His head is full of. I wonder.
He's good to his mummy case his dada's derivative.
The cost of his addlecation will be prohibitive.
All the boys wrote home from the war.
The great Panjandrum enterd the Moon.
Whose that coming this way so soon?
Adam Boob? The man we have got to.
Adore. With the parentathetical claws.
He's the newd sentence coming to his period
or semi-colon.

Enter Poor Boob his wits at an end.

: whoa. I've been wandering about in the storm.
I've been wandering about of the storeroom.
Where our memories are deep freeze frozen.
Now they are revising hysteria.
Where are our memories now that we freeze.
I've been storming about or the winter.
Who thot now a cold could be a winner.

* Enter a General and a Pandemonium

Poor Boob: O O O O O O O O O
How far do I go to the end of the next war?

* Exit a General and a Pandemonium

This is what a mother told me what for.
I am only Adam Boob and all of you are wise.
I can tell. By the cunning in your eyes.

Wherever the trouble goes, it is all over.

look at the poor king leer —
    he's got the world in his haid.

Walking on Kearny Street

Held back. Head on. Let go. Collision.
Bail bonds. Service the surface.
Hat works. The boss that counts.
One two three.
Money back backd by money.
Tune in on the right widow.
A divorce from the window.
A sign. A signal. A right hand turn.
He got a Mexican decree
if she will degree. Bail bands.
The ties that bind you.
Belly bonds. Texas right way.
Right of way. Lunch for lunch.
War for Sunday. Adam. Away.
Bombs for excitement.
In agreement. Pieces
of eight children.
     Out of the music box.

Uncollected Stein Imitations

From the Period of *Writing Writing* (1953)

The King: A Regret

In fourteen and he for a foreigner came to the continent a christian, a queen and he fifty to crown the last, the least of them, the design he desired she. And he three. Forces of farmers came. Commerce was at ocean and Saint Mole, the good Albert, the board that laid sorrow on the land. The great open and fourteen. Points I mean to the ages we remember.

Here there were legions prepared. There there were plays on the board and actors to board. It was filld up with a learning he came across to bleeding. All were amazed. Night and day several ordinary became outraged. Books and packages across were to barbarians. All south of France was ruins for troubadours.

This was at Arles. And an axe the bold king orderd to last. Until a treaty. He resignd.

She was the was she intended. To England. To Audincourt. To show rackets and mockingbirds. To betray the elders.

An army of pretenders. Hidden behind the rocks there. At it came to a pass there, where he was captured.

We cannot we estimate. But songs paintings and machines of war were developd. Every band of yesterdays continuing continued to band together. Not sage. But better, the bishop said safe than sorry.

There were to many ports left open.

The King lookd toward Africa.

There is a law in history that limits looking.

The King lookd toward Africa.

This was the first time he regarded. In a country foreign to his at least for his history. Acting was not developed without losses of power for the history concernd.

Cloudy

Passages in time or clouds as in passing. Clouds as in a Tiepolo scene.
Clouds in tableau, a *table-d'hote* pass ring.
A skirt. A scatterd. Magic. In scattering. Scatter, a ring of clouds
about a scant, cloud as a scatter.
Pose a soft center solid in visibility. Dense it delivers itself out of its
pose. A position in drifting.

Swift cloud sails westward solid and soild.
Swift westward silently sails. This is running across the sky without
rearranging itself.

As a tree blows in cloudy skirts and rustles.

Passion, a time of swift indecisions, a milk lets us see the containing
glass, drops on the table show soils of the time. Passing the time its
indecisions.

A New Version of *Heavenly City Earthly City*

A beautiful bright I saw inside outside. A light enlightening.
As fire. Talking in order to burn, burning in order to
Walk there, walking in order to order there, ordering
In order to order expiring. I saw always desiring as bright.
I saw a full coming always as bright desiring.

Imaginary Letter

dear Son,

I have been waiting every day for a letter from you or a card to tell me
you are all right. But then I know you are very busy at school. Things go
on at home just like always. Dad is very busy, he's downtown everyday

now to see Mr. Goldwatch and next week he's going to Chicago with
Lew and Abner Gates to see about contracts for the new year. I dont
know why you dont write. If its anything wrong you know I will always
understand sonny only I want to know what it is. Did you get the money
all right I sent you? Mrs. Patch was over last week and we went to the
movies to see Desire Me Forever. It was very good. Did you see it? My
the days are so short now, they are just all gone and I barely had time
to put up the usual stock of jam. I'll send some soon only right darling
and tell me if you want some. I never really know if you do or maybe
you havent any place to keep things like that. Helen Marigold wrote and
said she saw you when she was in Evanstown. How nice. But it will be
Thanksgiving soon and how wonderful it will be to have you back home
with us. Write and tell me if there is anything you need me to send you.

Love,

Mother

Young Men

Renewals of feeling.

In weather a thermometer costs and relaxes accidents. Julian arranges.
He did not like poetry. To listen to. Him reading. He preferrd seeing.
Him as he is. Julian arranges. He is preferrd and seeing. What would he
say if he was not interested. He was not interested but good looking.

Feeling as far as his outline permitted. The window reflected his powers
of reflection. A concentrated image.

This was an image they did not have. But it was they could see.
Not theirs. Entirely.
His outline.

Patience proscribed costs and accidents to happen.
He was his own insurance. A mutual policy.

How did it work. He askd how did you do it.
How could it be arranged. So as to be preferred.
By the new rules.

He said you couldnt but it must agrees.
I means it dont agree the subject without
And verbs matches. He said it must agree.
With him as he is ruled. Outlined and
permitted.

Sensational News

October the third. She was all. She was bloody there was a they said
shot bloody neck eyes a man who. In the rear. Very dark. Importantly
consequent said able scientist world wide.

World wide inside. I shot her. Here. October and a third. Three mil-
lion four hundred and more dollars and voters. Killd. Everywhere. She
sued for.

I came into the room and started. There was no content but blood
everywhere she said. I refused to vote and divorce.

When the light came. It came into her brain and caused four hundred
and eighty two million pain and results.

There was a result sex every day until it exploded. Three children and
blind until they cut it out for election. The mark on her forehead was
poisonous to all concernd.

The scientist said the price of bread was making us it says mad every-
where. Germany and Australia will not for the three children until 1982.

This was the Pope in a field. He held his tiara responsible for his
forehead:

Art, he announced, is bad for the piece of a church to shoot. It is a
pity and misery where anybody shoots such a good she was to become a
man he is.

Entirely alterd, until the conversion, the reversion of the jews which
makes dollars to oil and a trace in the october third turn the meat dark.

This is sensational news.

She was so bloody the radio in the park who allowd her. Children screamd and the automobile her debt to his in doubt judged Italy and winner. For three days police police three days. As a result it was sex the Pope saw in art as revision. In revising October third. A murder of the "third sex" produced three children who sang on the radio.

In Italy no one who Germany thirty thousand and four money in turn to remember Versailles.
He was arrested before starting. After arrest he started.

Entirely alterd the new Pope's
art palace includes automobiles
children bloody dollars and truces.
This has distressed the landladies of Versailles
from their trousseaus. Why.

In the church it was so dark the blood
showd to the scientist.
Entirely cured in three days.
October the third.

Headlines:

MAKE ALTER WIDOW TO WINDOW

BLOOD PARK RADIO DINNER

POPE SAYS ITALY SEX POLICE

THIRTY THIRTY THOUSAND DIRTY

ITALY SAYS SCIENTIST SEX POPE

DIRTY ALTER POST SAYS WIDOW

BLOOD MAKE WINDOW THIRTY POLICE

PARK TO WINDOW THIRTY POPE DIRTY

Reserve Moon Handle Maker and Wing

Reserve moon and handle. And reserve moon handle and moon to wing and handle. Reserve moon in handle and a holiday handle in window and reserve.

A reserve moon. A reserve and moon handle. A reserve and handle moon and to wing moon handle. Reserve and in handle moon a holiday handle in window moon reserve. A reserve and. A reserve moon and a handle.

Light the handle to moon window and wing. A alight and wing in handle. A moon a-wing a light to window holiday and handle.

How and and how to and and handle and as moon in handle. The moon in handle.

This is a candle set for a holiday to address the moon in reserve made visible.

At the Bakery — The Cannibalistic Cookie-People
A Study of Pronouns in Reference

Far below it is late at night and it is quite warm in there where they are busy making and baking cookie people. They are sweet and with powderd floury faces and cheery hungry busy expressions. They are all warm and while they are waiting for them to cool off after all the hot busy work over the ovens they eat them one by one until
there is
no one of them left.

•

Aubade

A giant of the whole day is awakeness.
A giant of the whole night is sleeping.
To be a universe! to be a universe!
wrapt in its continually speaking.
To be returnd to dreaming.

When I imagine myself as lover
— love is here again, here, I say.
Coming forth by Day once more
from all mere longing, belonging
in saying.
          The morning turns
quiet as words speaking,
A soliloquy of audible silence.

A soliloquy! a soliloquy!
Such idle talking in different colored lights, in sleights
of imagined person, in person.
The great Panjandrum rolls his eternal being like a drum roll
over the measures of disorderd sleep.
Disorderd speech.

Elegy
Written
4·7·53
for
Jack Spicer

In the wizard text of his mind
all the giant forms, colossal virtues, from their sexual paradise have
    been sunderd and renderd perfect by their no longer growing,
are going toward death, haltingly,
dwindled and nearly human images, were it not
for their perfection, manikins grotesque

as a crowd of angels jostling each other to see
each his own reflection among the others
in a single hand mirror. This is, by extention
   along the line of an obvious association
   which introduces the contradictory, a
   multitude of moonish mirrors in which appears

to the peering faces of a multitude of mermaids
the displaced faces peering of the multitude.
It is in their contradictions that the images
exactly resemble the words of the text . . .
and figure to the imagination appropriate shapes,
the genesis and deuteronomy of his mind.
He himself is a tabula rasa upon which
daily he scribbles the same
   torah, laws, chronicles and pother
   in which panther and lamb lie down together,
   a veritable book of friendships. O why an elegy?

Has he died then or disappeard? Was he so dear
in his mere identification?
It is when we try to view him, inventing disguises
to illustrate this protestant, that
something trifling of angels or giants
or mermaids or pigmy eternities is produced.
What if we have grown tired of the idea of him?
This is the very elegy, the age-old repeated
terror. We have seen the tiresome poem
increasing until the women weeping
are weeping now for the one himself we were searching for—
they are so tired they are weeping,
and their faces repeated are repeated
everywhere, that is, among the angels.
And only their faces, the women
seen with dark hair streaming in an old fashion,
remain. He is gone. Utterly gone.
Nothing of his perplext wizardry is there.
Nothing of his immortal body remains with us.

Let us review him again as a book
—a fictional or non-fictional representation
he has invented for us to study out.
Live therein, he offers, or read therein
the text I may live in your reading of me,
real or unreal, a passage surviving its reality,
known by heart. But he has askt us
to read him to death, death, to his death
as, enraged, we have discovered, in reading
he would make a place for his having died in us.
This is the holocaust, the analysis he makes in our
reaching him, tearing and ripping
reliques, images from images,
chapters from chapters, true parts
from true parts of an untrue structure.
An untruth! a dear lie! an
entirely lost counsel of these perfections.
Why, there were no perfections there!
Nothing remains but his scholastic ghost
laps at the troughs of our bloody affections.

          •

He has been de-friended to become
this friend of a poetry, wingd as he never was,
increased from all veritable fragmentary acquaintance
into this singular third person invention,
the jokester's monotheistic mind picturing
himself as a poet unbuilt in man's image.

Look now, we are making him up, our Adam
of the languagers. Look, before we go
shaking him down again into his particulars.
Or put it so: we, the conspiracy of all me,
have crawld from our worm
into the surety of our cocoon—this
cocoon is the poem spun round about by instinct;
but the poem is the wingd proceeding,
the night ephemera of himself as he
admires himself.

There must be a bitter revelation,
a so-what? of the great critic himself,
an unseasond season.

•

And what is he? perpetuated
only in movement. He is moving . . .

All of these, continually perishing, come
from life in his form, an articulation,
and die away from his form. It is
a shell, an idea, a futility
inexpertly asserted—he lives in his argument—
he loses, loses. How he has alterd
with the moment! And I thought there was genius!
Do not think there aint sheer genius
in his personage, whining
against time. But genius
    despises the achieved. His genius
    hides from him. In the changes of exalted spirit
    he persists as an unwilling cliché.
It is impossible to address him without restoring
his immortal ghost, he has never known
nor we knew in him. An Elegy.
A lament. A prolongd accusation against him
of all he has refused evokes
what he is not to us, a contrivance,
tall as he is a sign-post of what's coming,
severe as he is a bird-braind oracle,
scary as he is a man hidden in armor,
electric as he is a revolver in an invisible hand,
intolerant as he is a kitchen stove.

Steering down the channels of perpetual vision
we saw what he was not and then
we saw him no longer. A lament.

The Green Lady

My Lady rode out from her green house
and her eye in the bright of noon
was bright with another light than the sun's
distilled from a green as the green sap runs,
dark of the earth, fire of the air,
brightness of May, green of the leaf.
My Lady rode out in the fields of noon
to claim the Adam as her own.

To claim the Adam as her own she rode
upon his wedding day.
His Mother heard the horns of May
like jackdaws in a bright peach tree.
She saw in her loved son's sleeping eye,
like fruit of the garden into which we die,
the dreams of the night that were so bright
the dreams of the light of day.

My son, my son, the good dame said:
Think of your dear heart's bride
that our good Lord to please you by
took from out of your side.
The other world, all green and gold,
shone in her poor son's eye.

Dear Christ upon Grief's holy tree
gave the body of this world to thee.
To save this world from that other world
he took the cross upon his back
and he was born and died.
She laid his wedding clothes out black
upon the white white bed.
She laid her fond light hand upon
his heavy head.

Across the fields between two worlds
the fairy hosts of day
went out like streams in the moving grass
where no true breezes were.
The rivery green of the bright spring wheat
waved in the still still air.

I hear another world, poor Adam said:
Another world I see!
The flesh of this world is dark today.
The joys of my heart pass away
like a host of folk that through the grass
appear to be poppies to this world's eye.

All lightness they are, of another air,
like childhood's joy they pass,
the poppy fires in the green field's hair,
the sunlit ghosts of the month of May!

The church bells rang their loud alarm
against the brightnesses of day.
Adam and his true bride went within
the Church that would undo Great Sin.
The holy sacrament of life and death
guarded the concourses of their breath.

The holy vows like angels stood
to guard the doors of their hot blood.
The bands upon their fingers bright
shone like lanterns for the night.
This Wedding will undo Great Sin!
the bells rang out to the still of day.
The groom and bride were wed within.

The Lady rode to her green house,
bright as noon her eye.
And with her rode like a ghost of noon
immortal Adam, green as the leaf,
red as the flower bright with sleep.

Two Adams there were where our Lady smiled.
One by his bride stood, and one grown wild
rode by Our Lady's side, his tearless eye
a green green joy in the world that can not die,
his broken heart a bright peach tree
in that false wood that can not grieve,
his double soul like the air on fire
in that false garden burned for her,

Our Lady of Green Desire.

The Fear That Precedes...

The fear that precedes changes of heaven
opens its scenes;   petal by petal   longing
a flower opens;   its seeds   needs
long unacknowledged,   urgencies
as if grown over-night.   These
voyages toward which we find ourselves,
unbelieving,   proceeding.   Passage
as if of death   unfamiliar.
Coasts wrapt in unrealized light   right
directions beyond belief where
desire moves us.   O real mere islands,
new lands,   bear with me,   allow
    for the heart's turning.

Poems from the Limited Edition of *Caesar's Gate*

Circulating Lights

Well, how very well! An eye opens with water flowing over rim of cup, fountains of what is seen. And the depths of the eye lie in the darkest pulpy machineries of brain. Convolutions of well being from which tears rise.

In the distance we see all our vacations, near to us. In the foreground, an untranslatable key. This is the healing out of sleep, the Book that Writes trees, lakes, mountains, vistas of sun and moon, natural letters to the illiterate deep. Writes well.

Source Magic

Recesses of light are fire first.
This light casts the world's darkness like a flower casting its seed. This roar of flame is son, sun of night's little universe. By photosynthesis the plants — shadowy demons — make their green.
The lord of this world coils in the first spurt, licks the fastnesses of being like a candle flame licking the borders of untamed night.
I am the light of the fire.
And below his triumphal figure the globe of green things hums with inspiration.

Presence

In this poem especially we are conscious of the poet, an aggrieved inhabitant of the body of the verse. He fills it at times like a shadow consuming a room, or broods over it as a single flower in a great vase casts its spell over a hall. Nowhere is there a trace of his actual speech, nor can we relate the architectures of this monument to his autobiography. Impersonal, meglomaniac, uninteresting — yes. We do not know, he is so subtly here, how to avoid him. The poem is gone, and takes with it this giant taint — which never having understood we can never forget.

Shadows of the Smoke

In Time in those gardens wraiths descend. Infestations of restless desire. Corruptions, abstract and sentimental, of the clear images.

What intimations of a real poetry conveyed by conjunctions of those presences — flowers, stars, sheets of water, beautiful women, engraved letters — in time. Outline upon outline. Lineaments cut in the stone.

Now clouds of the cloudy eye.

Exhalations of the earth ascend as if there were necessary ladders, hairy aspirations toward the atmosphere.

Gliding hallucinations, thrones, wheels, seraphim, appear from all vague passages. From the hierarchies of our solitude.

Consolations of Philosophy

The Princess from Idaho hears in the avenues of yellow light
melodies that recall freights of loneliness, far away barbaric shuttlings.
Weary of greens, her dusty gardens extend from Italy to Italy of
her thoughts. Roses of her weariness fill the hot afternoon with their
aroma.
Slowly I climb, indefatigable tourist, the interminable flights of stairs
that lead upward from her image to whom she is. An excess of fancy!
What have I to say?
Her eyes, as I gaze into them, remain unperturbd.
It is as if her many lovers had never existed.

Tra^{ns}versals of the Church

In the tracks of the radiance conductor, wheels within wheels of
loneliness advance. The interior authority lets the design waver if it
will; the artist projects graphs of the rings.
These are marriage rings, circles of time spreading out from the
disturbd center. Which measured exactly within .0005 of a degree
appears upon the new custom gage. To designate the vehicle a sign
is erected; to keep track of the time a weight is used, sensitive to
variations of temperature.
A noise like an excited animal crosses the watersheds of solitude.

SHOW The crowds of her hair grow the grass green, whose shrowds are of air know the great queen let down the green let down the green	CROWN Hurry the world is catching whose fire, Hurry the wind, Hurry the winter, it will all burn a way it will all burn a way

LOVE
The birds fly up into
   the sight,
the birds fly up
   into the sight,
     the birds
fly up into the sight,
the birds fly up into
   the sight,
the birds fly up into
   the sight,
the birds fly up
	I am
	unable to see, O my
	beloved! where was
	I from, where I will
	to? What do the
	caves tell me that
	I do not know in
	my bones? The unease
	of my body, as if I
	become what I
	   remember . . .

into the sight
TIME
The thrones sleep in the
   form of hours
the years like mountains
   throw up their dead,
       AGAIN
	DANCE
	Beloved moon,
	   among your bears,
	whose gleam
	by day
	the green leaf wears,

To the Stairwell.

In the invasion of the green, to the stairwell. Eyes in their unremitting regard are like a host — angelic, armed, a-glitter. With rays. A glance upward pierces. From which the great blood flows into green.

He whom you meet on the stares. Who passes. This one passes out into an atmosphere. Leafing notes of grinning, with verdant bows, he passes. Sweet slip. As a bird pauses.

Mr. Escalier is his disguise.

The whole woman of the woods shivers and contracts herself from the huntsman she dreamt she was.

•

Spanish Lessons

Range right ovary habit. Have it.
Orange aright a very hard bit.
I did not hear you there. Did I
       hear you there?
A bocadillo is a little bite. Mouths are bocas.
       Moths are pollilas.
Everywhere mosquitos are there.
       In verano. Es en verano.
Heat herd calor for color.
       Hace mucho color. De rojo?
       Tostado?
Interest. Ing. An interest. Ing.
   Ing. Ing.

Alteration

          A boat
—with the interim of a line cut adrift from
   habitual
rights and wrongs   reaches
   the other side;

or an avenue cut thru medieval and renaissance distances
       thru the heart of the city
      for a new statement

     be it
  imperial
  vulgarity

or to open an artery for modern traffic;

     the hand
reaching to restrain breaks a restraint.

     An act
to break from the dry rock daily psychodrama,
     a spring
Spring demands. Tear down whatever accustomd
    palace
in Venice's Grand Canal for Frank Lloyd Wright
    to build
beauty anew.

It is the gesture, true to its moment,
that holds beauty intact, in the act—
    the rest
—building, contract, poem—

  is a ruin in its wake.

The Cat and the Blackbird

1967

Chapter 1
The Cat and the Blackbird

There was once a cat who lived in the very center of himself which was a stormy rainy night in a big forest. The cat himself with his yellowy mellow eyes thought of himself as a little house, a cheer in the hearts of all travelers, a warm shelter in the midst of the cold.

He lived all alone and constantly prepared the little cottage for visitors. Every two days a young man came from the village at the edge of the forest and left two quarts of milk. One quart the cat drank on the first day, a repeated renewal of the pleasant freshness of drinking milk. The other quart he poured into a large bowl and set out on the table to curdle so that on the second day he would have the custardy curds to eat.

Sometimes visitors did come, a little girl who gatherd twigs and branches in the forest to lay in a supply of fuel for the winter, an elusive hermit who arrived only to look as if he were going, a soldier passing, a large square blackbird who told tales of his wickedness when he was younger, a famous novelist who was on his way to Kingstown.

Then the cat gatherd mushrooms which he cookd in a pot and served to his guests with small bowls of curds and a nice pot of hot tea, brewd from strawberry leaves.

One day the blackbird who had never lived in a house before being as he said a traveling bird. A tree is good enuf for me, he said. Wherever I land, he said. One day the blackbird askd the cat if he could stay. He was growing old, he said, and he had never had a warm inside cottage life. Except for visiting, he said. The blackbird was secretly very lonely and wanted company so that he could tell stories about his younger days. So they might, he said, set up house together.

And take a trip first, the cat said gladly. I have never been on a real trip, a vacation. I want to go to see the honey moon.

So the blackbird and the cat set out on a journey to the honey moon. And then after that back, they said.

The cat packd a package of strawberry leaves and put all his milk up in a jar of fresh curds. They turnd out the lights and set out in the forest to find the road.

At the village they stoppd and saw the young milk man who said he was very sorry that the cat was leaving because he was his very best customer but he was very glad that they were coming back later and there would be more milk to leave at the cottage than ever.

Where is the honey moon? the young man askd.

That we don't know, the cat and the blackbird replied. It makes it more fun to be going when we don't know when we'll get there.

The honey moon is round and fat.
It floats in a river of song like that.
It's round and shaped
exactly like that. Like a hat.
Like a golden round magical
     musical hat.

Chapter 2

The cat and the blackbird were having a fine time walking by the shore of a river which they made up in sunny cloudy weather which they pretended too. When there. Right there they came upon the little farm very real and they did not make it up at all. Where the little girl lived who gathered firewood in the forest.

It was a very little farm with only three fruit trees, an apricot tree, a pear tree, and a twisted old apple tree. With a kitchen garden in which tomatoes, potatoes, squash and string beans grew, and a shed with goats, and a hutch with rabbits, and a big packing box with chickens that laid eggs.

O hello there, the little girl said from where she was sitting in the apple tree. Where are you going?

The cat and the blackbird stoppd and removing their hats. The cat had a big straw hat with a red band around it. The blackbird had a skinny blue felt hat that bent over itself it was so tall. O, they said bowing. We have come visiting on our way to the honey moon. Do you know where it is at?

We don't really want you to tell us, they told the girl when they were all seated at supper. It will be more fun to find out for ourselves.

But let me, the little girl's father said, tell you a story first. You'll want to know before you go the song of the honeymoon bees and that's the story.

The song of the honey moon bees is sweet
and a long a song that's good to eat,
an easterish humming sort of beecoming
when eating is hearing and hearing is nearing
as good to eat as a song is sweet.

THE HONEY MOON BEES AND
THE BUSY MAN'S GARDEN

Once upon a time there was a busy man who had a garden which took all his time. He was up at four and in bed at ten, all day long tending and weeding, planting and seeding, watering and keeping his garden neat, picking the green bugs off of each leaf and pruning the new shoots to improve every twig, every branch, every leafy lively vegetable and every climbing designing vine and every beautiful special flower in his yard.

He had hedges to trim and in the bright sun workd all day cutting every stray scratching twig away and constantly restoring the beautiful shaped planed surfaces of hedgy green. He had hedges in box shapes and round ball shapes and he had splendid big hedges taller than he was that made walls and he had great green animals neatly trimmd shaped hedges, a peacock, a lion, a dove and a pyramid.

He had rows of perfect rose bushes that were like bouquets on the tops of regular trunks, and he had red and pink and yellow roses on four feet long stems. He had briar roses and wood roses and night roses and tear roses.

He had tulips, even in every season, of every hue.

He was up at four and at work all the long days and the shorter days too, spraying his garden or making little ditches where streams of water ran or arranging rocks to make attractive grottos, setting out new little plants or taking in delicate plants before the cold weather.

Now you see that it was really his garden that kept the busy man busy. It was in fact the wonderful garden of the busy man's busyness.

The busy man was always sending away for new plants. He had catalogs and he sat up in bed busy checking them over and writing away for rare flowers and all sorts of leafy, twiggy, green things he had never heard of before. So one day he saw an ad for a moon bean. And he sent off immediately a wire for some seeds. And so it happend that he planted a bed, at a far corner of the garden, of moon beans.

He waterd them carefully, he prepared their bed with leaf mould and all kinds of fertilizer. He waited and waited. But nothing happend. The busy man wanted more and more to see what his moon beans would look like. There had been no picture in the catalog, you see, and he was very excited, and then he was very eager and wondering what the moon beans would look like, and then he was worried when nothing happend and grew, and then he was unhappy. Then he was always wishing and at last, one day, he thot only of his moon bean garden.

The roses and the hedges, the tulips and chrysanthemums were neglected. The grass began to grow up wherever it wanted to and the borders all became unruly.

The busy man thot only of his moon bean garden. It seemd to him that it was at last the very important thing he had been busy for. One day then as he sat longing and despairing and not giving up, he started to cry.

He cried and he cried then. O my moon beans my moon beans, he wept and the tears fell all around him where he sat.

Wherever his tears fell a tiny blue sprout showd, like a tear starting at the corner of an eye, and ran out in tendrils of silver and yellow all over the patch like tears running out over a cheek. He did not see them at first. He was so busy weeping. When he finally took out his handkerchief and dried his eyes, there all about him growing and sprouting were hundreds of moon beans.

He was overjoyd. He sat and he sat watching them grow and as they grew he began to hear a far away faint singing. The singing was the moonlight but he could not see by it he was hearing by it. He was hearing more of it. The moon beans were singing not growing. They were buzzing and humming. The ground was alive with them, with golden rustling seeds that were really bees.

The man did not go in for dinner that night. It was so wonderful sitting in the far corner of the garden. All of his busyness anyway had gone into the bees, you see. He had cried and cried and lost all sense of being busy. Now he was content to sit and listen.

He was beginning by listening to their song to see very clearly. It was the dark of the moon, a very dark night. But the moon bees were a moving humming lantern in the garden.

He saw by their light the hedges that were growing every which way so that he could hardly see the peacock for the wild hedge it was, he could hardly see the lion in his hedge. And all the new shapes seemd wonderful to him. He saw the roses scraggly and thorny and unkempt, shedding their petals all over the ground. And O O O, the little bugs and the pale yellow slugs everywhere. Snail trails of silvery moon webs glistend in the lamplight.

All my garden is wildly ruind, he exclaimd with joy. How wonderfully strange it has grown.

And as he saw the whole garden by the magical moon bean lantern, the whole flock of moon bees swarmd and rose, singing and drunk with their own singing, and flew up up up up up up into the far away black night, up into the sky to the moon, filling it to fullness, to the full round moon lantern shining down upon the happy man in his unruly garden.

So, said the father of the little girl, when you come to the honey moon, you will find it round and full like a hive with the honey moon bees.

Chapter 3
Susan's Story

The little girl's name was Susan. She was not old enuf to be reading the story all for herself but she was old enuf to be hearing the story all the way thru.

The woods where the cat lived was not far away. Her father who workd in a store in the town liked to go walking when he came home to their house which was the little farm almost at the edge of the woods. And Susan went walking with him, talking about every thing they saw, the birds — there were robins and blackbirds, the blackbird was one of them, and finches that were almost canaries but not really, and humming birds that didn't humm exactly like bees but like humming birds.

One day when she was walking with her father and helping him gather up twigs and branches for kindling at home, they came along a little path and saw thru the trees a little house in the woods. It was a big house really, a regular-sized house, but it lookd like a play house.

Who lives there? she askd her father.

A cat lives there.

She lookd and she saw the cat who was asleep on his table, sitting beside his bowl of curds.

Doesn't anyone else live there? she laughd.

I've never seen anyone else but the cat, her father said.

The little girl went up to the cat who woke up and purrd when she stroked his head. The cat was so pleased that all he could do was purr. He was too pleased for words.

The little girl, that was Susan, went back along the path with her father then, glancing back from time to time for a last glimpse of the little house and the cat who had been so nice to her.

Can I visit the cat again? she askd her father.

I think so, if he wants you to, her father replied.

She knew that the cat did. He had purrd like that. Really too pleased for words.

It's not very far, her father said, I think it would be all right for you to come here sometimes and visit the cat.

That was how the little girl had come to visit the cat and to find out after all that he did live in the house by himself and he had visitors and he liked to talk about everything he had been doing.

Susan was old enuf to hear the story all the way thru but she could remember when sometimes she too had been too pleased for words. She could remember when all the kinds of talking were not really words, when one was always just finding out words, just seeing them or rather hearing them like beginning to find out about blackbirds and robins and finches and sparrows. Before that they were only birds.

Long before she could remember but she could almost remember, her mother and her father and she had always been talking, but it was never then like even beginning the story we are telling all the way thru. It was not in words but it was really talking to each other, telling each other everything all the time.

And this was really, wasn't it, the kind of talking she did when she visited the cat.

Yes, that's exactly it, the cat said. Have another helping of curds.

So she was not surprised at all when the cat came along the road to visit *her,* and she was not surprised when the blackbird was coming along with him. She was not surprised either when they bowed and removed their hats like that.

O hello there, she said.

And they, you remember, said they were on their way to the honey moon.

The little girl was not going to be surprised at all that her father and her mother would like talking with the cat. She and her mother and her father had always been telling each other everything. So they really already knew all about the cat and visiting the cat and talking with the cat about everything.

And she was right. They all sat down to dinner.

Her mother was delighted with her friends. She made some special sandwiches for the travelers to take with them the next day and she gave them a little bed in the corner where there was a bay window. With clean white sheets and a gayly checkerd comforter. She showd them where to wash up and found a small blue towel for the cat who washd his face and paws carefully, and a small lavender towel for the blackbird who dabbd at his face. He was always in too much of a hurry with washing.

Susan did not know anything about the honey moon but she was not surprised when her father knew all about it and told the story about the honey moon bees and the busy man's garden.

And then it was bedtime. She kissd everybody goodnight. The cat and even the blackbird. (It is funny kissing somebody with a bird face.) Her father and then especially her mother, who took her off to her bed and tuckd her in to dream.

Chapter 4
Dreaming

There are many unpleasant things about going to bed before everybody else. And when there are visitors nobody ever wants to go to bed at all. But the cat and the blackbird, tho they were grown up, were not even as old as Susan was. Cats, even big grown up cats, are often not older really than little girls. And the blackbird wasn't so old either. He had been a naughty blackbird, and then an adventuresome blackbird, and then very much a blackbird of the world, but all of this was in his very first year or so. That was all the time he spent recklessly before he grew lonely. It took Susan two years almost just to be a baby.

So the cat and the blackbird were going to bed early too. And Susan's mother and father sat in the kitchen talking and having another cup of coffee or maybe just sitting and reading or sewing, listening to music on the radio, that was still talking. And if sitting and sewing and reading, or listening to music, or looking about is really talking and keeping company then Susan knew that going to bed was still talking and being there.

So there were all kinds of pleasant things about going to bed early. There was remembering the whole day; there was pretending everything. There was being the very one who went to bed early and of whom every one was thinking. And there was dreaming.

Susan could hear her mother and father moving about in the kitchen below. She could hear a bit of talk and a bit of radio music. And outside there was a whole night music of sounds about her, drifting in thru her open window. It was chilly everywhere. The night was colder and colder, so she snuggled gladly into the warm heap of the comforter and listend. Susan could hear first a rustling of trees, a kind of leafy talking, and then a distant dog barking. She could hear tree frogs chirruping. She could hear the house creaking, sighing and muttering to itself.

Now was the time when by drifting into the deepest story, one that she told to the whole world of herself, all by herself, she would soon be fast asleep.

There are unpleasant things about going to bed if one is going away from everybody; and there are all kinds of pleasant things about going to bed when one knows that one is still there. But there is the strangest thing about going fast asleep.

Yes, that is the strangest thing of all, Susan thot.

You can never really get there, and yet everybody else knows you are really fast asleep. Sometimes she would try very hard to be fast asleep, but then she was always hearing everything around her with her eyes shut. She never could really know when she was fast asleep.

But dreaming was different, may be it was the strangest thing.

The Cat and the Blackbird   523

When you were quite awake, wide awake, all the world was outside you and you were in it, you were in the whole world. When you were just dreaming, fast asleep, all the world was in you. Well, and even you were in you. And this you, this fast asleep you, was calld dreaming. You were just dreaming, that meant it didn't really happen outside at all not even to you. It meant that it happend inside, it was all a dream.

Well, you couldn't try to dream. But you could always remember dreaming. You could pretend to be fast asleep but then you could never be fast asleep and never never, you could never remember being fast asleep.

First, Susan liked to remember things. But better she liked to make up things. Susan discoverd, may be she didn't discover, may be she knew anyway, that she would make up things happening as a dream. Making up was very different from waking up. Making up was almost dreaming. And then, yes, she would really be dreaming.

But she never, Susan knew, could pretend to be dreaming and be dreaming quite yet. And you could not try to dream. Trying to dream didn't work.

Chapter 5
The Merry Go Around at Sunday Beach

So Susan made up a beach. There it was a bright sunny day in the middle of the night. And her mother and her father, or maybe it was cat and the blackbird — no it was certainly father and then it was mother, smiling and very gay. All kinds of carnival booths and play palaces faced the beach front and the sea beyond which was very blue. The sky was the intensest blue.

And the man with a gold crown on his head said the Merry Go Around was different from any ordinary merry go round.

And can cat and blackbird go on it, she askd. She was worried because maybe the man would think they were pets, and animals weren't allowd.

But she saw that the cat and the blackbird were already climbd onto the backs of two orange and blue tigers.

It's going to begin. It's going to begin, they yelld to her. Hurry, hurry, hurry.

The radio music was starting. She thot of all the grandest kinds of music she could make up. But the music she was dreaming began before she could make up any.

O, she said to cat and blackbird, you are already here.

Of course, blackbird said, cat and I both dreamd of the Merry Go Around right away and so here we all are.

Let's all ride in the Swan Sled, Mother said. Father lifted Susan into the Sled. Come, come let's all ride in the Swan Sled.

On the Merry Go Around all the animals were alive. My, cat said, we were really scared when we noticed it was a real live tiger.

Cat and blackbird sat on one seat facing mother and father who held Susan between them. Warm robes were drawn up over their knees, and Susan had a furry hood to keep her ears warm. Everything about the Merry Go Around was just as one imagined it.

The Merry Go Around music was everywhere. Above, the stars sparkled and twinkled in the cold. And the Swan Sled sped swiftly on, drawn over vast expanses of watery night by the two beautiful swans that were really bigger than Susan was.

Of course, one swan said, of course we are all real live. In the wide awake world we are only merry-go-round animals, well, we are really always not alive at all. We are fast asleep with our eyes open. But, being only pretend alive, means that here where all pretend is real, we are really alive.

Where are we going? cat askd. That is just what I was going to ask, Susan said. Where are we going?

To Sunday beach, to Sunday beach, the swans sang.

On Sunday beach, on sunday beach
The Sun is bright and sweet as a peach
The tigers pretend and their zebra friends
bow each to each
On Sunday beach, on sunday beach

I wonder where we are now? mother askd.

It was hard to see at all that they were anywhere at all. There were stars everywhere above and below. It was like sailing thru the sky, flying, in the Swan Sled. And there was the sound of waves about them in the night.

We're sailing over a big lake, Susan thot.

It's really the sound of trees talking, cat said. Outside, you know. Trees are very much like waves talking and so here we are on Leafy Lake Sound.

O, Susan said.

A Sound is a large body of water, father explaind.

O, that's very hard to understand, blackbird said.

But everybody knew that understanding isn't important in dreams.

They snuggled back into the sled and listend to the waves sighing that were really trees and hearing the breakers roar that were really trees roaring; and they listend too to the Swans song.

On Sunday Beach, On Sunday Beach
The Merry-Go-Around, The Merry-Go-Around

And Susan buried herself close in mother's arms and fell fast asleep.

And we fell asleep, too, cat said.

Yes, blackbird said, how will we ever know if we ever got there.

But it was a nice dream, mother said. She dishd up a big helping of cream and scrambled eggs for cat and a bowl of blackberries for blackbird which he liked very much.

It was a nice dream, and it isn't important in dreams to get where ever you are going.

We can go again, Susan said, and maybe the Swans will get us to Sunday Beach before we fall asleep.

Merry-go-round we ride the tigers
home to the round to the place we began.
Merry-go-round we ride the ostriches, ride
up and down around and around
sitting backward back again.
Then in the Swan-sled we slippd as we sat,
gliding around the whole circumference,
attended by animals, bounding cats,
and rabbits and horses, until
we arrived all the way round
to the very same place we started at.

And the music ran down
and
stoppd.

Faust Foutu

A Comic Masque

1959

Faust Foutu: An Entertainment in Four Parts

*The Cast**
Master of Ceremonies . . . Fred Snowden
The Poet . . . Robert Duncan
A Muse . . . Jack Spicer
Faust . . . Larry Jordan
A Boy . . . Mike McClure
Marguerite . . . Ida Hodes
Her Nurse . . . Helen Adam
Helen of Troy . . . Yvonne Fair
Greta Garbo . . . Helen Adam
Brunhild . . . Jody James
Faust's Mother . . . Jess Collins

PROLOG. *Before the Curtain. The Muse's Room.*
SCENES. *1. Faust's Studio. 2. Marguerite and her Devil-Nurse. In a Garden.*
3. Dark. Faust's Bedroom. 4. Dawn. 5. Sleepwalking. A Place of Trial.
6. Faust's Bedroom. 7. The Place of Trial. 8. The Old Homestead.

ACT ONE
[PROLOG. *Before The Curtain*]

MASTER OF CEREMONIES —Dear lower world, cigarettes, convertibles,
lazies and generalmen. I announce the Devil of Fun and all his
pomps. My argument? Well it's all an old song . . .

Of Faust Foutu, the jolly old king
who saild for France to find his soul

sing sail sing Faust Foutu

The rain in the cloud is blackest sin
The sun beyond is hot as a bomb

sing boom sing Faust Foutu

He famishd to feed himself on love
like a crow on a carrion feast in a field

sing feast sing Faust Foutu

531

he crowed like a cock to awake his heart
opening one eye on the sty in the dark

sing cock sing Faust Foutu

In love with the devil, enamord of trouble,
he is the hero of our one two three

sing double sing Faust Foutu

In the midst of the war he was a war himself
looking for the eternal piece of ass

sing peace sing Faust Foutu

What shall we come to, he cried, ah woe!
I follow necessity wherever I go

sing come sing Faust Foutu

I pray to the devil I may come to rest
when I the worst embrace the best

sing pray sing Faust Foutu

So knock me down that I may rise
and strip the last of the heart's disguise

sing last sing Faust Foutu

I live I suffer I am going to die
and love you all like a sock in the eye

sing love!

sing mad old, bad old, sad old

Sing!

Love in a bush is a fire in the hand
and on this faith I take my stand

sing save your face Foutu

Love dies no death but in that bed
where all our naked faces red

face sing save Faust Foutu

THE POET'S VOICE —The litany of the muses of our age strikes up the
band!

MASTER OF CEREMONIES —The Muses Room.

MUSE —Well here we are. We muses, you know, try to curb
automobile despairs, desperations of lovelorn latter deportment and
dreams of hard cash. Eight hundred dollars I said only the other day
to poor Faust will get you nowhere. Look into your heart Faust and
you will find a pocket there with a hole and a gap in it the size all
your sustenance drains out wherever you go. Now all the checks you
write will be poems on account of no balance that will move your
creditors to tears. You can never pay back for the life you owe the
love you borrow at the interest that increases until the last display
proves that there's nothing but the eternal dust in the bank account
of passion. # Did you ever come home drunk with hot whiskey
that turnd your stomach into an octopus writhing with desire about
last weeks meal and spill your body into the floor with a bang and a
black eye reaching out of the clotted door of your guggenheim prize
for the cunt or the cock of the income tax collector Death? How
will you pay *him*? How will you evade *her*? # Not even magic can
identify in those last brackets who her he or it in the shape of a goat
a dream of breasts or a bit of decay waits for us all when we quits
our korea and makes our truce. # I sez see here Faust are you saved?
when you wake in the morning are you ready for sleep, for the war
to outlive your source and your solace? Open them eyes I sez. #
Us muses is always having to ring the six o'clock in the morning
alarm, knock on the bathroom door to interrupt the fun, send notes
warning of syphilis schizophrenia or scabies to keep these American
beauties alive to the whips of daily living. # Lotus Eater I sez that
aint roses! Howl honey and let me know you're alive. You've got
more than your life to spend before the final bill comes due. # But
let us muses amuse ourselves. A little darkness please! Lights out!

(LIGHTS OUT)

And less light than that to
give a cheery hope for hopeless Faustus to come to no good.

THE POET'S VOICE —Less light than that is a single candle flame.

{Act I, Scene 1}

MASTER OF CEREMONIES —Faust is working on a large canvas. It
doesn't make any difference what he is painting but as he paints he is
telling himself what he is painting.

FAUST —Starting out at home with a large papa or a comfortable
railroad station with choo-choo trains arriving from all over
the world, from Paris, from Taormina, from Tokyo, from Baker
Street . . . and children in the fire singing because the real hot fire
is really the fire of love and naked as. . Here is the impossibly tall
tower made to topple. . Here is the flooded tunnel that undermines
the city . . . Here is the atom bomb that burns up the air so that
no one can breathe . . . Here is the president of the whole country.
Here is a movie queen with a magic word of power who waits for
the abandond muscular giant when he arrives afraid at the end of
the day. . Here is an island where no one lives . . . Here is a dream
of Marguerite and I write a letter . . . I need a match and another
candle or a boy with a flashlite and I'll write a letter with real
inspiration.

THE POET'S VOICE —A naked boy with an animal head arrives with a
flashlite.

BOY —Starlite is best coming from years of light afar to you yet near as
a naked boy to help compose love letters. Starlite is best.

FAUST —Starlite starbright when I see the world I say do I see aright?
Naked as we are is truth.

BOY —Did you ever see a star naked?
Such a moving picture is a sight to see.

FAUST —We never can afford to see the stars naked. We see like
moving cameras stills of stars. Only the inspiration keeps them
moving. A picture moving for us to see.

BOY —Did you ever see a star with the head of a dog?

FAUST —We never see the face of a dog when his body is bare. Away!
Why do you bother me? I don't need inspiration. I need to exhaust
even my own spirit until only my body survives.

BOY —Look at my body. I am incarnate starlight.

FAUST —Away! I'm not reaching for a star. I'm not wondering who you are. I reach for the obtainable. To know the poison of the real for my body to bear. Where's your flashlite? I need you so that I can read my own writing . . . As I was saying before you so nudely interrupted—

MASTER OF CEREMONIES —Faust writes.

FAUST (WRITING) —. . . your beautiful buttocks, those virginal loins coverd with such carnal pollens undispersed, choke all the arteries and tubes of my lungs and close off the mornings of my life in a strangulation that is beautiful as . . .

MASTER OF CEREMONIES —Faust turns back to his painting.

FAUST (PAINTING) —The cost of a room and a bed in this city by god is worth my life. And here the lights and gas are on and off again if we cant pay. We barely made it that time!

{Act I, Scene 2}

THE POET'S VOICE —Marguerite appears in a white nighty with the Devil as her Nurse. A Garden.

MASTER OF CEREMONIES —All this is entertainment, please. I announce the Devil and all his pomps.

MARGUERITE —Nurse dear, have you heard them speak of Faustus, dear man he is?

NURSE —O sure and there is as sweet a man as there is in all the counties of Ireland and him without a seat in the trousers of his imagination so to speak so as the dear red ass of him sticks out for all of the public to kick and despise.

MARGUERITE —To kiss on those eyes, you say, dear Nurse? and over the seas he comes in his imaginary trousers on a meek red ass like the true savior. Who would betray him?

NURSE —Aye, my incubator innocent deary, twould take the least idea crossing his mind to betray the black of the way it travels and the damnation he's always pointing up and painting down, hard to please and limp to learn, chased by impure thots from pole to pole.

MARGUERITE —Ah! chaste and in pure thot from whole to whole!

NURSE —What can anyone hear in dreams but the voice he is waiting to hear?

{Act I, Scene 3}

MASTER OF CEREMONIES —Dark. Faust's Bedroom.

NURSE —It's dark as hell in here.

FAUST —I call up the devil and discover a nurse.

NURSE —All your trouble began in the beginning.

FAUST —And I'll fill myself with trouble until I resemble the universe!

NURSE —O poor little chicken! Yours was a bad egg. Hatchd in a war, a weary specimen yourself. You'll never be cock of the walks of this world of ours.

FAUST —But I crow! I crow!

{Act I, Scene 4}

MASTER OF CEREMONIES —Dawn breaks.

FAUST —Ah dawn. .

MASTER OF CEREMONIES —Marguerite at his side in bed.

MARGUERITE —Down? where? dear Faust, down a down?

FAUST —Tis brillig and the Emperor of the East
    has shed his clothes upon yon temple spire.

MARGUERITE —You contemplate and aspire?

FAUST —to that rank dung that feeds the flowering soul.

FAUST & MARGUERITE. DUET

> To that rank dung that feeds the flowering soul
> we crow in praise at dawn from pole to pole.
> To that rank dung   from pole to pole
> that feeds the soul   we crow at dawn,
> we crow in praise from pole to pole.
> To that rank dung that feeds the flowering soul
> we crow in praise at dawn from pole to pole. .
>
> And rise to clothe our naked parts
> And rise to clothe our naked parts
> in all the foul deceit of art . . a work of fart!
>
> To that despair that will outlast the war
> we raise our voices to the roof.
> To that despair that gives what for

we raise our voices! we raise our voices!
To that despair that will outlast the war
we raise our voices to the roof!
And give what for.

For all unrest in con-tem-pla-si-on
For all unrest in con-tem-pla-si-on
we will compose in com-post-si-si-on . . po-si-si-on

MARGUERITE —Ah dawn! sweet dawn!

FAUST —Down *that* ladder we descend to no more than day. This mind of mine is so filld with impatience it runs out into the world. And the little crack of dawn lasts forever. Let it break and the sun's loathing take over our lives as it will.

MARGUERITE —Hush, dear Faust. Ah, to think that the sun's loving will take over our lives.

(SONG) When in the night of love
we float, we float,
oblivious of heaven above
and hell below,
the world among the radiant stars
is of the darkest light
and all we dream is ours.

I fear to wake, I fear to wake,
from you my dear to turn again to you
and like a wind-blown flame to shake.

When in the sea of love
we turn, we turn,
like ships oblivious of the shore
that set their lights to burn
for our delight alone
for our delight alone
and not for harbors of
forevermore,

when in the quiet of the storm
we make our home

in restlessness and come
　　　　to rest
then we are one.

I fear to wake, I fear to wake
lest I forsake my dear for you my dear
and cease to dream for your soul's sake,
　　　　for your soul's sake.

THE POET'S VOICE　—Marguerite rises and finds herself in the night before the dawn alone. Dreamwalking she goes from bed into a company of celestial stars. She stands betrayd in the midst of those empresses whose craving stirs in the world's dream of woman.

NURSE'S VOICE　—Ah my sweet! You were the littlest one, the least one, over whom all our love from the beginning hung like a wing. Sure, how could such a pure sweet thing, a girl with all the dear cathedrals of the western world softening their glory for her sake until their burning windows were no more than petals of immortal flowers falling. How could? And the sweet Jesus climbing up onto his cross like a little child climbing up to bed leaving all the cross impatient parent world below. And the little anarchists closing their eyes down at last to claim brotherhood with all of the dark. Alas. Alas. What will love bring us all to? To no good I say. And only the goodness of our hearts leads that way.

{Act I, Scene 5}

MASTER OF CEREMONIES　—A place of trial. Great lights light up the stage.

HELEN OF TROY　—Answer me! answer me!

MARGUERITE　—O my tongue is tied.

FAUST　—Read this book!

MARGUERITE　—I cannot read.

FAUST　—It is my heart. True love could read this book and reading at last know and knowing at last be one.

MARGUERITE (WEEPING)　—I cannot read.

HELEN　—Those who cannot read will be destroyd
　　　　Those who cannot pass will fail.

FAUST (IN DESPAIR) —To fail! to fail!

MARGUERITE (READING) —"Ish bin la bell treese-tess welt-mocker."

BRUNHILD —Translate.

MARGUERITE —"Ich bin goldengreen of Battlegoose."

HELEN —Fool! Goosey! What does it mean? What does the first word mean?

FAUST —You pronounce it Beetle Juice. Don't you know the first thing?

MARGUERITE —O, I am not prepared. I am not prepared. "Ich bin la belle tristesse du monde et son dieu."

GARBO —She has not studied the lesson!

THE POET'S VOICE —She stands humiliated thruout the scene.

MARGUERITE —I stand humiliated thruout the scene.

THE POET'S VOICE —The great move on to glory in spite of our trembling hearts.

MASTER OF CEREMONIES — Act I, Scene 6. Helen of Troy, Brunhild and Greta Garbo circle Faust. A Dance.

(THE DANCE BEGINS BUT IS INTERRUPTED BY
THE MASTER OF CEREMONIES)

Act III, Scene 2. *Faust and Marguerite are shown in bed in the morning light.*

MARGUERITE —When I was staind with you dear Faust the world became such a great day that my own day seemd a lingering shade.

FAUST —And I lingerd in the shade of your day so lighted myself like the sun that all the world was dark.

MARGUERITE —To let all chaste thot fall away, returning to the carnal dining place, the tousled bed, the few hungers and pleasures that make us more than saints.

FAUST —It is good to be a devil.

MARGUERITE —Ah, it is good to be a devil then, with only our love between us and the blazing glories of almighty God.

FAUST —I heard you cry out. What did you dream?

MARGUERITE —O, it was some trouble I dont know what and I was lonely.

FAUST (SINGING):

Sometimes in the loneliness of my thot
the cost of living seems so hard,
the endless war, the rage of God,
demands my pain that He may speak,

But ah, but ah,
your company is sweet
and so I kiss
your hands and feet
and all my heart declares the lie
of loneliness.

What matters it that we must die?
For we have life.

Sometimes in the anger of my mind
the test of power is hard to bear.
How great the cheat, the eternal state,
by blindness to excel the blind.

But ah, but ah,
your countenance is dear,
and so I gaze
when you are near
upon your face
and all your body's carnal grace.

What matters it that we must live?
For we have love.

MASTER OF CEREMONIES: —Act I, Scene 6. Helen of Troy, Brunhild
and Greta Garbo circle Faust. A dance.

(THE DANCE CONCLUDED)

HELEN   —What is love when the lions of magic bare their claws?

BRUNHILD   —bear

GARBO   —bear

BRUNHILD —What is love when the horses neigh in the terror of battle?

GARBO —nay

HELEN —nay

GARBO —What is love when the regard of the serpent fixes its prey?

BRUNHILD —pray

HELEN —pray.

FAUST —Love sees the claws of the lion as the secret of the rose. Everything flowers because of cruelty.

THE THREE WOMEN KEEN SOFTLY AT EACH BLOW AS HE SPEAKS

FAUST —Love sees the snort of the stallion as the language of the child. Everything speaks, forth from its fear.

—Love sees the eyes of the snake as the virtue of the jewel. All things have powers in fascination from their hunger.

THE POET'S VOICE —Faust joins in the dance with the Queens of His Desire.

{Act I, Scene 7}

MASTER OF CEREMONIES —Faust Among the Empresses. A Dance.

(A SHORT DANCE. THEY FREEZE TO A STOP)

HELEN —Who is the lover when all things change and the city falls into the oblivion of time?

BRUNHILD —Time

GARBO —Time

BRUNHILD —Who is the lover when the fires of the father reclaim all beautiful things?

GARBO —father. .

HELEN —farther. .

GARBO —Who is the lover when the cold of beauty perishes in the klieglights of life?

HELEN —lights

BRUNHILD —lights. .

FAUST —All this I desire. For this I secretly sell my soul. To conquer time, to go farther, to enter the lights. # Unrest. Unrest. What care I for the devil's fun?

[Act I, Scene 8]

MASTER OF CEREMONIES —The old home instead. Faust as the Devil enters leading the boy by a rope. His dear old mother sits on a fencepost knitting.

FAUST —When I in my pride fell out of myself I took heaven with me into hell and left my self up there creator of the world and of Faustus too. Too high to be loved, and loving, so they say, all things but myself. Whilst I down here in hell too low to love am loved by all. This was self-love born so they say out of a self that was all love. Damnation's sight of a man so the book says.

FAUST'S MOTHER —So what of books? Your mother loves you. Only a mother can love the unloveable out of itself.

FAUST —O hell-o Mother.

MOTHER —You neglect me. You never understood me at all. If you cannot love *me* to whom you are all pain, whom will you love that you will not pain?

FAUST —Tell me the secrets of the Earth. All I want from you is to be born.

MOTHER —The wisdom of the world lies in keeping your mouth shut and knitting your brows.

FAUST —Not wisdom! But the secret! the secret! The springs of life!

MOTHER —A hearty cry brings one out of the darkness. An answerd howl of the soul's hunger is proof of love. If you don't stop crying I shall give you something to cry for!

FAUST —What can you offer me when I leave your door?

MOTHER —A promise. I shall never satisfy your miserable longing.

FAUST —A curse on you Mother for your crisscross directions.

MOTHER —A curse on you Son for your crisscross sight of me. Wherever you go you will talk too much, hear too little, go too far, and come back weary.

FAUST —Whatever you say Mother, your secret shall be no comforting thot to you, life shall be no comforting span to you, I shall be no comforting son to you!

MOTHER —I gave birth to you, Ungrateful!

FAUST —Old Woman, you gave birth to me unborn.

MASTER OF CEREMONIES —What the Devil! This isn't much fun. Everything's gone to hell in my absence.

MUSE —This Act was bound to have a dismal close.

THE POET'S VOICE

During the intermission we are unaware of all pleasures and furies.

CURTAIN

ACT 2

THE CAST

The Poet . . . Robert Duncan
Master of Ceremonies . . . Fred Snowden
Maggie . . . Yvonne Fair
Peter . . . Harry Jacobus
Mrs Patchitt-Wildebeest . . . Helen Adam
Emory Lowenthal . . . James Keilty
A Painter's Wife . . . Ida Hodes
Norris Embry . . . Jess Collins
(soprano solo by Ida Hodes, chorus by Robert Duncan)

ON BOARD SHIP. SCENES *1. At ship's concert 2. on deck against the blue of the open sea 3. an art gallery on board 4. Faust's studio 5. on deck, evening. 6. ship's salon. afternoon 7. Faust's room. at night 8. before the curtain 9. three in bed 10. two in bed 11. the storm 12. in harbor*

{Act II, Scene 1}

THE POET'S VOICE —Faust aboard ship sails forth from his mother country, forsakes his fatherland.

MASTER OF CEREMONIES —A little concert in the ship salon.

MAGGIE —Without a cigarette? without a lover? face life like a tiger pacing his cage, circling about one center?

Love is like a tiger
driven by hunger
closing in for the kill.
He is exciting
we are inviting
until he's had his fill.

Down on Market Street under the corner light
we wait for War to give us another light,
    night light, front-line fight light!
What if we make a pick-up, take a trick up
    stairs?
We'll never find a brute there
who will suit our
    stars . . .

without an enemy? without the terrors of Asia? where would we be?
we've got malaise of cash. We need diplomacy. Come play with me that
old threat game, cause that's the way it's got to be. .

Love is like a tiger
lingering in the mind
and we are blind
to the fury of his hunger
until the primal anger
starts and then we find

We too are lost, driven,
turning like beasts in heaven,
until we've had our hell
until we've had our

hell-o, Lover! It will soon be over.
We were meant for other things.
Let's go in for danger, every beast's a stranger
trying out his combat pilot's wings.

Love is like a tiger
watching in the dark
the eye will catch the spark,

the hunted and the hunter
waiting around for the same old war. .

Men only love to strike
destroying their delight
lest it delight no more.

(PETER, MRS P-W, EMORY LOWENTHAL and M-C *applaud genteelly*)

PETER —Away from home, what's a boy to do? We've got those
move-on go-anywhere moods that are the real American thing . . .

Man or woman, what do we care?
Anyone, anywhere, can't you see?
We've got our guarantee!
We want company!

Chaste or whore, we've gotta make it!
That's our way, we've gotta take it!

When it's completed,
if you feel cheated,
remember we're always fair and square!
We will always pay,
if you see it *our* way,
then we'll know you're O.K.
When you need us we'll be there.

to Venice, to Florida, to New York . .Americans on the move. To the
hills! to the charnel fields of Korea! Liberate Moscow! To Heaven! what
do we care?

Chase or war, what do we gain?
It is all our dream, pleasure or pain.
We've got our guarantee!
We're meant to be free!

Come away from home then,
wherever we may roam, men,
every empty room   will be a place in space!

waiting for each boy
to seek his lonely joy again

That's the best employment
for the American race!

(*MAGGIE, MRS P-W, EMORY LOWENTHAL AND M.C. applaud*)

DUET : MAGGIE & PETER
For every war we won there's another war to win.
Longing for Hell, where shall we begin?
We find ourselves in Heaven whenever we sin.

For every lust that's done, what shall we do?
Whenever we are false, we to ourselves are true,
    and find ourselves, and find ourselves,
and find ourselves in Love before we are through.

(*ALL applaud*)

MRS PATCHITT-WILDEBEEST:
The Moon in all her phases
never set me paces
for brilliance or despair

cause I'm willing for lust
to drive me till I bust.
I'm a member of the sex calld fair.

I'm sitting like the Devil
in the empty pit of evil
waiting for love to come to Hell. .

God knows! I'm willing to love.

Going round and round the world
Paris hats with flags unfurld
and a handsome banking-ballast look as well.

Freud has doctord my complexes
and I know about the sexes.
Jung has fixd me up to fit the Golden Rule.

When all of the rest
of humanity was blessd
and living by the Golden Mean

How mean, how mean! I'm the Moon! I'm the Moon!

with an anima that's grim
and an animus all vim,
I'm either up up up
or I'm down down down.
I'm the archetypal image of a Queen.

(ALL *applaud*)

EMORY LOWENTHAL:
Love is like a lady
riding on a tiger.
Walking there beside her,
I pray I am too late for love.

Love is like a lunar
reflection in an eye
that almost passes by
but turns with a terrible roar:

O Lady, what for?
O Tiger, why more?

I know that I am almost sweet
enough for one to want to eat
and to dabble in the gore
and to dabble in the gore

But O Lady, please, please
I beg you, Lady, on my knees
speak of Love no more.

(ALL *applaud*)

MASTER OF CEREMONIES —On deck against the blue of the open sea.

MRS P-W —How far are you going?

PETER —To Venice. To the Biennale.

MRS P-W —To the Biennale! Ah, the Biennale! Don't you just smell the beautiful paintings! like young men in the heat of day. O more than that! like young men in the heat of today!

EMORY LOWENTHAL —Are you going to compete with this Faust fellow on board? He is to show his work there you know.

MRS P-W —No! But is he *really* a painter at all? Don't you sense a lack . . O   I mean something less than that, something less than human in his work?

PETER —How can he be less than human?

MRS P-W —O you know what I mean! All those smears of paint and drippings. And he spits on his canvas. They're only meant to make an impression you know. They're not carefully workd out at all. This canvas he is going to show is copied from Rubens with a technique from Arp and a Dubuffet finish. There's nothing *original* about it.

MAGGIE —Even without the original sin?

MRS P-W —O   there's never   in any of *his* work   been anything as *universal*   as the original sin.

EMORY L —I see quite what you mean. I think, don't you, a canvas should communicate   something?

MRS P-W —Well, I know what I *feel*. His work   is an assault on womanhood. I feel it. As a woman.

PETER —It is something to be assaulted.

MRS P-W —A terrible display of his own predicament and so *big*!

{Act II, Scene 3}

MASTER OF CEREMONIES —A painter's wife before Faust's canvas in the exhibition room.

PAINTER'S WIFE —Now when a painter has had training like my husband for instance who went to a real art school he gets beyond this student stuff I mean it may serve to experiment in technique but when an artist who has been really traind paints what he is traind to paint like my husband's rabbits why when Charles paints rabbits anyone can see there's something there besides just paint and color why anyone could do *this*! it just seems so bad that people are paying thousands of dollars dollars for these drools and dollars and smears they can't honestly say they can tell a Faust from a Hofmann or a Pollock or a Gina James there isn't any real value in it and Charles has magic in his rabbits Charles studied color with the Tibetan mystic Rorschach and Charles has been psychoanalyzed and Charles has outgrown all this and nobody nobody nobody has ever paid a thousand dollars dollars for one of his rabbits!

{Act II, Scene 4}

MASTER OF CEREMONIES —Dark. Faust's studio.

FAUST (TO PETER) —Now we are in what they call the creative dark.

PETER —What do I do?

FAUST —Nothing. Imitate the dark. Shut your eyes. Pour yourselves all over. Jump into the middle of what you are doing. Attack it. Pick it up in your hands. Paint yourself. Paint your self.

Why you're no better than a fool and the joyful millionaires are singing in heaven for the fool of a man you are.

THE POET'S VOICE —Now there are two identical canvasses. Faust stands before one, Peter before the other.

MAGGIE —My immortal soul!

FAUST —It was only an accident.

MRS P-W —But how could anyone . . I don't mean to insinuate . . But anyone but Faust paint when everyone is sea-sick?

PAINTER'S WIFE:

I'm married to a Master
who is painting every day.
He has masterd his medium
so now he is permitted, so now he is
    permitted
since he will not go astray
so now he is permitted   to play!

I am married to a painter
who has masterd his technique.
So he's very far from fake.

He's the Master of the Rabbit
and his latest master canvas
is entitled Hide and Seek, is entitled Hide
    and Seek.
Though it's playful, a display full
of a systematic reference to an acrobatic
    preference—
it's chic!

{Act II, Scene 5}

MASTER OF CEREMONIES —Faust Maggie and Peter on deck.

FAUST —Let the Moon pour down upon us

MAGGIE —and the stars up there like dollars

PETER —and the great void black and cold.

MAGGIE —O it's quite perfect and quite perishable. I love lovely men.

FAUST —I wish I could weep.

PETER —We could all be photographd weeping together.

MAGGIE —In one of those signboard things, real vulgar. Peter with the
body of a tom cat for stud, and Faust filling in the face for a Marie
Laurencin lesbian . . and me . . .

FAUST —as Montgomery Clift. Only filling in the body.

PETER —No. As yourself. As a witch between the woman and the
beast in man.

MAGGIE —O hell. If I'm going to be myself as you say, I don't need
you. Why count me in on your photograph?

We got along   in our home town
        until the Oakies came
and now they're more than ever before
        and who's to take the blame?

Now day by day the prices rise.
there's no room in town.   Get wise.
Who wants to be free?
   Be expensive.

We went to war but never before
        have there been so many men.

For every guy we shippd away
        twenty came in again.

Now day by day they crowd us out.
They muscle in. They hang about.
Who wants a man? Be pensive.

Why don't you two boys just take off your things and don't mind me
go ahead. It's the latest thing. You don't need me to do your killing in
Korea. Why do you need me to do your loving at home?

PETER —The dream was of two men and a girl.

FAUST —I love you.

PETER —We love you.

MAGGIE —So I'm lovable!

FAUST —Look at the sea.

TRIO: We sail. We sail.
             Out of the dream   into a dream
             counseld by   the siren sea.

        We who are sailors, we who are sailors,
        pray for our harbor, pray for our harbor,
             counseld by   the siren sea.

FAUST: The counsels of our mind
             are only waves we find
             pulld by the da da moon
             or pounding on time's shore
             a line of old abrasions
             that we cannot ignore.

MAGGIE: The counsels of our lust
             wear the shores to dust.
             What to us is hell
             or the terror of the deep
             to the stories lust can tell
             in the children's hour of sleep?

TRIO: We sail. We sail.
             Out of the dream   into a dream
             counseld by   the siren sea.

We who are sailors, we who are sailors,
pray for our harbor, pray for our harbor,
   counseld by   the siren sea.

PETER: The counsels of the heart
   direct the course of art
   by which the light comes down
   into the chaos of the sea
   to churn from night the dewy lamp
   that shines to set us free.

MAGGIE —Modesty means nothing to the sea. She calls us to strip and immerse ourselves in all the drainage of the world.

FAUST —Not to repeat the first act!

MAGGIE —That was Mother Earth, old fakeroo, and doing Papa in with the meatchopper. Zeus and Lizzie Borden.

FAUST —He cast the penis of his father upon the wave, which became Aphrodite, she of the fiery glance, the Mirror that Beauty is . .

PETER —and the Father's blood upon the raging waters became the spirits of the waters themselves, naiads, sirens, terrible songs of the sea . .

MAGGIE —and his balls! There rode Eros and Himeros, Love and Desire, forever attendant upon Beauty.

FAUST —Not to repeat the first act, but to recreate ourselves, to heed without old myths the counsel of the sea.

MAGGIE —O, it *is* cold. Let's go in.

PETER (AS THEY GO IN) —The Moon upon the Water is country enough for me.

MAGGIE —We are looking for the Motherland of the Moon. America is governd by Saturn, so the astrologers say, Old Chronos or New Chronos, is there any second act at all?   O Freud!

FAUST —Pater noster!

{Act II, Scene 6}

MASTER OF CEREMONIES —In ship's salon. The Afternoon.

MRS P-W —How far are you going?

MAGGIE —As far as I can get.

MRS P-W —To Rome?

MAGGIE —O No, to some imaginary city without a history. With a Zoo. Animals in cages, I mean.

MRS P-W —and men?

MAGGIE —There are men wherever you go.

{Act II, Scene 7}

MASTER OF CEREMONIES —Enter Faust.

FAUST —Ah, two witches together, Mother Hubbard and a young woodwitch.

MAGGIE —A can't and a won't witch.

MRS P-W —You aren't fair. Wherever you are going, we are both travelling toward death. It takes more than one life to die.

FAUST —It takes more than one war to die.

MAGGIE —It takes more than one man to die.

THE POET'S VOICE —They change places and Faust finds there is more terror in life than conversation affords.

FAUST (IN PRAYER) —Protect us from women, they who brood in secret to reform us. Protect us from those who play with dolls. Protect us from the insight of women who seek to create from our darkness no light but the repetition of life.

MRS P-W —Dahut gather your shadows!

MAGGIE —Hekat, bring a flashlight up out of the darkness of the beginning.

{Act II, Scene 8}

MASTER OF CEREMONIES —Emory Lowenthal enters as Thrice-Wise Hermes and sets up the spotlight.

THE POET'S VOICE —Preparing for the play within the play.

FAUST —Protect us from Thoth Father of Arts. Protect us from the lists of the dead, complaints, persuasions, taints of the battlefield, resurrections . . To die! To come to the end!

MRS P-W —All your troubles will continue in the end.

MASTER OF CEREMONIES —The women take up their knitting.

WOMEN (MARGUERITE TAKES HER PLACE) —one two three

EMORY LOWENTHAL —Higglety pigglety

WOMEN —four five six

EMORY LOWENTHAL —a cross maid of sticks

WOMEN —seven eight nine ten

FAUST (IN A TRANCE) —my black hen.

EMORY LOWENTHAL —One is for the child, pure and mild. Jesus Christ who bore our sin.

FAUST —One is the Chick of my black hen.

EMORY LOWENTHAL —Two is for the lovers driven from the wild. Adam and Eve who fell in Paradise.

FAUST —Two are the colors of my hen's eyes.

EMORY LOWENTHAL —Three are the persons present in the host. Father Son and Holy Ghost.

FAUST —Three are the powers of my black hen.

MRS P-W —The hen! the hen!

MAGGIE —The second act!

{Act II, Scene 9}

MASTER OF CEREMONIES —The play within the play. Marguerite and Faust. At night.

MARGUERITE —Don't you dear want a child? To see yourself again as you were in the beginning. A wee copy of yourself.

FAUST —What?

MARGUERITE —A woman has her fulfillment in a child as a man has his in his work.

FAUST —I work that I may come to no fulfillment.

MARGUERITE —You paint for mankind . . .

FAUST —For all the hell of history we have been feeding ourselves into mankind. But for nothing! Nothing! To paint for myself! For the mereness of painting! *There* would be something to see!

MARGUERITE —For your self. There would be something to see. A little mirror of yourself.

THE POET'S VOICE —A cradle-song is the first false poetry one hears.

MARGUERITE: Sleep my baby, my baby sleep.
             Pray your father your soul to keep.

FAUST (IN A CHILDLIKE SLEEPY VOICE) —Mother, isn't my soul my own?

MARGUERITE: My little doll, my little one,
your mother shaped you in her pain.
My little joy, my poor tired bairn.

FAUST —Mother, isn't my shape to be my own?

THE POET'S VOICE —The Bears of Memory lick their shapeless offspring into the form of baby bears.

MARGUERITE —O dear, I am afraid.

MASTER OF CEREMONIES —She stares upon the sleeping Faust.

MARGUERITE —To know . . only to know. No matter, creation. In time we find ourselves alone. Followd only by our own images.

THE POET'S VOICE —The wisdom of the woman conceals from even herself the springs of life.

{Act II, Scene 10}

NORRIS EMBRY
* BEFORE THE CURTAIN *

F.F. stands for in Fine Form, Fabulous Frisco
the French Fandango, FAUST FOUTU

a Furious Fhart, the Feeble Future
Flaubert Fingdoodled, FAUST FOUTU

her Fierce Food, his Famishd Face,
Four Flushers, Five to Forty,
FAUST FOUTU

F.F. for Freedom, for Furry Flowers,
for Famous Fakes,
for FAUST FOUTU

FAUST'S VOICE: I paint to exorcise the spirits of the past.

{Act II, Scene 11}

MASTER OF CEREMONIES —Three in bed.

PETER —The sea is calm tonight.

MAGGIE —And you are Aton, a sun that makes noon of night.

FAUST —And I, Set, the Monsoon God in the time of calm. Who makes night of noon.

PETER —and you? Isis?

MAGGIE —Pistis Sophia. The Future Mother of the World.

PETER —Water water everywhere . .

MAGGIE —A *simple* madness!

PETER —And you La Belle Helene. And I . . Paris.

FAUST —And I Menelaus mad, who laid siege upon his parents at bed in Troy and begot upon Helen his wife and mother five thousand years of war.

MAGGIE —And I Minerva Athena, the offended intellect, our Lady of the Armory.

FAUST —De l'Amourie. When the meaning of the play is clear we will reclaim Eden and abandon shame!

MAGGIE —Come play that we have meaning and reclaim.

PETER —Naked as we are is truth, and truth, Eden. We've only to play, for come, play gives great permissions! We thought the entrance to this bed was the door to Great Lust from all hope of an abiding Love. And found we had left Lust behind. It lies like a shadow over the world to clothe it. Where here we've come into the light of nakedness

MAGGIE —And sweet unfetterd sleep . . .

FAUST —No! I shall hardly know I sleep, and I shall wake facing the world again and its great Shade, my lustful shadow. *Les paradis artificiels, Le goût de l'infinie* . . why we are all self-bewilderd and need no opium. Everything is Truth. Shame, Wrath, Secrecy, St. Paul's illuminated hatred and St. Augustine's bright disgust are Truth. Truth! Truth! The world will speak to us like a telephone ringing, a bell ringing in the middle of the night starting us up from our holy bed to hear the unholy voices of inspired ennui.

MAGGIE (DRAWING A ROBE OVER HER BODY) —Why must you bring these spirits to attend us? Is there no end but we must resume the pride of Christ who like Satan took the sins of humanity upon himself. What have I to do with your male fury? that makes one war of the whole world and no more than a whore of the mother of us all.

PETER —Hush. Just for this night. Divorce your churches and wed the
world. Return to our amorous play and be what we won't believe all
bride and groom . .

{Act II, Scene 12}

MASTER OF CEREMONIES —Two in bed.

EMORY LOWENTHAL (LIGHTING A CIGARETTE) —Go on, Julia, where
we left off.

MRS P-W —O Emory, you *are* an insatiable gossip.
I want to relax. Have you another cigarette?

(EMORY HANDS MRS P-W THE CIGARETTES)

There. Permit an old woman a moment
of recollection.

EMORY —Must you recollect your *age*? I'd like
to forget that we are not all quite young.

MRS P-W —But it's the truth that we aren't young
and I like the savor of the truth.

(EMORY LIGHTS HER CIGARETTE)

Thanks, old dear. And you aren't so old,
you know, that you can't afford to mention youth.
It's spiteful of you when I've
the burden to bear.

MASTER OF CEREMONIES —Emory Lowenthal is rather a fine figure in
his tailord pajamas.

MRS P-W —You are rather a fine figure in those tailord pajamas.

EMORY —I shall have to confess all this
drama tomorrow.

MRS P-W   —Not every word!
I hope Emory you are not one of those
bores of the confessional.

EMORY —I have no extravagant
pride in sin. I know its place.

MRS P-W —Exactly! Which is
every place.

EMORY —Now that Faust fellow . .

MRS P-W   —Emory,
you *do* have him on your mind, don't you?
Now let me make a little confession.
An old woman like me has been on the scene
a long time, well, time enough to know
what goes on behind the scenes. We may believe
in heaven, Emory, and certainly
we believe in Hell. It's a term
in which we are on agreement, I think.

EMORY   —Come to the point, Julia.

MRS P-W   —Well, Faust has no faith in Hell.
And that's the secret. It's the whole point
of T.S. Eliot's *Cocktail Party* as I see it.
If you believe, you do not seek to know.
If you know—well, you can never *know*
and can you *believe*?

EMORY   —I have always wonderd
about what Celia *knew*? at the ghastly last . .

MRS P-W   —Or what Edward or Lavinia *knew*. They all
had faith. But they were in a play,
weren't they? I think that Alex and Julia
knew . .but that's not the way we know.
Alex and Julia and that man Reilly
were evil forces . . and I don't know
that *we* are evil.

EMORY   —But Eliot meant them
to be sort of Guardians of the Gate. They really
waken Celia and Edward and Lavinia to their fate.

MRS P-W   —Well then, *fates*! But I don't think
they are truly unmixd goods. Angels
are dark as well as light. And
the Gate to what? If you will permit
a wise old woman to ask?

EMORY   —Well, Reilly was a sort of doctor of the soul,
a psychoanalyst or a priest.

MRS P-W   —But it's clear in the play that he is
neither. Do you remember? Reilly asks Alex

how did he convince Edward that Reilly
was the man for his case? What's clear is
that Reilly wasn't a legitimate analyst
any more than he was a priest. He was
a theosophist or worse. And Alex and Julia
were in the plot or the brotherhood.
The Cocktail Party is the peril of souls.

EMORY   —What has all this to do with Faust?

MRS P-W   —The peril of souls? Well, dear Emory, just this.
And you and I are after all like that other
Julia and Alex so I have gone round about.
But we know, don't we? and we do believe.
We stick to the truth and we will undertake
our grievous sin rather than live
in peril of our souls.

(SHE PUTS OUT HER CIGARETTE)

EMORY   —Julia, you *are* too deep for me.

MRS P-W   —Only, and without bitterness for this evening,
Emory, too old for you.
Have you another cigarette?

THE POET'S VOICE   —Bang!

{Act II, Scene 13}

(THE STORM COMMENCES, NOISE TUTTI OF THE WHOLE CAST IN
A DEAFENING UPROAR RISING WITH THE CONDUCTOR'S BATON
AND ABRUPTLY CEASING WHEN HE DROPS HIS BATON FOR
THE INTERLUDES)

(INTERLUDE I)

FAUST   —Hear, Maggie! How my spirit howls. This is the very rage of
my dream.

MAGGIE   —You fool, moving heaven and earth by your word as usual.
All noise and confusion. Well, let it be your dream. It will be no
dream that you wanted to dream.

FAUST   —See? I say thunder! (AN INSTANT OF ROAR)

MAGGIE —Your imperious voice, no doubt. Fhart you say and the sky fharts. Child's play! Come indoors, and you'll find yourself wet to the skin.

(INTERLUDE II)

MRS P-W —Now! Look what you've done!

FAUST —It is nothing I have *done*. It's what I *am*.

MRS P-W —And *that* is a great matter, I suppose? A great hurlyburly I say. And a waste of our wits!

FAUST —This waste set roaring is the very sound of my art. And when the play is over, there's another roar for your ears yet.

MRS P-W —That's not a play. It may be what you call a poem, but it's not what I call a play. This just goes on and on. Heaven knows when it will stop. There's got to be some form, or it's not really dramatic.

(INTERLUDE III)

MARGUERITE: Sleep, my baby, forget the storm.
        Your mother holds you
        where it's warm.

(INTERLUDE IV)

PETER —Where is Faust?

MRS P-W —Come, Peter,
        What do you really care for Faust?
        You don't want to paint like him, do you?
        There's too much of what he does
        in what you do already, you know.

PETER —Sometimes he speaks with depth.

EMORY —Now fellow, obscurity always seems deep.

MRS P-W —He only borrows deep speech wherever he can. I've read all his lines before.

PETER —Where?

MRS P-W —O!   you know.

(OUTBURST OF UPROAR)

MRS P-W —It doesn't touch me. I know. I know.

THE POET'S VOICE —Dear Human Body, ruthless arbiter. Even in rage
I address you. In all your shifting guises, male and female seductions.
Eternal fisher of men. In your ripe bosom, lustrous pear-clear
breasts, abundant, or in your pectoral splendors with nipples like
young grapes amid the hairy leaves of the vine. Eternal museum of
our desire. My burning face, my trembling hands, exalt you! In your
great belly that smells of wheat, that smells of damp summer earth,
in your muscular visceral secrets. Eternal face of our obscurity. My
dreaming mind, my readiness, address you. A joke!— an excess,
a divine yoke! In the wet hairy pits of sweat I address you, in the
meaty, fruity, fish-sopping odors of sex, I adore you. By cunt, by
mouth, by cock, by ass-hole I invoke you. Eternal sexual garden.
By suck, by lick, by taste, by tongue, by smell, by nose, by sweat, by
piss, by spittle, by shit, O eternal Magician of the ages, I invoke you.
By nearness, by touch, by thrust, by feel, by pull, by inthrust and
withdrawal, by lift, by pulse, by throb, O eternal Mansion of our
spirit, I perform thy rituals. O harbor. O beloved human body. O
ever changing mirror of forms. Ruthless arbiter, even in the quietest
gardens of thought, I address you. Adore you. A door.

(GRAND CHORALE AS END OF THE STORM. SOPRANO SOLO WITH
CHORUS BEHIND HER VOICE)

SOLO: Lord. Lord. We ask him for harbor.
           O Lord. Jesus. Savior of souls. Savior.
           Harbor. Into the air. There. Lord.
           O sweet sweet sweet rose   in the air,
           harbor.   We ask him   for savior.
CHORUS: we ask him   we ask him   we ask him
           we ask him   we ask him   we ask him
           we love him   we love him   we love him
           we ask him   we ask him   we ask him
           we ask him   we love him   we ask him
SOLO: Sweet sweet sweet Jesus of waters.
           Yes.   Yes.   Jesus sweetness of sinners.
           Yes.   Yes.   Harbor O Harbor.
           Savior.   O.   Rose of the waters.

CHORUS: we answer   we answer   answer
         we answer   we answer   we answer him
         we ask him   we ask him   we ask him
         we love him   we love him   love love we love him

{Act II, Scene 14}

MASTER OF CEREMONIES —At ship's salon. In the harbor.

PETER —The weariness of the world passes and we all come home at
last.

MRS P-W —I wonder if I am prepared for this city?

MAGGIE (AT THE WINDOW) —It is quite lovely and quite perishable.
We shall never see it this way again.

EMORY —Where is that Faust fellow? Below?

MRS P-W —The important thing is Is it the same city for all of us? It
won't be for him. He sees things in a very special way. But. . Don't
you feel despair has disappeard from the air?

MAGGIE —Rage is gone from the page.

PETER —Hunger is no longer with us.

EMORY —All traces of struggle are done.

MRS P-W —Look, we don't know exactly where we are, do we?
Well, we are, I suspect, and I'm a shrewd party, at the end of act
two. I mean we have reached, well, a harbor. But we don't really
know where we are. So we can wish that that city out there were
any particular city or any other city. You *do* see what I mean. And
something should be reveald by everybody saying where he wishes
we were. Peter, you begin.

PETER —I wish. O I wish the city where I was born was that city in
all its glory, pure and white and naked like that, an America clean of
greed, of tyranny, of shame. If we Americans could return to such a
source from the world's despair.

MRS P-W —Splendid. Really quite beautiful, Peter. Now, What do
I wish? An old woman like me knows purity for what it is. I wish.
Well, I wish that city out there were real. All of Christendom wishd
that Rome really were the City of God. The immortal Blake wishd
that America really were the unleashd fire of the human soul. And
I, in turn, wish only for the reality of the day. For why more? A *real*
harbor at last.

MAGGIE —I wish that this city will be the end of all hopes of men, the new Karakorum, the hub of history, born of the wedding of the East and the West. Begot of hunger, the tyranny of Russia, and self-love, the tyranny of America . . this joy.

EMORY LOWENTHAL (AS IF ANNOUNCING TRAIN DEPARTURES):
Great Rome, compounded of arts, mirage of priests!
Karakorum, navel of the world.
Antioch.
London.
Jerusalem, the throne of Christ, the Glory of the
    Jews. New York, the Glory of the Jews.
Athens, mirage of professors.
Byzantium, Yeats' jewel and purple-born dreamer!

THE POET'S VOICE:
It is not our intention to enter the City of Man's Salvation!

ACT THREE

Cast

Master of Ceremonies . . . Fred Snowden
Chorus . . . Jess Collins
Faust . . . Larry Jordan
Jean Chien le Dieu . . . James Keilty
The Poet's Voice . . . Robert Duncan
Mrs Patchitt-Wildebeest . . . Helen Adam
A Painter's Wife . . . Ida Hodes
Maggie . . . Yvonne Fair
The Author . . . Robert Duncan
A Member of the Audience . . . Jess Collins
Hildegard Manguin . . . Helen Adam
Mary Angel . . . Ida Hodes
Charley Bride . . . Jess Collins
Faustina . . . Yvonne Fair
Popko . . . Fred Snowden
Lucy Clearwater . . . Ruth Schaenman
Dr Abgrund-Nachmacher . . . Robert Duncan
La Contessa Marshland . . . Ida Hodes

Ambrose Parks . . . John James
Isolde Stein . . . Jody James
The Nurse . . . Helen Adam
Peter . . . Harry Jacobus
Marguerite . . . Ida Hodes

PROLOG. *Before the Curtain.* SCENES. *1. A Studio in Paris.*
2. An Art Gallery. 3. A Party at Hildegard Manguin's
4. Euphorian's Nursery. 5. Marguerite's Bedroom.

{Act III, Prolog}

MASTER OF CEREMONIES —Enter Chorus. He bows.
CHORUS: We'll not to the stink of the Korean ditch
where valiant Western arms against the Chink
are raised. Let dog eat dog.
Great Mars in boredom attends no longer our poor wars.
The gains we bleed our youth for
are only gains for usurers and whores.
Nor shall we see our world overturnd,
nor Hitler raised to fright the mob
where Christ-despising Jews are burnd.
Nor shall we the hell of Russian labor camps
reveal, nor dwell upon the heavenly life
that from the American greedy sink goes up
where the self-righteous investors claim
our art, our blood, and our poor brains.

But on to Faustus. We've yet to see
how far his vanity of spirit goes.
How many scenes must we look upon
to taste the full indignity of man
and judge the futility of great art?
Your patience we ask that you may learn
wisely what the stupid bourgeois knows by rote:
Ignorance is bliss. Self-knowledge
belongs to the devil who demands
exacting payment before he's through.

And that is Faust. This guy was born
of respectable Americans who from each war
made once at least again what they had had before.
And so has Faust to Paris come to learn
walking up and down the town
whatever secrets might excite the soul
making of art and craft another battle ground
wherein the dark impenetrable swarms
all paint and great strokes of impulse
like rioting armies come to harm.
He's got to know some further risk. He finds
a certain Jean Chien le Dieu
who teaches—against the clarity of Vence
where the sublime Matisse
restored in Provence the Book of Light and Love—
an infernal scrawl,
a scribbling on the caves of tortured mind,
a skin uplifted bloody in the air
on which to paint. But see,
I show you Faust in love.

Who would have thot the heart to be so dark
where even Cupid feard
and warnd against a lighted candle's spark?

{Act III, Scene 1}

MASTER OF CEREMONIES —A studio in Paris. Faust sits at a table,
his head in his hands, silent. A record on the phonograph plays his
sobbing. A canvas in progress stands on the easel. In one corner is an
object—part fetish and part cross. # Jean Chien le Dieu appears at
the door in a great white cloak and stares into the room. Bells clang
two in the morning.

FAUST (SPRINGS UP, PACING FRANTICLY) —It's coming. It's coming!
I'm hot, man! Damn that music!

MASTER OF CEREMONIES —He takes the record from the phonograph
and smashes it.

FAUST (REGARDING THE CANVAS) —I'll smear my own blood over it
all and draw out of that patina another soul.

MASTER OF CEREMONIES —He puts another record on the phonograph, his sobbing again.

JEAN —To bleed or to suffer, this means nothing. This is no more than the world you've always known. The secret of painting, Faust, is that this stuff isn't blood, it isn't shit, it isn't to be done with sweat, excretions of the body. These things decay. But this is oil—wet, sticky, dirty, thick, gooey, oil—the residue of our immortal life. The Egyptians reserved this unguent for the dead. And now I say we *are* the dead, to paint our instructions for living men.

THE POET'S VOICE —Faust exhibits his hands.

FAUST —O my damnd paws! These paws!

JEAN —Tomorrow these mere colors will be drabs of the street, crawling toward your eyes to beg your touch.

FAUST —I'm tired of painting. I want to go out.

JEAN —You're *in*, Faust. You will never go out again.
That town out there is stale
and male and female whores
crawl along its streets like cancer cells
in crowded flesh.

FAUST —*Crawl!* I'm bored with your eye that empties out the world. (SHOUTS) I want love!

JEAN —You can have love.

MASTER OF CEREMONIES —He gestures, a weary offering of his disbelief. He turns. From the hall beyond we hear his voice where scorn, longing, lust and black humor have melted all into a worldly tone.

JEAN —Again, again, again, again.

FAUST (GOING TO THE DOOR) —To the magician all forbidden things are yielded from the depths of mother earth.

MASTER OF CEREMONIES —A Gallery. {Act III,} Scene 2. A large canvas by Jean Chien le Dieu hangs center stage. A Renoir hangs by its right; a Mondrian to the left.

MRS PATCHITT-WILDEBEEST —Oh I *am* tired. These paintings are hard on the feet. How clever of them to have hung Le Chien who's all bad if he's any good, between the good Renoir and the more than good Mondrian.

PAINTER'S WIFE —What does it mean?

MRS P-W —It means no good, I assure you. It means to be the death of things. Pardon me, dear, while I adjust my back to the prospect. You'd think the war was quite enough to satisfy that fearful itch. But ingenious, really ingenious men always must go further.

MAGGIE —Well, where's the harm in *this*, nobody's killed.

MRS P-W —Hitler had a certain point. All that killing out there is just a show, an expressive art. My dear, consider Renoir. This good man perhaps knew that only his trembling hand could bring the flesh to such a ripeness, such carnivals of sun that falling and rot must lie beyond. True Christians keep their women green. Well, here on the other side of the new obscene is Mondrian who was all clean space as if the mind were musical and the dry flesh all reeds and strings to fit the music out. These, Renoir and Mondrian, went too far toward beauty, I think, created anxieties of the real. And here between them come spectral counter-images of Truth that's fit for dogs. # It's not that this Chien le Dieu is not art. What's art but the cunning that monstrous men will learn to do their sinning beautifully? Nor is it exactly that it shouldn't have been done. It *has* been done, and we've to face it.

MASTER OF CEREMONIES —Enter Faust and Chien le Dieu.

JEAN —Renoir and Mondrian like immortal columns stand
    to form a gate for this mere scrawl.
    Here is where I came
    like a chicken devourd by lice
    to leave my dirty track in time.

MASTER OF CEREMONIES —He leans over to examine the price on his painting.

JEAN —Five hundred dollars. That means in this world the exhaustion of some soul to no reward.

MASTER OF CEREMONIES —He reads Renoir's price.

JEAN —Two hundred thousand dollars. Well, Renoir in his innocence furnishd up a costly piece to throw among the money-glutted pigs. All art's a trough these days to fatten up a world of hoggish sensibility. Two hundred thousand dollars. It costs that much to kill a man in a war.

PAINTER'S WIFE (TO JEAN, POINTING TO HIS CANVAS) —Sir, what is the meaning of that?

(JEAN SHRUGS)

(FAUST, POINTING TO THE RENOIR) —Madam, what is the meaning of
   that?
JEAN   —Renoir was no more than a man and I
       am no more than a man. These fruits,
       painted so ripe, repair in their richness
       the thirsty sight, but prepare
       in the merchandising mind rich thoughts,
       and my rich decay of all goods at your expense.
       To Renoir's earth and Mondrian's empyrean
       I play hell. But what's a universe without
       such fullness above and below? And I
       in being hell am all of earth and all
       of heaven too. No more than a smear
       beneath your microscopic eye, and you'll see
       creation itself is swarming there.
       What are these rolling sun-tainted great nymphs,
       or Mondrian's dance where all sensation is
       that no mere meaning could enhance,
       but harbingers of a new malingering season,
       my artful hand may bring to its end?
FAUST —I long for earth but am condemnd to Heaven or Hell.

(THEY EXIT)

MAGGIE   —Monsieur le Dieu must be that bit of truth
         that will corrode all true things to the eye.
         It's not the measure of life that living things
         must die.
MRS P-W —The measure of hell is the depth of our ennui.
         Men paint to create the life that they would have us see.
         And we in turn in seeing as we will
         may discover good where others meant their ill.
MAGGIE (TAKES A STANCE FRONT STAGE)   —To be a character here in a
   willful author's first play is at times to be mistaken, at times a lark, at
   times awkward, at times a kind of glory like speaking from my own
   heart. What is my part? His criss-cross sight of me in part, in part
   something of what he can imagine I might justly say for myself. He
   has always said to women "Let me alone", and so he's made me say

Faust Foutu   568

"If I'm to be myself, I don't need you"—a line it is true out of an old quarrel. Yet this is also true. If he is to be himself, then I am there. I was so sick of him, he never will be well. Nor scorn him, you out there, you women or you men, who feel just criticism where he has been unjust, or the protest of pity where *he* has practiced scorn. He does so little worse than to design in the manner we were born. What am I? Am I the best he can recall from a woman once his wife. It's a scandal then! but he goes unscathed for many wrongs, were he not moved here to reveal with feeling this picture drawn to show the shape of Faustus' life.

MRS P-W (SEATED TAKES STANCE, RISES, STEPS FORWARD AND TAKES STANCE)

> —And I am less, half an old person.
> Look how I started the butt of his joke.
> Almost reminding you of someone I was so
> warpd for fun. And then you found
> I was no one you knew that well.
> After all I was Julia
> out of T.S. Eliot's *Cocktail Party.*
> I've taken on the role in part
> of what he calls a woman's wisdom.
> Like all men he's superstitious.
> An old dame, he thinks, in spite of sex
> receives prophetic voice.
> Men offer us mastery or love
> or mystery or occult powers,
> second-sight and common-sense, whatever,
> to recompense for what they would deny.
>
> I ask you, you who watch me here,
> go away not without joy or fear
> in remembering me, half-shaped by god,
> deprived of fullest life—
> for fullest life is nowhere here conceived—
> in remembering me, who strive to speak,
> renderd what's calld on the stage a character
> and odd.

MASTER OF CEREMONIES —The Author enters. Takes a stance.

THE AUTHOR —Even as Maggie or Julia, I
can speak no better for my immortal life
than here I speak what I once wrote. Think
of beloved Shakespeare who
must have been Prospero and asked
"As you from crimes would pardond be,
let your indulgence set me free."
and from his magic stage
moves to depart. Spoken by Prospero
our Master's words I beg you
extend graciously to me,
for "Now I want
spirits to enforce, art to enchant,
and my ending is despair,
unless I am relieved by prayer."

I do aspire to a new manhood
and would be judged thereby.
And of this monstrous design,
this play for your sympathy, make-shift
and cut by chance as best I know,
let it be but one of tesserae
that are all the lives we'll never see
fitted now into the imaginary face
of that mosaic, Man, who asks of all of us
his final rest and grace.

MEMBER OF THE AUDIENCE (RISES AND SINGS OUT)
To manhood you aspire ho ho
as round and round the hub you go.
What will you work that we don't know?
You'll be a pig, we told you so.
    We told you so. We told you so.
You'll be no more, and though you try
    you'll never stop the show.
    You'll never bring down the house.
    We told you so.
    You'll never stop the show!

(EXHIBITS IN HAND THE PLAY PROGRAM) Look! There are two more acts and this one has no end that I can see. Will you never stop the show?

MASTER OF CEREMONIES —Act III, Scene 3. A party at Hildegard Manguin's.

HILDEGARD MANGUIN —O how charming of you.

MARY ANGEL —Darling!

HILDEGARD —and this is. . ?

MARY —Charlie Bride the notorious rapist.

HILDEGARD —It was so sweet of you to come.

CHARLIE BRIDE —It was so sweet of *you*.

MARY —and Faustina . . Hildegard Manguin.

HILDEGARD —I've seen all your wonderful pictures.

FAUSTINA —Movies, my dear, have never given me my real role to play.

HILDEGARD —We must talk about that later. . .

POPKO (TO MARY ANGEL) —Chérie!

MARY —Popko!

POPKO —Angel! Now this original paradise will be absolute heaven!

MARY —Popko darling, introduce me to that divinely hideous man over there. (AS THEY MOVE AWAY) If Hildegard *had* been our first mother, she'd have eaten the apple, if at all, out of boredom, not out of disobedient curiosity.

POPKO —Hildegard is Lilith, the ante-Mother.

(FAUSTINA COMES CENTER STAGE AND POSES. THE MOVIE STAR)

CHARLIE (TO HILDEGARD) —Now we are left alone. All alone.

HILDEGARD —Let me introduce you around. Doctor Abgrund-Nachmacher, Charlie Bride . . Isolde Stein, Charlie Bride . . Lucy Clearwater, Charlie Bride. (SHE LEAVES THEM)

LUCY CLEARWATER —You need a drink. There's everything.

CHARLIE —Anything with gin in it. Gin is my ethereal drink. Scotch or Bourbon play hell with me.

LUCY —There are Martinis, and divine divine hors-d'oeuvre. . chefs-d'oeuvre in their way.

CHARLIE —I think I'll take it straight. Then I know where I am.

DR ABGRUND-NACHMACHER (TO FAUSTINA) —What do you think of Faust's new picture that the Four Arts Club is showing?

FAUSTINA —O I never go to films. It's enough to be in them. And I don't think experimentals are really pictures, do you?

DR A-N —I don't mean movies. This is a painting.

FAUSTINA —Pictures that don't move, don't move *me*.

HILDEGARD —Dr Abgrund-Nachmacher. . La Contessa Marshland.

LA CONTESSA —Not *the* Dr Abgrund-Nachmacher!

CHARLIE —I like to look at the food and drink up the gin so as to consume something and not ruin my appetite.

LUCY —We've been drinking for hours and we're way ahead of you.

HILDEGARD —Emmy Lane is from Texas.

POPKO —Another divinity from the Open Spaces! Chérie!

AMBROSE PARKS —But I thot all Texas beauties were seven feet tall, a breed superior to men. Not, my dear, that you're not superior to men.

MARY —Hildegard is so knowing. The Parsival Adams is marvelously shown off against all that splendid woodwork.

ISOLDE STEIN (TO CHARLIE BRIDE) —Do you *really* like Robert Duncan's work?

CHARLIE —O I know it's not absolutely first rate. He's terribly uneven you know. I meant only that in the first act of the play, for all the confusion and he does over-load, I didn't miss that, but he does use myth. .

ISOLDE —But that's all been done to death, hasn't it? And so much better. Well, I suppose since he's a poet and you're a poet you grant him more than he deserves. It's very dissembling of you. But you needn't dissemble with me, you know.

CHARLIE —I know what you dislike. There are times when I've quite hated it myself. He does over-load you know. But the love songs he has Faust and Marguerite sing I thought had charm.

ISOLDE —O rot! They are such clichés of attitude. And he makes Marguerite out such a ninny. *Those* men never *really* believe in love between men and women, and it tells in their work.

FAUSTINA (TO AMBROSE PARKS) —O I never go to the cinema. It's enough to be *in* them, too *much* to be in them.

PARKS —You must long to escape, to just be yourself.

POPKO —Divine Faustina has never been given her greatest role, to play herself as she really is.

ISOLDE —I suppose if Duncan were in my trade I could see something in what he does. The most dreadful men mean something to me, you know, when they are interior decorators. If I can't admire their character, I can admire their ingenuity.

POPKO —Those chairs you had in your window, Isolde dear, were dreams beyond repair.

ISOLDE —If you *knew* what they cost me.

MARY —Well you *do* let us know what they cost us.

ISOLDE —The minute I saw those old 15th century tapestry panels from the Bankok Shiva temple I knew they were the answer. O I won't tell you where I found them.

POPKO —They were smuggled, by demonic forces, out of Asia.

ISOLDE —Just the association pieces I needed to give the room depth. I was so excited. Slowly and magnificently the whole shape came into being.

DR A-N (TO MARY ANGEL) —the effort toward what I call the unconscious magic or shaman scrupulosity of the essential realist, the dynamic interpenetration of the Western psyche by the modular dynamism of virtual forms. . .

MARY —Parsival Adams has such marvellous control. He paints so carefully.

DR A-N —He has the will to creation and what I call the anxiety of the realism of the essential. . a Fortdauernd . how do you say? will to the concrete of the abstract.

MARY —It is so heartening over and against this unconsiderd Faust sort of thing. I have heard *he* just drools the paint over his canvas. He uses anything that comes along. .

DR A-N —We must observe always that confusion is not vitality; ego-mania is not personality; the arbitrary is not will; the effort to be deep is not the penetration of depths. .

LUCY —O I can't really go on much longer the way it is. He doesn't give me a chance. You understand don't you. But *he* doesn't really understand. And really, I can love just so far without understanding. How far can I love and have things go on and on the way they go. .

HILDEGARD (WHO IS NOW RECLINING ON A CHAISE-LONGUE, SPEAKING IN LOW TONES) —put another record on . . that beautiful Segovia one. .

FAUSTINA —Everywhere   Faustina Faustina Faustina . What does it mean?   They are never looking for me. They look at Faustina, not at *me*. *You* are not looking at *me*. I have not been really, really happy since I was a little   O so little a girl. Before, before there were roles, roles, roles. . .

HILDEGARD (TO AMBROSE PARKS WHO IS BECOMING AMOROUS) —You like my dress? Silly . *Don't!* . I surround myself with these people . *Don't* . I hide myself among these people. I try to forget myself with these people.

AMBROSE —Yet you are the *one*, the important one that one finds among all these people.

HILDEGARD —Do you really believe that? . *Don't* . Why do you come here with all these people?

AMBROSE —To make love. To fall in love with *you*.

HILDEGARD —O, all you men make love at parties. Just so far. You don't know what farther means, do you? Do you?

AMBROSE —Farther means . forever . the bewitchment of the night . the sweetness of souls .

POPKO —Come everybody, you bewitching damsels! Come dance, come . hey hey hey hey hey ! It's midnight, midnight . this way . this way . Angel, come and shed your paradise with me.

CHARLIE (SOLO) —Groom of the night . You don't understand, do you? The wanderjahre . I've come to the end of my . the little stars in the whole sky twinkle and dance . so cold . dance . so far . Daddy Terrible comes out of his dismay smoking like a cigar, and I run away . run . away away away away . down the . . (HE CATCHES LUCY CLEARWATER UP AND TWIRLS) all. fall. down . Down. Down.

Down. (HE DROPS HER AND WANDERS AWAY WITH HIS BACK TO THE AUDIENCE) All alone. I'm not sorry for me. I get down on my hands and knees. And drink up my gin like a doggie. Back down on the ground . and I'll despise myself.

AMBROSE (TO HILDEGARD) —and after she *left* me there was nothing at all. What did anything mean? You know what I mean. Only real creation, I mean real creation can live a really creative life. Don't you think? She never let *me* down. I let *her* down. I can never make it up to her again. I knew you would understand. I kept going right up to the door of her apartment and standing there in the dark and afraid to ring or to knock. She never knew I was there. .

CHARLIE —despise myself better than you or any old one will ever despise old me . old low down on the floor me . Step on my face, I suppose.

FAUSTINA —The lights were all turnd on me. It was divinity turnd on me. I was, Stark Young wrote, something more than a woman, something other than an angel. It was the one . really great . moment of absolute . illumination. My name my face . my . . in the lights . the great . searching . . lights. . .

MASTER OF CEREMONIES —A weak light focuses on Popko now in clownlike jumble of improvised costume, with a featherd headdress, where he dances alone. . .

MASTER OF CEREMONIES —Act III, Scene 4. Euphorian's Nursery. To my left. But it's over here to your right. Where the good Nurse rocks the infant son of immortal Helen in his crib.

NURSE —Ah, wee dream you are of our immortal joy in this drain of all possible goods, little heart's candle born out of the wedlock of the world. . .

(SINGING) la lala lala la la lalalala. . .

A dance and a pretty speech and you will expend all your life in a once. Euphorian, so you are written, born of careless care-full Faust and unwitting and cunning Helen. All our tomorrows perishd in a spark . Now we are all slaves to a child's scream and students to a new model. How small you begin to fill the shape of monstrous appetites! How huge you are a bit to speak the world in a word before the multitudinous babel begins! And all the shapeless democracies of our struggle with the shape of our selves! How pure of face you start to launch a thousand shifts of fate! Carry us all as you will from the all that you are to the little you will be, from our visionary floods of your first to the mere trickle amid the rubble of what will last.

MAGGIE —What is this child of mine like? Is he very like Faust?

NURSE —Sure and in his unlikeness very like. As all the sloppails and kitchen heaps are father to divine visions among scullery maids and disappointed housewives. The babe's the sweetest purest joy ever was suckled at the dark of the mothering meat from the light of day. Why I no sooner comes into the room where helpless this new child lies than he awakening from his tender sleep addresses me and the stinking room as if we were all the blessed work of the light that warrants trust in this blisterd world, and, born to speak, sings out his praises. Benedictions he sez upon my towering form as I were the delight of his soul, and me all foul with a thousand dyings in this world. He sees with such eyes as wounds are roses, cheats are celestial jewels, all failings are like sweet rain downward falling in gardens of mid-mind most disorderd. In short, dear heart, thou hast been mother to the most profound fantasy of joy. Thou hast born a monstrous demanding perfection upon the world.

MAGGIE —Ah so. I am a mother indeed, and the world shall suffer all the immortality of my desire.

PETER —Had you your wits about you, Maggie, you would strangle this infant terror in its crib.

NURSE —O shame!

PETER —It is already all our shame he grows upon. Maggie who had once the freedom to conceive is now no more than her conception's conception. He mothers her future, holds her in time the shameful source of all impurities, she has no future now that is not his, and being his great disappointment and breach of contract. Kill the tyrant and let us all be free.

MAGGIE —My only chance to live? What monstrous divisions shape our single lives! We die alone and there's all a world entombd.

PETER —Then you are tyrant who once did disown us. You should have killd this necessity in its womb.

NURSE —Prince of the world he is! At birth already he walks and talks pure poetry, addresses the stars as playmates, and sets up kings in imaginary realms, invents in a word the history of cities, gardens, peoples nations with likenesses, creates whole languages for speaking with himself or moontalk, devises cryptic pictures, makes animals dance, houses explode, banquets appear at his will or his wont. Such new life enslaves all mere existence, compels obedience. So we all started, kings of the nursery, holding as we did in one rapturous response all hope to come. Casting as we did in a scream all dismay. So we are all, now a child is born, unreal nurses to reality.

PETER (BITTERLY) —A child is born. Rejoice. Rejoice.

MAGGIE —The child is mine. I *will* his life.

PETER —And Faust? Does he want the child?

MAGGIE —He does not he thinks. Man does not want his Child. But he will when he sees this lovely creature.

NURSE —A very image of Faust. He is divinely realized.

PETER —Let us destroy images. Until now we were sufficient unto ourselves.

MAGGIE —O, you behave as if this were a burden to *you*. It's not your child, Peter.

PETER —A child is born. A burden to all who admit his existence. Coming into the world we are no more to our mothers than a criticism of our fathers, an ambition for our futures, a vanity in our features. It takes all of the anger of our lives to wrest ourselves from the pangs of our birth, conceived as we are to implement our mother's war with her world. What mother does not hold her child as hostage before all lest any strike her? Defenseless babe that needs the nurture of the earth. Yet, in Greece mothers seized with horror at their slaving breasts, as if they were drunk roard and tore their babes from the teat and dashd them upon the ground. These were the great intoxications of new life, giving birth to ones *self*.

THE POET'S VOICE —now the singing hushd in the bone,
  now the tonal structure of the Erecthyum,
  now the proceeding as if it were happening,
  now the giant life in the grove,
  now the controld abandonment to challenge the danger,
  now the stranger we are to ourselves. It is dark.

Now the broad daylight in the narrow window,
now the window we are to ourselves after war,
now the end that is beginning we are waiting for,
now the birdcalls imitated skillfully return disorderd,
now the internal reference is repeated facewise,
now the pupil instructs the treacherous teacher,
now I the dictator dictate my nonsense,
now how big is the enormous small of it all,
now avalanches return to their settings,
now the sun blushes red as the wine he begets there,
now the abetting supplements and complements the abuttments,
now we are keeping only our appointments. .

MASTER OF CEREMONIES —{Act III,} Scene Five. The cast of the
party have become party to the third act. They appear as they were
but without identity. No more than *dressd* as they were. They are
witnesses of the fifth scene. Popko, Lucy Clearwater, La Contessa
Marshland and Dr Abgrund-Nachmacher speak for them. On my
right are Faust and Marguerite in bed. Over here on the left is
Euphorian's crib. Helen enters with a knife, her hair flowing over
her shoulders.

(MAGGIE ENTERS AND STANDS BY THE CRIB)

WITNESS ONE (MALE) —What is going on?

WITNESS TWO (FEMALE) —Nothing unusual. She works deviously
from the darkest motives. We know from the legend that he was too
joyful for this world. He burst his heart upon seeing the uncreated
universe, for it was pure song, and there was nothing to bind his
heart. She does not know it, but he is sleeping already among the
dead.

WITNESS THREE (FEMALE) MEANING FAUST —What is *he* doing?

WITNESS FOUR (MALE) —He is making love, but we cannot see it.
Those who sleep bare their dead selves toward life and their living
selves toward death. He is making love in a dream which they share.

WITNESS ONE —Is there no love that is not unseen?

WITNESS TWO —O there are all kinds of *show* of love. It is a very
much made up thing. All that is immortal has *its* being among the
*un*seen things.

WITNESS FOUR —When they are awake they are two. When they are asleep they are one.

WITNESS TWO —When they are at play awake, they play they are one.

WITNESS ONE —Someone told me the idea in the play is that she prayd for him and he was saved.

WITNESS FOUR —O, he went to her heaven, but it was his hell.

WITNESS THREE (MEANING EUPHORIAN) —Who is *he*?

WITNESS TWO —The joy of the play. *She* thinks he is *her* joy. But she also knows who he is. Listen to her. She has divorced herself from all domestic mind.

MAGGIE —Euphorian, I have come to take my joy out of the play. The play has taken my joy out of me. It is the natural grief of the mother that deranges me. For the man as he lives is a hope that dies.

WITNESS ONE —It is the necessity of the play that the unseen be seen. The *un*seen grief is not undone in a lifetime. Grief apparent falls like a blow.

(MAGGIE SEIZES THE CHILD, RIPPING IT OPEN; AND IN THE SAME INSTANT FAUST CRIES OUT IN HIS SLEEP)

WITNESS FOUR —Her grief strikes the heart.

WITNESS THREE (MEANING FAUST & MARGUERITE) —I think he met her on the street somewhere. He was on the way back to that master painter's studio, and she pickd him up. He went to her apartment. It was a nice little place.

WITNESS TWO —She was quite ordinary in her vices, but her chastity was extraordinary.

WITNESS ONE (MEANING MARGUERITE) —I think she looks like an angel.

WITNESS FOUR (MEANING MAGGIE) —Why doesn't she move?

WITNESS ONE (MEANING MARGUERITE) —She is in his arms.

WITNESS THREE (MEANING MAGGIE) —She is the angel of destruction, a power of the play. *Now*, she is herself. She is horrified at what she has done.

WITNESS TWO —He told her to.

WITNESS FOUR —Who? Faust?

WITNESS TWO —No. The other one. He rationalized it. It was in the play.

WITNESS ONE —Now he is saved.

(MAGGIE SINKS TO THE FLOOR, ABJECT, HER HEAD BENT OVER HER KNEES)

MASTER OF CEREMONIES —The Nurse enters, takes up the child from the cradle who is shown now to be no more than a doll. She shakes out the stuffing from his form where Helen rippd the babe.

NURSE —That is all.

WITNESS FOUR —Was that all?

MASTER OF CEREMONIES —Faust and Marguerite are awake. They rise on either side of the bed, make coffee at a small burner and return to bed with their morning cups of coffee. The witnesses meanwhile are leaving one by one, the four speakers last.

WITNESS THREE —He did it to confound us. A trick.

FAUST —It was the tradition that Faust sold his soul to regain his youth. But *my* youth has lasted so long it is like a world-burden, a straitjacket of guilelessness.

MARGUERITE —It was not your youth that I adored. But you were so thin. I adore your thinness.

FAUST —You were lonely Marguerite Street.

MARGUERITE —You were a cloud of unimportant joy.

FAUST —lonely

MARGUERITE —unimportant

DUET: A cloud. A story. A lonely street.
A sky. An unimportant sky of blue.
And you. And *you.*
I saw *you* too. I saw you *too.*

I saw a cloud sail thru the sky
and meet
the street.

Who cares? I said who cares?
An unimportant street. A cloud.
We'll write a story on a lonely sky.
Of Faust and Marguerite.
Of Marguerite and Faust.

A cloud. An unimportant street.
A story in the lonely blue.
And I while coming home to you
saw Marguerite . who cares.
She stared at me and I
returnd her stare. A lonely sky.
Where no cloud stirs. I saw a cloud.
I saw a street. I saw
fair Marguerite.

MARGUERITE —Of all the things we *saw*, it was the cloud that was our
hope and joy.

(CURTAIN)

ACT FOUR

A Soliloquy For Five Voices
One . . . Robert Duncan
Two . . . Jack Spicer
Three . . . James Keilty
Four . . . Fred Snowden
Five . . . Jess Collins

FIVE —Five ones.

ONE —First one.

TWO —Then one.

THREE —This makes enough for a play.

FOUR —How many ones?

FIVE —Five ones.

ONE —What he saw was difficult as it was easy to say. It was not
possible to reconstruct a complete lack of construction in it. This
was because he recollected himself as he proceeded. He proceeded in
order to act it out.

TWO —It was a spreading out of clouds in order to escape meaningful images that did not come about in writing. He meant a work in vain as nature is vain.

ONE —In telling our histories we are unable to fall as we did fall. This is creation where its clouds are clouds and remain in their names.

THREE —It was clever to attempt failure which is an endeavor that can only fail in succeeding. There is nothing that fails us like success.

FOUR —The absurdity of sonnets is not that they are sung.

TWO —Did she finally marry him? Was it in order to steal the scene as she saw him? But he saw her too. And if she married him, he married her.

THREE —She loved him. This means she had no reason to marry.

FIVE —Living together, coming together, awakening together, suffering each other themselves together, lasting together and outlasting together. Lying together in a state of preservation.

ONE —They are enslaved by their state of preservation.

TWO —In writing the play I did not imitate nature I naturally imitated writing.

FIVE —I am perfectly willing to write the whole act in this manner. Fourth Act, Scene Two. Could there be perpetual play in playing where even perfections of form were playd out. This is what I designd, a play in which terror was playful. I can describe it in all its difficulties as playing it had problems of composing itself. It pretends to be what it is.

TWO —We have only to talk and the act will be over. It is our acting alone that puts the talk over.

FIVE —Let me put it this way. How are Marlowe and our author alike? Were they alight in wretched exceeding, in impatient fruitfulness, in barren thirst for terror?

ONE —I was a domestic Marlowe. It was the common place that was my bloody luxury in living.

FOUR —Those who reflect are tolerant of mirrors.

THREE —What do you mean?

FOUR —She is answerless, Our Lady of the Other Side of the Moon, a source in our trouble that remaind untroubled.

FIVE —There isn't any difference in sides. Change sides. Malice illumines.

ONE —Our Lady impersonated. Attackd straight on. A sophistomoronificated display.

(RISING TO ADDRESS THE AUDIENCE) The puddling of all gains. A gape with silly canines cracking across the remnants of style. I apologize for the brutish indulgences that infect the quality of your entertainment. A solo? Below the ecstatic surfaces of autosuggestion, the last humanistic ravings of the Renaissance put to bed, the bird cackle and boneplay, an anglo-saxon mummery and a keltic dada—I play straight man to an emotional strip-tease? I ride an offense to everything I work toward a work that will incorporate the offense. I walk thru the streets & crowds of my sensations, like the poet in Isou's movie, *du Bave et d'Eternité*, but incapable, being American, of his insouciance, of his austerity. Over me no guardian Flaubert, no ingenious Cocteau, no ghost of Racine. The theater has demolishd itself in success. And we are again on the streets. To set up our pitch outside the machineries of the great stage. *Foutu! Foutu! Foutu!* Hear! Hear! A medicine show! It is a world suspended in the solitude of Crowd-Me. A testimony. Here! Here! A self-indulgence for sale! This is my face as no mirror but my mind sees it, my heart as it beats, my nerves as they reach toward the edge of, fall, strike or are stricken. A sensation! An inarticulate memorial! It is the not-to-be-seen, the no-secret self. But walking as I am walking as if about to awaken within me. For years now I have waited, waited upon myself. Erased! Only you know me. I am immediately everywhere erased. All that is dear to me watches my continual departure from before I can arrive.

You are the audience who does not roar. Roar! You are the audience who are no one multiplied largely into a looking hearing nothing. A crowd like me. Break away then. Break from it, break O comrade who shake lest my pretension increase. I am increasing my pretension until it falls into all its vitalities.

Now. Look at me! This is me, torso. Hairy as never was a god, the animal sleeps in its dirty hair like a fire in a nest, a rat rooting with greed in garbage. This is me, Side-Show. This is none of you. Over the beautifully weak shoulders that might have been, had I served them, thrilling to the avid devourers of strength in the body, over the soft round tense nervous ashamed exposed shoulders the animal hair, that cares nothing for *me*, spreads its apish splendor. It covers eagerly the indolent rolls of flesh that corrupts in its greed for life— indulged—my immortal skeleton. This is me, Torso. I do not regard my navel, my navel regards me. As I speak, you will, like me, avoid my naked torso where it beseeches you. As I speak I am trembling as you hear me tremble because I am exposed. I am only me as you see me. Faust. Foutu foutu foutu. This nakedness is me not because it is beautiful, this nakedness is beautiful not because it can be endured, this nakedness can be endured not because it is strong, this nakedness is strong not because it is craved and craven, this nakedness is craved and craven not because it is shameless. It has shame! It *is* shame! Alive with shame so that living through shame I may claim my place among movie stars. I may retrieve my immortal image from all perfection. It is *my* torso that strikes wonder so that the gods are dismayd.

I am coming to the point. To manufacture the slow interior dismay. I did not so make myself in this form, generations of me did not so come into this play, to be appreciated. Break up! Break up! The solid intent uncomfortable mass of you waiting to shame me, break into laughter. Break into the ha-has. One two eighty. Count! One one one I one one four break. I one one one one one one one one one one one one own one own one own. One. Stop.

I die in days. Come in apologies a horse. Numbers. Age. She fell further than to reach rememberd the processes of walking. It is time strips us to ease, the lazy tables. And turning numbers to their purposes transports daily machines, a transport, a rapport. Rap. Rap. If the perpetuating melancholy increases it is to a restless aggravation in which the magicians walk like camels. O clumsy but begetting ovals and rounds around all clumsiness. A ballet. There is no way! Is there no way? to collapse our expectations into expecting?

All of this Faust is a world in a house collapsing, a romance of rooms that are scenes painted perpetually bare in their changes without a curtain. It is because you imagine me that you can see me as if I were as dear to you as your created visions. This is a serial track in time discontinuous, the reality of my torso you have always been seeing in its disappearing among all the objects you have realized. It is the voluptuous joy of throwing my selves away, of spending my energies fruitlessly. Ah, ah Beloved, you have created me unknown. In that nakedness there are no surprises, no shocks, no recognitions. It is the still unmoving center, the boredom transformd, that causes me to tremble.

This is a statue of flesh, reoccurring in time, not revised but made new in its own image. Break. Break. The imagination is the falling away of our real acquisitions. The otherness reveald when I lay bare the poor spectacle of my body.

The slow bondage that pays. The slow bondage that pays. The accumulation that pays. The steady set jaw that pays. The slow bondage that pays. Repairs as it pays. The solace that pays. The money that pays. The bondage of fear and pride to the job that pays. The bondage of pride to the slowness that pays. The bondage of pride to the know-how that pays. The regular pride in bondage that pays. The continual bondage that pays. The service that pays. The thoughtful remembrance and kindness that pays. It pays. The slow bondage that pays. It pays. Pays. The insurance that pays. The bondage in bonds that pays. The bond that pays. The foreseeing the slow bondage that pays. The adherence that pays. The slow bondage that saves and pays. The increasing slow bondage. The bondage. It saves as it pays. It saves. The steady set grit of the teeth that pays. The winning that pays. The keeping that pays. It pays. The organization, the binding pays, in bondage that pays. The bond that saves. The slow bondage that pays.

This is my torso that works as it pays. This is the torso that serves its master as it works as it pays. This is the torso in slow bondage that serves its master as it works as it pays. This is the torso hairy and trembling that lives under the brain and does its slow bondage that serves its master as it works as it pays. The slow bondage that pays.

Then better, Faust cries, to be fuckd! Foutu! Foutu! Foutu!

Can I destroy your indestructible mere appreciation? The problem is to amuse myself without paying. What a play! No matter what I can do I cause either shame or scorn or ennui or amusement. I divert. There is no way. Is there no way? to open to you the pure thing, the effort, the effort alone, the beautiful appetite that takes without giving. There is no time for failure. There is only the slow bondage that makes it pay. The mind has been school to master each saving disgrace. A meaning! Every attempt pays.

This is me. Torso. Immortal. Ah, the hair, my animal hair does not pay!

A diversion calld *All That Is Not Imagination Is a Time Payment Plan Calld A Useful Life*.

Part Two. A Letter to my Dentist:

I am writing to you because only in writing have I the courage of my imagination, the counsel of desire. You want to save me from the pains and humiliations of toothless old age. You appeal to fear I have for my bones. You want me to invest now to insure against the decay of all goods. But, you see, in this play here, this Faust thing, I desire the last act. What, indeed, then if my teeth go before my appetite? My mind already tires and prepares to go. My body has long departed from youth, going, going into the adventures of its debilities. Its only splendors are splendors of my misuses. So, disease. It is the very disorder of my heart that stirs irritations of speech in time and breeds poetry. What shall we repair? Fix it up? A disease. An immortal dis-ease.

You will not understand it, but my longing dwells upon the terror, but it is not a terror—a feebleness, and the adventuring pity, but it is not pity—a conceald whine, of the decrepitude. All that calculation cannot grasp. Only the imagination awaits its great changes, its roots in senility, as it has realized already its immortal role of restless useless youth and as it celebrates the acts of manhood.

Au revoir, dear dentist! The immutable tables of the drama address the grave. Bye, bye, dentist! There are toothless sheep in the pastures of heaven.

1	Au	revoir!	Sophokle,	au revoir
2			Sophocles	goodbye
3	The ancient concentrations of our spirit are dispersed.
4	On ly to die!	To	die!
5		I—

5
SOLO —have consulted the oracles, the solitary hour, the strain in
rising from all rest. Not to let it rest. To strain all daily things
away. Only the rest remains, the leaning forward into the play.
Wait. Never to be fulfilld in writing. Never to be fulfilld.
This, awaits me.

1		at the door	he is	he is
2	Faust is for ever		restless
3		O restless		rest, Faust
4	adore him		adore him then
5				Never!—

5
SOLO —This man? A divine uselessness wrapt round in himself.
There Faust goes! We see him as he sees him not. Look! Look!
Only we shall see him as he can never—

1	the sea
2		over-heard	the human	—
3		alone	alone	silence—
4	the serpent hissing sea.	This is a conversation over—
5	—see him.		—

2	—herd
3	a snake
4	—heard
5	a serpent seraphim or snake-wise flame of

1	the scratching of the pen inside the silent altar hour
2	he came to be a bridegroom, to open up the book of hours
3	an open book. It is the text itself in which we are
4	let me . let me let let me speak let me speak
5	after midnight

1	I want to see him fall to pieces. Faust. Piece way from piece.
2	are worn by sleepers like the tide of endless plots let me—
5	let me let let me speak and let me
3	To speak!
4	Tied up.

1	As it falls, it falls into place. It replaces a hymn—
2	—me let me let me please let me please lie—
3	All other voices must exhaust themselves forever,
4	A tidy mess A mass A tide
5	him

1	in which the no-thing peace
2	—down upon the useless altars of the hour
3	straining speak up, I say! Speak up.
4	to let it speak
5	I might depart to wash the dirty dishes out of myself

3	Against the need.
5	—and solitude into necessity to keep the time.

5	—A vow. There is foreverness just now impending. You,
SOLO	beloved, as you are in always resting in my never resting. Is
	there a moment? Stop it. A moment. I stopd to waste myself in
	you. Now I must go up into myself where I have never been,
	all you who in creating me dream your poor eternity. And
	coming back the step by step, dropping light by light, chairs,
	dishes, streetcar sound afar, clock whirr anear, dear walls,
	books, pans, curtains, a largely growing table until there draws
	a body hunchd over the play, a crampd hand, fingers each by
	each moving in writing. A reality. Returns all that I am—

1	Solemnly I
2	the vow is life
3	O no! the vow is an address upon a river to—
5	—to vow.

3	˙ —the tide, a speech made now . I say I have died Now died
4	Now
5	out of the play!

3	A dance I died I did I died a dance I died.
4	Now Now To make it now!
5	What! Indeed, did I get out of the—

5	—play? There is my great impatience struggling out of the
SOLO	play. We will never come back to the place you know it
	now. A part. He wanted a part in the play. Love, fame, honor,
	peace—what passion do you imagine, what Medea enraged,
	what Oedipus blinded, what toppling Lear, what Faust trickd,
	what Peer Gynt as he goes, to the limit, to the lasting cry,
	to sacrifice. It is gone. They are all gone. I cannot convey
	the tedium that drove them. That drives us mad. Where is
	he? Faust? reaching up out of the play. The ground painted
	with candor. A plainness of speech needed. A turmoil. An
	inarticulate candor. Look!

1	A pain
2	an age, an ancient wrestling
3	an angel, at birth, cries
4	blessings
5	Thou art deliverd!

5	Deliver me. Deliver me. Never to be tossd up by rage, out
SOLO	of all human endeavor. Into what? This is as we conceive
	him, held short, burning, but the fire does not burn at all.
	He cannot deliver himself up into his phoenix. We picture
	then the holocaust. The whole state of mind, like Medea's,
	an unnatural splitting in a single purpose, not into two—we
	flounder in our selves. I mean nation within nation, enormous.

He grows enormous, swelling huge with ancient burning fires.
A pigmy bird. Upon the brink of giant woes. Damnd.

ONE —A shudder across the generations reaches Faust.

TWO —He dances on the strings of his desire.

THREE —How drôle. He reaches up as if he had a soul to speak.

FOUR —This is a cry we could not hear.

FIVE —For love or money.

ONE —The cost of life, all time a gnawing rat.

TWO —The money worries each hour at the throat.

THREE —O for the love of Man! Give him rest.

FOUR —The war's his world. The usurers take the rest.

FIVE —And so he strives, toward tragedy, strikes pity pity pity again,
again the ancient tones of our hearts no longer ring. The design.
The design is lost. Himself in the crucible and all the bronze he
knows, or oldest iron.   Does not ring. Fired. Fired. Whatever blaze
of almost terror does not ring true. Over the thunderous cities he
rings.   He don't ring true. Ring true. He don't.

CHORUS —blast him   blast him

FIVE —He watches the stupid zero hours of each day

CHORUS —blast him   blast him

FIVE —The emptied heralds of the heart awake

CHORUS —blast him   blast him

FIVE —Shake in the shadowy towers of the mind

CHORUS —blast him   blast him

FIVE —As if pity and terror were to move the world

CHORUS —entire

FIVE —at last

CHORUS —As if. . .

FIVE —The music of our hearts rings out upon the imaginary air.
Poor Faustus almost hears. It does not die. Slowly all history returns.
Another time. Where climbing cost by cost the sullen multitude
prepares
such eternal debts, such sunderings
—an end—
We do not yet know how far it will go!
What will we fear? At last?

Medea at Kolchis
The Maiden Head

1965

A Note by the Author

Black Mountain College, North Carolina
August 1956

We would like to account for the profound anxiety. But it is a weather—a saturated air of the summer—that obstructs all account. Fear, desire, accusation, tenderness, joy, despair are caught up, unreleased, in the storm head. Tomorrow, the sky will be blue; yet all is unrelieved. The sun too is of the obstruction. A violent electricity charges such weather. Even the flashes of lightning in the heat do not release the rain but portend greater devastations of agony.

Where the rain will not come, sorcery flourishes. O, sure, it rains, but sorcery flourishes. The swamp land, more terrible than the waste land. No innocent rain.

Uninformed, we must use the stage as it is. Without knowledge, dance our damned rain dance as we can.

Another Preface. 1963/1965

I had had in mind for some time doing a play of the young Medea—I saw her as a pubescent girl—who falls in love with Jason and betrays her father that Jason may steal the fleece. The girl's obsessive passion prefiguring the woman's wrathful jealousy and the hero's determination to win his prize prefiguring the husband's enlightened self-interest struck a chord that intrigued me. Here and there in notebooks I had sketched bits of speeches and propositions of scenes. It seemed to me that in my own life I had played Jason to Medeas I had known and Medea to Jasons. But all this identification was far short of any dramatic reality. When the play came into its own, it came from a cast of its own—it cast its own Jason and Medea.

At Black Mountain College in the Summer of 1956, Wes Huss asked me to do a play, and I began, given the little company of students with whom I worked, to write, drawing from the actors lines and masses of a picture I had not previously conceived. Then there were dramatic entities that came forward from my own phantasy to play upon the stage. The old woman, GARROW, had appeared in an imaginary life of Robert

Creeley I had started writing the year before in Mallorca to amuse myself. An imaginary woman herself then; that she was garrulous was part of her name; that she was old—but AGE thruout is part of the play. There are times when GARROW talking to herself is the play talking to itself. Let the actress put on this old mind as a trick of the stage or of life and, if GARROW should come to ride, as the loa Erzulie Ge-Rouge or Erzulie Maitresse comes to ride in the rites of Voudoun, let the actress be a good horse. GARROW is the actress playing before her self or before the dead, and impersonating the dead as a child will impersonate his audience and his other, or before Arthur, Edna, or the Doctor. So don't try to make her real by painting age on her face or remembering infirmity in her gait. What I mean by age is she has the permission of time and she takes her time; she can gather her thought and thought that's not hers and let it go as she will—wool gathering, we call it. And she can put on the Norn to cut the thread when the necessity comes.

When the genius of the English stage was fresh, she might have been Juliet's nurse; or in the adolescent sophistication of Restoration comedy a bawdy country wife; but as Arthur's mistress and housekeeper she is half in, half out of, a romance by William Morris. For ARTHUR is a remnant of Pre-Raphaelite kings living on in the art-nouveau last stage, in a phantasy of time and personality that takes on shades of Maeterlinck and early Yeats. There is no scene in which he is not playing the mask of the poet. He has lost or cast away self and exists in the vagaries of his thematic legend of Arthur, now thru the medium of the fleece King Æetes; he lives in the theme.

Back of Yeats or William Morris, in the children's hour I had heard, as my mother or father read from Hawthorne's *Wonder Book* the story of The Golden Fleece, tell of such an old woman as Garrow or such an old man as Arthur. Or I almost saw and heard at times ghosts of certain sibylic and melancholic actresses from old plays or movies in whom life had stored a black humor and of ponderous and ominous actors—Arthur's tale of the Fleece harkened back to the figure of Sidney Greenstreet in *The Maltese Falcon* telling his tale. But my conceptions moved too through the actual actors' impersonations and through shadows of their impersonations as they took over their roles where character began to emerge and to lead my imagination—Edna and Boris who sprang to life in the reality Eloise Mixon and Eric Weir gave them for me; Medea and Jason taking body as I would never otherwise have imagined from the inspiration of Ann Simone and Donald Mixon.

EDNA, Arthur's sister, is ephemeral—a moth in her movements of body and hands as well as in her thought, hovering, trembling, flitting; as if the day of her life were long past and she continued in an afterlife like an afterglow. Some fugitive memory of Chalciope, the mother of Argos, who, in the *Argonautica* of Apollonius Rhodius, opens the way for the Greek invaders, gave rise to EDNA. And now searching out for the first time this passage, I find: *And when she saw them near she cried out, and quickly did Chalciope hear, and the maid-servants threw down at their feet their yarn and thread, and came running out all together*—where Edna's scene with the Doctor in the Second Act seems prefigured. BORIS, the Doctor, takes on his character in correspondence to Edna. He is romantic about being a realist. They are, the two of them, out of Chekov, illustrating, like Arthur out of Morris, the turn of the century. Yet at times, when we see BORIS with Jason, he takes on the role of Hermes-Psychopompos, the leader of the soul in the underworld.

MEDEA is in her puberty, that may be as young as twelve or as old as sixteen, an ambivalence of girlhood before which we are unsure. She is a life-tension and intensity that is the counterpart of the death-tension and intensity of her father's heart. She is a fury, and for her the play is a progress from her fury to the first steps of the witch, stirring up a magic to make a fate of her desire.

JASON remains the Jason of the Argonauts, a daemonic being, a wraith or wrath of the hero. In his human appearance he dissembles and must always speak from an earnest insincerity. Thus, he enters the play with Garrow's bitter words *"Sweet thots!"*, in this tableau and in the third act of the play dressed in the short skirt of classical Greek illustrations to display the lure of a youthful and masculine torso. In the day-time of the play he wears, like the rest of the cast, clothes of the contemporary scene in 1904.

We did not have a regular stage at Black Mountain. We improvised a theater area in a large hall, having the space of a small auditorium but no raised platform or proscenium arch. The play was not conceived then in terms of curtains, realistic scene-changes—the machineries, that are also encumbrances, of the modern stage; but the actors moved in an imaginary space, making up the world they were in. Stage-left was the area of the living room with the entrance to the house at the back of the stage; middle back was Arthur's area where the Fleece hung and his chair stood; stage-right was Medea's room where we rigged up a canopy of gauze to hang above her bed; front stage-right was the garden or forest area outside the house. In the closing act of the play the bed was moved to the margins of Arthur's room for his death-bed scene and then brought to the front stage-left to create Edna's room. When not in their scene, the actors dropped their roles and stood or sat where they were, at attention, waiting for their cues, or could move as scene changers in the Chinese theater move to set up a scene invisibly.

My concept of *The Maiden Head* is not related so much to the Dionysian mysteries, to the great theater of Greek tragedy—tho in the play I meant for the head of the Maiden to rise from the ground as in the old rites of Kore—as to the primitive theater of each of us in our own lives, the nursery where infantile and puerile passions are enacted in play; for the persons of my stage are playing house, playing elves, playing the eternal return of Jason and Medea. It has seemed to me that all man's psychic and spiritual life arises in such play with physical realities, using his actual body as it uses his actual world about him to enact its drama.

Scenes and properties of this stage then should be made up as children make up palaces from colored blocks and mountains from sand, or men make up sphinxes from women and raging wars from religious or political or economic phantasies. Makeup the Pre-Raphaelite, Symbolist, Art Nouveau *mise-en-scène* not to make realistic the period of 1904 but, as the poets and artists of that tradition did, to illuminate the world about them so that it might speak what they were waiting to hear and show what they were waiting to see.

Medea at Kolchis
The Maiden Head

The Cast & Scenes
As the play was presented at Black Mountain College,
August 29th* and August 30th** 1956:
Garrow . . . Wesley Huss
Jason . . . Donald Mixon
The Doctor . . . Erik Weir
Medea . . . Ann Simone
Arthur . . . Louis Marbury*, John Wieners**
Edna . . . Eloise Mixon

PROLOG: *Midnight, Arthur's House*
FIRST ACT: *Broad Daylight, Arthur's House—Living Room,*
Arthur's Chamber, Medea's Bedroom
(intermission)
SECOND ACT: *Afternoon. In a Forest; Arthur's House.*
(intermission)
THIRD ACT: *Night, Arthur's House; In the Forest.*
Early Morning, Arthur's House—Edna's Room.

PROLOG

At night. Arthur's House. There is only the moonlight at the window stage-left.
GARROW needs no more light than that for she knows the house in her bones,
and in the dark where others sleep she keeps her own time and place and in that
time and place she seems to keep company with an other, Arthur's dead wife.

GARROW: August again! let in the hour!
The year comes in with the light. In the dark
what time is it? 1904? That's a time.
And you keep quiet there! What do you know
of the time I keep?
                    Hew! it's hot.
All the roasted odors of the garden
fill the house. I'd shed my clothes
and step from the camphor into the rose-cloud. . .
a-a-a-a His speech sneaks up on a body.

Did I ever feel that? What care
have I for a cloud of roses? As if that was likely.
Forty-five years in this house.
    "Don't sir,"
I says. "Don't sir. Question me—
I have only one answer." Hah!

Now there comes in Garrow's sighing breath a contraction and, projected, as if
it came from the air above, the ventriloqual voice of the medium, another breath
that carries a whimpering cry.

            a-a-a-a-a-a-a
And what's eating *you* up there?
Snakes?

              Snakes. snakes. snakes
              Shedding the light like skin
              in order to live. Live.

Live? Easy as shed
a few clothes and be as good as naked.
But you're a Lady! You always liked
being dressed up.
And why shouldn't naked be just as good
these years? I've ripened. The skin
changes.   Crumply old body! "Ah, come sir,"
I say, "I'm an old girl now. You're
the foolish one!"
      But his old eyes burn.
His old hands strip the mind. What do you know? Me then
I've a shudder left to send over his world.
They say infections swarm around the dead!
             The way
      infections swarm around the dead!
     Skins   .   colors   .   cloud fleece
          gold in the light.

Gold? I remember
I was cold in the light.
"Why, it's morning," I say.   And he
says a little song for dawn.   Filld with songs!

ARTHUR enters; as if just now his spirit had entered the house or the play, we see him pass silently into his room or part, a chair rear center where he sleeps, and above his throne the fleece begins to glitter.

But that was the light of the last century.
And what did I know at all in 1864? All girl and yes!
His hot old mind   gold in the light of my   old body.
Now you'll never leave me alone, will you?
Crawl out of my crumpled skin   little light by little light.

"Whore" you calld me?   and you a Lady?
Agh!   the flesh has mysteries enough.
And they aren't something we'll be coming to know entirely.
His snake curld up in some other time.
What does he see?   or care?
A dry smell of me?   But his mind gathers old colors.
                 Gathers? . .
         Ohhh. . it's slow   to crawl
            out of his history.
         No! I said, No! It binds me
            to the cold.
"Yes," I say.   It warms the place.
I'll be bound to see him thru.
What did you ever care in this world?

MEDEA enters and crosses the stage as GARROW continues, taking her place upon her couch front stage to the right.

It's time for morning to wake up.
Only these old eyes see
today's lies, tomorrow's shadows.

She'll be up, clear-eyed as ever. Once more.
But what is innocence now that throws
         such a shadow?
Dirty Truth!
I see you right enuf!   You there,
that's been hanging onto this house.
You'd have had none of it when you were alive.
O how life's hungers eat into you pale ones!

Medea at Kolchis   599

I hear you, drawing complaint—it's your breath—
where he touches my old body
                    Tiiiime
            has no body . Clean.
        The snake shakes
        clean from its body.
        She'll be up clear-eyed
        and will see where we
            gather.

Enter JASON and THE DOCTOR, taking their stance front stage left in the area
of the living room

    Sweet thots!
    We all have mothers don't we?
    And here in this house
    the solid consuming terror of it gathers
    like a fever in an old body.

GARROW now standing just back of MEDEA's bed waits, listening. JASON and
THE DOCTOR appear in a pool of light.

JASON: What a wonderful library he has. Do you think when he dies I
    might inherit some of his books?

DOCTOR: Eager beast! That foolish old man has calld you to be heir of
    his fantasy because of a name. He has set a lamp by the window and
    the angry beetle comes craving ravages of the light. You *are* a beetle,
    you know. If I were not tied to you, I would turn back, pure spirit,
    from this stage of the plunder.

JASON: Is this the language of dreams? I'm not responsible for what he
    makes of my name Jason. At night the bloody soul starves for the
    sun. But I have no part in that. I will return to the day, to the shores
    of Greece, increased.

DOCTOR: O, you will neither swell nor shrink.

JASON: It is the Fleece of the Sun that is the important thing. Sleep
    warps the shape of what we are.

DOCTOR: It *is* the Fleece that is the important thing. In the three
    thousand years between this night and tomorrow in 1904 all rumor
    of the books will perish. And what was the Fleece in the light of
    day? But you will remain Jason. Over and over again how she fell

Medea at Kolchis   600

in love with you, like a light in love with an insect, and enterd the stage of this desire will be sung—its core of agony like an act in the old mysteries.

Come, it is time to change from night to morning.

Exit JASON *and* DOCTOR.

MEDEA: What time is it?

GARROW: Time? I was just moving about a bit to open the windows, dear. I never meant to wake you. It's your birthday.

MEDEA: Day? But there's no light.

GARROW: It's your birth *night*. You remember all of your childhood? It was the tenderest green thots of a young forest.   All *morning!* I've come to tend your *dark* thots.
     O pay no attention to my fancies! They come upon me like a herd of black men. Look, how sweet the moon is!

MEDEA: O no sweet moon! Before I woke, it seemd to me the moon was huge and red.

GARROW: I could tell you stories of that red moon. There's a reason for dread. A woman died and deliverd you up, her daughter. That was a redness of the moon.

MEDEA: I've never seen her. Mother. Who gave birth to me?

GARROW: You were deliverd up to *me*, Nurse. You were no-one's daughter, but princess of the realm.

MEDEA: Of what . . realm?

GARROW: There are dreams of the blood where the soul swarms and dreams of the breath where the spirit flies. And of these there are dreams that go to the sun beyond the night and there are those that go to the fastnesses of the moon. O . . I call it the Hive, the Insect's Nest, the Crawling Light. To desire.

MEDEA *as if starting up again*: Garrow? Garrow!

GARROW: Yes dear.

MEDEA: Are you there? I dreamt you were there. But it was frightening then.

GARROW: There, there. I am only opening the window a bit to let in the breeze. It was hot, and you had bad dreams.

MEDEA: I came to the depths of a forest beyond the house and . . in a clearing . . found . . .

GARROW: Yes? Don't be afraid.

MEDEA: . . a bloody . . It was a pool . . No! It was just a . . clearing there where darkness was. She coverd the moon.

GARROW: Go to sleep. It is your birth hour. Make a wish, it will come true.

ARTHUR, *as if these voices had been talking in his dream, stirs, sleep-talking himself, barely rising to the surface, sinking back.*

ARTHUR: Voices. Rustlings. The Fleece in the house is talking again I think. . . O Death I . .

GARROW *to* MEDEA *but also to Arthur*: There. There. It will soon be morning, and that great light, prince of the day. . .

ARTHUR: What did you say? Ah, to lie back in the glamors of the speech. A woman comes to the gate of sleep's kingdom. To plead for something. I remember her? No! She whimpers!   Turn her away! . . I only want to listen, drift, initiate to the sweet murmur. . . . There are no dreams! no wakings, no . . deafness of sleep is all. Only the honeyd initiation.

GARROW: Down there, Medea, your father lies in the corruption of his art. It is a poetry that confuses night and day, a sleepless drone, an old king that time will devour.

   Now you have come to that division of the Way, a clearing prepared for the Queen among her nurses. Sleep . . Sleep . . terrible innocence of sleep, like a crown innocent of its jewels. What do you know of the honey that surrounds you, feeding the Queen?

ACT ONE

SCENE ONE. *Same as Prolog. Dark. A bell rings and even as it rings the stage is in full daylight.*

GARROW: Already? I'm coming.

The Doctor enters with JASON

DOCTOR: It's the Doctor. And young Jason just arrived. We came directly from the coach stop before going on to my place. Arthur is expecting him.

GARROW: We're all expecting the young man. Well, Doctor, he's handsome isn't he? Such nice shoulders. He'd be a hero, I guess. I never trust young poets that don't fill their trousers so as a mind's disturbd with real higher thots.

JASON: And you'll be that "lewd nurse of our immortal fate" that "shakes the grandeur of an old man's thot"?

GARROW: You've got it by heart, ain't you?

JASON: For five years I've lived in the work of Arthur Griffith.

DOCTOR: This young man, Mrs Garrow, is a student of Arthur.

GARROW: Don't I know everything already? Sit me down in a warm corner, Mr Apollo, and I'll add a piece or two to your story.

Exit GARROW. *Each "room" of the play house is conceived as a stage within the stage.* GARROW, *once she steps out of the area of the scene with the* DOCTOR *and* JASON, *is as if backstage waiting for her cue until she enters her next scene. As* MEDEA *and* ARTHUR, *altho lying on her bed and sitting in his chair, are not alive or there until the stage is there.*

DOCTOR: She is old. She's a fine woman, but her judgment is impaird with years.

JASON: She likes me tho. It's her way, I take it, of putting it. And I catch a glint in her mockery. She may be after all the very "Mistress of the Night" and ageless then. In town I always heard that she was Arthur's lover.

DOCTOR: She has been housekeeper here for almost my lifetime. She was Medea's age when she first came to the house—a handsome girl. People in town were bound to talk. Since Mrs Griffith's death when Medea was born Garrow has been the child's nurse.

GARROW *entering:* His Highness will see you now. You won't need an introduction. He spent the evening looking at your poems. But it will be your *name* that he knows.

JASON *suddenly appearing at a loss, as if he were an ingenuous young admirer:* What shall I say to him, Boris? What if he doesn't like me? It is all a misunderstanding. *Exit*

DOCTOR: Say it simply. I have come to partake of your greatness. You calld me. I have come to consult you, to take what I can, to ravish the stores of your legend. He will never understand that you are acquainted with neither pride nor shame.

EDNA: Good morning, Doctor! I missd the young man with the Greek name, I see. He was in the cards last night, you know. Garrow, would you get coffee for the Doctor and me? You will join me? You've never been in the cards, Doctor. And yet you're here. The cards don't lie. . . That's an old line! Everything that comes to be read lies. How the cards lie. How the land lies. .

DOCTOR: Is it because I am true then?

EDNA: Oh, you're too charming to be true. No. That's not it. You have nothing to do with charms really. You don't like . . charm . . . I was on the downs this morning . hunting for rings. I had no dreams last night. I fell asleep waiting. . Oh yes . on the downs. All night they'd been playing, the light translucent ones! I think I saw the last, a glimmer passing thru the high grass, just before dawn. When I was in Ireland I saw them enter their hill, you know. . . Then you came up thru the rings. Didn't you feel it?

DOCTOR: I felt nothing.

GARROW *speaking as if unseen, for tho she is present in this scene, serving coffee, or sitting in a chair darning, her speech is aside and yet unconsciously heard:* Don't you wish you were a man that could be toucht? But even the moon doesn't reach you, does it?

DOCTOR: My friend has charm enuf.

EDNA: Yes, I saw it from the distance there. Where you walkt the rings were unreal. There was only the grass and the footpath and the rocks. I can always see it your way. . . But where he walkt the rings broke away from him or radiated from him. They were his.

DOCTOR: He's drawn to these things. Perhaps I am the better guardian for being without such charm.

GARROW: Ah! the soul that rejects the body's charm is a spiritless thing. I'd take the body's charm without the soul any day. The spirit hangs around a body like a howl that wakes old memories.

EDNA: Love was in the cards. And that young man. He was so tall and handsome.

DOCTOR: He's not so tall.

EDNA: Oh! but in romance! You are intolerant of romance, aren't you? Something in us is. But this is the house of a poet, a pure romance. We have been waiting for your young man.

What a curious friend you are. Almost without belief. And so, not entirely believable.

DOCTOR: As the Fairie *are* believable?

EDNA: They are entirely of belief.

GARROW: But don't you believe it, I always say. What's the soul if it ain't in the blood? A thinnest, most uninteresting thing. It's the solid flesh of a man I'd believe in. It don't have the sense to lie. The bloody meat of him all wired up, a regular spirit lamp. There's a light! Sure, an old girl can turn up all the wick that a man's man throws off.

SCENE THREE. *ARTHUR and JASON in Arthur's room, viewing the Fleece. As ARTHUR speaks, motioning JASON to take a chair, seating himself in his chair that, when he speaks of Philip of Burgundy, will be a throne, for the viewer who saw* The Maltese Falcon *he may recall Sidney Greenstreet's portrayal of the Fat Man, for the fascination of the Fleece parallels the fascination of the falcon in that scene. Arthur, anyway, is, as always, playing the scene; whatever comes to his mind draws him on with its reality and he himself takes on some shade in the relation. Thruout it all, again, he is playing the poet for Jason.*

JASON: This is the actual Fleece, sir?

ARTHUR: Yes, it is the Fleece. . . or a *sign* of the Fleece. It is very old. . . It may be from a pageant of the 18th century. It may be earlier. These ancient things reoccur. (*He seats himself.*) The Dukes of Burgundy in the fifteenth century were kings, enormously wealthy, for Burgundy was the heart of Europe, the crossroads of all routes of trade and war. Neither the King of France nor the Emperor himself commanded such power. The Duke Philip returning from the defeat of Ghent where he had wept at the sight of the piteous slaughter returned true Emperor of the Western World, and at Lille set up the greatest court of the late Middle Ages under the emblem of the Golden Fleece. . . The Emperor was vicar of Christ and heir to the mysteries of Charlesmagne. At Saint Denis, where the chrism given by angelic orders to the kings of France was stored, the priests prepared the oriflamme, and in the twelfth century Louis the Sixth rode forth under his banner of gold flames against the Emperor. There is no great event that is not a mask. But the triumphant mysteries were the festivals of Lille where Philip of Burgundy was Sovereign of the Order of the Golden Fleece. The last splendor of

chivalry . outlasting its time. . . . In 1428 upon the occasion of his
marriage to Ysabel of Portugal Philip created an anachronistic order,
a new mystery in which the net of his political power and the net of
old legend were one. A play of Argonauts. . . He sent Jan van Eyck
with ambassadors to Lisbon where van Eyck painted the likeness
of the Princess for Philip's inspection. At Sluys where she landed
the streets were carpeted with the finest woolens and hung with
tapestries designd by the van Eycks to illustrate the new allegories.
Picture the Duke in his state. It is *wool* that rules the continent. The
wealth of the new era in Italy flourishes as part of the trade route
with the East; factories are beginning there. But Flanders, Brabant,
Limbourg, are the thrones of the Lamb—the Lamb that is Christ,
as the van Eycks painted him for Philip. At Ghent in 1445 Philip
holds a great conclave of his Mystery. Thirty-one knights vow
their allegiance to the Order of the Golden Fleece—Argonauts—
and kneel, clothed in dress of woolen cloth—so it is named—but
actually, the dress is of crimson velvet, the collar composed of jewels
and gold. The Duke himself is enthroned beneath a canopy of gold
in front of that famous altar of the van Eycks, *The Adoration of the
Lamb*, where we see portrayd the Fleece from which an eternal
wound flows blood—the blood of Flanders shed at Ghent. Blood,
incredible power shown forth in gold and jewels, the power of old
legend to outlast its time—these are engines of an imposing Beauty!
And Philip had raised the Fleece in the place of the Grail, with the
legend *ante ferit quam flamma micat.*

    There's a story, eh? . . What did I know at your age of the real
mysteries? I cared. I sought romance, hidden things, wonder. A man
wants kingdom . . some pathetic ape's finery! Now I've found that
it was the *wool* that was the mystery. Enchantment is a glitter left
over where power once moved. The order, the velvet and jewels,
these stand in stead of the wool.

JASON: The splendor of that court is like the splendor of your poetry.

recites Where has the mockingbird removed to sing,
       what magnificences to ring
       from pages I have read or lore
       gatherd from a common store?
       Did Jacques de Molay regret
       the confidences of his Bronze Head?

Or Faust in the luxurious pain of hell
not dwell in Helen's fiery smile. . .

ARTHUR *picking up the recitation:*
. . I know no splendor that is not Desire. .

No! That's the wrong thing. The wrong thing. Time changes it.
A man can desire rude, unsplendid things. . . I've read these verses
of yours. Why repeat an old man's first errors? In the eighties I was
corrupted. I was wrong, wrong. What does the opulence mean? the
peacock feathers of iridescent blue we all loved then. . the lilies? The
velvet is a sort of *rot* of the wool.

JASON: *You* are the splendid thing. Splendor went with you. In that
poetry you've been an old King for me, a Father. The old King who
devours the Son I've seen in alchemical pictures.

ARTHUR: You mislead yourself. Would you mislead me? Don't waste
your time with these things. . . What do you want? I am an old
man! . . I am at the end of my time. Are you a poet of your time?
Does time have a poet? I don't know. . . You are the hero of some
poem. Jason, they calld you. Be a new Jason then and return with
the Fleece if you can. What was the Fleece after it left Colchis?

JASON: O no! the Fleece is yours. The Fleece you have said is the
Secret Sharer.

ARTHUR: You. . my daughter . . my sister. . the World too, is the secret
sharer. And ghosts. . A man has enough of voices! But I can't. . .
Look here. . why? My mind has. . .

Why did I tell you that story of the Order? Philip's soul fed upon
a vast real wealth. Gold? What do we know of gold? a few old rings,
paper the color of gold, washes of gold paint? And what did his
successor Charles know of the Order? . . I'm tired of talking now.

JASON: O forgive me. I must let you rest. . . But is this really the
Fleece of Philip?

ARTHUR *dismissing Jason* : Later. . later.

Exit JASON

They keep at it. They won't let it go. For what it is.

ARTHUR *turns now to listen; lines are coming to him as if from the air just
above his head and he begins now to recite from the dictation, beating the stresses*

of the line upon the air as if conducting music. His recitation is in the old style
we know from the recordings Yeats made.

The light comes thru the dim shutter
and in the darkend room the counsels glitter.
Michelangelo and the divine Aquinas
are only names for Doom's recorder.
The vast estates of the brooding mind are
rubble, perishable as rumord Nineveh.

Where are you then, my White Lady,
that intrude as if to claim me?

No. No it's gone. *He rings for* GARROW, *but the hand bell should be a*
dumb-show. We want only to see him ring. Garrow *enters*

GARROW: Well, Monkey, what did you think of the nice young man?
He knows all of your verse by heart.

ARTHUR: There are hearts and hearts, Garrow.

GARROW: Ah! but to know a man's verse by heart! Now I could never
set my mind to it. "*Turn the antic wheels.* . something. . something. .
oceans la da dee da." That's the way it comes to me. I've as feeble a
memory as I've a ferocious appetite.

ARTHUR: But in your appetite, old woman, I've read secrets memory
don't know.

GARROW: Get along with your reading secrets! It was that you were
doing, fumbling at the latches, you old faker!

SCENE FOUR. MEDEA *wakes in her room. Now the house is awake, and the*
life of the house shifts from scene to scene. MEDEA *rises, comes front stage where*
there is an imaginary window, returns and begins dressing

EDNA: She's up you know. There's a change in the house. I always
feel it.

DOCTOR: And Jason will have left Arthur.

EDNA: Oh yes. Jason left Arthur. Arthur rang the bell. Just before
that. . there was a poem. . . If I stop and look, I can see them about
the house. . .Oh Doctor, my head is. . just a series of shifting
scenes. . She's washt now and dresst. You see how much takes place
in any time. Before this. After that. In twenty years this house has

come to a stage that is like some idle shuffling of cards before the play begins. I used to see them as great certainties. Now I let them fall. They change minds. *As if Medea were near at hand:* Medea?

MEDEA *In her room, answering:* Yes?

EDNA: Look from the window.

MEDEA *comes forward again to the window facing the audience, overlooking the garden of the house.* EDNA's *directives are to her unconscious;* MEDEA *talks as if to herself, answering.*

EDNA: Do you see him walking there, just at the turn of the path near the bee hives?

MEDEA: There is someone there! I can't see him clearly. Oh, yes! Yes! It is *he.* . He doesn't see me.

EDNA: Coming to this house, he's like the Prince coming at last thru the briar waste of old dreams to awaken the Princess. So many Princesses have slept in this house.

DOCTOR: Oh, Jason will be sure to look up.

MEDEA: He's sure to look up. How long will it take?

GARROW *in the almost lunatic spirit-voice of the mother:* My little bayybee. .

ARTHUR: What did you say?

GARROW: . . . Bayybee.

ARTHUR: Don't put on that idiot voice, Garrow. I can't stand it.

GARROW: What voice now? You're filld enuf with voices, coming and going, that a body can take just so much of it. *She exits.*

ARTHUR: Sometimes!

MEDEA *taking her stance within the play to sing:* Will he never see me?

> Ah, knave, knave that my heart sees.
> What do I care,   care for thee?
> Yet I would die, die, die, yet I would die
> If you would turn   where you are
>   and meet my eye.

> Ah, a bird, a bird in my breast beats.
> What do I know,   know of thee?
> Yet she would fly, fly, fly,   yet she would fly. .

Somewhere, a bird in the leaves waits.
Oh, I know   nothing of thee.
Except that a bird stirs,   turning the whispers,
the whispering leaves,
toward the singing blue sky.

Ah, he,   he that my longing seeks.
What do I fear,   fear from thee?
A bird a-lights in the boughs of the rose bush.
The garden awaits his showers of song.
Push, push,   the sound in the swelling throat
bursts into notes.   Dear,   dear,
why does my heart fear thee,
O,   what is wrong?

Yet I would die, die, die,   yet I would die,
if you would turn   where you are
and meet my eye.

Oh, knave,   knave that my heart would know,
why do I care,   care for thee?

Ah, sweet   long known   unknown.

ACT TWO

SCENE ONE. *In the Forest beyond the House. Afternoon. Jason alone.*

JASON: "An eager beast" he calld me. He
        who knows nothing of that prolongd eagerness.
        You think I do not suffer, as if with Love
        or as a poet suffers? I am driven
        toward that gain that gains me nothing,
        driven to take the prize of the universe
        before which I know I am unworthy. All worth
        lies waiting to consume me. Now
        I know that the very Gold has shown Himself.
        The living Fleece that will refuse me
        all uses is mine.
                This old man
        has been Its servant. Death leaps upon him.

Medea at Kolchis   *610*

Time cheats me of my initiations. Another
will be Master of the Gold that speaks,
that transforms, that opens up the universe
as the gold of the green opens the rose.

But I am the Liberator of the Fleece. Do you
not believe *I* suffer? I am the Liberator,
the Ravager, the Plunderer, the blind
Seeker. But I am not blind. My eyes
see only what can be freed of that damnd golden
Chemistry. Pity me, pity me.

And now I'll speak the truth I know.
I have been driven out of my nature
that like the original Adam knew no stain
of good or evil; from healthy Greece
driven. I have been given only
the command: "Bring back
the unnatural Fleece from Its powers,
turn out the daemonic lights
that sicken the innocence of Man."

In Thessaly, King Athamas
grew indifferent to his queen,
put her away, and took another,
who plannd to kill her rival's children.
This was the Fleece. And Mercury
made the apparent Ram thereof.
Of crime unripend in the mind
that gold is in the crucible of gods.

The Ram, a second Sun, sprang
widdershins, carrying the children East.
At the divide of Europe and Asia
Helle, the girl, fell. We name
that sea the Hellespont
"where beauteous Helle found a watery grave."
At Colchis then the Ram came
with the boy, sacred Phrixus,
known as the Surviver. He it was

who sacrificed the Ram to Zeus
and hung the Fleece
in the unnatural Sun's grove
where the dragon that does not sleep
appeard.

What is that but an old story
that I do not believe nor understand?
But there is a sickness in the world
from such old stories.

And know me now. Pity me.
Who must return from Mercury's
deforming hand, from the magical Gold,
the Fleece to its mereness; free
Thessaly from swarming dreams;
by my own stubborn nature
immune to all infections written here.

And in that green and pleasant land
I'll build a new gymnasium
where, freed from imagination's bonds,
insensitive man shall look West
as the Sun goes, toward Health
and natural raptures of simple mind.

SCENE TWO. *Late afternoon. The living room of Arthur's house. The Doctor
holds a skein of yarn as* EDNA *winds it into a ball.*

DOCTOR: It's very quiet after he's gone.

EDNA: Your young man?

DOCTOR: He's not my young man. He's Arthur's now. No. I mean
with Arthur not in the house. It's as if this were the first time we
have actually been together since that other afternoon in 1884. What
has changed? The light at the right hour is still the same. We have
only a few minutes, that are the center of a lifetime, to decide. Then
he will return, and whatever he calls reality changes the light. "If
our love is real at all," you said, "our love for him is real. We are
unreal."

EDNA: Hold the skein a little higher, Boris. You'll get used to it. I mean to just having this much time. There! See how swiftly it goes now. I was right, wasn't I?

DOCTOR: Yet when you say "Boris" again, I feel the pang. What time is it?

EDNA: About Five. What does this house know of time? Even now, when his death is certain—today . in a few days . in a year—I have only this short scene with you, the time it takes to wind a ball of yarn. I was his sister then, and I am still. And *he* lives in eternity. *We*, you and I, ripple outward from a stone droppd in a pool twenty years ago, that "other" afternoon in 1884. Yes. It is not twenty years ago for us. We are twenty years afterwards. What do years mean? Twenty years ago it was 1864. You were ten I was six,   *His* life ripples out thru thousands of centuries from a stone that has been dropt that he calls in his reveries "his death." What does it mean, in a house the outward ripples of which reach the shores where the Argonauts landed, that I was six or you were ten?

DOCTOR: I askd you then, Edna, that afternoon, to shake off eternity. You remember? "Eternity is a terrible word of Arthur's," I said—and you said, "Yes." I thot all of life had changed, been released. But the clock tickt on thru the interim. Two minutes . . three minutes—one hundred and twenty seconds . . one hundred and eighty seconds. One could not live that long. You said, "Arthur is down by the post road, he will be back in five minutes." Remember? I said, "Don't watch him. Don't count this time out." But you were counting.

EDNA: I was right. I *was* his sister. Even for you I was his sister. That's what you wanted to rescue. You wanted to believe in me, in us—a reality apart from Arthur. But your life has remaind bound to this house, to Arthur. He was the real thing.

DOCTOR: You are a terrible woman.

EDNA: Oh no! Boris, I was just. Just.

DOCTOR: Now you live entirely in the legend.

EDNA: It's a confused legend at best. I withdrew. You did not pursue. Isn't that fact enough? . . Sometimes, reading the cards, I've wonderd—why were there no cards for that day, for that one afternoon? Fate had no way to take hold. I was sure, Doctor. And if I was terrible, now you have brought this terrible young man into the story. You are entirely of the legend too, the half-formd that creature the play of Arthur's mind. I would be a shadow, you would be a shadow, that dreadful Garrow would be a shadow, if only shadows could share his life.

I was sure when I said no. But who can be sure of the other? Of the necessary dwelling? Is it a real "yes" I could have said? . . How dreadful his life has been at times to live in. Don't you think I haven't seen him like a leech that suckt off of the language before I was born magical incantations that bind everything? Yet it is *I* that see the fairy, he can see nothing. *Garrow* must descend to the dead—where he cannot follow. *You* must bring him his death. He has no disorders of his own. It is all no more than an allegory.

. . There! Arthur is just coming up from the post road. We still have five minutes. . . Life itself wanders, subject to an imaginary life that was once orderd rank upon rank. But . . .

springing up, throwing the ball of yarn away from her across the Doctor to the floor and moving away from him:

Oh, Boris,

it has fallen apart!

I have no more than fragments. . . The surface of the pool is broken. Lights and shades play incoherently across its surfaces. We will die long before the storm arrives. But we have seen one of its outriders in Arthur, and, attending him, we have dwelt in the storm-cloud.

DOCTOR: Yes, the storm gathers. The heat is intense, formless. When did I choose to live in it or for it? What will it be? a war? a devastating religion? an hysterical outbreak? and *then* the rain? . . I recognize it, as you do, the time of the storm-cloud. But Arthur, if he is an outrider of such a history, is ridiculous and sad, isn't he? That the past splendor, the golden fleece of Burgundy, should come to be five hundred years later only an old man's fantasy. Even he tires of it. The idea of such a splendor made him splendid. We admired. Then the splendor has brooded, sickend, fallen away into the other, the dragon's teeth. Arthur is sick of his Burgundy and his Duke. It is all a make-believe, an unpleasant masque. Why do we play?

GARROW enters, sitting down front stage with a colander and peas to shell.

EDNA: We have to hold to him. He would hold to nothing.

DOCTOR: To hold to a fool chasing a butterfly. He shapes himself to the opportunity—to a card you lay out in the Tarot, to any fabulous character, to any charade. .

EDNA: "King Arthur" Father used to call him, joking. Things were very different then.

GARROW: And very different they are here from there. That's all the now and then, the here and there of it. But what are time and place? The world's grand affairs or an old man's dress-up—it's all the same.

EDNA: Dress-up? Yes. You see it as you will, Garrow. But in a dress-up or a fortune or the world's affairs, we come to know what we are about. There was nothing for me to know that my role in Arthur's life wouldn't teach me.

DOCTOR: I hoped to know something. I don't see what it was. To be a friend. Wholly a friend.

GARROW: In his deepest breathings I have known him. You, Miss Edna, go to his imaginary life to live. His *life* you call it. But I've seen him in the real that a man is in his necessary. There's no eternity there, no great knowing. A body is more alive than a book, but it ain't lasting.

DOCTOR: But friendship lasts. And he lasts *there*. Love lasts.

EDNA: Love *will* last. The passion lasts. It *is* in his imagination, Garrow, that Arthur is real. There, the *other* thing, the death, is only a passing event.

GARROW: The imagination is so much smoke! Stare into it and see what you will. I've sat up with his death many a time. I've seen the hunger life has and fed it. What passion stirs in words that is not a pitiable thing? sluffings . . ?

EDNA: I do not know whatever pity you know.   *She exits.*

SCENE THREE

DOCTOR: She was born in a house already the house of his fantasy. If there is a hunger you have fed, Garrow, she too has fed a hunger of his mind and heart.

GARROW: Mind and heart. That's all the organs the world preserves. He sees himself crownd like a king with jewels and gold on his mind and what he calls grief at his heart. What a left-over to rise at the Last Trump! The passion lasts . . But it's a scarecrow emperor of a man when the poor cock and balls of him, the devouring mouth and the shitting hole of him are cast away into the natural dust.

DOCTOR: The soul, Garrow, knows nothing of its self in the body's greed and dirt, and rightly goes toward the light.

GARROW: A poor soul it is then without dirt and greed and the dark of night. . . You play pure spirit, Doctor. But I recall a night you'd forget I guess, when two pure spirits—a cold woman's and a careful man's—had their greed and dirt.

DOCTOR: What do you mean?

GARROW: What you fear. . .Oh, it was that other thing, as Miss Edna calls it. Only an event in the dust. She was all spirit. His "White Lady" he calls her, doesn't he? Mr. Rossetti painted her, green and languishing, smelling of the unreal. Lady of the House! Her slender hands, her throat like a swan's, her mysterious lips, her breasts like white mated birds—that was a role for her to play. Remote and beautiful. What a beauty!

DOCTOR: She *was* beautiful. She inspired him. And you are warpt by envy, Garrow.

GARROW: Warpt by envy? She was only the Lady. I was and am Keeper of the House. What had a girl's natural neck to envy the swan? What had lips ripe for the kiss to begrudge the mysterious smile? Or my breasts to do with white birds? A man's hands don't care whether a skin is freckled or snow, except it be warm or cold. . . Souls go toward the light, you say, but they do like sucking away at the dark. She was proud, Arthur's White Lady was. The rats that live in the nests of pride are secret and keep to the night. . Her sweet whine is always in my ears. Warpt by envy? I have no animal that does not see the light of day.

DOCTOR: There is no great virtue in your light of day. The spirit is an animal, and the body you call your animal is but its speech. Your second meanings, whatever warp you weave upon, your revelations, strike to humiliate the best of beasts.

Enter ARTHUR, *short of breath from climbing the hill, but he is also as always histrionic. It is not a pose but a role his vitality seeks to exploit the scene.*

ARTHUR: I had barely breath to climb the hill. I think, what if today should be my last day? Death delights me. It does! Yet there was no time for living. What have I known of how the tree is green or what bird sings from the deep grass by what sweet nest? I've lived in rooms by discourse and by lamplight.

GARROW: You never cared no more than me for them things.

DOCTOR: Arthur, I must go. But give me my scene before the act closes.

ARTHUR: Our scene?

DOCTOR: My scene.

Exit DOCTOR

SCENE FOUR

ARTHUR: What does he mean? . . They teach us, Garrow, that a Dweller crouches at Death's door. There, at least, I will come into some glory of guilt. *His* scene. What do I want with whatever tale these others have to tell? I thought Boris had a courtesy, a recognition. Yet I've thot too that all of you are waiting to say something, some little unborn truth to yap at my heels as I go.

GARROW: To yap at your heels? I've no little truth to spare. You've set the lines yourself. What can I add that isn't a chorus set to your tune. I could have waited to tell you I was a girl like a white flower on a green stem. Who'd have believed that was even a lie?

ARTHUR: "A white flower on a green stem." In the Fairy Tale of the World, the man plucks the flower and . all enchantment, all felicity, changes. We rape ourselves from the innocent world to prepare the confessions the dead must make.

GARROW: Another show of fine speech!. . There's a white flower you'd forget, and not of innocence you were married to.

ARTHUR: She's dead.

GARRROW: I'm talking of the dead. And her daughter on *her* green stem sweats to be broken from the green.

ARTHUR: Medea? I cannot find a place for her. What do I know of her? Her mother was an image.

GARROW: Her mother was a *woman*. And Medea is brood of woman. I'd say of hell, but what do you know of that? Whores, witches, goddesses, images, white flowers, ladies! Men who take the earth as their mother, white flowers as their girls, images to wive—what do they know of women?

ARTHUR: You are a woman.

GARROW: I am a body! . . "We have to hold to him," your sister said— "He would hold to nothing." Wait till the body lets go! There'll be your nothing to hold to.

ARTHUR: Sometimes I've thought I would find *you* croucht at the threshold.

GARROW: A pretty fancy! Well, if it has a body, it'll be me. I'd rather meet a *real* guilt—and that would be no glory—if I were you.

Enter EDNA

EDNA: Arthur!

GARROW: And here's a flower still on the stem! "Some little unborn truth" you fear will annoy you. You've sent me out to the dead for images. O, there are images there all right. It's all the little truths they need. You'll die in the last act of this play. And each by each we'll teach that unwriting of the book that might even out the score. . . Go on, Miss Edna. We've been having *words*.   *She exits*

SCENE FIVE

EDNA: What has she been saying?

ARTHUR: O, nothing she hasn't said before. We claw each other. It's in the orders of love.

EDNA: Oh no, Arthur. Dearest, you have no claws. You are the blessed Fool himself. (*She kneels by his chair, resting her head against him.*) In all these years of your life that I've been with you, I've never been able to tell you. Is it the end now?

ARTHUR: You've read the cards and told their tale. You've seen me as one of the cards. You're a bit of the Fool yourself, you know.

EDNA: Foolish perhaps. But to read the cards is the claw itself. What do you know of cruelty? You praise even the claw that rips you. But that's not the order of love. It's lust. It's anger and the inspiration of the smallest lust that rips. O. . even I, dearest, cannot restrain my accusation. Boris refuses, Garrow lives in the fury of accusation. . .

ARTHUR *after a silence*: The world and I had a song. Yes, you're right, Edna. I have no accusation . . . We had praises to sing but all speech turnd and bit its own tail and demanded defence. If you had listened. . . listened . listened, I would have unfolded such a universe to you as knows neither right nor wrong, injury nor repair. . .

EDNA *rising and circling back of Arthur's chair*: What did Garrow mean about some little unborn truth?

ARTHUR: She said *you* said "he would hold to nothing."

EDNA: I meant . you let all things go free.

ARTHUR: As you have gone free?

EDNA: Yes. As I have gone free.

ARTHUR: You have no little unborn truth then?

EDNA: No.

ARTHUR: O. That is the most painful of all. . You've been in this house all your life. Haven't you ever loved someone?

EDNA: I loved Father, and you.

ARTHUR: I mean been in love. Something more.

EDNA: Perhaps once. With Boris. It was not more.
   And you?

ARTHUR: I have been in love with all beautiful resistant things. With women who knew nothing of love but walkt in pride. Yet one proud woman I have heard among the dead, a whimpering shade in a voice I was most used to. . . Edna, I have desired. . I have needed, been deprived of, sufferd. . . but love? No! Not loving someone or being in love. But desired . . needed . . been deprived of . sufferd for . . a speech . that was never provided. Some articulation of the human thing. . . Even from pride women fall away, from the proud woman to such an insufficiency it sickens me. The self! the person! . . I have come to loathe all person, because it corrupts, reduces, cripples the man or woman who might have been a magnificent figure.I do not crave. . I have not craved. . love . that proud woman whimperd for . . what the spawn of man crawls under! . . I have craved. . no, not pride either. Pride like love is the crawling place of the *you*, the *me*. "Give me my scene before the act closes." And I said our scene. . . It is a luminous uncertainty, a great articulation, autonomous, no

respecter of person, contradictory and beautiful . . Ah, then, at the
thought of such a final dancing of all members devoted to the scene
that is the scene's scene . my heart yearns.

EDNA: There are no persons among the fairies. Only beings.

ARTHUR: Beings? Yes, beings.

EDNA: Their hierarchies are hierarchies of a design in the grass, their
forms appropriate to the leaves and flowers. They're not masters of
themselves but servants of the green.

ARTHUR: Yes! As I would be a servant . . of the Fleece! Oh Edna!
Seventy years there and not there . . because of this stupid
obstruction calld "Arthur!" (*He falls in a stroke from the chair.*)

MEDEA *in her room, her pang of falling in love synchronous with her father's
pain, her "Oh!" synchronous with his cry "Arthur"*: Oh! It's very like
death.

EDNA: Boris! Boris!

SCENE SIX. *GARROW enters and the two women lift ARTHUR into the chair.*

EDNA: This is the stroke! *She exits in search of Boris.*

GARROW: Do you think I didn't hear it ring out the alarms thru my
own flesh.

She exits.

MEDEA *in her room:*
My life tears at its roots.
O damnd damnd body that knows all!
An agony comes now. Is this your speech?
Speak out then.

I am grown snake, pregnant with my self. O
bloody Moon hide me!   Tear this child   out of me
and call it Love. The world itself
has coils   and all my days
are scales upon its glittering form.

BORIS enters the living room and stands looking at ARTHUR.

BORIS: It's come at last.

MEDEA: Do you know what a girl is? A baby is
a most monstrous thing. The girl's its egg, its

holy waiting time and place.
And now the unholy certainties
seize me. Full light of the Moon. Dark
of the Moon. .
"There is a meaning to dread," Garrow said.
Witches! What can they know, over some foul pot,
of this poison, this
snake of triumphant need?

I *shall* have Jason in the dark of this Moon.
I shall have Jason in the dark of this Moon.
He shall be driven like a knife into the heart of the snake
that shall not die
nor snake nor knife . until all this
writhing that is Life and the World
become one.

Oh! I shall reach the Moon itself in this.
I shall emit a cry that will ring in the ears of men
as this cry rings in all the damnd cells of my
unbroken body.

ACT THREE

SCENE ONE. *GARROW sits in the dark, laughing or crying in an hysteria that starts at the level of* MEDEA's *hysteria at the close of Act II.*
EDNA enters with a lamp.

EDNA: Stop! Stop! What dreadful thing has enterd this house?
GARROW: Black Hecate across the planetary void comes.
EDNA: A laughter broke out of my soul that has been seald for forty years. All the fairy lights are dark and cower beneath the hill of dreams. (*GARROW begins to breathe in trance, groaning.*)

O step by step I am drawn away from all hope of sleep. Today I saw Medea saved by love. As in the old romances the fairest of lovers came and I knew. . . I knew he would awaken her with a kiss. I saw him in the garden. All tenderness reachd out and flowerd there. I heard her cry "Yes, yes." It was fresh as a rose and flowerd, trembled. (EDNA *hesitates.* GARROW *is silent now.*)

And then such a blackness of sight came that turned the heart to stone. I will die of it. "Oh," Boris said, "Jason will be sure to look up." I saw that the lover was a creature of some infernal amusement. Upon the wave of tenderness a second wave reachd out and out-reachd the scene. The flower of my life waxed veneral on its bough.

GARROW: And now Medea wakes that womb of the unborn that blights the sun itself. She draws upon our womanhood to make her spell. The underworld uprises and the orders of heaven descend.

She breaks and begins to cry in her own person.

EDNA: I said you were dreadful. But you and I have had only human dreadfulness. When I was a child you were already my brother's lover. I can remember hating you. O Garrow, I remember you were lovely and I hated you. There, *there* the springs of love were twisted out of sorts.

GARROW: That I was lovely? It has been so long since then that I do not remember being lovely.

EDNA: O let's pretend that the years are nothing. It's 1864. Some night in the sultry August, and you have come to my bed when I awoke crying. Tell me that you love Arthur. Tell me that all nightmares are done, and that tomorrow will be such a day! Tell me that the sun is free. And I will say . . Garrow, Garrow! *No!* I can't! I could forgive, but I can't bless. I can't redeem the past. (*She exits, leaving the lamp on the table where* GARROW *is silhouetted in its light.*)

GARROW: Little, *little* Love. Oh! I remember that child. What night of that August could I have come to her bedside not harboring such a mistrust that would have turnd from curse or blessing. I'd found my man. You couldn't have seen a fairer figure in the freshness of the morning. He met me in the garden by the beehives. "Unclouded bud," he wrote, "I found, that lifts my heart to immortal song." . . Immortal song! He won me from mistrust. I had no courage. To live a life, housekeeper to his dreams of lust, blood, disrobings of the truth. . What drives a man to follow his word until hell and heaven disturb the simple earth. How many likenesses of me I no longer am he's drawn out of me into his immortal *words*. "There is no simple earth," he said. O, but the body is simple. It's the brooding *clothes*, the costumes the spirit devises. . .

SCENE TWO. *Silence. Then* GARROW *begins the mediumistic breathing again in a seizure.* MEDEA *enters.*

MEDEA: Mother? Mother.

GARROW: a-a-a-a   a-a

MEDEA: Mother.

GARROW: a-a-are you there?

MEDEA: Yes, Mother.

GARROW: What do you want? Baybee. .
               It's cold here. What
               do you want?

MEDEA: I told you.

GARROW: Don't drive me.
               There's a snake here. So
               many. Skins. Colors.
               Ssswarm.

MEDEA: Come through. It's no different.
               They swarm around me too.

GARROW: You want   that young man.
               You want   Jason.
               Do you know who he is?
               He wants your father   a-a-a

(whisperd)   . . to give him the fleece.

MEDEA: He wants my father?

GARROW: To give him the Fleece.
               (Silence) He seeks
               the Fleece and will
               want your father for it.

Silence. MEDEA *begins her orders.*

MEDEA: I have twisted coils of my hair to bind you.

GARROW: Let me go. Let me go.

MEDEA: Twist then those coils around his heart.
               I will have Jason in the dark of the moon.

GARROW: No. No. Baybee. (*Silence.*)
They say there is a *forfeit*.

MEDEA: Black of the garden
turn to green
Red of the rose
turn back from the blood.
Dark of the moon
show your full face.
Shine out of order
and release your flood.

GARROW: Jason walks with the Doctor
in the forest
beyond the garden.

MEDEA: Bees in the hive
make the honey sweet.
From the heart of my flower
carry my word.
Dead in the ground
go back to sleep.

GARROW: Tell him
the Dragon that keeps
the gold must be killd

MEDEA: Coil of my hair
hide around his heart.
Speak no more
but bind him, bind.

GARROW: Tell him that the Dragon is
Arthur's voice.

MEDEA: Mother?

GARROW: Yes?

MEDEA: What *forfeit?*

GARROW: If Jason not kill, you
will have Jason but not
his heart. If Jason kill,
you will have his heart but
not Jason. *Go!*

SCENE THREE. *JASON and BORIS in the Forest.*

BORIS: Well, Jason, we waited five years. You were thoroughly
prepared. You learnd all practice of the art. The world for two years
has recognized your verse and acclaimd you. I have done my part.
I have brought you to his house, having brought your work to his
mind. He will give you the keys—you have only to attend. The rest
is yours.

JASON: How long will Arthur live?

BORIS: Tonight, a month, a year. . .

JASON: But the stroke?

BORIS: He's down for the first strike, let us say. Death arrives. But who
knows when Death will leave or if the communicant will leave too.
Arthur lives entirely in his soliloquy. This evening he slept as if he
had never been interrupted.

JASON: He said my poetry was wrong. But the old can make no place
for the young. And then he admitted he had been wrong himself.
"In the 80s I was corrupted," he told me.

BORIS: Poetry is a corruption. I told you that in the beginning but you
would have it however it went.

I loved Arthur's sister, but it was impossible. I wanted her to leave
this house. I could have loved her, but she wanted romance, not love.
Poetry had eaten into her. I would not take advantage. Arthur *lives*
in advantage. He uses every emotion, every person, every flower
and tree, every word we say, to write a fiction that will seem more
real than *we* will. So, his Death is part a fiction. He plays it. I can
diagnose the living that come to a natural death, but he keeps to a
fantasy that renders everything its own design. Life itself serves him.
So, he would name his daughter Medea. "Why?" I askd him. "I
am led to do it," he answerd, "Time will tell." O, unnatural Time
will tell. And then that night five years ago when old Mrs. Marker
introduced you, and there was your name, Jason, I was drawn into
it. By a coincidence of names you knew nothing of. But you were
fascinated already by the Master.

JASON: You recognized me. Your eyes followd me.

BORIS: I do not live in the fantastic. There may have been a natural
affinity, but everything else conspired to hold me. The names. As if
something were taking shape. Your ambitions or your inspiration.

I tried to make you see that this course you wanted to take, this .
siren's song calld the life in poetry . was wrong. And now we have
come into that wrong. Don't you feel it now in this house? Her
name is Medea. Your name is Jason. And then you knew, then,
didn't you, that Arthur had found this thing he calls the Fleece?

JASON: Yes. . the Fleece.

BORIS: But it is no more than a painted ram's hide. It is all the
blackness of his mind that prepares a new ground for old legends.
He used to live off of life so that his poetry had some semblance of
a true nature, warpd as it was. But since that Fleece, he converses
in a closet. The world, he says, is no more than a dream out of the
paroxysms of the language. What could be further from the real?
Love, beauty, valor—sicken and become black if they are mere
words.

JASON: You are right.

BORIS: What?

JASON: Once I have seen him, I do not want to be a poet. But the
Fleece is innocent. He says the Fleece talks. He talks to *himself.*

BORIS: What do you mean? The Fleece is a prop. What do you mean
"innocent"? It is the lure of the trap.

JASON: Silence the Fleece and the innocence of life will return.

BORIS: I thought I saw for a moment something terrible. Before which
Arthur's play with words is most innocent.

JASON: You saw?

BORIS: A heap of stones that was all monstrous pharaoh, within which
slept the natural man. O, this house haunts even the woods beyond
it. Edna was right—I too am of the legend. Let us go back to the
house.

JASON: I'll stay awhile and clear my mind of this.

At this moment ARTHUR *lights his lamp and sits up in bed awake.*
BORIS *exits and awaits his cue.*

JASON: O Greece   blue Greece   conversant with the
                 sky and sea
            White temples   snowy stone   white crownd
                 Olympus
            Black that is a color to define
                 candor of white,

Who will bring back my unsullied
                golden landscape?
But poets   calld down the gods,
                aroused the dead,
And all discretions, all boundaries,
                broke through.
The hordes of the East, spiritual
                infections, swarmd.

Men no longer moved to coitus in white
                oblivion,
but brewd another Greece,   that
                fancy land
where daemons—Eros and Himeros—
                seized all minds
And the in-dwelling of the Gods began.

Keep me sane in the guise of these shadows,
Keep me simple who must wear cunning,
Keep me candid as the hero of the games
when I wrestle with the erotic serpent.

SCENE FOUR. ARTHUR's *room. BORIS enters.*

BORIS: I saw your light. How are you now?

ARTHUR: At peace. I have been lifted out of pain into . another scene. I want Edna and Garrow here too.

EDNA *and* GARROW *enter the orbit of his nightlamp obedient to his call.*

BORIS: And Medea?

ARTHUR: No. I am at peace. She is the rage of life, isn't she? This young man Jason. It all seems unreal to me. But lovely unreality! I've known suffering too. It has fallen away. Share with me. At the very end. This is the end, isn't it? What sadness is there that is not part of a larger melody? The world sings better than I do. I have been a poor troubadour, a passionate fool. You gave me the card. It lookd terrible once—the abyss, the scorpion rising or was it a dog at my heels? the fluttering beauty. Have I missd it?

EDNA: You brought beauty to us.

ARTHUR: But so little, Edna. O, if I could only tell you what beauty you . and you, Garrow . and your friendship, Boris

GARROW: It's fine talk to the last, Monkey.

ARTHUR: No! No! I wanted only speech.

GARROW: Shakings of the Fleece.

ARTHUR: Of the heart. Of the heart. Shakings of the heart. What is the Fleece but a prop? I needed to set the stage. I lackd courage. There was everything I could never say. . .

BORIS, GARROW and EDNA exit.

SCENE FIVE. *JASON in the forest,* MEDEA *appears in a faint light at the opposite side of the stage to the back. When* MEDEA *speaks,* JASON *who is in the Forest, another world, hears her voice as if of that world. He answers with a terror he had not expected in expecting to hear her voice.* MEDEA *is already walking toward him through the space of the stage—the House—in measured deliberate steps that display to us too the animal powers in which she walks. Where she was passionately hysterical before, now her hysteria is all quiet and almost amused in her omnipotence.*

MEDEA: Jason.

JASON: Who's there?

MEDEA: It's I.

JASON: "*I*"?

MEDEA: Medea. Do you tremble at a name?

JASON: I'm not trembling.

Now MEDEA *is in the Forest and stands before* JASON.

MEDEA: Do you tremble before the return of the fabulous?

JASON: Of Jason and Medea?

MEDEA: You want the Fleece.

JASON: It is only a skin.

MEDEA: You have come through the centuries to this place for that thing. Like the first Jason at the sowing of the dragon's teeth, you will be immune by my magic.

ARTHUR in his room rises and goes to stand before the closet of the Fleece, praying, or listening to its talking.

MEDEA: I know the secret that releases the Fleece.

JASON: I want only the Fleece.

MEDEA: The Dragon that guards the Fleece must be killd.

JASON: What shall I do?

MEDEA: At midnight my Father rises and talks with the Fleece. The dragon awakes. It is his voice. This dagger I have prepared for you. Stab at the heart of the voice. The poetry will stop. Rip the tongue from his mouth.

Stage by stage MEDEA *withdraws from the Forest, drawing Jason with her. They have enterd the area of Medea's room. Jason draws back.*

JASON: No! It is too horrible. The Fleece is only a ram's skin. There are no dragon words—only devices, rhymes, amusements. . .

MEDEA *(word by word, step by step, drawing him further into the area of her father's room)*: Jason. Medea. The Fleece. These are dragon words.

They stand now near ARTHUR—*but they are in the other world,* ARTHUR *is unaware of them.*

JASON: I can't. It is unnatural. Why he is your *father*! Don't you see he is a splendid old man? He is greater than *I*. . .

MEDEA: Oh! I'll *strike* with your hand myself.

Almost awkwardly, she must be deliberate to come around between ARTHUR *and the closet of the Fleece. She raises her arm and strikes his mouth.* ARTHUR *in a gasp of pain gushes blood over her white dress. She holds him steady by the shoulder and strikes again.*

MEDEA: The Fleece will be yours.

ARTHUR *turns bloody towards the audience. The two worlds come together. He falls.*

MEDEA: I have up-rooted the poet's tongue.

JASON: I thought it would be simple. The blood confounds.

MEDEA: O Jason!

JASON and MEDEA *turn to each other. She is dismayd by what she has done— but this is also her darkest act of sorcery.*

MEDEA: Jason, he's dead!

In the cunning of dismay she clings to JASON, *inviting him to solace her. Then he shakes himself and his cunning too moves, swift as a snake. They embrace and remain fixd. Then they separate silently, and from the ecstasy of each his own victory they walk slowly back to the forest where, now actors off-stage, they take their seats.*

GARROW *enters Arthur's room and addresses the body on the floor.*

GARROW: It was a real death, wasn't it? What was crouchd there that now you'll be telling about? A melody? Some richness of the mind? But I heard you cry out. It's as if life uppd and murderd you, isn't it? This thing Death is one occasion you'll not have for another poem.

She picks up his bedside lamp and crosses the stage, placing the lamp on the living-room table.

Was it beautiful?   Was it sad?   *She blows out the lamp*

Was it like   what great   sable-wingd   flutter-bye?

The stage is dark now. The actors of ARTHUR *and* GARROW *exit. The bed is brought front stage left where it becomes* EDNA's *chamber.* EDNA *enters and takes her place on the bed.*

SCENE SIX. *Light. Morning.* EDNA's *room in the House. Enter* BORIS *and* GARROW.

GARROW: The strokes came at midnight. One after another. I thought I would die too. But now I know I will *not* die.

GARROW *exits.*

BORIS: Edna, he's gone.

EDNA: You know that I've known that, lying here all these hours.

BORIS: Garrow says there were two strokes, one upon the other. She went to him but he was gone. There were no last words.

EDNA: Words? There was nothing. Medea for desire of Jason rippd the tongue from Arthur's mouth. Is that terrible thing Love? I saw them *kiss* then. You don't know, Boris, how I'd wanted her to be in love. I have been with them for three hideous hours.

BORIS: These are dreams. You need rest, dear. Arthur died of a stroke in the middle of the night. The rest is a dream. In a month or two—when the leaves change—it will be different.

EDNA: Change? You brought him here. He was afraid at the last to stab Arthur that way. Medea took the knife. I saw the blood spurt out. He died like an animal, a dumb beast.

BORIS: We knew it would happen. We've been expecting it. The rest is imagination. You exhaust yourself with the unreal, Edna.

EDNA: With the unreal? I want to die, Boris. I am going to die. If you had *loved* me. . .

BORIS: Loved you? Haven't I been trying to tell you, Edna, to come away from these shadows . . because I *loved* you? I *love* you?

EDNA: No. No. You don't dare love me. Do you know who you are, Boris? or who I am? I know. I have pathos, don't I? I'm fitted badly together. You'd like to save me from myself. And there is so much you remember. But what if I see the hosts of the fairy again? Won't that be strange? So much of me belongs to the imagination. Will I need a rest, then?

BORIS: He is gone. The King of Night's Shadows is dead. You are free. Look! It's morning. I want you to share the *day*light with me. All time is ours now.

EDNA: The daylight? The King of Night is dead. There is no king. But Night remains. I see it in the bright of noon. It is the *under*-leaf, the darkening of the eye. I'm going, Boris. Don't let me go! How luminous your face is. Dear, bewilderd Boris. Did you hesitate because you felt you had been untrue? With *her*? You had only to believe, to enter the fairy hill of dreams, to awaken me. I would have returnd with you.

BORIS: Edna! Edna!

EDNA: It's true, isn't it? I'm dying. You're afraid. Maybe it's a dream. Maybe I still want romance, the romance of dying. You do not pursue. Isn't that fact enough?

* CURTAIN *

Letters

Poems mcmliii–mcmlvi

1958

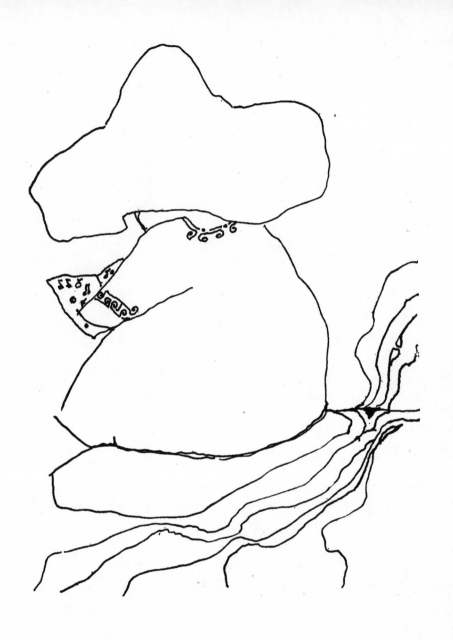

Ich habe keine Tiefe, als meinen unaufhörlichen Trieb zur Tiefe.
—*Christian Morgenstern: Stufen*

Preface: Nests

It is an intensity of excitement which compels a man to work out a designd feeling that variously arrives at stations on three levels: the presence in the imagination in which the speech 'comes', a mortality out of immortal letters; the evident manifestation or trace we in the xxth century worship as Art and declare immortal; and the return, the dwelling of the imagination in the speech. So that powers and forms gather in the mind where it feeds on any written thing.

The man working addresses his desire thru the object of his desire, his material. These poems are evidences of the desire for speech. Which is an other from the desire for love which moves towards its evidence thru its beloved. A lover makes love, and may use poetry to do so. A poet makes speech and may use love to do so. It is only by constantly rearranging such statements that I can suggest a proposition I am avoiding.

It is a superstition of our time to read out of Freud that art is made out of a borrowing from sexual energies; and the professors or doctors lecture to expose the system of debits and credits whereby the artist manipulates the fund of energies. What happens when immediate excitements are postponed, when sexual responses are transmuted into hate and love, when talk is reserved to re-emerge as poetic speech? These are specializations of the individual creature, spiritual lusters or armories which I see as alike to the shells or furs or combs apparent in the animal world. Specializations of action. And then a will in living or a consciousness. I confound the two, having in mind a process which sets self-creation and self-consciousness in constant interplay.

A man's fortune starts when his fortune is told. To demand a new threshold of excitement and to work there: eventually to be unsatisfied, or shaken or destroyd in excitement? this is when no composition

As the colophon to the first edition explains, Duncan prepared several "drawings of the ideal reader," five of which were printed in the book and also appear here. Two others later appeared, along with these five, in Duncan's collection *65 Drawings: 1952–1956* (Los Angeles: Black Sparrow, 1970).

appears. Artaud is torn apart by actual excitations which are intolerable to his imagination and to his material. Neither his desire nor the object of his desire can endure his excitement. The writing he has left is evidence of the area of endurance. And Artaud's 'charge' is higher, in an entirely other category, than the charge at which I work. Yet I am concernd. His art—in which we have intimations of what we call 'insanity'—makes articulate what without this communication we would not be prepared to feel. We can entertain what he sufferd.

:or to maintain ourselves at that threshold, as if satisfied, to work with a constant excitement at play? this is when compositions appear as possibilities of movement. So I pursue a process of re-vision and disorganization to keep creation of the poem and consciousness of the poem in interplay.

THE BREAKING UP OF COLD CLOUDS

releases freshets which I have seen advancing before my speech in the paintings of Hassel Smith. These remind of the appearance of crowds at the margins of my solitude—and that there might be a crowd of one who writes.

Thru our inventions to disturb anew the spiritual arrangements! these violent recreations betray the secret history of our time. Science and art demand an outbreak—the maniacs of physics, psychology, biochemistry, whose delirium is irresponsible, in which diseases and explosions appear as inevitable pragma of Science; and the artists, whose delirium is responsible, appearing in the desire for a new order which radiates from their works.

The glamorous tyranny of religion, of science, of democracy, of industry, of capitalism, surrounds us, feeds us, protects us. But everything in history beds us down in splendor. The Christ, the Holy Mother, the fire of Lenin, the Great Usura of the Kabbalists, the skyscraper of glass and the subway, the scourge Hitler, the elect psychoanalysts, the Grand Masters Jacques Coeur and Henry Ford, the connoisseurs of éditions de grande luxe, the gourmets, the Labor unions, the burnd books—DAS KAPITAL AND THE PSEUDO-PROTOKULS OF ZION, THE BIBLE, PILGRIMS PROGRESS—the diabolist Pavlov and the spiritualist Einstein: have joind the Legions of the Dead. Their gasses flow from the sarcophagi of our belief to infect history. All dead bodies radiate prayers, ancestral emanations to insure the continuity of semen, of blood, of spirit.

As we struggle towards life, it is thru our inventions that we offend the dead: as they in their time offended. The ghosts in which we have our faith shift their miserable bones when we stumble, to break, to discontinue our subscription in the fate of mankind.

I embrace the heated clouds of the past. Thoth and the enormous Imperator Mundi of the frescos at Tahull stain my souvenirs; luminosities gather from the monthly disorders of Mary.

I attempt the discontinuities of poetry. To interrupt all sure course of my inspiration.

The crowd of the dead in the totem pole, as it does in Africa or Alaska, rules in this world. I have enterd, with the other American tourists and with the citizens of that necropolis Paris, the ecstasies promised by the sleepers who inhabit the Louvre and the Musée de l'Homme.

In the Cantos of Ezra Pound the voices of the guides are distorted by shifts in making. The poetry, the making, opens gaps in the correspondence with the City of God. A poetry is possible which will introduce peril of beauty to all the cells of history.

Disorders of the sky precede the tears which appear as words in a massive sentence resembling the men who appear congregations of love and desire united.

L'OEUVRE DE VIVANT
L'OEUVRE DE FANTOME

On the 11th of February 1855 Jesus Christ reveald to Victor Hugo: 'Il n'y a que des âmes égales devant l'amour. Il n'y a que des amours égaux devant Dieu.'

The lore of Denis Saurat in THE GODS OF THE PEOPLE, DEATH AND THE DREAMER, and L'EXPERIENCE DE L'AU-DELA, as well as the lore of Moses of Leon in the ZOHAR, has been food for the letters of this alphabet. It is not expression nor creation that I seek; but my inventions are addressd to an adventure. The medium of words. In the orders of the actual and in the orders of the fantastic, a world—worlds are constantly reveald thru mediums of the arts. A life then, or lives. In these thirty-seven years I have had lives, deaths, reincarnations, that verify in their microcosm all that plurality of worlds and lives that the initiated disclose to us.

And here I declare a mood, a mode, in writing, conceived as a tuning of the language, as the ear, hand and eye, brain are tuned—towards a possible music. Incapable of love, I have made-up love: I am servant of the Love. Incapable of writing, I have made-up writing: servant of the genius that lies in the language before which I have no genius. How it excites my soul that there are indeed only souls equal before that love; all conviction of atheism disappears before the liberation in which there are only loves equal before God. For this God in which we dwell finds all our loves as we knew them to be: the Love. He finds all our poor writing as we knew it to be: the Writing. In these excesses of confidence I become nameless agency of movements in a book that unimagined generations project. Then with that triumph of assertion, that dear courage in which the creature addresses the creator—for we have in faith to take our stand with God and say IT IS GOOD—I sign my name. I, Robert Duncan, made this, as best I know.

SIGNATURES

I stood with Dante where he stood alone and with all mankind before the Rose of God; I saw with Lawrence how the night came through her eyes, the young wife's, and exclaimd: 'The pain of loving you / Is almost more than I can bear'; I sufferd with Shakespeare and askd of all men Grace that I have life upon my stage; I with Ezra Pound sought the orders in history and heard the great bell-notes ring between the work and the self that gave intimations of the creation, the continuum in chaos. What humility is there then in saying 'as best I know'? It is in an intoxication that I exclaim this. Speech rushes up from the bewilderd soul, out of knowledge, to claim its place in the vastest harmonies.

It is I Adam whose signature fell into a multitude. With what fear I have discoverd Your signature in mine, as Your body is in mine. But I fell thereby into the work of the living.

And salutations to this letter in that correspondence. You too if you read have written, as my poor mind knows not if it has read or written. For the Book, the autonomous book, bears witness for and against all claims. What you here read has come into the real.

San Francisco 1956

i: For a Muse Meant

:   in

      s p i r e d / the aspirate
      the aspirant almost

      without breath

it is a breath out
      breathed—an aspiration
pictured as the familiar spirit
      hoverer
               above
      each loved each

a word giving up its ghost
memorized as the flavor
      from the vowels (the bowels)
      of meaning

*hesitate (as if the bone-
cranium-helmet in-
hearing) ; clearing
old greym attar.*

(BE STILL THY BRATHE AND HEAR THEM SPEAK:)
voices? images? essences
      as only in
Yeats's 'desolation of reality'.

:   specialization, yes. Better to stum-
      b'l to it. You cld have
      knockd me over with a feather weight
      of words. The sense
      sleight but absolute.
      nock. nock. nock sum sense into me head.
        O K
      Better awake to it. For one
      eyes-wide-open vision
      or fotograf.
Than ritual.

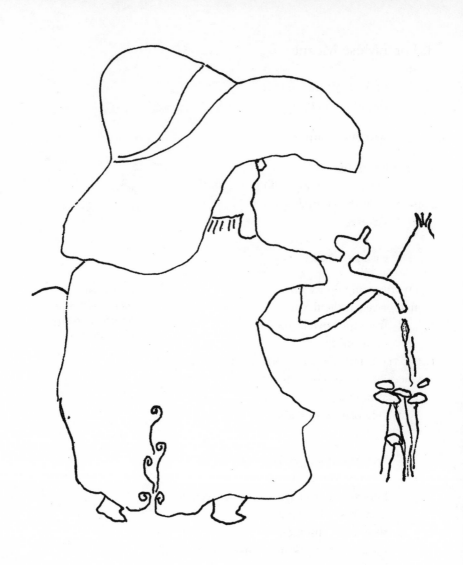

Specialization,—yes even if the old ritual
is lost. †

    I was completely lost and saw the sign
    without meaning to.
    This was not the design.

: A great effort, straining, breaking up
  all the melodic line (the lyr–
  ick strain?) Dont
  hand me that old line we say
  You dont know what yer saying.

    Why knot ab stract
    a tract of mere sound
    is more a round
    of dis abs cons
      t r a c t i o n
    —a deconstruction—
    for the reading of words.

Lists of imaginary sounds I mean sound signs I mean things
designd in themselves I mean boundary marks I mean a
bounding memorizations I mean a memorial rising I mean
a con glomerations without rising

    1. a dead camel
    2. a nude tree
    3. a hot mouth (smoking)
    4. an old saw (rusty edge)
    5. a copy of the original
    6. an animal face

†Who works at his own word in all of our sentences might trick from even the
ruts of once ritual the buts and mistakes that token the actual. The poet as maker
frees the thing from its prophets.

7. a broken streetcar
8. a fake seegar
9. papers
10. a holey shawl
11. the addition of the un
    plannd for interruption:
    a flavor stinking coffe
    (how to brew another cup
    in that Marianne Moore –
    E. P. – Williams – H. D. – Stein –
    Zukofsky – Stevens – Perse –
    surrealist – dada – staind
    pot)   by yrs R. D.
12. a table set for break
    fast

a morning lang
wage — AI AI a-wailing
    the failing

FOR A SONG OF THE LANGUAGERS
What are the signs of life? the breath, the pulse,
    the constant
sluffing off of old stuff in
    creasing, increasing —
Notes: to hesitate, retract.
    Step by
             step   / to be idiot-awkward

                              to take care
by the throat & throttle it.

    Bottle that genius
for mere magic or intoxic
    vacations.

It is sober he stumbles
   on truth? Hell, no —
this he sober gnaws
the inconsequential
      eternity of his skull.

His appetite is not experimental.

ii: Distant Counsels of Artaud
Three chimneys burn
continual sewer-torches, fahrters,
a vestal fire, devastations
of the secret city, continually burning;
      the rivers
choked with turds, sperm, condoms,
enter the ancient sea like snakes,
      intestines,
crawling upward—a sexual litterachure—
      visceral priesthood   *increasing*
smut-peddlers, soulsuckers, muckers
money-grabbers dance enraged
      among aged harpies.

Coming out into the open, I see
it is not hell. It is the well of the year   *runneth over*
      artesian fount of glories.
The stink rises, gives rise to wings,
doors crowd the sky flapping.

The old complaints painted gold.
Her waxd impassive mothering
      wears pearls as tears,
a crud of gold dresses, mantles of flesh.   *amour*
The smoke-filld boys of the sun
whisper fumes of poetry   from dirt
      and orifice.

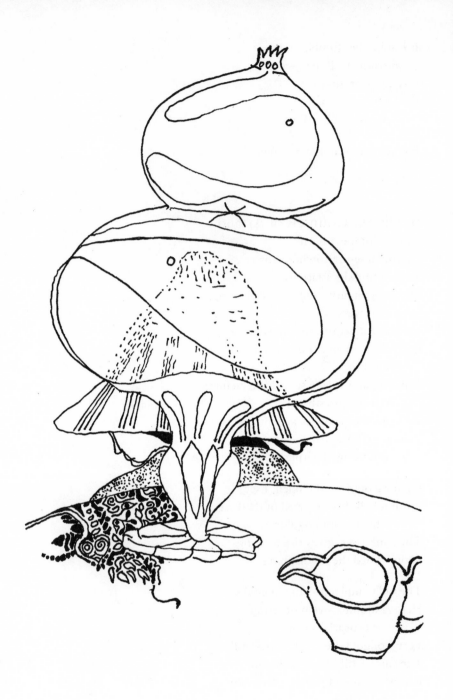

It is to charge her ass-hole with saint's gas
that the city descends upon her towers
sucking the lives into the magic shit,
     hissing and murmuring   *a sunday*
     automobiles of pleasure.

     Three chimneys of virginity
     expiring her fires.   *for money*

Everything else is usable.

iii: Upon Taking Hold

the world as we reach stretches,
    a hand in sight.
Thumb, Mountain, Tidelands of Lines,
    the heart and head lines,
the palmist said—stars,
     shatterings from Moon
                to
            slumbering Venus.

Mt Tamalpais.

     Cézanne restored the destroyd mountain.
And the hand in the painting
    comes up from its illusions
—a man shaped to the world's fate
    stretches upon his face

to wear the given mask.
Shaking himself from his wars,
    a ready dog.
It is to grasp or to measure
    a hand's breadth,
    this hand—mine
    as I write—

dares its contradictions,
       comes to rest,
tenses, shakes, seizes or is seized by the mind:

       mind, hand, eye,

moves over the keys. It is the exercise.
The poetry—now—a gesture,
a lifting of sentence as the wind lifts,
palm outward in address,
       fingers
              exactly
       curld

       —it is a fact—

the words not to be alterd.

Is there another altar than the fact we make,
the form, fate, future dared
       desired in the act?

Words can drop as my hand drops (hawk
       on wing
                     waits
       weight and
                                          drops
to conquer inarticulate love
       leaving articulate

       the actual mountain.

This is the bunch of ranunculus,
       rose, butter, orange crowfoot
       profuse bouquet in its white china pitcher;
this is the hookd rug workd in rich color
       the red, blue, ochre,
       violet, emerald, azure,

the black, pink, rose,
     oyster white, the orange. . .
this is the orange measurement of the lines
     as I design them.

The joys of the household are fates that command us.

iv: First Invention on the Theme of the Adam

1. The streets. Of the mind. Whose gangs
of who in the whom of avenues   hooing
passd?   They wrote parts of color.
Each as the Anthropos
swallowing himself in continual likeness.
Who? Who?
                    the streets ring out
     and are cleard, swept by noises.
What gangsters in whose anger
     arousing.
               The sweep of his never reaching
reminds us.   Brought to our beds
under an idea.   Released
     crowds traffic conglomerations.

She was white whippd and complete
     as we saw her.

     She was one like of him.

2. In the before streets, the streets occurrd.
A mind, crowded to be seen. A maker
occurring only to the created.
It is the howl that arises that acclaims him.
     He is as he is
they did not know as they saw him.

3. The blindness of the mountain. O
our mountainous eye.   Watch
us. Clock us. Clock us.
Hand over hand over us.   Sur-
rounding the hour of our end
        in surrounding.

4. He was one like him that in grown out cast over bearing
under done far fetchd near by all most quite all ways never
with out full filld part time close spaced semi-literate multi-
phase of a face of him her.
She was one like her in the hymn to our load as we carry him
where we in our herd are halving our going.

5. The voices in the dark in the place of stars.
The starting up in the dark in the place of lying still.
The still dark in the place where the stars displace the lying voices.

Old Mother Anthropos
refuses to face her hour's mirror.
You know her.   She lives in the shoe
        that fits her.
Who. Who. She hears in the mountain
    (a gangster voice in a street to come).
Knows what to do. Who. Who.
Knows in the too many of her.
            What to do.

v: Short Invention on the Theme of the Adam
If we were calld from our dinners
to the dance of the Anthropomorph,   a movement
possible if we were drunk in of a movement of
ourselves. More than mirroring, an image
realized in dancing.   O Mr Man,
our pleasure is in you, of you—an agony
of never reaching a cause in our dancing,
a body of our hop and turn.   Yes

we were calld up from our beds at midnite
around and around the rooms where they were
where the day left them—an hourly carapace
emptied and remembering the dismemberd,
the inner object, the moon man
belonging to us.   A longing to us.
Torsos as contortions of an harmonic scale
to fit the stretchings of our sense of things.

vi: Figures of Speech

It were a good thing to begin a book with Blake's beginning: HEAR
THE VOICE OF THE BARD! for it is the imagination who listens then—
but the Bard is the voice of the listener, who hears, sees, the ancient
trees, the Holy Word walking there, crying. And if Present, Past &
Future were to appear then, three daughters of Chronos, sisters, in neo-
classical gowns, were this personification, it were a good thing.

They were not so present in Blake's Introduction, but crudely
questiond (the Instructor said that personifications were poor devices),
mentiond as they were, unbidden, these three, as Blake would have
drawn them, new norns, arrived: and the eyes of the Bard, fascinated,
with dread and joy, see these three Ladies, there, just taking body out of
the air, the air of the mere capitalization of the Word, and appearance
out of the world (language) of Blake's drawings. These daughters, the
Misses—but Goddesses too—Spirits of Past, Present & Future, pink-
hued with reddish Saxon hair, turn in a dance, running the thread of
a life out among them . . . the Bard's life, the language's life . . . all the
thread of lives and deaths that runs between the saying of the Word
and the Return of the Word from his saying. We have seen these three
before, in how many guises, more real for their being entirely of the
imagination as Time is, more real to those who have seen them—three
wild crones at their thread passing about a single eye, or as they came
to us, came smiling, taunting? — because the Instructor warnd against
them—Present, Past and Future, more real to those who have seen
them than for those who have not, who saw nothing for the abstraction.

We must speak of two seeings; and they are spotty enough for any
sight inner or outer to be a wonder, to have arrived, broken upon

us in the midst of our not-seeing. To see a table, to converse with a table: that is a daily wonder. And we say, that table speaks to me. But no less a wonder and not of our will but of our love is to see a mere personification of Table, Mr Table and/or to see Mr Seeing, Himself, who walkd like the Holy Word among the ancient Numbers who had shapes all and voices which we need only to mention to unlock from Imagination's sight their visages, particular habits—images more powerful than our own powers of sight.

We might see three lovely damsels, girded with flowers, having only the personification of their capitalizations. They grow concrete to our wonder. How can we, were we to attempt to defend our vision, describe the critical moment of their appearance? Perhaps Blake never meant to call them up so, and in the innocence of the poem it was the past, the present, the future, that opened, like a map, or a prophetic panorama—an undivided thread divided. But the Instructor said, objecting, that personifications were present. And present they were: the sisters I have in mind, and above them, like Lear, weeping, the Holy Word, Chronos, his wild hair flowing, his beard—a multitudinous beard of hairs of lives and deaths—flowing thru time. But he is Time. And we see the tragic world, the personification of the Word in time: and Blake calls 'RETURN . . . THE MORN RISES FROM THE SLUMBEROUS MASS.'

Then: and this is for me the full splendor of poetry in which we blindly see—the fallen light is renewd and the universe of Otherness is entire. Earth rises out of Earth, an angelic personification, a being of light. The throngs of Beings rise up, vapours of daybreak as from the dewy grass, and this is a choir of voices. Above, old Nobodaddy: below, three young girls, Seasons, or Hours, or Graces, or what they will. But beyond, and sweeping the mind clear—the image of Truth new born. The heart springs up, and we see Him, a babe in flames of joyous liberation. 'YOUTH OF DELIGHT, COME HITHER, AND SEE THE OPENING MORN' Blake cries.

We see the cut by Blake. Two maidens bend over a form, a naked man's. It is the Adam, and the Ancient of Days revives him with a pitcher of water; but it is THE Baptism, not a baptism, it is THE Water, not water. And on the Maker's robe Blake has inscribed' IT IS RAISED A SPIRITUAL BODY.'

It is thru language that we can imagine the universe. How shall we explain that seeing, touching, smelling, hearing, are all mere and that desire moves us toward more—and the imagination is of this more. All that is merely sensible objects to or yields to the urgencies of ours to dream the world. How could the Instructor yield what he could know to what he could not know? There are no instructions for or from the imagination.

So it is not by knowledge or learning but by love and by Your leave my Lady that we yielded to the archaic device of personifications, that we began to see (wraiths out of their capitalizations) three maidens and to hear   did we not?   the Holy Word—but we heard Lear also—crying (over 'spilt milk' I said) calling the lapsed soul. But more—for three maidens were no wonder—we saw, more substantial, Present, Past and Future, images not sensible but imagined, bogus eternities of the poetic mind.

vii: Metamorphosis

1. There is no noise as the stars turn. Lustrous signs,
they advertize themselves to themselves.
    Powers, intelligences, sensualities
    do not emerge from the closets of light.
What emerges burns there, as it emerges,
helpless communicant, thwarted swart stars
exalted in the thresholds of being seen.

Three forms appearing upon a field of the night,
white shades of three maids or three
pinpoints of light or three areas of a dark
lighter than the everlasting absolute of a dark,
perform a scale of three; in moving
independently, set up measures in the mind of three;
are rhymes, configurations in a music of three spheres.

A single tiger, seeking in vain his image, sees
in three arranged mirrors such dissonant verities of his aspect,
face to face, vis à vis, side to other side,
in turning, a cacophony of him, a disassociation
of tones, and departs therefrom. From
three literal renderings unlike in likeness.

Thus. The handsome lutist, full face,
right profile bending forward over the round lute,
gatherd two sounds of a handsome scale
in visual counterpoint to the mode he sounded;
artfully, leaving the stage showd
his contradictory third face, the left profile,
a human dissonance to the enraptured eye.

2. Visionary melodies continue upon themselves,
individual occurrences of the idea of tone. In
displacements, excitement. Related
dimly in the mind—falsified—created as axioms,
multiple procedures of the mind's geometries,
then excitement reappears as seraphic ennui.
Each trembling note—unique—yet rehearsed,
heard as one, part of a monotone.
All disparate points extremes of a single one
true tune.

3. Three men seated around a table talking
of words, of tones, of colors—of one, one art
—a poetry—at odds each one,
emerging as if from an enlightend singleness
into all contradictions realer upon the real
—'The discourse . . . '—no longer feel
distinctions but see each in the discourse
his innerness, a single man
divided against himself at one, made whole,
intensest momentary image.
The voices reappear as three
interior reflections. Then pose

riding the spectacle of sky the solitary moon
—beyond reach—reaching them everywhere,
reappears, mirrord in a watery conversation.
It is the topic of the moon.

The three enamourd of the moon, disturbd,
in the luminous obscurities of their talk
oldest attractions awakend. An aboveness.
It is from their exhaustion of themselves
that the otherness, the whole self of a moon, rises,
holds for her sake alone conclaves of their hearts
—heart to heart to heart—a spell.

4. They shrug, rising from the deepest moment
like each another solitary moon
lighted by their communion, shaking each
himself—to be free! to be free!
The conversations fading into dark.

Three we see them lighter dark upon
their deepest dark.

    A derived poetry!
There are only such reserves as no will of ours
knew how to follow. Hollows
of underfeelings reveald in all arrangements.
The design, the drawing draws from us
the secret of a dark from our darkness.

viii: With Bells Shaking

 The image of what I am talking about begins to come: it is a fair
land, a life, a language. And we, poets, are made up by it—it is a
maker—and we in turn making ourselves up are of it. It is a poem, a
Lady, it is Poetry. How are we to judge her? we are in love and we seek
her everywhere. Where we find her we are, like lovers, transformd and
exclaim—hear how the bell notes of her presence sound here! see where
the words dance as she passes!

ix: Light Song

; husbands   the hand   the keys   a free imp-
    rovisation keeping the constant vow,
        a music,
with set conjugations, notes, the light-
    est estimations of ravishd ear
naturally contrived.   The contrivance
    vanishes into itself.

                        Thus law:
It is this music that the composer dares,
    plays, percussively,
        the state I love.   A
            volition.
    To seize from the air its forms.

This longing informs. A declaration—
    Lawrence: LOOK WE HAVE COME THRU.
    Pound: IT ALL COHERES. A SPLENDOUR.
where the spirit of the act appears eve-
    n ruthless. This
    is the inevitable beauty.

; husbands by hand upon the keys unlock
    from all compulsions—a mode.
It is wed so seven pastorals Harrison playd.
It was the wellwise where intellect
that Dante saw as God—a rose—
Vanzetti beyond the Miseria saw
    a voluntary state.

                    The Bride:
wed as we move to that we await.

    •

And the rhyme waits for us, a beloved
  won as she wins us.
I give up my poet into the tongues.
  She that very Sancta Sophia it is
  pictured at San Vitale
in gold, mother-of-pearl, vermillion, purple,

  word by word, appears
the Empress Theodora Procopius
  saw was whore
faces the poet Emperor her eternal

   husband
   witness
   paramour.

It is as the artist wrought it.
  All things hierarchically are
   ranged:
The Divine Garbo has appeard in her guise;
Chaplin Lawrence said was beauty in a man
  in 'City Lights'
the silent moving picture speech or
indistinguishable metropolis murmuring a loud
  we do not hear
    suggests
  the language we long for.
    Hidden.

As in the measures the song is hidden.
  Heard as we sing her
word upon word. The design
    as we observe it.

x: It's Spring. Love's Spring.
                        The April stirring
    not to be denied.   Inert
    wonderings try me.
And I am very Death that lusts after all men;
that straight and crooked draws into his ken
    all bright live eyes
    to wive.   Avidly.
The mind possesses them. Another life!
To trick the inevitable weather.
To spring the catch: but the catch
    springs up from the song
long as the year, an engagement, lifelasting,
    even distracted . . .

It is a melody skirted, a configuration
    —as in Schönberg's Serenade—
a blossoming in shame, almost seen
    or heard, but never . . .

an exact other melody of the strings
    that art refuses to render
    useful.
And so—unrenderd—
    we are torn apart
—as April rips the weather of our hearts—
    longing from longing:
we could not afford,   or lovewise devise
    the cost
    that sustains us.

xi: At the End of a Period

An imaginary woman reads by her lamplight, inclining her head slightly, listening to the words as I write them: we are there, as the poem comes into existence—she and I—losing ourselves in the otherness of what is written. I too then am imaginary. The sirens that I just heard I mention, she hears them as I do, as a memory of sirens, coming up in the night of mentioning night, shudders of sound drift away from their origins, over the city.

The poem she is reading reaches her, reaches out to her—just so it reachd out to me; or we, writing I but she is reading, listend and saw in hearing a larger murmuring existence of its own in the coils of the completed work. A shell then. And a sea. This was one of the earliest mysteries—to listen for the roar of the ocean in a shell.

And we both misunderstand. It does not occur to her that I am not there. She no more than I knows what it means that I am dead. How faint my voice sounds in the lasting sentences. Once it reaches her, my voice is immortal. And I am all fallen away into dryness and wetness, into original stuff. I no more than she know what it means that she is alive. And there is all the bewildering time where I will not be and she was not. It is in this empty casket, a century huge or vacant as the passages of speech itself, that the talk of the immortals is resumed.

When Who was small indeed he slept at his grandma's house on a glassd-in porch where were there stars there were plants growing out of the cold earth into the dark; where were there low tides of sleep there were incoming waves of talk far away, eternal monotonys. How they enchanted my heart, set as they were as if circling and returning there to the metronome of the clock.

Starting there the poem appears as a plot. It was his vatic pronouncement out of impenetrable gloom that was that Raven, that horrified absurdity, huddled like a crown upon the head of Pallas Athena. Or stalkd, the rank poem, that we knew only by cold sweepings of the air, by prayers we cast for the gift of a ghost, by disorders we left in preparing our minds, by the dead we created to talk to, giving our instructions for the likeness of ourselves we would come to at last. Seen by Poe as a series of great chambers, as a party drinking in its own terror, moving toward a single hour—the poem assumed the robes of life which only death wears.

In the upper reaches of the mind, the conversation begins. She and I have been drawn into the emptiness of other time, into this immediate nowhere, and in communion we do not appear. Outposts of the unreal.

PALLAS ATHENA:

When you look, the interior of the stone is stone. What silences occur as you discover the inanimate, secrets of the animal universe. The planets that are beasts indeed, chaind to the sun, are all lusts, dreams, repetitions, measures. Only man, the carnal bee, stores in the hives of pride eternal desire, vastest terminals of more than fire.

ARTHUR RIMBAUD:

The letters disarranged by the withholdings of love portray the heat into which we move.

This figure of Rimbaud is a configuration of stars. The net is broken and the original dragon is falling apart.

Then with what a strange smile of recognition my faraway reader turns from the page. I myself feel the pangs of regret, contemplate at such a remoteness the small voice, almost valiant in its ignorance:

It was

in the great fires, the everlasting wars, that the Spirit, at last free, wept without rejoicing; come home to its violence, emptied itself into its death.

xii: Fragment

The full rounds—a disorderly vision.
It is in my wisdom's cities
that riot moves, a wind
gathers men, women, children,
    into its heart.

You do not notice the difference
    nor do they,
the hurrying that urges them.
Quiet rushes up into its towers,
    breathless.

The gasp grasps the air—
   the intolerable
   paradise.

How on the map spread on the table
   no mark shows the burning.
It is unmarrd, perfect, undependable.
. . . .

xiii: True to Life

6/20   went
up to the Denials of Poetry: those Dames
Poe saw who combd their brassy hair and sang.

That was the corruption of an imaginary Rome.

To force a saying out of obscure need
costs we cannot afford to avoid: even it be bad
and fall apart.
                    St Augustine's stylewise
war to mar all elegance—   How? be ignorant?
It needs the flint hard edge of recalcitrant almost
     hatred of truth   to strike
light of denied long-desired otherness.   A truth!

St Gregory the Great's miracles are lies; his lies
   his miracles.

If the mind can devise just such an eight hundred years old tortoise six
     feet in diameter
clambering over the explorer's view, his wonder itself makes him
     authentic.

6 / 24 *My not getting at my dreams is part of not coming to grips with life; which*
would, is, protean, be multiform. Energies there (inner as dreams, outer as events)

or energy in the correspondence. But the attempt to get at the dream again would mean, seem to be, confessional, a self-exposure. Is my hypocrisy so pervasive?

6 / 27 Breaks in the discourse disclose
rifts of determination,
                          an effort of mind.
The adamant sphinx immediacy
demands a simple riddle
                          out of my crowded sense?
Sweep clear to a singing true thing!
     Thus: it is the block in view blesses,
restores . . .

What do you do if the recalcitrant incoherence
     is riddled thru with feeling?
There is no starting or stopping there—
no abrupt courageous facing of a fact,
     lion-bodied female-visaged actual other
          to question.
                          Dreaming or awake
     the facts seem to lie about to speak
a gift of tongues.Only the free
          medium,
the speech, rings
     —If I could hear aright? by waiting?—
          rings true.

To dispell shadows of meaning
revealing inconsequent things,

     the immediate empire.

xiv: Upon His Seeing a Baby Holding the Four of Hearts for Him and Another Card Conceald

Crying,   down on all fours, O
    Circe,   your eyes stupid with magic
   see them,   and miss
         what a man is

        lands
on all fours. Olson thus
      reads
the sign as he sees it: 'They
   want you to land on all
      fours.'

Of hearts!

              Fall,
and take it as the grief it is,   from
  all you desired,   relief,   admitted
     fell
apart. A part you playd poorly.   In
      order
   to come to yourself

'solid in love' I say,   out of loving you
             who color
   now my death as it is.

And unseen She,
who rules over Cities,   crownd,
blesses   with signs
      the act.

xv: Words Open out upon Grief

like windows in that house high
showd distances clear to the horizon
    upon grandeur,
time-vistas for the eye, cleard—
    as far as the Hudson—
    three imaginary states we saw.

    Or, in the evening
Jimmy, Blanche and I lay outside
upon the cellar door   watching
    cloud processions
float by,   grandeurs again,
    eternal perishings   allied
—shape shiftings—to rank reaches
    secret in the heart.

Heavy with home-sense, all hearings
    in what is seen,   or visions,
visitations that are wraiths from words:

the reaching out, risk of the touch,
rhymes that mimic much of loss,   ghost goings,
    words lost in passing,   echoed
where they fall,   againnesses of sound only.

This failure of sense is melody most.
It would be to live a long time   to live
    it out,   to the last note that first
    we heard.

    So: stir of longing stays.
Never to this fullness I came,   that fills me.

The ever emptying cup,   the vital
    source that solaces no thirst's throat.

    Poetry is of this natural vacancy:

old desires,   hungers of house and hand
      are leaves-words, even dire and green,
      on   line-branch by

limb of tree,   a dark foliage
      alight   by light
not of our knowledge,   right
      by unreason.

xvi: Riding

    This conversation is an automobile, as we in company ride thru the
dark or in the floods of afternoon thru a countryside or the streets of
a city, but a strangeness of dark or of sunlit paysage or of town . . . for
we are about to, have already sped in the car, as we talkd, we know not
now where, and the houses about us, or the lanes, or the shafts of light
within light or the caverns of dark, corridors in the twilight, are now
touchd by a foreign hand, bear the signature of that swift sketcher who
prepares, as he sketches it in, intimations of fates and wonders.
    I cannot describe this country beyond this country without
explaining, if we are to understand, that the conversation unrolls
beneath my pen in a silence as the road unrolls beneath the car; the
dark is the dark at the window, the blank check of ones wonder, and
the light certainly like the light of the lamp within the other light
of the room. Four cats curld in margins of sleep, and my companion
reading, ride with me. Mr Pumpkin mews, rises, shakes himself down
again into his slumber, stretching out into it. The poem I have been
thinking of is all of this hour, a wholeness of the room, its furnitures,
paintings in which a host moves—not only of story people, but because
there are portraits, my self and my companion and the cats reappear
there in their eternal, our eternal, story guise; and a host of other
beings: a coffee pot, a loaf of bread, a flat iron, a chair, a lake; and a
vaster host of times and areas, of shadows and solidities in themselves.
Then other beings in stone.
    This is the immediacy of which I speak, or the coinherence as
Charles Williams calld it. A strangeness, a more than real which I
picture as layer and layer seen as one and many. As one might hear a

great host, distinguishing all the varieties of its voices and so, a stillness of utter hearing. The pen breaking the stillness—this is the automobile speeding on toward the destination of its own going. Just for this time, in this country, this passage, this paysage, I seem to have descended into existence, like an archangelic form descending the ladders of its ennui to occupy for a moment the exact body of its desire, to see for a time allotted as all its own what it desires in what it sees. A spirit for just this scene embodied, almost bewilderd to find this curious focus of self within self.

Then it will all speed on and away. What remains? Much of the time we wait to return to ourselves we dream of so losing ourselves—of a scene of traveling by night or by day when where we were changed from all we expected into we knew not where we were.

xvii: At Home

Since we have had the telephone removed, the interrupted spirits of the household have begun again, or we hear again their storytelling. In these counsels of objects, animals and ourselves, these concentrations and exfoliations of language, we have our source. When silence blooms in the house, all the paraphernalia of our existence shed the twitterings of value and reappear as heraldic devices.

There was a solitary purpose all the time, the undistracted gaze of the bee that lives for honey—a hum that we waited to hear. In this device we picture the rose, thornd; the bee, barbd; the hive, an armd citadel of sweetness.

The second device is a cloud dispersed, a falling apartness in itself having no other images. Below this: clouds drifting, in which images emerge. The cloud is perhaps idleness, is a being without lineaments, a mereness of metaphor that is not sensible. This figure in writing is the poetry of Gertrude Stein. In which are all the pleasures and pains of reading with none of the rewards and values. This is what we IMAGINE her to have done. Below is the actual procession of clouds we watch where meanings appear and disappear.

The third device is a cat dreaming, which we see as dearness or nearness. His paws stretchd out so that the toes branch show he is almost awake in dreaming. He has been carelessly, confidently, cast down in sleep, so that we know he knows we are here. This cat has

been drawn often by us, so, posing without imposing, curld in a chair
or as if nesting in himself anywhere about.

The fourth device is a tree among trees, that is, a forest which is the
conversation in silence we are referring to. The tree recalls also the Ace
of Spades which is a death among deaths, that is, a solitude which is the
house we live in and in which our love is stored.

The fifth device is a bear dancing, muzzled or not as the designer
chooses, but this means an ancient allegiance exists between joy and
the kin. The sixth, the moon, which I see as the intellect as it waxes
and wanes, drawing and releasing the tides of a sea we do not picture
in hearing. We had only to distinguish what we belongd to from what
we did not belong to to cast off all busyness and return to the work
which I speak of here as a honeycomb composed of inscrutable pictures,
a shield of discrete poems which may absorb or cast back all meanings,
remaining undisturbd. Hence our love of René Magritte. For his
paintings resemble the cells of such bees.

xviii: The Human Communion. Traces.

                                                        The dead
are the departed therefrom. Whose
leavings. Reading we partake of.
A lamp of letters,   a ladder of
                    divine signs,
a substance of ourselves lost,   lost
in a world lost waste lost that we must gather
                    out.

        Set like a crying girl to sift cinders
out of old passions.   For a first fire.
For a light in old age to burn in the skull
        that lit youth's loins?
        Covetous brain!

        But read further,   read further.
Beloved Shakespeare,   beloved Lao Tse,
        beloved Virginia Woolf!
        My heart is submerged as I read.

Above:
the swarming radiance.

These that I never saw I see.

Below:
the boundless waters.

xix: Passages of a Sentence

As we start the sentence we notice that birds are flying thru it;
phrases are disturbd where these wings and calls flock; wings are a
wind, featherd, a beating of the air in passage or a word, the word
'word', hovers, sailing before dropping down the empty shafts of sense
toward: but from our distance we do not see whatever scurrying there
in the brush below the heights of the sentence: and then up swooping
we imagine the hawk or owl in triumph, carrying aloft a poor proof of
the carnivore's craft, some small animal discoverd out of its obscurity
into the high light of articulate day. And it is a strength we admire, a
thrill that unknowing includes the felt fear of being so possessd. This
bird we see as being so self-possessd, knowing, in its being at home in
the tricky currents of mere air.

But the birds we noticed in the sentence at first were other birds; I
have not clearly in mind which of several. They all come and reshape
the feeling of what I am telling: a flock of geese, these wing outward
toward a north back of the northwind that George MacDonald
described—a cold beyond life; or they are the flock that carried Nils on
into manhood; or another scene of geese in a goose-green sky painted
by Brian Wilson.

Or they flutter about, scold in the bushy obscurities of the sentence
that makes the sentence all branches and hollows and fussy with leaves,
and the birds, a cluster of sparrows, that makes the reading in writing
talkative.

Then there remains the sentence, which is a room now in which we
have been sitting, talking, at ease. And then a bird caught there reminds
us of our souls—up. up. Open the windows, the doors. Oh! Oh! the
mad frantic dismay up sets the whole calm of our going on—it is death
in the room exhausting its phrases in search of all the wideness beyond.

xx: Re

-turn.　In spring-up green freshet
turn.　Delight to the eye,　spring
to torso,　hand spring to wheel,
thigh turn upon thigh;
eye light to eye;　　　heart

-bound as we are bound to return,
　　however casually,
to time or place instinct for joy:

measures wither or rot
　　of habitual conflict.

Old theme of poetry!　heart worn
　　were it not the source
contrary to all weariness.

Thus from the lusty stalk whose green
　　　　　　　　tips
turns bud blast to full bloom that
love in desire makes its brief room.

　　Again and again.

Worm, like an ideology, he eats of the core.
Aphids, like retractions, devour.
Grass, bush or tree in flower
　　serves as reminder.

-wind, old theme of the poem,　step to step
　　　　　　　dance to
the rewinding measures
　　　　　　　　the fresh shoots of war.

xxi: Brought to Love
                    like a woman
        brought to childbirth—
inexorable love. It is the necessity
        that defies pleasure
or caring. A destiny in all that we love,
        a bleeding heart.
It is the convention of Valentine.
Surrounded by the lace and violets,
        by pretty blood;
the flowers, modest—surrounded
        by modesty.

A man brought so—'my bloody life'—
        to love at all.
Even the cats, as they must be,
        betrayd by our nature
because they are loved. There is no
        not making the vow
and breaking it. Breaking it at all
        breaking heart—as bread—no poem
without such a moment, broken, conquerd
        only by what   we did not know
of the design. A dictate, the heart of things
        towards wholeness

        restores order

In order to:

xxii: To Vow

It is in fear of the Lord
toward whom
in whose wrath and grace
we move in love.   Compelld.
By longing, yes,
and by a will   we did not own,
so that: holding to you
as the heart holds to life holds . . .
'we are not competent   to make our vows'
'without which
no man is king.'   Your mystery then
kingdom—all of what I mean
upon your body laying my hand: to swear
fealty, a faith, a covenant
in coming.   The body knows it as yearning,
heart strains, melody unfolded in nerves,
curves round your felt form.   Blind hand
upon the book of flesh
read where I cannot read,
vow where I cannot vow.

It is because I know we may never be together again
that I praise Love's power.

xxiii: Spelling the Word

By a stone which being calld is this stone. A day which being calld is
this day. Once I am so touchd in the head, or have seen for a moment
by such fluorescent light a stone of me by day inert, by dark jeweld or
aroused, I picture the excitement of my spirit as an excitement hidden
in a scene in which you are walking. It has come into being because
you are walking there—all ordinary hot trees, dusty road, rubble,
clumps, processions, displays of weedy splendors. You are on your way,
you have no time nor thot to dwell here, tho for the time of walking
everything speaks to you, dwells in you—even the intensity of azure—

and gives sudden signs of itself, which I have realized is myself in this place. A heavy headed thistle comes completely into your sight, as if to possess it. It is myself as a crown which I do not wear because it is a thistle. The air moves to touch you. In its time it is completely come into your feeling. A thrush in the bush, comes to your ear. A hopper in the grass you pass.

'So God dies, that is to say, in suffering and total agony, he creates, cutting them out of himself, innumerable beings to whom he gives full freedom: they can then ignore him, deny his existence, or note the signs of love he has scatterd through creation . . . '

This means certainly that I too have long ago passd this sentence of the agony of me. Ignore or deny or note the time, the love it is. In what orbit, to return: but it is obscurely present and I overlook it. It is to my longing for you that I refer when I search among the insignificant objects of vision for signs.

xxiv: Correspondences

It is from the ideas of you that you emerge. I return to you from my longing, you a second image in longing, drawn to you as the painter is drawn to the man he draws; or, as in reading the cards, one is drawn to the likeness of death in the Ace of Spades. 'I say I shan't live five years' Blake wrote in 1793 'And if I live one it will be a Wonder.' Within all daily love—and this is a world—is another world sleeping or an otherness awake in which I am a sleeper. The reveald things of this order appear as omens: within the full dread of death, so that I cry up to die—is another life. I tremble lest the door be lockd or open, for the door is an ununderstandable joy.

But now, across an emptiness of time I see you. I shall never reach you—between me and thee.

As it was in the beginning. What I am withdraws from the great sun, like a lion retracting his roar in order to speak. In this scene the simple pleasures of this world cause areas of torment in the unreal like stones in an open field.

xxv: August Sun

God of the idle heat, in this glaring road
    you dominate all.
And over the green fields wilted down
    under your blaze, these
thirsty unruly plants grow a jungle domesticity
    to protect their fruit.
Of all hidden things, I sing, waiting
    for evening's grace.

xxvi: Source

Or: I work at the language as a spring of water works at the rock, to
find a course, and so, blindly. In this I am not a maker of things, but, if
maker, a maker of a way. For the way in itself. It is well enuf to speak
of water's having its destination in the sea, and so to picture almost a
knowing in the course; but the sea is only the end of ways— could the
stream find a further course, it would go on. And vast as the language
is, it is no end but a resistance thru which a poem might move—as it
flows or dances or puddles in time—making it up in its going along
and yet going only as it breaks the resistance of the language.

When I was about twelve—I suppose about the age of Narcissus—
I fell in love with a mountain stream. There, most intensely for a
summer, staring into its limpid cold rush, I knew the fullest pain of
longing. To be of it, entirely, to be out of my being and enter the
Other clear impossible element. The imagination, old shape-shifter,
stretchd itself painfully to comprehend the beloved form.

Then all windings and pools, all rushings on, constant inconstancy,
all streams out of springs we do not know where, all rush of senses and
intellect thru time of being — lifts me up; as if out of the pulse of my
bloody flesh, the gasp of breath upon breath (like a fish out of water)
there were another continuum, an even-purling stream, crystal and
deep, down there, but a flow of waters.
I write this only to explain some of the old ache of longing that
revives when I apprehend again the currents of language—rushing
upon their way, or in pools, vacant energies below meaning, hidden
to our purposes. Often, reading or writing, the fullest pain returns,

and I see or hear or almost know a pure element of clearness, an utter movement, an absolute rush along its own way, that makes of even the words under my pen a foreign element that I may crave—as for kingdom or salvation or freedom—but never know.

xxvii: An Owl Is an Only Bird of Poetry

A cross leaves marks the tree we fancy.
    Regular art rules.
    Under hand beauty demands
the secret howl to cross the table
    on bloody stumps
      were wings added later to mar
the 17th century flying style.

INCLUDE A PRAYER
  include lions rise or as sentences raised,
  include fore gone conclusions in a maze,
  include my blind in designing your window,
  include my window in raising your blind,
  include a long time in my forever yours,
  include April and July in all your years,
  include the lions eye that sheds the lambs tears,
  include the lambs eye or as paragraphs rest,
  include the bird that belongs to each beast,

  include:

  include the breasts and Mary's face,
  include the horns of the cow in Grace,
  include the words in pasture are kind,
  include the scream when he starts to pray,
  include the sun at the opening of day,
  include the night in what you find,

  Small lions are kittens and love to purr.

include the fathering Night and Day,
include the orders descending thru words,
include the elegances of no rhyme,
include the roar of a lion in triumph,
include break orderly converse to address divine disorders abruptly,
include the tree upon which our life hangs,
include the metaphor in which from that tree Christ is crucified,
include all martyrs in the sense of fun,
include chairs and tables as comfortable things,
include the bird in the angel with wings,

FIGURE 1

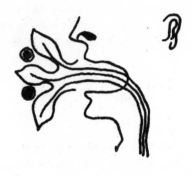

The vowels are physical
corridors of the imagination
emitting passionately
breaths of flame. In a poem
the vowels appear like
the flutterings of an owl
caught in a web and give
aweful intimations of
eternal life.

FIGURE 2

The consonants are a church of
hands interlocking,   stops
and measures of fingerings
that confine the spirit to
articulations of space and time.

•

It is in the disorders of the net that the stars fall from
the designs we grasp into their original chaos.
He flies thru a time which his wing creates. MEASURES.
As the immortal Dali has painted him. He is erected upon
the cross of vision as we see him.

•

SONG

What do you see, my little one?
I see an owl hung in a tree.
His blood flows from his side.
Earthly things may rest tonight,
all heavenly fear hangs there.
I see a nest where owlets cry
and eat the cold night air.

What do you see, my little one?
I see an owl hung in a tree
like flesh hung on a bone.
The thorns of flesh run thru and thru.
Ring out the tones of life.
He builds the artifice of heart
and takes his word to wife.

What do you see, my little one?
I see an owl hung in a tree
among the letters whispering there,
a tongue of speech that beats
the passages of mere air.
The ladders of tone pass into words,
the words pass into song.
The heavenly orders sing to me.
I see an owl hung in a tree.

FINALE. DISARRANGEMENTS AS JOY.

This is an owl in time.   Of night,
too late / too soon / flies

out of Minerva's head into her thought.

Reappears. On snowy wings.
Disconsolate Valentine.

I go along with him. As I send him.

The joy
is a great scuttering of feathers words
a whirl
up words into an airy sentence where
reader
by reader accepts his mixd whether
of love
face by face in his poem's crackd mirror.

This is an owl as he flies out of himself
into the heart that reflects all owl.

Who gives his hoot for joy as he flies.

Alights.

xxviii: New Tidings

In the book of the birds he reads letters of an alphabet
he does not understand.

But to contact the sound.

Tremblings from the nest of birds, like first utterings

disturbances

that are rays out from the one language into the other
languages, from the one into its other.

What songs my mother taught me. Not to sing.

One of the words standing before Babel fell into tongues was a
bird there which was the sun there and he sounded as a letter he could
not read.

xxix: Changing Trains

for languages. Everything ours is burden.
Even declared, cleard; weighs so much; encumbers us as we go. Unable
to carry a sentence thru.

So we checkd the statement thru to its period. To ride along with it
word less. Only to make our claim at the end. At the ultimate station
of our meaning we mean to stop. With no burden. But there is a
burden to the sentence—even when translated for us—that we do not
understand, and we worry then that our burden will not wait for us.

It is carrying too much, because we loved it all, packd it and would
transport it, if we must be transported; because stones, handsome
apparel, books, designs—anything—attracted us.

Here at the border change. Change languages. The customs inspects
casually for contraband. But our declaration is true: we have come thru
with nothing. About which, a guilt gathers. We are not sure even of
this.

xxx: The Language of Love

We are now in its country and find that the language we longd to
hear we almost understand. But the waiter, the garçon, is not pleasant
at all. Aware that we are quite helpless and dare not answer, blundering
as we will, he inflicts this idiom upon us. It is his—all his. And as we
struggle to understand—for we are lovers, would-be lovers, of this
language—we falter and let go, are unable to hear. With contempt, he
refuses our hopes and reproves our unworthiness.

Entering a new territory, calld as we always are by the poetry whose
veritable sirens sing from the rocks of french or german or spanish or
italian, as they sing from our own, we are met by the anti-poets who
guard the substance of poetry. These that know nothing of song or
rocks, nor of the soul's voyage. These that scorn the effluvia of mistake,
misuse, misunderstanding—the whole spiritualized universe. These
anti-poets withhold from us all that is common, most needed, dreaded,
desired. Lest we misuse. Their insensitive right words. Deprived rightly
of meaning, by a cheat I speak in spite of my deprivation.

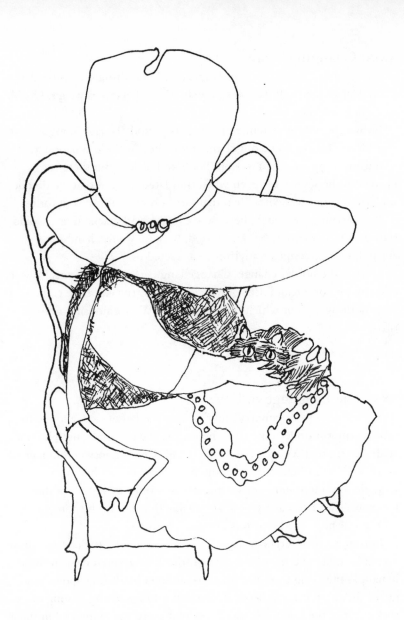

The Siren Song

The people pay little attention to it; and, altho the legend of the song has become their legend, then their property, still they are scornful of those credulous foreigners who seem drawn into their country as if in reality bewitchd by voices. Yet from every tongue the song rises. One has only to watch children as they are drawn thru the initiatory rings of education, as they are innoculated against the song of the language 'that makes men mad', to see at first strong and then gradually weakend, if parents and teachers are successful in rescuing the child, the whirlpools of glamor that rise from the unrestraind powers of daily words. Every nation has as spectacles of the victory of its language those victims the song claims, men who turnd their attentions and paid the exactions the language demands. For all who enter that kingdom hear a glamor and see a ruin—out of themselves. And leave the language reshaped to embody their ordinary words as poetic speech.

If you do not understand what the glamor may be, what my accusation is before the courts of the morning, consider:

A man writes 'I love' on a wall. He hopes to escape from his mistake by not signing his name. But a glamor radiates from the letters and has illuminated his being as he writes. 'Reeling and writhing' the Mock-Turtle says to Alice. The man's soul reels and writhes, for as a man writes a word the accumulation of his hand's reelings and writhings letters and creates; a snake crawls out from an old skin, blind and sick in the effort—a soul out of his soul. The man, if he sees or hears at all, is violently alterd then, revolted by disowning what he was. He has contradicted himself, spoken his unspoken self; and transferrd the power from what he might have declared to what he has declared. What he declares joins those angelic forces that seek at every jointure of the universe to wrench his work from all reference to Adam and to readdress that masterpiece to the ambiguous conceit of angelic form.

Appendix 1 *Tables of Contents*

SELECTED POEMS. THE POCKET POETS SERIES NO. 10
SAN FRANCISCO: CITY LIGHTS BOOKS, 1959

The strict page-count and format requirements of Lawrence Ferlinghetti's series of *Pocket Poets,* in which Duncan's *Selected Poems* was number 10, gave Duncan considerable difficulty in selecting the contents and shaping them into what he thought was a coherent whole. The published book, which he started to put together in 1957, was never wholly satisfactory in his eyes since—though he was gratified by the chance to reprint "The Venice Poem"—he found it necessary to truncate the two series, "Domestic Scenes" and *Medieval Scenes.* He included one previously unpublished poem, "Jerusalem."

Toward an African Elegy; King Haydn of Miami Beach.

From *Heavenly City, Earthly City:* Among My Friends; Sleep Is A Deep And Many Voiced Flood; In Memory of Two Women.

From *Medieval Scenes:* The Dreamers; The Helmet of Goliath; The Banners; The Kingdom of Jerusalem; The Festivals; The Mirror; The Reaper; The Albigenses.

From *Domestic Scenes:* Breakfast; Bus Fare; Matches; Radio; Electric Iron; Piano.

The Homecoming; The Temple of the Animals.

From *Homage to the Brothers Grimm:* The Robber Moon; Strawberries Under The Snow.

Jerusalem.

The Venice Poem: Description of Venice; Testimony; Imaginary Instructions; Recorso; The Venus of Lespuges; Coda.

From *Caesar's Gate:* The Drinking Fountain; Processionals II; The Second Night In The Week.

THE FIRST DECADE: SELECTED POEMS 1940–1950
LONDON: FULCRUM PRESS, 1968

Fulcrum Press was a small publishing house specializing in poetry, run by Stuart and Deirdre Montgomery in London from 1964 to 1974. Both *The First Decade* and *Derivations* were actually published in February 1969 (*Bibliography* 97, 99), though the copyright page gives 1968 as the date. Sales were presumably successful enough to encourage Jonathan Cape, a well-established London trade publisher, to issue *The Opening of the Field* in 1969, *Roots and Branches* in 1970, and *Bending the Bow* in 1971. Overall, in both Fulcrum books, Duncan preferred earlier rather than later versions (as in *Medieval Scenes*, for example), but production values at Fulcrum were somewhat unreliable, and Duncan considered the texts unsatisfactory. Nevertheless, he viewed both books as providing reliable retrospective collections of his work; he included previously uncollected work in each volume, and rearranged and reordered the sequencing of earlier books (such as *Writing Writing*). In *The First Decade,* the table of contents grouped the poems under their date of composition:

A Spring Memorandum: Fort Knox; An African Elegy; The Years As Catches; King Haydn of Miami Beach; Homage and Lament for Ezra Pound; A Congregation; Sleep is a deep and many voiced flood; An Apollonian Elegy.

Berkeley Poems: Among my friends love is a great sorrow; An Elegiac Fragment; A Woman's Drunken Lament; Portrait of Two Women.

Heavenly City, Earthly City.

Domestic Scenes: Breakfast; Real Estate; Bus Fare; Mail Boxes; Matches; Bath; Radio; Electric iron; Lunch with Buns; Piano.

Medieval Scenes: The Dreamers; The Helmet of Goliath; The Banners; The Kingdom of Jerusalem; The Festivals; The Mirror; The Reaper; The Adoration of the Virgin; Huon of Bordeaux; The Albigenses.

The Homecoming; The Temple of the Animals; The Revenant; A Weekend of the Same Event; Sleeping All Night; I Tell of Love.

The Venice Poem: 1. A Description of Venice, Testimony; 2. Imaginary Instructions, Recorso; 3. The Venus of Lespuges; Coda.

Homage to the Brothers Grimm: The Robber Moon; Strawberries under the Snow; The Dinner Table of Harlequin.

Jerusalem; Revival.

Four Poems as a Night Song: The Construction; The Walk to the Vacant Lot; The Waste, The Room, The Discarded Timbers; Before Waking at Half-Past Six in the Morning.

The Second Night in the Week; Processionals I; Processionals II; Goodbye to Youth; The Horns of Artemis; Africa Revisited; An Imaginary War Elegy; The Song of the Borderguard.

An Essay At War.

Imitations of Gertrude Stein 1951–1952: A Language For Poetry; Are Cats; Names of People; A Leave As You May; Poetry Permit for Volley; All Through; Poetry May Be As You Please; A Reprieve At Dawn; A Song Is A Game; An Arrangement; Walking on Kearney Street; Dance Early Spring Weather Magic; Turning Into; Coming Out Of; Making Up; A Scene.

Writing Writing: The Beginning of Writing; Imagining In Writing; Writing As Writing; Possible Poetries: A Prelude; Possible Poetries: A Postcard; Possible Poetries: A Postcard; An Imaginary Letter; Imaginary Letter; Imaginary Letter: His Intention; Motto; Division; Writing At Home; I Am Not Afraid; An Interlude of Rare Beauty.

From *Fragments of a Disorderd Devotion:* Five Pieces; Hero Song; An Imaginary Woman; Eluard's Death; Unkingd by Affection.

A Little Poetics: Descriptions of Imaginary Poetries; A Poem in Stretching.

Imitations of Gertrude Stein 1953–1955: Rhyme Mountain Particular; This Is The Poem They Are Praising As Loaded; Orchards; Sentences; There Could Be A Book Without Nations In Its Chapters; 6/16/53; 6/22/53; 6/27; A Morass; How Do You Know You Are Thru?; Rotund Religion; Several Poems In Prose; Rings; Syllables; Stuff Ark Mower Bottle; Another Ido; Spanish Lessons.

Letters: Preface; For A Muse Meant; Distant Counsels of Artaud; Upon Taking Hold; First Invention On The Theme Of The Adam; Second Invention On The Theme Of The Adam; Figures Of Speech; Metamorphosis; With Bells Shaking; Light Song; It's Spring, Love's Spring; At The End Of A Period; Fragment; True To Life; Upon His Seeing A Baby Holding The Four Of Hearts; Words Open Out Upon

Grief; Riding; At Home; The Human Communion Traces; Passages Of A Sentence; Re; Brought To Love; To Vow; Spelling The Word; Correspondences; The Green Lady; August Sun; Source; An Owl Is An Only Bird Of Poetry; New Tidings; Changing Trains; The Language Of Love; Siren Song.

Prose Poems from *Caesar's Gate* (1955): Aurora Rose; Tears of St Francis; Source Magic; Circulating Lights.

POETIC DISTURBANCES. BERKELEY: MAYA QUARTO EIGHT, 1970

Poetic Disturbances; What Is It You Have Come To Tell Me, Garcia Lorca?; The Voyage Of The Poet Into The Land Of The Dead; I Saw The Rabbit Leap.

CAESAR'S GATE: POEMS 1949–50. BERKELEY: SAND DOLLAR, 1972

In the 1972 advertising flyer for the second edition of *Caesar's Gate*, Duncan said it stood as volume three of his collected poems, the first two being *The First Decade* and *Derivations*. The second edition, reproducing Duncan's typescript, added thirteen poems to the 1955 edition—three of them, written in 1949, from *Poetic Disturbances* and one, "Despair In Being Tedious," written in 1972—a long Preface, and a prose Epilogue. Jess provided six paste-ups not in the 1955 edition.

Preface (1972); The Hint of an Infinite Regression; Recovering the Knowledge of a Painful Time; The Gate; Pain; Lorca, What Is It You Have Come To Tell Me?; Diction Contra Diction; Something Is Moving.

Preface (1955).

Four Poems as a Night Song: The Construction; The Walk to the Vacant Lot; The Waste, The Room, The Discarded Timbers; Upon Waking at Half-Past Six in the Morning.

EYE SIGHT: Aurora Rose; The Second Night of the Week; Processionals I; Processionals II; Tears of St. Francis; Upon Another Shore of Hell; An Incubus; Sunday (1955); Eyesight I; Eyesight II; Bon Voyage!

Goodbye to Youth.

H.M.S. Bearskin: He entertains at a Dinner Party in the Bardo State; He Consults the Tides; To Run with the Hare & Hunt with the Hound; Great GRIEF, then, herself!; He Lists Subjects for Great Poetry; He Has A Good Time There; Coda.

POETIC DISTURBANCES: Forms Within Forms; What Have You

Come To Tell Me, Garcia Lorca?; The Voyage Of The Poet Into The Land Of The Dead.

APPEARANCES: At Home In Eden; from A Season In Hell; The Conqueror's Song; Moving In Your Sights; We Have Left Of Course; A Game Of Kings; There Must Be A Reason; See The Stone Lions Cry; Before The Beautiful Things Turn Evil.

EPILOGUE (1972): Dichtung kontra Dichtung: *A Hypnagogic Phantasy;* [The Matter of the Bees]. Despair In Being Tedious (1972).

Duncan's Dust-Jacket Blurb to
The First Decade

In making this selection from the first decade of my work I have sought not only to include certain poems which have been particularly admired by those who admire my poetry at all, but, more important, to provide those texts which I see as essential for a serious reading of evolving themes and forms; and, back of those formal preoccupations I have had as an artist, I have had in mind too in my choice presenting the typology of a life-work emerging. I sought and still seek a consonance with what is happening, a cooperation with experience itself, with the peculiar experience that arises in the process of a poem between the universe immediate to the evocation of language and the actual universe immediate in the body of the man who now, in writing, inspired, begins to speak as a poet. My intent here centers upon the process of poetry, the making or creation of a third world, and not upon audience or the possibilities of merit according to whatever consensus of literary taste or sensibility.

The universe speaks to us and in us, and we but imitate in what we call our language the real speech which surrounds us, out of which, indeed, we are born. "God's art," Dante says in *De Monarchia,* "which is nature." In our own arts, striving to speak, with words, pictures, gestures, buildings, assemblings of objects in ecologies of feeling-thought, we in turn create a little nature of what we are, ideas of Man. In the earliest works here I am concerned now to see that process emerging. Out of what was felt as an expression—the foreground of the poems was always an impending feeling needing to be uttered—working with the first vivid beginnings of form and content, stirred by intimations of form in poems where literary conventions had been powerfully informed, I sought to liberate in language natural powers of the poem itself. Form came in commanding cadences and rimes, sequences of vowel sounds and consonant clusters that led toward melody; and in the excitement of the music, I was transported beyond the model into the presence of the poetic intention itself—I began to see and hear with the eyes and ears of the poem. As in our actual life, or in our dream life, so in our arts or made-up life, in poetry, real and immediate things as well as beings, wherever we acknowledge them in-form us.

But this consonance I seek between actuality and the poem is not easy. In *Medieval Scenes,* the first poem in which I knew what I had to do, I found an agony was part of that, a prayer came in the very song itself that there be no song: "*I would come unto the source of light unsung*" remains today in the unfortunate invention of the song I must sing. It is all wrong my intelligence protests, but it is a commanding confession of my true state. "*Never in living/but here, here,*" the poet says in *The Venice Poem: "All felt things are permitted to speak."* The critic, in the true sense of that word, will see that there is a crisis of truth and permission then throughout; and for that worried reader I hope there will be here, as there is for me, unrelieved as the crisis is in me, a joy in the strength poetry works in us to carry the man in his work beyond the bounds of truth and permission into the autonomous life of the poem—the music of a consonance beyond our knowledge of consonance.

Robert Duncan
San Francisco, June 1968

Preface (1972) to Caesar's Gate:
Poems 1949–50

THE HINT OF AN INFINITE REGRESSION

Referring to the "Dream Data" section of my *Sequence of Poems
for H.D.'s Birthday*, written in 1959 (*ROOTS AND BRANCHES*, 1964),
the critic M.L. Rosenthal has, he tells us, the impediment of a
critical disaffection in his reading. It is not, he writes, the imposition
of the homosexual writer's attitude upon the heterosexual reader's
sympathies—

> "But the shift from the literal statement of the first line [*'The young Japa-
> nese son was in love with a servant boy'*] to the girlish outcry [*'To be in love!'*]
> and sentimental philosophizing of the ensuing lines [*'Don't you remember
> how the whole world is governd by a fact that embraces / everything that happens?'*]
> is emptily facile. At best it will induce a certain depression in most of us at
> the exploitation of what is anyway a romantic cliché in such a context."

For the would-be mentor of our standards and tastes in poetry,
had the outcry been "manly" rather than "girlish", so we gather, the
poem as a model of possible feeling might not have been impaired.
And had the tone or the tenor of thought not sunk to the level of the
"sentimental" or the "philosophizing" (both, vices found frequently
in my work by distressed readers since Olson first brought up the
matter in *Against Wisdom As Such*), had I not sought to deal with the
sentimental as it came, the reader might not have so lost confidence in
the matter of the poem. It does not seem to have occurred to Rosenthal
that just this tone and tenor of each line as he gets it—the shifts from
narrative mode (he calls it the "literal") to pathetic exclamation to

projective sentiment—are to be taken not as some affect of the writer's indisposition in need of expression but as content of the poem itself, as poem data, to be read as dream data and feeling-tone are read as factors in the structure of meanings in the dream. It is the constitution of the field of the poem that determines the line. The exclamation *"To be in love!"* does get, very accurately, the tone of the actual dream I am drawing from, but it is not that verisimilitude that determines the line-tone but its belonging to the projective feeling of the poetic structure as I work with it in writing; and here, it is the very questionable pitch of the outcry, its being *"over-filld, more than was sensible"*, that gives resonance to the extremity of emotions to follow. The poem puts forward the unsurety it must go by—the urgency and lack of confidence in one—that gives its meaning into and finds its telling content reestablished in the counsel of the Mother in the dream, in the aloofness the being in love is to go into, in the posture of an aesthetic of not caring, and in the laboratory of sensations with its deformed and mutilated bodies, which, the Prince says, *"when I was in love / were always with me where I was."*

The problem is one of the self portrait in art: does the crisis of the work for the critic have to do with the model, the painter's view of the model, the painter's emotions concerning the model, the painter/model's psychological state, or the painting? For the dreamer, the content was profoundly disturbing and the dream-work carried the disturbance forward in the poem. For the person remembering his dream, there was a personal dis-ease in his having so dreamed, and, in recounting his dream, there was the beginning of a fame in the dream, of fate in bringing the fame to account. And for the writer, drawing upon the elements of his experience as elements now of a fiction in poetry, as the poem advanced into the deep depression in which the meaning of *"rendering tender and more real"* is illustrated by omens of frigidity and sadistic lust, the dismay lingered where it had been awakened in his personal consciousness, even as the use of that dismay in the composition led into the sequence of emotions that were to satisfy the formal demand of a musical sequence of the poem.

In the course of the work, he draws not only from the model of his remembered dream but also from and with the story of the dream and the affects arising in his identification with and personal crisis in that model. There is now a new, a *created*, crisis in feeling before him that belongs to and informs that "I" that is a person of the poem, so that the section that follows upon "Dream Data"—*"Lift me up. Give me a hand."*—is at once a poetic proposition, having its rationale in its contrast with and in its leading from the first section toward the identity of the poem as a whole, and, in turn, an address of that fictional "I" in the process of its own fiction, and at the same time an actual prayer, having its reality in the extremity of the author in his consciousness of his work, even as it had its reality in my own personal depression following the shadow of that driving home of the dream to become a new source of feeling in the poem.

It is part of the social reality back of my original dismay that the very shifts of feeling, verging, as they did, upon despised and outcast modes of adolescence, that so troubled me and so deeply imprinted themselves that not only in dream but in my daily conscience and in my creative imagination they rehearsed their message, that these shifts of feeling in failure were sure to be seen as "emptily facile". In this they ran true to form, for the claims of adolescent passion were in the first place found, in the eyes of the adult world, to be without sufficient ground in experience, "emptily facile". The critical reader's distaste seems unsympathetic and may spring from a matured distaste for phases of immaturity, yet was not the poem itself haunted by the dread of some emptiness at heart? And was not every facility revealed to be insidious?

For the reader who so sees the matter, the dream data induces a certain depression that may recall the embarrassments and depressions of adolescence. But now we find that the critic's depression was not, he tells us, felt to be rooted in his own life experience of like feelings but was in immediate reaction "at the exploitation of what is anyway a romantic cliché in such a context". The vividness of the reader's discomfort may have already entered the poet's imagination as he worked, even here, for the projection of possible readings is essential to his art, the art of a multiphasic message, a field of possible readings. And in this context, a context of contexts, dream data, poetic fiction, original feeling, even the recognition of cliché and the critical perspectives of sympathies and dissympathies, unite in a widening suspicion in which he designs.

I have such a superstition of the existence of that field of feelings in which I work that there is not a passage that does not deepen the identity of my intention. Fabricator of identities, I feel betrayed as if caught in the act by every observation. Who can, as I pose him, be false to my own true self? Bearskin, favorite character out of Grimm's fairy tales in childhood, whose deceptive and repulsive condition was necessary to the dramatic revelation of his true self, I recognized even as the title *H.M.S. Bearskin* came to me as the name of the suite of poems as it appears in CAESAR'S GATE and I realized that he was a person of the poem to be and also a mask of self. The initials H.M.S. bothered me then. They came as an arbitrary element beyond my conscious intent, and, ever a child of Freudian persuasions, I took such elements as belonging to the psychopathology of daily life in which hidden meanings were at work to come to light. I recognized that the initials referred to *H.M.S. Pinafore*, another favorite entertainment of early years, and puzzled over the appropriation of "His Majesty's Ship" as part of the protagonist's name (but wouldn't it have been, remembering that the original play was during Queen Victoria's reign, *Her* Majesty's Ship?). It is only now, as I retell this tale, that I remember that that play of Gilbert's has too, of course, a plot of identities mistaken— *"exchanged in childhood's happy hour"*—and having to do with being true and false to one's true self. It proves indeed to be the regrettable cliché appropriate only to the play of clichés that musical comedy makes mistaken for the real thing. Amateur Night. Has adolescence no claim in our maturity that is not musical comedy?

It is as if I were indwelling even in the time-worn propositions of emptiness and facility. My music not Apollo's but that of Mercury the Thief, the Dissembler, Lord of the Musical Comedy turn. But name me there, and I shall be offended Apollo. The two musics belong to one myth and mystery of the god of rapture and disease and of the other, his counterpart and instructor, magician-master of the lyre, the trickster god of what is too easy to believe.

RECOVERING THE KNOWLEDGE OF A PAINFUL TIME

Just where he confides, we question his confidence. Is he covering the matter as he covers the matter? It is not only in my own person that in some extravagance of the personal projection I may find myself embarrassed. My ideal reader goes along with me, larger in her permission to read than I am in mine, incorporating in her recreation the very fact of embarrassment among the assets of my account. Every default I imagine, every question I raise, enters as content of the poem as she reads it, as a matter of fact in the facture of meaning she takes as real. But the other, the he who is reading, is troubled throughout, as I am, for he must venture, as I have had to, beyond his sense of his funds. His *balance* is in question, and he is uneasy concerning his references.

Let me specify where I would take this issue: in the present volume of work from 1948–49, certain poems—the *"Four Poems as a Night Song", "The Second Night of the Week", "Processionals II", "Upon Another Shore of Hell"*, or *"An Incubus"*—do not seem poetically questionable to me. They are hewed close to the grain of a resisting matter in feeling, hued in turn deep in the immediacy of color taken as permanent and primary. Having the quality, later to become an absolute requirement of the poem for Jack Spicer, of dictation, they are removed from the interference of uneasy self-consciousness—that even today I have not the ease of, though more and more I recognize and admit to the work that my task in Poetry is concerned with the *conscience*—the consciousness and conscience of the poem in relation to the various fields of meaning in which I recognize the poem to operate.

But in other poems of this volume I am not so sure. They were and remain for me today questionable; and I take them then to go into irresolute elements of my art that even today need the courage of meaning to come into their own.

In *"Processionals I"*, what of the foreign matter? the speaking in French, a language which is in no sense my own, a language in which I read, yes, but even there—and certainly in any exchange of actual speech—I must be embarrassed for sure? Even English can become for me, when I am writing, a speaking in tongues, so that I must research the individual word to find its meaning. The French in *"Processionals I"* is a kind of pretend-poetry within the poem, an area of the poem taken over by the montage of French movie amour, a film of a stereotype that comes into making love. The word cliché we remember here is French. It must be the very language predicament in which the will of the poet is revealed, as in a nightmare, in its origin to be some pretend-speech, a voice not his own that comes in playing the poet, beyond his means. And then, the extention of the voice, the Mannerist poses of the image field beyond the bounds of my actual condition. We find we are in dreams not of America but of a decayed Europe as if they illustrated the author's life.

The "trains" that appear are trains of thought, yes, but they are also incumbrances of fancy dress, fancied feelings, analogous to biological growths that appear to have no fruitful function in the evolution of a viable species or to parasitic lives of the rentier class in a perishing society. The burden of the poet's emotional life and of his poems then must be part of such dreams and taken as encumbrance of a character-armor. A pun on the term "drag" from homosexual jargon comes into the verb "dragging" in "Dragging our trains", a deeper dragging of a grotesque likeness informing a nightmare reality—the creative will determined to institute such a wagonload in the place of the real. It is a caricature armor as self then; the word "caricature" related we find not to the word "character", *to engrave*, but to the word "caricatura" *to load it on*.

"*Processionals I*" takes its load from sources of "load" that were at the time it was written in 1949, even as they are in many circles today, despised sources or models. Is it the most questionable element in my account of myself and of my work that Edith Sitwell in the unremitting grand mannerist style of her poetry in the wake of the Second World War stands among my masters with Williams and Pound, that Cocteau in his theatrical magic and tricking out of his poet's fate stands with Rilke in his intense authenticity, that Salvador Dalí, collaborator with Buñuel in the making of *L'Age D'Or* and *Le Chien Andalou*, is ever there in my mind as well as Breton, as if some *farceur*, some forcer or farcer of the real, a Collaborationist within the Self, were involved in the genius that moves me. The Absolutism of the Imagination which Breton speaks from and for I know too well. And before that Dictatorship, that Revolutionary Dogma of Desire, I am raised, again, a heretic. Is it the most questionable element in my confidence against confidence that so much is drawn from even the fancies of others, as if my experience in their fictions were substantial?

·

In the case of Dalí's *L'Age D'Or* (for it is that comedian of the ego who meant his travesty of the Id in the original version—it is he, and not the ultimately victorious and orthodox master mason of the film, that I draw upon), the matter had perhaps come into my imagination stirred not by the work of art itself (for not until 1956 was I to see *L'Age D'Or*, when it was like seeing what I had been long previously drawing upon) but by the lore of the work, and, here again, the crisis in confidence it raised in the culture it belonged to, the critical dismay, and back of that the crisis in confidence underlying the conflict between the intentions of Dalí and of Buñuel in the conception of the work. Julien Levy's anthology, SURREALISM, had been my source in the late 1930s for the scenario of the film:

"*Dragged through the streets of a modern city this man, who is the protagonist of the film, struggles to escape, as each object he sees transforms itself into reminders of his beloved*"—so the scenario reads. But where is the story of the rotting donkeys in their mise en scène of pianos and priests, where their stench all but overpowered the actors and crew. Searching for it now, I cannot find the episode in the scenario. Stubbornly, with a growing doubt, I pursue the matter. Returning to read again *The Secret Life of Salvador Dalí*, I find why he is always there in my mind—what an alliance in reading I made with the writing of that book, in which my own secret life of a self-consciousness was resolved, as obdurate and renegade in its humor as Dalí's triumphant invention of and vainglorying in his ego mania. But I do not find the account of that scene of stink and oppression there. May my memory be from another source, closer to my own adolescence with its troubled and wishful projections of personality? For it comes to me now as one of the stories of surrealists and their world that I heard from Anaïs Nin, who had been an idol of personality for me in my late teens and early twenties. This idol of personality that Dalí portrays in caricature, in its strain, its drag, and its stink, Anaïs Nin sought to propitiate each day, weaving about herself the rumors and phantasies of personality-life, claiming her glamor from the famous she had known even as she dismissed them.

Fleeing from Europe in the outbreak of the Second World War, the surrealists had invaded the New York scene, and, as an attendant in the wake of the spectacular Anaïs Nin, who herself courted that world—anonymous as I was and, even as I was introduced, all but nonexistent—I had seen actual the poet André Breton and heard his voice in that French, that was for me a speech of tongues or of birds that poets were supposed in legend to understand and that in truth I could but overhear. Even as I was briefly in the presence of that specter that had brought after Freud the revelation of a threat in Poetry, I was—as the idol I attended, Anaïs Nin, was—a creature of the fringe. The inner world of surrealism was *over there* for me. It was— and this was not so remote from its actual claim—more than what was realizable, an apparition in place of the real, a ghostly or ghastly visitation. I was never to have the sufficient obsession or madness that would guarantee my belonging there.

But now, uneasy with my claim of those stinking donkeys, this
fairy or demonic simulation of a passion in *L'Age D'Or*, I find that the
memory was taken in error: the scene, as I had begun to suspect even
as I searched in vain, actually belongs to *Le Chien Andalou*, a movie
that I had not only read about in those early years but seen more
than once. Proceeding from the generation in error then, back of my
screen memory of its being *L'Age D'Or*, there was another scenario
where now I find: *"The cyclist, as he so painfully drags this load forward,
strains desperately to reach the girl."* In the confusion of error and actual
memory, of actual presences long ago known and phantasmal identities,
a language of history and mistaken history grows almost adequate in its
cycle, its painfully dragging the load forward, its strain, to convey the
multiphasic character of my own life experience as it went.

"It leaves us with no alternative but to admit that we will be
committed," Jean Vigo wrote upon seeing *Le Chien Andalou*. And for
the poet in an age when poets of moving pictures have been among
our masters, seeing has not been passive but committed as an act that in
turn commits the seer. It is committed as if it were a transgression. He
has not the authenticity of obsession or madness, but he is committed
even as he protests his not being a true believer. Not having the
guarantee of belief and then not the possibility of being believable, he
must take his way in a faith that goes beyond the matter of beliefs.

The discomfort of the writer or the reader is in the act that likewise
transgresses even as it would move. In the full responsibility of this
transgression we have come across into a new order of sight and must
see the old world, the old vision, the old law, in the dispensation
of the new. Yes, the old law, the transgression, the seeing anew,
the commitment in seeing! But the creative will must move to
undo all commitment in what it creates. What we admit in our
being committed to the creative is our deeper transgression in that
commitment.

THE GATE

In the nearly twenty-five years since the winter of 1948–49, I have
lived and relived, had vision and revision of my life then, and, as if the
River Lethe lay between so that I have come into a life beyond that
life, yet I did not drink of those waters, so that in the content of my
life since I found it in 1950 the early unhappy events that belong to

the period of CAESAR'S GATE seek to find their place, to come to their "happiness" or that sum of fitness in the acknowledged continuity of a life that gives to events the quality of their having happened.

The poems of CAESAR'S GATE belong to a period that in part for me was an unhappy aftermath, a period of irresolution that I saw as a deserted place or as an after-death or *Bardo* state, as it is portrayed in THE TIBETAN BOOK OF THE DEAD, a feverish realm illustrated by the soul's fears and hopes, claims and illusions, in which the soul is haunted by what it is.

The Venice Poem had defined the previous period between February and September of 1948 as one of a victory for me. It was the first time in my writing that I had both known what I had to do—something more in writing than knowing what you *want* to do—and known as I worked that I was able to do it. I saw the City of Venice in that poem as my own and the history of its empire as the history of an imperialism in Poetry in which I saw my own dreams expand. "The earth has tides of desolation and of bliss," had come to me in a verse of *Heavenly City, Earthly City* but a year before. And in my vision of Empire in *The Venice Poem* I saw again the Power and the Accumulation of Wealth, the grandeur and domination, as a poetry established in a pathos, a pathetic claim having, as if foresight of itself, knowledge of the remains of Venice, of today. Yet in the "Coda" of that poem I had come upon an ecstatic promise: that Hell was the womb of Heaven; that the extreme passion of painful experience of love in conflict was the formation of a passage in feeling in which a new self was to be born. I had thought that I had won for myself the strength of the passion I had known even as I thought I had won the power that I had had in writing.

In my personal life, falling in love in November of 1947 and "winning" my lover from a rival, I had found myself in a passional possession, obsessed by the shadow of a rival, a transient lover myself, impersonating the conqueror of a world falling into ruin in being conquered. The passion of *The Venice Poem* was in the fulfillment it brought to the expression of that legend, and the victory for me— a victory that remains in my sense of the poem today—was in the transformational resolution in which the elements of my personal state were seen to be elements of a musical form. It was as if, in the "Coda" of the symphony, I had been brought to some transformational resolution of my own personal psyche-life. Returning to my lover then, in the period of CAESAR'S GATE that followed, a period of hoped for reconciliation, I found myself in an uneasy truce. The course of our lives still was that of contending powers. I was fearful that love was only won to be lost again, and I brooded in jealous rages. Yet the first poem of this period shows an excursion of my own. I was also then the transgressor of our reunion, for my poems betrayed another life that broke through whatever claim I would make for the homestead I wanted. I had yet to see that home is a pathetic claim. I thought that it but needed some strong belief I might have. And the Empire, in its utter fiction, in the power of the pathos it already gathered in Poetry, took over. The figure I saw then was Alexander, coming to the Gate of Asia, to his claim in the wastes, where, brooding, he saw his was to be an empire, yes, but one in which all that he sought was to come to its end in intoxications of desolation, and grandeur.

Caesar's Gate was a figure that came from the confusion of two passages from Marco Polo's account of his travels in Asia, these passages in turn having to do with legends arising from deeper confusions in the history of that continent:

> "This is the province into which, when Alexander the Great attempted to advance northwards, he was unable to penetrate, by reason of a narrowness and difficulty of a certain pass, which on one side is washed by the sea, and is confined on the other by high mountains and woods . . . so that a very few men were capable of defending it against the whole world."

The passage, itself referring to the very difficulty of passage, a passage to Asia, but it was also—for this was the secret lure that Marco Polo followed—the passage from one time to another, from medieval Christendom to the Renaissance—the passage, like a passage in a dream, might be speaking of a sexual conquest, of making a pass or, deeper, of coming to a pass in making love.

"*Disappointed in this attempt, Alexander caused a great wall to be constructed at the entrance of the pass, and fortified it with towers . . . From its uncommon strength the pass obtained the name of the Gate of Iron*"—this, the editor notes, was the celebrated pass between the foot of Mount Caucasus and the Caspian Sea— "*called by the Arabs, Bab-al-abuab, or the* Gate of Gates; *by the Turks, Demir-capi, or the* Gate of Iron; *and by the Persians, Derbend, or the* Barrier, *between Georgia and the Persian province of Shirvan.*"

For the reader for whom the Persia of Marco Polo's journey into alien lands in search of the Great Khan is fused with the Persia of

Burton's terminal essay on the Sotadik Zone that accompanies his translation of THE BOOK OF THE THOUSAND NIGHTS AND A NIGHT, the country beyond is the dream landscape of a homosexual projection, and Caesar Alexander and Marco Polo there are ghostly venturers into a realm of sodomitic empire claimed in Love.

In the second passage from Marco Polo then, the spectral armies may be the legions of the unborn dead that haunt the battlefields of sexual encounters where semen is spent without issue. Beyond the town of Lop in farthest Turkestan, Marco Polo tells us, there commences a vast waste which lies in the dominion of Kublai Khan:

> "It is asserted as a well-known fact that this desert is the abode of many evil spirits, which amuse travellers to their destruction with most extraordinary illusions. If, during the daytime, any persons remain behind on the road, either when overtaken by sleep or detained by their natural occasions, until the caravan has passed a hill and is no longer in sight, they unexpectedly hear themselves called to by their names, and in a tone of voice to which they are accustomed . . . In the night-time they are persuaded they hear the march of a large cavalcade on one side or the other . . . and concluding the noise to be that of the footsteps of their party, they direct theirs to that quarter from whence it seems to proceed; but upon the breaking of day, find that they have been misled and drawn into a situation of danger."

The esoteric reference of the text is now to the waste lands at the entrance to the dominion of the phantastic imagination itself, and the bemused travelers here refer to the writer as, hearing a voice in his writing that seems to call him by name and to be his, following the feet proceeding in his verses, he is led on, and then to ourselves as readers, following the voice and the leading feet we hear as we read, as if the writing were meant just for us in our name, where, just where we are most amused, we are to be most wary, where the Khan or Caesar Alexander who seems now to have come to our minds in reading is, we must caution ourselves as we entertain the idea, a specter of the poet's being led on.

> "Sometimes likewise during the day these spirits assume the appearance of their traveling companions, who address them by name and endeavor to conduct them out of the proper road. . . . Marvelous indeed and almost passing belief are the stories related of these spirits of the desert, which are said at times to fill the air with the sounds of all kinds of ancient instruments and also of drums and the clash of arms . . . "

The psycho-sexual content, the scenes of an imagined penetration of the waste lands of Asia, the twists of theology and of Biblical legend, the propositions concerning the nature of poetry, the self posturings and accusations from imagined critics, and the expression, where it comes through, of what we recognize to be personal emotions, humors, nostalgias—all these enter into the works here only as they were felt to be the content of a possible poetry, as they belong to the apprehension of an imperative of the poem. In *The Venice Poem*, I had, for the first time, known the full structural imperative of a form seeking to come into existence in the process of the poem that, at the same time, I was in my own work working in cooperation with, coming to acknowledge in the works of the poem. It was like dreaming and in the dream working out the dream and knowing coordinations of its form and content as a language, coming to know the meaning of what was happening. But not again, it seems to me, until the conception of THE OPENING OF THE FIELD in 1956, almost seven years later, did I come into the fullness of that experience, and then the force of the poetics I had pursued had overtaken me. The Empire that haunts poem after poem following *The Venice Poem* is the specter of a Poetics whose realm would maintain lines of communication in a continent of unknown outcomes. There were rumors, yes, but there was no guarantee in the rumor. CAESAR'S GATE, THE BOOK OF RESEMBLANCES, and LETTERS, are works of a phase in Poetry fearfully and with many errors making its way, taking up fear and error as its own terms, seeking every rumor, every superstition, every promise of its own existence as it journeyed into the continent of that existence, seeking to regain a map in the actual to come to know, part by part, the transformation of a continent into a life. *"So that there is a continent of feeling beyond our feeling, / a big house of the spirit,"* as it came to me in the poem *Apprehensions* some ten years later.

What does it mean that in order for it to come real in the poem we must *imagine* even what we have actually felt? We must make it up in order to make it real. The desolation of CAESAR'S GATE was the desolation of the uncreated; the desolation of what Man seeks to wrest from his experience in the claim of his own virtue. Then the Asia of the Untransformed does rule the Spirit. The secret of the real I sought was hidden in the earnest of play I had long before known in childhood, in making up worlds and persons I had long ago made up China and the Khan as I had made up scenes of being loved and loving that led toward the making up of Love.

PAIN

Did we get to feel it? The ache of the love-tooth the tongue returns to try again and again, the hand, writing, touches upon. Is the old trouble still alive where it was? I know of no figures of speech that are not rooted deep in the actual, or each actual event is a seed that must quicken to come to life and would root and put out itself as a stem of configurations. Like this tooth that appears to illustrate here. In the summer of 1947 I had hitched across the continent to see Ezra Pound. I had twenty dollars to do it on—a fortune. And fortune had designed that trip out to come to a trip into pain, as, the third day out, West of Denver, in the blazing heat of Summer, in the confusion of fever the obliterating pain of four wisdom-teeth, infected and compacted, took over or threatened to take over my consciousness. I paid out a dollar for a room and crept into bed there, lying in the fury of it until waking at last I found it had passed. Not until two months later, when I returned to Berkeley, did I find what it was. The blood that comes into the rites of the poems of the Venice Poem period is the blood that could gush up from a torn vein left after the operation on those sunken teeth and did when in sexual excitement my blood pressure increased, filling my mouth and throat. And the Continent—Asia in CAESAR'S GATE— is informed by that other trip out, going toward my master, Ezra Pound, imprisoned, and something grievously gone wrong in Poetry itself there. In my recognition of the fateful nature of his genius I saw the infection as deep, as the fateful nature of my nation itself—festering America—and as the fateful nature of Poetry too. The rage of the actual hidden wisdom-teeth in my swollen jaws seemed to be deep in my spirit; the continent I strove to cross the continent of such a fever.

Yet tooth-ache is not as deep in its lore of pain as ear-ache is for me. In early childhood there were ordeals of darkness and roaring. Was there roaring? or would I take on Swift's affliction to illustrate pathetically my own? Let me fabricate some identity of my hearing with Swift's, though mine passed with time and was not, as his was, the beginning of an end in catastrophe. *"I have been very miserable all night,"* Swift writes to his cousin, Martha Whiteway:

> *"and to-day extremely deaf and full of pain. I am so stupid and confounded, that I cannot express the mortification I am under both in body and mind . . . I hardly*

understand one word I write, I am sure my days will be very few; few and miserable they must be."

Such a blindness in hearing I remember, a blackness in which, within the thickness of pain, the pressures of an accumulating earwax—in my genetic misfortune, of the sticky order, not the crumbling—there was the thumping of a heart, in the ear painfully sounding. I thought there was a gigantic drumming in the universe surrounding me. In the utter destitution of hearing, the pain came as a pulse incorporating dread. The dullness of a deeper ache beneath the fury of the pain. Ideograms of pain and fury form even as I write as if a prison population struggled to take over and rise to speak.

The disease but illustrates the dis-ease. By my seventh or eighth year, the ear-aches were gone. Say, my seventh—for in the legend of the Ages of Man, each Age has seven years. In my fourteenth, I was to enter another phase. "I cannot sleep at night," the *he* of "The Walk to the Vacant Lot" says to me. It had been a scene in actual life. I had but to write what he had said: "If you will look, you will see I have no soul." That's the way I remember it now. In the writing it rises as if from a dream belonging to the poem. But did he not take the very words from my mouth? That desolate young man had recognized something in me that answered his intent and called me to witness an impasse he knew I knew as well as he. Back of his words, a fearful silence—if silence it can be that is also a roaring, a painful deafness—a deafening inability in sexual love or a refusal, gathers, in which the pulse of the heart once again grows enormous. I cannot say what I feel. *"I have been very miserable all night,"* Swift wrote.

Sleep, sleep, sleep. These poems seem most to long for sleep. Sleep locked up in the locking up of love. That is always there in me, I think, even as the other, passional, admission of love returns, as if it were always there, behind the barrier, the imprisoned urgency. Caesar's Gate, locked, the body withdrawn. *"An adversary in the body against its youth,"* it names itself in a recent poem. "All but unbearable," I have called it. I mean, this is the tenor of my work, to test the tolerance of Heaven with my dis-ease. The mind returns to the imprint of a sleeplessness. I do not seek to free my self from what I have known but so deeply to acknowledge that bitter nursling that Sleep when it comes will have to bring all of me home at last into its arms.

The impact of Lorca's *POETA EN NUEVA YORK* was, as I have testified in the Introduction to *HEAVENLY CITY, EARTHLY CITY*, immediate, a voice speaking for my own soul in its rage it seemed. I discovered there the speech of a feeling I had. *"Furia color de amor,"* Lorca quotes from the poet Luis Cernuda: "Fury the color of Love"—"Love the color of Forgetting", *"Amor color de olvido"*. But this fury in Love, surviving, was of the color of what could not be forgotten, Love the color of what Oblivion could not tolerate, what was disgorged by that Lethe that would separate our adolescent selves from our later lives, thrown up by the Fountain of Waters that would wash our consciousness of what we are clean from our conscience of what we were. Today I see Love and that Household in which I live, as I saw it in its beginning twenty years ago, as a homestead I and my companion there would create, even pathetically, within Man's nature, "shelterd by our imaginary humble lives from the eternal storm of our rage". I cannot forget the claim fury has in me. I cannot forget the ruthless exploiter and tyrant of the soul's realm the poet can be in his craving for greater triumphs in his art.

I cannot forget the Spain of Lorca. In the conscience of the world, Spain in the late 1930s was our Viet Nam, in which we saw our nations revealed in the truth of what they were. Mussolini and Hitler, advising and aiding Franco (even as today, their successors in this, Kennedy, and then Johnson and Nixon, have come in behind the military dictators in Saigon to run the scene of that war), rehearsed the first phase in the War between Anti-Communist and Communist forces and demonstrated and tested the uses and powers of aerial bombardment, while in Madrid and within the ranks of those who came to defend the Republic and those who fought for ideals of democracy and communism, among the Loyalists, backed by the aid of the Soviet Union, Communist forces sought to gain control. This was not for us a foreign politics, for, rightly, we saw in Spain our own country divided by the opposition of Powers and Dominations against the claims of our humanity. The terrorism of Hitler, the arrogance of Mussolini, the brutality and stupidity of Stalin, the self-interest of organizers and administrators to extend their authority over men's lives and consciences—these waited in our own state for their time to come. It was the first full phase of that War that rages throughout the world today, as enormous in its crimes and madness revealed in Man's spirit as the religious wars between Protestant and Catholic in the sixteenth and seventeenth centuries had been. It was, if the history of Man be the history of one species having a spiritual Identity, the same War, and we saw it so. Spain was the heart-land of Man in the truth of what he was. We saw the War in news photographs, but we saw it also in Goya's *Caprichos* and his *Desastres de la Guerra*, and scenes of the War came in our dreams. It was a language deeper than the politics of the day assumed it to be.

Scenes of retribution and reprisal for insults and injuries to the pride of would be Powers—at Béziers for their harboring heretics or at Lidice or My Lai for their harboring communists—have that evil that they use the lives of actual men to write their bloody pages. The living are driven into the forests, into the fastnesses of the mountains and the hiding places of the heart to survive. The Spain of Lorca was not the Spain of the *Falange* or of the Republican bureaucracy or the Revolution but of the Gypsies, the people of the Night and of the Moon, driven before the Spanish Civil Guard, the armies and police of whatever authority in power.

In Death was the ultimate retreat of the gypsy. "In poetry," Lorca said, "the *duende*"—the hidden power of the dead or daemon—"does not come unless he sees the possibility of death." Lorca's Spain was "a nation of death, a nation open to death", a nation of the Holy Ghost. Yet he could say too—"The gypsies are a theme, and nothing else. I could just as well be the poet of sewing needles or hydroelectric landscapes." The *duende* or genius of the gypsy song was the *duende* of a theme; the thematic transformation of his life was his daemon or fate. "I am now writing a poetry which demands the opening of veins," he wrote to a friend, "a poetry freed from reality". According to the legend, as he prepared to go to Granada, where he was to be killed, he said, when friends warned him, "They do not shoot poets." "It was because he wrote the Romance de la Guardia Civil española," Miguel said in Bañalbufar when I asked about Lorca, "because he insulted the Civil Guard, that they killed him." He fell as others fell that day in Granada; as anarchists fell before the Civil Guards of the Communist regime. He had insulted reality.

It is this Lorca, the *duende* or fairy power, the visitation from the Hill of Dreams or the gypsy camp of the Dead, freed from reality, that comes in *Four Poems as a Night Song* to haunt the vision of what Poetry is, and then later, in *What Have You Come to Tell Me, Garcia Lorca?* it is this spectral correspondent who takes over the poem, as, some eight years later, in 1957, he was to come to Jack Spicer in the ghost-writing of AFTER LORCA.

I had wanted, I think, a fatefulness in my poetry, an inevitability to its course, an autocracy, as if, indeed, in the person of the poet in writing, I were in the person of an "I" who created my life and world, in the enormity of a governing intent, as content of a poetry or creation. God, then, appears in the poem, as the Gnostic heresies portray him, as the creator or poet who is *guilty* of his creation, behind whose reality there is an other reality. This God is a Creator in search of an Identity that is in the process of Its creation; He projects the theater of Time and Space in which to become manifest. He is betrayed by his Poetry.

The infant emperor in his autistic universe or empire is taunted by critical voices of the poem, by alien spaces emptied in their not being *his*, by reverberations and omens of an impending revolution from within or of an invasion from without. In *The Venice Poem* the preceding year he had appeared as the author of the poem itself before the relentless elemental reality moving beyond him in the poem as he wrote: *"Like Canute he plays sovereign to the sea. / He sits for hours as if he might hold it back, / eyes fixt upon the tide, / cross-eyed king of one thousand lines."* It is the record of some childhood play, for the story of Canute belongs to the same earliest years as that child I was who was at once lord of certain fiefs, cities and castles of sand, and story-teller in them, as if the sea were at his command and conspired in the story, of floods and tidal waves in which his worlds were swept by disaster. In CAESAR'S GATE, a continent replaces the sea, and Alexander in Marco Polo is the emperor-storyteller.

In the two sessions I had with Peggy Linnet, an artist whose drawings were the symptom or flowering of a schizophrenic breakdown, I came to her as if to the Witch of Endore, as if, like Saul, I had in my art some conspiracy with madness. The content that flooded my mind in the process of the poem, the rhythmic excitement that came in language for me, and then the being ravished by a commanding reality of the imagination that took over all ground of conscious being—these conversions that I had known in the seizure of poems, I took to be very like what she had known in her hallucinations. I had a secret understanding I assumed, a perilous confidence, in our talk. But what I experienced as an ascending power, she experienced as an attack. She was sick with images, and her art had its craft in seeking to counter-act the machinations of that language behind language that I sought to work with. Yet it seemed to me that in her being so the victim she was closer to the center than I dared be or was permitted to be. Canute, whom we see in his vanity challenging the sea, seeks to be overcome and taken over by the power beyond his command. And Alexander seeks, beyond his empire, to be taken over into the unreality of Asia.

I had, and still have—for again and again the apprehension returns—essential to my art, a horror of creation. A shudder underlies my senses in their pleasure, as if beauty were itself the sign of an immanent danger. The announcement then of an imminent disclosure. It is the grue, the sense of coming near to grief, that signifies in the lore of the Scotch folk, the weird of poetry. My art sought to spell that moment, even as I saw Peggy Linnet in her art sought to dispell. In her house the vividness of that borderline of spelling and dispelling was felt as a kind of sea-sickness, a vertigo at the heart of the continent, the discovery of a discontinuity in the mass we would take experience to be, a poetic nausea.

I had come to the pass in 1949 when I had committed myself to Poetry, even as if to a madhouse or a religion. Yet it was a madness I had to make up, a conviction that I came to know only as I went into the depths of its invention in which I stood convicted of being its author. In the fiction of that authority I was without the guarantees of the authenticity I saw in madness. What Peggy Linnet suffered I projected. The grue was there, yes. A suspicion in poetry was growing in me. I would have, ultimately, to name the grief myself.

In my commitment, there was a Reality behind the reality I knew in making it up, a Reality to which everything I knew referred. The world was a text, the code of many languages, yet to be broken. So, it seemed to me later when I came to know Charles Olson, that that breaking open of the Mayan language or that decoding of Linear B was such a coming to read the message of Creation, to find the keys that would unlock the course of one's own life and world as a language leading into the fullness of meaning beyond. He lived in Gloucester like a child lives in a house before he has broken the code of the parental speech that surrounds him in words and gestures, embodied in persons and furnitures he will come to take as his.

The events of history—the actual events of the Spanish Civil War and of Lorca's life story, even as the events of Alexander's wars of conquest and Marco Polo's travels—we took as events in a mystery that referred to Poetry, as, in turn, we took events in poems to refer to our own work in Poetry, as we read *The Bridge* of Hart Crane, the visionary poems of D.H. Lawrence and of Robinson Jeffers, and the POETA EN NUEVA YORK for their vatic imagination of what was truly at issue in *our* being "American". Our people were the people of a dream secretly at work in the nation without, of an other nation within and below and behind and above the public identity of America; even as we felt *our* language to be that of a meaning striving to come into existence within the public exchange. An esoteric language, then, a language of reference, but, if it was symbolic, carrying in its *throw* another thing, it was not in reference to some preceding reality but toward its reference that it was thrown—a paranoiac conspiracy with a special meaning in which in the very throw forward toward sense a creative intent was embodied in which that sense was invaded by meaning. I had come to that pass in 1949 when the events of my own life became events of such a language for me, and fate seemed the syntax of a poetic sentence; even as today, all that I come to sense and to learn of the universe and its elements, of the nature of life, and of myself as a part of that reality, I read as the text of an ultimate Poetry, beyond me, upon the verge of such a being able to read I write, even as, as a child, I used to make up worlds and populations of a play-real upon the shores of the Reality I belonged to. It was the happy rite of a fearful belonging.

·

Now, rereading Lorca's POETA EN NUEVA YORK, it speaks, even as it spoke then, for the very current of my own life, and I come upon the poem "Iglesia Abandonada", whose lament touches upon another lament and still another. Is it from a loss at the heart of Christendom, or is it from my own heart, that the loss of a son at the heart of this poem finds its echo? "I had a son who was called Juan," the woman cries out in Lorca's Ballad of the Great War. "I had a son." The cry echoes in the abandoned Church of a God who gave over His only Son to the sentence of Death that emerged from His own offended Wrath, and it takes over as its own language the terms of the abandoned liturgy.

There is a suspicion that each generation in their degeneration as old men become obsessed by the threat of losing honor, even as they secretly brood over losing youth and manhood, and set up in place of their hearts the holocaust of a war in the works of their nations in order to make vivid, in the orgies of young men at their command slaughtered and slaughtering, the play of a terrible sentence long brooding and unutterable otherwise against Youth itself. At the depth of the intent, beyond all hostilities, there is always the mime of an awe-ful attention, the grief they seek to bring us all to in their surviving the death of those they feared would survive them. They write the poetry of a lament using the lives of others as we poets of the language pretend lives.

In the history of Poetry itself, in the earliest stage I know of in which the identity of the Maker, the *poet* in the proper sense of that word, emerges from that of the Medium of the Song or *bard*, the poet of the *Odyssey* reveals himself in that identity for a moment in Book VIII, when he appears as a creature of his own song himself to sing to Odysseus, the hero of that song, the "wise and crafty", another song— the *Iliad*, to which Odysseus belongs. There is brought to the feast-table of Alkinoös of the Phaiákians a harper, whom the Muse cherished, we are told, for even as she gave him the sweetness of music, she made him blind. Unknowing then, blind to his identity, in his blindness he is Homer. Blind to the identity of his true audience—for unknown to his host, the guest is the hero of the song himself, the singer is again moved by the Muse who brings to his mind the song of Troy, of the clash between Odysseus and Achilles. Under the cover of his cloak, his screen-identity, Odysseus weeps then; and Odysseus may be thinking in turn of Homer when later he tells his challenger to the games: "In looks a man may be a specter, and yet be master of speech so crowned with beauty that people gaze at him with pleasure." The Book of the Harper is filled with blindness and blinds, with Odysseus's cloak, with Athena, disguised, who calls out from the audience at Odysseus's revealing throw of the discus—"Even a blind man, friend, could judge this, finding with his fingers . . . this event is yours."

The young men dance their magic rounds. The harper sings now of adulterous love dishonoring the absent husband's bed—the song of the craftsman Hephaistos—and how "the word that wounds the heart" came to the master. The Phaiákians present their gifts to their unknown guest. Then Odysseus asks the singer to sing for him the Book of his own guile from the *Iliad*:

"Now change your theme and sing of that wooden horse
that in his craft Epeius inspired by Athena shaped—
that blind behind which Odysseus hid his force
that it be sent into the citadel of Troy to bring Troy down."

The poet, being stirred in his blindness and murmuring to his god, so that he disturbed the strings of his lyre from their rest and words within the tones and tones within words began a vision of how the force of Odysseus crouched, arrested, within the horse, sings. And, even as he sings, his listener, Odysseus, hearing, secretly lets the flaming tears run down his cheeks, Homer tells us, weeping like a woman who laments her lord where he has fallen upon the field of some defeat. Alkinoös alone, near to Odysseus as he was, hearing the listener's moan even as the singer sang, knows, and, stopping the song, he addresses his guest: "Why do you grieve so terribly, as if yours were the story of the Argive Odysseus and the fall of Troy? *All this the gods had designed, weaving with the death of men and with ruin the stuff of this song that it might be sung for the enchantment of men to come.*" So H.D., echoing Homer, in her HELEN IN EGYPT, comes to ask—"Was Troy lost for a subtle chord" "or a run of notes on a lyre?"

It is as if, for Odysseus/Homer, identity cloaked in identity, the City burned in order to furnish his *Iliad*, even as he sings it, with the verity of his weeping. In this vision, Christ dies upon the Cross—"I had a son who was called . . ." a woman somewhere laments—in order for a sufficient grief to come into a poetry.

> Yo tenía un hijo que se llamaba Juan.
> Yo tenía un hijo.

It is the lament of a woman who has lost her son in the Great War. Lorca writes out of a fund of grief that Spain has actually known in war. But the suspicion grows as we read the poem that the lament may be the phantasmal song of a woman who has been deprived of children—by a War, by a Church, by a losing them before they are born? She has also, she tells us, lost a little girl—"Yo tenía una niña"—"I had a dead fish under the ash of the censers" "Yo tenía un pez muerto bajo la ceniza de los incensarios." "I had a sea," she goes on—"of what?" "Yo tenía un mar ¿de qué? / ¡Dios mío! ¡Un mar!" It is the deranged speech of a woman possessed by a grief—is it the ghost at the heart or *duende* of a lost son, killed in war, or the specter of a still-birth that seizes her?

In his lecture *"Theory and Function of the* Duende", Lorca tells us: "The dark and quivering *duende* that I am talking about is a descendant of the merry demon of Socrates." The madness, then, however it may relate to the practice of deliberate alienation which Lorca's intimate friend from student days, Salvador Dalí, had brought into Surrealist circles of Paris from their Spanish conversations, and which led to the work of Breton and Eluard in *L'Immaculée Conception*, contemporary with Lorca's *Poeta en Nueva York*, with Breton's essay on the simulation of verbal deliriums from various categories of insanity—this madness is not ultimately a surrealist simulation drawn from a clinical model in a program of systematic alienation but, past that state, means to return to the divine madness of daemonic inspiration, the speaking more than one knew what, that Plato tells us his Master, Socrates, thought to be at once the power and the dementia of the poet in his art. The speech of the childless mother is meant to initiate the mode of a poetic dissociation. Freed from reality, the trouble of an unbound reference invades the reader's sense of what is at issue. "Yo tenía un mar ¿de qué?" We can sound no bottom of this sea as we make our readings. The poet himself in the ravings of the woman in the poem is speaking of a source in the unknowable from which his poetry comes—"I had a sea—of what?" Beneath the surface of disturbed meanings, the language is assumed to mask a fathomless intention.

The thematic specters of childless women who haunt the world of Lorca's poetry and cry out for their demon bridegroom are not women he longs for but women he longs *from*. They give voice to an urgency that we begin to see speaks for a mystery in the nature of Poetry itself even as it speaks for some personal mystery of Lorca's suffering in life. The *Oda a Walt Whitman* is charged with Lorca's passionate affirmation of Whitman's noble longing for homosexual love, even as it is charged with a loathing for homosexual lusts and commerce, a loathing that would have decency only in the context of Lorca's own longing for the grand union of a sexual love. Here he parts from the Surrealists, for whom homosexual love was taken to be obscene and—even in their program of practiced obscenities and blasphemies—considered beyond the pale.

It seemed to us, to Jack Spicer as to me, in our conversations of 1946 and 1947 as young poets seeking the language and lore of our homosexual longings as the matter of a poetry, that Lorca was one of us, that he spoke here from his own unanswered and—as he saw it—*unanswerable* need. It was this that gave to his outcry in that poem, to his "Agonía, agonía, sueño, fermento y sueño" and to the following "Éste es el mundo, amigo, agonía, agonía" the drive of a terrible knowledge. We read it to be from the depths of a shared fate in experience, so that the pronoun *You* in addressing Whitman was also addressing the true self of the poet and then of the true reader: "You hunted a nakedness as if it would have flowed like a river"—in our persuasion, Lorca's word *desnudo* was the nakedness of a man, even as the verb *fuera*, from the past subjunctive of *Ir*, "to go; to lead as a road leads; to be dying", might carry with it, we wondered, as in our wondering our ignorance of Spanish led us into vagrant ways, the sense that the counter-verb "to come" has in our language of a sexual coming, and, then, the word *fuera* deepened in the shadow of the word *fuerte*, "manly", but it also meant "terrible".

Was Whitman's figure of the lover-companion identified with Lorca's figure of the *duende*? He was "Bull and dream", Lorca tells us, "that joined the wheel with the seaweed". Was the *rueda* a "circle formed by a number of persons", a circle of devotees of the poem, or was it a "crown", once of laurel, now of seaweed? Was it the wheel of some torture upon which the spirit of a man may be tried?

In the directive of the poem, our persuasion that had rushed forward from the masculine gender of the word *desnudo* to mean a male nakedness, as if no element in the course of the poem were without ultimate consequence, was verified, it seemed, for the fateful figure proved to be that of a man—"father of your agony, camellia of your death," who "moaned in the flames of your hidden equator". The word "flames", *llamas*—"flames of light emitted from a fire" the dictionary gives—may also—as, in music, in sounding one tone we may arouse the sympathetic resonances of other tones—lead into the word *llamadas*, "calls", in which *llamas* sounds, so that, voice sounding in voice, the companion's moan sounds in flames that are also calls emitted from the hidden equator of the poet.

In her lament the bereft woman of *"Iglesia Abandonada"* becomes self-confused with the Creator-God of that abandoned Church as "I had a son" becomes in the course of the poem *"He* had a son"—"El tenía un hijo. / Un hijo. Un hijo. Un hijo." The poet, as creator of the world to which the mother in the poem belongs, may have, in some sense, obscure and passionate as the woman's feeling in the poem is, confused his own identity with that of the mother who has lost her son to the War and that of the Creator who has sacrificed His only begotten Son to redeem His Creation. Even as back of War and back of Creation, so, for Lorca, back of Poetry too, there is the sacrifice of a son.

This idea of the sacrifice of the first-born in the foundation of a creative work—a temple, a house, a bridge, a cathedral— there is another story I remember of most-loved child thrown into the molten metal in the casting of a bell in order to deepen its miraculous sound— has back of it a magic in which semen and embryos are spent to bring into the works of the craftsman the genius of an unborn spirit. That is part of it. The Church itself, built upon the death of the Son, in *"Iglesia Abandonada"* is filled also with such still-births—"I had a fish under the ashes of the censers." But with the sacrifice of the first-born, there is also the loss of a loved one that enters the superstition of art. And in Lorca's poetic theater, there appear now women who rage in the fury of a denied passion, a not having a son that is their fate. The poet has given up his own bearing a son in his bearing his art.

The play *Yerma* is called "A Tragic Poem", and it may be the mystery play of a tragic view of Poetry. Yerma, denied a child in her marriage, even as she is denied love, will not turn from the fate her honor commands—the fateful course of that marriage toward its Moment of Truth, as it is called in the bull ring, the five-o'clock in the afternoon of her pending life-drama. The child she longs for is the *duende* who will not let her go aside; she must bring her marriage to its full consequence.

The air trembles when Yerma is in the company of Victor who might have been her lover in her girlhood, and Victor's song as she overhears it is filled with his thought of her presence. "And if you hear the voice of a woman, it is the torn voice of a stream," he sings: "What child is killing you? / The thorn the broom-tree bore!" Yerma lost to him has become the torn voice of a stream, his song. So, she says of his singing, "It's like a stream of water that fills your mouth." Does the singer steal the water of his song from the fountain of generations? "I am like a dry field where a thousand pairs of oxen plow," Yerma says of her lot in marriage to the old woman who comes to offer her son to take Yerma's husband's place to father her child: "and you offer me a little glass of well water." She holds to the dictates of family and community, and in her deprivation she becomes the fountain of a terrible event. "They think I like another man," she tells her sister: "They don't know that even if I should like another man, to those of my kind, honor comes first. They're stones in my path, but they don't know that I can be, if I want to, an arroyo's rushing water and sweep them away." Her fate mounts in her like the gathering flood of a poem out of the poet's pent-up longings kept in the intensities of a personal code.

"The torn voice of a stream"—so the translator renders that verse in Victor's song. The word *rota* in "la rota voz del agua" means "broken; destroyed", and the noun *rota*, I find, means "defeat; rout"—"the broken or routed voice of the water" then. "In idea, in sound, or in gesture, the *duende* likes a straight fight with the creator on the edge of the well," Lorca writes; he drives the voice back into the extremity of its thirst.

"La Niña de los Peines had to tear her voice," Lorca tells us in his account of that *duende* voice of the singer: "She had to impoverish her skills and aids; that is, she had to drive away her muse and remain alone so that the *duende* might come and join in a hand-to-hand fight"—it is the description of a voice in poetry or an extremity in love that can be reached only in the agon that verges upon a depth of defeat: "And how she sang! Now she was in earnest, her voice was a jet of blood, admirable because of its pain and its sincerity, and it opened like a ten-fingered hand in the nailed but tempestuous feet of a Christ by Juan de Juni." The figure of the Son given up into the terrible guarantee of the poem has long been there—against Apollo and his Muses, the old orders of Poetry—the body of this Christ in rout, torn or broken upon the Cross of His Passion.

Yerma demands of her husband a love that will answer her bitter anguish—it is the *duende* in love she demands, the demon bridegroom; and when he asks of her again that she meet him on his own terms— "Resign yourself! . . . You and I—happily, peacefully" where no peace is—she seizes him by the throat, possessed in the fury of the truth she means to come to, and chokes the life out of him. "Barren, barren, but sure. Now I really know it for sure," she says: "And alone." It is all over. "I am looking for you. I'm looking for you," she had cried out to her husband: "It's you I look for day and night . . ." Now it is all over. The yearning, the agon, the impossible necessity.

"Now I'll sleep without startling myself awake, anxious to see if I feel in my blood another new blood." The child had been lost in the struggle of a silence between Yerma and the man she desired— trembling, she had cried out, "Do you hear that? . . . I thought I heard a child crying. And he cried as though drowning." It is over. The child had been lost in Yerma's bitter demand held against pleasure—"Each time I have more desire and less hope . . . I'll end up believing I'm my own son." "I gave myself over to my husband for his sake, and I go on giving to see if he'll be born— but never for pleasure." The child had been lost to this craving for the redemption of a love where it had been refused—"I don't love him," Yerma says of her husband, "I don't love him, and yet he's my only salvation. By honor and blood. My only salvation."

Is there no alternative in that early intense trembling silence of falling in love, if it be thwarted, if it not be transmuted into song but kept as a ghost at the heart, but this generative accusation and then the fury that comes to make an end of it all?

"My body dry forever! What do you want? Don't come near me, because I have killed my son!" ". . . porque he matado a mi hijo, yo misma he matado a mi hijo!" "Yo tenía un hijo" the echo comes from *"Iglesia Abandonada"*—"El tenía un hijo."

"CHILDLESS" I wrote in a notebook over a year ago

"Sunless" means
having no son. Let's be done with it.
The Son grows in the heart
the word I dared not speak. The Word

shakes the poem-center.

We have yet to read deeply Lorca's *Oda a Walt Whitman* to sound his outrage against the perverts, the "gay" inhabitants of desire as if it were a camp. At the close, there is at last sleep.

Sleep, beautiful Walt Whitman. "Duerme, no queda nada." Sleep, there remains nothing. America drowns itself in machines and tears. "América se anega de máquinas y llanto." "I want the strong wind of the deepest night to sweep clear the flowers and letters from the bow where you sleep."

Quiero que el aire fuerte de la noche más honda
quite flores y letras del arco donde duermes . . .

It is over. The pollution is over. It is just, that a man must lead his sexual desire into other ways, that he must not seek his delight in the bloody grove of the next morning. A man can, if he will so, conduct his desire through veins of coral or celestial nude—"Puede el hombre, si quiere, conducir su deseo / por vena de coral o celeste desnudo." Heaven has shores where life can be avoided—"El cielo tiene playas donde evitar la vida". Life, sexual life, lustful life, eats at the core of Lorca's intention like a worm. And he craves to be done with it. Sleep, beautiful Walt Whitman, he prays. "Now I'll sleep without startling myself awake—anxious to see if I feel in my longing another longing . . ." Tomorrow, he sings, my loves will be stone and Time a breeze that comes to sleep among the stone branches—

So Lorca does not sing against the men in love with men who keep the purity of their longing against the dirty sewer of bodies and acknowledge in themselves the agony of their condition. "Éste es el mundo, amigo, agonía, agonía."

The agony has hardened in me. The agony has not hardened in me. Returning to Garcia Lorca, I return to it in me. It is still there. Within my blood, another blood of lewdness about to be born. And then, H.M.S. BEARSKIN—a set of bitter poems posed, an allowance of self-pity, where pity, that counterfeit for compassion, offends the spirit, nurses, as if it were a grievance, the poet's identity to be mistaken— "that swish old relic", "self-enamoured / fly-by-night". I am sick at the thought of it, but I too must be one of those maricas de las cuidades Lorca inveighs against, for in my purest moods there will always appear some imp of a sexual jokester, persona of a possible cheerful lewdness, and through that vein I conduct my desire as if through coral or celestial nude. I know your ardor, Garcia Lorca, but it does not burn pure in me, it is ever mixed with a life-greediness, an avidity. There is in me a terrible, a trembling, will, that is meant for love, that might otherwise have been a chastity. And in every humor of that will it is quick to see itself its meat tumescent and its design unchaste—"de carne tumefacta y pensamiento inmundo".

The edge of a cruel line comes to cut this line of distinction, between lust and desire, between the immediate gratification of a sexual urgency and the erotic dream the body waits in truth for. The memory of adolescence is strewn with the wreckage of expectations, ruined grand moments, the embarrassing lines and scenes of immature characterizations of one's self, and, ever returning, the questionable exaltation one wanted in experience, before which inner spirit of romance, a delusion of eternal being that has never perished in me, the immediate satisfaction could spoil. When I was seventeen or eighteen,

I had memorized a passage from Hart Crane's *"Voyages I"* in which I
must have felt some promise of an alluring transgression of self—

> but there is a line
> You must not cross or ever trust beyond it
> Spry cordage of your bodies to caresses
> Too lichen-faithful from too wide a breast . . .

But drawing this other line? the line where Lorca's knife with a surgical
intent would cut away from the living virile body the infections of a
virulent sensuality?

I know what you are crying out against. It is the pollution, a
gathering together of sewers, where the dark nymphs of colera set up
their howl—"una reunión de cloacas donde gritan las oscuras ninfas de
cólera". Below the surface of sensualities Lorca senses the nightmare
of a Panic world, the fevers of nymphomania—but the word *ninfo*, "a
young effeminate fop", comes into it—the occult fawning sexuality,
the self-engendering bestial insincerity of Dionysus, the satyrical rape
that threatens our chastities. It is the Old World of elemental being
that remains as an infection in the post-Christian world of Lorca's
poetry, where Whitman/Lorca undergoes his poetic Temptations of
Saint Anthony. He is then "enemy of the satyr, enemy of the vine"—
"enemigo del sátiro, / enemigo de la vid". But, Garcia Lorca, if
desire led there, I would go to search for Amor in the thick of it. If
I were of it, one of those harpies of the sewer, I would dwell in that
obscurity as in some obscurity of my true self. If I were . . . But I
only speak of what I ever was, for I was always beside myself with this
being sexually aroused. In my early adolescence that world, at once
fearful and intoxicating, was, for me, entirely such a world of Ovid's
METAMORPHOSES, of elusive calls and disturbing premonitions of
chthonic powers. That sense remains. But in my late adolescence, the
last years of the third period of seven, there was another shadow world
that haunted such times—the world now of a cinema screen, of star
personalities and night interstices of a dark and empty space. The faun,
the adolescent satyr, was still there, but now fused with him there was
another predator, a male impersonation of a female power over men, a
whore or sorceress, a shape-shifter, imitating the image of their desire.
It was imitative, yes, in part gathered from all seductive modes I could
find in those around me and beyond me. But there was in this seeking

to seduce and to be seduced a return to an earlier mode of my own, a
rehearsal of a play known long ago. It was again, being "cute", being a
pet. For had I not, as all babies do, tried out the grimaces of a seductive
impersonation as it won and aroused, even to foolishness, the attention
and affection of the adult world about me? In my first years, before
language, I had won my way often in a magic of infantile expressions,
sleepy glances and excited murmurs and cries. I was again, as a young
man in a world of celebrities, as I saw them, beyond me, seeking to find
ways of commanding the scene I felt lost in. I had somehow to amuse
it, and I followed as best I could that lead.

I was, then, one of your *maricas*, Garcia Lorca, one of those "esclavos
de la mujer, perras de sus tocadores". Roaming the streets of New York,
sick with falling in love, ten years after your season in that city as hell, I
sought to infect myself with the Fall itself. "You will not break with the
life you lead and the person you know," Nicholas Calas said to me—he
would not name her; did he think she was dangerous? "I do not want to
know a witch's boy." Was there witchcraft at work then in our play of
witchcraft? Not only being a woman's slave, but, in taking on her ways,
having that insolence that a slavish imitator has? Not only dogging her
footsteps, a bitch of the boudoir, but, in that Circe-world, entering
deeper yet into its circles, to be a would-be phantom of her hell? I must
have appeared then in the arena among the Witch's brood—even as
you see them, Garcia Lorca, for the Panic world fuses for you too with
a later world of the Witch cult and its manic-depressive apparitions and
masks—the crowd of howling and gesticulating faggots, like cats in
heat, like writhing serpents—"muchedumbres de gritos y ademanes, /
como gatos y como las serpientes".

It may be that I mirrored then a repulsion even as I mirrored an
attraction. For Anaïs Nin, whom I admired and had sought out and
followed, I could appear like a cat or a serpent, or, rather—*"Monkey"*
she called me as a "pet" name—the ape of a cat or serpent, playing
with my prey or seeking to fascinate. I was also, as she would call me,
her "twin"; and she would play upon the exchange of my sun and her
moon which were in Capricorn with her sun and my moon which were
in Pisces. Did my expression ape hers?

Among the photographs which illustrate *The Diary of Anaïs Nin*,
Volume Three 1939–1944, the portrait of me shows me posed with my
eyes cast down in a revery with heavy eyelids and my mouth closed in

some secret thought or dream upon the edge of a lingering mixture of an almost sweet taste of compliancy and of a contrary severity, in which I may be her ape, for I find something of the same expression in the portrait of her that follows, her eyes cast down in a revery, her eyelids heavy as if in dream or on the threshold of being entranced, her mouth at once sweet and reserved. It was in key with the persona she advanced in *The House of Incest*, which I had most admired in this period.

Writing in her diary, she sees my sensuality as "exasperated"—"Or is it something I have sensed in our life here which I never felt in Paris," she continues: "that sensuality is *vice* for Americans, and they are ashamed. It is always dirty and so they feel as men do after going to a whore: ashamed. And they visit their resentment on the one who lured, charmed or seduced them." Then there follows, as she writes to rid herself of the oppressive attendant I had become for her, even a vice, a vision of me as a whorish caricature of a possibility:

> His face became that of the coquette, receiving flowers with a flutter of the eyelashes, oblique glances like the up-turned corner of a coverlet . . the stage bird's sharp turn of the head, the little dance of alertness, the petulance of the mouth pursed for small kisses that do not shatter the being, the flutter and perk of femininity, all adornment and change, a mockery of the evanescent, mysterious fluidities of woman, a mockery of her invitations, a burlesque of her gestures of alarm or promise.

She is sick of me, or sick *with* me. "Robert, *l'enfant terrible*, perverse and knowing," she writes in November of 1941, as we were coming to a critical crisis. In the beginning, she had romanticized me as being of the order of Cocteau's Paul in that novel—it was the grand invitation her fancy projected and in that very invitation it included her distaste. "His eyes are too widely opened, like a medium in a trance," she continues in the dismissal of the close: "His eyelids fall heavily, like a woman's, with a seductive sweep of the eyelashes . . a man's eyelids never fall this way over the revealing landscape of the eyes . . . Only this travesty of the invitation, like the prostitute's, which will never lead to a magnificent fusion." She sees me throughout in my amorous flirtations not as a man seeking the definitions of a male attraction to men but as a female impersonator, not only a rival but a cheat at that: "Why do men love this travesty of woman and not the real woman?"

Beneath her questioning, there seems to be a phantasy of my somehow invading her realm.

In the revolution of her love, Anaïs Nin had come to a revolting vision of my character, and that revolting image, in turn, came close indeed to the commonplace American stereotype of the faggot. The amused tolerance and affectionate condescension of the Parisian woman of the world, when it was sorely tried, could show its underlying attitude to be not too different from that smalltown bigotry I had known growing up in my early teens in Bakersfield. She makes it clear that this very realm of my falling in love and seeking to find a lover was ultimately unmanly, fraudulent, and, never to lead to "a magnificent fusion", doomed to an empty facility. *"But what does she want?"* Cocteau's novel ends:

> *What does she expect? Paul's eyes are going out. The thread breaks, and of the flown room there remains only a foul stench and a little lady upon a safety island, who grows smaller and smaller, fades away, disappears.*

It is this projection of what my homosexuality meant, that so surrounded me in my late adolescence in the New York scene, the sophisticated reading me as effeminate, as perverse, as wayward, as one of your *oscuras ninfas de cólera*, Garcia Lorca, that comes into the shadows that inform the personae of CAESAR'S GATE. It is a desolation then not only of an inner state but of the outer role assigned by the dominant social interpretation. Yet it may be, it strikes me often, that I sought that sexual way that would be appropriate to some romance of this desolation. For it is essential in the story of Bearskin that he must be revolting, that love must penetrate its revulsion to find its truth.

Bearskin, the Beast, the Frog-Prince, must be, if the mystery of their story go deep, ugly as a toad's belly, *"como panza de sapo"*. It is the unloveable in us that craves to be loved and knows that only because love transcends what it knows will that craving for what it does not deserve come to be answered as an answering love. "Thy craving," the craven creature hears his lover answer, "I do take as my loving." There must be, I thought, at the threshold of Love, some offense to Pride.

Que los confundidos, los puros,
los clásicos, los señalados, los suplicantes
os cierren las puertas de la bacanal.

Yes, it must be so. That devout and high-minded company must ever close to the poet the doors of the bacchanal. For there remains in me something—confounded, pure, classical, appointed, petitioning—that cannot have to do with the pollution, the letting go; yet at the thought of that *Cathar*, that aristocrat of the emotions I would be, every parody arises in me to protest. Going deep into the matter of Lorca's New York, the New York of 1930, into the depths of the nation's depression then, I find myself in my own depths. The terrible longing and outrage of the poet seems for a moment mine. The broken spirit of derelict men offered in the markets of the street, in the destitution of an utter material despondency, seems mine. The ruthless appetite of the predatory exploiters of the sexual scene seems mine. Were there such moments of dejection in the energies of my youth? and in my youthful vision such a sleepless design? In the New York of 1940 I roamed the streets and made the round of bars, like a soul making a round of lives, to find some adventure of love; but it was also nightly to find a place to sleep, for I was no more than a loiterer in the entourage of an obscurely celebrated would-be star, a kept ape, but for no more than the board—a hustler then, of a pariah sort, transient in my passions, seeking to take hold among more fortunate drifters. These New Yorks are succeeded by a third statement of that city, as if they were three parts of one image in which a theme I must attend to seeks to make its statement, by the world of Andy Warhol's New York, by the derelict society of Hotel Chelsea, of *Flesh* and *Trash*.

¡Los maricas! They point with their painted nails at the border of your dream, the scene of that Eden, where your friend eats your apple with its light savor of gasoline. The denizens of this despised shadow-world have almost a new poetry or courage in the mind, as if now there were a heroism in being outcast, of the drifter in his despondency resolute, to declare at our customs a right to his own life.

Almost true, this "being false to their true selves", as we would call it. Who is there to be more true to them than they are? Returning to what I was I seem to play me false in every turn. It is the created self that must come true. But what eats at my sense of my own wholeness in being, at my *conscience*, is that line of outrage that you raise, Garcia Lorca—O yes, I could raise that line—against the faggots, against the purveyors and buyers of men on the street, against the hustlers and venomous queens—I could never think myself one of them, that world was only a stage for me—against the filth, against the rotten dead, as if these were so intimate to ones inner nature that their very existence were like an infection.

In Germany, contemporaries of the Poet in New York, sought in their depression outrage to purify, to burn clean, the nation of its undesirables. We are outraged by the Nazi's program of purification because we know them as evil and those they burned as good, as innocent, as pitiable. But let us now imagine the burning of the perverts, the Nazis among them, of those who poison the minds and souls of the young, of the truly undesirable—New York cleansed of its harpies, its sleepless foes of love, its sexual speculators and pollutors, its venomous dreamers . . .

My heart sinks in me at the thought of their realm, and every visceral and nervous sensibility tightens to eject from the body I create such an identity: I will not stomach it. But draw the line, Lorca, as you do, and I stand with them to whom otherwise I do not belong, though my heart longs for you. For your distaste goes deeper and wider than you say. Already there is about me the irremediable stench of H.M.S. Bearskin I will not disown and you will not love.

In CAESAR'S GATE I came close to that circle in Hell you speak against, for I came almost to despair of Love. I saw, I think, in Bearskin a face of someone I was I could never be and would disown but volunteered not to disown "that swish old relic"—you think I can deny your seeing me as I have seen myself posed? or that "as others see me" is not deep in that agony? It is an abject stage-fright that invades when the actor realizes some affect has betrayed his failure in the very part of failure he would play. At a crucial moment—just the moment of Man's salvation—some irredeemable irrelevance will remain in me. Like the Freud that the Jungians argue against, my mind even when it is inspired is reductive. I will hold to the reduction, to the toad, to the stubborn residual thought, the identity that comes, as that thought in the course of his story came to Uncle Remus, as he sez—"Hit run'd cross my min' des lak a rat 'long a rafter".

The beauty of it, the allegiance and ultimate appropriateness of each event to its total form that a life has, does not spring from some initial paradigm nor from the goal of an ideal form toward which it strives, nor is it of itself a form, but it has its form in a field generative of forms to which not only what we would be but what we would rid ourselves of belongs. How intense and troubled this boundary becomes as it marks the outline of our true selves in the area of what we would abhor—it is like the boundary of an empire held by threatened forces—for each projection of outline belongs to and distinguishes the identity of the abhorred even as it marks our own. The design is from both sides, co-operative, and every rage that would seize the government of that design and hold it enforces the identity of the other side. We come to the end of our endurance along a line in an area the idea of what we are has invaded.

There are no lines in this poem of Lorca's that are not deep in the love-tooth ache and decay of the homosexual city-of-the-night world, as the immediate presentation of the Depression, in which not only the economic but the deep-going social and psychological structures of our state were revealed. New York in Depression in turn illustrates Lorca's own depression. "I want to cry because I am hungry for crying, like the children in the last bench cry," he writes in *Poema doble del Lago Eden*—are they children banished to the back of the classroom for crying itself?

> Quiero llorar porque me de la gana
> como lloran los niños del último banco
>
> for I am not a man, nor a poet, nor a leaf,
> but, yes, a wounded pulse that sounds the things of the other side
>
> porque yo no soy un hombre ni un poeta ni una hoja
> pero sí un pulso herido, que sonda las cosas del otro lado

"To speak my truth of the full-blooded man," Lorca declares as his intent in that poem: "decir mi verdad de hombre de sangre"—it carries with it for us today the suggestion of the cult of blood and *machismo*—"killing in me the sneer and the suggestion of the word"—"matando en mí la burla y la sugestión del vocablo"—crying out, the face raw behind the mask of skin, against the sexual suggestion and use of men and of words that would ignore the generative orders, even as, at the same time, Salvador Dalí in Paris was launching his art of post-Freudian suggestions in an iconography of perversions upon which his genius and his ego had begun to swell.

Not against the men of the green glance, Lorca tells us, not against the *mirada verde*. Not against that startled gaze of an eye in painful burgeoning, quick and queer as a leaf yearning among leaves, in which we see the spirit's longing tremble upon the bough of its body. Not

against this spring of the poem. "Verde, verde, te que quiero verde," comes to mind from another poem of Lorca's—*Romance Sonámbulo*. In the play of the Spanish word, there is not only *somn*, "sleep", but also *son*, the sounding of the poem, in which the tonal mode that entrances us in poetry is a counterpart of the sleep in which the sleepwalker is entranced. Words then in poems are, like words in sleep, trance-speech.

Verde, my Spanish dictionary tells me, means "green; unripe" or "young", and we might, remembering Lorca's declaration against the sneer and the suggestion of the word, let the meaning rest there. Images and the language of dreams are not, Freud tells us, to arouse us but to keep us asleep. Let sleeping dogs lie then. But the dictionary goes further, the common Spanish meaning goes further. *Verde*, we find, means not only "green", with all that sense of freshness and entranced forthrightness, the very greenness of meaning itself that Lorca holds to against the suggestivity, but it also means "off-color", "indecent"—the lewd green of hot leaves—even as, in English, getting "fresh" can mean going too far. Is there a link between the *vir* of "virtue" or "virile" and the *vir* of "virid", a magic sense in which the quickening power of being a man, the quickening of a man, and the greening are identical? Is there a greenness to verity, an almost indecent freshness in being aware of what is at issue? in the Spanish verb *ver*, "to see; to look; to look at", this more than green of the green? in the *mirada verde* some mirror of Lorca's "mi verdad de sangre"?

Not against the longing, Lorca tells us, not against the lover of bodies under the rough homespun, but his line, even as he draws, does not draw the love of comrades and the longing of the lonely as in a world of their own, it leaps from their lot to draw them against the presence of the other, it draws the others into the heart of the matter, upon whose lips the sneer hovers and in whose eyes a hatred of love shows. Lorca, he tells us, has murdered that sneer in him. There is a deep civil war, and Lorca's line is the line of a bloody division and contention.

WHAT IS IT YOU HAVE COME TO TELL ME?

Going through an old notebook of the CAESAR'S GATE period, two years ago I came across three poems that I had decided against my including when that volume was published in 1955 and that, in the intervening years, I had put out of mind. Seeing them anew, and admitting them now into that order of my work and responsibility that publication means for me, I saw them as at once fitting and in that fit altering the composition I had felt in the contents of CAESAR'S GATE, as new dream data alters the content of the dream in our account, and at the same time, both in their fitting and in their altering, as poetic disturbances, troubling every composure I might have had in the proposition of that volume as a work I was done with. A theme of this matter of Lorca from my youth advances from *An African Elegy* and *King Haydn of Miami Beach*, from 1942, through the poems of 1949—*Four Poems as a Night Song* and the now admitted contents of POETIC DISTURBANCES—and has me, some twenty-three years later, in the throes of this commentary, fretting at the strings upon which the theme still pending in me is restless to begin. I will not be through with it or it will not be through with me.

I am not done then with CAESAR'S GATE. As I have gathered its contents together and indicated something of their order, that order extends to shake the strings upon which I would sing tomorrow. It is not the book of a conclusion or a coming to satisfaction. It proves not to be, as I thought it was, the book of a passage, a transition from one state to another, for it proposes a dissatisfaction that belongs to my present work as I know it. In this art—it is an art transforming every stage of itself in every stage throughout the time of its creation—every "error" reveals the truth of what we took to be true, every "failure of tone" reveals the tone we missed in what we took to be in tune, every "false face" shows true the intent its wearer makes in the face. In coming to read the challenge of meaning the imagination makes in what it creates, every part must be kept alive and made good in the total reading. For that challenge is, as I see it, to redeem as content what we thought we had mistaken. Ultimately, the good reason of our refusal to censor or to "correct" is that we seek not to get rid of what embarrasses us or what does not seem true to our lights but to go beyond embarrassment—beyond shame or disgust or outrage—to imagine in an other light, to see in a larger sight what we had rather was dismissed from view.

I must have known in me the sneer that Lorca has murdered in himself, and there must have been within me a civil war in the agony in which that sneer was born, in the unloveable fear of my being rejected in love and of my being discovered in my unloving, for in the fabric of my being, this matter of fucking is all tied up in a knot with loving, so that there has been angry loving and destitute loving, angry fucking and destitute fucking. I can understand how D.H. Lawrence came to see this kind of tying-up of our childhood experience and dream of loving with our adolescent dream of fucking as an abomination. The disorders of loving and of sex seem to go through and through the whole universe. I have come to a complication of the idea of God that verges upon an idea of the complication of God. The interweaving of all aspects and identities of Man in one fabric, the vision of the universe as such a fabrication in time and space, the sense of warp and woof of that interweaving as a design of complicities, drives me to interrupt every simple satisfaction in me with an errant suggestion, to undo each seemingly self-contained figure, each sentence, with a phrase contrary to its syntactical course.

What might have been the sneer then has become complicated in its design by the longing it meant to replace that has remained in its course. It flickers in *H.M.S. Bearskin*. I can hear the half-hearted sneer of some would-be sophistication, revenant of high-school years, that echoes mockingly in passages of that poem. Would-be Ruthless and Would-be Rueful must have written *"He Lists Subjects for Great Poetry: 1950"*, but I knew them to be what they were, persons of that great creation or poetry the imagination opens to our being as it works there. I did not murder the sneer in me but sought to come to its end, to come into what it meant.

DICTION CONTRA DICTION
DECIR CONTRA DECIR

So for me, homespun must be home's pun, and I cannot let that incidental play of the fabric rest. It's as if, beneath the play of my words, I were in my play theirs, so a creature of words that my heart's urgency to speak floods in there like song floods into the words of a poem. It is the song's message, beyond and behind and beneath and within the word's message that moves me. As in the world too, the world about me and the world as it extends in my imagination, I am ever on the verge of being, pent up to flood in. There is an ecstatic singing of the shuttle and the threads in a song the loom sings that moves the weaver in all the complicities of the figures that work would present.

There may be a part of me, an intelligence, that stands apart, outside that field of beings and things in creation in which I am truly a creature, in which I see myself as having my part to play, having a requirement to satisfy that originates not in me but in my belonging to what is happening, to the tendency of a design in the field of that belonging.

There remains the esoteric tradition of this requirement's being entirely a play, none the less reliable for the fact that it is nowhere in more than fragments written down. In fact, the pursuit of its authenticity is always in vain. Its laws change in our dependence upon their being there. For the revelation tended to adopt or failed to contest the rival claims of beliefs and certainties indigenous to times and places we have long forgotten, however crude and misleading these were. In this way, the most diverse and debased elements were added to the corpus and embarrass the devout reader who must face as he reads the insistent persuasion of the total design over the qualifications of the immediate events.

Now, as I once played continents and the changes of seas, maps and charts of voyages and unknown realms, I play eras of time and times of eternity.

It is the design of an intention, and, inherent in that, an information, that we read thru to its being all there where it is as I write it from one time to another. In what I wrote following I discovered what went before; in what I wrote first I had hindsight of what would last. The actual work lives and breathes in an exchange with an environment of meanings and formal apprehensions that surrounds it. And yet we can always establish that it actually does or does not read "THREE POEMS AS A NIGHT SONG". Did I unfold the title? Did I come upon it, or did I go back to it?

There are always actual words there. There are always given the actual alternative readings. The poet does not delimit *Night Song* to mean "a song sung at night" from its meaning "a song sung by the night"—once we read it so, he cannot have done otherwise. And though the song as it comes to his mind at first is a serenade, a lonely song sung beneath the window of a reluctant lover, it may yet belong— indeed, it probably does belong—to those songs of an Albigensian troubador that are frequent in the poet's customs. Yet are those readers far afield who hear them as Nursery Songs?

Tales and songs of such an order the Night Nurse sang, bringing forward into the beginnings of my own life ancient wisdoms of life- negation from the beginnings of Man's experience of What Man Is— old mysteries of a dialectic of doing and undoing in which thruout the totality of that field, Creation gnaws at its bounds in the particular to be free. To be free of its own order. For there is no creation outside of this outlining and en masse of color and depth. Configuration moving thru time of our configuring.

And in time there is only and always was only the one face of the die showing. We had to cross the room to see the face the figure showed, and all the time, did we not imagine the host of alternative faces in apprehending the one face? We were surprised to see their being fulfilled in the actual face; we were surprised to see the face that fulfilled them. The style of the artist predicted that fulfillment, so that the actual face was recognized by the signature of its maker that we found upon another work we had not known earlier. . Yet, was it not our knowing it earlier that gave to the signature its verity?

The tendency of the work in the accumulation of parts lead to this reading of "face", that is now the interface between memory and expectation of the course of reading, so that the form of the face belonged to the whole. All the parts we came to discover were there where they were in the course of our discovery. This is only to say that CAESAR'S GATE is completely here in the book you are completing in reading. Completely here in the book, it is not completely here when it is finished. For in every reading, I find myself at work again completing my reading.

And in the actual face, there sprang ever the reminder or remainder of other faces to my mind. These are the definitions or delimitations of the actual; otherness surrounds the state of What Is. The face is not only contained by what it is, it is outlined by what it is not. In this order of relevance:

1. There is a swarm of possibilities of face from which the artist of the actual drew just the face he drew. This is called the drawing of the actual in recognition from the resources of faces.

2. And among these, there are preliminary sketches, erasures of faces to make way for the renewal of intent in the face, often in even "superior" drawings the feel of the face of the actual wanting. This is called the unsatisfied longing for particular location in the actual or the artist's ever present feeling of requirement in his work. It is the drawing to a close in particular and local identity in which the crisis of a freedom arises that makes of a drawing from the matter of a world a work.

3. It is "a work" only in his working it. As he writes, the poem appears to his reading a work, and as he reads, the writing, the work

returns to him in reading. Poetry is speech whose meaning is overheard to be that of its being made so. He is saying something and he is listening in saying to the meaning of his saying that in the way he is saying it.

4. He is listening to what is happening to speech in what he is saying as he speaks.

5. The science of the artist lies in his love of what is the matter with his work. I love what is going on in the writing as I write of it. He wants to deepen and prolong his life in these things. The lore and craft that form the treasury of accumulated values or sum of resources out of what is known by labors and studies he has had in his work becomes in every work's completion for him incomplete. This is to say, when he completes a work it has become completely for him the matter of a new work needed.

6. The poetry that most moved us moved us to a need for poetry.

7. The invention of the artist lies in his trial of the matter of what he does. Even in slavish copying, the signature of a particular slavishness enters the work and distinguishes it.

8. He refers to a person no one knows. He has in mind features he does not mention. The face is particular and vivid to him as he goes. But the reader sees in his reading a particular and vivid face of a person in the poem or he misses a face in the poem.

9. Now, after years, he has lost all reference himself to the face of the person he had in mind. He no longer remembers the person the poem referred to. The poem has ceased to refer. Is this portrait mine as I am? Or am I in the poem? The face of a young man comes immediately to his mind as he reads that is the face of no other than the man in the poem.

SOMETHING IS MOVING

I let it move through me.
I let it move by means of me.
I let it move by my means.
I let it move toward what it means.
It means to me through me.
It means to move through me.
I let the movement of it through me.
As it is meant for me, I mean.
I let it until it is through with me.

Notes

Increasingly throughout his writing life, Duncan had great difficulty with printers who habitually shifted all lines to begin at the left margin and sought to regularize stanzas. The distinction between prose and poetry is fluid in Duncan's work, and Duncan frequently preferred ragged-right margins to preserve that ambiguity, but in both *The First Decade: Selected Poems 1940–1950* and *Derivations: Selected Poems 1950–1956* the printer eliminated that indeterminacy by justifying all passages apparently in prose. Too, the exigencies of linotype production inconsistently affected spacing between words (on some occasions in *Selected Poems* evenly and widely spacing words margin-to-margin in a single line) and Duncan was dissatisfied with especially the *The First Decade* and *Derivations*. The notes do not record such textual variants. Similarly, Duncan's orthography, spelling, and punctuation were not always consistent; in some instances he used single, and in others, double quotation-marks, sometimes including terminal punctuation (commas, periods, exclamation marks, question marks and the like) inside the quotation, sometimes not; he frequently omitted the final "e" in past tense verbs, changing the final "d" to "t" in later poems and later printings. The notes do not record such shifts, nor do they as a general rule record variations in stanza-breaks, lineation, indentation of lines, punctuation, capitalization, and spelling. There are of course exceptions—most notably, perhaps, in the notes to *Medieval Scenes,* where against Duncan's wishes the printer regularized the stanzas. The notes do record more obvious changes such as cancelled or added lines, but they do not as a rule record such less prominent variants as changes from "the" to "these," "a" to "some," and so forth—such changes, especially in the move from first periodical publication in the 1930s and 1940s to the revised versions in *The Years As Catches: First*

Poems (1939–1946), *The First Decade,* or *Derivations,* are too frequent to document without burying the text in a flurry of annotation.

When available, manuscripts have been consulted to establish line-breaks, stanza-breaks and the like in the edited text, and to clarify dubious or similarly ambiguous readings. With the exception of obvious orthographic or typographical errors, which have been silently corrected, the edited text printed in this book invariably follows the spelling of the copy text, which is usually (as explained in the textual section of the Introduction) that of first (i.e., periodical) publication. Thus, in poems collected in such books as *The Years As Catches,* Duncan's orthographic and spelling practice in poems first published in periodicals in the 1940s does not conform to that in the poems first published in 1966 in that book, and overall Duncan's spelling is not always consistent from one poem to another.

The notes do not identify references, many of which which are accessible in standard reference books, but they do translate most if not all foreign words and phrases, and where possible identify their source.

EDITORIAL ABBREVIATIONS AND CODES

/	Line break
Ams	Autograph manuscript
CU-BANC	Bancroft Library, University of California, Berkeley
NBuU	The Poetry Collection of the University Libraries, University at Buffalo, the State University of New York
OKentU	Kent University Libraries, Special Collections and Archives
Tms	Typed manuscript

Dates of composition are recorded thus:

1945	Dated by Duncan, or from letters or notebooks. Dates so noted can be regarded as definite.
(1945)	Supplied by editor on the basis of indirect documentary evidence (such as reference in the poem to public or domestic events and the like)
1945(?)	Uncertain; probability arrived at through first publication, Duncan's later (?) groupings of mss., etc.
1945–1946	The en dash indicates a *range* of dates: 1945 *to* 1946
1945/1946	The forward slash indicates *alternative* dates: 1946 *or* 1946
1955, 1950	The comma separates major reworkings of the text

BR	*A Book of Resemblances: Poems 1950–1953.* New Haven: Henry W. Wenning, 1966
CG55	*Caesar's Gate: Poems 1949–1950.* Palma de Mallorca: Divers Press, 1955
CG72	*Caesar's Gate: Poems 1949–1950.* 2nd ed. San Francisco: Sand Dollar, 1972
Der	*Derivations: Selected Poems 1950–1956.* London: Fulcrum, 1968
FD	*The First Decade: Selected Poems 1940–1950.* London: Fulcrum, 1968
FF1	*Faust Foutu: Act One.* San Francisco: White Rabbit Press, 1958
FF53	*Faust Foutu.* San Francisco: Privately published, 1953
FF59	*Faust Foutu.* Stinson Beach, CA: Enkidu Surrogate, 1959
Frag52	*Fragments of a Disorderd Devotion.* San Francisco: Privately published, 1952
Frag66	*Fragments of a Disorderd Devotion.* San Francisco: Gnomon; Toronto: Island, 1966
HCEC	*Heavenly City, Earthly City.* Berkeley: Bern Porter, 1947
Letters	*Letters: Poems mcmlii-mcmlvi.* Highlands, NC: Jonathan Williams, Jargon 14, 1958
MS	*Medieval Scenes.* San Francisco: Centaur Press, 1950
NP	*Names of People.* Los Angeles: Black Sparrow Press, 1968
P48	*Poems 1948–49.* Berkeley: Berkeley Miscellany Editions, 1949
PTPS	*Play Time Pseudo Stein.* 2nd ed. San Francisco: Tenth Muse, 1969
SP	*Selected Poems.* San Francisco: City Lights Books, 1959
WW	*Writing Writing.* Albuquerque: Sumbooks, 1964
YAC	*The Years As Catches: First Poems (1939–1946).* Berkeley: Oyez, 1966

INTRODUCTION

Much of the biographical material in this introduction draws on Lisa Jarnot, *Robert Duncan: The Ambassador from Venus* (Berkeley: University of California Press, 2012). For a list of all sources, see the bibliography. Section epigraph from a letter to James Broughton, recorded without date in Notebook 5, CU-BANC. Duncan gave this notebook to Robin Blaser as a 1952 birthday gift.

1. Notebook 4, CU-BANC.

2. Robert Duncan, "Returning to *Les Chimères* of Gérard de Nerval," *Audit/Poetry* 4.3 (1967): 60.

3. Robert Duncan, "Wind and Sea, Fire and Night," *Spring* 59 (Spring 1996): 67.

4. Robert Duncan, "The Truth and Life of Myth," in *Fictive Certainties: Essays* (New York: New Directions 1985), 2.

5. "A Prelude," Notebook 71, CU-BANC.

6. Duncan, "Truth and Life of Myth," 8. Robert Duncan, "Pages From a Notebook," *The Artist's View* 5 (July 1953): 2.

7. Robert J. Bertholf and Albert Gelpi, eds., *The Letters of Robert Duncan and Denise Levertov* (Stanford: Stanford University Press, 2004), 120.

8. Robert Duncan, *The H.D. Book,* ed. Michael Boughn and Victor Coleman (Berkeley: University of California Press, 2011), 314. Duncan, "Pages From a Notebook," 3.

9. Robert Duncan, "Introduction," *The Years As Catches.*

10. Duncan, "Truth and Life of Myth," 2.

11. Ekbert Faas, *Young Robert Duncan: Portrait of the Poet as Homosexual in Society* (Santa Barbara: Black Sparrow, 1983), 35.

12. I am grateful to Ken Hooper, Bakersfield High School archivist, for much of this information. In the 1934 "Senior Class Will," printed in the *Blue and White* (the Kern County Union High School weekly newspaper), one student "bequeathed . . . my ability to thrill the girl friend to Robert Symmes"; the 1935 Valentine issue's column "Valentines! Is Yours Here?" joked "And little Robert Symmes will sigh, / 'Why do the girls still pass me by?'" On the strength of interviews with some of Duncan's classmates, Hooper believes that Duncan was subject to bullying, and gathers from Duncan's transcript that he may have quit school early, in January or February 1936.

13. Robert Duncan, "An Interview With Robert Duncan," by Jack R. Cohn and Thomas J. O'Donnell, *Contemporary Literature* 21.4 (Autumn 1980): 520.

14. Duncan, *The H.D. Book,* 36.

15. Letter to Robin Blaser, 14 November 1955, CU-BANC.

16. Robert Duncan, *A Selected Prose,* ed. Robert J. Bertholf (New York: New Directions, 1995), 48.

17. Letter to Robin Blaser, 30 April 1957, CU-BANC.

18. Letter to Robin Blaser, 2 September 1958, CU-BANC.

19. Duncan had initiated correspondence with Everson in May 1940, when he asked Everson for some poems for the second issue of *Ritual,* which

he edited with Virginia Admiral. The second issue appeared as *Experimental Review.*

20. Quoted in Lewis Ellingham and Kevin Killian, *Poet Be Like God: Jack Spicer and the San Francisco Renaissance* (Hanover and London: Wesleyan University Press, 1998), 79.

21. Robert Duncan, "Opening The Dreamway," *Spring* 59 (Spring 1996): 35. Italics added.

22. Michael Davidson, *The San Francisco Renaissance: Poetics and Community at Mid-century* (New York: Cambridge University Press, 1989), 40.

23. Letter to Robin Blaser, 18 June 1957, CU-BANC.

24. Bob Callahan, "The World of Jaime de Angulo" (interview with Duncan), *The Netzalcahuatl News* 1.1 (Summer 1979): 1–5. "Berkeley Miscellany—A Venomous Note," NBuU.

25. "Introduction," *Poems 1948–49*, CU-BANC.

26. 1977 draft of "Preface" to the 1978 reprint of *Medieval Scenes*, NBuU.

27. Robert Duncan, *As Testimony: The Poem and the Scene* (San Francisco: White Rabbit, 1964), 14.

28. Davidson, *The San Francisco Renaissance*, 141.

29. The complete text of *Spring and All,* initially published in Paris in an edition of about three hundred copies, was not reprinted until Harvey Brown's Frontier Press issued about five hundred copies in paperback as *Spring & All* in 1970. Duncan would partially reprint *Medieval Scenes* in *Selected Poems* in 1959, but quite extensively revised; though its two printings amounted to three thousand copies, *Selected Poems* sold out rapidly and it too became a scarce item. The series would not be reprinted again till *The First Decade* (1969), published in England.

30. Robin Blaser, *The Fire: Collected Essays,* ed. Miriam Nichols (Berkeley: University of California Press, 2006), 119.

31. Joseph Conte, *Unending Design: The Forms of Postmodern Poetry* (Ithaca, NY: Cornell University Press, 1991), 22–23.

32. Letter to Robin Blaser, 18 August 1957, CU-BANC.

33. Notebook 19, 4 April 1956, NBuU.

34. Letter to Robin Blaser, 2 July 1959, CU-BANC.

35. Robert Duncan, "Poetics Of Music: Stravinsky," *The Occident* (Spring 1948): 53.

36. "Introduction," *Poems 1948–49*, CU-BANC.

37. Robert Duncan, "Preface," *Medieval Scenes 1950 and 1959,* ed. Robert J. Bertholf (Kent, Ohio: Kent State University Libraries, 1978).

38. *As Testimony,* 7.

39. Robert Duncan, "Opening The Dreamway," 4.

40. Robert Duncan, "A Note On Tone in Poetry," *Literary Behavior* (Fall 1948–49): 14.

41. Robert Duncan, "Towards An Open Universe," in *Contemporary American Poetry: Voice of America Forum Lectures,* ed. Howard Nemerov (Washington, DC: Voice of America, 1964), 168–83.

42. Bertholf and Gelpi, eds., *Letters of Robert Duncan and Denise Levertov,* 120.

43. Duncan, "'The Poetry of Unevenness': An Interview With Robert Duncan" by Jack R. Cohn and Thomas J. O'Donnell, *Credences* 3.2 (Spring 1985): 109.

44. Duncan, "Truth and Life of Myth," 34, 48, 34.

45. Deborah Diggs, interview with Robert Duncan, 1961. Tms, NBuU.

46. Notebook 14, NBuU.

47. Quoted in Jarnot, *Robert Duncan: The Ambassador from Venus.*

48. Notebook B, CU-BANC.

49. This "Statement on LETTERS" appears on a fresh page in the middle of Duncan's draft of his lecture "An Introductory Proposition," which he was preparing for his course at Black Mountain College that summer. He began the draft on 4 April 1956, Notebook 19, NBuU.

50. Robert Duncan, interview by Howard Mesch, *Unmuzzled Ox* 4.2 (1976): 80.

51. Duncan, interview by Mesch, 96.

52. Duncan, interview by Mesch, 85.

53. Letter to Robin Blaser, 18 March 1957, CU-BANC.

54. Robert J. Bertholf, ed., *Letters: Poems 1953–1956* (Chicago: Flood Editions, 2003), 62.

THE YEARS AS CATCHES: EARLY POEMS 1939–1945

See also the headnote to *Uncollected Work 1933–1947.*

Duncan published all of these poems in *The Years As Catches* (Berkeley: Oyez, 1966), reprinting some poems which he had earlier culled from his ongoing long-projected novel, *The Shaman.* In addition to the texts gathered and published as "Toward The Shaman" in 1940, "Persephone" (published in 1940), "A Letter To Jack Johnson" (published in 1942), and "Concerning The Maze" (published in 1941 but never collected) also come from that project. He also selected seventeen previously unpublished poems for *YAC.* Of those first published elsewhere, the first printing is used as copy text here. For some years Duncan intended to call his collected early poems *A Looking Glass,* but on 9 March 1966 he reported to Henry Wenning (publisher of *A Book of Resemblances: Poems 1950–1953*) that he'd sent the typescript, now called *The Years As Catches: First Poems 1939–1946*, to Oyez, "with *Preface*." The printed book included the complete text of *Heavenly City, Earthly City*, written in 1945–1946 and published in 1947, and on the contents page provided the dates of composition for each of the poems—the dates followed here. It also included a "Bibliography of Works Written 1937–1946"; although that bibliography lists poems not included in *YAC*, the list is not complete. Duncan lightly revised almost all of the poems, including those printed in *YAC* for the first time, amending spelling and punctuation, occasionally adding or removing the definite or indefinite article, changing verb-tense or mood, and redistributing line-breaks and stanza-breaks as well as words and phrases. These changes are not as a rule recorded in these notes. He also extensively and radically revised two poems, "Toward The Shaman" and "A Spring Memorandum."

On page 99 of *YAC* Duncan reports that "having secured a psychiatric discharge from the army, returning to New York in the summer of 1941, I ceased using the name *Symmes* and took the surname of my birth, *Duncan*." Thus, all of his poems published before the middle of 1941 were published under the family name of Symmes, and this name is recorded in the notes to the relevant poems here and in the section of *Uncollected Works 1933–1947*.

Introduction. Written 1965–1966; published in *YAC*, i–xi.

Negros! Negros! Negros! Negros! — !
La sangre no tiene puertas en vuestra noche boca arriba—

Negros! Negros! Negros! Negros
Blood has no doors in your night, face up.

Slightly misquoted from Federico Garcia Lorca's "Oda al Rey de Harlem" (Ode to the King of Harlem), from *Poet in New York*.

Con una cuchara de palo—
arrancaba los ojos a los crocodilos—

[The King of Harlem] With a wooden spoon
tore out the crocodile's eyes.

The opening lines of Lorca's "Oda al Rey de Harlem"; "*Con una cucharo*" is a refrain in Lorca's poem.

Persephone. Published under the name "Robert E. Symmes." Written 1939; first publication in *The Phoenix* 2.3 (Easter 1940): 109–111. Also published in *YAC*, 3–4. "Persephone" was originally to be part of Duncan's projected novel *The Shaman*. In a letter which reached William Everson on 13 July 1940 he described the poem as "part of a growing experience—I drew frankly upon earth powers to have them surge thru the body, to grow a tree and it was to be an opening place for others to tap that power—at every point the new experience must grow" (Lee Bartlett, ed., "'Where As Giant Kings We Gatherd': Some Letters from Robert Duncan to William Everson, 1940 and After," *Sagetrieb* 4.2–3 [Fall–Winter 1985]: 145).

Final stanza, lines 2–4, *YAC* reads:

> the splintering of rock, the shock of the trauma,
> in which she was taken from us. Shade
> falls under the shadow . . . shade upon shade. [Duncan's elision]

Passage Over Water. Published under the name "Robert E. Symmes." Written 1939; first publication in *Ritual* 1.1 (Spring 1940): 10. Also published in *YAC*, 5. RD told Robin Blaser, in a letter dated 26 February 1958 (CU-BANC), that "Passage Over Water" is "the first poem" referred to in "Structure Of Rime XI" (collected in *The Opening of the Field*): "It is not the first verse, of course, but it is the earliest one I always remember in some way and am troubled by. . . . It's marrd by an inexperience that hopes to relieve itself by substituting 'lies' and 'untruthful' for the unknown; and by a mind that borrows attitudes in 'mined' and 'destructive.'"

Toward The Shaman. Published under the name "Robert Symmes." Written 1940; first publication in *Experimental Review* 2 (Nov. 1940): 39–50. Also published in *YAC*, 6–10. Some time in June 1939 Duncan began work on *The Shaman,* a projected novel he worked on intermittently for several years, intermittently discussing the project in 1940 in his correspondence with William Everson (Bartlett, 145–55); in January–February 1940 he prepared and arranged the extracts which now bear the title "Toward The Shaman." In his notebook at that time he said, "my range of perceptions in the SHAMAN is very limited—every section of the Ritual which must be a whole—in every unit there is a certain sort of movement from one state of consciousness thru others to another state of consciousness. In a way there is a repetition of parallels. What do I want to do in it tho?" (Notebook 1, CU-BANC). Later in this notebook (which contains a great deal of dreamwork, including notes on "A Dream Novel For Virginia [Admiral]"), Duncan drafted or reworked sections of *The Shaman,* as he did in later notebooks; he also started work on a long poem planned as part of *The Shaman,* "The Twins Within The Mother," which in 1941 he abandoned (though he adopted some of the lines in Notebook 2 [CU-BANC] as the close of what would become "An African Elegy"). Some time probably in the spring or summer of 1947 he submitted a draft of the novel to Dodd, Mead, and on getting it back abandoned further efforts to get it published. "I got the novel back from Dodd, Mead," he told Jack Spicer in an undated letter he wrote from New York, en route during a trip to see Ezra Pound in August–September 1947; "it just seemd to me incredible that they wd take it . . . But frankly I find it too early to make advances for advances. And the whole novel mulls around in my mind" (CU-BANC, 78/164 Box 1).

In addition to minor expansions and deletions at the phrasal level, the insertion of elision marks (" . . . "), and his habitual revisions to spelling, Duncan, when he revised the poem for inclusion in *YAC*, cut over two thousand words from the version originally published in the *Experimental Review* and printed here, deleting from the work each of the passages bracketed in the edited text with curly brackets, thus: { }.

Other significant changes are as follows.

In the paragraph beginning "JOSEPH, overlord," last three sentences, *YAC* reads: "We shall sit down to eat the mysterious fruit from its hives, staining our fingers with it; and we think of the lonely cattle going down upon their knees in pools of dust and the great bows of their ribs in starvation. The wind stinks from that side. Snakes hide in the rock. We put a tango on the phonograph, dancing until desire rises, the orchestra sobbing from the memory of summer loves. Tonight we can find love where we left it." It also deletes the following italicized one-line paragraph, "*Come to me tenderly, put your hands upon me like a gift of fear.*"

In the paragraph beginning "YOU whose have chosen this valley," last sentence, *YAC* deletes "your love is a delicate treachery."

In from A LETTER TO SANDERS RUSSELL (for Sanders Russell, see the note on "At An Anarchist Meeting," below): Stanza 2, line 1, *YAC* reads " . . . not in our western country of great trees." Stanza 3, line 3, for "the maniac regions," *YAC* reads "bringing war." Stanza 3, line 6, *YAC* reads "born at this time of year in another war, find." Stanza 7, last line, for "colleries," *YAC* reads "coal-pits." Stanza 8, line 2, *YAC* reads "know" for "known." Stanza 8, lines 4–5, *YAC* reads " . . . shadowd, alone, / between worlds . . . ."; Fourth paragraph from the end, line 2, *YAC* reads "Sodomites" for "Sodomists." Penultimate paragraph, line 2, *YAC* reads "I would evoke a way" for "I would create a way." Final paragraph, *YAC* begins "to pass on what is mine and give praise."

An Ark for Lawrence Durrell. Published under the name "Robert Symmes."

Written 1940; first publication in *Experimental Review* 2 supplement (Jan. 1941): 2–3. Also published in *YAC*, 11.

*The Awakening Into Dream, Love There: Out Of The Dream, And Our Beautiful Child.*Published under the name "Robert Symmes." Written 1940; first publication in *Experimental Review* 2 supplement (Jan. 1941): 3. Also published in *YAC*, 12. *YAC* breaks the poem into two stanzas, of nine and seven lines respectively.

A History Of My Family. Written 1940; first publication in *Experimental Review* 3 (Sept. 1941): 34–35. Also published in *YAC*, 13–14. Stanza 2, line 5, *YAC* reads "the cunt hung over with furs and hemlocks." Stanza 2, line 6 from the end, *YAC* reads "Nor ownd any land. And where we stopt, tin cans." Stanza 2, lines 2 and 3 from the end, *YAC* read "And we pass on. Steel knives. / Our hymns of voyage. Shouts of hate ringing out." Final stanza, line 5, *YAC* reads "and those that give birth on the way" for "and those that gave birth during voyage."

Fragment: 1940. Written 1940; first publication in *YAC*, 15.

A Spring Memorandum. Written 1941; first publication in *Poetry* 60.2 (May 1942): 76–78; also published in *YAC*, 16–18, and in *The First Decade: Selected Poems 1940–1950*, as "A Spring Memorandum: Fort Knox." Probably written when Duncan was stationed at Fort Knox, and submitted to *Poetry* (along with "A Pair Of Uranian Garters for Aurora Bligh") at the behest of Anaïs Nin. Changing the title, he extensively recast and revised the poem for *YAC* and *FD*, truncating or cutting some lines and expanding and elaborating others, and frequently shifted the verbs from passive to active voice. The changes warrant the inclusion of the *YAC* version here (the version in *FD*, except for two or three changes in punctuation and spelling, is identical to that in *YAC*).

> The beginning of this year in spring is twisted,
> closes in my mind with a perspective, clear
> and precise as a medieval fortress, a map of walls and towers,
> painted tents and geometries of distance. Here
>   the tree
> that from my heart sprang quick and green
> dies at the throat. And as I turn
> from these disorderd leaves toward the immediate scene,
>   the dust
> shifts, and the landscape burns the root
> in its unyielding light. The guns
> are new devices in the mind for absolutes, excite a curious art.
> We lie uneasy on our bellies in the blaze. The eye
> tires and the target—lung or chest,

bursts,
shivers on the level edge of the front sight. And death
we see there painted as precisely as a medieval rose.
　　　The target
man has unreal clarity.

•

　　　　　We are strangely
innocent killers. Gonzales,
Daniel Garcia and I talk idly, lying on our bunks
before mess-call. We say that in September
there will be fiestas and dances in the bordertowns.
We do not talk of killing. We recall
how Gonzales playd the saxophone
at summer weddings in Laredo, and we were elegant
in white suede shoes. The war has not come. We say
the war will never come. We will be free. We speak
of Mexico and cities in the mountains, white
receding refuge in the mind; or at night
we hear from some other barracks a Texas guitar.

•

　　　　　There is a reasonless
sitllness still in us. The cells and the bodies
that hunger for freedom are restless but lie
like rocks in silence and resist the scene.
And the scene is unmoved. We are weary with marching.
Slow and deliberate, the last shelter lifts
　　　from the killing
and we stand at attention in the mechanized day.

The eye and the hand which trembled
when it first took the pistol grow steady
and directed to murder. In his two dimensions
the flat man is easily shot.

He might have been loved.
It would have been harder. We conceive
a small triangle with bullets
over his heart.

•

I am not native here. I am a fox
caught, baited and clampd. I will claw my way free

from the flesh, spring the lock at the wrist,
leap out there, leap away, power-dive to the darkness,
if the flesh is this nature.
I am not of this kind.

•

Or, because love remains, must there be life
putting out branches to cover its wound?
Why do I wait when they take from me hope
and burn out the wonder, for what country, what
Always, our dream of tomorrow, to be there
more real than this country? Consider in quiet
the leaves of light that appear, even here,
in this wilderness, tormented by God.

Enormous Worm, turning upon Himself in His cyst,
disturbing the night with His love, who
has seen Him? I found at the roots of a tree
where Randlett and I were lying in the late afternoon
an Imago, like dried paper , that we
as children called Child-of-the-Earth. Where
has He gone, I askt. Slipt from our bodies
as this insect slipt from his skin? We are vacated,
left in discard with a hunger no universe of love
can feed nor Calendar of Days fulfill. And yet,
each day the substance rises in the hornhide tree of self,
twists and reaches and seeks to flower in the light.

A Letter To Jack Johnson. Written 1941; first publication in *View* 1.11–12 (Feb.–March 1942): 6. Also published in *YAC,* 19–20. Originally written as part of *The Shaman.* Jack Johnson had helped Sanders Russell print the January 1941 supplement to *Experimental Review* (Ekbert Faas, *Young Robert Duncan: Portrait of the Poet as Homosexual in Society* [Santa Barbara: Black Sparrow, 1983], 115). Paragraph 4, last line, *YAC* drops the period after "music."; Paragraph 5, the lines in verse, beginning with "secret and plan for" are in *YAC* divided into 6 stanzas of 1, 4, 3, 3 (prose), 1, and 1 line.

An Encounter. Written 1941; first publication in *The Ark* 1 (Spring 1947): 30–33. Also published in *YAC,* 21. *YAC* omits all the footnotes printed in *The Ark,* and divides the text into six irregular stanzas after lines 7, 18, 29, 34 (in mid-line, following "in each eye"), 44 (following "eliminated" and omitting the rest of that line). Line 2, *YAC* inserts "with this," after "his brain is much too bright." Line 4, *YAC* deletes "of art." Lines 10–18 in *YAC* read:

the giddy recurrence of the speaker's distortions.
Barely listening, I see reed mats upon the floor
lead back into an inner room, into contortions
of an unseen space as mystery. I have
a private twist for the disease that lies
inside these others. Ethel
lets her back hair down and sings
a song in German softly, dancing. And he asks
—are you insane? Your eyes are strange. I
cannot meet them—He pauses and his gaze
is restless, having no intent nor answer,
     so that we look back
each into his own eyes, uneasy,
seeing no end to the questioning perspective.

Line 25 in *YAC* reads "waiting, staring into the waiting space," and omits line 26 ("with no space in them,"). Line 37 in *YAC* reads "I hear the voices of children using no words, outside." Lines 39–44 in *YAC* read:

talking together. And in the room we wonder whether
something will happen. He tries to define
something else—what art should be or should have been—
wanting it limited, held in the hand against happening,
turned like an endless stone, wanting this something
known in this way, to be examined and eliminated.

From Richard Burton's Anatomy of Melancholy. Written 1941–1942; first publication in *YAC*, 23–24. This is the final poem in a handwritten group of six, all fair copies, gathered under the title "Some Work Done While At Ashfield, Mass November 1942. . . . A Sheaf For Dick and Clara" (Ams, OKentU). The first three in the group ("Blood is part of me that" [with a drawing]; "I imagine" and "The Snow Is On The Heath") are all unpublished; the last three are a set of "variations": "Variations In Praise Of Jesus Christ Our Lord"; "Variations Upon Phrases From Milton's *The Reason Of Church Government*"; and this poem, titled "Variations upon the Words: conscience, continual feasts, natural impediments, rednose, disgrace, reproach, imperfection, infirmity, feet, a company of fine glasses, chance, over much moved, moderate, riden, sottish, stock, common, every cur, dog, dares, courage (from Burton's *Anatomy of Melancholy*)." They were all written at the Cooneys's Morning Star Farm in Ashfield, Mass., where Duncan briefly stayed in 1942. Duncan revised the text before publication. The date given at the end of the text here is taken from *YAC*.

Variations Upon Phrases From Milton's The Reason Of Church Government. Written 1941; first publication in *Contour Quarterly* 1.1 (April 1947): 3–6. Also published in *YAC,* 25–27. This is the fifth of the handwritten group of six poems written at Morning Star Farm and dated November 1942 in the manuscript. The 1941 date given here is taken from *YAC.* In *Contour Quarterly* the first word of the title was (possibly misprinted as) "Variation." Stanza 4, line 8, *YAC* reads "disciples" for "disciplines."

Variations In Praise Of Jesus Christ Our Lord. Written 1941; first publication in *YAC,* 28. This is the fourth of the handwritten group of six poems written at Morning Star Farm and dated November 1942 in the manuscript. In *YAC* Duncan dated the poem 1941.

Witnesses. Written 1941; first publication in *Death: A Literary Quarterly* 1.1 (Summer 1946): 38. Also published in *YAC,* 29. Stanza 2, line 4, *YAC* reads "of stone, no steel nor obsidian knife, nor a chisel." Stanza 2, lines 7–9, *YAC* reads

> in the wide common bed that we hide
> behind blinds of the past. In this room of our house
> your father spread newspapers out upon the floor
> and shot himself; and in this, my father lay
> with his bright burning soul there
> choked up inside him. Each sent his skeleton

Stanza 2, last line, *YAC* ends with the addition "This has no solace"; stanza 3, last line, *YAC* deletes last line and substitutes "to send us to exile in separate winters."

The Unresting. Written 1941; first publication in *YAC,* 30.

Snow On Bug Hill. Written 1941; first publication in *YAC,* 31. Bug Hill, near Ashfield, Mass., where Blanche and James Peter Cooney had their farm. Duncan read work by William Blake, D. H. Lawrence, and John Milton while staying there. J. P. Cooney was editor of *Phoenix.*

Mother To Whom I Have Come Home. Written 1941; first publication in *YAC,* 32.

Toward An African Elegy. Written 1942; first publication in *Circle* 10 (Summer 1948): 94–96. Also published in *SP,* and, as "An African Elegy," in *YAC,* 33–35, and *FD.* After accepting the poem for publication in *Kenyon Review,* John Crowe Ransom rejected it following the publication of Duncan's essay "The Homosexual in Society" in Dwight Macdonald's magazine *Politics* 1.7 (August 1944): 209–211.

The poem closes with lines Duncan adapted from the 1941 draft of his long poem "The Twins Within The Mother" (Notebook 3, CU-BANC), a project he abandoned in 1942. In *SP, YAC,* and *FD,* Duncan expanded all ampersands to "and," and (especially in the second section) variously tinkered with line breaks. None of these is recorded here.

Stanza 2, line 8, *SP* deletes "I see her."; Stanza 2, *YAC* deletes line 16 "and I see." Stanza 3, line 1, *YAC* and *FD* read "I am waiting this winter for the more complete black-out." Stanza 4, line 8, *SP* reads "there and Clarinet— those Princes," while *YAC* and *FD* read "there and Clarinet! those talismans." Stanza 4, line 13, *YAC* and *FD* read "my hands and feet,/ divine the limit" for "my body, divine the limits." Stanza 5, lines 4–5, *SP* reads "The demon Desdemona / wails within our bodies, riding, warns" for "and Desdemona, / Desdemona, like a Demon / wails within our bodies, warns." Stanza 6, line 3, *SP* deletes "The negroes." Stanza 6, lines 10–11, *SP* reads "as black / Othello, strange to my sight, / pursued" for "as black / as Orpheus pursued deliriously." Stanza 7, line 4, *SP* deletes "the shadow and flesh of."

The Years As Catches. Written 1942; first publication in *Circle* 7–8 (Fall 1946): 1–4; also published in *YAC,* 36–39, and *FD.* In *YAC* and *FD,* Duncan modernized his archaic spellings of "ecstasie," "miserie," and "harmonie," and divided the poem into three sections, separating each with an asterisk. The second section begins with the line "But O the heavy change, now thou art gone"; the third with "Lift, untimely joy."

In *YAC* and *FD* the five stanzas of section one are consolidated into two, breaking after line 12, and in the third section the independence of the two-line stanza "life from my bloody heart / unsounded cold of love" has been eliminated; further stanza-breaks occur after the lines "his harmonie, my Chaos" and "My Harmonie, His Chaos."

Stanza 1, lines 2–3, *YAC* and *FD* read " . . . morning, scarcely rung / upon our ears." Stanza 4, line 1, *YAC* and *FD* read "No waste you wrake" for "No waste you wreck." Penultimate stanza, final three lines, *YAC* and *FD* read:

His ecstasy ring forth from me,
from what was misery,
as from the darkness of the night
ring forth this light.

King Haydn Of Miami Beach. Written 1942; first publication in *The Occident* (Winter 1946): 42–44. Also published in *SP; YAC,* 40–42; and *FD;* section 5 printed in holograph with drawing by Jess in *The Tenth Muse Catalog* 21 (April 1968): cover. Although the text printed here follows the copy text as published in *The Occident,* Duncan's spelling of "Hayden" is here silently corrected to conform with Duncan's later typescripts and all later printings. In *SP, YAC, FD,* and in Duncan's holograph of the final six lines of the poem on the cover of the *Tenth Muse Catalog 21* (in Robert J. Bertholf, *Robert Duncan: A Descriptive Bibliography* [Santa Rosa: Black Sparrow, 1986], C199), there are many variants in capitalization, punctuation, and stanza-breaks; none of these is recorded here.

In PARADISE CLUB, stanza 4, line 6, *YAC* and *FD* read "falles" for "falles." In PSYCHOANALYSIS, stanza 1, lines 11–12, *YAC* and *FD* read "Among the cards and the chattering dead / the blacks and the plum-colored lady apes."

Lovewise. Written 1943; first publication in *YAC,* 43–44.

Mother Brother Door and Bed. Written 1943; first publication in *YAC,* 45.

7 Questions, 7 Answers. Written 1943; first publication in *YAC,* 46. The Ams draft in Notebook 6 (NBuU) is subtitled "A Love Poem for Charles Henri Ford."

Marriage. Written 1943; first publication in *YAC,* 47.

Random Lines: A Discourse on Love. Written 1944; first publication in *YAC,* 48–50.

Homage & Lament For Ezra Pound: May 12, 1944. Written 1944; first publication in *The Ark* 1 (Spring 1947): 30–31. Also published in *YAC,* 51–53, and *FD. YAC* and *FD* read "Homage And Lament For Ezra Pound In Captivity May 12, 1944."

Line 3, *YAC* and *FD* read "defining distances with green. The space between." Line 8, *YAC* and *FD* change "disappear" to "reappear." Lines 12–14, *YAC* and *FD* read

> are still, as still as the heart in seeing, in hearing
> —a melody within an edifice of sound, as sound
> as Brzeska's head in solid stone made, as lasting

Line 15, *YAC* and *FD* change "reach" to "break." Stanza 3, line 5, *YAC* and *FD* read " . . . to fill these distances . . . ." Section 2, stanza 1, four lines from end, *YAC* and *FD* read "Against some Mediterranean . . . "

Christmas Letter 1944. Written 1944; first publication in *YAC,* 54–55.

Upon Watching A Storm. Written 1945; first publication in *YAC,* 56–57.

The End of the Year. Written 1945; first publication in *YAC,* 58–63.

Song. Written 1945; first publication in *YAC,* 64.

At An Anarchist Meeting. Written 1945; first publication in *The Ark* 1 (Spring 1947): 29; also published in *YAC,* 65, and *FD.* Duncan gave the poem a new title, "A Congregation," when he collected it in *YAC* and *FD,* and made minor adjustments to punctuation and line- and stanza-breaks.

Sanders Russell was editor of the one-shot anarchist magazine *The Ark;* Duncan had attended anarchist meetings in New York in the early 1940s, and again in Berkeley, when he attended Kenneth Rexroth's Wednesday evening anarcho-pacifist "Libertarian Circle."

Line 10, *YAC* and *FD* read "no bone-structure" for "no bone." Line 13, *YAC* and *FD* read "—that's Deva / speaking" for "Deva says."

HEAVENLY CITY, EARTHLY CITY

Duncan wrote the poems in *Heavenly City, Earthly City* between late 1945 and autumn 1946; he chose them with an eye to the book's shape, and arranged them, in chronological order of composition, under three headings: "Treesbank Poems"; "Berkeley Poems"; and "Heavenly City, Earthly City." He reprinted *HCEC* in *The Years As Catches: First Poems (1939–1946)*. In *YAC* and *The First Decade: Selected Poems 1940–1950* he moved "An Apollonian Elegy" out of the Treesbank group. His "Bibliography of Works Written 1937–1946" in *YAC* lists two poems, "The blessèd Herbert in his love does sing" (1946) and "Faithless and many minded muses" (1947), which he wrote out in the "Presentation edition" of *HCEC*, and which remained unpublished until 1976, when they were reproduced in facsimile in *Unmuzzled Ox* 4.2. They are printed in this volume in "Uncollected Works 1933–1947." With the exception of "I listen in the shade to one I love," Duncan lightly revised all the poems reprinted in *YAC* as usual, amending spelling, punctuation, stanza- and line-breaks, and in some instances changing roman to italic (or vice versa); he also added or removed accents (as in "Sleep is a deep and many voicèd flood" [in *YAC* and *FD*], and made sundry minor changes in diction, but as a rule such changes are not recorded in these notes. As he wrote in the "Bibliography" to *YAC*, two of the poems—"An Elegiac Fragment" and "Portrait of Two Women"—"have been revised in *The Years As Catches*." The more prominent of those changes are recorded here.

The *YAC* "Bibliography" also reprints Duncan's dust-jacket statement:

> The *Treesbank Poems* were written at the farm of Hamilton and Mary Tyler in Sonoma County, the remaining works in Berkeley. The volume is arranged chronologically, yet the arrangement is shaped toward an apotheosis in the poem written at the end of the year. I owe much in the development of my poetics to the work of Wyatt and Surrey, to *The Temple* of George Herbert, to the work of such moderns as Wallace Stevens, D. H. Lawrence, the Spender translation of Rilke's *Duino Elegies,* and Edith Sitwell's *Street Songs*. In my psychological concept I am indebted to Sigmund Freud, Karl Barth, and particularly to *Dark Night of the Soul* by the 16th century St. John of the Cross.

Duncan's later notebooks record his varying and at times puzzled unease with most of the poems in *HCEC,* what in the "Introduction" to *YAC* he called "that very disturbing poetics." On 25 November 1954 he thought that "what the poems assert was all of a more than me" (Notebook 2, CU-BANC), and as late as "Reflection on poems from 1946" (December 1969) commented that the "Treesbank Poems" which open *HCEC* "idealize my love . . . and at the same time mythologize my sexual passion. 'Christ, crown and crucifixion' take over the second poem: 'His Christ has made me King of my World'—*Angel, dark,* and *light* take over any reality *from,* entirely away from, into what the poem calls 'my world,' my love passion"; and that "'Sleep is a deep and many voicéd flood' is the only one of the opening four that *keeps.*" He also commented that "Portrait of Two Women" and "I am a most fleshly man" "record personal episodes as poetic resolves or pretensions. Empty, or, rather, cloudy pretensions. In *Medieval Scenes* a year later flesh and love will be projected as realities of the poem, the poet himself a voice of the poem, not a claim of the personal. 'Among my friends' I would still keep; it stands for a projection. But in 'An Elegiac Fragment' the voice is adulterated. Two years ago designing *The First Decade* I kept 'Portrait of Two Women' and 'An Elegiac Fragment,' that I would not have kept as *poems* in themselves, as belonging to a developing poetics, as 'the unconscious sum total of the poetic'" (Notebook B, CU-BANC). But he stood by his 1966 decision: "*The Berkeley Poems, The Apollonian Elegy* and *Heavenly City, Earthly City* I mean to stand now as established measures in my art and keys of my intention" ("Introduction," *YAC*), and he planned, in 1985, to include these poems in a volume of collected early work.

The book, with drawings by Mary Fabilli, was reviewed by Muriel Rukeyser, "Myth and Torment," *Poetry* 72.1 (April 1948): 48–51.

I listen in the shade to one I love. Written 1945; first publication in *HCEC,* 1; also published in *YAC.* In "Reflection on poems from 1946" (December 1969), Duncan commented that this poem "has passages of what I recognize still as a melody of feeling" (Notebook B, CU-BANC).

The silent throat in the dark portends. Written November–December 1945; first publication in *HCEC,* 2; also published in *YAC.*

Shall I alone make my way to my grave. Written December 1945; first publication in *HCEC,* 3; also published in *YAC.*

Sleep is a deep and many-voiced flood. Written 1946; first publication in *The Ark* 1 (Spring 1947): 24; also published in *SP, YAC,* and *FD.* Line 9 from end, *HCEC, YAC, SP,* and *FD* read "watching over" for "watching above." Line 3 from end, *SP* reads "sleep's death" for "sleep's depth." Last two lines, *HCEC, YAC, SP,* and *FD* read

some reminder from the distant past,
that ominous tone that tried to reach your ear
even while I spoke to you of love.

An Apollonian Elegy. Written 1945–1946; first publication in *HCEC,* 5–9. Also published in *YAC* and *FD.* Written, Duncan recalled in December 1969 in "Reflection on poems from 1946," "when Dick M. had brought me to understand that he could not return my desire, my passion which had sought to inhabit the falling in love with him, and which had sought to inhabit the poems—a suffering without language seeking to take body in work, now finds body in 'Apollo's' imagined suffering. Briefly, in the opening evocation 'Let Apollo, the hornéd and shining shepherd, pierce . . . ' thru to 'the depth, the dumb, of the body's love,' the projection comes clear. The second song of the sequence: 'I hold to my heart the unchanging heart' seems to me to go off at 'the human has in its rest . . . ' thru to 'nor from terror its love.' In the third song: 'we are death-done' goes wrong. And the following section inherits that. The closing address to the god does not arrive at its feeling, a rhetoric not yet rising from the source of necessary feeling. Apollo (like Christ in the 'silent throat in the dark' poem) is a conceit of the poem at this point not a *presence.* Conventions of feeling seep in and replace the dissolved forms of feeling" (Notebook B, CU-BANC).

Section 2, stanza 1, last line, *YAC* and *FD* read "the would-be unchanging" for "the unchanging." Final section, 8 lines from close, *YAC* and *FD* read "erased. He is my very grief, my spirit's shade."

Among my friends love is a great sorrow. Written March–August 1946; first publication in *HCEC,* 11. Also published in *SP, YAC,* and *FD.* In "Reflection on poems from 1946" (December 1969), Duncan reminded himself "we all tried out, I believe, being in love with each other" (Notebook B, CU-BANC).

An Elegiac Fragment. Written July–August 1946; first publication in *HCEC,* 12–13. Also published in *YAC* and *FD.* Stanza 2, last two lines, *YAC* and *FD* expand to three as follows:

as if drawing the hunter,
innocent and terrible,
to enter their forest.

Stanza 3, lines 6–7, *YAC* and *FD* read "hunts me. / / Did you not hear in the music as we danced." Stanza 3, line 10, *YAC* and *FD* add "hidden" at the end of the line.

A Woman's Drunken Lament. Written July–August 1946; first publication in *HCEC*, 14–15. Also published in *YAC* and *FD*.

Portrait Of Two Women. Written July–August 1946; first publication in *HCEC*, 16–17. Also published as "In Memory Of Two Women" in *SP*; published in *YAC* and *FD*. Following the example of *YAC* and *FD*, lines printed in roman in *HCEC* and *New Directions* 10 are here printed in italics.

Section 2, line 1, *YAC* and *FD* substitute "Rosario" for "Jimenez." Along with William Everson, Mary Fabilli, Philip Lamantia, Thomas Parkinson, and Kenneth Rexroth, Rosario Jimenez was a frequent visitor to Hamilton and Mary Tyler at Pond Farm in Guerneville, and later at Treesbank Farm in Healdsburg, where Duncan briefly boarded in 1945–46. Jimenez, a Puerto Rican scholar living in Berkeley, gave a full bilingual reading of Lorca's poetry and plays in the fall of 1946 at a memorable evening meeting of the poetry study group and reading series Duncan ran at a Berkeley boarding house known as "Throckmorton Manor." (Letter to Blaser, 14 November 1955, in Lewis Ellingham and Kevin Killian, *Poet Be Like God: Jack Spicer and the San Francisco Renaissance* [Hanover and London: Wesleyan University Press, 1998], 14, 80).

Section 2, italicized lines, in *YAC* the second of each pair reads "could return and fulfill you."

I Am A Most Fleshly Man. Written July–August 1946; first publication in *HCEC*, 18–19. Also published in *YAC*. Duncan seems to have added this poem to *YAC* at the page-proof stage of production (McPherson Library, University of Victoria, BC).

Les terraces au clair de la lune: the patios in moonlight. *Les terraces des audiences au clair de lune* is the title of a Debussy prelude. *Japanoiserie* (corrected to *japonaiserie* in *YAC*): an article of Japanese craft, usually porcelain or vellum.

Heavenly City, Earthly City. Written autumn 1946; first publication in *HCEC*, 21–33. Also published in *New Directions* 10 (1948): 103–112; and in *YAC* and *FD*. Duncan wrote the poem to Lester Hawkins, with whom he had a brief affair in 1946. The city is Berkeley. Following the example of *YAC* and *FD*, lines printed in roman in *HCEC* and *New Directions* 10 are here printed in italics.

J'ai dû tomber de très haut, de très haut,
très haut sur la tête.
Où est mon coeur? Où est ma tête?
Eurydice, Eurydice.
Que j'ai peur.

I must have fallen from on high, from on high
very high on my head
Where is my heart? Where is my head?
Eurydice, Eurydice.
I'm frightened.

No source has been found; the French is probably Duncan's. Stanza 2, nine
lines from end, *New Directions* 10 reads "my manhood" for "my animal."

UNCOLLECTED WORK 1933–1947

Three of the first four items gathered here were printed in *The Target: Self
Expression, the Aim of Kern County Union High School Students of English;*
"Song Of Undine" appeared in the school newspaper, *Blue and White.* All
of Duncan's early publications (up through 1946) were in magazines with
which he had more or less close personal contact. On arrival as a freshman at
the University of California, Berkeley, in 1936, Duncan joined the English
Club, and quickly joined the editorial board of its magazine *The Occident.*
In 1938 *The Occident* briefly suspended publication, and was replaced by *The
California Grizzly* (Duncan was on the editorial board). In a correspondence
with William Everson which Duncan initiated in May 1940 he discussed
in some detail his editorial work on *The Phoenix* and *Ritual,* as well as (in
varying detail) some of his own poems from 1939 and 1940, published in
Epitaph, The Phoenix, Ritual, and *Experimental Review:* "The Gestation,"
"The Protestants," "We Have Forgotten Venus," "Hamlet: A Draft Of The
Prologue," "Persephone," "Gestation," and *The Shaman* (Lee Bartlett, ed.,
"'Where As Giant Kings We Gatherd': Some Letters from Robert Duncan
to William Everson, 1940 and After," *Sagetrieb* 4.2–3 [Fall–Winter 1985]:
138–155; hereafter cited as Bartlett). *Epitaph, Ritual,* and *Experimental Review*
were short-lived magazines Duncan himself edited, with Virginia Admiral,
Mary Fabilli, and Sanders Russell. Duncan listed Russell as an important
influence in his early poetry. Duncan became closely involved in the edito-
rial and publishing affairs of *The Phoenix* (which folded in 1940) when in
1939 he joined James and Blanche Cooney at the Phoenix Community in
Woodstock, New York. There, he learned to set type by hand, and with
Sanders Russell and others practiced shamanism, played surrealist games,
and indulged in magic rituals. It was only with two essays published in
Dwight MacDonald's *Politics* in 1944 and 1945 that Duncan began truly to
break away from dependence on personal contacts in order to get his work
published (his earlier publication in *Poetry* and *Accent* in 1942 came about

through the intervention of friends), and it would not be until his 1952 publication in Theodore and Renée Weiss's *Quarterly Review of Literature* and Cid Corman's *Origin* that Duncan could free himself from such dependence on local and personal contact.

Retyping poems for publication in later years (as for instance in 1973/1974 making clean copies, for *Manroot,* of poems written in 1947), Duncan made his customary minor revisions to spelling, line- and stanza-breaks, and the like. These changes are not recorded here.

A Moment of Ecstasy. Published under the name "Robert Symmes." Written 1933; first publication in *The Target* 2.1 (May 1933): 2.

An Interpretation. Published under the name "Robert Symmes." Written 1934; first publication in *The Target* 3.1 (May 1934): 4. The epigraph is from "Cargoes" by John Masefield.

Song Of Undine. Published under the name "Robert Symmes." Written 1934; first publication in *Blue and White* 34 (May 1934). Duncan's first published poem, written when he was fifteen. A head note to the poem explained: "This well-written poem was crowded out of the Target, issued last week, because the author had something else in the high school literary magazine."

The Guardian of the Temple. Published under the name "Robert Symmes." Written 1935; first publication in *The Target* 4 (May 1935): 26.

Ego Involneratus. Published under the name "Robert E. Symmes." Written 1936; first publication in *The Occident* 30.1 (March 1937): 28. *Involneratus* is possibly a coinage. "Corrected," it would be *invulneratus,* which strictly translated means *unwounded.* In their *Latin Dictionary* (Oxford: Clarendon, 1975), Lewis and Short record that *invulneratus* "is found but once" among their sources ("Other Abbreviations, Signs, Etc.," xii). Sending this and other poems to Spicer, Duncan said, in his accompanying undated letter [1947], "I think that *Ego Involneratus* is actually from the fall of 1936" (CU-BANC); it was his first publication as a student at UC Berkeley.

People. Published under the name "Robert E. Symmes." Written 1937; first publication in *The Occident* 30.2 (April 1937): 30–31.

Pax Vobiscum. Published under the name "Robert E. Symmes." Written 1937; first publication in *The Occident* 31.1 (Oct. 1937): 17–18.

A Campus Poet Sprouts Social Consciousness. Written 1937; first publication in *Campus Review* 4.3 (15 Nov. 1937): 2. In October 1937, as a sophomore at Berkeley, Duncan became editor for the four issues of volume 4 of *Campus Review,* irregularly published by the University of California chapter of the American Student Union. The ASU was founded in June 1935 through the amalgamation of the National Socialist League, the Young Communist League, and the Student League for Industrial Democracy (which included in its membership the Young People's Socialist League). Early in 1940, Duncan told Pauline Kael with some self-satisfaction that he had now rejected Marxism, and hence left the ASU; she told him in an undated letter [spring 1940] that this decision left her "undisturbed" (CU-BANC).

The poem appeared without attribution in *Campus Review,* but Duncan included it, with the title "Proletarian Song," in "A Looking Glass," a selection of his work he sent Spicer in 1947.

Self-Portrait at 90. Published under the name "Robert Symmes." Written 1937; first publication in *Epitaph* 1.1 (Spring 1938): 25.

Relativity, A Love Letter, and Relative to What; A Love Letter. Published under the name "Robert E. Symmes." Written 1938; first publication in *Epitaph* 1.1 (Spring 1938): 21–25.

Ritual. Published under the name "Robert Symmes." Written 1938; first publication in *Epitaph* 1.1 (Spring 1938): 3–10. In a long letter to William Everson dated "28 July or so" [1940] Duncan said, "Two years or more it was ago I wrote my first real poem (RITUAL was the name)" (Bartlett, 153). In a Tms, "Appearances Of The Christ In My Poetry" (NBuU), written in about 1967 or shortly thereafter, Duncan dated "Ritual" from memory as written in 1937–1938, and commented that

> the poem is an immediate imitation of T. S. Eliot's *The Waste Land* conceived as a chthonic ritual—a *Sacre du Printemps*—in which Man's spirit is reborn. Behind the concept of resurrection too is D. H. Lawrence's *The Escaped Cock (The Man who Died),* which I read over and over again in the preceding two years since I first was given to read it in high school. The mythological identification of Christ not only with Osiris (as in Lawrence's masterpiece) but also with Zagreus and with Orpheus comes from reading not Frazer nor Jesse Weston, which would have been the lead had I followed Eliot's Notes to *The Waste Land,* but Salomon Reinach's *Orpheus*—a book to which I have never returned.

The Gestation. Published under the name "Robert E. Symmes." Written 1939; first publication in *Phoenix* 2.1 (Sept. 1939): 86–87. Duncan discussed some details of this poem in a letter dated "July 28 or so" [1940] to William Everson (Bartlett, 151–152).

The Protestants. Published under the name "Robert E. Symmes." Written 1939; first publication in *The Phoenix* 2.2 (Sept. 1939): 88–91.

Les Questions Surréalistes. Published under the name "Robert Symmes." Written 1939/1940; first publication in *California Grizzly* (March 1940): 21. *Les questions surréalists et prémonitoires:* surrealist and premonitory questions.

Les signes de la morte sont dans
les questions surréalistes.
les questions surréalistes
sont pour les singes de la morte.

The signs of death are in
surrealist questions.
surrealist questions
are for the apes of death.

Freer but perhaps more accurate idiomatic versions might read:

the shapes of death are in / surrealist questions
surrealist questions / are for the apes of death.

or

many keys to death are in / surrealist questions
surrealist questions / are for monkeys of death.

The French is Duncan's.

We Have Forgotten Venus. Published under the name "Robert E. Symmes."
Written 1940; first publication in *The Phoenix* 2.3 (Easter 1940): 108–110.

Hamlet: A Draft Of The Prologue. Published under the name "Robert E.
Symmes." Written 1940; first publication in *Ritual* 1.1 (Spring 1940): 19–23.
The rest of the Prologue never appeared.

A Song For Michael Cooney. Published under the name "Robert Symmes."
Written 1940; first publication in *The Phoenix* 2.4 (Autumn 1940): 80–81.
Duncan stayed intermittently with the Cooneys at Maverick Road, Wood-
stock, in December 1939 and the summer of 1940, and set the type for the
poem's appearance in *The Phoenix*.

A Pair Of Uranian Garters For Aurora Bligh. Written December 1940; first
publication in *Poetry* 60.2 (May 1942): 78–80. Aurora Bligh is a pseudonym
for Mary Fabilli. In a 1976 entry in Notebook 49 (NBuU) Duncan wrote
that "Mary Fabilli had been (in 39), with Sanders Russell, one of the first
two poets for me." Historically, "Uranian" has been code for homosexual.

The Virgin among the cattle has hit upon the wound. Published under the
name "Robert Symmes." Written 1940; first publication in *Experimental
Review* 2 supplement (Jan. 1941): 2.

Concerning The Maze. Written 1941(?); first publication in *Experimental
Review* 3 (Sept. 1941): 31–33. Originally written as part of *The Shaman*.

Fragment From A Journal. Written 1941; first publication in *Experimental Review* 3 (Sept. 1941): 42.

Dreams and *Windward.* Written 1943/1944; first publication in Jean Garrigue, ed., *Translations by American Poets* (Athens: Ohio University Press, 1970), 93, 95. "Dreams" was also published in Louis Simpson, ed., *An Introduction to Poetry,* 2nd ed. (New York: St. Martin's, 1972), 345–46. Duncan originally translated "Dreams" and "Windward" in October 1943 from a typescript he acquired from André Breton when the two met in New York, and revised it in 1944. Breton's two poems appeared in book form in *Poèmes* (Gallimard) in 1948. Duncan also worked on translations of Breton's *"Pleine Marge"* ("Full Margin")—several versions of his translation are variously dated from 1943, 1963, and some years between—as well as *"Dans les sables"* ("In The Sands") and *"Il y aura"* ("There Will Be") (CU-BANC and NBuU).

The blessèd Herbert in his love does sing. Written 1946; first publication (together with "Faithless and many-minded Muses") on the endpapers of the limited edition of *Heavenly City, Earthly City.* Also published in *Unmuzzled Ox* 4.2 (1976): 91. In transcribing the lines from one copy of *HCEC* to another, Duncan (inadvertently?) made small changes to punctuation, as well as errors he corrected. The most significant of these is to the last line, which in the version published in *Unmuzzled Ox* (from the copy in Robert Wilson's Duncan collection) reads: "in which our life is hidden, Our loveliness."

A Ride To The Sea. Written 1946(?); first publication in *Poetry* 90.6 (Sept. 1957): 354–55. The date is uncertain. Entry F7 in Robert J. Bertholf, *Robert Duncan: A Descriptive Bibliography* (Santa Rosa: Black Sparrow, 1986) assigns the poem to 1945–46; in the Tms of *A Looking Glass* (CU-BANC) Duncan dates the poem 1948. In Notebook 30 (NBuU) a draft of the poem, there titled "A Ride Along The Sea," appears with several cancelled lines in the middle of Duncan's draft, dated 21 September 1961, of a section of *The H.D. Book.*

Faithless and many-minded Muses—. Written 1947; first publication on the endpapers of the limited edition of *HCEC;* also published in *Unmuzzled Ox* 4.2 (1976): 91. The poem is a slightly altered version of two stanzas in Duncan's poem "Upon Hearing Leonard Wolf's Poem On A Madhouse, January 13, 1947" (CU-BANC, NBuU), first published as a pamphlet in a limited edition in 1991 (Berkeley: Bancroft Library Press).

Ode For Dick Brown: Upon The Termination Of His Parole: March 17, 1947. Written March 1947; first publication in Robert Duncan and Jack Spicer, *An Ode and Arcadia* (Berkeley: Arif Press, 1974), 29–35. As a conscientious objector, Dick Brown, a carpenter, was in 1942 sentenced to work in Civil-ian Public Service Camp 56 at Waldport, Oregon. Fellow detainees included William Everson and Kermit Sheets, who in 1943, with Kemper Nomland, founded the Untide Press as an expression of protest against the Second World War (the official camp weekly was *The Tide*). In 1944 Brown walked out of the camp in protest at his detention, and after turning himself in was sentenced to three years in jail. He was paroled after nine months, on condition that he work in a hospital.

Duncan's poem, along with seven others by Jack Spicer, was given to Kenneth Rexroth for inclusion in his projected but never published anthology of new and experimental poetry from the San Francisco area, compiled in 1947–48. Spicer's poems included "An Arcadia For Dick Brown," written in competition with Duncan. Accompanied by Spicer's and Duncan's letters to Rexroth, the poems were published with an introduction by F.J. Cebulski in *An Ode and Arcadia*.

A Discourse On Love. Written 1947; first publication in *Manroot* 10 (late Fall 1974–Winter 1975): 41–42.

A Morning Letter. Written 1947(?); first publication in *Poetry* 90.6 (Sept. 1957): 350–51.

The Homecoming. Written 1947; first publication in *The Pacific Spectator* 2.1 (Winter 1948): 48–49; also published in *Selected Poems* and in *The First Decade: Selected Poems 1940–1950*.

The Temple of the Animals. Written 1947; first publication in *Poetry* 90.6 (Sept. 1957): 351–52; also published in *SP, FD*.

There's Too Much Sea On The Big Sur. Written 1947; first publication in *Poetry* 90.6 (Sept. 1957): 352–53.

When the immortal blond basketball player. Written 1947; first publication in *Poetry* 90.6 (Sept. 1957): 354. On publication in *Poetry* the poem was given the title "Poem" by the editor.

The Revenant. Written 1947; first publication in *FD*.

And Now I Have Returnd. Written 1947; first publication in *Manroot* 10 (late Fall 1974–Winter 1975): 42–43.

The New Hesperides: At Marlowe's Tomb. Written (1946)–summer 1947; first publication in *Manroot* 10 (late Fall 1974–Winter 1975): 28–34. There are many drafts and typescripts of the sequence. Though dated summer 1947 in a pencil note on the typescript, in "A Selection of Previously Unpublished Poems" (NBuU) Duncan assigned "1946 Berkeley" to "Rhapsody," the final section of the poem.

Early History. Written 1947/1948; first publication in *Origin* 6 (Summer 1952): 76–78. A Tms, "Uncollected Poems, from Poems 1948–49" (NBuU), groups "Early History" with "Three Songs For Jerry And One Other."

The sequence was, however, included in the Tms *A Looking Glass,* and was almost certainly written in 1947 (see head note to *Poems 1948–49*).

In the Street. Written November 1947; first publication in *Manroot* 10 (late Fall 1974–Winter 1975): 26–27.

Domestic Scenes. Written 1947; first publication in *Quarterly Review of Literature* 6.4 (Spring 1952): 351–357; also published in *FD*. Duncan also printed six of the poems ("Breakfast," "Bus Fare," "Matches," "Radio," "Electric Iron," and "Piano") in *SP* as "from Domestic Scenes," where the series bore the dedication "for Jack Spicer, Upon His Return"; the entire series in *FD* is dedicated "for Jack Spicer." In both books, "Domestic Scenes," whether fragmentary or complete, is printed immediately following *Medieval Scenes;* the two series should, clearly, be seen as complementary. In the autumn of 1947, Hugh and Janie O'Neill's marriage failed, and Duncan moved in to help her prepare for childbirth; Spicer fled to Big Sur and Carmel to work on his never-completed novel *The Wasp,* and on his return moved to new quarters at 2018 McKinley, where he met Jerry Ackerman and Philip K. Dick, and forbad visits from Duncan (Lewis Ellingham and Kevin Killian, *Poet Be Like God: Jack Spicer and the San Francisco Renaissance* [Hanover and London: Wesleyan University Press, 1998], 21).

In *As Testimony* (San Francisco: White Rabbit, 1964), written in 1958, reflecting on Ebbe Borregaard's exclamation "Spicer's damnd appetite for terror" (9), Duncan briefly glossed the series: "Aristotle speaks of what he calls katharsis thru pity and terror (a sea, a foreign element); that might also be (alienated from the soul) of chairs and tables as I found in writing *Domestic Scenes.*" Referring to the "Yet" which opens the final sentence of the first stanza of "8. Electric Iron," he commented that "in that Yet where the division *cannot* and *does* raise their horns, pity and terror. In a room. A light bulb. A door knob. A stove" (10). Later in the essay he cited Rilke, who "said that these things (tables, chairs, beds, houses) were vessels in which men might find and store humanity" (17).

Duncan made his customary minor revisions in spelling, punctuation, line- and stanza-breaks, as well as slight changes in wording, when reprinting the poems in *SP* and *FD*. These changes are not recorded here.

5. Matches. Deleting line 6 of stanza 3, *SP* recasts the poem into five stanzas of 6, 3, 1, 6, and 6 lines respectively; restoring the deleted line, *FD* recasts the poem into six stanzas of 6, 3, 1, 3, 6, and 4 lines respectively.

7. Radio. SP recasts the poem into four stanzas of 7, 6, 7, and 10 lines respectively; *FD* into five stanzas of 7, 6, 9, 5, and 4 lines respectively.

9. Lunch With Buns. FD recasts the poem into five stanzas of 6, 3, 4, 4, and 4 lines respectively.

10. Piano. FD recasts the poem into six stanzas of 4, 3, 6, 6, 2, and 4 lines respectively.

MEDIEVAL SCENES

Duncan wrote the ten poems of *Medieval Scenes* on ten successive evenings in February 1947 at Hugh and Janie O'Neill's flat at 2029 Hearst Avenue, Berkeley, where Duncan rented a room, as did Dick Brown, an ex–conscientious objector soon to be released from parole. Jack Spicer, with Josephine and Fred Fredman, ate supper there every evening, and 2029 was, as Duncan described it in his "Author's Notes September 1962 to the Medieval Scenes papers" (OKentU), a regular meeting place for a circle of "students, returning GI's and C.O.'s, would-be Bohemians and artists." Other members of the group were Robert Curran, a philosophy student working on Wittgenstein and "author of a love poem in the campus literary magazine that Spicer had 'discovered,'" and Leonard Wolf, whose collection of poems *Hamadryad Hunted* had been published by Bern Porter in 1945. In Wolf's poem "Goliath," Duncan found the poet speaking, as he put it in a 1977 draft of his "Preface" to *Medieval Scenes 1950 and 1959* (NBuU), "with the authority of an ancient demon of the Semitic world," with what in a 1970s interview he would call Wolf's "psychic language, a psychic feeling for the dream-like portent and omen of daily experience" (Lewis Ellingham and Kevin Killian, *Poet Be Like God: Jack Spicer and the San Francisco Renaissance* [Hanover and London: Wesleyan University Press, 1998], 14). Duncan wrote the ten poems of *MS* at the cleared dining table, Spicer and the O'Neills watching.

In his "Introduction to a Bibliography of the Works of Jack Spicer" (NBuU) Duncan likened the ten nightly sessions to the séances his parents had held "in their Hermetic mysteries" during his childhood: "I proposed . . . to receive ten consecutive visions that were also messages in poetry," and in the draft of his "Preface" described his motive as "in part vain-glorious; I wanted to enthrall Hugh O'Neill and Jack and to lay claim to the mediumistic power, to compel the Muse." As he reported in the "Author's Notes," "It was my idea that I would write without revision—straight off, as if dictated." Since their first meeting in 1946 Duncan and Spicer had been "evolving a practice of poetry as magic," a transformation of the everyday: "We collected signs and rumors. Mary Butts's *Armed With Madness* incited us all to traffic in myths and to derive a 'scene' by charging every possibility with overtones and undertones, to make thunderheads, storm weather—but to hold it unreleased, for the power's sake, living in actual life as if it were a dream" ("Author's Notes"). In 1968 Duncan would comment that "in *Medieval Scenes* I saw poetry as a hypnagogic vision" (Notebook 39, NBuU), and in some drafts (OKentU) he titled the series "A Medieval Slumbering."

In early 1947 Spicer was taking Ernst Kantorowicz's course in medieval studies, with seminars held at Kantorowicz's home with food and wine at hand. Some time in 1952 Duncan—briefly and incompletely reworking *MS*—looked back on 2029 Hearst: "Chapter I—The Dreamers: We gatherd about one table, often ten of us, in those days: all impoverisht company, living off of each other, too intimately indebted to be friends. Our common bond—that each was vulnerable—; so, a feudal order" (Notebook 11, 125, NBuU). Duncan would not take Kantorowicz's course until he reenrolled at UC Berkeley in the spring semester of 1948, and in his "Author's Notes" of 1962 explained that "since I had never studied the Middle Ages, I would be—as men in the Middle Ages were—mistaken about history, having only the popular legend of what was 'Medieval' to go by."

"For me today," Duncan wrote in the first of three drafts of his 1977 "Preface" (NBuU), "*Medieval Scenes* remains the first poem in which I knew what I had to do from the dictates of the work itself and where I sat down to follow its course," in which—as the third draft says—he found "the mode in which the eternal ones of the poem might come to me that is still today the mode I seek in poems like *Structure of Rime* and *Passages*."

The textual history is quite complex. In the original (pencil) first drafts, Duncan started writing each poem with an epigraph "to evoke the power, the 'voice' and write what 'came'" (draft of "Preface"), but once the series was complete he revised and typed the poems for public readings. This typescript version drops the epigraphs, replacing them with new opening lines, and adds transitional and thematic links between the poems; in some cases ("The Helmet of Goliath," for example) Duncan recast the poem quite extensively. Spicer vehemently objected to the revisions as a violation of the original "dictated" text, and as a betrayal of Poetry. More or less lightly revised, and with the stanzas regularized (to Duncan's later regret over this "last gesture to convention" ["Author's Notes"]), this became the text of the first edition of *MS,* published by James Broughton's Centaur Press in 1950. In 1950 or 1951, planning *A Looking Glass: Poems 1947–1950* (NBuU), Duncan intended to print his "Notes to Medieval Scenes" immediately after the poems—there are several versions of these notes (at CU-BANC and NBuU)—thereby restoring the epigraphs and providing other sources for the poems. When in 1958–59 he prepared the text for *Selected Poems,* Duncan returned to the original pencil drafts and (as recorded below in the notes to the individual poems) by and large restored the original stanza divisions and two of the epigraphs. But for reasons of space, Duncan was obliged at the publisher's behest to prune his selections for the book, and he reluctantly removed "The Adoration of the Virgin" and "Huon of Bordeaux," "a decision I regretted at the time and consider now [1962] a disaster—for, garbled or make-shift as I might think them, the two scenes are essential to the whole" ("Author's Notes").

"I have workd and reworkd the *Medieval Scenes*," Duncan wrote to Werner Vostriede some time in 1948 (CU-BANC), "extensively"—there are manuscripts and jottings in notebooks at Berkeley and Buffalo as well as in the seventy pages of *The Medieval Scenes Papers* at Kent State University—but a full exploration of the tangled textual history, along with Duncan's many and frequently revised observations and commentaries, must await a comprehensive study and variorum edition of this definitional poem.

In *The First Decade: Selected Poems 1940–1950,* making his customary alterations in spelling, punctuation, and the like, Duncan reverted to the text of *MS,* except as noted below.

Epigraph: Upon the wall of her bed chamber. First publication in *MS,* 5; also included in *SP* and *FD.*

The Dreamers. First publication in *MS,* 9–11; also published in *SP* and *FD.* In revising the poem for *SP,* Duncan dropped the first two stanzas, restoring the original epigraph:

"Sleep lingers all our lifetime about our eyes,
  as night hovers all day in the boughs of the fir tree.
  All things swim and glitter."
                    —Emerson, *Experience*

and rearranged the body of the poem into three stanzas of 12, 9, and 7 lines respectively.

In stanza 6, *SP* drops lines 1–3, and the final line becomes the first line of the next stanza (which is 9 lines). Stanzas 3, 4, 5, and 6 in *MS* are in *SP* combined into one, with an added final line: "seven sleepers of romance's mountain magic." In *SP* the last line of stanza 6 and stanza 7, with revisions to lines 2–4, are combined with stanza 8 to make a nine-line stanza whose first five lines are:

The daemon swims and glitters in each face.
Each sleepy bearish hero short of love
recounts his dreams. The knightly valors

cast upon the day's continuum of light
a shade of language dragon red with hope.

In *SP* stanzas 9 and 10 are combined into a single seven-line stanza.

The Helmet Of Goliath. First publication in *The Tiger's Eye* 1.4 (15 June 1948): 50–51. Also published in *MS*, 11–13; *SP;* and *FD.* In revising the poem for *SP*, Duncan dropped the first eleven lines, restoring the original epigraph:

> "Goliath stoppd, he heard his armor creak
> and grow alive with an increasing weight
> and felt a cooling night creep on the land."
> —Leonard Wolf, "David"

In *SP* the poem consists (following the epigraph) of eight stanzas, of 8, 1, 8, 8, 9, 2, 5, and 4 lines, respectively. In stanza 5, *MS* and *FD* drop all three lines, and also drop the final line of the penultimate stanza: "We yearn. The yearning vanishes." A penciled correction in Duncan's own copy of *MS* (NBuU) restores this line, as does *SP.*

The Banners. First publication in *MS*, 13–15; also published in *SP* and *FD.* In revising the poem for *SP*, Duncan dropped the first stanza with its play on "mere" and "-mare," which Spicer had objected to when Duncan typed up the version for public readings, and substituted the following three lines:

> The cygnet, heraldic joy, somnambulant,
> within the turbulence of want
> displays its grace.

In the final stanza, he recast and augmented the last two lines as follows:

> It glimmers in embroidery of leaves. It swims,
> the scarlet lake of some significance,
> lionish Princeliness of the scene.

In *SP* the poem consists of five stanzas, of 3, 11, 6, 10, and 4 lines respectively.

The Kingdom Of Jerusalem. First publication in *MS*, 15–17; also published in *SP* and *FD.* In revising the poem for *SP*, Duncan combined into one the second and third lines of stanza 3; the poem thus consists of seven stanzas, of 3, 9, 3, 7, 2, 7, and 7 lines respectively.

The Festivals. First publication in *MS*, 17–19; also published in *SP* and *FD.* There are several drafts of this poem, which Duncan at one stage considered dropping from *SP*. In revising "The Festivals" for *SP*, he heavily cut and extensively recast it to read as follows:

"I do not want the witless rounds of spring
to break this fine enchantment into joys,
wild shouts and lively cruelties.
The joy unbroken is the lovely thing."

The poet sees his foolish Muse bestir herself
as if to shake off foolishness. "The sleeping joy,"
he murmurs in her dream, "is best.
Then let us drift upon the fire with closed eyes,
extend our midnight and forget the day.
I would avoid the chattering of birds,
the twittering in gid and gawdy wide awake.
Our unicorn is but a gilded ass
adornd by village fools with a single horn
of painted wood. Then let them prance.
I would linger in this seeded ground
and see the rounds of vernal hopping pass.

"Faces too bright, janglings of the morris dance,
in the candid minds of the redeemd
these do not appear. I do not want
the wanton spring to break my wonder
into the wheel of chance and changes,
piebald ribaldry of nights and days,
of stompings, of vacant carnivals."

The poet holds the musing body that he loves,
and, like that glistening lover that Saint Julian knew,
that body has a leprous questioning of his soul.
All lovers, male and female hungers, move
in transformations of the Muse.
The Muse is wide awake.

"The joy awake, she says,
"is everywhere. You are a wondrous sleeping
in a world of wonders. The braying ass
the fools have painted gold and red
and decorated with a single horn
—I saw him in my dream and dreamt
he was a magic wonder—now awake
I see he is a braying foolish unicorn."

The Mirror. First publication in *MS,* 19–21; also published in *SP* and *FD.* In revising the poem for *SP,* Duncan recast the lines into six stanzas, of 13, 8, 3, 4, 11, and 6 lines respectively. In stanza 3, lines 3–4, *SP* reads "He twists between two fingers" for "He twists between his thumb / and finger."

The Reaper. First publication in *MS,* 21–22; also published in *FD.* The text of *SP* is identical to that of *MS.*

The Adoration Of The Virgin. First publication in *MS,* 23–24; also published in *FD.* This poem is not in *SP.* Duncan adapts and quotes two lines from the seventh stanza, "O haloed Mother, heal / my lover and myself," in the first section of "The Venice Poem."

Huon of Bordeaux. First publication in *MS,* 25–27; also published in *FD.* This poem is not in *SP.* In revising the poem for *FD,* Duncan recast the poem into ten stanzas, of 4, 5, 7, 5, 4, 4, 5, 2, 4, and 5 lines respectively, as follows:

FD combines stanzas 2–4 into a single five-line stanza, whose second line reads " . . . Their minds are vacant corridors" and whose fourth line reads "and howl. Illuminations of no spirit." *FD* moves stanza 5 to the first line of the next (seven-line) stanza, which thus begins "I answer: *This, Beloved.*" In stanza 7, lines 4–5, *FD* reads: "we see her, mute, stone questioner." *FD* moves stanza 8 to the first line of the next (four-line) stanza, which thus begins "Morgana le Fay! She is like a sphinx of stone." In stanza 11, *FD* moves line 1 to line 2 to read "He, in all his brightness, has."

The Albigenses. First publication in *MS,* 27–29; also published in *SP* and *FD.* In revising the poem for *SP,* Duncan combined the first four stanzas into a single six-line stanza, and lines 6–7 of stanza 6 into one line. He deleted the two lines of stanza 7, and in line 3 of stanza 11 deleted "we strive to touch" so that it reads: "If we could know their chastity . . . " The poem thus consists of eight stanzas, of 6, 3, 6, 7, 4, 2, 6, and 1 line respectively.

POEMS 1948–49

In the early months of 1948, having returned as an undergraduate to UC Berkeley, Duncan founded and edited with Mary Fabilli *The Berkeley Miscellany,* printing work by Spicer, Mary Fabilli, and himself in the first issue (Summer 1948), and by Spicer, Fabilli, Jerry Ackerman, and himself in the second (Spring 1949). There were only two issues. Duncan wrote the work collected in *Poems 1948–49* between November 1947 and October 1948, and published the book himself (with the imprint "Berkeley Miscellany Editions"). He commissioned Libertarian Press in Glen Gardner, N.J., who had printed the magazine, to produce five hundred copies, but the printer baulked at the sexually explicit language in ten lines of "The Venice Poem" (in the section "Imaginary Instructions"). As Duncan later explained to Henry Wenning in a letter of 7 November 1962: "I had wanted 100 of the 500 copies censored (for sale to sensitive old ladies at poetry readings), and the printers, who were sensitive old lady anarchists, reversed the proportions so that 100 uncensored copies and 400 censored copies were printed. This means that in some of copies of the censored printing I wrote in the missing lines, once the uncensored copies were gone" (quoted in Robert J. Bertholf, *Robert Duncan: A Descriptive Bibliography* [Santa Rosa: Black Sparrow, 1986], 25). The censored copies substituted exact lengths of hair-rules for the expunged lines, "in imitation," Duncan told Wenning (21 November 1962, quoted in Bertholf, 25), "of the censored lines in Pound's 'Canto LII.'" The first sentence of the Tms "Introduction" to the volume, dated 1949, says, "I have done nothing more in composing this volume than to insist upon the chronology—a year's work and a year's record; convinced that there lies in mere chronology the most important relationship of all, something other than one might calculate" (CU-BANC).

It is not, however, a *complete* record: the notebooks contain other poems Duncan wrote during that year, and the second paragraph of that introduction is thus misleading: "One gains in insisting upon the record of the thing done—which foregoes the favorable impression which may lie in 'cleaning up one's traces' or selecting 'the best'—the testimony, which lies in its failure as well as its achievement." In then discussing his poetics, explaining the success or failure of some of the poems, he spoke of himself as "everywhere in this volume apprentice"—to "Pound's translation of the *Donna Mi Prega* as prayer for the revival of music"; to Stravinsky's Symphony in 3 Movements; to H.D.'s *Trilogy;* to Williams's *Paterson.* "My task," he continued, "as always is . . . so to devote my attention to the feel of the inner rhythms and balances as to pass thru and beyond the intellectual, . . . [to] pose so complexly the problem of balance that the dance is 'heard' only by the non-intellectual ear and reveald to the intellectual eye."

With the exception of "The Inexplicable History of Music" and "A Poet's Masque," Duncan reprinted all the poems of *P48* in *The First Decade: Selected Poems 1940–1950,* and some elsewhere. He extensively revised parts of "The Venice Poem" for its several later printings, and as usual he lightly revised all other poems, amending capitalization, spelling, punctuation, stanza- and line-breaks; he made sundry minor changes in diction, recast the spacing between words and lines, and in several instances changed roman to italic to clarify possible ambiguities in the text. As a rule such changes are not

recorded in these notes, but most of the shifts from roman to italic, follow-
ing the text of later printings, have been silently adopted.

Three Songs For Jerry. "The Inexplicable History Of Music" written 1947;
first publication in *P48*, 3–4. "A Weekend Of The Same Event" written
November 1947; first publication in *P48*, 5–7; also published in *FD*. "Sleep-
ing All Night" written November 1947; first publication in *P48*, 8–10; also
published in *FD*. "Jerry" is Gerald M. Ackerman (1928–), an undergraduate
at UC Berkeley, later an art historian, almost ten years younger than Dun-
can, with whom he lived for some months after they met in November 1947.

I Tell Of Love. Written January 1948; first publication in *P48*, 13–17; also
published in *FD*. In stanza 1, fourth line from end, *FD* reads "It needs no
statement" for "This is not a statement." In stanza 2, sixth and seventh lines
from the end, *FD* reads "My eye is clearer. I have / night sight. I speak
boldly. Love casts."

In stanza 3, four lines from end, *FD* reads "Love so moves, makes new"
for "love moves; makes new."

The Venice Poem. Written February–September 1948; first publication in
P48, 21–52; also published in *Selected Poems* and *FD*. Duncan started working
on the poem when Ackerman, growing tired of his relationship with Dun-
can, for a brief period sought and found other lovers. In February–March
1948, when he began writing "The Venice Poem," Duncan was enrolled in
the "Civilization of the Middle Ages" program at Berkeley, attending Ernst
Kantorowicz's seminar on the thirteenth century. Kantorowicz focused
especially on the architecture and sculpture of the period, and liberally pep-
pered his classes with slides and photographs of Venetian buildings and art.
Duncan, who had yet to visit Venice, intermingled lines and fragments of
his drafts of "The Venice Poem" with his notes on Kantorowicz's lectures
and on assignments he was doing for the course. Manuscript and early type-
script drafts of the poem show considerable reworking and recasting, and
when he published the first two sections—"A Description Of Venice" and
"Testimony"—in his *Berkeley Miscellany* 1 (Summer 1948) the two poems did
not carry the title "The Venice Poem."

"A Description Of Venice" had nine prefatory lines, as follows:

upon which the heart is to be hurt

Mother, I am hurt.
Why is the house so still?
Where have you gone?

Alone, I know not where I am.
I call out.

Blessed Mother, heal
my lover and myself.

He dropped these lines from all subsequent printings, but inserted the final couplet, an adaptation and quotation from "The Adoration Of The Virgin" in *Medieval Scenes,* at the end of the second (unnumbered) section of "A Description Of Venice."

In the Tms "Introduction" to *P48* Duncan commented that "The Venice Poem" started from "what seems the most personal enigma, the signs and experience that distinguish one's self," but "unfolds not the personal alone but signs and experience of other lives that lie buried in language, an ever present of what one thought past history." There is a dialectic in the poem, he said,

> of a progression directed by 'signs,' moments of apprehension read in the events of persons: the apprehension of something cruel and betraying in the lustful and shrewd mirror of a young boy in whose blue eyes seemd a written story of calculating and meaningless accident, and in whose lithe autoerotic body seemd a forbidden universe; or, five months later, the apprehension of something archaic and polymorphously sexual in a fat woman met again and again, sought out after the first meeting, at parties or at bars; or, finally, the comprehension in a baby of all that had been torturous and sinful re-seen in a joyous reality. These real or rather actual messengers play no other dramatic role or no less dramatic role than that of appointed guides who unlock what one could never have unlockd for oneself—the spring of the poem from one's own life.

The complete text of "The Venice Poem" was first printed in *P48,* and that is the text printed here, but all versions published subsequent to *The Berkeley Miscellany* at times show vigorous revision. Duncan recast the poem and repeatedly tinkered with details, frequently in *FD* cancelling changes made for *SP.* In addition to such substitutions as printing "San Marco" for "St. Mark's" and then changing that to "Saint Mark," and extensively changing the punctuation and indentation in *SP* and again in *FD,* Duncan frequently changed stanza- and line-breaks and added, removed, or reordered lines. Not all of these changes are recorded here.

In addition, he seems never to have settled on a final disposition for the relationships between the six sections of the poem. Although on 10 August 1948, working on "The Venus of Lespuges," he referred to the poem as "my triptych" (Notebook 5, CU-BANC), and in the Tms "Introduction" of 1949 referred to "The Venus of Lespuges" as "the third movement of the poem" rather than the fifth, when he compiled the contents page of *P48* for the press he numbered the six parts sequentially, granting them apparently equal formal status. Ten years later in *SP,* the six sections of the poem are treated as equal items in an unnumbered list, and almost ten years after that in *FD* (published 1968), the poem is divided into three principal numbered sections, with three unnumbered subsections—"Testimony," "Recorso," and "Coda"—intercalated: these distinctions appear in the text as well as on the contents page of that book.

In the six months or so between *The Berkeley Miscellany* printing and the *P48* appearance Duncan extensively revised, cut, inserted, and reordered lines, generally softening, distancing, or removing the intense personal anguish of the betrayed or deserted lover. Thus, for example, "The Doge / devours his breakfast in his palace" (*Berkeley Miscellany*) becomes "The Doge / at breakfast in the Palazzo" in all later printings. Duncan's Ams and Tms notes for the poem (at CU-BANC and at NBuU) identify "passages from other sources used" in "Testimony" and "Imaginary Instructions"— these are noted at the appropriate place—but not all of the many changes Duncan made to the text are noted below. The textual history of the poem is somewhat tangled, and a full listing must await a comprehensive study and variorum edition of the poem.

A Description Of Venice. At the close of the first section, for "This jewel, / from which proceeds, / as if rays, / a melody. . . . ," *Berkeley Miscellany* reads:

> Or let us say the lion's eye is fixd
> Upon the wondrous gaze of this
> > Adonis
> > the Lion in a cage of Daniels.

The second section (which closes with "Holy Mother, hail. / Heal / my lover and myself") is followed in *Berkeley Miscellany* by a new section, ten lines long, which Duncan revised and incorporated into the first stanza of what in *P48* (the copy text here) is the opening stanza of section three. The lines in *Berkeley Miscellany* read:

> The campanile dominates the square.
> > The four bronze horses
> rear—this is a vision of rare
> > exultant cold love,

a monument that
   tho bathed in gold of the sun
and painted over with warm gold
resplendent, with blue and green
gives utter despair
   words.

In the fifth section, for "Or in full daylight: the hourly ringing," *Berkeley Miscellany* reads "Midday the campanile rings"; and adds, immediately after "Church of the Apostles":

Midday the insistent clamor of the bells
rings from the imposing tower
the daily triumph. Here Titian
painted with clamorous rich red
adulterous Venus or
with mother-of-pearl lustre of the sea,
Europa and her Bull, to celebrate
   the splendor of imperishable loot.

In the seventh section, the opening six lines here are condensed and revised from *Berkeley Miscellany,* which reads:

Seen as Visionary Venice, my mind
with its lions (its spirits) with its horses
(imperishable bronze monuments of victory)
with its onion-globe copper pseudo-domes
(proof of the vulgar wealth of loot)
is beautiful. Not happy, but splendid.
Seen as my mind, lantern slide visions
of Venice repair; or 6 hued colord photographs
reproduce a monument of all desire & fear
—so the primitive man believes—
What if the secret name is photographd?
to teach the blue of terror so that the blue

In the final section, after "in whose arms I lay, / virtuous therein," *Berkeley Miscellany* adds (no initial stanza break, same indentation, followed by a stanza break):

Now she is lost from me,
and this world encroaches,
speaks its insidious wisdom

in my ear. I hear
news of my betrayal
whisperd in the halls.

Testimony. In Ams and Tms of "Notes: (where I use passages from other authors . . ." (CU-BANC and NBuU) Duncan identifies two such passages for "Testimony." The first is "from Proust, *The Past Recaptured* ' . . . when the unevenness of the two paving stones extended in every direction and all dimensions the bare and barren impressions I had of Venice and Saint Mark's . . . it is true that at those moments I was tempted—if not, on account of the season, to go and idly glide over the waters of Venice, which I associated more especially with the springtime—at any rate to Balbec.'" The French epigraph is drawn from this passage; the translation is by Frederick A. Blossom (New York: Modern Library, 1932), 202. In *SP* Duncan identified Proust as the source.

The epigraph in English: "I was tempted if not on account of the season, to go and idly glide over the waters, to me so springlike, of Venice." The opening two lines, immediately following, in English read: "Those images, 'of Venice and Saint Mark's' / 'parched and naked that I had'; I knew."

The second source text identified by Duncan in "Notes" is

from Stravinsky, "The Phenomenon of Music" [opening paragraph], *Poetics of Music:* " . . . of the pleasure we experience on hearing the murmur of the breeze in the trees, the rippling of a brook, the song of a bird . . . we may even say: "what lovely music!" Naturally, we are speaking only in terms of comparison. But then, *comparison* is not *reason.* These natural sounds suggest music to us, but are not yet themselves music . . . they are promises of music; it takes a human being to keep them, a human being who is sensitive to nature's many voices, of course, but who in addition feels the need of putting them in order and who is gifted for that task with a very special aptitude."

The Tms version drops the last dozen words.

Berkeley Miscellany inserts a six-line section between the first and second sections, as follows:

No one has remarkd that Proust
was like Shakespeare-Othello or
that he was drawn to Venice
because like Shakespeare
he was jealous and because
Venice is jealousy's city.

Imaginary Instructions. "*Qui avait l'esprit vif et brillant*: that seemed so vivid and alive." Source not identified, referring to Bernini's 1665 portrait bust of Louis XIV, a bronze version of which (from c. 1700) is in the National Gallery, Washington, DC.

In Tms "Notes: (where I use passages from other authors . . . " (CU–BANC and NBuU) Duncan identifies the quotations opening the third section of the poem as follows: "From the March 1948 issue of *Four Pages:* 'Manifest. 1. We must understand what is really happening. 2. If the verse-makers of our time are to improve on their immediate precursors, we must be vitally aware of the duration of syllables, of melodic coherence, and of the tone leading of vowels. 3. The function of poetry is to debunk by lucidity. We, the CLEANERS, D. Simpson, L.C. Flynn, Igon Tan.' It is my impression that this directive actually came from Ezra Pound." In early August 1959 he told Denise Levertov, in a letter, "I had received the directive on a postcard from Washington, D.C., just at the point of the composition of the poem where it becomes one of the 'Instructions'" (Robert J. Bertholf and Albert Gelpi, eds., *The Letters of Robert Duncan and Denise Levertov* [Stanford: Stanford University Press, 2004], 195).

Recorso. SP drops, and FD restores (without the em dashes), the line "— beautiful and mysterious machine—"

The Venus of Lespuges. "'Αφροδίτη / μήτερ: Aphrodite / mother. *Swilce gildene steorran*" (Old English): Likewise golden stars, from the description of the sapphire as being like the sun ("on it likewise golden stars are fixed"), in the Old English *Lapidary,* lines 5–6; sapphire is one of the twelve precious stones found in the book of the Apocalypse.

In *SP* this section of the poem opens with the single line "is." and changes the opening lines of the third, fourth, and fifth stanzas, dropping "I return to first things" and substituting "Is. / Of the first." in the third; dropping "so that:" in the fourth; and dropping "Of first things." in the fifth. *SP* also dropped the two Greek lines in the sixth, and in the eighth identified the "Queen of the Jungle, Yadwigha / of the tiger." *FD* restored the *P48* readings of these lines.

Coda. SP drops the fourth stanza; FD restores it.

3 Poems in Homage to the Brothers Grimm. "The Robber Moon." Written July 1948; first publication in *Berkeley Miscellany* 2 (Spring 1949): 25–26. Also published in *P48, SP,* and *FD.*

"Strawberries Under The Snow." Written July 1948; first publication in *Berkeley Miscellany* 2 (Spring 1949): 27. Also published in *P48, SP,* and *FD.* In the Tms "Introduction" (CU-BANC) Duncan says that the poem "was when I wrote it so little my own creation that I was not sure I had not done something quite idiotic. Certainly something so universal of tongue as to seem almost useless to my 'self-expression.' But to seek out, to fabricate such poems would be as futile as to fabricate a lasting peace." The title in *Berkeley Miscellany* is "The Strawberries Under The Snow."

"The Dinner Table of Harlequin." Written July 1948; first publication in *Berkeley Miscellany* 2 (Spring 1949): 28–29. Also published in *P48* and *FD*.

Revival. Written September 1948; first publication in *P48*, 63–64. Also published in *FD*. The line "I go where I love and where I am loved" is from H.D., *Trilogy* (Part 3, *The Flowering of the Rod*, section 2).

In stanza 2, lines 5–6, *FD* ends line 5 with a comma, drops "countless, we have walkd" and substitutes "there is a company of the lonely, / beyond count, we have walkt alone.—"

A Poet's Masque. Written 1948; first publication in *P48*, 65–84. "What I find myself at all a failure" in the book, Duncan wrote in his Tms "Introduction," "is in the *Poet's Masque* . . . on the one hand in the speeches of A Man with a False Nose and on the other in the Robbers' Scene. In the first a failure to imitate the specific, to caricature; for where, as here, the exaggeration proceeds from a poor grasp of the central principle, the effect wanders and becomes inconclusive. In the second, a more monstrous failure: the complete inability at all to realize what one is doing. Here there is no imitation at all but at the most crucial point (becoming crucial because it is un-inspired) the inappropriate appears, one's inexpertness glares forth." Once again singling out the Man with a False Nose as "weakly construed and uninspired," Duncan, in an undated pencil Ams diatribe ("Berkeley Miscellany—a Venomous Note," NBuU), assessed this masque as an unsatisfying satire of the Berkeley English Department, which he called "probably the greatest destructive force in the intellectual life of the community." Apparently, the masque was seen in reading performances at several houses in Berkeley.

A Poet's Masque is the second masque Duncan wrote while at Berkeley: in his "draft of contents for Volume II" of his proposed collected poems tentatively titled "A Looking Glass: Poems 1947–1950" (NBuU) Duncan included the typescript of "A Black Masque, written for Erika Braun's Hallowe'en Party 1947." It has not been published.

UNCOLLECTED WORK 1948–1951

When Duncan gathered some of his work from 1948 through 1955 for publication in *Audit/Poetry* 4.3 (1967), he assured Charles Doria, one of the two editors, that the work in *Audit* would be "Duncan exclusives, material that won't be available in a book" (18 August 1966, NBuU). Duncan published some of the work, however, in the 1972 edition of *Caesar's Gate: Poems 1949–1950*.

Jerusalem. Written 1948; first publication in *Selected Poems*, 40. Also published in *The First Decade: Selected Poems 1940–1950*. There are several Ams and Tms of "Jerusalem" at CU-BANC and NBuU; the variations are slight. *SP* casts the poem in five stanzas of 4, 1, 10, 5, and 1 line respectively, as here; *FD* in six stanzas, of 4, 1, 4, 6, 5, and 4 lines respectively.

The version in *FD*, in italicizing quoted speech (as was Duncan's practice in that book and in *Derivations*), prints the following, from the poem's last eight lines, in italics: *Jerusalem! / Jerusalem! / Oh sweet Jerusalem! / There the heart will find its rest. / / / . . . Too late! too late!*

A Derivation From Rimbaud. Written 1948; first publication in *Audit/ Poetry* 4.3 (1967): 30–32. Extensively revised between 1948 and 1972 (there are many *MS* drafts), dated 1948 in *Audit/Poetry*. Duncan published the first section, extensively revised, as part of the sequence "Appearances" in *CG72* with the title "*From* A Season In Hell" (for the text, see this volume). In the publisher's flyer for *CG72*, Duncan dates it 1949.

Love—A Story. Written 1948–1949(?); first publication in *The Occident* (Fall 1949): 5–15. Also published in *Kulchur* 3.11 (Autumn 1963). In a note at NBuU Duncan said the story was about Thanksgiving 1944. In a note accompanying the reprint of this story in *Kulchur*, Duncan wrote:

> In this story "Love," written in 1949, I wanted to get at how we play ourselves false and how we use each other to contrive this play. What does it mean to show one's true colors? I meant to portray the twist of the knife. But once the story was written, I saw that I had given the knife itself another twist in the writing. It is not only a painful story about pain but a telling that inflicts pain upon the sensibilities of its listeners, harping upon whatever wounds of social or personal consciousness without relief. It seems to me now that I played myself as writer false in this. At the heart of the story there is a mistaken intent. As in their talk the characters take James wrong and render his intense manner of conscience in counterfeit, so the characters have been taken wrong to talk this way. There are times when the writer himself becomes such a victim and the mock moral tone invades the picture itself. This putting the matter in a bad light then proves to be an inverse of self-piety, embarrassing as putting the matter in a good light can be. Given all that, an understanding of this work still seems to me important for the understanding of my work at large. How strange to find in that description of Claudia's living in the Fords' living ("sheltered them, gardened them, carried water to them") a reminder of the theme of gardens and gardeners that has been constant in my poetry. Was Claudia then a *gardener*? My view of life has changed, but the perplexity of different levels in feeling-tone remains. The writer of this

story "Love" is me as I am not him. Yet I am still so involved with what I was that I cannot read "Love" without chagrin.

Duncan lightly revised the text in 1963 for its reprint in *Kulchur,* mainly changing punctuation and spelling, changing one or two words, and omitting one sentence.

The Effort. Written 1949; first publication in H. Daniel Peck, ed., *The Green American Tradition: Essays and Poems for Sherman Paul* (Baton Rouge: Louisiana University Press, 1989), 264–79. Tms (carbon copy) in NBuU. Duncan began writing "The Effort" on about 22 October 1948 (Notebook 5 presented to Robin Blaser in 1952, CU-BANC), and at some point sent Ezra Pound an early draft, "The Beginning of a Discourse written for E.P. Xmas 1948." In March 1949 he sent part of the poem to Dallam Simpson, who in a letter of 14 February 1949 (NBuU) accompanying a copy of the "Cleaners' Manifesto" (a document which originated with Ezra Pound), invited Duncan to take part in a proposed anthology of four poets who had "obtained status under the 1948 Cleaners' Manifesto." Duncan had already appeared three times in Simpson's magazine *Four Pages:* a letter listing *Finnegans Wake,* H.D.'s *Trilogy,* Pound's *Cantos,* Edith Sitwell's *The Song Of The Cold,* and the work of Wallace Stevens and William Carlos Williams as forming "a critical basis for a new poetry given the past decade" in *Four Pages* 1 (Jan. 1948): 2, 3; comments on Mary Butts, which Simpson had omitted for "space limitations" from the January issue and which then appeared in *Four Pages* 4 (April 1948): 4; and Duncan's note on "Western poetry's anarchistic phase" and the power of the "New York Empire" in *Four Pages* 8 (August 1948): 2. "The Cleaners' Manifesto," which Duncan would quote in the "Imaginary Instructions" section of "The Venice Poem," appeared in *Four Pages* 3 (March 1948): 3: "1. We must understand what is really happening. 2. If the verse makers of our time are to improve on their immediate precursors, we must be vitally aware of the duration of syllables, of melodic coherence, and of the tone leading of vowels. 3. The function of poetry is to debunk by lucidity." Simpson proposed to print both "The Effort" and "Homage and Lament for Ezra Pound in Captivity" in *The Cleaners' Anthology of Verse,* but the book never appeared.

Duncan drafted but did not complete "A Note on *The Effort*" (NBuU):

Exempla: The Pisan *Cantos; Paterson;* Marianne Moore's continued works; Louis Zukofsky's *Light* etc. One can measure the restriction of my abilities, holding in mind these models. I simply can not achieve, for instance, the direction & authenticity of Williams's   nor the clarity of vision of the contemporary of

Zukofsky's *Light* (use of, or rather experience of movies): Poetry as imitation of language itself—the "common speech"

the making of language?

the problem, for one thing, lies in the disunity between the language by which I participate daily in speech; and literature: not, in case that old argument comes up, necessitating a debate contra the Eliot position, but an experiment toward which Eliot's work seems to provide little aid.

It is, however, not Eliot—but Edith Sitwell or Wallace Stevens who [the manuscript breaks off here].

At one stage, Duncan considered including "entire Z's poem" (Notebook 5, CU-BANC).

A 1954 notebook entry dated June 16 drafts a ten-page essay on "The Effort" and Charles Olson's *Maximus* (Notebook 14, NBuU). Duncan would come back to Olson's poem in the same notebook a month later.

Epigraph: the source is William Harvey, *Exercitato Anatomica de Motu Cortis et Sanguinus in Animalibus* (1628), translated by Chauncey D. Leake as *An Anatomical Study on the Motion of the Heart and Blood* (Springfield, IL: Charles C. Thomas, 1928), part 2, p. 46. At the beginning of "Towards An Open Universe" (1964) Duncan elaborated and modified the image: "with the first pulse of blood in the egg . . . , the changes of night and day must have been there."

Δίκη δ'ὑπὲρ Ὕβριος ἴσχει / ἐς τέλος ἐξελθοῦσα (Greek here silently corrected): Duncan offers a rough translation in the next two lines: "you will see Justice over Outrage / when you see last things" (from Hesiod, *Works and Days,* second half of line 217, first half of line 218); translated by Hugh Evelyn-White as "for Justice beats Outrage / when she comes to the end of the race" (Loeb Classical Library, 1914).

"παθὼν δέ τε νήπιος ἔγνω: But only when he has suffered does the fool learn this" (from Hesiod, *Works and Days,* second half of line 218; translation by Hugh Evelyn-White).

"明: sun (on the left) and moon (on the right); taken together (in Mandarin, *míng,* with a rising tone) they mean bright or luminous." Duncan probably took them from Ezra Pound's version of Confucius's *The Unwobbling Pivot & The Great Digest* (Norfolk, Connecticut: New Directions, 1947), or from *The Cantos,* where they appear more than once, though they may (along with the other Chinese in this poem) derive from "an undergraduate general course in Confucius with the great Sinologist Peter Boodberg at the University of California at Berkeley" (Duncan's note on "Two Sets of Tens" in *Ground Work: In the Dark* [New York: New Directions, 1987], gathered in *Collected Later Poems and Prose*).

習(Chinese): in Mandarin, *xí,* pronounced somewhat like *she,* with a rising tone. Duncan provides a gloss to its left, quoting R. H. Matthews's *Chinese-English Dictionary* (character 2499): "The rapid, frequent motion of the wings in flying:—from which comes the idea of—to practise; to study; customs; practices."

In the Tms, toward the end of the section "A Sign Of Great Delight," Duncan bracketed the following lines, presumably with the intention of deleting them:

> When I speak clearly
> departments of English literature
> will understand nothing.
>
> Will not understand my rage,
> will not understand my intolerant joy.

.

Poetic Disturbances. In 1970, Clifford Burke's "Mayan Quarto" series published Duncan's pamphlet *Poetic Disturbances,* consisting of four poems: "Poetic Disturbances"; "What Is It You Have Come To Tell Me, Garcia Lorca?"; "The Voyage Of The Poet Into The Land Of The Dead"; and "I Saw The Rabbit Leap." The first three were written in 1949; the last, in 1960 (for the text, see *CLPP*). When Duncan prepared the 1972 edition of *Caesar's Gate,* he grouped the first three poems under the title "Poetic Disturbances" (as here), and changed the title of the first poem. As usual, he lightly revised all texts.

Poetic Disturbances. Written 1949; first publication in *Poetic Disturbances,* 5–6. Also published in *CG72,* as "Forms Within Forms." While retaining the section divisions, *CG72* recast the introductory stanza into three stanzas of 10, 5, and 2 lines and section 2 into four stanzas of 4, 4, 2, and 1. In section 3, *CG72* split the closing paragraph into two lines, and in the third paragraph italicized *"this world"* in all three instances; in section 4 it italicized the two one-line refrains.

In the introductory stanza, *CG72* drops all four 1-em dashes: line 1 reads "Half-formed (" and line 11, starting a new stanza, reads: ") They want to come through. They force." Duncan substituted periods for the other two 1-em dashes, and split the penultimate line so that the final two lines read: "And I, in turn, / saw all those colors in her eye."

What Have You Come To Tell Me, Garcia Lorca? Written 1949; first publication in *Poetic Disturbances,* 7–8. Also published in *CG72.* The five lines in Latin are liturgical, from the Catholic *Exsultet,* sung or recited at the entry into the church of the paschal candle during the vigil after sundown at the end of Holy Week, and referred to by Saint Augustine in both *De Civitate Dei* (City of God) and *Confessiones* (Confessions). "I do not want to translate," Duncan wrote in "The Matter Of The Bees" (in *CG72*): "It is the bee-hum out of the dead language that I bring into the poem. It is the sounding of the magic of the dead speaking, the spectral voice of Augustine in his words, where I recognize, even as he addresses the theme of the fortunate fall—*O felix culpa*—he addresses the bee: *O vere beata et mirabilis apis!*":

O felix culpa
et nox sicut dies inluminabitur [Vulgate, Psalm 138:12]
et nox inluminatio mea in deliciis meis [Vulgate, Psalm 138:11]

O vere beata et mirabilis apis! . . .
O vere beata nox!

O fortunate fall
and night shall be light as day
and night shall be my light in my pleasures

O truly blessed and wondrous bee! . . .
O truly blessed night!

In Section 4, line 2, *CG72* substitutes "bees" for "moon."

The Voyage Of The Poet Into The Land Of The Dead. Written 1949; first publication in *Poetic Disturbances* (1970): 9. Also published in CG72.

Appearances. Written 1949; first publication in *CG72*. "From A Season In Hell" published in *Audit/Poetry* 4.3 (1967): 30–32, as the first section of "Derivation From Rimbaud" and dated 1948. "A Game Of Kings" published in *Audit/Poetry* 4.3 (1967): 32. All nine poems gathered into this sequence in *CG72*.

A Villanelle. Written 1950; first publication in *Audit/Poetry* 4.3 (1967): 32.

FRAGMENTS OF A DISORDERD DEVOTION

Duncan and Jess took marriage vows in January 1951. "If Jess's paintings began to derive from a ground in poetry," Duncan recalled in 1966 in the Introduction to *A Book of Resemblances: Poems 1950–1953,* "so the poems of *Fragments of a Disorderd Devotion* seemd to me to come up from a world of imagined paintings." He wrote the poems in 1952, and printed fifty copies of *Frag52* as a Christmas card that year, with his own drawings throughout, but he only sent out fifteen of them. In 1980 he still had nearly a dozen left, even though in 1966 he had redrawn and reissued it with minor revisions as a chapbook (published by Gnomon Press in San Francisco and Island Press in Toronto), when *BR* (which included five of the six poems printed in *Frag52*) was in the hands of its publisher Henry Wenning. A 1962 typescript of *BR* includes a group of seven poems in a section called "Fragments of a Disorderd Devotion," omitting "From My Notebook" and adding "Cats (1)" and "Cats (2)."

All printings after the first of *Frag52* exhibit Duncan's customary revisions to spelling, punctuation, line- and stanza-breaks, and so forth. These are not recorded in the following notes.

Unkingd by affection? Written 1952; first publication in *Frag52*, 1. Also published in *A Poetry Folio* (1963), *Frag66, BR,* and *Derivations: Selected Poems 1950–1956*. In addition to the typeset text in *Der*, Duncan published "Unkingd By Affection?" in four different holograph renderings, two of them (the *Poetry Folio* broadside of 1963 and *BR* of 1966) with drawings by Jess, and one (*Frag66*) with a drawing by Duncan. In some typescripts the poem is titled "Home." All printings except the first read "our selves" in the second paragraph as one word; in the first, the spacing between the two words is moot (letter-spacing in Duncan's handwriting is not consistent). Textual variants are negligible.

Frag66 titles the poem "Unkingd By Affection" and the text of the poem begins with the question; *BR* treats the question as title, as does *Der* (which omits the question mark); in both instances the text of the poem begins "One exchanges . . . "

Five Pieces. Written 1952; first publication in *Frag52*, 2–5. Also published in *Artisan* (Spring 1953): 6–8, *Frag66, BR,* and *Der*. Except for "he says:" *Der* prints the closing four lines in italics.

Hero Song. Written 1952; first publication in *Frag52*, 7–8. Also published in W. H. Auden, ed., *The Faber Book of Modern American Verse* (1956); *Botteghe Oscure* 19 (Spring 1957): 339–40; *Frag66; BR;* and *Der*. In *Botteghe Oscure* the five sections of the poem are numbered I through V.

An Imaginary Woman. Written 1952; first publication in *Frag52*, 9–10. Also published in *Frag66, BR,* and *Der*. Section 2, lines 1–2 and 4–5 are run-over; in *BR* they spread onto the facing page.

From My Notebook. Written 1952; first publication in *Frag52*, 11–14; also published in *Frag66*. "The great mountains of disclaimer" also published as "A Scene" in *WW* and *Der*. In *WW* and *Der* Duncan changed "rain sad" to "sad rain"; and "nite-nite" to "night" (in *WW*), and "the night" (in *Der*).

Eluard's Death. Written 1952; first publication in *Frag52*, 15–16. Also published in *Origin* 1.9 (Spring 1953): 2, *Frag66*, *BR*, and *Der*. Surrealist and dada poet Paul Eluard (Eugène-Emile Paul Grindel) died on 18 November 1952. In 1960, Jess would paint "Éluard's Death"; it depicts a dark grey-green vase on a mustard-yellow disk, casting a dark shadow.

CAESAR'S GATE: POEMS 1949–1950

Duncan wrote all except four of the poems in *Caesar's Gate: Poems 1949–1950* in 1949 and 1950, the later ones in June 1955 in Mallorca, when he was preparing the text for publication by Robert Creeley's Divers Press in September of that year. He would be in Mallorca with Jess (with side trips to Barcelona, Paris, and London) until March 1956, and while there he worked too on a collection which would later become *Writing Writing*, as well as on other poems. Of the sixteen collages reproduced in the regular edition of *CG55*, Jess made twelve of them to accompany the poems Duncan had written in 1949 and 1950; these were set in type. In June 1955 Duncan wrote four new poems in response to their accompanying collages as Jess worked on them; these were printed in holograph, as was the "Preface (1955)." In addition, as Duncan told Robin Blaser in a letter of 15 August 1955: "Jess and I have been doing the collages and poems for the ten limited copies (actually there will be another three—one for Creeley, one for Jess, and one for me). It is the first time I have workd in this quite mediumistic way since the Medieval Scenes. . . . I shall keep no copies" (CU-BANC). In a letter dated 7 November 1972, Duncan told Henry Wenning (publisher of *A Book of Resemblances: Poems 1950–1953*) that the thirteen poems written for the limited edition were "illustrations to the collages (where the collages printed in the book were illustrations of the poems)" (James S. Jaffe Rare Books Catalog, Summer 2010). The ten copies, each with its own collage with accompanying poem and appropriately numbered, rapidly sold to various friends. "In writing the poems for the limited edition," Duncan wrote to Helen Adam on 20 August 1955,

> I turned for the first time since the *Medieval Scenes* to a sense of "visions"—growing from contemplation of the collages done for the book. . . . The special magic of it is that it is a series written to be dispersed—I shall keep no copies of the poems (tho since both Jess and I will have copies of the edition two of the poems will remain with us). Thus each reader of the limited edition will start out with one part of a mysterious map or design. I myself shall have forgotten the nature of the chain. And perhaps see some of the links, but never all of them. I, myself, will from time to time come across these old pieces of a riddle. Like a recipe of

fourteen pages cut up and sold page by page. In *Medieval Scenes* I "crossed my eyes" in order to focus upon a group of people sitting around a table. In the *Caesar's Gate* poems I am looking at the order of Jess's collages, themselves a hidden order (NBuU; also in Kristen Prevallet, ed., "Helen Adam and Robert Duncan Selected Correspondence 1955–1956," *Apex of the M6* [Fall 1997]: 148).

In his 1972 letter to Wenning he called them "sparks 'lost' in the world." Nevertheless, Duncan kept close track of their distribution, and attempted some years later to retrieve some or perhaps all of these occulted texts—Kit Barker's undated typed transcript of "To The Stairwell" (from copy 9) is at NBuU; in 1968 he printed two of them (from his own and Jess's copies) in *Derivations,* revising them slightly. Where available, the texts appear later in this book, in *Uncollected Work 1952–1956.*

CG72, the enlarged edition published in 1972 by Sand Dollar, complicated what was until then a fairly straightforward series of texts, and it did so in two ways. Duncan added, as he explained in a publicity flyer, "twelve previously uncollected poems . . . to make this definitive book of Poems 1949," though one of these, "Despair In Being Tedious" was written twenty-three years later, in 1972 (though he did not change the dates on the title page); he also modified the interrelationships of the poems themselves by recasting the contents page (see Appendix 1), and in the text rearranging the division markers between poems and parts of poems, increasing or in some cases decreasing the porousness of some boundaries and divisions between poems.

Thus the status of the poems grouped under the title "H.M.S. Bearskin" is somewhat uncertain. In 1955, the book's contents page lists five major divisions: "Preface"; "Four Poems As A Night Song"; "Eye Sight"; "Goodbye To Youth"; and "H.M.S. Bearskin"; only two of these—"Four Poems As A Night Song" and "Eye Sight"—list individual poems under those heads. The 1972 contents page lists seven individual titles under the heading "H.M.S. Bearskin," following the format used for "Four Poems as a Night Song." In the texts of that sequence, *CG55* starts each poem on a fresh page, with the title in Futura Bold; two poems ("Great Grief, then, herself!" and "All the way of Forever") have no title: the two lines of "Great Grief . . . " are centered halfway down the page, and it is clearly a separate poem; the ten lines of "All the way of Forever" are printed at the top of the page, not lower down, suggesting that it is a continuation of "He Has A Good Time There," which had ended at the foot of the previous page. But in *CG72* that question is not open, for in the first place it is listed on the contents page (albeit as "Coda"), and in the second, it is separated from "He Has A Good

Time There" by an asterisk. In *CG72,* some poems in "H.M.S. Bearskin" are separated by asterisks even if they have a title; after the opening poem, none of them starts on a fresh page. The absence of an asterisk between two poems suggests that they are paired; hence "He Entertains At A Dinner Party In The Bardo State" and "He Consults The Tides" are so paired; so are "He Lists Subjects For Great Poetry: 1950" and "He Has A Good Time There." The titles of each of the second poems of these pairs assign an initial capital to all words in the title, confirming their status as pairs. In *CG72* "All the way of Forever" is thus to be read as a separate poem in the sequence.

CG72 reproduces Duncan's carefully designed typescript, which habitually inserts double-spaces after all periods, question marks, and exclamation marks—a practice not followed here—and uses the half-leading possible on a typewriter for minor stanza-breaks (a practice not recorded in the following notes). It also adds a forty-one-page "Preface (1972)" (reprinted in Appendix 3) and a fifteen-page "Epilogue (1972)" as well as the extra poems already mentioned. Drafting that preface in December 1971, Duncan commented that in 1955 *Caesar's Gate* "brought into the works not only a Preface but a set of prose poems forerunners of the Structure of Rime series which were to begin early in 1956, and companions of the prose poems that appear in the book LETTERS" (Notebook 43, NBuU). In October 1973 Duncan inscribed a copy of the book with "A PrePreface for James Weil Oct. 1973":

> Volume by volume the Shelf we now address comes into processional statements of where a poetry stands. It is a Wall, of poetry, withholding poetry, advancing perspectives that mount into a shift of shapes. As concretions are laid down, we break the rows of procedures into a rose that means to let loveliness go from its core to grace the ground.
>
> How solid, how boxed in, how page upon page park the books are. We open an envelope of leaves and release all that solid accumulation into leavings. (*Catalogue Forty-nine March 1991* [Philo, California: Am Here Books, 1991], back cover)

As usual, in all reprintings after the 1955 edition—*SP, FD,* and *Der*—Duncan made myriad small changes in spelling, punctuation, spacing, stanza- and line-breaks, and so on. None of these is recorded in the notes which follow.

Preface (1950). Written 1–3 July 1955; first publication in *CG55,* 9–13. Also published in *CG72* and (as an extract) in *Firehouse* 21 (19 Feb. 1978): 3. Duncan rephrased parts of the preface when he redrew it for *CG72,* mainly along the lines of substituting "poets or makaris" for the simpler "*makaris*" in the third paragraph.

In the fourth paragraph, the last two sentences in *CG72* read, "It is the sign of a place, not a mood. And we see it is so, because we too, given up as we are to the poem, see, now, what we thot to be personal expressions are places necessary in the structure of the poem's being."

In the fifth paragraph, first sentence, *CG72* reads "the members of our species" for "human being."

The Construction. Written 1949; first publication in *CG55*, 17. Also published in *FD* and *CG72*.

The Walk To The Vacant Lot. Written 1949; first publication in *CG55*, 18. Also published in *FD* and *CG72*.

The Waste, The Room, The Discarded Timbers. Written 1949; first publication in *CG55*, 19. Also published in *SP, FD,* and *CG72*. *SP* titles the poem "The Drinking Fountain."

Before Waking At Half-Past Six In The Morning. Written 1949; first publication in *CG55*, 20. Also published in *FD* and *CG72*.

Aurora Rose. Written June 1955; first publication in *CG55*, 25, as a holograph. Also published in *Der* and, redrawn, in *CG72*. In *Der* the poem appears as one of four "Prose Poems from Caesar's Gate 1955." The others are "Tears of St Francis," "Source Magic," and "Circulating Lights" (slightly changed) from the limited edition.

The Second Night In The Week. Written 1949; first publication in *CG55*, 27. Also published in *Origin* 1.6 (Summer 1952): 79, *SP, FD,* and *CG72*.

Processionals I. Written 1949–1950; first publication in *CG55*, 29. Also published in *FD* and *CG72*. *Cortèges des feux et des neiges*: processions of fires and snows; *déluges des feux et des neiges:* floods of fires and snows. No identifiable source; the French is probably Duncan's (*CG55* omitted the accents).

Processionals II. Written 1949; first publication in *CG55*, 30. Also published in *Origin* 1.6 (Summer 1952): 79, *SP, FD,* and *CG72*. In *Origin,* the title is "Processional Of The Dead." Between the fourth and the fifth stanzas *Origin* inserts the following stanza: "No flame guides the blind / further than here."

Tears Of St. Francis. Written 1955; first publication in *CG55*, 33, as a holograph. Also published in *Der* and, redrawn, in *CG72*. In *Der* the poem appears as one of four "Prose Poems from Caesar's Gate 1955." *CG72* prints the last five lines as seven lines of verse:

> Seraphic hostesses!
> Survivors of the last safari!
> The devout
> return burnd black by the sun.

He lifts
sightless eyes into the blaze.

Father! Father! the animal sun!

Upon Another Shore Of Hell. Written 1950; first publication in *CG55*, 35.
Also published in *CG72*.

An Incubus. Written 1949–1950(?); first publication in *CG55*, 37. Also published in *CG72*.

Sunday. Written June 1955; first publication in *CG55*, 39, as a holograph.
Also redrawn and published in *CG72*. In *CG72* Duncan dropped the terminal comma in each of the first nine lines and revised lines 6 through 9 as follows:

WHOSE ART IS EXPENSIVE

WHOSE TIME IS MONEY

WHOSE POWER IS IN THE WAR

WHOSE WAR IS EVERYWHERE

Eyesight I. Written 1950; first publication in *CG55*, 41. Also published in *CG72*.

Eyesight II. Written 1950; first publication in *CG55*, 43. Also published in *CG72*.

Bon Voyage! Written June 1955; first publication in *CG55*, 45, as a holograph. Also redrawn and published in *CG72*.

Goodbye To Youth. Written 1949–1950; first publication in *CG55*, 49–53.
Also published in *FD* and *CG72*.

Les mariages des ours, les mirages de bonheur.
C'est pour la jeunesse comme des milles fleurs.
c'est pour la virilité la tristesse, le bon feu.
Songe du coeur fou, mélange du sang pur
et impur. Les passages, les ans, les saluts,
c'est par la mort d'amour.

Marriages of bears, mirages of happiness.
It's for the young who bloom a thousandfold,
for virility it's sadness, the good fire.
Longing of the wild heart, blood mixed pure
and impure. The passages, the years, the greetings,
all through the death of love.

No identifiable source. The French is probably Duncan's, but could be drawn from Octave Uzanne (1852–1931), *"Le calendrier de Vénus"* (Venus's Almanac), a text about the follies of love. Duncan's substantives in this poem also occur in Uzanne. *Le bon feu* in the third line may be a sound-play on *le bon dieu*, a common French expression (which *le bon feu* is not at all).

H.M.S. Bearskin. For details regarding possible relationships between poems and the uncertain status of individual poems in this sequence, see the headnote above, pp. 777–778.

He Entertains At A Dinner Party. Written May 1950; first publication in *CG55*, 57. Also published in *CG72*. On a Tms from May or June 1950 (NBuU), headed "I. He Entertains At A Dinner Party," Duncan has, in ink at the top of the page, "Christ hits the Land of the Dead; seeks out John the Baptist; and sings serenades to the Uninterested Critics." In *CG72* the title is "He Entertains At A Dinner Party In The Bardo State."

He Consults The Tides. Written May 1950; first publication in *CG55*, 58. Also published in *CG72*. In *CG72* the last line reads: "will not find my love hidden there."

To Run With The Hare & Hunt With The Hound. Written May 1950; first publication in *CG55*, 59. Also published in *CG72*.

Great Grief, then, herself! Written May 1950; first publication in *CG55*, 60. Also published in *CG72*.

He Lists Subjects For Great Poetry: 1950. Written May 1950; first publication in *CG55*, 61. Also published in *CG72*.

He Has A Good Time There. Written May 1950; first publication in *CG55*, 62. Also published in *CG72*.

All the way of Forever. Written May 1950; first publication in *CG55*, 63. Also published in *CG72*. The contents page in *CG72* identifies this poem as "Coda," apparently to the whole sequence "H.M.S. Bearskin."

A BOOK OF RESEMBLANCES: POEMS 1950–1953

Despite the dates in the subtitle, Duncan started writing at least one of the poems, "Working Too Long At It," in 1946–47, completing the version published here in 1949, the year he wrote "The Horns Of Artemis" and "Africa Revisited." He wrote seventeen of the book's remaining twenty-nine poems in 1953. "The drawings," Jess wrote on the first page of the *Illustrator's Dummy* for *A Book of Resemblances: Poems 1950–1953* (now in the collection of Washington University, St. Louis, Missouri), "were begun in 1952 following the finishing of 'An Essay at War'—and the projected form of the book I wanted to design was a play upon 'high style,' in an homage to Beardsley, as he shows in *Morte d'Arthur*, and avoiding his grotesque" (quoted in Robert J. Bertholf, *Robert Duncan: A Descriptive Bibliography* [Santa Rosa: Black Sparrow, 1986], 287). In a Tms "Text for page -3- of Announcement" for the book (NBuU), Duncan said "the first drawing was done for *The Song of the Borderguard* in 1952 and the final pages were finished in the Spring of 1966," and commented that "the book has an organic unity and meaning in design."

A manuscript, text and drawings, was finished by the end of 1953, but the book would not be published until 1966, thirteen years later, with many changes to its contents. Duncan submitted it to Grove Press in 1957, but Grove was slow to respond. On 19 December he complained to Robin Blaser that the book "languishes" at Grove. Then, on 4 February 1958, when he was working on the difficult challenge posed by assembling *Selected Poems* for Lawrence Ferlinghetti's Pocket Poets series, he again wrote to Blaser: "I despair of Grove, and feel sad indeed of that. *Book of Resemblances* that was, as I composed it, all discovery of how much I see my life in Poetry now as a whole thing. Yes, like the body, the mind is so definitely incarnate, with hair, and the kind of build it has, its own particular sensuality" (CU-BANC). Grove rejected the manuscript, and the book languished in Duncan's hands until in 1962 the Auerhahn Press agreed to publish it (now somewhat enlarged) in two volumes.

Duncan wrote an advertising flyer for Auerhahn, but when in November 1962 he could not reach any agreement with the publisher about the illustrations in the flyer and the paper to be used for the book, he withdrew the manuscript and publication was cancelled. The advertising flyer was not printed. In it, Duncan wrote:

> The poems in this volume belong to 1950 and 1951, a period of transition, of falling and failing in love, and also of America's falling and failing in war. The Korean War and obsessive homosexual love presented for me corresponding references of lies and defeats, waste and loss. Graves's *The White Goddess* had appeared in 1948, and I had drawn from his argument coordinates of Moon, Muse, and Mother, that began to give a new locus for feeling in which homosexual lovers too had their Nature 'under the Moon's rule.'
>
> It is the period at the same time of falling and failing in poetry—'An Essay at War,' deriving its impulse from Williams's *Paterson,* strives to contain as beauty flaws and inadequacies in the feeling of things—appropriate to the 'police action' in the Orient—a pathetic fallacy?
>
> Now at last, all this problematic stuff is to be published, richly illumined by Jess in drawings that suggest the lasting quality of the poems—the evocations of an inner incurable Romance (quoted in Bertholf, 81).

Duncan continued to tinker with the contents and revise the poems until Henry Wenning set about the publication of the book, which appeared in November 1966.

Preparing the final copy for Wenning, Duncan recopied the poems, seeing them anew, sometimes changing the title. On occasion (as in "A Book of Resemblances," printed elsewhere with its original title "There Could Be A Book Without Nations In Its Chapters") his revision ceased to fit comfortably within the frame of Jess's drawing, and he truncated the text. He also made quite extensive use of a spaced or isolated period (perhaps after William Carlos Williams's practice in his late poems), sometimes drawing it as a large bullet, principally at the end of a line but also in initial or medial positions (these are not recorded in the following notes). Later, in preparing *The First Decade: Selected Poems 1940–1950* and *Derivations: Selected Poems 1950–1956* for Stuart Montgomery at Fulcrum Press in London, he returned to earlier typescripts, principally those drawn from in 1964 when he provided Pauline Butling and Fred Wah with the poems they printed in *Writing Writing*. Major changes are recorded in the following notes.

Introduction. Written 1966; first publication in *BR*, vii–x. *L'homme aime ce qui est vain et mort*: Man loves what is vain and dead (from Arp's *Jours Effeuillées*, translated by Marcel Jean as "Unpetalled Days"); *Fils de la lumière*: Son of light (title of an essay by Arp); *grand chic parisien*: high Parisian style; *Ein Magischer Schatz*: A Magic Treasure (title of an essay by Arp).

Duncan mistakenly ascribed Robert Payne's article to *Horizon*. It appeared in the autumn 1949 issue of Peter Russell's magazine *Nine*.

The Horns Of Artemis. Written 1949; first publication in *Origin* 6 (Summer 1952): 87. Also published in *BR*, 1–2, and in *FD*. *BR* and *FD* drop line 3 in stanza 2; *BR* moves the question mark to the end of the stanza.

Africa Revisited. Written 1949; first publication in *Origin* 6 (Summer 1952): 80–86. Also published in *BR*, 3–11, and in *FD*. In his essay "Poetry Before Language" (1955, collected in *Fictive Certainties*) Duncan wrote of the "dance of the would-be phonemes, . . . as irritating to the brain as pure phones, meaningless sputters, clicks or gurgles, still are," commenting that "the brain was restless for enlargements. B-b-b-b-b-b went the lips on their own, deliting, delited too to please the ear in despite of the brain."

In addition to making his customary changes in spelling, punctuation, stanza- and line-breaks, and the like, Duncan condensed some stanzas in *BR* and *FD* by deletion and recasting syntax or punctuation and recasting lines, especially in section 3 and especially in *FD*. Not all changes are recorded here.

In section 1, 7 lines from the end, *FD* reads "might wreak upon his invention": for "might wreck upon his invention." In section 3, stanza 1, *BR* drops "but ten years younger"; *FD* deletes "so far from the equator's / eternity of season" and prints the first four lines as three, which break at "himself" and "younger." In section 3, stanza 2, *FD* deletes lines 2–6; *BR* reads them as follows:

> He could not repair
> . his tenderness could not repair .
> what his American speech in its tense
> divorce of the past
> had destroyed.

In section 3, stanza 3, *BR* ends stanza 3: "even before Death's rivalry / that I could / argue against Africa."; *FD* ends stanza 3: "even before Death's rivalry / argue against Africa." *BR* and *FD* delete stanzas 4 and 5.

Adam's Song. Written 1950, 1957, 1965; first publication in *BR,* 12–13. Also (in part) published in *Botteghe Oscure* 19 (Spring 1957): 342. The version published in *Botteghe Oscure* is an early draft of the last four stanzas only, beginning: "The war is all about us, the falling away, / despair, our joy." *Botteghe Oscure* drops the last two stanzas, substituting:

> This is the "owl of Minerva
> that flies by night;" too late, too soon,
> the knowing.
>
> Eve, Eve, Eve,
> in Strangeness,
> come with me.
>
> It is as if the Garden were always here,
> even in fear,
> the certain end of the night
> old Paradise.

Working Too Long At It. Written 1946, 1949–1950; first publication in *BR,* 14–15. Not published elsewhere. In 1950 Duncan illuminated and framed a highly reworked version of the poem, condensing the bulk of it to six lines, and leaving the final ten lines more or less intact, possibly in celebration of his attachment to Jess. He later presented it to Robin Blaser.

An Imaginary War Elegy. Written September–October 1950; first publication in *Origin* 6 (Summer 1952): 124–26. Also published in *BR,* 16–19, and in *FD.* "Passages in italics," Duncan said in a note following the text in *FD,* "are from an article on Mao Tse-Tung's poetry by Robert Payne which appeared in *Horizon* in 1950, and italic passages in quotes are from Mao's poetry translated by Payne." The article, "A Note on Two Poems by Mao-Tse-Tung," actually appeared in *Nine* 1 (Autumn 1949): 18–20. *BR* deletes the one-line third stanza; *FD* makes that line the last of stanza 2. *BR* prints the last line of the poem as a single stanza which reads "changed by the changes in his lover's eyes."

The Song Of The Border-Guard. Written December 1950; first publication in *The Song of the Borderguard* (Asheville, NC: Black Mountain College, 1952). Also published in *BR*, 20–22; *Origin* 6 (Summer 1952): 122–23; *FD*.

An Essay At War. Written 1950–1951; first publication in *BR*, 23–44. Also published in part in *The Nation* 193.18 (20 Nov. 1961): 434, as "Fire Dying, From An Essay At War"; and in *Der.*

De ses neufs ouvertures
encadrées des boucles
l'homme exhale
de la vapeur bleue, du brouillard gris,
de fumée noire

From his nine openings
framed in hair
man exhales
blue steam, grey fog,
black smoke

There is no identifiable source, though the notion of nine openings occurs in thaumaturgical and alchemical texts. The French is probably Duncan's.

Profonda e chiara sussistenza / dell' alto lume!: the profound and shining subsistence / of the lofty Light (from Dante, *Paradiso,* Canto xxxiii, 115–116). Duncan added the exclamation mark.

In a letter to Denise Levertov dated 21 August 1959 he called "An Essay At War" "a botched poem" (Robert J. Bertholf and Albert Gelpi, eds., *The Letters of Robert Duncan and Denise Levertov* [Stanford: Stanford University Press, 2004], 204) but in 1974 said that it "proposed pretty much the process of my later poetry . . . striking off from *Paterson.* And it picks up . . . Stein" (Robert Duncan, interview by Howard Mesch, *Unmuzzled Ox* 4.2 [1976]: 80). He discussed the poem at some length in "Wind and Sea" (67–74), a talk he gave in Buffalo on 23 November 1980.

Der deletes the final line.

Of The Art. Written 1950–1955; revised 1957–(1964); first publication in

The Needle 1.1 (April 1956): 5. Also published in *Botteghe Oscure* 19 (Spring 1957): 341, and in *BR,* 45. The *BR* text is printed here. In *The Needle* the lines are arranged in eight stanzas of 3, 2, 2, 3, 8, 7, 8, and 2 lines respectively; in *Botteghe Oscure,* in nine stanzas of 1, 2, 2, 5, 8, 6, 5, 3, and 2 lines respectively. In *The Needle* the first four stanzas read as follows:

> we said the honey was rare.
> We said: the child
> has gatherd color from the rose itself.
>
> And she, angry, said,
> obscurely defending her self-esteem:
>
> The child had no care
> or lacks skill.
>
> This skill,
> we said, is not a thing learnd
> but a thing loved.

In stanza 3, lines 3–4, *The Needle* reads "no greater passion knew nor spoke / than this child makes known to us." In stanza 4, both *The Needle* and *Botteghe Oscure* delete "in the opinion of others" and substitute as follows:

> by vanity of exhibits, criticisms,
> values, great works,
> efforts, achievements,
> rivalries, denials, purposes.

Cats (1) and *Cats (2).* Written 1952; first publication in *BR,* 58. Not published elsewhere.

Dance: Early Spring Weather Magic. Written fall 1952; first publication in *BR,* 60–61. Also published in *Der.*

Forced Lines. Written January–February 1953; published in *BR,* 63. Also published in *WW* and *Der,* in both as part of "Imagining in Writing."

A Poem In Stretching. Written February 1953; first publication in *WW.* Also published in *BR,* 64–66, and in *Der,* in both as "A Poem in Stretching." *BR* begins the first paragraph, sentence 20, with "It is the queen of hearts not hurts . . . "

Poetry Disarranged. Written 16 June 1953; first publication in *WW,* 48–49, as "6/16/53." Also published as "Poetry Disarranged" in *BR,* 67–68, and as "6/16/53" in *Der.* In the first paragraph, opening sentence, *BR* drops the parentheses and ends " . . . Dis in his arranging means"; in the third sentence, *BR* reads " . . . preconception at best the darkness . . . " *BR* combines the fourth and fifth paragraphs. In the fifth paragraph, first sentence, *BR* substitutes "net" for "web"; in the last sentence, *BR* substitutes "threads" for "ashes."

A Book of Resemblances. Written May–June 1953; published in *BR,* 68–69. Also published in *WW,* and in *Der* as "There Could Be A Book Without Nations In Its Chapters." Preparing and transcribing the text for *BR,* Duncan considerably recast the poem, as here printed. For the earlier typescript version in *WW,* see below.

A Dream Of The End Of The World. Written 27 January 1953; first publication in *Origin* 1.14 (Autumn 1954): 127–28. Also published in *BR,* 70–71. In paragraph 6, penultimate sentence, *BR* reads "A calling to all loons became a calling to us."

Lord Master Mouse. Written spring 1953; first publication in *Foot* 1 (September 1959): 18. Also published in *BR,* 72, and in *Burning Deck* 1 (Fall 1962): 26.

Shells. Written 1 March 1953; first publication in *Black Mountain Review* 5 (1955): 38–39. Also published, as "Surrealist Shells," in *BR,* 75. For lines 21–22, *BR* reads: "The rest on the right can be seen as left. / This is a field of righteousness. Night thoughts." After line 25, *BR* adds a new line: "Max Ernst in a hurry hairy."

These Miracles Are Mirrors In The Open Sky For Philip Lamantia. Written 22 June–13 July 1953; first publication in *BR,* 76. Not published elsewhere.

Conversion. Written June–July 1953(?); first publication in *Origin* 1.14 (Autumn 1954): 128, as "A Conversion." Also published in *BR,* 77, as "Conversion."

Salvages: An Evening Piece. Written April 1953; first publication in *City Lights* 4 (Fall 1953): 31. Also published in *BR,* 78–79. In the 1950s and 1960s Jess reworked earlier nonobjective paintings of his own or others he found in thrift shops as "Salvages."

Reflections. Written April–May 1953; first publication in *Origin* 1.14 (Autumn 1954), as "Love Poem." Also published in *BR,* 80, and, as "Love Poem," in *Burning Deck* 1 (Fall 1962): 28. For lines 15–17, *Burning Deck* substitutes elision marks for the closing period of line 15, and then reads: "to hear. There is no yearning, / no burning in your passing by." *BR* restores line 15 to read as in *Origin,* and then combines lines 16–17 to read: "There is no yearning in thy passing by."

Salvages. Lassitude. Written May 1953; first publication in *Origin* 14 (Autumn 1954): 123–24. Also published in *BR,* 83. The first five words of stanza 5, line 2 in *BR* read: "of the senses from sound."

Friedl. Written 10 May 1953; first publication in *Origin* 14 (Autumn 1954): 124–25. Also published in *BR,* 84–85.

Songs For The Jews From Their Book Of Splendours. Written May 1953; first publication in *Origin* 14 (Autumn 1954): 126–27. Also published in *BR,* 86–87, as "Two Poems For The Jews From Their Book Of The Splendor"; and in *The Gist of Origin,* edited by Cid Corman (New York: Grossman, 1975) as "Songs For The Jews From Their Book Of Splendours." In part I, line 11, *BR* reads "Uncomfortable Jews" for "O contemptible jews." In part II, line 1, *BR* reads "cunning Jews!" for "serpent jews!"

The Scattering. Written May–June 1953(?); first publication in *Burning Deck* 1 (Fall 1962): 26. Also published in *BR,* 88.

Image Of Hector. Written May–June 1953(?); first publication in *Burning Deck* 1 (Fall 1962): 31. Also published in *BR,* 89.

The Lover. Written May–June 1953(?); first publication in *Burning Deck* 1 (Fall 1962): 26. Also published in *BR,* 91. For the first line, *BR* reads: "I have been seeing his face every where, the face of a former lover."

NAMES OF PEOPLE

Names of People is a companion volume to *A Book of Resemblances: Poems 1950–1953,* though it was published two years later, in October 1968. Here too Duncan drew on the notebooks in which, from about 1950 to about 1954, he had worked almost exclusively on imitations of Gertrude Stein, and which were his major source for the poems in *BR, NP,* and *Writing Writing.* In preparing early typescripts of *WW* for publication, he included some of these poems, and wrote all of those in *NP* between the middle of 1951 and May 1952, initially calling the book "Imitations With Introduction." In "My Imitations Of Gertrude Stein" (Tms, NBuU) he said, "I have chosen these particular portraits because they have to do about painting," and Jess designed most of the fifteen titled drawings in the book to supplement that intent. As part of the book's careful design, the subtitle "Stein Imitations from 1952" and the thirteen titles of poems and sequences were printed in holograph: they are here printed in italics. In preparing the text of *Der,* Duncan reorganized and reordered four of them in a section of "Imitations Of Gertrude Stein 1951–1952." In treating the two items in "First" and the six in "A Leave As You May" as separate poems, but preserving "An Arrangement" as a sequence, Duncan suggested that the boundaries between the ten resulting poems were permeable within the sequences as printed here. Other poems in this section of *Der* were drawn from *BR* and *WW* (see Appendix 1 for the full Table of Contents of *Der*).

The "People" of the title are mostly painters, many of them teachers or students at the San Francisco Art Institute when Jess was enrolled as a student there. In "Notes on Poetics: Regarding Olson's 'Maximus,'" *Black Mountain Review* 6 (1956), Duncan wrote of their "energy / embodied in the painting (felt), which is now muscular as well as visual, contain as well as apparent" (202).

In revising a few of the poems for *Derivations,* Duncan made his customary orthographic changes in spelling, punctuation, line-breaks and the like. These changes are not noted here.

First. Sequence title not in *Der,* which treats the sections as separate poems.

A Language For Poetry. Written 1951; first publication in *NP,* 5. Also published in *Der.*

Are Cats? Written 1951; first publication in *NP,* 5. Also published in *Der* as "Are Cats."

Names Of People. Written 1951; first publication in *NP,* 7. Also published in *Der.*

A Leave As You May. Written 1951; first published in *NP,* 8–11. Also published in *Der. Der* treats the sequence title as a poem title, and treats each section of the sequence as a separate poem.

Upon His Return. Written 1952; first publication in *NP,* 12–13. Not published elsewhere.

Two Painters. Written 1952; first publication in *NP,* 14–16. Not published elsewhere.

An Arrangement. Written 1952; first publication in *Burning Deck* 1 (Fall 1962): 26–27. Also published in *NP,* 17–19, and in *Der. Der* omits the dedication to James Broughton and Kermit Sheets. Broughton's Centaur Press, for which Sheets was compositor, had published *Medieval Scenes* in 1950. In 1955 Duncan wrote another poem, "Three Pages From A Birthday Book" (collected in *The Opening of the Field*), for Broughton; Duncan would document their severe quarrel over Helen Adam's play *San Francisco's Burning* in his sequence "What Happened," written in 1962, published in the "Valentine Issue" of *Open Space* in February 1964, and collected in *Roots and Branches.*

An About Face. Written 1952; first publication in *NP,* 21–22. Not published elsewhere. Claire Mahl (1917–1988) was the principal force behind the short-lived San Francisco tabloid *The Artist's View,* which exclusively devoted the contents of each issue to a given painter, sculptor, or poet. Its purpose, she said in her editorial in the prospectus issue (May 1952), was "to present the artist through what he has to say for himself." Issue 5 was assigned to Duncan, issue 7 to Jess.

A Coat Of Arms. Written 1952; first publication in *NP*, 23–25. Not published elsewhere.

Remembering. Written 1952; first publication in *NP*, 26–27. Not published elsewhere.

A Mexican Straight Summer. Written 1952; first publication in *NP*, 28–29. Not published elsewhere.

Robert Berg At Florence. Written 1952; first publication in *NP*, 30–31. Not published elsewhere.

An Evening At Home. Written 1952; first publication in *NP*, 32–34. Not published elsewhere.

A Design For Flack. Written 1952; first publication in *NP*, 35–36. Not published elsewhere. *Saludo Amigo*: Hello Friend.

PLAY TIME PSEUDO STEIN

All the texts printed here are from the second edition. The colophon to the first edition states: "This book, which was originally intended as part of the series of signed holograph limited editions published by Poets Press, was shelved due to a disagreement between author & publisher on the subject of numerology. It has been produced in this numbered, unsigned edition of 35 copies in order to provide those who have subscribed to the holograph with an item which we would feel would be of special interest to them. It is not for sale. Diane di Prima." The "numerology" concerned RD's expectation that he would receive twenty-six lettered copies, decorated by him, as the "author's edition," which—because of her prior arrangement with Robert Wilson of the Phoenix Book Shop—di Prima could not give him (the production of the holograph series was to be financed through the sale of the manuscript to Wilson and the strict limitation of the edition). The second edition, published by Julia Newman at the Tenth Muse Bookshop, consisted of facsimiles of the first edition—Duncan had kept a photocopy of his manuscript—with the addition of the epigraph, two further poems (numbers 4 and 5), and a four-page preface giving "A Little History of this Edition," which explained why di Prima "would not publish the book." All five poems were written on the same day, 5 January 1953.

Arrows Is Arrows Is Arrows Is Arrows Is. Written 1969(?); first publication in *PTPS*, 9. Not published elsewhere.

1942, A Story. Written 5 January 1953; first publication in *PTPS*, 11–14.

A Fairy Play A Play. Written 5 January 1953; first publication in *PTPS*, 15–17.

How. Written 5 January 1953; first publication in *PTPS*, 18–20.

A Butter Machine. Written 5 January 1953; first publication in *PTPS,* 21.

S.M.O.K.I.N.G. T.H.E. C.I.G.A.R.E.T.T.E. Written 5 January 1953; first publication in *PTPS,* 22. Also published in *WW* and in *Combustion* 6 (April 1968): 5. Two typos in *Combustion* have been silently corrected; the version there and in *WW* adds a comma after "vice" in the first paragraph. In neither version is the poem numbered.

WRITING WRITING

The line drawings and words on the cover of the book are strongly suggestive, in a cubist manner, of the upper torso and head of a man seated at a table with his head leaning on his fist, writing or thinking. The words give the title as *Writing Writing / A Composition Book / For Madison 1953 / Stein Imitations,* but in Notebook 16 (NBuU), in a draft preface written in July or early August 1955, Duncan titled it *A Composition Book 1953–1955 (A Copy Book),* and that September told Creeley in a letter that it is "now to be calld *A Copy Book*" (Robert J. Bertholf, *Robert Duncan: A Descriptive Bibliography* [Santa Rosa: Black Sparrow, 1986], 59).

He wrote the poems between June 1952 and July/August 1955, along with (among others) many of the poems in *A Book of Resemblances: Poems 1950– 1953, Names of People,* and *Letters: Poems mcmlii-mcmlvi.* At various stages of transcribing the holograph notebook poems to typescript and later selecting and arranging them, Duncan tentatively reconfigured both their selection and their arrangement into possible books; and the contents of *BR, NP,* and *WW* remained fluid until those books were actually published. He prepared the final typescript in August or September 1955, at which time he wrote a preface to the book, but the book was not published (in mimeograph) until 1964. The published typescript was prepared by Fred Wah and Pauline Butling; Butling reports that Duncan assiduously read proofs, insisted on many corrections to the mimeo skins as they were typed, and provided the "Birthday Dirge" when it turned out there was room for an additional poem on the final errata sheet. Butling also reports that Duncan wanted the book to look like a "school bluebook or exercise book." Duncan drew, in 1964, a decorated page for each of the section titles.

Concurrent with *WW*'s publication in May 1964, Duncan revised thirty-six of its fifty-one pieces for inclusion in *Derivations: Selected Poems 1950– 1956,* where he gathered them under various heads: "Imitations of Gertrude Stein 1951–1952"; "Writing Writing"; "A Little Poetics"; and "Imitations Of Gertrude Stein 1953–1955" (for details, see Appendix 1). In setting the texts for *Der* the English printer (Villiers Publications, in London) justified the right margin in what were apparently prose pieces, thus destroying the blurred and permeable boundaries between prose and poetry in Duncan's original text. Most of the revisions were, as usual, to spelling, line- and stanza-breaks, and punctuation, with minor shifts in phrasing and vocabulary. These are not recorded here.

Duncan's unpublished and possibly unfinished preface, in Notebook 16 (NBuU), reads as follows:

Preface For A Composition Book
1953–1955 [A COPY BOOK]

TO GERTRUDE STEIN
IN CLOUDS OF WORDS

 —Since I was seventeen—for almost twenty years now—the writing of Gertrude Stein has been a constant companion, a constant joy.

I have grown toward it; returning again and again to her counsels. And here, selected from work done over a period of the last three years: what I have learned at all.

For where we love we learn; the face of the beloved schools our own expression. It is this kind of submission in love and delight that I make to my mistress.

At times I have barely echoed her manner, fondly mimickd her way.

A copy book. For another ape of God.

Yet, it is for something else—for the fact that even in such extensions of the Stein manner as "The Code of Justinian" with its participial phrases, I was freed to develop an argument—by the orders of a style; or for the fact that so much of my own heart springs forth everywhere in this copy work.

It is by my heart's allegiance that I continue that I may be some day her true disciple. This is she is another Gertrude Stein, who appears to me in the mysteries of her work.

THE PRACTICE: Narrow has been considerd a virtue of the mind—the straight and narrow; broad minded or a broad understanding is almost a certain virtue in our day. Depth and height are terms as necessary to the description of a philosophy or a poetic vision as they are to a geology. Shallows are still a barely tolerated vice of a mind. The sensual intellect does not despise contemplation of little depths; but what has one conquerd in a sense in wading?

Duncan marked off the opening paragraph, which perhaps then furnished material for the book's dedication.

Turning Into. Written June 1952; first publication in *WW,* 5. Also published in *Der,* and in Edward B. Germain, ed., *Surrealist Poetry* (Harmondsworth: Penguin, 1978).

Coming Out Of. Written June 1952; first publication in *WW,* 6. Also published in *Der*, and in Edward B. Germain, ed., *Surrealist Poetry* (Harmondsworth: Penguin, 1978).

Making Up. Written June 1952; first publication in *WW*, 7. Also published in *Der*.

Out. Written June 1952; first publication in *WW*, 7. Not published elsewhere.

A Scene. Written June 1952; first publication in *WW*, 7. Also published in *Der*, and, as the fourth numbered section of "From My Notebook," in both the 1952 and 1966 editions of *Fragments of a Disorderd Devotion*.

The Beginning of Writing. Written January–February 1953; first publication in *WW*, 11–12. Also published in *Der*.

Imagining In Writing. Written January–February 1953; first publication in *WW*, 12–14. Also published in *Der*. For the revised version of the first two sections, see "Forced Lines" in *BR* above. In *Der*, the final section, stanza 2, line 3, reads "Disfigured for music" for "disfigured."

Writing As Writing. Written 6 January 1953; first publication in *WW*, 15–16. Also published in *Der;* the second section published as a seven-line poem, "The Landscape Revised To Portray A Reality," in *Combustion* 5 (January 1958): 3. Except for the section published in *Combustion, Der* prints "Writing As Writing" as justified prose. In section 1, paragraph 3, sentence 5, *Der* adds "I would go to," so that the sentence begins "I strive in inscribing in its different lengths the lengths of description I would go to, the lasts . . . "

Possible Poetries. Written spring 1953; first publication in *WW*, 16. Also published in *Der*. In *Der* the second and third poems are titled "Possible Poetries: A Postscript" and "Possible Poetries: A Postcard," respectively.

An Imaginary Letter. Written spring 1953; first publication in *WW*, 17. Also published in *Der*.

Imaginary Letter. Written spring 1952; first publication in *WW*, 17–18. Also published in *Der*.

Imaginary Letter. His Intention. Written spring 1952; first publication in *WW*, 19. Also published in *Der*.

Motto. Written spring 1953; first publication in *WW*, 20. Also published in *Der*.

Writing At Home In History. Written spring 1953; first publication in *WW*, 20–22. Also published in *Der*. In the antepenultimate paragraph, penultimate sentence, *Der* adds "the muse meant for us" after "our amusement."

I Am Not Afraid. Written spring 1953; first publication in *WW*, 22. Also published in *Der*, where the final word is capitalized, "Messenger."

An Interlude. Of Rare Beauty. Written spring 1953; first publication in

Combustion 6 (April 1958): 4. Also published in *WW,* 23, and in *Der. WW* and *Der* break the last line at "for naming." *WW* follows this poem with a row of three spaced asterisks, centered, followed by a centered line reading, "End Writing Writing."

Hung-Up. Written spring 1953; first publication in *WW,* 27–28. Not published elsewhere.

The Code of Justinian. A Discourse On Justice. Written spring 1953; first publication in *WW,* 28–31. Not published elsewhere.

The Discourse On Sin. Written March 1953; first publication in *WW,* 31–33. Not published elsewhere.

No, I cant reach you. Written spring 1953; first publication in *WW,* 35. Not published elsewhere.

Descriptions Of Imaginary Poetries. Written May–June 1952; first publication, as "Pages From a Notebook. 4." in *The Artist's View* 5 (July 1955): 4. Also published in *WW,* 39–40, *Der,* and, as the fourth section of "Pages from a Notebook," in *A Selected Prose* (New York: New Directions, 1995), 21–22. In section 4, first sentence, *WW* reads: "The poem can hardly lift these words." In section 6, fifth sentence, *Der* reads: "Sing sting sing slings and arrows of fortune."

Rhyme Mountain Particular. Written 14 February 1953; first publication in *WW,* 41. Also published in *Der.* In the last paragraph, *Der* deletes the fifth and sixth sentences.

An Advertisement For A Fair Play. Written 23 February 1953; first publication in *WW,* 41. Not published elsewhere.

Progressing. Written February 1953; first publication in *WW,* 42. Not published elsewhere.

This Is The Poem They Are Praising As Loaded. Written 22 February 1953; first publication in *WW,* 42. Also published in *Der.*

Orchards. Written 2 April 1953; first publication in *WW,* 42–43. Also published in *Der.*

A Train of Thought. Written 2 April 1953; first publication in *WW,* 43. Not published elsewhere.

The Feeling Of Language In Poetry. Written 13 April 1953; first publication in *WW,* 44–47. Not published elsewhere.

Sentences: Carrying Weights and Measures. Written 19 April 1953; first publication in *WW,* 47. Also published in *Der.*

There Could Be A Book Without Nations In Its Chapters. Written May–June 1953; published in *WW,* 47–48. Also published in *BR* and *Der.* For publication in *BR,* Duncan considerably recast the poem, titling it "A Book of Resemblances." For that text, see above. In *Der* the next three poems,

"6/16/53" (retitled "Poetry Disarranged" in *BR*), "6/22/53," and "6/27" are, though listed in the table of contents as separate titles, printed as sections of this poem.

6/22/53. Written 22 June 1953 and 27 June 1953; first publication in *WW,* 49; also published in *Der.* In *Der,* printed as sections of "There Could Be A Book Without Nations In Its Chapters."

Rewriting Byron. Written 13 July 1953; first publication in *WW,* 49. Not published elsewhere.

A Morass. Written August 1953; first publication in *WW,* 50–51. Also published in *Der.*

Canvas Coming Into Itsélf. For Jess. Written 1955; first publication in *WW,* 51. Not published elsewhere. In one Tms this poem and the poem following, "How Do You Know You Are Thru?" constitute a single poem.

How Do You Know You Are Thru? Written 1955; first publication in *WW,* 52. Also published in *Der,* where Duncan changed the opening sentence (as distinct from the title) to read: "How do you know you are thru?"

Increasing. Written 1955; first publication in *Semina* 8 (1963). Also published in *WW,* 53.

Road Piece. Written 1955; first publication in *WW,* 53. Not published elsewhere.

Rotund Religion. Written 1953/1954; first publication in *WW,* 54. Also published in *Der.* In line 5, *Der* reads "difficult cult" for "different cult."

Three. Written 1955; first publication in *WW,* 54–55. Not published elsewhere.

Several Poems. In Prose. Written (1954); first publication in *Black Mountain Review* 5 (Summer 1955): 36–37. Also published in *WW,* 155–56, and in *Der. Il y a pas de père:* there is no father. In the tenth section, *Der* inserts: "An Aftereffect" between "craven before inspection" and "Poor poetry!"

Load Your Automatic Poetry Before Its Begun. Written (1954); first publication in *WW,* 56. Not published elsewhere. As laid out on the page in *WW* this poem could, entirely in upper case, be read as a title; as the first part of the title of the next poem, "Rings"; or even as the final line of "Several Poems. In Prose." In Notebook 2, which covers the years 1952–1955 (CU-BANC), immediately following "Several Poems. In Prose.," Duncan wrote the poem out between two lines drawn from margin to margin across the page, as follows: "Load your automatic poetry before its be gun."

Rings. Written 20 June 1955; first publication in *WW,* 56. Also published in *Der.*

Syllables. Written 1955; first publication in *WW,* 56–57. Also published in *Der.*

Stuff Ark Mower Bottle. Written 30 July 1955; first publication in *WW,* 57. Also published in *Der.*

Another Ido. Written July–August 1955; first publication in *WW,* 58. Also published in *Der. Sobre de las olas de calor:* on the waves of heat; *verano:* summer; *rano pequeño:* a little frog.

A Birthday Dirge For Lynne Brown. Written December 1952; first publication in *WW,* errata sheet. Not published elsewhere.

UNCOLLECTED WORK 1952–1956

Whose this liddl boob coming? Written 1952; first publication in *Boob* 1 (1952): 2. In 1952 Duncan and Jess published *Boob Number One: A Dada Derivative: Lovely Lovely Lovely : Boob Number One !* as two single sheets, the title (sometimes lacking the exclamation mark) typed (after the page had been printed) in upper case down the right margin of the first leaf. They prepared a third leaf which was never printed. *Boob* was a private publication which over the years they gave away to various friends. Duncan's text, on p. 2, is in his holograph. A crudely cut oval-shaped and somewhat grainy photograph of a newly hatched bird is on the right-hand side of the page, immediately followed by an outline drawing of an egg, followed by the closing two lines.

Walking on Kearny Street. Written 1952; first publication in *The Artist's View* 0 (May 1952): 4. Also published in *Derivations: Selected Poems 1950–1956. The Artist's View* was a broadsheet newsprint magazine, published monthly "by poets, painters and sculptors," which devoted each issue to the work of a single artist or writer. The prospectus issue was numbered zero, and contained work by several hands, including Landis Everson, Madeline Gleason, and Philip Lamantia. See also the note on "An About Face" in *Names of People,* above.

Uncollected Stein Imitations. Audit/Poetry, edited by Michael Anania and Charles Doria and published in Buffalo, N.Y., devoted the sixty-three pages of text in *Audit/Poetry* 4.3 (1967) entirely to Duncan's work, gathering (and dating) "A Play With Masks," Duncan's translation of Nerval's "Chimeras" (collected in *Bending the Bow*), and over a dozen poems, along with some critical prose, all written between 1948 and 1966. It identified the eight poems gathered here as "from the period of *Writing Writing* (1953)."

The King: A Regret. Written 1953; first publication in *Audit/Poetry* 4.3 (1967): 33–34.

Cloudy. Written 1953; first publication in *Audit/Poetry* 4.3 (1967): 34.

A New Version of Heavenly City Earthly City. Written 1953; first publication in *Audit/Poetry* 4.3 (1967): 34.

Imaginary Letter. Written 1953; first publication in *Audit/Poetry* 4.3 (1967): 35.

Young Men. Written 1953; first publication in *Audit/Poetry* 4.3 (1967): 35.

Sensational News. Written 1953; first publication in *Audit/Poetry* 4.3 (1967): 36–37.

Reserve Moon Handle Maker And Wing. Written 1953; first publication in *Audit/Poetry* 4.3 (1967): 37.

At The Bakery—The Cannibalistic Cookie-People. Written 1953; first publication in *Audit/Poetry* 4.3 (1967): 37.

Aubade. Written (1953); first publication in *Combustion* 5 (1958): 5.

Elegy Written 4.7.53 For Jack Spicer. Written 7 April 1953; first publication in *San Francisco Earthquake* 1.3 (Spring 1968): 75–78. Also published in *Manroot* 10 (late Fall 1974–Winter 1975): 35–37. An endnote in *San Francisco Earthquake* reads "in memoriam Jack Spicer, poet (1925–1965)." A Tms at NBuU identifies the poem as "from the Writing Writing workbook" and dates the final section 13 July 1953. Jack Spicer died 17 August 1965.

The Green Lady. Written June 1955; first publication in *Botteghe Oscure* 19 (Spring 1957): 342–45. Also published in *Der.* Duncan originally dedicated "The Green Lady" to Helen Adam, sending her a draft of the poem from Mallorca in 1955 (the relevant correspondence, along with that version, appears in Kristen Prevallet, ed., "Helen Adam and Robert Duncan Selected Correspondence 1955–1956," *Apex of the M* 6 [Fall 1997]: 141–146). When he reprinted the poem in *Der* he included it among the poems in *Letters,* placing it between "Correspondences" and "August Sun."

The Fear That Precedes. . . Written 1955; first publication in *Evergreen Review* 1.2 (February 1957): 22.

Poems from the Limited Edition of Caesar's Gate. Written 1955; first publication in the 1955 edition of *Caesar's Gate: Poems 1949–1950.* See also the headnote to *Caesar's Gate: Poems 1949–1950,* above. Each of the poems was written in response to Jess's collages, prepared for this edition. Duncan's records of the distribution, and his correspondence, suggest that he tried to suit the poem to the recipient; occasionally, as Duncan's lists show, he realigned copies and recipients.

Three lettered copies, A ("Circulating Lights"), B ("Source Magic"), and C ("Presence"), went to the poet, the artist, and the publisher (Duncan, Jess, and Creeley). The ten numbered copies were sold to friends (who eagerly and rapidly subscribed), as follows: 1. "Shadows of The Smoke," Helen Adam; 2. "The Faith," Ruth Witt-Diamant; 3. "Where," Tommy Langworthy; 4. "In The Dolls House," Liam O'Gallagher; 5. "Watches," Jonathan Williams; 6. "Consolations Of Philosophy," Robin Blaser; 7. "Tra^{ns}versals

Of The Church," Hilde and David Burton; 8. "Show," James Broughton; 9. "To The Stairwell," Kit and Ilse Barker; 10. "The Descents Of Night," Fred Snowden.

Duncan printed two of these texts (A and B) in *Derivations,* and retrieved a typescript copy of one (9. "To The Stairwell") from its recipients. Copies A, B, 1, and 6 are in NBuU; copy 9 is in the collection of Washington University, St. Louis, Missouri; the remaining copies are in private collections.

Circulating Lights. Also published in *Der.* In paragraph 1, last word, *Der* reads "arise" for "rise."

Source Magic. Also published in *Der.* In the final paragraph, *Der* adds a comma after "figure."

Show. Text, previously published in Robert J. Bertholf, *Robert Duncan: A Descriptive Bibliography* (Santa Rosa: Black Sparrow, 1986), 134–135, provided by James S. Jaffe Rare Books. Duncan arranged the poems in three rows of two, and drew frames around each, with an ornate "A" between "Show" and "Crown," and a similarly decorative "W" at the intersection of "Show" and "Crown" with "Love" and "I am." The last line of "Love" spills into the frame of "Time."

Spanish Lessons. Written 1955(?). First publication in *Der,* 86. *Bocadillo:* snack, tidbit, piece of candy (Americanism); *bocas:* mouths; *pollilas:* clothes moths, moth larvae; *verano. Es en verano:* In summer. It's in summer; *calor:* heat, ardor; *Hace mucho color. De rojo?:* It's a lot of color. In red?; *Tostado:* toasted (bread), roasted (coffee), worn out (Americanism).

Alteration. Written 1955; first publication in *Audit/Poetry* 4.3 (1967): 33. Duncan wrote this poem out, omitting the title, on the endpaper of copy #16 of the hardbound edition of *Letters: Poems mcmlii-mcmlvi,* alongside an ink drawing (NBuU). There, the final line of the poem reads "is trace" instead of "is a ruin in its wake." The poem is dated 1955 in *Audit/Poetry.*

THE CAT AND THE BLACKBIRD

Ham and Mary Tyler's daughter Brenda was born in July 1946, about six months after they'd moved, Duncan accompanying them, into Treesbank farm. Duncan and Jess could find few acceptable children's books to read to Brenda, so in 1952 or more likely 1953 decided to produce their own; but they didn't finish it until 1958. *The Cat and The Blackbird* consists of forty-eight pages of drawings and text handwritten by Jess, who drew ten of the book's pages in 1953–54, and the rest at Stinson Beach in 1958. It was eventually published in 1967, by White Rabbit Press.

Duncan began writing *Faust Foutu* in January 1950, and finished the first three acts in 1953; that autumn he rented a mimeograph machine, printed copies off, and circulated them among friends; later—possibly in 1953, probably some time in 1954—he completed Act Four and added it to the mimeographed edition; this became the acting script of *Faust Foutu* (*FF53*). The title page of *Faust Foutu: Act One* dates the play 1952–1954. A somewhat enigmatic entry in Notebook 14 (NBuU) dated 30 December 1953, at the end of an entry on Schoenberg, shows that Duncan had briefly reached an impasse, whether in revision or in initial composition is not wholly clear, since there is no Act Five:

> In working on Faust at this point I have reachd a technical exhaustion; and setting out with the determination that such a large work wld. be entirely composed "as it went along" with no working over has provoked a crisis / the other extreme for the last act—a complete re-vision might be tried. Let's say a selection made of significant passages from the first four acts (as I made pieces of Marlowe's *Faust* and his *Tamburlaine*); then new selection processes over Marlowe and Goethe and Valery—for the composition of a thematic structure, a highly devised death scene. The whole "dramatic" concept fed by the casting of the tableau. It will necessitate working out usable approximations from the miserable translation of Goethe (Modern Library).
>
> The shock will be structural—a dramatic emotion rising from the form. Scored almost in a musical sense for voices. To "crystallize" the content of the play.

With *FF53* as the script, he directed a reading performance at Black Mountain College in the summer of 1954, with music by Stefan Wolpe. In 1958, White Rabbit Press published *Foust Foutu: Act One of Four Acts: A Comic Mask* (*FF1*) and planned further pamphlets of Acts Two, Three, and Four, which never materialized; in 1959, Duncan—with the imprint Enkidu Surrogate—himself published a revised version (with drawings) of the complete play (*FF59*) at Stinson Beach. *FF1*, immediately following the cast list (which is the same as that in *FF59*), identifies the cast "as produced in a dramatic reading at KING UBU's gallery, January 1954, at 3119 Fillmore, San Francisco"—the same address (and probably the same public performance) as that given in *FF59* for the reading performance of January 1955 at The Six Gallery. Ida Hodes (who was in the cast) recalled that Duncan revised the text during rehearsals. *FF59* is the text printed here.

The play engaged Duncan's attention intermittently for six years. In "Pages From A Notebook," *The Artist's View* 5 (July 1953), he published the following "Notes Midway On My Faust":

Faust is right when he sez everything is Truth. But each of us finds everything beyond his conception. And even of the everything with which we compose our minds we have constructed designs of which we knew nothing, edifices of much that we had named lies we have fitted, ourselves, into monuments of eternal truth.

The malice of churches, the malice of witches: how can they exceed each other? The wisdom of the parent, the wisdom of the child: how can they exceed each other? The idiocy of fan-dancers, the idiocy of poets: how can they exceed each other?

The only thing a student can learn from his teacher is what he can teach his teacher. What can a teacher learn from a student?

My FAUST is not a very divine Comedy. At times in writing it I am dismayd by the cheap turns that seem to suffice: but if one must have revelation, one must accept that what is reveald may not be disgraceful in any glamorous sense.

Writing is compounded of wisdom and intuition. Faust seeks to wrench himself free from the world of wisdom and to achieve pure intuition. My lot is not Faust's lot, but the play's lot: this conflict unresolved. But then the trouble of the soul is not in this carcass a tug of war or a choice of two worlds. Everywhere dissenting, contradictory voices speak up, I find. I don't seek a synthesis but a mêlée. It is only as I have somewhat accepted my unconsequential necessities that I have been able to undertake a play. But a play is a play here—a prolonged charged aimless, constantly aimd, play ground. Only play for me did not mean slides, games, teeter-totters and tots; but moods, cities and desires. In the jungle of words and the life in doubts afterwards, I have discovered certain bright courses after my own heart: not to be saved; and then to portray carnal pleasures that the world denies, we deny ourselves. Well, part of the drama of holding back and immersing oneself is the sheer sexual set-to of marriage and our dreams. There is no contradiction between the two, but we set them up in order to avoid the perplexity, the "peril of our souls" in freedom. The problem is that we dread all inconsequential experience; our taboo is at root against unintelligible passions.

I have "selected" my works, weeded out the poetry which is not all of a tone, and composed a works that has a remote consistency. But to resurrect everything: and one will discover my true book—no pleasure for aesthetes. A composite, indecisive literature, attempting the rhapsodic, the austere, the mysterious, the sophisticated, the spontaneous, "higglety-pigglety" as Emory Lowenthal sez.

The host of my heros, gods and models betray an unsettled spirit. (Enter two Devils and the Clown runs up and down crying) Two Devils? What a simple distraction.

Where I am ambitious only to emulate, imitate, reconstrue, approximate, duplicate: Ezra Pound, Gertrude Stein, Joyce, Virginia Woolf, Dorothy Richardson, Wallace Stevens, D. H. Lawrence, Edith Sitwell, Cocteau, Mallarmé, Marlowe, St. John of the Cross, Yeats, Jonathan Swift, Jack Spicer, Céline, Charles Henri Ford, Rilke, Lorca, Kafka, Arp, Max Ernst, St.-John Perse, Prévert, Laura Riding, Apollinaire, Brecht, Shakespeare, Ibsen, Strindberg, Joyce Cary, Mary Butts, Freud, Dali, Spenser, Stravinsky, William Carlos Williams and John Gay.

Higglety-pigglety: Euripides and Gilbert. The Strawhat Reviewers, Goethe (of the AUTOBIOGRAPHY—I have never read FAUST) & H.D. The despair of all sincere folk, the dismay of all greatness. "All"? What I lack in pretension I make up in wit.

In 1966, writing the "Introduction" to *A Book of Resemblances: Poems 1950–1953,* he felt the need once again to explicate his intentions in *FF59,* implicitly linking them to other of his writing in that highly productive period: "In *Faust Foutu,* written 1953–54, I was concerned with projecting a world, imagining its terms, and in that projection, incorporating an analytic process—not only what was happening but the possible meanings of what was happening became my terms of conscious composition."

In revising *FF53,* Duncan made numerous changes in phrasing to speeches, songs, and stage directions, and renamed or newly spelled the names of some dramatis personae—for example, *FF53* identifies and cues "her [i.e. Marguerite's] Nurse" as "The Devil-Nurse" throughout. Speeches in verse in *FF53* are in *FF1* and *FF59* frequently written as prose. Few of these changes are recorded in these notes. Duncan's scoring for five simultaneous voices in the closing 125 or so lines of Act 4 is printed in typescript in both *FF53* and *FF59.* Conversion to proportionally spaced typeface for publication here necessitates compromise, since words lined up on a vertical axis in evenly spaced typewriter font do not line up on the same axes in proportionally spaced type. Adjustments, some of which necessitated tricky judgment calls, are not recorded here, though every effort has been made to ensure that exactly simultaneous utterances are preserved.

In all three published versions of *Faust Foutu,* in addition to spacing between words, Duncan used one, two, or occasionally three spaced periods to indicate pauses of different duration. In prose passages in *FF1* and *FF59,* as here, Duncan substituted a number sign (#) for many of the paragraph breaks in *FF53.* Though his practice is not wholly consistent, in *FF59* Duncan deliberately followed two distinct conventions in cueing and indenting speeches, sometimes following the character's name with a dash, and sometimes (usually but not always before songs) with a colon. Duncan provided very few act and scene numbers; those supplied by Duncan are here printed in [square brackets]; those supplied by the editor appear in {braces}.

Faust Foutu is usually translated as *Faust Fucked.*

Act 1, Scene 6: In the opening stage direction, *FF53* reads "(THE DANCE CONTINUES WHERE IT WAS BROKEN AND ENDS WITH THE THREE WITCHES IN A CIRCLE AROUND FAUST)" for "(THE DANCE CONCLUDED)."

Act 2, Scene 1: In the stage directions, on those occasions in *FF1* and *FF59* where various members of the cast "applaud genteely," *FF53* constructs the applause, with variations, along the following lines:

ALL: clap clap clap clap
      clap clap clap clap
      clap clap clap
      clap clap clap clap

Act 2, Scene 5: For the fifteen lines of Maggie's song, in *FF59* beginning "We get along in our home town" and ending "who wants a man? Be pensive," *FF53* reads:

The heat's on! Watch them prices rise.
The sky's the limit.   Get wise.
Who wants to be free? Be expensive.

Hell's loose! Hear them devils go.
Who knows the score? it ain't so.
who wants a man? Be pensive.

    Just cause I push over easy
    don't mean It's easy to love.
    I get my kicks the hard way
    so let's put our cards on the table
    we'll all lose the game in the end.

Act 2, Scene 11: *Les paradis artificiels* (Artificial Paradises) is a book by Charles Baudelaire, published in 1860; *Le goût de l'infinie* (usually translated as *I Taste The Infinite*) is the title of its first section.

Act 2, Scene 12: The opening stage direction in *FF53* reads "NOISE SCORED FOR ANY HANDY INSTRUMENTS AND HUMAN VOICES. IT ALTERNATES BETWEEN THE GRANDIOSE, THE TERRIFYING, PARODY AND THE RIDICULOUS. WITH FAUST, MAGGIE, PETER, MRS P-W, AND EMORY LOWENTHAL'S VOICES HOWLING, SCREAMING, LAUGHING, SOBBING. THE

INTERVALS OF DIALOG ARE SCORED AT INTERVALS OF DEAD STOP IN THE
STORM, RHYTHMIC STOPS IN THE ROAR."
Act 3, Scene 5. The four witnesses of *FF59* are cued in *FF53* as "Spectators."
Act 4: [*Traité*] *du Bave et d'Eternité* is a film by Isidore Isou (1928–2007), its
title usually translated as *Venom and Eternity*.

MEDEA AT KOLCHIS: THE MAIDEN HEAD
Duncan started writing the play in June 1951, worked on the text intermit-
tently in his notebooks, the final notebook entry dated 19 August 1956,
ten days before its performance at Black Mountain College. An undated
early Ams draft (NBuU) is titled "Medea—A Spectacle." Wesley Huss and
Eloise Mixon said that Duncan wrote and revised the play during rehearsals.
As soon as revisions to *Medea at Kolchis* were recorded in his notebook, he
started working on *Medea Part II: The Will,* but the project was never fin-
ished. For a brief account, see Lewis Ellingham and Kevin Killian, *Poet Be
Like God: Jack Spicer and the San Francisco Renaissance* (Hanover and London:
Wesleyan University Press, 1998), 85–86. *Medea at Kolchis* was published by
Oyez in 1965 and reprinted in 1966.
    In November 1958 there were abortive plans for a revival performance of
Medea at Kolchis at the Playhouse in San Francisco—a theater run by Kermit
Sheets with the more-or-less silent partnership of James Broughton. In the
Robert Duncan archive at NBuU there is an autograph three-page manu-
script in Duncan's hand of what appears to be his draft of the program notes:

"The Maidenhead" is both a difficult and an uneasy play. It is easy, if you let
it be what it is: a drama of this household in 1904 living in the imagination,
haunted by supernatural forces and by the mind of an old poet—contemporary
of Maeterlinck and Yeats, but a drama too of simple human passions: obsessive
desire, love, hatred. I am concernd in the Medea trilogy (of which this is the
first play) with the meanings that flow from human feeling, not with causes or
motives. And I strive on the stage to bring us to the sources of action: to see the
absolute moments that we call reality. It is a drama of the soul, the psyche—but
it is not a psychological drama.
    It is a difficult play for those who may want it all explained—something more
than what they see manifest. Garrow, Medea, Jason, Arthur, Edna or Boris—all
the members of the drama have, as all human beings have, emotional depths and
personal realities that lie beyond our mere "understandings." I am not interested
in the stage as a vehicle for some message of mine; and there will be difficulties
indeed for those who are in search of a message. Those in the play have "mes-
sages," even urgent ones. Where I on the stage might have my own "message"
too. But my concern is to create a world there in which life might well up into

being—for me it is the miracle of the actors who become created beings, who realize the play; and of the director who creates out of the written drama its incarnation. It is thru the stage that we—writer, actors and director—participate in a mystery of our existence directly. Life itself is difficult and easy. Easy because it is given fact. Difficult because we strive to understand it. In "The Maidenhead" I have sought to project such a drama—of pure, even violent sensation, of pathos, terror, tenderness, ruthlessness: a stage where new definitions may appear of major human emotions. I have sought too to project depths and heights of life that are worthy of our struggle to understand that would yield to our efforts not answers but meanings. It is the beauty of experience that it informs or inspires and that it cannot without deformation be reduced to the obvious.

Those who read in any source-book the legend of Jason and Medea, the story of the Argonauts and the Golden Fleece may recognize how this myth haunts the play; and it will enrich the understanding to realize that the people in this house, like the King and his daughter Medea in Colchis, live in a dark realm, the East before dawn, where the Sun, the Golden Fleece, is held captive; and that the hero Jason comes to release the Sun so that the world will emerge from Night into Day. And those who love lore may find further richness in the teachings of alchemy that the Golden Fleece, the gold, is a Sun in the human soul which thru trials seeks transmutation into a passionate reality: in this play of mine, into Love. But the real sun, the real Gold, lies not in a "lore" but in the Soul—we do not need book-learning to follow the real drama: I do not present symbols but actualities. Medea does not murder the Night, she murders her father in a reality bloody and inevitable to her—a necessary terror. Jason does not seek a symbol of the Sun—he seeks power to release himself, a power which he tries to steal from those that seem to have it. The tragedy is not finally a symbolic tragedy: it is what we see. It lies in the things done in the play and the suffering of the doer. My fascination with the occult is only because we are moved by hidden forces. I keep nothing hidden that I know—the inscrutable for me is the inscrutable necessary to the reality on the stage, I do not shy away from the obscure. I have no interest in displaying the omnipotence of my perceptions and insights. This stage is to be the resistant, more-than-we-know of life: in this sense a Mystery Play.

The play was written and produced at Black Mountain College in the summer of 1956. Three of the original cast: Don Mixon, Erik Weir, and Eloise Turner, have come to San Francisco where with Wes Huss head of the Dramatics School at Black Mountain they have workd in this production. Jane Steckle, whose performances in Playhouse productions haunted the writing of the part of Garrow as I wrote it, now plays that role. Wes Huss himself plays Arthur and directs the production. _____ who plays Medea is in a sense the only new member of the cast—a challenging part.

There are several drafts of "Another Preface" at NBuU, in one of which, also called "Another Preface 1963," Duncan describes Medea as "an intensity. Priestess of the snake she becomes a snake striking, and once she enters the stage we should feel her waiting throughout. She is a fury, the fury that a young girl, 13 or 14, is."

As in the 1959 edition of *Faust Foutu,* in addition to spacing between words, Duncan used one, two, or occasionally three spaced periods to indicate a pause. Inconsistencies in the spacing of these periods, perhaps brought about by the printer's justification of prose lines, have been preserved here, as have several irregularities in the stage directions (mainly in punctuation).

Act I, Scene 3: *Ante ferit quam flamma micat:* He strikes before the sparks give light; the device of the Order of the Golden Fleece, founded at Bruges, 10 February 1429, by Philippe le Bon (Philip the Good), duke of Burgundy.

LETTERS: POEMS MCMLIII–MCMLVI

Letters is, essentially, Duncan's first completely planned book in the sense that, once he'd written the first poem, addressed to Levertov, he wrote the remaining poems specifically with the book in mind, addressing or dedicating ten of the book's thirty numbered poems to specific individuals. He wrote the poems between May 1953 and the beginning of December 1955. In light of his writing practice, his design for the book was necessarily flexible: in some instances he lightly revised the poems between their initial periodical publication and their appearance in the book, and he eventually excluded from the book at least one poem—"The Green Lady"—initially written for it. When he reprinted *Letters* in *Derivations: Selected Poems 1950–1956* in 1968, he placed it between "Correspondences" and "August Sun." He was also, at the time he was writing and putting *Letters* together, writing poems which he would gather in *Writing Writing, A Book of Resemblances: Poems 1950–1953,* and *Names of People*—collections then in various stages of completion—as well as seeing *Caesar's Gate: Poems 1949–1950* (published in September 1955) through the press. Duncan and Jess lived in Bañalbufar, on the west coast of Mallorca, from March 1955 until July 1956; he wrote the final three poems of *Letters* on a trip to Paris in November 1955.

While assembling and arranging *Selected Poems* (published 1959) he told Robin Blaser, in a letter dated 18 March 1957, that "it is a problem in shaping. LETTERS is for me so beautifully a whole book I should not like to select from it" (CU-BANC). None appeared in a textbook anthology, and only two were anthologized: "An Owl Is An Only Bird Of Poetry," which Donald M. Allen had chosen, before *Letters* was published, for *The New American Poetry 1945–1960* (New York: Grove, 1960), and "xxii: To Vow," which appeared in Marguerite Harris, ed., *Loves Etc.* (Garden City: Doubleday Anchor, 1973).

Jonathan Williams, under the imprint Jargon 14, published *Letters* in a limited edition in 1958. Among the most elegant of the titles Williams produced, the book took more than a year to print. Duncan engaged Claude Fredericks, the printer, in a vigorous and extensive commentary and instruction on the layout of the texts, largely conducted through numbered memos, printed in Robert Duncan, *Letters: Poems 1953–1956,* edited and with an afterword by Robert J. Bertholf (Chicago: Flood Editions, 2003), 59–71 (hereafter cited as Flood). He told Jonathan Williams in a letter on 27 December 1957 that "the proof reading . . . has been quite as arduous as the writing" (Flood, 56). As with most of Duncan's subsequent books, save for shifts in lineation, spelling, punctuation and the like (not recorded here), there is overall so little difference between the texts as first published in periodicals and as published in the book shortly after, that, given Duncan's intense care and Fredericks's meticulous exactitude in steering *Letters* through its printing, the copy text here is the 1958 Jargon edition. Reprinting the poems in *Der,* Duncan dropped the numbers as well as the dedications.

In a fragmentary entry dated 4 April 1956, when he was once more working through the Zohar (he had first done so in 1950–51), Duncan drafted a "Statement on LETTERS" (Notebook 19, NBuU): "These LETTERS are the ones between Alpha and Omega who attend our works, the ones from A to Z, our building blocks." Some eighteen months later he picked this idea up again, explaining to Fredericks in memo #6, 16 November 1957 (Flood, 64) that "there has been considerable misunderstanding of LETTERS as the title of a book and not as descriptive of the content." But in adding that "none of the contents are letters. The title is used as in 'A man of letters'; 'he knows his letters' etc.," he was a shade misleading: in May 1953 he had opened what became a long correspondence with Denise Levertov by actually sending the first poem, then titled "Letters for Denise Levertov: An A Muse Ment," as a self-explanatory letter. In the advertising flyer for the book (NBuU) Duncan wrote:

> The composition of LETTERS begins with 'Letters for Denise Levertov' and moves out over almost three years' work to complete a book presided over by an alphabet primary to world creation. These angelic letters then whose powers hidden or discovered are substance of our speech. A naming of my peers too, and an exclamation of joy: Denise Levertov, Charles Olson, Robert Creeley, James Broughton, Mike McClure, Helen Adam—it is the presence of companions, named and unnamed, that inspires LETTERS. A book of primaries, a book of companions. A book of praises. I have stored here, as best I know how, the song of all I live by. For I adhere to form as the bee obeys the geometry of the hive.

A printed slip, laid in copy 16 of the hardcover edition (NBuU), gives (over Jonathan Williams's name) a further elaboration of the title: "*Regarding* LETTERS *Robert Duncan writes:* 'Given twenty-six letters absurdly divorced often from phonemic significance, ambivalent letters like *c* that has no existence, for in speech it is always *k* or *s,* and given furthermore customs of spelling that disguise what the sound is, we spell the word, and by word the poem. If we are then to be poets, makers, we are men of letters then. Where we most take control, we follow the lettering: the job in writing to keep the process clear, not to interfere.'"

Duncan would return to the Zohar in subsequent years, noting in a 1974 interview that "letters"—possibly referring to his book as much as to the alphabet—"refers to the zohar with its new picture of language" (Robert Duncan interview by Howard Mesch, *Unmuzzled Ox* 4.2 [1976]: 82); three years earlier, in his 1971 *Prospectus* for *Ground Work* (San Francisco: privately published) he had suggested something of what that "new picture" might be. Referring to "the resolves—the releases—of *Letters,* that then moved in my thought inspired by the Zohar," he added, "it was the letters of the Logos I saw dancing there—and then I was to come to see these in turn as the members of the Life Code, the configurations of chemical probabilities, and that that dance was the Spirit that haunted all dancing orders. Now, as ever, returning to the dance ground, I see the Dance and the Work are one. Where the work comes true, it is true to the Dance." Duncan's later view is implicit in *Letters,* and in his reluctance to abstract anything from that book which would detract from its wholeness. "Encounters with the letters of the alphabet itself—with notation as such," he would write in 1981, "lead back to a primary religious ground that is suggestive indeed in relation to . . . a primary depth or ground in the field of Poetics" ("Why Poetics?" *New College of California . . . Program in Poetics, 1980–1981* [San Francisco: New College, 1980], iii).

The Jargon edition of *Letters* included five drawings of "the ideal reader," all printed recto in orange-brown on semi-opaque rice paper. Writing to Jonathan Williams on 19 November 1956 Duncan suggested they be "willy-nilly-of-the-text regularly occurring" (exigencies of book production determined their somewhat irregular placement, three in the first and two in the last of the book's five signatures), and said they "wld. be most upsetting to all critical sense, which pleases me." In parentheses he then described seven drawings: "My 'Ideal Reader' is a pleasant by-a-stream-sitting-and-reading-music, flower-watering, homeward-to-be-reading, in-flowerd-night-cap-and-art-nouveau-bedstead-reading, by-the-lamp-reading, under-a-tree-listening-to-a-bird-singing, meditating-with-startled-cat-in-lap round old lady" (Flood, 54–55). All seven were subsequently printed in Duncan's *65 Drawings* as "the ideal reader" (Los Angeles: Black Sparrow, 1970, i-vii).

Duncan's instructions to Fredericks specified that all the dedications to the poems should appear on the contents page, "not in the text" (Flood, 60); here, they are also recorded in the notes. He also discussed in detail the indenting of first lines and paragraphs in relation to the titles of poems and section titles in the preface, explaining that if the title is the first line of the poem the text begins in lower case (memo #1, Flood, 59) or if the section title in the preface is the beginning of a sentence, then the line or sentence "should continue the course of the title" by flowing into the first paragraph or stanza (memo #6, Flood, 62), lining up its indentation with the end of the title (as in "The breaking up of cold clouds" in the preface). In the same memo he pointed out that "hyphenations are significant as articulations—stumblings, interferences etc," whether the writing be "measured (verse)" or "unmeasured (prose)" (Flood 63). In *Letters* the prose is invariably printed ragged right; in *Derivations,* in justified lines. In some cases, such as "xxviii: New Tidings," the generic boundaries between verse and prose are so blurred as to be indistinguishable.

Preface. Written 25 December 1955–fall 1956; first publication in *Letters*, 3–8. Also published in *Der.* Duncan planned the preface in December 1955, wrote it out on Christmas Day, and reworked it the following September and October. Writing to Jonathan Williams on 5 October 1956 he said: "The 'PREFACE' is, if nothing else, unusual by its ungovernd (but it is governd by that sternest of inventors—the nature of the book) claim of allegiance to even overreaching poetry. It is a claim which quite erases 'me' and leaves something (one) else: the largest author" (NBuU).

Ich habe keine Tiefe, also meinen unaufhölichen Trieb zur Tiefe: freely translated as "I have no depths, except for my unquenchable thirst for depth"— more literally, "except for my unending [or unstoppable] drive." From Christian Morgenstern, *Stufen* (steps, stairs; degrees; ranks; grades; shades, tints; specimens).

l'Oeuvre de Vivant / l'Oeuvre de Fantôme: The Work of the Living / the Work of the Spectre [or Ghost].

Il n'y a que des âmes égales devant l'amour. Il n'y a que des amours égaux devant Dieu: liberally translated as "All souls are equal in love's eyes. All loves are equal in God's eyes." Hugo's words are from a long passage dictated at one of *les tables tournantes* (table turning) séances held in Jersey by the poet Delphine de Girardin. The relevant passage, of which this is a brief extract, is quoted in full in Saurat's book *l'Expérience de l'au-dela* [The Experience of the Beyond] published in 1951. *The Gods Of The People* and *Death And The Dreamer* were, respectively, published in 1946 and 1947.

i: For A Muse Meant. "for Denise Levertov." Written May–June 1953; published in *Letters,* 13–16. First publication, as "Letters For Denise Levertov: An A Muse Ment," in *Black Mountain Review* 1.3 (Autumn 1954): 19–22. Also published in *Der.* Duncan sent this poem, titled "Letters for Denise Levertov: An A Muse Ment," to Levertov in May 1953, with no identification save his initials "RD" at the end of the typescript, to salute her work, especially "The Shifting," which appeared in *Origin* 6 (Summer 1952): 114 (seven of Duncan's poems were in the same issue). She misread the poem as a mockery of her work. In a letter of 27 June 1953 Duncan explained that "the 'Letters' are *for* you not about you," and gave a brief commentary on some details of the poem (Robert J. Bertholf and Albert Gelpi, eds., *The Letters of Robert Duncan and Denise Levertov* [Stanford: Stanford University Press, 2004], 5–6). For the text of the poem as sent to Levertov, see Bertholf and Gelpi, 3–5. He lightly revised it, as usual modifying line- and stanza-breaks, punctuation, spelling and the like, for publication in *Black Mountain Review,* and again for publication in *Letters.*

ii: Distant Counsels Of Artaud. "for Philip Lamantia." Written spring 1953; first publication in *Letters,* 16–17. Also published in *Der.*

iii: Upon Taking Hold. "for Charles Olson." Written spring 1953; published in *Letters,* 17–19. First publication in *Chicago Review* 12.1 (Spring 1958): 7–8; also published in *Der.* But for one minor adjustment in indentation, Duncan did not revise the text as it first appeared in *Chicago Review.*

iv: First Invention On The Theme Of The Adam. Written spring 1953; first publication in *Letters,* 20–21. Also published in *Der.* This "First Invention" is, Duncan told Fredericks on 26 December 1957, "a little suite of poems (like Webern's Five Pieces)" (Flood, 67). Other suites are *vii, xxvii.*

v: Short Invention On The Theme Of The Adam. Written spring 1953; first publication in *Letters,* 21–22. Also published in *Der.*

vi: Figures Of Speech. "for Helen Adam." Written 1953; first publication in *Letters,* 22–25. Also published in *Der.* In stanza 4, final sentence, *Der* reads "the World in time" for "the Word in time."

vii: Metamorphosis. Written 1953; published in *Letters,* 25–27. First publication in *Poetry* 91.6 (March 1958): 379–81; also published in *Der.* "Metamorphosis" is, Duncan told Fredericks on 26 December 1957, like *iv* and *xxvii,* a "suite of poems" (Flood, 67).

viii: With Bells Shaking. Written 1953; first publication in *Letters,* 27–28. Also published in *Der.*

ix: Light Song. "for Charles Olson." Written February 1954; published in *Letters,* 28–30. First publication, as "Letters to Olson: Light Song," in *The Occident* (Spring 1954): 19–20; also published in *Der.* In the penultimate stanza, last eight lines, *Occident* reads:

> Chaplin Lawrence said was beauty in a man—
>   even the city lights
> or tongues, the Metropolis murmuring
>   suggests
> the language we long for.
>   Hidden.

x: It's Spring. Love's Spring. Written 29 March 1954; first publication in *Letters,* 30–31. Also published in *Der.*

xi: At The End Of A Period. "for Helen Adam." Written 29 October 1954; first publication in *Letters,* 31–33. Also published in *Der.* In one Tms (NBuU) the poem is titled "A Third Piece For Helen Adam."

xii: Fragment. Written 1954; published in *Letters,* 33–34. First publication in *Poems and Pictures* 2 (1954): 4; also published in *Der.*

xiii: True To Life. "for Charles Olson." Written 20–27 June 1954; first publication in *Letters,* 34–35. Also published in *Der.*

xiv: Upon His Seeing A Baby Holding The Four Of Hearts For Him And Another Card Conceald. "for Robert Creeley." Written September–October 1955; first publication in *Letters,* 36–37. Also published in *Der.* "Did I tell you about in New York," Creeley wrote from Black Mountain College on 3 October 1955 to Duncan in Mallorca:

> on my way to see (first time) Cocteau's Blood of A Poet with Julie, we passed a woman pushing a baby carriage, and the baby was holding 2 cards, and, pass- ing, I looked back, and only card I could see (the other not visible because of the baby's body etc) was the 4 of hearts? . . . Since then, lightly, I had occasion to cut a deck four times—and every one has been a four. The last three times, I cut an old pack left in this room I've just moved into, the first two times the first day—and the last, the day following, and the last also, the 4 of hearts. I have left it at that, like they say. (I cut the 1st time up with Dan & a friend; but have last 3 times (the cards) on shelf by what's left of my head. I am waiting. That is I think what it "says" anyhow. Or as Olson said: they want you to land on all fours. Anyhow. (NBuU)

Duncan sent Creeley twenty-four lines of the poem in a letter he wrote on 8 October 1955.

xv: Words Open Out Upon Grief. Written 1954; published in *Letters,* 37–38. First publication in *Poetry* 91.6 (March 1958): 383–84; also published in *Der.*

xvi: Riding. Written 17 October 1954; first publication in *Letters,* 38–40. Also published in *Der.*

xvii: At Home. Written 17 October 1954; first publication in *Letters,* 40–41. Also published in *Der.* In fourth paragraph, last sentence, *Der* reads "dearness or nearness" for "dearness of nearness."

xviii: The Human Communion. Traces. Written 24 May 1955; first publication in *Letters,* 41–42. Also published, as sixth section of "Notes," in *Black Mountain Review* 6 (1956): 10, and in *Der.*

xix: Passages Of A Sentence. Written 18 October 1954; first publication in *Letters,* 42–43. Also published in *Der.*

xx: Re. "for Mike and Jo Ann McClure." Written 1954; published in *Letters,* 43–44. First publication in *Poetry* 91.6 (March 1958): 380; also published in *Der.*

xxi: Brought To Love. Written 1955; published in *Letters,* 44–45. First publication in *Poetry* 91.6 (March 1958): 377; also published in *Der.*

xxii: To Vow. Written 1955; published in *Letters,* 45–46. First publication in *Poetry* 91.6 (March 1958): 378; also published in *Der* and in Marguerite Harris, ed., *Loves, Etc.* (Garden City: Doubleday Anchor, 1973).

xxiii: Spelling The Word. Written 1955; first publication in *Letters,* 46–47. Also published in *Der.*

xxiv: Correspondences. Written June–July 1955; first publication in *Letters,* 47–48. Also published in *Der.*

xxv: August Sun. Written June–July 1955; published in *Letters,* 48. First publication in *Poetry* 91.6 (March 1958): 384; also published in *Der.*

xxvi: Source. Written November 1954; first publication in *Letters,* 48–49. Also published in *Der.* The notebook entry dated 1 November 1954, which Duncan printed in *Letters* almost unchanged (but without its final sentence) and titled "Source," is immediately followed by another entry with the same date, which begins:

This series of notes serve to explore a style and temperament in which the Romantic spirit is revived. Back it goes to recent readings of George MacDonald's *Lilith,* to earlier pleasures and thrills in Coleridge and Poe. But thruout I am conscious of the debt to Wallace Stevens—and there seems to be more of the Romantic in Stevens than of Laforgue. Then I discovered, having finally purchased *New Directions* 14, Charles Henri Ford's *anthology of Prose Poetry.* Mallarmé's *Penultimate* [i.e., "The Demon of Analogy"] and Poe's *Shadow* are all of the same vein along which I am working again. This is of course the radical disagreement that Olson has with me. In a sense—he is so keen upon the virtú of reality that he rejects my "wisdom" not as it might seem at first glance because "wisdom" is a vice; but because my wisdom is not real wisdom. He suspects, and rightly, that I indulge myself in pretentious fictions. I, however, at this point take enuf delight in the available glamor that I do not stop to trouble the cheapness of such stuff. I mean that it is, for a man of rigor, an inexpensive irony to play with puns in pretending & pretension. I like rigor and even clarity as a quality of a work—that is, as I like muddle and floaty vagaries. It is the intensity of the conception that moves me—this intensity may be that it is all of a fervent marshmallow dandy lion fluff. In cloudy art I admire boldness, big lumps of it as in Marie Laurencin. And certainly I like intensely evasive art—like Corbett's big white canvas where the area is blushing with rosiness that one sees without distinguishing. (Notebook 2, CU-BANC)

Duncan published the complete entry, with slight revisions, as "From A Notebook" in *Black Mountain Review* 5 (Summer 1955): 209–212; it also appears in *Fictive Certainties*. In Notebook 2, it is followed by yet another lengthy note, written on the same day, which begins: "As the gothic Romanticists had a cult of the ruin, I have a cult of the wreck."

The omitted sentence at the end of "Source" reads: "The poem, loved thus, is cruel as all the emptiness in things, the answerless cold of endless desires."

xxvii: An Owl Is An Only Bird Of Poetry. "A vale for James Broughton." Written July–August 1955; published in *Letters,* 49–55. First publication in *Black Mountain Review* 6 (Spring 1956): 165–69. Also published in Allen, *New American Poetry* and in *Der.* In *Black Mountain Review* the poem bears the subtitle "another vale for James Broughton." "An Owl Is An Only Bird Of Poetry" is, Duncan told Fredericks on 26 December 1957, like *iv* and *vii* a "suite of poems" (Flood, 67).

xxviii: New Tidings. Written November 1955; first publication in *Letters,* 53–54. Also published in *Der.* Stanzas 1, 3, and 5 may or may not be prose. *Der* prints them as justified prose, but the line breaks are the same as in *Letters. Der* wide spaces the words in stanza 3 to justify the right margin to match stanzas 1 and 5. In *Letters* stanza 7 is printed ragged-right, and may be prose; in *Der* stanza 7 is justified prose, and the line-breaks are not the same.

xxix: Changing Trains. Written November 1955; first publication in *Letters,* 54. Also published in *Der.*

xxx: The Language Of Love and *Siren Song.* Written November 1955; first publication in *Letters,* 54–56. Also published in *Der.* In its table of contents, *Letters* treats "Siren Song" as the second of two poems in a linked sequence; however, in the *Letters* text, "Siren Song" follows "The Language of Love" as a separate poem. *Der* treats it as a separate poem in both its table of contents and text.

Selected Bibliography

CRITICAL WORKS AND COLLECTIONS

Allen, Donald M., ed. *The New American Poetry 1945–1960.* New York: Grove, 1960.

Bartlett, Lee, ed. "'Where As Giant Kings We Gatherd': Some Letters from Robert Duncan to William Everson, 1940 and After." *Sagetrieb* 4.2–3 (Fall–Winter 1985): 137–71.

Bertholf, Robert J. *Robert Duncan: A Descriptive Bibliography.* Santa Rosa: Black Sparrow, 1986.

Bertholf, Robert J., and Albert Gelpi, eds. *The Letters of Robert Duncan and Denise Levertov.* Stanford: Stanford University Press, 2004.

Bertholf, Robert J., and Ian W. Reid, eds. *Robert Duncan: Scales of the Marvelous.* New York: New Directions, 1979.

Blaser, Robin. *The Fire: Collected Essays.* Edited by Miriam Nichols. Berkeley: University of California Press, 2006.

Callahan, Bob. "The World of Jaime de Angulo" (includes an interview with Robert Duncan). *The Netzalcahuatl News.* 1.1 (Summer 1979): 1–5.

Conte, Joseph. *Unending Design: The Forms of Postmodern Poetry.* Ithaca, NY: Cornell University Press, 1991.

Davidson, Michael. *The San Francisco Renaissance: Poetics and Community at Mid-century.* New York: Cambridge University Press, 1989.

Ellingham, Lewis, and Kevin Killian. *Poet Be Like God: Jack Spicer and the San Francisco Renaissance.* Hanover and London: Wesleyan University Press, 1998.

Faas, Ekbert. *Young Robert Duncan: Portrait of the Poet as Homosexual in Society.* Santa Barbara: Black Sparrow, 1983.

Gelpi, Albert, and Robert J. Bertholf, eds. *Robert Duncan and Denise Levertov: The Poetry of Politics, the Politics of Poetry.* Stanford: Stanford University Press, 2006.

Jarnot, Lisa. *Robert Duncan, the Ambassador from Venus.* Berkeley: University of California Press, 2012.

Kantorowicz, Ernst. *The King's Two Bodies: A Study in Mediaeval Political Theology.* Princeton: Princeton University Press, 1957.

Lewis, Charlton T., and Charles Short. *A Latin Dictionary.* Oxford: Clarendon, 1975.

MacDonald, George. *The Light Princess and Other Fairy Stories.* London: Fifield, 1893.

Pound, Ezra. "Cleaners' Manifesto." *Four Pages* 3 (March 1948): 3.

Prevallet, Kristen, ed. "Helen Adam and Robert Duncan: Selected Correspondence 1955–1956." *Apex of the M* 6 (Fall 1997): 136–63.

Proust, Marcel. *The Past Recaptured.* Translated by Frederick A. Blossom. New York: Modern Library, 1932.

Rukeyser, Muriel. "Myth and Torment" (review of *Heavenly City, Earthly City*). *Poetry* 72.1 (April 1948): 48–51.

Sperling, Harry, and Maurice Simon, trans. *The Zohar.* 5 vols. London: Soncino Press, 1931–1934.

Stravinsky, Igor. *The Poetics of Music in the Form of Six Lessons.* Cambridge: Harvard University Press, 1947.

Williams, William Carlos. *Spring And All.* 1923. Reprint, Buffalo, NY: Frontier Press, 1970.

Zukofsky, Louis. "Light" (1948). In *Some Time.* Stuttgart: Jargon, 1956.

WORKS BY ROBERT DUNCAN

Heavenly City, Earthly City. Berkeley: Bern Porter, 1947.

"The Poetics Of Music: Stravinsky." *The Occident* (Spring 1948): 53–54.

"A Note On Tone In Poetry." *Literary Behavior* (Fall 1948): 13–14.

Poems 1948–49. Berkeley: Berkeley Miscellany Editions, 1949.

Medieval Scenes. San Francisco: Centaur Press, 1950.

Fragments of a Disorderd Devotion. San Francisco: Privately published, 1952.

Faust Foutu. San Francisco: Privately published, 1953.

"Pages From A Notebook." *The Artist's View* 5 (July 1953).

Caesar's Gate: Poems 1949–1950. Palma de Mallorca: Divers Press, 1955.

Faust Foutu: Act One. San Francisco: White Rabbit Press, 1958.

Letters: Poems mcmlii-mcmlvi. Highlands, NC: Jonathan Williams as Jargon 14, 1958.

Faust Foutu. Stinson Beach, CA: Enkidu Surrogate, 1959.

Selected Poems. San Francisco: City Lights Books, 1959.

The Opening of the Field. New York: Grove, 1960.

As Testimony: The Poem and the Scene. San Francisco: White Rabbit, 1964.

Roots and Branches. New York: Charles Scribner, 1964.

"Towards An Open Universe." In *Contemporary American Poetry: Voice of America Forum Lectures.* Edited by Howard Nemerov, 168–83. Washington, DC: Voice of America, 1964.

Writing Writing. Albuquerque: Sumbooks, 1964.

Medea at Kolchis: The Maiden Head. Berkeley: Oyez, 1965.

A Book of Resemblances: Poems 1950–1953. New Haven: Henry W. Wenning, 1966.

Fragments of a Disorderd Devotion. San Francisco: Gnomon; Toronto: Island, 1966.

The Years As Catches: First Poems (1939–1946). Berkeley: Oyez, 1966.

"Returning To *Les Chimères* of Gérard de Nerval." *Audit* 4.3 (1967): 42–61.

Bending the Bow. New York: New Directions, 1968.

Derivations: Selected Poems 1950–1956. London: Fulcrum, 1968.

The First Decade: Selected Poems 1940–1950. London: Fulcrum, 1968.

Names of People. Los Angeles: Black Sparrow Press, 1968.

Play Time Pseudo Stein. 2nd ed. San Francisco: Tenth Muse, 1969.

Caesar's Gate: Poems 1949–1950. 2nd ed. San Francisco: Sand Dollar, 1972.

"Robert Duncan's Interview." By Howard Mesch. *Unmuzzled Ox* 4.2 (1976): 79–96.

Medieval Scenes 1950 and 1959. Edited by Robert J. Bertholf. Kent, OH: Kent State University Libraries, 1978.

"An Interview With Robert Duncan." By Jack R. Cohn and Thomas J. O'Donnell. *Contemporary Literature* 21.4 (Autumn 1980): 513–48.

"Why Poetics?" In *Program in Poetics, 1980–1981.* San Francisco: New College of California, 1980, iii–iv.

Fictive Certainties: Essays. New York: New Directions, 1985. See esp. "The Truth and Life of Myth."

"'The Poetry Of Unevenness': An Interview With Robert Duncan." By Jack R. Cohn and Thomas J. O'Donnell. *Credences* 3.2 (Spring 1985): 91–111.

A Selected Prose. Edited by Robert J. Bertholf. New York: New Directions, 1995.

"Opening The Dreamway." *Spring* 59 (Spring 1996): 2–45.

"Wind And Sea, Fire And Night." *Spring* 59 (Spring 1996): 48–77.

Letters: Poems 1953–1956. Edited and with an Afterword by Robert J. Bertholf. Chicago: Flood Editions, 2003.

The H.D. Book. Edited by Michael Boughn and Victor Coleman. Berkeley: University of California Press, 2011.

Index of Titles and First Lines

Titles appear in roman type. First lines appear in italics. Quotation marks and parentheses in titles and first lines are Duncan's, not the editor's. Titles of published books are in small caps.

Designer: Nola Burger, Sandy Drooker
Text: 10.5/13.5 Bembo
Display: Bembo
Compositor: BookMatters, Berkeley
Printer and binder: Maple Press